Companion Encyclopedia of Middle Eastern and North African Film

Companion Encyclopedia of Middle Eastern and North African Film

Edited by Oliver Leaman

London and New York

First published 2001
by Routledge
11 New Fetter Lane, London EC4P 4EE

Simultaneously published in the USA and Canada
by Routledge
29 West 35th Street, New York, NY 10001

Routledge is an imprint of the Taylor & Francis Group

Typeset in Times by Routledge
Printed and bound in Great Britain by TJ International Ltd, Padstow, Cornwall

British Library Cataloguing in Publication Data
A catalogue record for this book is available from the British Library

Library of Congress Cataloging in Publication Data
Companion encyclopedia of Middle Eastern and North African film / edited by
Oliver Leaman.
p. cm
Includes bibliographical references and index.
1. Motion pictures–Arab countries–Catalogs. 2. Motion pictures–Middle
East–Catalogs. 3. Motion pictures–Africa, North–Catalogs. 4. Motion
pictures–Arab countries–Biography–Dictionaries. 5. Motion pictures–Middle
East–Biography–Dictionaries. 6. Motion pictures–Africa,
North–Biography–Dictionaries. I. Leaman, Oliver, 1950–
PN1993.5.A65 C66 2001
791.43'75'0956–dc21   00-068390

ISBN 0–415–18703–6

Contents

Illustrations

Figures

Tables

Notes on contributors

Roy Armes received his Ph.D. in Film at the Slade School of Art, University College London, and is Professor of Film at Middlesex University. Over the past thirty-five years he has written widely on European and, more recently, African cinemas. His sixteen books include *Arab and African Film Making* (co-written with Dr Lizbeth Malkmus), a bilingual *Dictionary of North African Film Makers* and a recent study of the Algerian film, *Omar Gatlato*. His work has been translated into a dozen languages.

Gönul Dönmez-Colin received her Masters Degree from the McGill University of Montreal, Canada and taught in Montreal for fifteen years and in Hong Kong for one year. She is the author of *Paylasilan Tutku Sinema*, a collection of her interviews with prominent filmmakers, published in Turkish and co-author of 'Die Siebte Kunst auf dem Pulverfass' (Balkan-Film) published in German. She has served on the juries of international film festivals and has also been artistic advisor to film festivals. As an international film critic and writer specialized in Asian cinema, she travels extensively in Asia to research for her writing. Her work, which is regularly published in eight languages, includes *Le Monde Diplomatique* (Paris), *Cumhuriyet* (Istanbul), *Cinemaya* (New Delhi) and *Blimp* (Graz).

Nezih Erdoğan teaches film theory and screenwriting at Bahcesehir University, Istanbul. He has mainly published on Turkish popular cinema. He has forthcoming chapters on the reception of Hollywood in Turkey after the Second World War from BFI, and on Turkish trash and Hollywood from Hampton.

Deniz Göktürk teaches German and Film Studies at the University of Southampton (UK) and at UC Berkeley (USA). She collaborates in an interdisciplinary research project on 'Axial Writing: Transnational Imagination and Cultural Policy' (funded by the Economic and Social Sciences Research Council 'Transnational Communities' Programme). Her publications include a book on literary and cinematic imaginations of America in early twentieth-century German culture: *Künstler, Cowboys, Ingenieure: Kultur- und mediengeschichtliche Studien zu deutschen Amerika-Texten 1912–1920* (1998) as well as articles on migration, culture and cinema. As a translator from Turkish into German she co-edited an anthology of contemporary Turkish literature and translated novels by Aras Ören and Bilge Karasu. She is currently working on *The German Cinema Book* (BFI, co-edited with Tim Bergfelder and Erica Carter) and other book projects on 'Transnational Cinemas', 'Multicultural Germany' and 'Ethnic Role-Play in Immigrant Comedies'.

Kiki Kennedy-Day received her Ph.D. from New York University in Near Eastern Languages and Literatures, specializing in Arabic, in 1996. She focuses on medieval Islamic philosophy, and has a deep background in art, having travelled widely in the Middle East and Central Asia visiting Islamic monuments. She studied Arabic in Syria one summer, leaving her with an interest in Syrian culture. She has taught in New York City and Istanbul, Turkey. Currently she is working on a book about the history of Definition in Islamic Philosophy.

Oliver Leaman is a philosopher and cultural theorist with a longstanding interest in the Middle East. He is author of *Evil and Suffering in Jewish Philosophy* (1997), *Brief Introduction to Islamic Philosophy* (1999) and co-editor of *History of Islamic Philosophy* (1996) and *History of Jewish Philosophy* (1997). He was the co-editor of the Jewish philosophy section and the editor of the Islamic philosophy section in the *Routledge Encyclopedia of Philosophy*.

Hamid Naficy is a Professor of Film and Media Studies and Chair of the Department of Art and Art History at Rice University in Houston. He has published extensively about theories of exile and displacement; exilic and diasporic cultures, films and media; and Iranian, Middle Eastern, and Third World cinemas. His English language books are *An Accented Cinema: Exilic and Diasporic Filmmaking* (Princeton University Press, 2001), *Home, Exile, Homeland: Film, Media, and the Politics of Place* (edited, Routledge, 1999), *The Making of Exile Cultures: Iranian Television in Los Angeles* (University of Minnesota Press, 1993), *Otherness and the Media: the Ethnography of the Imagined and the Imaged* (co-edited, Harwood Academic, 1993), and Iran Media Index (Greenwood Press, 1984). He has also published extensively in Persian, including a two-volume book on the documentary cinema, *Film-e Mostanad* (free University of Iran Press, 1978–9). His forthcoming book is *Cinema and National Identity: A Social History of Iranian Cinema* (University of Texas Press). His works have been translated into many languages.

Judd Ne'eman is Associate Professor at the Department of Film and Television at Tel-Aviv University. He has produced and directed feature films and documentaries for cinema and television, among which are *Maasa Alunkot / Paratroopers* (1977); *Mered Hayamaim / Seamen's Strike* (1981); and, *Streets of Yesterday* (1989). Recent articles include: 'The Metallurgic War Machine in Schindler's List' (Hebrew); 'Fields of Dominant Fiction' (Hebrew); 'The Death Mask of the Moderns – A Genealogy of *New Sensibility* Cinema in Israel'; 'The Empty Tomb in the Postmodern Pyramid: Israeli Cinema in the 1980s and 1990s'; 'Jew and Arab Chronicles in the Israeli Cinema'. He is the co-editor of an anthology: *Fictive Looks – On Israeli Cinema*.

Viola Shafik, German-Egyptian film-maker and scholar, received her Ph.D. in Middle Eastern Studies at Hamburg University, teaches Cinema Studies at the American University in Cairo. She is the author of *Arab Cinema. History and Cultural Identity* (1998). She directed experimentals and documentaries, among others *The Lemon Tree* (1993) and *Planting of Girls* (1999).

Amal Sulayman Mahmoud al 'Ubaydi is Dean of the Faculty of Economics and Assistant Professor in the Department of Political Science, University of Garyounis, Benghazi, Libya.

Preface

I should like to thank my colleagues for having worked hard on producing what we hope will be a useful source of information about a variety of cinema which is not as well known outside the area as it ought to be. It was not an easy task to collect information on what was often little discussed in some of the countries we have included, and a lot of effort has been spent on trying to gain access to facts which are useful in throwing light on the topic. We have tried to be objective and not to allow our aesthetic and political preferences to distort the text. But of course we have had to select and that involves leaving many things out which are no doubt important, and we hope that readers will forgive us if they find that their favourite films have been omitted or little discussed.

The authors of each section are clearly indicated. I have edited all the sections, written some of the entries and helped translate the entry on Libya. I am also responsible for the preliminaries, the structure of the volume as a whole, the indices and the selection of the images, the latter with the assistance of the contributors, of course.

Oliver Leaman
April 2000

Introduction

The first question to be raised here is why some countries have been included and others excluded. The geographical area in the title is so vague that it is difficult to justify any such exclusions, but it was necessary to limit the coverage in order to make possible a degree of precision and focus in the treatment. We could have included Sudan, Somalia, Chad and so on, but had we done so there would have been arguments for extending coverage to many other North African countries, and then we would have been entering what has tended to be referred to in the literature as specifically 'African' cinema. By contrast, what we have referred to here as the 'Middle East' has been interpreted quite widely to extend to Iran and Turkey, and even further to Central Asia. In many ways the cultural background of Central Asia is far more closely linked with the former Soviet Union, of which it was until quite recently a part. On the other hand, the cultural and linguistic ties between Central Asia, on the one hand, and Turkey on the other made it reasonable to include Central Asia in this volume.

There is no attempt here to argue that there is any essential core to the different traditions of film which have been included here. It is always tempting to try to find some idea around which a whole variety of cinema is constructed, but this is not feasible. Readers will be interested to find that the histories of film in all these different regions are often very distinct. Of course, there are degrees of resemblance on occasion, but there are no useful generalizations which can be drawn to cover the whole area. What is understood as a constant presence in many of the treatments here is the significance of film as part of popular culture. For example, it is interesting how the Egyptian film industry, so dominant for so long in the Arab world, should have for a time succumbed to the pressures of satellite television and video; yet lately there has been something of a revival of interest in Egyptian films of an earlier time through the growth of video and retrospectives on television. To go to Iran, another country with a very strong film tradition, it is intriguing that the reforming President Khatami should have done so much to foster the modern Iranian cinema during his period in charge of cultural affairs, at a time when to act in this way was regarded as provocative by the more conservative religious forces. The cinema is the perfect vehicle for a gentle widening of the options offered by the state, since it seems both of little political significance and yet capable of making surreptitious announcements of independence from local political restrictions. Those who would argue that film is an insignificant cultural force clearly know little of the Middle East. In the two years before the 1979 revolution in Iran, for instance, there were numerous attacks on cinemas, which were regarded as representatives of Western and hence Pahlavi values;

after the revolution the number of cinemas in the country almost halved. To give another example, many films produced in Israel have adopted a critical attitude to Zionist ideology, representing ironically the clichés in earlier and more ingenuous cultural products.

Having claimed that there is no common factor in the traditions of film-making in this region, I should like to point to one factor that might come close to serving as such a common factor. This lies in the ways in which film has advanced the acceptability of the colloquial languages and idioms of the area. There are often vast inequalities in the region between levels of income and education, and the formal kinds of language which are used in high culture can be very different from those in general use. Film also allows for the representation of 'ordinary' ways of life, which has no doubt been the source of much of its popularity. It is difficult to explain to a Westerner the gasp of admiration and surprise from an audience in the Middle East in reaction to films that represent ordinary forms of life and speech. This is hardly surprising in what is after all popular culture, but for many in the Middle East and North Africa even popular culture is quite distant from the general population in both form and content, yet with film the audience is invited to identify with what is portrayed. It is this emphasis on the ordinary that has led some Iranian and Turkish films to become popular in the West, along with the desire (perhaps influenced by orientalism) to portray the exotic and the 'other'. How films from the area are viewed outside the area is an interesting issue, but not one dealt with here except in so far as communities from the Middle East and North Africa now live outside the region and work in film there. Another interesting issue is how the Middle East and North Africa are represented in films made outside the area, and there is a growing campaign (especially in the United States) to try to challenge the stereotype of the Arab and Iranian as terrorist and/or criminal. We do not touch on these issues in this volume. The concentration here is entirely on how film in the Middle East and North Africa sees itself. The aim is to present an account of this important area of film-making as much from within as we could. I hope that readers will find this as fascinating a topic as we obviously do.

How to use this book

The book is organized in terms of areas, and topics are discussed within the context of those areas. Film names are in *italics*; the names of directors, actors and others involved in the cinema are to be found in the Index of Names; the titles of films are to be found in the Index of Films.

Transliteration

Many of the films in this volume have Arabic titles and these have not been presented here in line with any consistent form of transliteration. This is because in many of the existing works of reference and the magazines which refer to these films, a whole variety of forms of transliteration is used; it was felt to be better to use a system in this book that comes closer to that used in other texts, rather than one according with a consistent system that is to be found nowhere else. I have tried to use a system which gives some indication of pronunciation.

Films from the Francophone Maghreb tend to use French forms of transliteration, which I have sometimes altered to make it easier for English readers to pronounce. So, for example, I have represented 'ch' with 'sh' (that is, *Weshma* as well as *Wechma*). I have not done this for names of people or for French spellings of the titles of films.

The letter hamza is generally represented by ', the letter ayn by '.

No effort has been made to distinguish between alef and ayin in Hebrew.

The pronunciation 'ch' in Persian is roughly similar to the English and is distinguished from 'sh'.

Turkish is presented in its full form, since it is now written in Roman characters.

Acknowledgements

All illustrations have been provided by the general editor and the contributors with the exception of the following. We are indebted to those listed below for permission to reproduce these photographs.

Many thanks to the Plato Film Production Co. for permission to reprint the still from *Propaganda*.

Many thanks to the Filmdirector's Guild of Azerbaijan for permission to reprint the still from *In A Southern City*.

Many thanks to IIan Moshenson for permission to reprint the stills from *The Wooden Gun*.

Many thanks to Misr International Films for permission to reprint the stills from *The Earth, Alexandria Why?*, *Alexandria Now and Forever*, *Mortal Revenge* and *Son of the Nile*.

Every effort has been made to trace copyright holders but if you have any queries please contact Routledge. Any omissions brought to our attention will be remedied in future editions.

Central Asian cinema

Gönul Dönmez-Colin

Central Asia's first known screening was in 1897 in Tashkent, the capital of Uzbekistan. The first documentaries were shot in Uzbekistan in 1920, in Kazakhstan in 1925 and in Tajikistan in 1929. Studios were first established and feature films first made in Uzbekistan in 1925, in Tajikistan and Turkmenistan between 1931 and 1932, in Kazakhstan in 1938 and in Kyrgyzstan in 1955.

From the time cinema was nationalized in 1919 by a Lenin decree, film production and distribution had been regulated by a government institution, the State Committee for Cinematography (Goskino), which gradually gained control over the film industry.

The majority of the films of the early period were didactic and directly linked to the problems of the times. The struggles against the rulers, landowners and religious traditions, and for women's freedom, were some of the predominant themes explored using cheap orientalism, Asian folklore, parades and, when sound became possible, oriental music. The language used was Russian.

World War II played an important role in the relocation of most studios to Alma Ata and Tashkent. The end of 1950s and the beginning of 1960s proved crucial for Central Asia, as for the rest of the USSR. A new generation of film-makers arrived in a climate that saw the dismantling of the ideological principles of Stalinism. However, a truly nationalist fervour did not manifest itself before 1960.

In 1986, the Fifth Congress of Soviet Film-makers challenged the lawlessness of the methods used by the bureaucracy to control the arts and proposed the principles of the free market as an alternative. It also undertook the responsibility of defending non-commercial, *auteur* cinema. The Soviet Film-makers' Union announced the end of Goskino's hegemony over the film industry and its intention of introducing new, independent economic and cultural policies. The real base of power gradually shifted from Goskino offices to the studios, now run by the film-makers themselves.

In the first phase of *perestroika* (1986–7), the newly created Conflict Committee released hundreds of films banned by the censors. The second phase (1988–90) eliminated censorship and the monopoly of the state altogether. Independent studios and co-operative film companies began to mushroom everywhere. The overall annual production tripled, despite the sharp increase in the number of films imported from the West, the video black market and a general loss of public interest in cinema.

A new horizon was opened up for young film-makers of Central Asia, most of whom were trained in VGIK (Vserossiyski Gosudarstvenny Institut Kinematografii – the All-Union State Institute of Cinematography) in Moscow and shared the same concerns and difficulties – such as the conservatism of their respective local authorities, poor equipment and inadequate working conditions. Despite the diversity of their backgrounds, they converged on a common film language. Abandoning the epic tradition and orientalism for a more Western outlook, they tried to develop a sociological and psychological approach in the treatment of their characters, as well as in reflecting their destabilized cultural roots. Subject matter was diverse, but fashionable themes (such as purging of the Stalinist past, sex and violence in youth subcultures) or obscure avant-garde narratives were deliberately avoided. Natural décor and non-professional actors were favoured. Native languages were employed instead of Russian.

Following independence, social, economic and ethnic turmoil swept all of the former republics – except perhaps Kazakhstan, whose capital Alma Ata (Almaty) had become the largest film centre of the USSR after Moscow, Leningrad (St Petersburg) and Kiev. Under the liberal policies of President Nursultan Nazarbayev, the country moved to a free-market economy faster than Russia, and banks and co-operatives did not miss the opportunity to publicize themselves through high-profile investments, which included investment in cinema. However, private capital soon lost interest when investments did not show the expected profit. In the old regime, films were made according to formulas dictated by Moscow, but Moscow supplied the finance and took charge of distribution; today state studios are not able to function due to lack of funds and film production has fallen considerably throughout the Commonwealth of Independent States (CIS). Many film-makers have settled in Moscow or abroad, others are in search of co-productions, while still others are trying to push the limits of their disadvantageous circumstances.

Women directors

It is still difficult to compete with men in the Muslim states. Kazakh Roza Orynbasarova, after her successful debut with *Jhertva Dlya Imperatora / Sacrifice for the Emperor*, moved to St Petersburg. So did Kyrgyz Dinar Asanova, whose *Klyuch Bez Prava Peredachi / The Non-Transferable Key* and *Patsani* were very popular in the 1970s. Tajik film-makers Margarita Kassymova, Maryam Yusupova and Gulbakhor Mirzoeva, who all began as documentarists, have moved to greener pastures. Kamara Kamalova continues to work successfully in Uzbekistan.

AZERBAIJAN

Cinema had a relatively early start in Azerbaijan. Projections began in Baku three years after Paris. The first film – *V Tzarstve Nefti i Millionov / In the Kingdom of Oil and Millions* in two episodes by Boris Svetlov (based on a work by Ibrahim Bek-Musabekov) – was made in 1916. Popular folk operas, such as Svetlov's *Archin Mal Alan / The Cloth Peddler* (1917), soon found their way onto the screen. In the 1945 version, which was the first film realized after the war, Rza Takhmassib and Nicolas Lechenko painted a very exotic city with narrow alleys and a bustling bazaar as the background for intrigues of love.

Mavi Danizin Sahilinda / On the Shores of the Blue Sea (1935), the first Azeri talkie, was shot by Russian Boris Barnet and Azeri Samed Mardanov. Armenian Amo Bek-Nazarov was a link among the Transcaucasian Republics: *The House on the Volcano* which he shot in Baku in 1929 is considered to be one of the first Azeri films on the multinational proletariat of the city at that time. With the fervour of revolution, such collaborations were quite common and undoubtedly beneficial to the formation of young film-makers such as Samed Mardanov, who made *Kandlilar / The Peasants* (1939) – a propaganda film about the peasant revolt of 1919 – using a new cinematographic language, evidently influenced by Eisenstein.

Political jargon became increasingly pronounced in the 1950s, as in *Bir Mahallali Iki Oglan / Two Boys from the Same District* (1957) by Ajdar Ibraguimov (scenario by Nazim Hikmet), but gave way to the dramatic films of the 1960s. *Bir Djanoub Sharinda / In a Southern City* (1969) by Eldar Guliev was a turning point, marking the change from the earlier comedy musicals and propaganda-laden *kolkhoz* (collective farm) stories. These new endeavours had serious difficulties with censorship.

With the emergence of good screenwriters, such as Rustam Ibrahimbekov (*Bir Djanoub Sharinda*), the themes of identity crises, conflict between the old and new orders, and social evils such as the mafia and corruption began to find their way into the films, as evidenced by *Hamyerli / The Fellow Countryman* (1987) by Valeri Kerimov and *Sud Dichinin Agrisi / The Pain of a Baby Tooth* (1988) by Gussein Mekhtiyev.

Following a period of typical *perestroika* films, almost all production stopped when the newly independent Azerbaijan cut all ties with Moscow. Seven years of war with Armenia left the country in an economic shambles. Film-makers of the new generation are now free to express their opinions, but private sources are reluctant to invest in unknown talents. Ayaz Salayev's *Yarasa / The Bat* (1995) was the first independently produced film to come out of Azerbaijan. The government began financing projects from 1994, but this has not been enough. A further problem is how to give

Figure 1 Bir Djanoub Sharinda / In a Southern City

future film-makers the sound education that was provided by Moscow in the old regime. Baku's seventeen cinemas (and the seventy of the whole republic) mostly show Hollywood films. There is also a video market. For the majority of the population, television is the most popular form of entertainment.

Filmography

Bir Djanoub Sharinda / In a Southern City

1969, 75 mins, black and white, Russian
Director:	Eldar Guliev
Producer:	Azerbaijanfilm
Screenwriter:	Rustam Ibrahimbekov
Cinematographer:	Rassim Odjagov
Editor:	Tamara Narimanbekova
Music:	Faradj Garaev
Sound:	Vladimir Savine
Leading Players:	Gassan Mamedov, Eldaniz Zeinalov, Gadji Mourad, Malik Dadachev

A young man is caught between the lifestyle of a big industrial city and the patriarchal ways of a provincial suburb, in this drama about friendship and betrayal.

Gumuchvari Furgon / The Silver Truck

1982, 61 mins, colour, Russian
Director:	Oktay Mirkassimov
Producer:	Azerbaijanfilm
Screenwriter:	Eltchin
Cinematographer:	Alesker Alekperov
Music:	Rafik Babev
Leading Players:	Gamida Omarova, Mamed Mamedov

A young woman, mentally strong despite marital problems and barrenness, makes carpets to express her feelings. One day, she meets a man working in the circus. He gradually helps her to improve her relationship with her husband and the carpets she creates.

Mavi Danizin Sahilinda / On the Shores of the Blue Sea

1935, 67 mins, black and white, Russian
Director:	Boris Barnet, Samed Mardanov
Producer:	Azerfilm, Mejrabpomfilm
Screenwriter:	Klimenti Mintz
Cinematographer:	Mihail Kirilov, M. Mustafaev
Music:	Niyazi
Leading Players:	Nicolai Krutchkov, Lev Sverdine, Elena Kouzmina

Story of unrequited love of two shipwrecked comrades, the blond Aliocha and the dark Youssouf, for beautiful Masha, the head of the 'Fires of Communism' *kolkhoz*, who loves yet another. The film renders blatant propaganda with delightful naïvety.

Yarasa / The Bat

1995, 87 mins, black and white / colour, Azeri

Director:	Ayaz Salayev
Producer:	Akhmedov, Inter-Turan
Screenwriter:	Kamal Aslanov, Ayaz Salayev
Cinematographer:	Baguir Rafiyev
Editor:	Rafiga Ibragimova
Music:	Nazim Mirichli
Sound:	Teimour Abdoullayev
Leading Players:	Mariya Lipkina, Rassim Balayev, Tolib Khamidov

A young woman is shot in a theatre while she is absently watching a film on which she finds herself reflected. An allegorical reflection on art and life, the film alludes to death in film (as subject), death through film (as theme) and the death of film (as idea), with the bat symbolizing blindness caused by exposure to too much light / beauty.

List of directors

Babayev, Arif (1928–83); Guliev, Djamil (1963–); Guliev, Eldar (1941–); Ibraguimov, Ajdar (1919–93); Kerimov, Valeri (1945); Mardanov, Samed (1911–39); Mekhtiyev, Gussein (1945–); Mirkassimov, Oktay (1943–); Odjagov, Rassim (1933–); Salayev, Ayaz (1960–); Seidbeyli, Gassan (1920–80); Takhmassib, Rza (1894–1980)

Major director

Guliev (Kuliev), Eldar (b. 1941, Baku, Azerbaijan)

Guliev won fame working in several film studios in the USSR, as well as in former Czechoslovakia. He explored the theme of old and new values in *Bir Djanoub Sharinda / In a Southern City* (1969) and *A Scoundrel* (1988), and made documentaries about recent events in Azerbaijan.

Selected feature films: *Bir Djanoub Sharinda / In a Southern City* (1969); *Esas Gorusma / The Main Interview* (1971); *Schastya vam Devochki! / Girls, the Happiness is for You!* (1972); *Babek* (1979); *Nizami* (1982); *Gumus Gol Efsanesi / A Legend of Silver Lake* (1984); *Vatana Yuruyus / A Stroll Outside the City* (1986); *A Scoundrel* (1988); *Sapma / Diversion* (1989)

KAZAKHSTAN

The origins of the Kazakh Film Studios go back to the 1930s. The first documentary was released in 1929, under the historical title *Pribytie Pervovo Poezda v Alma Atu / The Arrival of the First Train in Alma Ata*, followed by Victor Turin's *Turksib / Stalnoi Put / The Steel Road: On the Building of the Turkish–Siberian Railway* (also 1929). A documentary film studio was set up in 1934, where newsreels under the title *Soviet Kazakhstan*, documentaries and a few feature films began to be made. During the war, Mosfilm and Lenfilm were evacuated to Alma Ata and a centralized studio was set up (1941). This was merged with the documentary studio after the war and came to be known as Kazakhfilm. Sergei Eisenstein shot two parts of *Ivan Grozyj / Ivan the Terrible* there between 1943 and 1945. *Djamboul* (1952), by Efim Dzigan, was the first Kazakh film in colour. Until *perestroika*, most Kazakh films were propaganda pieces, historical dramas stressing Communist views or love stories with predictable endings.

Well-known Russian film-maker, Sergei Solovyov, organized a workshop at VGIK in 1984 with promising Kazakh talent such as Rachid Nugmanov, Serik Aprimov, Ardal Amirkulov, Amanjol Aituarov, Talgat Temenov and Darejan Omirbaev. The collective effort of the workshop, *Belij Golub / The White Pigeon*, was awarded the Special Prize of the Jury in the 1985 Venice Film Festival. Nugmanov's diploma film, *Ya-Ha* (1986), became an underground cult classic that foreshadowed the 'new wave' of Kazakh cinema. With his first feature, *Igla / The Needle* (1988), which dealt with drug addiction, Nugmanov emerged as the aesthetic voice of a counter-culture. Omirbaev's short film *Letnaya Zhara / The Summer Heat* (1988) laid down the model for Kazakh 'new wave', balancing the feature-film and documentary modes.

Most post-independence films reflect an innate pessimism about the future. Talgat Temenov's *Byegushaya Mishen / The Running Target* (1991), Bolat Kalimbetov's *Ainalayin / Darling* (1991) and all of Darejan Omirbaev's films are pessimistic portraits of youth who are victims of the times they live in.

Filmography

Ainalayin / Darling

1991, 72 mins, colour, Kazakh
Director: Bolat Kalimbetov
Producer: Kazakh TV, Kazakhfilm Studio
Screenwriter: Alisher Souleimenov
Cinematographer: Talgat Taishanov
Leading Players: Sana Zhetpisbaeva, Farkhad Saifullin, Erbulat Ospankulov

Adolescents try to grow up in a society that has turned into a desert. Their teacher is a cynical drunk. Military planes violate the tranquillity of their village. Lake Aral is drying up. The loss of a culture and a civilisation is effectively symbolized by a scene in which the lovers sit inside the skeleton of a rusted truck and discuss life and death.

Figure 2 Amanjol Aituarov's *Kanchu Ikial / The Light Touch*: the 'new wave' of Kazakh cinema

Kairat

1991, 72 mins, black and white, Russian
Director / Screenwriter: Darejan Omirbaev
Producer: TO 'Alem' Kazakhfilm Studio
Cinematographer: Aoubakir Souleiev
Leading Players: Kairat Makhmedov, Indira Geksembaeva

In this psychological love story a young man, Kairat, is caught cheating during the
university entrance examinations and loses his chance of a better life. The girl he loves
chooses another. He is beaten up by a lout, whom he has masochistically provoked.
He dreams of death.

Kardiogramma / Heartbeats

1995, 73 mins, colour, Russian
Director / Screenwriter: Darejan Omirbaev
Producer: Kazakhfilm Studio
Cinematographer: Boris Troshev
Editor: Rima Beljakova
Sound: Andrei Vlaznev
Leading Players: Jasulan Asauov, Saule Toktybaeva, Gulnara Dusmatova

Figure 3 Byegushaya Mishen / The Running Target

The problems faced by linguistic minorities are portrayed through the experiences of a monolingual Kazakh boy from the country. He is sent to spend a month in a sanatorium in the capital where the majority speak Russian.

Poslednie Kanikuli / Last Holiday

1996, 65 mins, colour, Russian
Director:	Amir Karakulov, Shinju Sano
Producer:	Studio 'D', Almaty
Screenwriter:	Amir Karakulov, Elena Gordeeva
Cinematographer:	Murat Nugmanov
Editor:	Yuliya Nilovaya
Sound:	Andrey Vlaznev
Leading Players:	Sanzhar Iskakov, Shalva Gogoladze, Anatoly Gapchuk

Kazakh Karim, Jewish Jacob and Russian Valera are classmates. Things take a bad turn when they steal an electric guitar from the bar of a famous Soviet skating rink. Valera's stepfather informs on him and he is badly beaten up by the police. The only medicine his friends can find to ease his pain comes from drug dealers.

Qijan | Konetschnaja Ostanowka | The Last Stop

1989, 77 mins, colour, Kazakh
Director / Screenwriter: Serik Aprimov
Producer: Kazakhfilm Studios
Cinematographer: Murat Nugmanov
Designer: Sabit Kurmanbekov
Leading Players: Sabit Kurmanbekov, Murat Akhmetov, Nagimbek Samayev

Erken returns to his native village after military service and becomes aware of the pitiful lives of the people he loves. He decides to leave the steppes forever. In seemingly random episodes, fragments of daily rural life are presented with documentary-style realism that borders on the surreal.

List of directors

Aituarov, Amanjol (1957–); Amirkulov, Ardak (1955–); Aprimov, Serik (1960–); Bolisbaev, Yedigue (1950–); Kalimbetov, Bolat (1955–); Karakulov, Amir (1965–); Nugmanov, Rachid (1954–); Omirbaev, Darejan (1958–); Shinarbayev, Ermek (1953–); Suleimenov, Timor (1959–); Temenov, Talgat (1954–)

Major directors

Karakulov, Amir (b. 1965, Alma Ata, Kazakhstan)

Karakulov's first film, *Razlouchnitsa | Woman Between Two Brothers* (1991), was based on a Jorge Luis Borges story applied to contemporary Kazakh life. The almost non-existent dialogue accentuated the personal isolation of the characters, caught in a love triangle. His second film, *Golubinyi Zvonar | The Dove's Bell-Ringer* (1994), was a reflection on the precarious nature of happiness as manifested through the personal tragedy experienced by the protagonist. His third feature, *Poslednie Kanikuli | Last Holiday* (1996), drew a non-judgemental and compassionate portrait of youth in Kazakhstan.

   Karakulov's simple, unpretentious films run like a visual dialogue in which images let the imagination work out what is left unsaid. He is often compared to Robert Bresson.

Selected feature films: *Razlouchnitsa | Woman Between Two Brothers* (1991); *Golubinyi Zvonar | The Dove's Bell-Ringer* (1994); *Poslednie Kanikuli | Last Holiday* (1996)

Nugmanov, Rachid (b. 1954, Alma Ata, Kazakhstan)

Leader of the Kazakh 'new wave', Nugmanov's diploma film *Ya-Ha* (1986) was a kaleidoscopic diary of the underground rock scene in Leningrad just before *perestroika*. His first feature, *Igla | The Needle* (1988), alternately burlesqued, embraced and rejected the conventions of the thriller genre. *Diki Vostok | The Wild East* (1993), which is reminiscent of John Ford westerns, was shot just as the Soviet empire was collapsing. Nugmanov now lives in France.

Selected feature films: *Igla* / *The Needle* (1988); *Diki Vostok* / *The Wild East* (1993)

Omirbaev, Darejan (b. 1958)

Omirbaev's first feature film *Kairat* (1991), about the irrationality of existence and the impact of unforeseeable events on one's inner life, was inspired by Kafka's *Castle* and won him the Silver Leopard at the Locarno Film Festival in 1992. *Kardiogramma* / *Heartbeat* (1995) depicted the pains of adolescence and the adolescent sense of total isolation with remarkable insight. His latest film, *Tueur à gages* / *The Killer* (1998), a co-production with France, is a realistic depiction of contemporary life in Kazakhstan.

Selected feature films: *Kairat* (1991); *Kardiogramma* / *Heartbeat* (1995); *Tueur à gages* / *The Killer* (1998)

Shinarbayev, Ermek (b. 1953, Alma Ata, Kazakhstan)

Shinarbayev's diploma film, *Karalisulu* / *A Beauty in Mourning* (1982), was a psychological drama about a young nomad widow. Its allusions to female sexual urges caused a scandal. He collaborated with the Korean novelist Anatoly Kim for both his first feature film, *Sestra Moia Liussia* / *My Sister Lucy* (1985), the story of a friendship between a Kazakh and a Russian woman, and in *Meist* / *Revenge* (1989), a multi-layered film epic about the tragedy of Koreans living in the Soviet Union. His fourth feature, *Azghyin Ushtykzyn' Azaby* / *The Place on the Tricone* (1993), was a psychological portrayal of youth in the former Soviet Union.

Selected feature films: *Sestra Moia Liussia* / *My Sister Lucy* (1985); *Meist* / *Revenge* (a.k.a. *The Reed Flute*) (1989); *Azghyin Ushtykzyn' Azaby* / *The Place on the Tricone* (1993)

Temenov, Talgat (b. 1954, Kazakhstan)

A former actor, Temenov's short film, *Toro* (1986), was praised internationally as a classic of Kazakh cinema in the style of Italian neo-realism. *Volchono Sredi Lyudei* / *A Wolf Cub among Men* (1988), a children's film focusing on the crisis of values in times of social and economic difficulties, narrated the friendship between two outcasts: a boy and a wolf cub. *Byegushaya Mishen* / *The Running Target* (1991) chronicled the aftermath of the bloody 1986 demonstrations in Alma Ata through a story of friendship between a hunted adolescent and a persecuted German woman (magnificently played by the Russian actress Nonna Mordjukova of *The Commissar* fame).

Selected feature films: *Volchono Sredi Lyudei* / *A Wolf Cub among Men* (1988); *Byegushaya Mishen* / *The Running Target* (1991)

Figure 4   Meist / Revenge (a.k.a. *The Reed Flute*)

KYRGYZSTAN

Film production began late in Kyrgyzstan. Kyrgyzfilm Studio was founded in 1942, but only got its name in 1961. During and immediately after the war, standardized documentaries were made. Important film-makers like Tolomush Okeev and Bolotbek Shamshiev began their careers in documentary. Between 1954 and 1960, Mosfilm Studios sent many film-makers to Kyrgyzstan: Vasili Pronin's *Saltanat / Sovereignty* (1955), for example, was produced there. Others from neighbouring countries with more developed cinema also arrived, which did not give Kyrgyz cinema a chance to develop its own identity.

Although *perestroika* arrived actively and in a democratic way, the road to a market economy proved to be difficult.

The Kyrgyz miracle of creation of a national cinema is attributed to Shamshiev and Okeev, whose protagonists are common men with everyday joys and sorrows. Another important figure is writer Chingiz Aitmatov. Many of his books were made into films and he often collaborated in writing the scripts.

A new generation of Kyrgyz directors is emerging, dealing with the problems of youth trying to break away from tradition. *Beshkempir / The Adopted Son* (1998) by Aktan Abdykalykov, a co-production with France, discusses the dramatic effects on a young village boy of the ancient custom of offering babies from large families to childless couples.

Filmography

Bakajdyn Zajyty / The Sky of Our Childhood

1967, 78 mins, black and white, Russian
Director: Tolomush Okeev
Producer: Kyrgyzfilm
Screenwriter: Kadir Omurkulov, Tolomush Okeev
Cinematographer: Kadircan Kidiraliev
Music: Tashtan Ermatov
Leading Players: Aliman Cankorozava, Muratbek Riskulov, Nasret Dubashev

An old groom's children have deserted their home for the big city. He tries to teach his youngest son how to herd horses to hold him back. But there is a new road being built.

Belyi Parakhod / Ak Keme / The White Ship

1975, 102 mins, colour, Russian
Director / Screenwriter: Bolotbek Shamshiev
Producer: Kyrgyzfilm
Cinematographer: Manasbek Moussaev
Music: Alfred Chnitke
Leading Players: Nourgazy Sydygalieva, Sabira Koumouchalieva, Orozbek Koutmanaliev

Figure 5   Beshkempir / The Adopted Son

In this adaptation from a Chingiz Aitmatov novel of the same name, a shepherd boy dreams of a white ship on the lake Issyk-Koul.

Boranly Beket / Snowstormy Station

1995, 90 mins, colour, Kyrgyz
Director: Bakyt Karagulov
Producer: Kyrgyz National Fuel Company, Katarsis
Executive Producer: Talat Kulmendeev
Screenwriter: Chingiz Aitmatov, Marat Sarulu
Leading Players: Kauken Kenshetaev, Abdrashit Abdrakamanov, Gulshara Ashibekova, Gulzinat Omarova, Ersaim Golobaev

Two former fishermen from the Aral Lake had spent World War II at a remote railway station in the steppes. When one of them dies, Soviet guards do not allow the other to bury him according to ancient Islamic rites and at a place sacred to Kazakhs that is now a military rocket-testing zone. Memories of his friend, a teacher and partisan who was persecuted during the Stalin era for the diaries he kept, haunt the hero. In his mind, he links the period of Soviet totalitarianism, which had threatened cultural and ethnic identity, with the Mankurts who, in ancient times, robbed conquerors of their memory by means of torture. Based on Aitmatov's novel, *The Day that is Longer than the Century*.

List of directors

Asanova, Dinara (1942–); Bazarov, Gennady (1942–); Karagulov, Bakyt (1950–); Kydyraliev, Kadyrjan (1936–); Okeev, Tolomush (1935–); Shamshiev, Bolotbek (1941–); Ubekeyev, Melis (1935–)

Major directors

Okeev, Tolomush (b. 1935, Bokonbaevo, Kyrgyzstan)

Okeev worked as sound engineer, scriptwriter and actor, staged plays and made documentaries, before becoming a feature-film-maker in 1965. A deputy and an ambassador, he is also the founder of Future, the private company that realized the multi-national super-production *Cenghiz Khan* (1991).

Selected feature films: *Bakajdyn Zajyty / The Sky of Our Childhood* (1967); *Al Alma / Red Apple* (1975); *Oulan / Ulan* (1977); *Altin Guz / Golden Autumn* (1980); *Potomok Belogo Barsa / The Descent of the White Leopard* (1984); *Cenghiz Khan* (1991)

Shamshiev, Bolotbek (b. 1941, Frunze, Kyrgyzstan)

An actor and a director, Shamshiev founded the co-operative Salamalek Film in 1990.

Selected feature films: *Karas-Karas Okujasy / Fireshots at Karach Pass* (1968); *Alye Maky Issik-Koulia / Red Poppies of Issyk-Koul* (1972); *Belyi Parakhod / Ak Keme / The White Ship* (1975); *Voshozdenie Na Fudzijamu / Ascent of Fujiyama* (1988)

TAJIKISTAN

The first film was made in Tajikistan by three Russian pioneers. It was about the arrival of the first train in the capital, Dushanbe, and was screened in November 1929. The first film studio, Tadjik Kino, was set up in 1930 to produce newsreels and films on collectivization. The newsreel *Soviet Tadjikistan* was started in 1935. The first significant feature film was *Pochetnoe Pravo / Honorary Right* (1934) by Kamil Yarmatov, dedicated to the Red Army. It mixed fiction and documentary, focusing on the period of collectivization when a 'middle' landowner ran away to Afghanistan but, unable to come to terms with the exploitative life there, returned to join a collective farm. The first talkie, *Syn Dzhigita / The Garden*, was made by Nikolai Dostal in 1939.

In the late 1930s, film-makers and actors were victimized. Production was negligible for nearly fifteen years. Only propagandist documentaries and newsreels were made. However, the late 1950s brought a new era with the Twentieth Party Congress' critique of the cult of personality. From 1965 onwards, new directors aimed at creating a new cinema – as had already been done in Georgia and Kyrgyzstan. Davlat Khudonazarov was the shining star of the period between 1965 and 1985.

With *perestroika* and the slackening of ideological controls, a variety of genres and styles began to be used to define an identity, to forge links with the past and to examine repressed cultural roots. Documentaries on Stalinist repression, on the plight of village women and on religion came to the fore. Feature films also began to take up similar themes: Anvar Turaev's *Bol Iyubvi / The Pain of Love* (1990) deals with Stalinist repression in the context of a collective farm.

Following independence, a civil war and economic crisis brought film-making to a halt. The Ministry of Culture, Press and Television, which is in charge of the film department, was left with no money. Private companies were left to seek sponsors at home and abroad, while many film-makers have emigrated.

Filmography

Bratan / Brothers

1990, 100 mins, colour / black and white, Russian
Director: Bakhtiyar Khudoynazarov
Producer: Tajikfilm, Soyuzfilm
Screenwriter: Leonid Mahkamov, Bakhtiyar Khudoynazarov
Cinematographer: Gheorgy Dzalaev
Editor: Tatyana Maltseva
Music: Ahmad Bakaev
Leading Players: Timur Tursonov, Firuz Sabzaliev

Bratan is a road movie with a number of heterogeneous characters. It brings together love, tenderness, solidarity, betrayal and sexual awakening on a long train journey through the stunning landscape of the Pamir Mountains.

Mavsimi Alafkhoi Zard / *Times of Yellow Grass*

1991, 65 mins, colour, Russian
Director: Maryam Yusupova
Producer: Tajikfilm, TPO, Soyuztelefilm
Screenwriter: Aleksei Katounine, David Tchoubinichvili, Saif Rakhimov
Cinematographer: Okil Khamidov
Music: Pavel Toursounov
Leading Players: Roland   Makarov,   Bobadjan   Kassadov,   Cherali
                             Abdoulkaissov

The people of a small village in the Pamir mountains are tired of the hardships of daily life. The day a dead body is found near the village is a cathartic event, revealing the diversity of characters, mentalities, traditions and morals of the village people. The film was shot on the eve of civil war.

List of directors

Aripov, Marat (1935–); Hamidov, Suvat (1939–); Khudoynazarov, Davlat; Khudoynazarov, Bakhtiyar (1965–); Kimjagarov, Boris (1979–); Mahmudov, Mukadas (1926–); Rahimov, Abdusalom (1917–); Sabirov, Tahir (1929–); Sadykov, Bako; Turaev, Anvar (1934–); Yusupova, Maryam (1949–)

Major director

Khudoynazarov, Bakhtiyar (b. 1965, Dushanbe, Tajikistan)

Scriptwriter, director and producer, Khudoynazarov came into the limelight with *Bratan* / *Brothers* (1990), a fresh approach in its choice of non-professional actors and an improvised style, owing much to Italian neo-realism. *Kosh Ba Kosh* / *We Are Quits* (1993), a fragmented story of a love affair set in a city divided by civil war, also used improvisation and authentic locations, giving it the realistic qualities of a documentary.

Selected feature films: *Verish Nje Verish* / *Believe It or Not* (1989); *Bratan* / *Brothers* (1990); *Kosh Ba Kosh* / *We Are Quits* (1993); *Luna Papa* (1999)

TURKMENISTAN

In Turkmenistan, cinemas began with newsreels. Elections, the inauguration of a monument to Lenin and the anniversary of the Revolution were the events that were filmed by the first chroniclers in the 1920s, followed by a number of educational films like *Sholk* / *Silk*, *Khlopok* / *Cotton* and *Karakul*.

The first fiction film was made by A. Vladycuk in 1929 (*White Gold*). Yuli Raizman made *Zemlya Zhazhdyot* / *The Earth is Thirsty* for Vostok-kino in 1930: the first version was silent, but a few months later it was given a soundtrack and presented to the public. During World War II, the Kiev Studio was evacuated to Ashkabad where war 'notebooks' were made. An earthquake destroyed the studio in 1948. In the post-war period, documentaries were made reflecting the main themes of socialist reconstruction, the reclaiming of the desert, the construction of the Karakum Canal and the new freedom of Eastern women. Turkmen cinema reached its peak in the 1960s and 1970s; the most renowned Turkmen director, Khodzakuli Narliev, releasing his best film, *Nevestka* / *The Daugher-in-Law*, in 1972.

Following government regulations, all Turkmen films are now made in the Turkmenian language, even though half of the country speaks Russian. Sergei Shugarev broke the tradition and introduced a Russian voice-over in *Ham Hyyal* / *Aromat Dzhelany* / *Fragrance of Wishes* (1996) – a film that drew attention, despite its obvious technical flaws, not only with its fresh perception of the world, but also with its refined depiction of events.

There is a tradition of children's films. Usman Saparov's *Angelotchek Sdelai Radost* / *Little Angel, Make Me Happy* (1992) received the most prestigious award in the children's category at the Berlin Film Festival in 1993.

How is it possible to produce films in Turkmenistan, where the Communist regime still seems to be preserved? Although the government has promised to finance five art films each year, as was the case in Soviet times, many good film-makers – from Narliev to Shugarev – have found themselves in conflict with the present regime.

Filmography

Yandim / *The Soul is Burnt Out*

1995, 75 mins, colour, Turkmenian
Director:	Bairam Abdullaev, Laura Stepanskaya
Producer:	State Cinema Viceo Co. of Turkmennistan, Turkmenfilm
Screenwriter:	Bairam Abdullaev, Laura Stepanskaya
Cinematographer:	Vladimir Spariskhov
Music:	Aman Agajikov
Sound:	Chali Annachalov
Leading Players:	Aman Channdurdiev, Aguljan Nijazberdieva, Artik Jalliev

Two brothers who live in Turkmenistan at the time of the Soviet Union have very different attitudes towards life and ways of behaving: one is a loyal supporter of the Soviet Union, the other – Sadik – questions everything. What does it mean and what does it take to be a human being? How can you remain loyal to your principles and not lose faith in the meaning of life? Before his death, Sadik contemplates the events of his life. Why have he and his brother chosen such different paths in life? Where did he go wrong? Did he choose the right path or could he have acted differently?

Yashlygymyn Destany / Destan Mojej Junosti / Legend of My Youth

1992, 70 mins, colour, Russian
Director: Biul-Biul Mamedov
Producer: Turkmenfilm, IO 'Ecran'
Screenwriter: Biul-Biul Mamedov, V. Lobanov
Cinematographer: Bayram Kovusov
Music: Redjep Redjepov
Designer: Ada Kutliev
Leading Players: Bairam Koboussov, Baba Annanov, Iusup Kuliev, Indira
                                        Quseinova

In the late 1930s, Maskat, a Red Army soldier, is in love with Ainabat, Achir's young wife. Achir is Maskat's class enemy. The young man's good-heartedness is troubled by the hate he feels for his rival. Intolerance mingles with a struggle for love which turns into a tragedy that Maskat is obsessed by for the rest of his life.

List of directors

Narliev, Khodzakuli (1937–); Mamedov, Biul-Biul (1950–); Saparov, Usman (1938–); Shugarev, Sergei

Major director

Narliev, Khodzakuli (b. 1937, in railway station no. 30, near Ashkhabad, Turkmenistan)

A public figure and artist, Narliev started to work in Turkmenfilm Studios as a cameraman for Bulat Mansurov. His first feature, *Nevestka / Daughter-in-Law* (1972) – the story of a young woman who is waiting for her missing husband – was a study in suffering, dignity and devotion in a harsh, inhospitable terrain. The fight of the new against the old in the field of morals, the value of a human life and the triumph of spirituality are some of Narliev's recurring themes, the motif of water playing an important role.

Selected feature films: *Nevestka / Daughter-in-Law* (1972); *You Must Dare to Say No!* (1977); *Derevo Dzamal / Jamal Tree* (1981); *Mankurt / Manwolf* (a.k.a. *Bird-Memory*) (1990)

UZBEKISTAN

The first Uzbek documentary was made in 1923. With the establishment of Boukhino, first feature films – *Pakhta-Aral / Pahta Aral* (N. Scerbakov), *Minaret Smerti / The Minaret of the Dead* (Viatcheslav Viskovski) and *The Muslim Woman* (Dimitri Bassaligo) – were realized in 1925. The following year, a big mosque was transformed into a studio.

Nabi Ganiev and Kamil Yarmatov are considered to be the founders of Uzbek

Figure 6   Yashlygymyn Destany / Legend of My Youth

cinema. Social and political issues gained importance with committed film-makers such as Ganiev and Soleiman Khodjaev. The latter's silent film, *Tong Oldidan / Before Sunrise* (1933) – which evoked the spontaneous rising of Central Asian workers against the Tsarist mobilization in 1916 – was his first and last, as it sent him to the gulag where he perished.

Sound appeared in 1937. During World War II, Russians came to Tashkent to realize their films, which resulted in very few prominently Uzbek films being produced. Post-war films were propaganda. For a long time, Uzbek cinema alienated people because of its schematic and superficial conceptions. The main aim was to make it to Moscow, which resulted in compromises regarding theme and casting, and a condescending attitude to everything national.

In 1961, Uzbek Film Studios became independent. The Uzbek 'new wave' was born in the mid-1960s following the Khrushchev thaw and the emergence of 'new wave' elsewhere in the world. Ali Khamraev, Shukrat Abbasov and Elyor Ishmukhamedov set out to create personal films about their country and culture. With the arrival of *perestroika*, a new dynamism manifested itself with provocative works from young directors such as Jahangir Faiziev and Zoulfikar Moussakov. Kamara Kamalova showed her determination to create works showing a woman's point of view.

Freedom also created confusion. In the effort to reach the new audience, some directors began to lean towards gimmicks. Thrillers and action films surfaced. Although narrative cinema with strong local social and political themes remains popular, there is a variety of genre and style today: irony and farce, traditional heroic folk tale, even science fiction.

Initially Uzbekfilm Studio did not make a fast transition to market economy. When the state reduced aid, film production began to decline. The public lost interest in local productions and many cinemas were closed. With renewed aid from the government through Uzbek Kino, a joint venture with the state, at least six films are made each year and these attract a large audience. Several directors are also involved in co-productions, which often favour historical themes.

Filmography

Atrof Qorga Burkandi / All Around was Covered by Snow

1995, 75 mins, colour, Russian
Director:	Kamara Kamalova
Producer:	Snod, Uzbekistan
Screenwriter:	Kamara Kamalova, Asap Abbasova
Cinematographer:	Rizcat Ubzagimov, Khasan Kadiealiev
Editor:	Olga Moova
Sound:	Zoija Pzedtechenskeja
Music:	Michael Jariverdiev
Leading Players:	Rano Shadieva, Seidulla Maidorhanov

Asal, a sensitive teenager, lives alone in a game reserve after her mother's death, which she believes was caused by a ghost who wanders the reserve in the shape of a wild dog.

Kamil, a hunter, works in the reserve and tries to understand the girl and the way she lives. The growing affection between them strengthens her and deeply touches Kamil.

Belye, Belye Ajsty / The White, White Storks

1966, 89 mins, black and white, Russian
Director: Ali Khamraev
Producer: Uzbekfilm
Screenwriter: Odelcha Aguichev, Ali Khamraev
Cinematographer: Dilchat Fatkhouline
Music: Ravil Vildanov
Leading Players: Bolot Beichenaliev, Sairam Issaeva, Mokhammed Rafikov

In a village called 'White Storks', a married woman, Malika, falls in love with Kaium. Their passion is misunderstood and rejected by the villagers. Some of them, like Malika's father, are torn between understanding the attitude of a beloved daughter and the burden of tradition.

Neznost / Tenderness

1967, 76 mins, black and white, Russian
Director: Elyor Ishmukhamedov
Producer: Uzbekfilm
Screenwriter: Odelcha Aguichev
Cinematographer: Dilchat Fatkhouline
Music: Bogdan Trotsiouk
Leading Players: Maria Sternikova, Rodion Nakhapetov, Gani Agzamov

An ordinary teenager in Tashkent sails down the canal that crosses the city on a tyre tube. One day he sees a fair-haired girl and falls in love with her, which changes his life. But she loves someone else. It is a film made up of three stories with the same characters, dedicated to adolescence.

Siz Kim Siz? / Who Are You?

1989, 85 mins, colour, Russian
Director: Jahangir Faiziev
Producer: Uzbekfilm, ASK
Screenwriter: Iouri Dachevski, Jahangir Faiziev
Cinematographer: Khamidulla Khassanov
Music: D. Ianov-Ianovski
Leading Players: Bakhtiar Zakirov, Elier Nassyrov, Toulkoun Tadjiev

Two intellectuals get arrested on a provincial road after they steal a watermelon. At the police station, tough negotiations start between the urban intellectuals and the country people, each group misunderstanding the other. The use of different dialects by various characters adds to the comic aspect of the film, which keeps going back and forth between the tragic and the comic.

Tashkent, Gorod Hlebnyji / Tashkent, Bread City

1966, 104 mins, black and white, Russian
Director: Shukrat Abbasov
Producer: Uzbekfilm
Screenwriter: Andrei Mikhalkov-Kontchalovski
Cinematographer: Khatam Faiziev
Music: Albert Malakhov
Leading Players: Vova Vorobei, Vova Koudenkov, Bakhtiar Nabiev, Natalia Arinbassarova

Based on the work of Alexandr Neverov. During the famine following the civil war, ten-year-old Misha is the only breadwinner after the death of his father. He leaves his village for Tashkent with his seven-year-old friend. Their journey is packed with trials and disastrous encounters with Bolsheviks, thieves and White Russians. In Tashkent, Misha works hard to earn the wheat to take back to his family. On his return, he discovers that his brother and sister have died. His weakened mother welcomes him with a resigned smile.

List of directors

Abbasov, Shukrat (1931–); Faiziev, Jahangir (1961–); Ganiev, Nabi (1904–52); Kamalova, Kamara (1938–); Khamraev, Ali (1937–); Malikov, Rachid (1958–); Yarmatov, Kamil (1903–78)

Major director

Khamraev, Ali (b. 1937, Tashkent, Uzbekistan)

One of the leaders and the most versatile directors of Uzbek cinema, Khamraev has left no genre untouched – opera, musical, western, children's film, comedy and history – to satisfy his curiosity and the demands of the authorities. In 1989, he founded a co-operative of independent films, Samarkandfilm, which co-produced *The Great Timur* (1997) with an Italian company.

Selected feature films: *Belye, Belye Ajsty / The White, White Storks* (1966); *The Red Sand* (with Akmal Akbar-Hodjaev) (1967); *Dilorom* (1968); *Crezvysajnyj Komissar / Extraordinary Policechief* (1970); *Celovek Uhodit Za Pticami / Man Follows the Birds* (1975); *Triptih / The Woman of Mevazar* (1978); *Telohranitel / Bodyguard* (1980); *Ja Tebja Ponni U / I Remember You* (1986); *Bo-Ba-Bu* (1999)

Further reading

Atwood, L. (ed.) (1993) *Red Women on the Silver Screen*, London: Pandora Press.
Brashinsky, M. and Horton, A. (1992) *The Zero Hour*, Oxford: Princeton University Press.

Dönmez-Colin, G. (1997) 'Cinema in Isolation', *Central Asian Survey* 16, 2 (June): 277–80.

—— (1996) 'Difficile survie pour le cinéma azeri', *Le Monde Diplomatique* (January): 4.

—— (1997) 'Kazakh "New Wave": Post-Perestroika, Post-Soviet Union', *Central Asian Survey* 16, 1 (March): 115–18.

Festival des trois continents, catalogues for 1990, 1992, 1995 and 1997, Nantes.

Goulding, D.J. (ed.) (1989) *Post-New Wave Cinema in the Soviet Union and Eastern Europe*, Bloomington and Indianapolis: Indiana University Press.

Lawton, A. (1990) 'Soviet Cinema Four Years Later', *Wide Angle* 12, 4 (October): 9–22.

—— (1992) *Kinoglasnost: Soviet Cinema in Our Time*, Cambridge: Cambridge University Press.

Passek, J.-L. (ed.) (1981) *Le Cinéma Russe et Soviétique*, Paris: Centre George Pompidou / L'Equerre.

Egyptian cinema

Viola Shafik

Egypt developed the first Arab-speaking local film industry, whose products were also consumed by the neighbouring Arab countries during and after colonial times. With a total output of more than 2,800 full-length films between 1924 and 1999, the Egyptian film industry created a commercial and export-oriented genre cinema which is based on a local star system and on private investment. Often referred to as 'Hollywood on the Nile', it has been repeatedly criticized for its low-standard commercialism and alleged plagiarism, and was moreover accused of hampering the development of other Arab film industries. However, its different stages reflected on all levels the specific cultural and socio-political conditions of the country.

Encounter with a new media (1896–1925)

In 1896, only a few months after the initial screenings in Europe, films by the Lumière brothers were shown in Egypt, first in the Tousson stock exchange in Alexandria and then in the Hamam Schneider (Schneider Bath) in Cairo. As early as 1897 the Cinématographe Lumière in Alexandria started to offer regular screenings. The construction of special sites for screenings followed soon. In 1906 the French company Pathé constructed a movie-theatre in Cairo. Three other *cinématographes* were run at that time in the capital and in Alexandria. It became, moreover, common to include the presentation of films in theatre performances. In 1911 eleven movie-theatres already existed in these two major Egyptian cities. Starting from 1912, they provided foreign films with an Arabic translation.

In general, the first cinematic activities, like elsewhere in the Arab world, were undertaken by foreign (mostly European) residents. Louis and Auguste Lumière ordered shootings in the so-called 'Orient', among others in Egypt. Their *Place des Consuls à Alexandrie*, by M. Promio, was the first film shot in Egypt in 1897. In 1906 the French-Algerian (*pied-noir*) Felix Mesguich travelled with his camera to Egypt and recorded its monuments. In 1907 the first 'native' Egyptian documentaries were shot by two acknowledged photographers from Alexandria: 'Aziz Bandarli and Umberto Dorès.

Before and after World War I the number of newsreels and short fiction films produced in Egypt increased steadily. In 1917 Umberto Dorès established (with the assistance of the Banca di Roma) the SITCIA film company in Alexandria, directed by Dorès. They considered the World War I period to be a good opportunity to exploit the native market, as well as the pleasant local weather conditions. Yet, after the creation of a studio and the production of three short films, the company went bankrupt. Its failure was due to the poor quality of the films and the producer's lack of cultural sensitivity. Their film, *al-Azhar al-Mumita / Mortal Flowers* (1918), for example, was banned by the authorities because it showed Arabic Qur'anic verses upside down.

Purely native interest in the media developed alongside foreign productions. In 1909 an Egyptian is said to have shot the funeral of the Egyptian leader and patriot Mustafa Kamil. Many short fiction films made in the following years by Europeans were realized in co-operation with Egyptian actors. The actor-turned-director Muhammad Karim starred in two films produced by SITCIA and was thus one of the first Egyptians to perform on screen. Others soon followed: Fawzi Gaza'irli starred with his troupe in Léonard La Ricci's *Madame Loretta* in 1919; Amin Sidqi and the popular theatre actor 'Ali al-Kassar performed in Bonvelli's short, *al-Khala al-Amirikaniyya / The American Aunt*, shot in 1920. The year 1923 witnessed the screening of Victor Rosito's full-length fiction, *Fi Bilad Tut 'Ankh Amun / In the Country of Tutankhamun*, shot by the native Egyptian director and cameraman Muhammad Bayyumi. Bayyumi, who was based in Alexandria, became one of most prolific film pioneers: In 1923 he founded his newsreel *Amun*, shot numerous documentaries and directed his short fiction, *al-Mu'alim Barsum Yabhath 'An Wazifa / Master Barsum is Looking for a Job*. Furthermore, in the following year Bayyumi adapted the popular play, *al-Bash Katib / The Chief Secretary* (1924) – taken in turn from *Charley's Aunt* and performed by Amin 'Attallah and his troupe.

The emergence of national cinema (1925–35)

In 1925 the first national attempt at organized investment in the realm of cinema was undertaken by Talaat (Tal'at) Harb, member of a nationalist-oriented group of entrepreneurs. As the founder and director of Misr Bank, he established in 1925 the Sharikat Misr li-l-sinima wa al-tamthil (Egyptian Company for Cinema and Performance), which was put in charge of producing advertising and information films. The company hired Bayyumi as its director, bought his equipment, founded a laboratory and issued the newsreel *Jaridat Misr / Egypt Journal*. The latter was directed by Hasan Murad and not by Bayyumi, who soon left the company.

The first feature film, *Layla*, was produced (not directed though) by a native Egyptian and released in November 1927. The Turkish director Wedad Orfi had persuaded the theatre actress 'Aziza Amir to finance the film. After a quarrel, Amir put Stéphane Rosti in charge of directing the film. (For a long time the appearance of *Layla* was considered the birth of Egyptian cinema, not least because the existence of Victor Rosito's full-length *Fi Bilad Tut 'Ankh Amun* fell into oblivion until the 1980s.) Only two months later, in January 1928, another full-length feature, *Qubla Fi-l-Sahra' / A Kiss in the Desert* appeared. It was directed by Ibrahim Lama, a South American of Lebanese origins who had settled in Egypt with his brother, the actor Badr Lama.

As production rates increased steadily following the release of these two movies, the years 1927 and 1928 may be considered the genesis of Egyptian cinema. Three full-length films made their way to the audience in 1928, including the adaptation of Amin 'Atallah's popular play, *al-Bahr Biyidhak Lih? / Why Does the Sea Laugh?* by Rosti. From 1927 to 1930 two full-length films were produced a year, five films were released in 1931 and six in both 1933 and 1934. Production in these years was, of course, still independent and not institutionalized – dependent on individual interest and moderate investment.

This is one reason why film-making was dominated at first by a considerable number of foreign residents, by indigenous minorities and, in particular, by women. 'Aziza Amir, Assia Daghir, Fatima Rushdi, Bahiga Hafiz and Amina Muhammad acted, produced and / or directed one or two films each. The Lebanese actress Assia Daghir, for example, produced her first film *Ghadat al-Sahra' / The Young Lady from the Desert* (by Wedad Orfi and Ahmad Galal) in 1929. For decades she remained Egypt's largest producer, with *al-Nasir Salah al-Din / The Victorious Saladin* (directed by Youssef Chahine in 1963) her most acclaimed and spectacular production.

Another characteristic of the genesis of Egypt's cinema was the close relation to popular theatre. The first genuine Egyptian production owed a lot to the activities of theatre actors, actresses and directors. It was not just that popular plays were among the first Egyptian films – like Muhammad Bayyumi's, *al-Bash Katib / The Chief Secretary* (1924), which starred Amin 'Atallah and his troupe – but also that many theatre actors and actresses invested in cinema – among others 'Aziza Amir, Fatima Rushdi and the actor, producer and director Yusuf Wahbi.

In the course of the 1930s, the stars of popular Egyptian theatre – Nagib al-Rihani, 'Ali al-Kassar and Yusuf Wahbi – attained great influence in the developing art of film-making. During and shortly after the pre-World War II era, they appeared in a large number of feature films which were developed to feature popular theatre characters. After the introduction of sound, these performers contributed to the formulation of film dialogue and partly also the script. Yusuf Wahbi even directed numerous films.

Sound, like elsewhere, was a decisive turning point for Egypt's film-making. It gave a unique chance to local production to use native language and music, and to develop film genres (such as comedy and the musical) which rely essentially on them. In 1932 the first two sound films appeared almost simultaneously: *Awlad al-Dhawat / Sons of Aristocrats* by Yusuf Wahbi and *Unshudat al-Fu'ad / Song from the Heart* by Mario Volpi. Although Mohsen (Muhsin) Szabo, an engineer of Hungarian origin, had succeeded in 1931 in constructing his own recording machine, the sound of the first Egyptian talkies was recorded in Europe. In 1935, however, with the inauguration of the fully equipped Studio Misr, films started to be entirely fabricated in Egypt. Hence, the following decade witnessed the rapid development of the national film industry.

Consolidation of the film industry and its heyday (1935–52)

The proper foundation of the Egyptian film industry was laid in 1934 when Misr Bank, under the management of Talaat Harb, established the Studio Misr. This studio, inaugurated in 1935, was actually not the first one to be established. The cameraman Alvise Orfanelli had already created a small studio in Alexandria in 1926, while in 1930 the tireless Yusuf Wahbi furnished a very modest studio in order to produce the literary adaptation *Zaynab* by Muhammad Karim. Moreover, in 1931 other places – like the studio Catsaros, as well as the Studio Togo in Alexandria – were used for shootings.

After 1935 and up to 1948 six further studios were built and a total of 345 full-length features had been produced since 1924. Moreover, the foundation of Studio Misr was responsible for shifting all film production from Alexandria to Cairo, which now became the main cultural metropolis of the country. New directors, mostly native Egyptians, appeared. The star system, as well as a variety of film genres – first the musical, then melodrama, farce and comedy, and the historical and the Bedouin film – emerged in this period.

Unlike the major studios in the United States, Studio Misr was not able to dominate the Egyptian film industry as a whole. It seems rather to have functioned as a catalyst for the rest of Egyptian cinema, as it set new technical and artistic standards. Its first production (released in 1936) was the musical *Widad* by Fritz Kramp, with the 'Star of the Orient' (singer Umm Kulthum) in the leading role. This film was the second historical spectacle produced in Egypt. It turned out to be a huge success, ran in cinemas for five weeks and represented Egypt in the Festival of Venice in the same year. The studio's next production, *Salama Fi Khayr / Salama is Fine* (1937) by Niazi Mustafa (starring the popular comedian Nagib al-Rihani), was also very successful at the box office. Moreover, in 1939 the Studio Misr produced *al-'Azima / Determination* by Kamal Selim (Salim), which has been considered by the Egyptian critics to be one of the earliest attempts at realism in Egyptian cinema. Directors who emerged through their work for the studio were Ahmad Badrakhan (later known for his melodramatic musicals) and Niazi Mustafa (the most prolific Egyptian director so far), as well as Kamal Selim (whose promising debut was terminated by an early death).

In contrast to earlier establishments, the Studio Misr was equipped with various workshops, a laboratory and sound studios that gave the opportunity to record sound and music. Moreover, it employed several European specialists, including (among others) two Germans – director Fritz Kramp and set designer Robert Scharfenberg – along with the Russian photographer Sami Brel. At the same time, it took care to provide native Egyptians with the required qualifications by sending them on scholarships to Europe. The directors Ahmad Badrakhan (Badr Khan), Niazi Mustafa and Salah Abu Seif (Saif) were some of the beneficiaries.

In spite of its importance, Studio Misr never became the strongest producer in the country, probably because of the sudden boom which started after World War II with the end of import restrictions and increased investment (undertaken by war profiteers among others) which transformed cinema into the most profitable industrial sector apart from the textile industry. Between 1945 and 1952, the Egyptian output doubled to reach an average of forty-eight films per year, an amount which was more or less maintained until the early 1990s. An industrial consciousness developed at that time which was reflected in the establishment of the Film Industry Chamber in 1947. Cinematic styles and techniques grew in sophistication. In 1950 colour was introduced to Egyptian cinema, with Husain Fawzi directing the first colour film, *Baba 'Aris / Daddy is a Bridegroom*. However, it took another fifteen to twenty years until the majority of Egyptian productions were shot on colour material.

Among the most important directors to appear during the 1930s without being linked with the Studio Misr were Muhammad Karim and Togo Mizrahi. Karim started his career with the literary adaptation *Zaynab* (1930) and later specialized in romantic musicals, while Mizrahi directed farces and comedies (and also some musicals). Yusuf Wahbi stuck almost entirely to melodrama. Other productive directors of that time were Mario Volpi, Alvise Orfanelli, Ahmad Galal and Fawzi al-Gaza'irli.

Melodramatic musicals, comedy / farce and, to a smaller extent, Bedouin films were the most prevalent genres of the time. Directors who appeared during the late 1930s and early 1940s and helped to develop these genres – apart from the Bedouin film which was primarily the speciality of Ibrahim Lama and Niazi Mustafa – were Husain Fawzi, Ibrahim 'Imara and Henri Barakat. The latter remained until the 1970s one of Egypt's most industrious and talented directors, known for some outstanding melo-dramas, musicals and realist films. Kamil al-Tilmissani and Ahmad Kamil Mursi showed a realist – if not socialist – orientation in works dealing with the economy and the working class, whereas Anwar Wagdi (who directed his first film in 1945) contributed a dozen light musicals to Egyptian cinema. He was one of those who introduced the rather syncretic genre that was so characteristic of the post-war boom, operating with a multitude of contradictory elements – such as comic acting in a basi-cally melodramatic plot – thereby creating a light and entertaining pot-pourri.

National independence and the nationalization of cinema (1952–71)

In 1952 the Free Officers, led by Muhammad Nagib and Gamal 'Abd al-Nasir (Nasser), seized power, abolished the Kingdom and declared the end of British inter-ference in Egypt. This also marked a new era in the Egyptian film economy, which was characterized by state interference in the arts and industry, and the advent of new genres and topics, including a 'Third Worldist' realist cinema.

This development can be traced back to the time before the nationalist *coup d'état*, when works with a clear nationalist anti-colonial stamp made their appearance – among others *Fatat Min Filastin / A Girl from Palestine* (1948) by Mahmud zu-l-Fiqar, dealing with the occupation of Palestine, *Mustafa Kamil* (1952) by Ahmad Badrakhan and *Yasqut al-Isti'mar / Down with Colonialism* (1952) by Husain Sidqi. Nationalism and the need for post-colonial cultural purification also generated a wave of religious films, initiated by *Zuhur al-Islam / The Appearance of Islam* (1951) by Ibrahim 'Izz al-Din and *Intisar al-Islam / The Victory of Islam* (1952) by Ahmad al-Tukhi. Both portrayed the appearance of a victorious Islam in the seventh century.

While the Bedouin film practically vanished during the two decades of the Nasserist regime, light music-hall comedies, gangster films and thrillers came to the fore. A small number of Egyptian film-makers, notably Youssef Chahine, Salah Abu Seif and Taufiq Salih, showed an inclination towards what came to be called 'Third Worldist' realism, and tried to realize it both within and outside the public sector. Their political and artistic commitment tried to raise issues ranging from foreign domination and social injustice to rationalism and gender equality, and created a kind of Egyptian 'Middle Cinema'. This realist cinema became highly appreciated at home and abroad. During the 1960s the production of realist and political films spread to a certain extent among mainstream directors, such as Henri Barakat and Kamal El-Cheikh (al-Shaykh): Barakat directed some of the most accomplished musicals and melodramas, as well as realist films, of the era; El-Cheikh's work also moved between the poles of gangster and political films.

Hasan al-Imam was entirely oriented towards the mainstream and specialized in musical melodramas, mostly featuring belly dancers. Director Hilmi Halim's name became linked to the popular musicals starring the singer 'Abd al-Halim Hafiz, whereas 'Izz al-Din zu-l-Fiqar, Ahmad Diya' al-Din and later Sa'd 'Arafa directed mostly romantic love stories. Hilmi Rafla and Fatin 'Abd al-Wahhab became known for their light comedies, and Kamal El-Cheikh for his sophisticated thrillers. In contrast, Husam al-Din Mustafa, who was described as the most vulgar Egyptian director, started his career with dramatic literary adaptations and ended it in the 1990s with espionage films. The commercial orientation of most of these directors persisted, despite increasing state interference in the cinema industry.

In 1953 the state created the al-Nil Society for film production and distribution, supervised by the officer Wagih Abaza. In 1954 a special information administration was founded, which in turn put the Service of the Control of Technical Affairs in charge of producing shorts and information films. Three years later even more concrete measures were taken. Special decrees were issued to reorganize the taxation on imported films in favour of national production and to found the Organization for Film Aid, whose objective was to raise the artistic standard of cinema and to support its distribution abroad. This organization laid the basis for the later national film organization. Eventually, in 1958, it changed its name for the first time to become the Public Egyptian Film Organization.

In 1960 the Misr Bank was nationalized, so were the Misr Company for Cinema and Performance, the Studio Misr itself, along with all the other private studios in the country and around one third of the movie theatres. The studios were placed under the supervision of the film organization which was encouraged to start production. It released the first public full-length feature film in 1963 after the organization had been restructured under the General Film Organization. It comprised four different societies, which held responsibility for the production of feature films and documentaries, for international co-production, for the administration of the studios and for the administration of movie theatres and film distribution.

The period of state ownership did not bring about a real rise in artistic or technical standards. In spite of the efforts in particular of Tharwat 'Ukasha during his period in office as minister of culture to promote national film culture, production remained dominated by commercial viability. In order to prevent the loss of foreign markets, the products of the General Film Organization followed the same commercial guidelines as the private sector, which meant that it lacked neither stars nor popular and entertaining formulas. Yet the nationalization policy led Egyptian, Syrian, Lebanese and Jordanian producers and distributors to withdraw from Egypt and invest in Lebanon instead. This resulted in a temporary increase of Lebanese production during the 1960s, which in turn made extensive use of Egyptian stars and technical talent.

The total number of productions decreased continuously after the foundation of the General Film Organization and reached its lowest level since the 1940s with thirty-two films produced in 1967. Eventually the total number of feature films settled at around forty films per year and did not increase until 1974. The film organization did not manage to produce more than thirteen feature films a year; the rest were private productions. Corruption and nepotism contributed to the wasting of public money. In 1971, the time when the Sadat government started reprivatization, the debts of the film organization supposedly reached seven million Egyptian pounds. This forced the public sector to withdraw completely from the production of full-length feature films that year. Only the production of shorts was kept on.

Under these unfavourable conditions, art films like *al-Mumya' / The Mummy: The Night of Counting the Years* (1969) by Chadi Abdessalam (Shadi 'Abd al-Salam) – striving for the development of a specific national film language and produced by the public sector – remained absolutely exceptional. In fact, some of the most talented

Figure 7 al-Mumya' / The Mummy: The Night of Counting the Years

and at the same time politically committed directors – primarily Taufiq Salih, Youssef Chahine (Yusuf Shahin) and also Henri Barakat – had such negative experiences with the public bureaucracy that they decided to leave Egypt as a whole; Salih went to Syria, and Chahine and Barakat to Lebanon. Thus, unlike the situation in Syria and Algeria, the Egyptian public sector did not become the godfather of a politically committed, modernist, anti-colonial Third Worldist cinema that was, in other Arab countries, consciously creating a distance from the products of the commercial so-called 'dream factory'.

Advent of electronic media (1971–91)

Although the reprivatization of the film industry has been discussed in Egypt since the 1970s, when Anwar al-Sadat came to power in 1970 and started the *infitah* or 'open-door policy', thus putting an end to Egypt's socialist orientation and its isolation from the West, one of the first steps towards reprivatization was the 1971 decision to termi-nate public feature-film production. On the other hand, the General Organization still invested in the industry: it inaugurated a colour laboratory in 1973 and started estab-lishing a modern sound centre in the Film City in Giza. In the following years additional attempts at privatization were made, which did not amount to more than the selling of some movie theatres. The rest of the technical infrastructure, including laboratories and studios have remained public property through to the late 1990s and are being privatized gradually. This situation represented, on one hand, a serious obstacle for the updating of technical equipment and infrastructure but ironically, on the other, served the interests of private producers who profited from the low fixed prices offered by state-run laboratories and have therefore always objected to further privatization.

Apart from the *infitah* and the accompanying attempts at privatization, two other factors shaped Egypt's cinema decisively during the 1970s and 1980s: the introduction of national television and the spread of the video cassette recorder (VCR). Egyptian public television – run by the Egyptian Radio and Television Union (ERTU) – started broadcasting in July 1960. It is not clear how much its introduction contributed to the drop in production mentioned above (ten to fifteen films less than the preceeding decade) and also to the closing of movie theatres. However, one of its positive effects was that it contributed to the preservation and dissemination of old Egyptian movies by constantly airing them, so it helped to transform them into a cultural legacy for following generations of film-makers.

In contrast to television, the introduction of the VCR doubtless had a strong economic and cultural effect on cinema. It did not only change habits of spectatorship, encouraging particularly women and families to stay at home instead of going out to the movies; the spread of the VCR in the Gulf region, primarily in Saudi Arabia where public theatres are still prohibited, also opened new markets for Egyptian cinema, leading eventually in 1984 to a boom of the so-called *muqawalat* or entrepreneur film. Directed by mediocre directors and featuring second-rate actors, these films were mostly shot and distributed on video.

Cinematically, the early 1970s were marked by various attempts at artistic innovations. Third Worldist cinema gave way to more individualist cinematic expressions. Young directors – like Husain Kamal, Khalil Shawqi, 'Ali 'Abd al-Khaliq, Ghaleb Chaath (Ghalib Sha'th), Mamduh Shukri, Sa'id Marzuq and Muhammad 'Abd al-'Aziz – made their first interesting experiments, though they were later to be absorbed by commercialism. In 1972, the huge success of *Khalli Balak Min Zuzu / Take Care of Zuzu* by the master of Egyptian melodrama, Hasan al-Imam, signalled the temporary economic revival of Egyptian mainstream cinema and a new increase of production rates, mounting to around fifty films a year.

At the same time, the composition of genres changed. The traditional musical and melodrama decreased in favour of action and gangster films, and a few low-quality karate imitations. Furthermore, more sexually permissive films, such as Sa'id Marzuq's *al-Khawf / Fear* (1972) or Abu Seif's *Hamam al-Malatili / The Malatili Bath* (1973) were released. This tendency, however, led to a clash between film-makers, public opinion and censorship in the early 1980s.

As during the late 1940s, some genres tended to merge in this period. Now it was melodrama, realism and the gangster film which combined and became a kind of 'social drama' that is still prevalent today. Nonetheless, the realist genre experienced a second revival during the 1980s. Heavy criticism of the *infitah* was expressed by the so-called 'New Realism' of Atef El-Tayeb ('Atif al-Tayyib), Khairy Beshara (Khayri Bishara), Mohamed (Muhammad) Khan, Daoud Abd El-Sayed (Dawud 'Abd al-Sayyid), the screenwriter and director Bashir al-Dik and, to a certain extent, 'Ali

Figure 8   Khalli Balak Min Zuzu / Take Care of Zuzu

Badrakhan, who had already made a name for himself in the 1970s. Screenwriter Ra'fat al-Mihi, who also directed a few realist-oriented films, later specialized in a kind of black and absurd comedy that was described by Egyptian critics as 'fantasy'.

Muhammad 'Abd al-'Aziz was one of the few directors who, after the demise of Fatin 'Abd al-Wahhab, still contributed light comedies of some quality to mainstream cinema. Sa'id Marzuq, Muhammad Radi and Ahmad Yahia worked on mainly social drama films, mixing action, realism and melodrama. In contrast, Nadir Galal and Samir Saif specialized primarily on action and gangster films – in the case of the latter, combined with comedy and farce. Muhammad Fadil appeared during this period too, but soon switched to television, for which he directed social and historical dramas.

The satellite era (since 1991)

The Egyptian film industry experienced a new serious crisis in the early 1990s. Production rates decreased dangerously: eighteen films were released in 1994, twenty-five in 1995, twenty-two in 1996, sixteen in 1997 and twenty in 1998. This development started first with the beginning of the Iraqi invasion of Kuwait in August 1990, which affected Egypt's foreign distribution to the Gulf countries for a few months. However, the major setback was the advent of satellite television at the same time, leading to a sudden growth of the electronic entertainment industry.

The number of Arab satellite channels – including those of the Egyptian ERTU, which are broadcast all over the Arab world and Europe – increased rapidly and have multiplied the need for new Arab serials, talk-shows and other television productions. Egypt's own first satellite channel started broadcasting during the Gulf War and was quickly followed by other foreign-language channels. Since 1992, the ERTU has also co-financed the pay-television Cable Network Egypt (CNE). In addition to that, it has increased the number of Egyptian satellite channels, profiting from the ministry's most recent investment: the first Egyptian satellite, Nile Sat, which started operating in 1998. Surprisingly, the film industry was unable to profit from this development. Due to insufficient trade regulation, Egyptian movies are still sold and shown for ridiculous prices, mostly not exceeding a few hundred US dollars.

Furthermore, the ERTU, supervised by the Ministry of Information, started competing with the private film sector. In addition to the large number of shows and serials (which are exported all over the Arab world), it financed expensive feature films, thus competing with the private film industry. In 1994 alone, five television productions were released in movie theatres. This boom has led to a serious shortage of studios, equipment and technicians. In 1995, for example, 80 per cent of cinema studios were rented to television and advertising productions. The ERTU has therefore invested millions in the construction of a huge studio complex outside Cairo – in the City of October Seven – which was partly operating by 1999.

The ERTU has only recently started to put cinema producers in charge of producing television feature films that are meant for cinematic distribution first. In 1998 and 1999 the first co-production between a private producer and national television was undertaken, resulting in Youssef Chahine's film *al-Akhar / The Other* (1999). The 1990s also saw an increasing tendency towards European co-productions. Apart from Chahine's most recent historical spectacles, *al-Muhajir / The Emigrant* (1994) and *al-Masir / The Destiny* (1997), young directors (such as Yousri Nasrallah, Asma' al-Bakri, Radwan al-Kashif, Khalid al-Haggar and 'Atif Hatata) have received Western support for their projects. However, none of the co-productions (except for Chahine's) have been really successful with Egyptian audiences.

The late 1980s saw the revival of old genres, such as the musical, along with the emergence of some new directors – among others Muhammad Shibl (Shebl) (who died in 1997) and Hani Lashin – who, despite their attempts to innovate and achieve a certain standard, remained marginal. Contrary to that, Sharif 'Arafa, as well as the female director Inas al-Dighidi, became the most successful mainstream directors of the present. 'Arafa's work stretches from light musicals and comedies to social dramas, including several box-office hits, whereas al-Dighidi focuses more on social drama. New Realism still found some followers in the 1990s, as expressed in the work of Muhammad Kamil Qalyubi, Usama Fawzi, Munir Radi and Radwan al-Kashif. Tariq al-'Iryan contributed two fast-paced police and gangster films, and the Sudanese Sa'id Hamid presented comedies starring Mahmud al-Hinidi, which became the greatest box-office hits of the late 1990s.

One of the peculiarities of the 1990s is the appearance of a 'Coptic' Christian cinema. Professional Coptic directors – among others Khairy Beshara and Samir Saif – have started since 1987 to direct devotional films produced largely by the Coptic orthodox church and some Protestant institutions. The majority of these videos – sixteen full-length films by the end of 1996 – feature the lives and ordeals of native

Egyptian saints and martyrs, thus echoing even in their *mise-en-scène* the Muslim religious films of the 1960s and 1970s. By law, they are supposed to be distributed only within the churches, thus creating a sort of confessional counter-audience.

Censorship and taboos

Every feature film produced in Egypt passes censorship twice. First the screenplay or, in the case of a documentary, treatment has to be submitted to the censor to receive approval. The latter is a prerequisite for acquiring shooting permission from the Ministry of the Interior. After completion, another official licence – a so-called 'visa' – is required in order to screen the film in public and to export it. Both steps leave much space for interference, as well as negotiation.

The most important taboo zones kept under state surveillance are religion, sexuality and politics. The latest censorship law, issued in 1976, forbids criticism of heavenly religions, justification of immoral actions, positive representation of heresy, images of naked human bodies and inordinate emphasis on individual erotic parts, sexually arousing scenes, alcohol consumption and drug use, obscene and indecent speech, and disrespect to parents, the sanctity of marriage or family values. Most importantly, the law does not allow films 'to represent social problems as hopeless, to upset the mind or to divide religions, classes and national unity'.

Vague notions like the prohibition of things 'that do not correspond to the normal' and 'embarrass the audience' open the door to official arbitrariness and unpredictability. This applies also to the question of national unity. Although many Christian directors work in Egypt, Christian characters rarely appear on screen and, if they do, it is mostly in minor secondary roles. Censors tended to reinforce this discrepancy by trying to secure national unity first of all through the exclusive representation of Muslim customs and convictions on the screen.

Of course not all prohibitions are respected. Film-makers do represent alcohol consumption, although it is often associated with immorality. Some restrictions are circumvented through negotiation with the censors. Another strategy is the codification of messages and actions by symbolic or stylistic means. For example, in his films *Iskandariyya, Lih? / Alexandria, Why?* (1978) and *Iskandariyya Kaman Wa Kaman / Alexandria Now and Forever* (1991), Youssef Chahine veils his protagonists' homoerotic inclination by representing sexual desire as murderous hate or, in another case, by replacing a man with a woman with masculine behaviour.

State interference in the realm of cinema dates back to the birth of cinema. A law issued in 1904 to regulate the press was also applied to cinema. In 1911 the Cairo governorate charged the chiefs of police to control strictly whatever was screened in the movie theatres. In 1918 the first case of censorship occurred, prohibiting *al-Azhar al-Mumita* because of wrongly reproduced verses from the Qur'an.

Official censorship was eventually begun in 1921 with a decree stating that all imported films had to pass the General Security Department of the Ministry of the Interior before projection. The religious-oriented censorship led by the al-Azhar institution (and university) interfered for the first time in 1926, when Yusuf Wahbi was asked by Wedad Orfi to represent the Prophet Muhammad on the screen. The al-Azhar protested so heavily that Wahbi withdrew his earlier acceptance of the role. Since then the representation of the Prophet, as well as the four righteous Caliphs, has

Figure 9 Iskandariyya, Lih? / Alexandria, Why?

been forbidden. This decision was underlined again in 1976 by the prohibition of representation of all the other prophets mentioned in the Qur'an, including 'Issa (that is, Jesus Christ).

The first cases of political censorship occured in 1937 and 1938. Bahiga Hafiz's *Layla Bint al-Sahra' / The Daughter of the Desert*, completed in 1937, was banned and only released in 1944 under the title *Layla al-Badawiyya / Layla the Bedouin*. By an unlucky coincidence, the film had presented the story of an unjust rapist Persian king in the same year that the Egyptian Princess Fawzia celebrated her wedding to the Shah of Iran. The second film affected was the Studio Misr production, *Lashin* (1938) by Fritz Kramp. It was also centred around a tyrannical sultan. After basic changes to the story and the addition of scenes that transformed the vicious ruler into a good one, the film was released at the end of the same year.

In general, the representation of the lower classes, social injustice and leftist or nationalist topics had to fear censorship in pre-Nasserist Egypt. The censorship law – the so-called 'Faruq Code', issued in 1949 by the Ministry of Social Affairs – excluded realism by equating it with subversive leftist trends and prohibited even the representation of 'oriental habits and traditions'. These regulations could be neglected by Egyptian cinema only after the abolition of the monarchy in 1952. In 1955 the revolutionary government issued a new censorship law, annulling some of the restrictions of the 1947 law. However, it declared also the new law's objectives: 'to protect public morals, to preserve security, public order and the superior interests of the state'.

In spite of the new limits set to democracy during the reign of Nasser, censorship was relatively permissive regarding foreign films. Many provocative art-films – like some of Pasolini's and Fellini's works – passed. Only a few cases of censoring local productions occurred, concerning among others *Allahu Ma'na / God is with Us* (1952) by Ahmed Badrakhan (released in 1955) and *Shay'un Min al-Khawf / Something Frightening* (1969) by Husain Kamal. Both were released after President Nasser had watched them with approval.

The most severe political censorship occured during the reign of Sadat, particularly before the October or Yom Kippur War in 1973. From 1971 to 1973, after Sadat's seizure of power, all films which addressed the Egyptian defeat by Israel were prohibited, including *Zilal 'Ala al-Janib al-Akhar / Shadows on the Other Side* (1971) by Ghaleb Chaath and *al-'Usfur / The Sparrow* (1972) by Youssef Chahine. Moreover, political films – like *Za'ir al-Fajr / Visitor in the Dawn* (1973) by Mamduh Shukri, addressing the abuses of the state security service – did not receive permission until 1975. *Al-Mudhnibun / The Culprits* (1976) by Sa'id Marzuq, which identified corruption and nepotism, was forbidden under a moral pretext. No film has actually been banned since 1984, but changes were sometimes requested: for example, the images of a Central Security Service (*al-amn al-markazi*) soldier protesting with a machine gun in his hands against the authoritarian and inhumane methods used in an internment camp had to be removed from the final scene of Atef El-Tayeb's film, *al-Bari' / The Innocent* (1986).

In general, the 1980s and 1990s were marked by a new morality on screen (in dress, behaviour and so on) and off screen (in public opinion). An important factor in this morality was Egyptian cinema's dependency on the Gulf States. Together with petrodollars, prudishness moved into Egyptian movies. While Husain Kamal's film, *Abbi Fawq al-Shajara / My Father Up the Tree* (1969), had been an attraction in 1969 because of its allegedly 100 kisses, today hardly a kiss passes on the screen. Female clothing has become more moderate in what it reveals.

The new morality reached one of its peaks in 1983 with an outraged debate sparked off by the prohibition of two mediocre productions of the same year: *Darb al-Hawa / Alley of Love* by Hussam al-Din Mustafa and *Khamsa Bab / Gate Five* by Nadir Galal.

Figure 10 Iskandariyya Kaman Wa Kaman / Alexandria Now and Forever

Most journalists and officials spoke in favour of the verdict and demanded more respect for traditions and good morals. In fact, since that time the press and the courts started to excel themselves in censorship, initiating furious media campaigns by suing certain films and their makers. In 1984 lawyers instituted proceedings against *al-Afukatu / The Advocate* by Ra'fat al-Mihi. Another spectacular process was initiated in 1994 by Muslim fundamentalists against Youssef Chahine after the screening of *al-Muhajir / The Emigrant* (1994), which was accused of representing one of the Qur'an's prophets. Noteworthy in these cases is the silence of concerned institutions, such as the Chamber of Industry and the Cinéastes' Syndicate – the latter being politically controlled since 1987.

A complementary phenomenon related to the new morality is the veiling of two dozen Egyptian actresses working in cinema, theatre and television. From 1987 to 1994 up to twenty-five actresses declared their retreat from show business and veiled themselves, complying with the calls of Muslim fundamentalist teaching. The reasons were various: a growing sense of morality, increasing family pressures, age and maybe even (as some newspapers suspected) bribery. Since 1994 cases of veiling have been rare.

Women

Egyptian women played a major role in founding national cinema, yet they were later gradually neglected and marginalized. Numerous artists and actresses such as 'Aziza Amir, Assia Daghir, Fatima Rushdi and Bahiga Hafiz worked at the end of the 1920s and through the course of the 1930s as producers, screenwriters and directors. The first full-length feature, *Layla*, to be considered entirely Egyptian was co-directed in 1927 by theatre actress 'Aziza Amir, who also produced and starred in the film. Amir had been trained in Yusuf Wahbi's theatre troupe Ramsis. In 1933 she directed her second and last film, *Kafarry 'An Khati'attik / Atone for Your Sin*.

In 1929 *Ghadat al-Sahra' / The Young Lady from the Desert* was screened. It starred the Lebanese actress Assia Daghir, who also produced the film. Later, she did not only act in many films, but until the 1980s also remained one of Egypt's important producers. The popular actress Fatima Rushdi, too, in 1933 directed her only film, entitled *al-Zawaj / The Marriage*. Bahiga Hafiz (who was a musical composer as well) starred in, produced and directed the 1932 *al-Dahaya / The Victims* and the lavish 1937 costume drama *Layla Bint al-Sahra' / The Daughter of the Desert*. Furthermore, the actress and belly dancer Amina Muhammad acted in, produced and directed her first and only film, *Tita Wung / Tita Wung* (1937). This was the last Egyptian feature film directed by a woman until 1966, when the actress Magda al-Sabahi realized the not very successful film *Mann Uhibb / Whom I Love*. Al-Sabahi had started acting in 1949, largely representing naïve spoilt girls. Her most interesting role was as a *mujahida* (resistance fighter) in Youssef Chahine's *Jamila al-Jaza'iriyya / Jamila the Algerian* (1958). She still works as a producer today.

For a long intermediate period that ended in 1984 with the appearance of Nadia Hamza's *Bahr al-Awham / Sea of Illusions*, no women succeeded in directing films for the film industry. But the following year, a total of three films by women were released: Nadia Salim's trivial comedy *Sahib al-Idara Bawab al-'Imara / The Doorkeeper Became the Building's Manager*, the odd *al-Nisa' / Women* by Nadia

Hamza and Inas al-Dighidi's '*Afwan Ayuha al-Qanun* / *Excuse Me Law!*. Subsequently, al-Dighidi has become the most prominent and talented Egyptian female director – though she is often dismissed as commercial and vulgar. Less successful were Nadia Hamza and Asma' al-Bakri. The latter's first film *Shahadhun Wa Nubala'* / *Beggars and Noblemen* (1991), adapted from an existentialist novel by Albert Cossery (Qusairi), was primarily well received abroad. So far, the most prolific of these directors have been Nadia Hamza and Inas al-Dighidi – in the case of al-Dighidi, directing more than a dozen feature films.

Most of the new female directors were trained at the Higher Film Institute and work according to the conditions of the film industry or, in the case of An'am Muhammad 'Ali, 'Ilwiyya Zaki and Sandra Nash'at, in the framework of television. They direct films covering a variety of topics and do not necessarily focus on women's issues. 'Ali, for example, directed the spectacular male-dominated war film, *al-Tariq Illa Aylat* / *The Way to Eilat* (1995). In fact, it is mainly Inas al-Dighidi who, although exploiting all the genres of cinema (ranging from crime to comedy), concentrates in her work on gender relations and abuse, as in her *al-Qatilla* / *The Murderess* (1992), *Lahm Rakhis* / *Cheap Flesh* (1995), *Istakusa* / *Lobster* (1996) and *Dantilla* / *Lace* (1998).

During the 1990s, female directors have still remained under-represented in fiction films. The reasons are various. Apart from the general lack of balance of women's representation in many professions, morality is certainly a decisive element. Cinema, showbusiness and, in particular, dancing and acting are followed with fascination (particularly by the lower and middle class) but are basically associated with immorality. A factor which might have facilitated the presence and activity of female pioneers in early cinema is their mostly privileged social backgrounds, which enabled them moreover to invest their own private money.

Hampered by traditional morality and lack of money, today's female film-makers have only succeeded in entering in large numbers the less expensive and more marginal field of short film- and documentary-making. One of the first women to direct documentaries for television was Sa'diyya Ghunim. Others followed in directing films for the National Film Centre, including Zaynab Zimzim, Farida 'Arman, Munnna Migahid, Firyal Kamil and Nabiha Lutfi. Documentary film-maker 'Attiyat al-Abnudi was even able to make a name for herself abroad and is considered one of Egypt's most important directors. Apart from that, numerous women have worked as screenwriters for television and ERTU employs many women in leading roles.

Education

One of the main opportunities to acquire the necessary expertise in film directing and other professions was through travel to Europe. For example, the first native Egyptian directors, Muhammad Bayyumi and Muhammad Karim, both went to Germany in search of training. At the same time, some local scholarly attempts were made to fill the gap. In 1924 Mahmud Khalil Rashid, author of several textbooks for correspondence education, published his book *The Dawn of Cinema*. The first attempt to institutionalize film education was undertaken by Muhammad Bayyumi, who in 1932 established his Egyptian Film Institute, offering courses free of charge in zincography, photography and film-making. One of the Institute's collective productions was

Bayyumi's feature film *al-Khatib Nimra 13 / Fiancé No. 13* (1933). However, the Institute had to close down after two years – probably for financial reasons. In 1945, another private film school opened in Cairo, but it too existed only for a short while.

The most fruitful contribution was made by Studio Misr, which proved to be very conscientious about educating its professionals. At the time of its foundation in 1935, it employed foreign specialists, such as the German director Fritz Kramp, the German set designer Robert Scharfenberg and the Russian photographer Sami Brel, who in turn trained Egyptian assistants. Another policy was to send aspiring young Egyptian talents abroad, mainly to France, for further training. Beneficiaries of this system included the directors Ahmed Badrakhan and Niazi Mustafa, the set designer Wali al-Din Samih and, later, the directors Kamal Selim, Salah Abu Seif, Kamal El-Cheikh and Sa'd Nadim. Many of them trained further generations, partly while working in the industry as teachers at what later became the Higher Film Institute. Until the opening of this school, film-makers and technicians were mostly educated by assisting others first. Only a few had the opportunity to travel abroad, such as Youssef Chahine (who studied in the United States) and Taufiq Salih and Husain Kamal (who graduated in France).

Eventually, in 1957, the Ministry of Culture started establishing the Higher Film Institute; it opened in 1959 and has until the present day provided the country with the necessary professionals, offering training in all relevant areas: screenwriting, directing, editing, production, sound, photography, animation, design, costumes and make-up. Almost all the Egyptian directors who started working since 1959 have graduated from this school.

In spite of an overloaded curriculum and deficient equipment, during the last decade the Institute has become the main producer of interesting and innovative short films (largely graduation projects), some of which were able to participate in and received awards from international festivals. As a whole (and seen together with the limits set by a commercial and industrial orientation) the Film Institute has certainly contributed to the relative homogeneity and continuity of Egyptian film-making, both in form and content.

Apart from the Institute, there are only a few other places in Egypt to study film-making: principally the public Television Institute and the private American University in Cairo. The studies at the latter are on a predominantly theoretical level.

Audience and movie theatres

Some of the major economic problems of the Egyptian film industry are related to its unbalanced distribution system. Although the number of movie theatres in Egypt has grown constantly since the construction of the first cinema in 1906, it remained always insufficient in relation to the population. It pushed, moreover, the Egyptian producer into a strong dependency on foreign distribution. Even in 1954, when the number of cinemas reached its peak, it did not exceed 454 theatres. Other sources speak of only 350 cinemas in the same year. In the course of 1960s – due to the introduction of television, on one hand, and the nationalization in 1963 of around one third of all cinemas, on the other – the numbers decreased continuously, as did revenues. In 1960, 80 million tickets were sold per year, whereas only 65 million were purchased in 1966. Although the General Film Organization tried at the same time to open up more cinemas, it could not prevent the technical decline and eventually the closing of theatres, particularly in the provinces. There public cultural centres started to fill the gap by hosting non-commercial cinemas. Eventually, in 1992, only 19 million tickets were sold in the remaining 208 theatres. A quarter of all cinemas were concentrated in the major Egyptian metropolises, Alexandria (sixteen theatres) and Cairo (fifty-two theatres).

Going to the movies in Egypt is, first of all, an urban means of entertainment. No movie theatres exist in the countryside. Film consumption in villages is confined to watching television and the VCR. In general, movie theatres are divided into three categories. The third class differs in programme and equipment from the first and second class: it does not present any first releases, but rather film packages that usually comprise one Egyptian and one or two foreign films; this package is repeated for days and the largely male audience enters the screening at any time, often knows the films by heart, interacts vigorously with the action and even repeats or comments on it during the projection.

First releases are offered only by first- and second-class theatres. They differ in ticket price, in the choice of programme, in furnishing and in the technical standard of its equipment and projection. The bulk of first-class theatres are in Cairo and Alexandria. They represent around 50 per cent of all cinemas there and around one third of the country's total. Since the late 1980s, the decline of movie theatres came to a temporary halt, expressed in the renovation of older cinemas (leased or sold to private entrepreneurs) and the construction of a small number of modern first-class theatres, equipped according to the most modern standards, with theatres in Cairo's affluent suburbs installing Dolby stereo and digital sound. Some of them are placed in the new shopping malls that have spread all over town. A ticket costs up to £E20 (around US$7), four to five times more than in a third-class cinema, yet they attract a highly mixed audience including many women.

The class system of movie theatres was further emphasized by the introduction of the VCR in the late 1970s. Already by 1982 some twenty-five VCRs were said to have been sold per 1,000 inhabitants. The middle-and upper-class audience – and in partic- ular women – have tended since that time to consume films at home. This development was accelerated by the bad condition of the old first- and second-class movie theatres, particularly in the inner city areas of Cairo and Alexandria. After the revolution and nationalization, their condition deteriorated to such an extent that they were avoided by the middle class, who also stayed away because these theatres attracted a predomi- nantly male working-class audience.

One setback for profitable theatrical exploitation in Egypt was the restrictive measures taken to support national Egyptian production, including the prohibition on releasing a foreign film in more than one theatre at a time, the heavy taxation of imported films and the obligation to show at least three Egyptian movies per year. In 1974 an extraordinary regulation was issued that prohibited the import of any karate and samurai films. In 1987 a law dating back to 1971 was finally implemented, requiring one Egyptian film to be exported to India for each imported Indian film, a regulation that resulted in an almost total halt in Indian imports.

Distribution

The existence of an international film distribution circuit represents a constant source of crisis for the Egyptian film industry. Foreign monopolies over international distribution and deficient domestic distribution prevent the investment of sufficient money in production, even though Egyptian cinema's growth was originally due to its opening up of foreign markets.

The export of Egyptian feature films started with the introduction of sound. One of the first films distributed in the neighbouring countries was Muhammad Karim's musical, *al-Warda al-Bayda' / The White Rose* (1933–4), starring the singer and composer Muhammad 'Abd al-Wahhab. His participation was certainly one of the reasons for the work's success in the Arab world. Like the other popular Egyptian singers of the time – Sayyid Darwish, Munira al-Mahdia and Umm Kulthum – 'Abd al-Wahhab's music had already been distributed on disc and radio outside Egypt before the rise of cinema, thus preparing fertile ground for its reception.

The songs surmounted one important obstacle in film distribution: the immensely distinct dialects of the Mashriq and Maghreb (*maghrib*) – that is, the Eastern and Western parts of the Arab world. The continuous consumption of Egyptian songs and films led the audiences of other Arab countries to acquire at least a passing knowlege of the Egyptian dialect. This process supported the distribution of Egyptian films and was an advantage that competitors from Tunisia, Algeria and Syria could attain only in exceptional circumstances. As a matter of fact, from the beginning film-making gave priority to the local Cairene dialect. With films directed at a partly illiterate mass audience, the use of sophisticated classical Arabic (primarily the language of the Qur'an, sciences and culture) would have been inappropriate. It was therefore only used for historical or religious films. Unlike the classical language, dialect offered an additional advantage in its ability to transport elements of popular culture. Thus representatives of popular Egyptian theatre used the colloquial in an imaginative way by introducing a popular and sometimes burlesque verbal comedy into early cinema.

The traditional markets for Egyptian films have been the Arab world and, to a certain extent, Muslim West Africa. In North Africa, Egyptian cinema did not only play an entertaining role, but also at times an ideological one. During the 1940s French productions in Morocco tried to compete with Egyptian products by releasing Arab-speaking orientalist films. In Algeria the distribution of non-Western films was marginalized until the 1950s by over-taxation and the concentration of theatres in French neighbourhoods. Nonetheless, Egyptian cinema remained popular, not least because of its symbolic meaning as an industry developed by an Arab people in spite of having been colonized. However, as a whole, export to the Maghreb has remained secondary, because of strong competition from Indian films and from Western films dubbed into French. In the 1980s the demand for Egyptian movies declined rapidly in some places due to increasing home production in these countries.

Until the 1970s the main market for Egypt's films was concentrated on the Fertile Crescent (that is, Lebanon, Syria, Iraq and Jordan), a fact which had enabled Lebanese and Syrian distributors to monopolize Egyptian distribution. This monopoly was challenged, on one hand, by nationalization and eventually terminated by the outbreak of civil war in Lebanon in 1975 and, on the other, by the Syrian boycott of Egyptian production. The latter was launched after the Camp David

Agreement with Israel in 1979 and lasted for more than a decade. In the 1990s the situation changed again: Iraq had to curtail its imports completely because of the Gulf War trade boycott, whereas the trade with Syria and Lebanon was revived in 1991 (although it never attained the importance of former times).

Today it is Saudi Arabia, Kuwait and the other Gulf States which represent the main customers. Half of all export revenues originate there. It is also companies from the Arab peninsula which monopolize Egypt's current distribution. This dependency developed during the video boom of the 1980s, when the introduction of the VCR resulted in an increasing consumption of the Egyptian mass product. Already in 1959, 155 of a total of 222 exported 16-millimetre prints were sent to Saudi Arabia. These films had been designed for private screenings only, as no movie theatres exist in the country. This increasing interest resulted in the development of the so-called '*sinima al-muqawalat*' or 'entrepreneur cinema', which was primarily used as a vehicle for advertising spots.

The most serious problem which arose from this foreign distribution system was the lack of reinvestment and the small margin of profit left for producers. It is due to a special financing system through which the producers take up production loans offered by the international distributors and in turn sell off the complete rights to the film. The loan's amount usually corresponds to the popularity of the involved stars. This system minimizes the financial risk for the producer, but reduces the profits to the limited and risky national box office revenues. As a result the budgets of Egyptian movies remain relatively constant and likewise small. Even the budget for a film starring the currently most expensive Egyptian star, 'Adil Imam, does not exceed approximately £E2 million (US$600,000). As a result, production tends to be dominated artistically, thematically and economically by the stars.

Stars

In Egypt the film industry lives like Hollywood on the creation of stars who exercise a quasi-mythical attraction. The Egyptian star system is organized pyramidically. A dozen highly popular and well-paid actors and actresses are positioned on top of scores of second- and third-rate performers. Today top stars hold a very powerful position in the film industry's economy, not only because the audience usually identifies films through the names of the stars and not directors, but also because of the production-loan system which depends essentially on a star's participation. As distributors turn out to be reluctant to finance a film which does not feature a known star, the whole star system suffers from constant stagnation. Meanwhile aged stars have to perform parts of much younger characters and younger actors age until they attain main parts. Moreover, stars interfere in the process of screenwriting in order to adapt narratives to their favourite persona and / or exclude stories which do not fit their age, like those centred around adolescents, for example. In addition, star wages are enormous in comparison to the total film budget. The average expenses for an Egyptian feature film are currently around £E1 million (about US$300,000). Up to 50 per cent may have to be spent on star wages (in a few particular cases even more), which means that little remains for props, set, costumes, transport and crew wages.

The first movie stars were taken from other branches of entertainment, either theatre or music. Some of them actively contributed to the formation of early

Egyptian genres – for example, the popular comedians Nagib al-Rihani and 'Ali al-Kassar, who decisively influenced comedy and film farce during the 1930s and 1940s. Each of them developed a specific persona, ranging from ethnic to social stereotypes – such as the average working-class little man and the naïve Nubian. The same applies to 'Abd al-Salam Nabulsi, representing the capricious aristocrat, Bishara Wakim the funny Lebanese and Mary Munib the terrorizing mother-in-law. They were substituted during the 1950s by the clumsy and ignorant gorilla-like Ima'il Yasin, the hot-tempered and sometimes vicious cross-eyed 'Abd al-Fatah al-Qusairi and the *Karagöz* Shukuku (an Egyptian Mr Punch), among others. During the 1960s and 1970s a more burlesque and silly performance style prevailed, presented by Muhammad Rida, the couple Shuwikar and Fu'ad al-Muhandis, and the Thulathi adwa' al-masrah (Theatre Lights Trio), comprising of George Sidhum, Samir Ghanim and Ahmad al-Daif. During the late 1970s 'Adil Imam, a theatre actor like most of the other comedians, introduced the nihilist young urban underdog. Denounced as trival, he remained the best-paid Egyptian star actor until the mid-1990s. His position is currently challenged by a younger sucessor, Muhammad Hinidi, in his role as the harmless, funny and pragmatic character. It is noteworthy that the comedians who appeared since the late 1960s were far less strongly characterizd in terms of specific roles and masks.

In contrast to their male colleagues, comic actresses rarely made it to the top. Mary Munib, for example, appeared in the 1930s and was followed by Zinat Sidqi and Widad Hamdi during the 1950s and 1960s. They used to represent female dragons, fat and far from attractive. Either dominant or silly, they always played supporting roles. Leading parts in comedies were usually performed by actresses who also possessed a melodramatic or realist repertoire, like the singer Layla Murad in the 1940s, Fatin Hamama, Shadia, Sabah and Su'ad Husni between the 1950s and 1970s, and Layla Ilwi and Yusra in the following two decades.

The stars of the early Egyptian musical coincided with the major representatives of contemporary Arab-Egyptian music – first the Kawkab al-Sharq ('Star of the Orient') singer Umm Kulthum, as well as the congenial singer and composer Muhammad 'Abd al-Wahhab. They were mostly involved in melodramatic plots. Layla Murad appeared during the late 1930s and embodied often charming and innocent aristocratic girls. She replaced – together with Sabah, Shadia, Farid al-Atrash and Asmahan (who died as early as 1944) – the first generation of singers. Farid al-Atrash continued to star in film serials throughout the 1950s, at a time when new singers like Muhammad Fawzi and Huda Sultan appeared. Sabah (Lebanese like Farid al-Atrash) performed mostly in light comedies during the 1950s and 1960s, as did Shadia, who was moreover a good-looking and talented actress.

The singer 'Abd al-Halim Hafiz was the idol of teenagers thoughout the 1960s and early 1970s, uniting an attractive appearance with musical and dramatic talents. He remained the last really adored music star of Egyptian cinema. His demise in 1977 and Umm Kulthum's death in 1975 terminated the golden era of the Egyptian musical. No remarkable singers appeared during the 1970s and 1980s. Commercially succesful, Ahmad 'Adawiyya (who starred in a few films during the 1980s) was considered vulgar and associated with the taste of the Gulf States. Eventually, during the 1990s, new singers and representatives of the new 'world music' – such as Muhammad Munir, 'Amr Diab and Muhammad Fu'ad – made their way onto the screen, largely performing young urban men aspiring for fame and a better life.

The most famous dancers of the Egyptian screen were Badi'a Masabni, Tahiyya Carioca, Samia Gamal and Na'ima 'Akif. During the 1940s and 1950s they elevated the belly dance to a respectable art form, whether on or off screen. Starting from the 1970s a general decline took place, however, with the appearance of Suhair Zaki, Nagwa Fu'ad and finally Fifi 'Abdu and Lucy, who gave belly dance an air of seduction and vulgarity that made it a complementary opposite to the new morality spreading in public. Some actresses – like Hind Rustum during the 1960s, Su'ad Husni during the 1970s, as well as Nabila 'Ubaid and Nadia al-Gindi throughout the 1980s and 1990s – who embodied at times the *femme fatale* persona, often performed the characters of belly dancers. A more positive film image had dancers who specialized in music hall, such as the little girl Fayruz (in the 1950s), her charming relative Nelly (since the 1970s) and more recently Sharihan.

Up to the 1960s the angels of the screen were Layla Murad, Layla Fawzi, Magda, Shadia, Camelia, Lubna 'Abd al-'Aziz, Mariam Fakhr al-Din and the megastar, Fatin Hamama. They starred in dozens of melodramas and their characters remained, particularly in Hamama's case, incorrigible even when they alienated spouses and spoiled other women's marriages. Stocky bourgeois-looking Mimi Shakib often played their vicious counterpart, mostly seducing others into immoral actions. In spite of the decline of classical melodrama since the late 1970s, endangered virtue remains an important theme to the present day, mostly represented by Ilham Shahin, Suhair Ramzi, Mervat Amin and Nagla' Fathi – the last two sometimes represented bourgeois or academic women as well. These actresses were often supported by Fardus Muhammad and Amina Rizq, playing less-attractive yet caring mothers and servants.

A subcategory of the virtuous girl developed to become the Arab Bedouin girl, mostly represented in Bedouin films and costume dramas – first by 'Aziza Amir or Bahiga Hafiz and later by Koka – and characterized as outspoken, courageous, generous and righteous, similar to the *bint al-balad* (literally meaning 'girl of the country'). This character appeared first in realist films and can be summarized as a loyal and kind-hearted but clever woman from the popular neighbourhoods, who supports herself independently but resepects traditional morals. This role was convincingly introduced by the dancer Tahiyya Carioca during the 1950s. More contemporary actresses who have at times performed this type are Ma'ali Zayid, Layla 'Ilwi and 'Abla Kamil.

Characters representing passive and endangered virtue have remained popular to this day (currently enacted by Ilham Shahin, Athar al-Hakim, Layla 'Ilwi and Nagla' Fathi), although they are now presented in a less melodramatic manner, instead appearing in the framework of social drama or gangster films. On the other hand, Berlanti 'Abd al-Hamid, Huda Sultan, Tahiyya Carioca and Hind Rustum (who starred between the 1940s and 1960s) and in particular Nadia al-Gindi (since the late 1970s) relied primarily on female charms and sex-appeal, expressed in dresses and manners, and were thus liable to by negatively characterized in the role of the vamp. Many actresses (like Nadia Lutfi, Su'ad Husni, Nabila 'Ubaid, Madiha Kamil and Yusra) have been flexible enough, however, to represent both sides – innocent despite their vices, mostly in the role of reluctant prostitutes or belly dancers.

The romantic lovers of the Egyptian screen were first represented by Badr Lama, 'Imad Hamdi, Husain Sidqi, later in the 1950s by Ahmad Mazhar, Kamal al-Shinawi and Omar Charif ('Umar al-Sharif) and in the 1970s by Husain Fahmi and Mahmud

Yasin. Their decent, slightly effeminate *noblesse* made them excellent romantic lovers, suitable for melodramatic victimization, in contrast to their strict, powerful and paternalistic counterparts – in other words the pashas, fathers and husbands, played by Yusuf Wahbi, Zaki Rustum, Yahia Shahin and later Mahmud Mursi. At the same time, Husain Riyad and Sulayman Nagib used to represent positive and tender fathers.

Physically strong, rude and rebellious men (among others Farid Shauqi, Rushdi Abaza and Shukri Sarhan) came to the fore with the gangster films of the 1950s and dominated the 1960s. Their agressive masculinity associated them sometimes with criminality and women of ill repute, but they also took positive roles as fighters who secure right and order. Pure villains were, in general, less attractive: for instance, Zaki Rustum and Stéphane Rosti (up to the 1950s), Taufiq al-Diqn (up to the 1960s) or the congenial Mahmud al-Miligi (who starred in many thrillers and gangster films from the late 1940s until the 1970s).

Some male actors were also primarily associated with virtue, like the 1940s actor Husain Sidqi and his slightly sour mimic, the always concerned-looking Salah zu-l-Fiqar, who appeared in the late 1950s. During the 1980s, with the appearance of New Realism, a new type of positive male character developed: 'heroes in blue jeans', young working-class men, roughly attractive and courageous, real social underdogs, best represented by Mahmud 'Abd al-'Aziz, Ahmad Zaki, Nur al-Sharif and, to a certain extent, 'Adil Imam, Mahmud Himida and Faruq al-Fishawi.

The most prevalent characters of Egyptian mainstream cinema are constructed according to a largely conservative moral system which is ruled by clear binary oppositions – good and evil, virtuous and vicious. The essential conflicts are often engendered by cathartic threats and dangers. In this context, males are likely to be threatened socially, whereas females are often exposed to moral dangers. Therefore, as Roy Armes and Lizbeth Malkmus noted, many film titles concerned with women 'imply the illegal (using such words as morals, licit, proof, law, arrest) and many of those concerned with men imply the asocial (bully, smoke, hashish, beasts, bums)' (Malkmus and Armes 1991: 106). Accordingly, women are more associated with emotions, love, passion and the body, and men with strength, power and violence.

Genres

All popular genres created by Egyptian cinema throughout its history shared the absolute determination to entertain and the permanent readiness to compromise in line with the oft-cited motto '*al-gumhur 'ayiz kidda*' (a colloquial phrase meaning 'the audience wants it that way'). Moreover, the Egyptian film industry favoured certain genres due to cultural as well as economic conditions, mainly the musical, melodrama, gangster films, thrillers, farce, comedy and realist films. Science fiction, horror, independent art-movies and even the historical spectacle were, by contrast, rarely produced.

In early cinema the musical played a major role, along with melodrama and farce which were temporarily joined by the Bedouin films. In the course of the boom that started at the end of the 1940s, a new popular formula crystallized. It was shaped by an entertaining mixture of genres that borrowed from all kinds of films, ranging from farce to melodrama, and was furnished with the obligatory happy ending. Dance, in particular belly dance, as well as music and songs in general, were considered indispensible. Elements of the American music-hall film moved into Egyptian cinema during the late 1940s. The adaption of successful Hollywood productions was quite common and, during the 1950s and 1960s, the spectrum widened further as new genres (like the thriller, gangster films, religious films, political films and melodramatic realism) made their appearence. During the 1970s and 1980s the latter, which was considered more serious than other mainstream genres, developed to become 'social drama' – mostly a mixture or gangster films and melodrama, furnished with social critique. In the same period, characteristics of the Asian karate film were adopted by some second-rate directors, while the old genres (like classical melodrama and the musical) increasingly retreated or were altered.

The musical

The Egyptian musical has contributed decisively to the success of Egyptian cinema. It has recycled both traditional native and Western forms of music and dance, and has thus developed a novel and genuine form of these arts. As a genre, the musical appeared always in alliance with other prevalent genres, be they melodrama, comedy or even realism.

The introduction of sound to cinema was an important factor in promoting the Egyptian musical specifically and the development of a national cinema as whole, not least because of the dominance of European and American products in the film market. Sound established a linguistic barrier between imported films and the regional audience that could be overcome only by dubbing or subtitling. Dubbing is still uncommon in Egypt, mainly because of the expense, and subtitling is problematic because of the high illiteracy rate.

Thus the soundtrack opened a new possibility for spectators to relate to their culture expressed in native music and speech. Therefore it is no wonder that one of the two first Egyptian sound films which appeared in 1932 was a musical: entitled *Unshudat al-Fu'ad* / *Song from the Heart*, it was directed by Mario Volpi and starred the singer Nadra. The first Egyptian movie to be successfully exported to other Arab countries was likewise a musical: *al-Warda al-Badha'* / *The White Rose* (1933). It was performed by Muhammad 'Abd al-Wahhab and directed by Muhammad Karim. The success of this film, in contrast to *Unshudat al-Fu'ad*, was not only due to 'Abd al-Wahhab's popularity (the same applied to Nadra) but also to a far better integration of the music into the narrative. Advised by his director, 'Abd al-Wahhab gave up the long instrumental introductions traditional to Arab songs and instead confined their total length to six minutes.

Although 'Abd al-Wahhab starred only in seven films, he remained a source of musical inspiration for cinema until his death in 1991, composing the songs for innumerable films. In his works he introduced new rhythms, both European and Latin American, which included the rumba, samba, tango and foxtrot. Moreover, he enlarged the traditional Arab *takht* (orchestra) – which consists of only a few instruments – adding Western instruments and increasing the number of all instruments, which gave him the opportunity to achieve bigger volumes and more musical variation.

He experimented also with the operetta-style in his films *Yahya al-Hubb* / *Long Live*

Love! (1938), co-starring Layla Murad, and *Yawm Saʿid / Happy Day* (1940), both by Muhammad Karim, by presenting the musical duet. Farid al-Atrash developed this kind of performance further in (among others) *Intisar al-Shabab / The Victory of Youth* (1941), with his sister Asmahan, and *Lahn Hubbi / Melody of My Love* (1953) – both films were by Ahmad Badrakhan.

Early musicals were mainly melodramas centred around a romantic love story, often featuring a young musician striving for recognition. This applies to ʿAbd al-Wahhab and to the singer Umm Kulthum, who starred in the first Studio Misr production, *Widad* (1936), which was also a musical. She largely represented a musically gifted faithful slave in love, as she did in not only *Widad* but also *Dananir* (1940) and *Sallama* (1945). Her mediocre acting was compensated for by her striking voice. Soon, however, other more attractive female singers appeared: first Layla Murad, who was discovered by ʿAbd al-Wahhab in their only common film *Yahya al-Hubb* (1938), and second Asmahan, who appeared in 1941. The latter's promising career came to an end with her sudden death only three years later. Her last film was *Gharam Wa Intiqam / Love and Revenge* (1944) by Yusuf Wahbi.

Al-Atrash continued performing on his own. He enriched his films with all sorts of music, ranging from Lebanese folksongs to Viennese waltzes, as can be heard in *Intisar al-Shabab* (1941) and *ʿAfrita Hanim / Lady Ghost* (1949) by Barakat, for example. Apart from him, few other singers and composers left a peculiar musical mark on their films, with notable exceptions being Kahlawi (the specialist in so-called 'Bedouin' rhythms), ʿAbd al-ʿAziz Mahmud and the composer and singer Munir Murad, Layla Murad's brother, who starred in Kamal al-Tilmissani's *Ana Wa Habibi / Me and My Beloved* (1953), among other films.

The songs presented were meant to convey the feelings of the heroes and heroines, although at the beginning they were poorly integrated into plot and action. The singers' musical performance was often static and retarded the flow of the action considerably. Niazi Mustafa was one of the first to provide a better integration of songs into the action with his film *Masnaʿ al-Zawjat / Factory of Wives* (1941); ʿAbbas Kamil made similar progress in his *ʿArusat al-Bahr / Mermaid* (1948), which starred Muhammad Fawzi. The coherence of plot, action and performance was developed further, particularly in backstage musicals like Barakat's melodrama *Lahn al-Khulud / Song of Eternity* (1952), which relied on parallel action and cross-cutting to create sufficient visual variety and secure a steady film rhythm.

Music was considered indispensable to early cinema. Between 1931 and 1961 Egyptian cinema produced 918 films, of which nearly a third were musicals (exactly 270 films). In some years, for example from 1944 to 1946, up to 50 per cent of the films belonged to that genre, with the result that the 1940s were seen as the decade of the Egyptian musical. Forty-six singers – including Huda Sultan, Sabah, Shadia, Nur al-Huda, Saʿd ʿAbd al-Wahhab, Muhammad Fawzi, Ibrahim Hamuda, Najat ʿAli and Fathiya Ahmad – are said to have appeared in them as main characters. Some singers starred in up to 100 films, among them Shadia, whose career lasted for almost thirty years.

Thus the initial attachment of the musical to melodrama slackened from the late 1940s onwards and opened up to cheerful musical comedies that often presented music-hall performances. Many of these films cannot be classified according to strict genre categories, as they rather form a *mélange*. The words of a typical film advertise-

Figure 11 Abbi Fawq al-Shajara / My Father Up the Tree

ment of the late 1940s may clarify this: 'a dramatic comedy love story with songs and dances'. Anwar Wagdi first of all specialized in this type of film, introduced among others with *Ghazal al-Banat / Girls' Flirtation* (1949), starring Layla Murad and Nagib al-Rihani, and developed further in the two films *Yasemine* (1950) and *Dhahab / Gold* (1951), starring little Fayruz. Its cheerful style was supported by the musical performance of comedians, such as Shukuku and Isma'il Yasin, who were made to sing some dialogues in a kind of melodious speech. A very cheerful example is found in *Ghazal al-Banat*, where Nagib al-Rihani performs a charmingly hilarious duet with Layla Murad during a car ride.

The 1950s gave rise to singers, such as the Lebanese Sabah, Huda Sultan, Shadia and 'Abd al-Halim Hafiz, who dominated the screen for the following decade. Huda Sultan, who is still performing today (although no longer as a singer), became one of the *femmes fatales* of the Egyptian screen and featured in films including the realist *al-Usta Hasan / Master Hasan* (1952), by Salah Abu Seif, but also starred in a few exceptional musicals along with 'Abd al-'Aziz Mahmud, such as *Taxi al-Gharam / Taxi of Love* (1954) by Niazi Mustafa, and in the classical melodrama, *Imra'a Fi-l-Tariq / Woman on the Road* (1958) by 'Izz al-Din zu-l-Fiqar.

Shadia also refined her acting to the point at which she was able to appear in films other than musicals. She started in musical melodramas and then switched to light comedy during the late 1950s and early 1960s. Some of her most hilarious films were by Fatin 'Abd al-Wahhab, including *al-Zawja Raqam 13 / Wife No. 13* (1962). By contrast, Sabah (who was also a talented singer) was not able to develop a more sophisticated persona. She starred mostly in light musicals featuring innocent or naïve girls.

The music and songs which stood most for that period were performed by 'Abd al-Halim Hafiz. The merging of songs with plot and action in his works was largely conventional, but he introduced an accelerated musical rhythm, backed, among other styles, by elements of beat music. In Husain Kamal's box-office hit *Abi Fawq al-Shajara / My Father Up the Tree* (1969), based on a *Dame aux camélias* motif, this tendency was further reinforced. Various songs and sophisticated lively group-dance choreographies seemed to correspond to the libertinage of the young characters and their permissive dresses, including scanty bathing suits and miniskirts. Thus, adapting the persona of the poor handsome and gifted yet unfortunate young man, Hafiz starred in a dozen melodramatic love stories, among others *Maw'id Gharam / Love Appointment* (1956) by Henri Barakat, *al-Wisada al-Khaliyya / The Empty Cushion* (1957) by Salah Abu Seif and *Hikayat Hubb / Love Story* (1959) by Hilmi Halim.

During the 1970s, a general decline of the musical took place and was expressed in two phenomena. First of all, no singer was able to attain the same fame as their predecessor on and off screen; this applies to Muharram Fu'ad, Kamal Husni, Najat al-Saghira, Warda al-Gaza'iriyya, Fayza Ahmad and Maha Sabri during the 1970s and Iman al-Bahr Darwish, Iman 'Abd al-Halim and 'Ali Himida during the 1980s. Even the commercially successful Ahmad 'Adawiyya, who starred in Muhammad Shibl's *Rocky Horror Picture Show* remake *Anyab / Tusks* (1981), was not highly valued in Egypt and was considered to be only appropriate to the taste of the Gulf States.

Moreover, the most successful musicals of the 1970s starred actors but not singers – for example, the box-office hit *Khalli Balak Min Zuzu / Take Care of Zuzu* (1972) by the master of melodrama Hasan al-Imam. Su'ad Husni was made to sing and dance, convincingly appearing as a young student, daughter of a belly dancer, who falls in love with an upper-class professor. The vivid, charming musical inserts and the melodramatic plot, brightened up with numerous cheerful scenes including a happy end for the couple in love, were responsible for the formulaic film's great success. Not successful, but one of the few interesting experiments on the musical and narrative level, was Youssef Chahine's tragic musical *'Awdat al-Ibn al-Dal / The Return of the Prodigal Son* (1976) – a politically relevant story about a disintegrating post-Nasserist family, which starred the Lebanese singer Magda al-Rumi and included several group dances and al-Rumi's music.

During the 1990s, in spite of the absence of charismatic singers, some talented and committed directors (notably Khairy Beshara, Daoud 'Abd al-Sayed, Mohamed Khan and Sherif 'Arafa) started reviving the musical. Khairy Beshara was the first New Realist to rediscover songs and dances. As early as 1986 he had included the Nubian pop singer Muhammad Munir in his realist melodrama *al-Tawq Wa-l-Iswirra / The Collar and the Bracelet*. Then, in his film *Kaburya / Crabs* (1990), he went further by introducing clear music-hall elements. In his more recent films *Ays Krim Fi Glim / Ice Cream in Glim* (1992) and *Amrika Shika Bika / Abracadabra America* (1993) he was able to integrate songs by the popular pop singers 'Amr Diab and Muhammad Fu'ad and is so far one of the first of his generation to represent a glimpse of youth culture in his works.

Beshara certainly inspired other directors to experiment too. Mohamed Khan, for example, applied the technique of using musical video clips in his film *Karate* (1996), where he made the popular actor Muhammad Zaki sing and dance. Daoud Abd El-Sayed, by contrast, did not rely on any pop or world music songs for *Sariq al-Farah /*

Wedding Thief (1994). He used occidental music for the songs, thus violating the traditional dichotomy between oriental and occidental music in Egyptian cinema, which usually assigned Western compositions to the background and oriental-inspired music to the songs.

Sherif 'Arafa, certainly the most mainstream among this group, produced a box-office hit in 1991 with *Sama' Huss / Silence!* (1991). The film presented several songs and, more importantly, a large variety of dances, ranging from belly dances to jazz and breakdancing. Some of the most recent musicals, like *Isma'iliyya Rayih Gay / Round Trip to Ismailia* (1997) by Karim Diya' al-Din, rely on the same melodramatic plots as the 1960s movies. This film starred Muhammad Fu'ad – in a typical 'Abd al-Halim Hafiz role – as a poor adolescent singer aspiring to fame. The music of the songs has meanwhile become even more syncretic, closely related to world music and including only a few oriental remnants.

During its long history, the Egyptian musical has always put emphasis on the song, whereas the dance was often complementary or secondary. In spite of the importance of belly dance – there is almost no mainstream film without at least an allusion to belly dance – it was in general more of a by-product, referred to in many films in a passing way. Apart from the films which were centred around a female dancer, it generally appeared (and this has not changed much even today) on a quite restricted number of occasions: in weddings, during private parties, in night clubs or in popular festivals. The *raqs sharqi* (oriental dance) presented in Egyptian movies in fact differs in dress, movement and presentation from the *raqs baladi* (dance from the country), the traditional belly dance that is still performed in the countryside.

Thus dance, including the oriental dance, was as syncretic as the music of the songs. In 1937, for example, Bahiga Hafiz presented in her film *Layla al-Badawiyya* supposedly oriental group dances reminiscent to those in Hollywood films of the time. Several girls wearing partly transparent dresses and waving their veils are made to spin around an ancient fountain while being observed by the fabulously dressed Persian king. This changed only slightly during the 1950s, when the music-hall film flourished most, but dance was given more space, grew in sophistication and the accompaniying music borrowed from everywhere: belly dancing, flamenco, Arab folkdance, tap dance and ballet, all were mixed up. The former circus artist Na'ima 'Akif, presented by director Husain Fawzi in (among others) *Lahalibu* (1949), *Fatat al-Sirk / Circus Girl* (1951) and *Tamr Hinna / Tamerind* (1957), and the little girl Fayruz, who starred in several musicals directed by Anwar Wagdi, were particularly successful in presenting this kind of mixture. Both, though not professional singers, were made to sing.

Badi'a Masabni was the first belly dancer to be given a major part, in *Malikat al-Masarih / Queen of Theatres* (1936) by Mario Volpi. Two other belly dancers who were trained at Masabni's variety theatre succeeded in cinema: Samia Gamal and Tahiyya Carioca. Samia Gamal even developed her own expressive style, borrowing from experimental Western dance. Tahiyya Carioca continued her acting career (even after she had stopped dancing) up to the early 1990s. The belly dance saw a relative decline, however, as the artistic level of new generations of dancers (such as Suhair Zaki and Nagwa Fu'ad during the 1970s and 1980s and Fifi Abdu during the 1980s and 1990s) decreased, along with their moral standing. In particular, Nagwa Fu'ad and Fifi 'Abdu linked belly dance to cheap seduction.

Lucy, who started her career in the 1990s, concentrated on acting and the very popular Sharihan is not considered a belly dancer in the true sense. She became famous because of her performances in the televised musical events that are broadcast during the holy month of Ramadan. Her performances are music-hall oriented and very syncretic in style. Her movies include *Suq al-Nisa' / Women's Market* (1994) by Yusuf Frinsis and *Crystal* (1993) by 'Adil 'Awad. Since the 1960s actresses have started to accept roles as belly dancers despite their insufficient skill – these include Hind Rustum in *Shafiqa al-Qibtiyya / Shafiqa the Copt* (1963), Nadia al-Gindi in *Bamba Kashar* (1974) (both by Hasan al-Imam) and Nabila 'Ubaid in Samir Saif's *al-Raqissa Wa-l-Siyasi / The Belly-Dancer and the Politician* (1990).

A special place was held by Farida Fahmy and the Rida Group, who starred together in several dance films during the 1960s. They specialized in folkloric group dances and mixed traditional regional peformances, including the belly dance (*al-raqs al-baladi*), with elements of ballet. *Ajazat Nisf al-Sana / Mid-Year Vacation* (1962) and *Gharam Fi-l-Karnak / Love in Karanak* (1967), both by 'Ali Rida, were to be their most acclaimed films. Farida Fahmy's performances did not suffer from their association with belly dance: they were placed in the framework of group dance – in other words, their were neither individual nor related to morally suspect theatres and night-clubs.

Farce and comedy

The majority of the narrative silent films were farce or comedy and they were mostly adaptations (or at least re-arrangements) of plays. Such films included *Madame Lolita* (1919), *al-Khala al-Amrikaniyya / The American Aunt* (1920), *al-Bash Katib / The Chief Secretary* (1924) and *al-Bahr Biyidhak Leh? / Why Does the Sea Laugh?* (1928), featuring the most popular comedians of the early Egyptian film industry, such as 'Ali al-Kassar and Nagib al-Rihani.

Drawing from the experience of improvised Egyptian theatre (*al-masrah al-murtajal*), in which the actors used to improvise *ad hoc* jokes and topical allusions around a loose plot, mere farce dominated during the first two decades of Egyptian cinema. 'Ali al-Kassar and the far less known Shalom, both presented by the director Togo Mizrahi, performed in series of films in which they developed specific masks. Shalom starred as a poor lower class Alexandrian Jew and 'Ali al-Kassar as the black Nubian 'Uthman 'Abd al-Basit. Togo Mizrahi directed all the works starring Shalom – including *Shalum al-Riyadi / Shalom the Sportsman* (1937) and *al-'Izz Bahdala / Mistreated by Affluence* (1937) – as well as for the majority of Kassar's most successful films – such as *al-Sa'a Sab'a / Seven O'Clock* (1937), *al-Tilighraf / Telegram* (1938), *Salifni Talata Gini / Lend Me Three Pounds* (1939) and *Alf Layla Wa Layla / One Thousand and One Nights* (1941). Unlike Kassar's output, the Shalom films were not very successful, probably because of their poor quality and the limited popularity of the actor.

The stories of these films were fragmentary, mostly focusing on sketches that were only loosely connected by a framing story. *Al-Sa'a Sab'a*, for example, focused on a nightmare of the Nubian in which he loses his employer's money and is chased for that reason by the police, yet the first third of the film is wasted on sketches before the main plot is even introduced. From the late 1940s the fragmentary style of farce became outdated or at least submerged by the dramatically stricter organization of comedy – although this trend was occasionally interruted by breathtaking nonsense films like Fatin 'Abd al-Wahhab's *Isha'it Hubb / Love Rumour* (1960) and more recently by *Sa'idi Fi-l-Jami'a al-Amirikiyya / An Upper Egyptian at the American University* (1998) by Sa'id Hamid.

Egyptian farce has kept to a relatively slow pace, with a few slapstick performances included. It has been rather verbally oriented, using a lot of jokes and wordplay, and relying on the generally clumsy behaviour of its protagonists and their schematized personae. Drawing from the regional tradition of the shadow play, it presented certain pre-defined cranky characters, often characterized by their ethnicity or accents, such as the European foreigner (*khawaga*), the Nubian and the Lebanese.

One of the first clear-cut comedies was *Salama Fi Khayr / Salama is Fine*, starring Nagib al-Rihani, which for its comic effect relied essentially on the plot – an errand boy is mistaken for a sultan – and the odd situations resulting from it. Other successful films starring Nagib al-Rihani, such as *Si 'Umar / Master Omar* (1941) by Niazi Mustafa, *Ahmar Shafayif / Red Lipstick* (1946) and *Lu'bat al-Sitt / The Lady's Game* (1946), both by Wali al-Din Samih, all had coherent plots and were spiced by Nagib al-Rihani's fine humour – expressed not only through his nuanced performances but also in the dialogues which he usually scripted himself. Moreover, al-Rihani's persona had no mask, like al-Kassar's; he rather chose to represent a middle-aged poor man who was badly mistreated by others, be they women or the rich.

One of al-Rihani's favourite themes was the experience of a socially misplaced person, as in *Salama Fi Khayr* where he played a lower-class Egyptian who is asked to replace a sultan. Similarly, in *Ghazal al-Banat / Girls' Flirtation* (1949) by Anwar Wagdi, he appears as a poor teacher who is hired by a pasha and has to live in the latter's palace. The sudden change of social position has been a recurrent motif of Egyptian cinema, starting with Togo Mizrahi's *al-'Izz Bahdala* (1937) and ending with *Sa'idi Fi-l-Jami'a al-Amirikiyya* (1998).

Al-Kassar's and al-Rihani's golden age ended in the late 1940s, marked by Rihani's death in 1949. The shift to light musical comedies which became a characteristic of the 1950s was already visible in al-Rihani's last work, *Ghazal al-Banat*, which co-starred the singer Layla Murad. It was typical of the new formula: a comedy slightly spiced with melodrama and enriched with songs and music-hall inspired dances. Director and actor Anwar Wagdi directed dozens of these works and starred in some of them himself. He presented not only the singer Layla Murad, but also the charming little girl Fayruz, who could dance and sing as well. Wagdi's most representative, if not always his most polished works, are *Ghazal al-Banat*, *Layla Bint al-Fuqara' / Layla, Daughter of the Poor* (1945) and *Dhahab / Gold* (1951).

The comedian Isma'il Yasin first appeared on the screen in 1939. He was initially, like many other comedians, assigned secondary roles, adding comedy to basically melodramatic plots like that of *Dhahab*, for example, where a young bourgeois woman is forced to abandon her child only to find her years later in the custody of a poor performer. Yasin subsequently became the star of a whole series of films dedicated to his persona. It started with *Isma'il Yasin Fi-l-Jaysh / Isma'il Yasin in the Army* (1955), by Fatin 'Abd al-Wahhab, and went on with Yasin in the police, the navy, the airforce, the zoo and so forth. His most accomplished comedy was *al-Anissa Hanafi / Miss Hanafi* (1954), also by 'Abd al-Wahhab, which evolves around gender reversals. Yasin's physiognomy – particularly his very big mouth – gave him a gorilla-like appearance, which he reinforced with his grimaces, and it led him to develop, just like al-Kassar's Nubian, the mask of a kindhearted but absolutely naïve clown who gets out of trouble solely because of his good luck.

Many of the Yasin films were directed by Fatin 'Abd al-Wahab, who is considered one of the best comedy directors of the period. In the 1960s he worked on light comedies, like *al-Zawja Raqam 13 / Wife No. 13* (1962) and *Mirati Mudir 'Am / My Wife is a General Director* (1966), that were well made on both the artistic and technical levels. These films were performed by dramatic actors and not comedians – in the first case Rushdi Abaza and the singer Shadia and in the second Shadia, again, and Salah zu-l-Fiqar. By focusing on gender relations, these films picked up on another comic theme prevalent since al-Rihani's *Ahmar Shafayif / Red Lipstick* and *Lu'bat al-Sitt / The Lady's Game*.

In both *al-Zawja Raqam 13* and *Mirati Mudir 'Am* macho men are taught a hard lesson. In the first instance, a young spouse discovers that her husband had already divorced twelve women and decides, despite being in love with him, to take revenge; in the second, a spouse is made director of the company in which her husband works, very much to his annoyance, yet eventually he has to admit her capabilities. Both films fed into the modernist discourse of gender equality that was popular in the Nasserist era.

Many comedies, however, were presenting shallow love stories that confirmed the most prevalent views: these included *A'ilat Zizi / Zizi's Family* (1963) by Fatin 'Abd al-Wahhab, starring the comedian Fu'ad al-Muhandis and the actress Su'ad Husni, and dealing with the love stories of three siblings. In this film the young female protagonist tries to convince a cinema director to give her a main part; however, he finally states that she is incapable of performing, but good enough to become his wife. This film, by the way, became al-Muhandis' most famous film. Otherwise, he starred together with his wife, Shuwikar, in several farces, such as Niazi Mustafa's *al-'Ataba Gazaz / Glass Threshold* (1969), which relied on al-Muhandis' exaggerated acting and on many silly awkward situations.

Like al-Muhandis, many comedians had to develop a specific mask and were thus assigned to mostly secondary roles, even in comedies starring dramatic actors. An example is 'Adil Imam, who spiced up *Mirati Mudir 'Am* as a supporting actor but took another decade to become a star whose name would carry a whole film. These second-rank comic actors had to fill the ranks of many musicals, like Isma'il Yasin in *Dhahab* or Samir Ghanim in *Khalli Balak Min Zuzu*, or even in primarily realist films and melodramas, like Mary Munib in *al-'Azima / Determination*, in order to temporarily relieve the viewer and the protagonists from their anguish. Beshara Wakim, Mary Munib, Siraj Munir, Hasan Shawqi, Zainat Sidqi, 'Abd al-Salam Nabulsi, Shukuku, Widad Hamdi, 'Abd al-Mun'im Ibrahim, 'Abd al-Mun'im Madbuli, Samir Ghanim, Muhammad Rida, Is'ad Yunis, Yusuf Dawud, Ahmad Bidir, An'am Salusa, Nagah al-Mugi and Muhammad Hinidi, among others, added humour to Egyptian films from the 1940s until the present time.

From the 1960s onwards, comedy was also combined with realism, as in *Bayn al-Sama' Wa-l-Ard / Between Sky and Earth* (1959) and *al-Zawja al-Thaniyya / The Second Wife* (1967), both by Salah Abu Seif and both, likewise, addressing social issues. The latter is a charming example of this kind of genre mixture: set entirely in the countryside, it tells the story of an old village mayor who forces a young farmer to divorce his beautiful wife in order to marry her himself, and has to pay a high price for his deed.

In spite of a relative decline of artistic and technical standards during the 1970s, comedy was increasingly used to express social critiques, as in the work of the directors Muhammad 'Abd al-'Aziz and his brother 'Umar. Muhammad 'Abd al- 'Aziz's first comedy, *Fi-l-Sayf Lazzim Tuhhib | In the Summer You Must Love* (1974), drew its humour from the sharp social contradictions displayed. 'Umar 'Abd al-'Aziz focused, in his *al-Shaqqa Min Haqq al-Zawja | The Flat Belongs to the Wife* (1985), on the housing shortage and the problems evolving from that for young couples about to marry.

Muhammad 'Abd al-'Aziz also directed one of the first 'Adil Imam films, *al-Mahfaza Ma'aya | The Wallet is with Me* (1978), which is considered one of the director's best films. The next film starring 'Adil Imam, *Rajab Fawq Sath Safih Sakhin | Rajab on a Hot Tin Roof* (1979), again by 'Abd al-'Aziz, became a major box-office hit and installed Imam as the 'King of Egyptian comedy' for most of the next twenty years. The film was centred around a peasant who goes to town only to end up in prison. Many of Imam's characters experience cathartic conflictual encounters, being confronted with an absurd 'centrifugal' social reality, 'everything flying apart, the widening of gaps between rich and poor, the impotence of institutions' and the destruction of the middle class (Armbrust 1996: 296). In an attempt to embrace society's immoral survival strategies, including theft and fraud, he often dismissed the whole system, as in *Ramadan Fawq al-Burkan | Ramadan on the Volcano* (1985) by Ahmad al-Sab'awi or *al-Afukatu | The Advocate* (1984) by Ra'fat al-Mihi – the latter featuring a corrupt lawyer who gets jailed, but supervises his illegal work from there just as comfortably as he had from the outside.

Throughout the 1990s 'Adil Imam, who had become the best-paid Egyptian star, dominated Egyptian mainstream comedy and worked with a variety of directors. He changed his original persona into a smart and tough lower-class man, and was thus able to take on roles in action and gangster films. Examples are *al-Mawlid | The Festival* (1989) by Samir Saif, *al-Mansi | The Forgotten* (1993) by Sherif 'Arafa and the historical spectacle *Risala Illa al-Wali | Message to the Ruler* (1997) by Nadir Galal. Collaboration between 'Adil Imam and director Sherif 'Arafa was particularly fruitful, resulting in one of the box-office hits of the 1990s: *al-Irhab Wa-l-Kabab | Terrorism and Kebabs* (1992). This work, which made its way also to Western audiences, dismissed the establishment as terrorphobic by presenting an average white-collar worker who is mistaken for a terrorist. Apart from his Imam films, Sherif 'Arafa succeeded in reviving the light musical comedy, with *Sama' Huss | Silence!* and *Ya Mahalabiyya Ya | Oh that Pudding, Oh!* (1991). Sherif's musical comedies are based on a similar formula to Anwar Wagdi's musicals, combining partly melodramatic, partly comic action with songs and dances.

One of the really exceptional comedy directors is Ra'fat al-Mihi, who scripted all his films for himself. With his Imam film *al-Afukatu*, sarcasm and black humour became his special trademark. One of his favourite topics was gender roles, which he successfully put into action in *al-Sada al-Rijal | Men, the Gentlemen* (1987) and *Sayyidati Anisati | Dear Ladies!* (1990), starring Ma'ali Zayid and Mahmud 'Abd al-'Aziz respectively. This topic has a long tradition, being first presented by 'Ali al-Kassar who, disguised as a woman, was sexually harrassed in the 1937 film *al-Sa'a*

Sab'a / Seven O'Clock. Others followed, such as *al-Anissa Hanafi / Miss Hanafi*, starring Isma'il Yasin. However, in contrast to the latter, in which everything is resolved happily and everybody takes back their rightful place at the end of the action, Ra'fat al-Mihi's narrations tend to be disturbingly subversive and irreversible. In *al-Sada al-Rijal* the woman-turned-into-a-man remains unhappily a man, forcing the former husband to think about a sex-change himself, and in *Sayyidati Anisati* the polygamous husband of four women becomes pregnant at the end.

Melodrama

Melodrama has a long tradition in Egyptian cinema, as well as in theatre. Its cinematic heyday stretched from the 1940s to the 1960s, at a time when the audience 'joined in singing with the musical comedies and cried hot tears with the abandoned heroine' (Wassaf 1995: 136). In Egyptian cinema melodrama was often combined with musicals, to name only some of the most distinguished these include *Dananir* (1940) by Ahmad Badrakhan, *Layla* (1942) by Togo Mizrahi, Henri Barakat's *Lahn al-Khulud / Song of Eternity* (1952), *Abbi Fawq al-Shajara / My Father Up the Tree* (1969) by Husain Kamal and Hasan al-Imam's *Khalli Balak Min Zuzu / Take Care of Zuzu* (1972). The narratives of these films usually revolved around romantic love prevented by insurmountable class differences, yet mostly solved by a surprising happy end.

The directors of the early musicals contributed decisively to the development of melodrama – primarily Muhammad Karim, whose name was linked with Muhammad 'Abd al-Wahhab after he had presented the latter as an unfortunate lover in *al-Warda al-Bayda' / The White Rose* (1933), *Dumu' al-Hubb / Tears of Love* (1935) and *Yahya al-Hubb / Long Live Love!* (1938). Ahmad Badrakhan, who presented Umm Kulthum in *Dananir* (1940) and *Aida* (1942), went on to introduce Farid al-Atrash in *Intisar al-Shabab / Victory of Youth* (1941), *'Ahd al-Hawa / Promise of Love* (1954) and other films. Henri Barakat, by contrast – as well as presenting some of the best musical melodramas, such as *Lahn al-Khulud* (1952) – also directed folkloric and realist melodramas, including *Hasan Wa Na'ima / Hasan and Na'ima* (1959), *Du'a' al-Karawan / The Cry of the Plover* (1959) and *al-Haram / The Sin* (1965).

Barakat often collaborated with the ultimate icon of Egyptian melodrama: the actress Fatin Hamama. Petite and girlish, with the face of an angel, she innocently lured scores of men into her arms. She also starred in works such as *Nahr al-Hubb / Stream of Love* (1960) by 'Izz al-Din zu-l-Fiqar, which introduced new sources of disaster to Egyptian melodrama. Director zu-l-Fiqar's characters were not so much mistreated by the social order, but rather by fate in general. Death, handicaps and disease engendered his melodramatic entanglements. He left many acclaimed melodramas, among them *Maw'id Ma'a al-Hayat / Rendevouz with Life* (1953), *Inni Rahilla / I Am Departing* (1955) and, most importantly, his patriotic melodrama *Rudd Qalbi / Give My Heart Back* (1957).

Despite the importance of women to melodrama, male characters were often placed in similarly passive and deplorable positions – negotiating not only the place of women relative to men, but that of the (male) parent relative to the children too. Their victimized position may have been one reason for the slightly 'effeminate' appearance and non-aggressive attitude assigned to the first generation of male Egyptian stars, notably Badr Lama, Muhammad 'Abd al-Wahhab and 'Imad Hamdi.

It was Muhammad Karim, in his *al-Warda al-Bayda'* (1933), who introduced one of the core narratives of Egyptian melodrama: a young and poor white-collar worker falls in love with the daughter of his wealthy employer. However, urged by the girl's father and even after his ascent to become an acclaimed singer, he gives up his wish to marry her because of his own inferior social position. The songs and the *mise-en-scène*, as well as the iconography of the film, strongly support the film's allegorical and melodramatic effect. Similar motifs were repeated in many other films centred around men, like *'Ahd al-Hawa* by Ahmad Badrakhan (starring Farid al-Atrash) or *Abbi Fawq al-Shajara* by Husain Kamal.

In these narratives individual happiness and love stood on one side, while tradition and family rested on the other. The main characters were the loving man or woman and the authoritarian father or a person related to that authority – a wicked opponent who tried to inflict the father's law – embodied by the bad cousins in, for example, *Sira' Fi-l-Wadi* / *Mortal Revenge* (1954) by Youssef Chahine and *Hasan Wa Na'ima* (1959) by Henri Barakat. Such adversaries have to die before the couple in love can reunite. *Sira' Fi-l-Wadi* condensed this conflict in one of the most legendary scenes in Egyptian cinema: a showdown in the overwhelming scenery of the original Temple of Karnak, where the beautifully matched couple in love hide from the villain and hug while actually threatened by death, an ultimate allegory for a violently suppressed sexual desire.

In association with melodrama, Egyptian cinema expressed a clear critique of the traditional family structure and arranged marriage, two major concerns of Egyptian modernists and feminists. In 1930 Muhammad Karim adapted, in his film *Zaynab*, a didactic novel by Muhammad Husain Haikal which told the story of the peasant girl Zaynab who is forced to marry someone other than her beloved with fatal consequences. Other films elaborated this motif too, such as the partly realist *al-'Azima* / *Determination* (1939) by Kamal Salim, in which the protagonist Fatima falls in love

Figure 12 Ghazal al-Banat / Girls' Flirtation

with a similarly young and poor man, while her parents attempt to force her into a marriage with a rich butcher.

Another major motif of Egyptian melodrama was seduction or, as Thomas Elsaesser puts it, 'the metaphorical interpretation of class conflict as sexual exploitation and rape' (Elsaesser 1985: 168). The first full-length feature film that depended on this topic was 'Aziza Amir's *Layla* (1927). It was centred around the village girl Layla, who gets seduced by her fiancé Ahmad. He leaves her later for a Western woman. After becoming pregnant, she dies. Bahiga Hafiz provided the same motif with an anti-colonial flavour in her *Layla al-Badawiyya / Layla the Bedouin* (1937). Layla, the daughter of an Arab Bedouin *shaykh*, is known for her beauty and is desired by many of her tribe. However, she is captured by the soldiers of the Persian king, brought to his harem, tortured and almost raped. Eventually, at the end of the film, Layla is rescued by her tribe.

Particularly during the 1940s and 1950s, the topic of the seduced or ruined – but nevertheless noble – woman became increasingly popular in Egyptian mainstream cinema. As a list set up by Galal El-Charkawi shows (al-Sharqawi 1970: 109), in the twenty-three films screened in the 1945–6 season alone, nine seduced and two raped girls appeared. One of the most accomplished melodramas that revolves around such characters is an adaptation of Taha Husain's novella by Henri Barakat: *Du'a' al-Karawan / Cry of the Plover* (1959). A young servant was raped by her master and subsequently killed by her uncle in order to clear the family's reputation. Her sister (performed by Fatin Hamama) seeks employment with the same master. She makes him fall in love with her in order to revenge her sister's death. Yet their mutual developing love–hate relationship rocks between powerful prohibition and deep desire, and mounts up into a dramatic crescendo in which he dies in her arms after being hit by a bullet meant for her.

Right up to the present day, morally or physically threatened women are indispensible to Egyptian drama. Seduction and rape re-occur in recent films like *al-Batniyya* (1980) by Husam al-Din Mustafa, *Ightisab / Rape* (1989) by 'Ali 'Abd al-Khaliq, *al-Mughtasibun / The Rapists* (1989) by Sa'id Marzuq and *al-Mansi / The Forgotten* (1993), but largely wrapped in a *mise-en-scène* oriented towards suspense and action with less melodramatic elements. Unjust violent husbands or criminal gangs, as in *al-Batniyya* (starring Nadia al-Gindi), are the main causes of female hardship in recent films, as opposed to romantic entanglements or inferior social status.

From the 1970s the melodrama seems to have lost its former emotional and psychological impact and sophistication, except for the work of the so-called 'master of melodrama' Hasan al-Imam, who has enjoyed considerable success at the box office with his highly voluptuous films. His stories mostly evolved around unhappy belly dancers or women of ill repute who, in a kind of *Dame aux camèlias*-plot, fall into impossible love with a young man from a respectable family. This is exemplified best by *Shafiqa al-Qibtiyya / Shafiqa the Copt* (1963) or his major success *Khalli Balak Min Zuzu* (1972). His late films, shot on coloured stock, were characterized by lavish filmsets and costumes, and corresponded to melodramatic emotionality of the plots and characters.

During the 1980s and 1990s the melodrama became more or less outdated. The tear-jerking music, dramatic lighting, emotional twists and romantic love were largely gone. What remained were a few exceptions, mainly dramatic plots of women cheated

and deceived either by others or by their own lack of ability, such as '*Atabit al-Sittat /
Ladies' Threshold* (1995) by 'Ali Abd El-Khalek. Here a childless woman seeks the
help of a supposed magician, but when she gets pregnant her husband repudiates her
in the belief that she has committed adultery. The main characteristic of Egyptian
'post-melodrama' is a realist-oriented *mise-en-scène*, as in *al-Jaraj / The Garage* (1995)
by 'Ala' Karim, which features a poor woman who works in a garage. She loses her
husband and has to give away her numerous children because she does not apply the
family-planning programme. In spite of the disastrous outcome, no emotional twists
are produced and the action is not underlined by any dramatic gestures or any dominant music.

One reason for the decline of melodrama is certainly the shift to more realist
perceptions on and off the screen which, although addressing similar issues (mainly
class difference and social injustice) favoured a less emotional approach. Moreover, an
increasing social mobility (particularly after the *infitah* of the 1970s) reduced the inclination towards melodramatic stories. This applies also to narratives that are centred
primarily around women, such as *Ahlam Hind Wa Kamilyya / Dreams of Hind and
Camelia* (1988) by Mohamed Khan, *Lahm Rakhis / Cheap Flesh* (1995) by Inas al-
Dighidi and *Ya Dunya Ya Gharami / My Life, My Passion* (1996) by Magdi Ahmad
'Ali. The women in these films are confronted with a multitude of abuses, but do not
succumb.

Bedouin films, gangster films and thrillers

The Bedouin films of early Egyptian cinema usually presented adventures, chivalry,
battle scenes and a melodramatic love story. They were probably inspired by the
American western and by films starring Rudolph Valentino, such as *The Sheik* (1921)
and *Son of the Sheik* (1926). Ibrahim Lama was the first to introduce this type of film
to Egyptian cinema, starting with *Qubla Fi-l-Sahra' / A Kiss in the Desert* (1928) and
ending with *al-Badawiyya al-Hasna' / The Beautiful Bedouin* (1947), all starring his
brother Badr. Wedad Orfi took up the genre in 1929 for *Ghadat al-Sahra' / The Young
Lady from the Desert*, as did Bahiga Hafiz in her nationalist allegory *Layla al-
Badawiyya / Layla the Bedouin* (completed 1937; released 1944).

Close to Bedouin films were the adaptations of Arab legends, such as the costume
drama *Abu Zayd al-Hilali* (1947) by 'Izz al-Din zu-l-Fiqar and the Italo-Egyptian co-
production *al-Saqr / The Hawk* (1950) by Salah Abu Seif. Niazi Mustafa's '*Antar Ibn
Shaddad* and *Faris Banu Hamdan* (both released in 1961) may be considered the last
films of a genre which seemed closer to orientalist fantasies than to the life of real
existing Arab Bedouin tribes in or outside Egypt. In general, Bedouin films focused on
love or minor adventures and were less suspense- and action-oriented than the thrillers
and gangster films which appeared during the 1950s.

The gangster film filled the place of the Bedouin film very quickly. During the first
two decades of its existence it was often centred around working-class gangs engaged
in different kinds of criminal action, like robbery, hijacking and smuggling. Some of
the most characteristic examples were *Qitar al-Layl / Night Train* (1953) and the
thrilling *al-Rajul al-Thani / The Second Man* (1959), both by 'Izz al-Din zu-l-Fiqar. The
latter featured an undercover agent who tries to reveal the identity of a gang leader.
From the 1950s up to the 1960s the gangster film also flourished in combination with

realism: some of its most remarkable examples are Salah Abu Seif's *al-Wahsh / The Beast* (1954) and *Raya Wa Sakina / Raya and Sakina* (1953), as well as *al-Liss Wa-l-Kilab / The Thief and the Dogs* (1962) by Kamal El-Cheikh. They differed by the largely sympathetic characters of their criminals, who were themselves victimized by society.

A subcategory of working-class gangster movies developed into what may be called the 'thug' (*futuwa*) film. It relied on a traditional character, the *futuwa*, a man who was originally associated with chivalrous nobility responsible for the protection of his neighbourhood. This original interpretation of the character became visible to a certain extent in Husam al-Din Mustafa's adaptation of a Naguib Mahfouz novel, *al-Harafish / The Racketeers* (1986). In the gangster film, this character was largely presented as a bully or racketeer, close to criminality, who often abused his power for exploitative or illegal actions; examples are Niazi Mustafa's *Futuwat al-Husainiyya / Husainiyya Thugs* (1954), Salah Abu Seif's *al-Futuwa / The Thug* (1957) and, later, *Futuwat al-Jabal / Mountain Thugs* (1982) by Nadir Galal.

Along with the gangster film, the thriller spread – in contrast often centred around upper- or middle-class characters. The genre was most skilfully developed by Kamal El-Cheikh, for example with *Hayat Aw Mawt / Life or Death* (1954) – the first Egyptian fiction to be shot primarily in the streets – and *al-Manzil Raqam 13 / House No. 13* (1952). The latter was centred around a Doctor Caligari-type of story in which hypnosis is used to incite a man to murder. Filled with crimes and intrigues, many El-Cheikh films are characterized by high psychological sophistication, as in *Tujjar al-Mawt / Death Traders* (1957) and in particular *al-Layla al-Akhira / The Last Night* (1963), starring Fatin Hamama as a woman who has been deprived of her memory and identity by her apparent husband, who turns out to be an imposter.

The 1960s are considered the heyday of the Egyptian thriller, characterized by a high standard of black-and-white photography, combined with dramatic lighting, sophisticated plots and editing. During the 1970s only a small number of remarkable works were produced, including the psychologically disturbing *al-Ikhtiyar / The Choice* (1970) by Youssef Chahine (about a man's confused identity) and Mamduh Shukri's political thriller *Za'ir al-Fajr / Visitor at Dawn* (1973), both shot in colour. Also politically oriented were *al-Muznibun / The Culprits* (1976) by Sa'id Marzuq and *'Ala Mann Nutliq al-Rasas / At Whom Do We Shoot?* (1975), written by Ra'fat al-Mihi and directed by Kamal El-Cheikh. The latter film, in particular, unfolded a panorama of society's corruption through a police investigation and was considered one of the highlights of the committed cinema of the 1970s.

Apart from the works cited, the genre started disintegrating by shifting from its former tight construction and clear genre rules to genre mixtures. It developed into social or political dramas, often including cheap chases and poorly staged action scenes, or offered remakes of earlier thrillers, such as two works by Ashraf Fahmi: *Washmat 'Ar / Sign of Disgrace* (1986), which remade Husam al-Din Mustafa's *al-Tariq / The Road* (1964), and *Layl Wa Khawana / Night and Traitors* (1990), which re-enacted *al-Liss Wa-l-Kilab*.

During the 1980s, kung fu and karate were used for action, along with chases and car crashes. However these elements were rarely presented in a convincing manner, due to the lack of technical facilities and finance. Specialists were also called in, such as the sportsman Yusuf Mansur, who (since the late 1980s) has acted in and designed some mediocre karate films, and the bodybuilder al-Shahat Mabruk, who appeared during the 1990s in several second-rate action films. In addition, the gangster film developed to become a sort of mafia film, taking up the *infitah* criticism of the early 1980s. Hence many works tended to feature businessmen and *nouveaux riches* involved in criminal acitivities.

It is hardly surprising that some of the New Realists borrowed, just like the directors of old realism, from the gangster film to make their films more attractive: for example, Atef El-Tayeb's *Katibat al-I'dam / The Execution Squad* (1989), in which his heroine takes violent vengance on corrupt gangsters. Mohamed Khan also directed gangster films, principally *Darbit Shams / Sun Stroke* (1980) and *Faris al-Madina / City Knight* (1992). Khan, however, was more interested in displaying social contradictions than in any kind of spectacular action.

Since the late 1980s two directors, Samir Saif and Nadir Galal, directed relatively persuasive action films – although they offered the usual genre mix. Samir Saif was particularly taken by the American model of speedy action, rapid cutting and physical violence. He directed largely thrilling, yet basically trival and comic films: for instance, his burlesque *Shams al-Zinati* (1991) – based on *The Magnificient Seven* by John Sturges (itself a remake of the Japanese original, Akira Kurosawa's *The Seven Samurai*) – and, more importantly, the gangster movie *al-Nimr Wa-l-Untha / The Tiger and the Woman* (1987), which is characterized by its fast-paced action. Both films starred the comedian 'Adil Imam. Nadir Galal also worked on some of 'Adil Imam's minor gangster films, among others *Jazirat al-Shaytan / Devil's Island* (1990), and the social drama, *Malaf Samia Sha'rawi / Samia Sha'rawi's File* (1988), starring Nadia al-Gindi. Top star Nadia al-Gindi featured, moreover, in several politically motivated espionage films that chose the Arab–Israeli conflict as a spectacular backdrop for their suspense- and action-oriented plots.

Realism

After the abolition of the Kingdom in 1952, Egyptian cinema showed an increasing tendency towards nationalism, anti-colonialism, modernism and so-called 'realist' representation. The developing Egyptian realism aimed to reflect the environment and daily life of the poorer classes, and denounced colonial oppression and social abuses. However, realist films were produced in an entirely commercial framework. They expressed the changed attitude of a segment of the Egyptian mainstream towards social reality. In Egyptian criticism, realism is primarily measured according to its *iltizam* or socio-political commitment and not its 'authenticity', because (to put it in Lizbeth Malkmus' words) 'a message about reality is mixed up with cinematic realism … ' (Malkmus and Armes 1991: 115). Thus no contradiction was seen in classifying a melodrama or an action film as 'realist', as long as it was set among the poor and addressed class difference and social injustice.

Before the Revolution in 1952, this kind of orientation was not welcomed. Not only did censorship (the Faruq Code in particular) discourage realist or socialist representation, but film-makers (such as the musical director Ahmad Badrakhan) also claimed that the audiences preferred to watch luxurious or uncommon surroundings. The first Egyptian feature film considered to be realist by the critics was *al-'Azima / Determination* by Kamal Selim (Salim), which was made in 1939. The director's original intention was to call the film 'The Alley' (*al-hara*), which was refused by Studio Misr who did not consider that kind of title effective advertising.

Indeed, *al-'Azima*'s realism was expressed less in the construction of its plot (which posits the upper class as the *deus ex machina*) than in its 'setting' – that is, in the environment of the protagonist. Set in a lower-class urban neighbourhood, it presents a barber's son who loses his job and wife because of an unlucky coincidence, but regains them in the end with the help of a friend – the son of a pasha. However, in the aftermath of *al-'Azima* Egyptian cinema saw the appearance of a first socialist orientation. In 1943 Ahmad Kamil Mursi directed *al-'Amil* / *The Worker*, which was about a worker starting to demand more rights for himself and for others.

Kamil al-Tilmissani's *al-Suq al-Sauda'* / *The Black Market* (1945) focused on structural problems in society. The film is set during World War II and revolves around the struggle of a young white-collar worker against the speculation of traders. Without any melodramatic tear-jerking, the director demonstrates the protagonist's plight through his attempts to uncover the blackmarketeers and to mobilize the inhabitants of his poor neighbourhood against them. The realism unfolds primarily in its accurate reference to the problems of the war economy. Salah Abu Seif's *al-Usta Hasan* / *Master Hasan* (1952), which focused on a worker as well, was more concerned with the worker's aspiration for higher social standing than with his actual condition – showing how he leaves his family and gets caught in the nets of an upper-class woman.

During the early 1950s the number of realist-oriented films increased, creating a kind of wave that was responsible for some of the most accomplished works of Egyptian cinema, including *Bab al-Hadid* / *Cairo Main Station* (1958), *al-Mutamarridun* / *The Rebels* (1966), *al-Haram* / *The Sin* (1965) and *al-Ard* / *The Earth* (1968). Interestingly, realism's qualitative importance was constantly confused with its actual marginality. Between 1951 and 1971 the film industry produced a total of 1,012 works. In addition to a dozen patriotic and political films, about thirty-two realist films were shot during the same period: that means just one-and-a-half films per year. After nationalization the annual average increased only slightly: between 1963 and 1971 two clearly realist films appeared per year.

In spite of the state's openness after the *coup d'état* of the Free Officers in 1952 to the interests of the underprivileged classes and thus to realist representations (albeit not for representations of topical politics), the genre remained at the mercy of the market. The nationalization of the film industry came only in 1963 and did not initiate any basic changes in the industry's commercial orientation. As a result most of the realist works were produced by the private sector and commercial interests were taken into consideration during their making. During the 1960s some mainstream directors (among others Henri Barakat, Kamal El-Cheikh and Husain Kamal) joined the realist wave for a short while. Otherwise it was confined to three directors: Salah Abu Seif, Taufik Salih and Youssef Chahine, who (apart from Salih) did not refrain completely from directing mainstream works.

The realist inclination of the time was not only linked to topics of class struggle and national liberation, but also to questions of development. Several films appeared which negotiated women's place in society and their right to define themselves: examples are Salah Abu Seif's *al-Tariq al-Masdud* / *The Closed Way* (1958) and *Anna Hurra* / *I Am Free* (1959), both adapted from stories written by Ihsan 'Abd al-Quddus. Henri Barakat directed *al-Bab al-Maftuh* / *The Open Door* in 1963, adapted from a novel by

Latifa al-Zayat, leading his protagonist out of a suffocating marriage to join the national liberation movement. This emancipatory interest continued also in the 1970s with Sa'id Marzuq's *Uridu Hallan / I Want a Solution* (1975), starring Fatin Hamama as a wife demanding a divorce in vain. This film attacked traditionalist Muslim personal-status legislation. Some other modernist issues were raised: for instance, family planning in *Afwah Wa Aranib / Mouths and Rabbits* (1977) by Barakat. *Qandil Umm Hashim / Umm Hashim's Lamp* (1968), a marginal but interesting work by Kamal 'Attia that was adapted from a novel by Yahia Haqqi and starred Shukri Sarhan and Samira Ahmad, was one of the few films to discuss the conflict between mythical and rational thinking, as experienced by a young doctor who returns from Europe to his home town.

Literature played a decisive role in establishing realist cinema in Egypt and resulted in the realization of some of the most accomplished works of Egyptian film history. The novelist Naguib Mahfouz played a major role in shaping cinematic realism – particularly the work of director Salah Abu Seif. The collaborations between the two started with the film *al-Muntaqqim / The Avenger* (1947). In the following years Mahfouz contributed to nine scripts by Abu Seif: among others, *Raya Wa Sakina / Raya and Sakina* (1953), *al-Wahsh / The Beast* (1954), *Shabab Imra'a / Youth of a Woman* (1956) and *Bayn al-Sama' Wa-l-Ard / Between Sky and Earth* (1959). They served as drafts for Abu Seif's most outstanding works.

Realism was entangled with various mainstream genres as well, such as with the gangster film, for example, offering action and suspense, and featuring thieves, monopolists and thugs – as in Salah Abu Seif's works *Raya Wa Sakina*, *al-Wahsh* and *al-Futuwa / The Thug* (1957) – without necessarily abolishing the binary moralism of mainstream genres. In only a few films (like *al-Liss Wa-l-Kilab* by El-Cheikh and *al-Wahsh* by Abu Seif) was the message clearly worked out that society holds responsibility for the hero's aberrations. In the latter film the protagonist is driven into criminality by the feudal structure of the countryside.

In contrast, Abu Seif's *Raya Wa Sakina* dwells on the spectacular nature of crime and moral antagonism to it, instead of explaining its social background. It features two sisters who kidnap women and kill them in order to steal their gold. The protagonists of *al-Futuwa*, which is set in a vegetable trade centre and addresses economic monopolization, are clearly split into good and evil. Morality and wealth define each protagonist's character: the poorer a character is, the more virtuous they are found to be.

By addressing class difference and social injustice, some realist films showed a clear melodramatic inclination – to name only two, these include *Bidaya Wa Nihaya / Beginning and End* (1960) by Salah Abu Seif and *al-Haram / The Sin* (1965) by Barakat. *Bidaya Wa Nihaya* is set in pre-independence times and features four siblings who suffer deprivation because of the loss of their father. The family's final disintegration is brought about by the sister, Nafisa, who was seduced by the wealthy grocer's son and turns to the street to finance herself and her younger brother's education. In a dramatic finale, the brother – performed by Omar Charif ('Umar al-Sharif) – forces her to commit suicide, then himself soon follows her lead.

Not only the film's style but also its motif – sexual abuse across the class divide, addressed likewise in *al-Haram* – places it close to melodrama. Moreover, in view of *Bidaya Wa Nihaya*'s tragic outcome, it is understandable why the attitude of some realist works to social conditions is considered fatalist. The individual is rendered helpless to circumstances and regards society as possessing an omnipotence similar to fate. The same applies to *al-Haram*. Its protagonist, a poor agricultural seasonal worker who had been raped, dies after having to deliver the resulting child in secret. Yet, contrary to the structure of a regular family melodrama in which the individual would have to bear their plight alone, the death of the woman incites the inhabitants of the village to develop solidarity with the seasonal workers to which the woman belonged.

Solidarity, not so much as an effect of oppressive conditions, but more as an aspect of emotional relief, was presented in some works – like Youssef Chahine's *al-Ard* (1968) – whose epic depiction of class struggle comes closest to the notion of social realism. Confronted with the selfish interests of large landowners, the small farmers of a village can only choose either to succumb or to unite and defend themselves. Although their resistance is crushed at the end, the film includes moments of group solidarity, where the farmers unite to save their cattle from drowning in the flood.

Apart from *al-Ard / The Earth*, it was *Sira' al-Abtal / Struggle of the Heroes* (1962), *al-Sayyid Bulti / Mister Bolti* (1969) and the extraordinary *al-Mutamarridun / The Rebels* (1966), directed and written by Taufik Salih, which addressed the issue of class struggle most intensely. They focused on peasants versus feudal authorities and workers versus capitalists. In *al-Mutamarridun* the conflict was depicted in an entirely allegorical and pessimistic way by following the story of a rebellion. A group of infected people, who are kept in a desert camp in quarantine, take over the camp's direction but build up the same unjust and authoritarian structure as the former administration.

Melodramatic features and the concept of social determinism with its victimized heroes started vanishing with the second wave of Egyptian realism – the so-called 'New Realism' of the post-Sadat era – and was replaced by aggressive accusations against the new materialism. New Realism developed in the early 1980s with the help of a new generation of directors, notably Atef El-Tayeb, Mohamed Khan, Khairy Beshara, Bashir al-Dik and Daoud Abd El-Sayed, nicknamed 'the children of Abu Seif, the street and *Coca-Cola*'.

The new wave appeared – at least with respect to its subjects – to be much more pragmatic than the old one, although it functioned according to the same mechanisms. It similarly borrowed from commercial genres, primarily the gangster film, could not do without stars and chose a similar milieu, mainly that of the urban petty bourgeoisie. It differed, however, in a stronger integration of original locations – partly by renouncing the studio. Director Mohamed Khan was the first to demonstrate this attitude in *Darbit Shams / Sun Stroke* (1980), which was almost entirely shot on the streets. Many of his films played on the idea of the road: among others *Ta'ir 'Ala al-Tariq / A Bird on the Road* (1981) and *Mishwar 'Umar / 'Umar's Errand* (1986).

New Realism evolved from changed themes, most of them related to the *infitah* that was initiated by the Sadat government: moral corruption, materialism, rapid social ascent, labour migration and political abuse. In fact, New Realism had been preceded by the gangster and mafia films in the choice of these particular topics. *Intabihu Ayuha al-Sada / Attention, Gentlemen!* (1980) by Muhammad 'Abd al-'Aziz and *al-Qitat al-Siman / The Fat Cats* (1981) by Hasan Yusuf were the first films to describe corrupt and criminal *nouveaux riches*. Close to realism in its stylistic and aesthetic qualities was *Ahl al-Qimma / People from the Top* (1981) by 'Ali Badrakahn. It told the story of a young woman who, under pressure from a former criminal businessman, complies with his wish to make her his wife. In spite of a bad conscience, she is urged by her need to escape the unbearable deprivations of her living conditions.

In order to tackle the moral corruption of the new era, many new realists concentrated on the family, whose members ideally should be loyal under any circumstances. The film *Sawaq al-Utubis / The Bus-Driver* (1983), by Atef El-Tayeb, was typical of this orientation to the extent that it was considered by some critics the real start of New Realism. Its story centred on a bus- and taxi-driver whose father's workshop is threatened with expropriation because the manager had evaded paying tax for many years. However, apart from the driver, none of the father's children are interested in keeping the workshop – they would rather make quick money out of it.

Thus new materialism seemed to endanger even the unity of families. Just like *Sawaq al-Utubis*, in Bashir al-Dik's *al-Tufan / The Flood* (1985) the grown-up children risk or even actively contribute to the death of their parents in order to enlarge their profits. Conflicts and competitive fights that erupt between relatives and friends are terminated in many cases by a bloody showdown, as in Daoud Abd El-Sayed's *al-Sa'alik / The Vagabonds* (1983), in which two former urban tramps who have jointly accumulated a great fortune end up killing each other.

Another characteristic of the 1970s, the emigration of labour (mainly to the Gulf countries), was expressed in Khan's *'Awdat Muwatin / Return of a Citizen* (1986) and al-Dik's *Sikkat Safar / A Way to Travel* (1986) in relation to consumerism and materialism. The depicted alienation of the heroes, their own and their relatives' aspiration to better social standing is characterized as a threat to traditional family unity and values.

Hence, New Realism discovered different enemies. Instead of the old landowners and pashas, unscrupulous businessmen, the corrupt *nouveaux riches* and thieves were attacked and the destruction of the middle class deplored. The conflict was often resolved in a bloody manner, as in *Katibat al-I'dam / The Execution Squad* (1989) by El-Tayeb, in which four people (including one woman) take revenge by killing a corrupt *infitah*-businessman.

Violence associated with abuse of power was also presented in *al-Takhshiba / The Arrest* (1984), *Malaf Fi-l-Adab / A Vice Squad File* (1986), both by Atef El-Tayeb, and *Zawjat Rajul Muhimm / Wife of an Important Man* (1988) by Mohamed Khan. While the latter had a rather political orientation, Atef El-Tayeb's works concentrated on the vulnerability of citizens (in these examples all women) to the executive apparatus.

However, some films pointed simply to the difficult living conditions experienced by the lower classes, without putting them into conflict with *infitah*-representatives. Such films include the family portrait *Yawm Murr Yawm Hulw / Bitter Day, Sweet Day* (1988) by Khairy Beshara or *Hubb Fawq Hadabit al-Harram / Love at the Pyramids* (1986) by Atef El-Tayeb, dealing with the housing problem which prevents young couples from getting married. Beshara also presented one of the few New Realist films set in the countryside: his beautifully shot *al-Tawq Wa-l-Iswira / The Collar and the Bracelet* (1986).

During the 1990s new realism declined in spite of the box-office hit *al-Kitkat* (1991) by Daoud Abd El-Sayed and the ascent of a new generation echoing the preoccupations of the 1980s. They included Radwan al-Khashif with *Lih Ya Banafsij / Oh*

Violets, Why? (1993), Magdi Ahmad 'Ali with *Ya Dunya Ya Gharami / My Life, My Passion* (1996), *'Afarit al-Asfalt / Asphalt Devils* (1996) by Usama Fawzi and *Hysteria* (1998) by 'Adil Adib. These films tried to remain faithful to lower-class reality, albeit with a slight twist. They largely focused on gender relations juxtaposed with social and sexual deprivation.

The political film

Addressing politics made Egyptian films more liable to be censored and so topical statements are in general avoided and relevant political allusions mostly either get encoded or are made retrospectively. Some films, however, were read by the censor as topical political statements, although it was not necessarily their intention – as was the case for *Layla al-Badawiyya / Layla the Bedouin* (1937) by Bahiga Hafiz, *Lashin* (1938) by Fritz Kramp and *al-Mutamarridun / The Rebels* (1966) by Taufiq Salih. In general, political films picked out (often retrospectively) many of Egypt's urgent problems, such as British colonialism, national independence, the Arab–Israeli conflict, official corruption and, last but not least, human rights violations.

Overt anti-colonialism and patriotism was first voiced in Ahmad Badrakhan's *Mustafa Kamil* (1952), which recounted the biography of one of the major Egyptian nationalists. The film moreover addressed the Dunshiway incident in 1906, in which dozens of villagers were arbitrarily hung by the British. In addition, it alluded to the events which led to the 1919 revolution. As a result, the film was released only after the *coup d'état* in July 1952. Other films which tackled British colonialism largely presented courageous resistance fighters at work; these included *Yasqut al-Isti'mar / Down with Colonialism!* (1953) by Husain Sidqi and *La Waqt Li-l-Hubb / No Time for Love* (1962) by Salah Abu Seif. Appreciated for its cinematic qualities was Henri Barakat's *Fi Baytinna Rajul / A Man in Our House* (1961) – starring Omar Charif, it was adapted from an Ihsan 'Abd al-Quddus novel about a middle-class family who accidentally hide a young resistance fighter. Colonialism and resistance stopped being addressed after Nasser's demise.

The earliest politically inspired Egyptian film was probably Mahmud zu-l-Fiqar's *Fatat Min Filastin / A Girl from Palestine* (1948) whose storyline was echoed years later in *Ard al-Salam / Land of Peace* (1957) by Kamal El-Cheikh. Both featured Egyptian fighters who are wounded in a military confrontation with Israelis, become the guests of Palestinians and are cared for by a Palestinian girl whom they later marry. Thus the Palestinian question was subordinated to genre rules and dealt with in an emotional – rather than analytical – way. Moreover, it seemed secondary in relation to the Egyptian–Israeli conflict, for the only Egyptian film that was entirely centred around a Palestinian character was the biopic *Naji al-'Ali* (1992) by Atef El-Tayeb, an expensive Lebanese–Egyptian co-production about the famous Palestinian caricaturist, yet weakened by Bashir al-Dik's shallow screenplay.

Works which touched upon the various military confrontations with Israel were more numerous and depicted the direct effects of military action on the Egyptian population, the heroic attempts to fight back and some of the reasons for the country's consecutive defeats. Early examples were Ahamd Badrakhan's *Allahu Ma'na / God is with Us* (1952), Niazi Mustafa's *Ard al-Abtal / Land of Heroes* (1953) and 'Izz al-Din zu-l-Fiqar's *Port Said* (1957). They tend to concentrate on human relationships and do not depict any elaborate battle scenes, except for *al-Rasasa La Tazal Fi Jaybi* / *The Bullet is Still in My Pocket* (1974) by Husam al-Din Mustafa, which featured a young villager who decides to take part in the frontier war (*harb al-istinzaf*) that lasted from 1968 until the Yom Kippur War (October War) in 1973 as a reaction against the corruption experienced in his home town. Another exception is the more recent television production *al-Tariq Illa Aylat* / *The Way to Eilat* (1995) by An'am Muhammad 'Ali, which re-enacts a sabotage operation carried out by Egyptian officers against the Israeli military forces and includes some sophisticated explosions and several underwater scenes.

Along with the war film, the espionage film appeared. The earliest film of that category was *Jarima Fi-l-Hay al-Hadi'* / *A Crime in the Calm Neighbourhood* (1967) by Husam ad-Din Mustafa. It depicted the preparations for the assassination of Lord Moyne, the British minister resident in the Middle East, who was murdered in Cairo by the radical Zionist Stern Gang in 1944. The more recent espionage films, *I'dam Mayitt* / *Execution of a Dead Man* (1985) by 'Ali Abd El-Khalek and *Muhimma Fi Tall-Abib* / *Mission in Tel Aviv* (1992) by Nadir Galal, were set on the eve of the Yom Kippur War (October War). In both works the Israeli intelligence service gets outwitted by its Egyptian adversaries. Extensive chases, physical violence (including torture) and sexual seduction are indispensable means to support the action. The same applies to the costume drama *al-Jasusa Hikmat Fahmi* / *The Spy Hikmat Fahmi* (1994) by Husam al-Din Mustafa, starring Nadia al-Gindi, whose action takes place during World War II.

Few political films surpassed the commercial formula to present less conventional and genre-oriented forms. Rather, they were concerned with the inner crisis of either society or individuals and pointed out corruption, nepotism and lack of democracy, correlated with Egypt's wars and defeats. *Zilal 'Ala al-Janib al-Akhar* / *Shadows on the Other Side* (1971) and *Ughniyya 'Ala al-Mamar* / *Song on the Passage* (1972) described both the inner crisis and ambiguities of its characters as reasons for the military defeat, as did Husain Kamal's *Tharthara Fawq al-Nil* / *Adrift on the Nile* (1971) – an adaptation of a Naguib Mahfouz novel – and Chahine's *al-'Usfur* / *The Sparrow* (1972). One of the more recent works, *al-Aqdar al-Damiyya* / *Bloody Destinies* (1982) by Khairy Beshara, displayed the disintegration of an upper-class family in the time of the 1948 war in Palestine.

Apart from military conflict with Israel, some works chose to address the Egypt's political system. Not all of them were critical. *Fajr Yawm Jadid* / *Dawn of a New Day* (1964) by Youssef Chahine, for example, glorified Nasserism and the new regime. Through the figure of a young student, the director characterized the new system as dynamic and progressive, whereas the pre-revolutionary bourgeoisie were shown as parasitic and unable to share in bearing the ideals of progress and social justice.

However, the critique of Nasserism increased gradually after 1967. *Miramar* (1969) by Kamal El-Cheikh (which was only released after Nasser's death in 1970) and Salah Abu Seif's *al-Qadiyya 68* / *The Process 68* (1968) dismissed the revolution and its party – the Arab Socialist Union. Moreover, during the 1970s film-makers started blaming the Nasserist regime for human rights violations. In particular, *al-Karnak* (1975) by 'Ali Badrakhan relied on the representation of torture and rape in his portrait of a student couple who are captured by the state security forces and tortured. However, the Sadat era was also accused of human rights abuses in, among other films, *al-Bari' / The Innocent* (1986) by Atef El-Tayeb and in *al-Tahwila / The Switch* (1996) by Amali Bahansi. Both films are set in desert concentration camps and convincingly attack the sadistic abuses of the officers in charge.

In contrast, *Za'ir al-Fajr / Visitor at Dawn* (1973) by Mamduh Shukri featured, in a very subtle and convincing way, political terror exerted by the state security – evolving his plot from the demise of a female journalist. This film is also counted as being among the most important Egyptian films on the formal level. The same applies to *Zawjat Rajul Muhimm / Wife of an Important Man* (1988) by Mohamed Khan. It was also less interested in the immediate portrayal of physical abuse and the critique of a specific government, than in the human and psychological dimensions of physical and political abuse. Thus the film portrays the development of an ambitious officer into an unscrupulous and fascistic personality that serves the interests of the regime, with the change mirrored in his wife, who experiences a total moral and emotional breakdown living at his side.

In general Egyptian cinema turned a blind eye to one of the most urgent current problems: confessionalism and increasing religious fundamentalism. Muslim fundamentalism was addressed for the first time in Sa'd 'Arafa's mediocre *Ghuraba' / Strangers* (1973). A more spectacular reception for a similarly mediocre film was waiting for *al-Irhabi / The Terrorist* (1994) by Nadir Galal (starring 'Adil Imam), which shows – quite naïvely – the coming to reason of a former terrorist who has been injured and hosted by a liberal upper-class family. This film was backed by the government and released in the movie theatres under heavy police protection.

The historical film

The number of historical films produced by Egypt has remained relatively low, even if those that are set in periods close to the film's actual production time and require as a result less changes in props and costumes are included. The main reason is certainly the high budgets required for this genre. Some examples, though, are *al-Ard / The Earth* (1968), set in the 1930s, and *Iskandariyya Lih? / Alexandria, Why?* (1978) and *al-Aqdar al-Damiyya / Bloody Destinies* (1982), both situated in the 1940s.

It is noteworthy that the ratio of costume and historical dramas was much higher during the early decades of the industry. Between 1935 and 1950 the country produced seven explicitly historical films. Another dozen costume dramas were shot during the same period and furnished with a historical touch, although they were basically popular fairy-tales or legends like ''Antar and 'Abla', 'Ali Baba and the Forty Thieves', 'Abu Zayd al-Hilali' and 'Juha'. With a few exceptions, such as Ahmad Galal's *Shajarat al-Durr* (1935) and Ahmad Badrakhan's *Dananir* (1940), most of the historical films were neither based on a literary model nor any profound knowledge of the cited epoch. They were furthermore made subject to genre rules: the melodramatic musical in the cases of *Widad* (1936) by Fritz Kramp and *Sallama* (1945) by Ahmad Badrakhan, and the farce in the case of *Alf Layla Wa Layla / One Thousand and One Nights* (1941) by Togo Mizrahi (starring 'Ali al-Kassar).

Unlike now, the first historical productions were essentially governed by business considerations. Producers seemed to be well aware of the legendary past's attractiveness. Some of the productions during the 1930s and 1940s, notably *Widad* (1936),

Layla al-Badawiyya (1944 – completed 1937), *Lashin* (1938) and *Dananir* (1940), were careful to use lavish props and costumes. The earliest productions of Studio Misr were historical spectacles: the musical *Widad* and the drama *Lashin*, both by Fritz Kramp. The Ummayad and Abbasid periods, which are considered the golden age of Islam, were the preferred temporal framework of many of these films.

From the early 1960s the number of historicals fell gradually in relation to total production. Some legendary stories were still brought to the screen, however: for instance, *'Antar Ibn Shaddad* (1961) and *Amirat al-'Arab / The Princess of Arabs* (1963) by Niazi Mustafa, as well as *Amir al-Daha' / The Artful Prince* (1964) by Henri Barakat. The most expensive and spectacular productions were *Wa Islamah / Oh Islam!* (1961) by Andrew Marton and *al-Nasir Salah al-Din / The Victorious Saladin* (1963) by Youssef Chahine. The latter is still one of the most remarkabe historical movies of Egyptian film history, due in part to Chahine's skill in handling fierce battle scenes but also to the careful set and costume designs of Wali al-Din Samih and Chadi Abedessalam. The film was not accurate in describing the crusades, but rather an apologetic nationalist statement, depicting the Kurdish warlord Salah al-Din al-Ayubi as a pan-Arab national hero who defeated the crusaders not just by his military skill but by his wisdom, righteousnes and dignity.

Apart from 'secular' historical spectaculars, twelve religious films were made, interestingly, during the Nasserist period (1951–72). Most of them were set in the time of the Prophet and presented the conversion of Arab pagans to the new teachings. These included *Zuhur al-Islam / The Emergence of Islam* (1951) by Ibrahim 'Izz al-Din, *Intissar al-Islam / The Victory of Islam* (1952) by Ahamd al-Tukhi, *Hijrat al-Rasul / The Emigration of the Prophet* (1962) by Ibrahim 'Imara and *Fajr al-Islam / The Dawn of Islam* (1971) by Salah Abu Seif. Most religious films, such as *Bilal Mu'azzin al-Rasul / Bilal: The Prophet's Muezzin* (1953) by Ahmad al-Tukhi and *Khalid Ibn al-Walid* (1958) by Husain Sidqi, were centred around historical personalities related

Figure 13 Sira' Fi-l-Wadi / Mortal Revenge

either to the Prophet or to Islam in general. Three films featured famous Sufi personalities: one was *Rab'a al-'Adawiyya* (1963) by Niazi Mustafa.

Many of the religious films were of poor dramatic or cinematic quality. They displayed the conventional binary morality of melodrama, livened up by some elements from war and gangster films. As in Western devotional fims depicting the martyrdom of early Christianity, they focused on the atrocities that early Muslim believers had been exposed to and endured patiently with a suffering expression and wrapped in indispensable white gowns. After 1972, no more religious films appeared.

All the cited works, whether secular or religious, were set in the Arab-Muslim past. Not a single Egyptian film dealt with the Coptic past and almost none with the Ancient Egyptian past. The reason was perhaps the marginal cultural identification with these two periods. Apart from Ibrahim Lama's mediocre *Cleopatra* (1943), the principal exceptions were Chadi Abdessalam's short film *al-Fallah al-Fasih / The Eloquent Peasant* (1970) and Youssef Chahine's biblical Joseph-story adaptation *al-Muhajir / The Emigrant* (1994). Moreover, in his *Iskandariyya Kaman Wa Kaman / Alexandria Now and Forever* (1991), Chahine alluded in passing to the Graeco-Roman period.

Only a few Egyptian films chose the eighteenth and nineteenth centuries as a background. 'Ali Badrakhan, for example, referred allegorically to present-day anomalies by depicting economic monopolization and exploitation in the nineteenth century. In *al-Gu' / Hunger* (1986) he portrayed, in accordance with the prevalent *infitah* criticism, the rise and fall of a speculator, while in *Shafiqa Wa Mitwalli / Shafiqa and Mitwalli* (1978) he told the sad story of two sexually and politically abused siblings by pointing out the ordeals suffered by Egyptian labour forced to dig the Suez Canal. Of similarly high cinematic quality was Youssef Chahine's expensive co-production *Wada'a Bonaparte / Adieu Bonaparte* (1985), which stands out for its unconventional story, its charming characters and its good set design. The film focused on three different brothers, whose stories are told against the background of Napoleon's failed expedition to Egypt. It furthermore addressed the encounter of the two cultures from an experiential perspective.

The most important Egyptian historical art-film is *al-Mumya' / The Mummy: The Night of Counting the Years* (1969), which is also set in the nineteenth century. Inspired by the famous discovery of the hiding place in the Valley of Kings of royal mummies from several dynasties, the film is centred on the quest for identity of a young Egyptian. It has a special place in Egyptian film history because of its aesthetic and narrative coherence and sophistication.

Experiments and young directors

During the 1960s and 1970s realist cinema was perceived to be in opposition to commercial cinema. This was, first of all, because it showed interest in the popular native environment rather than the Westernized upper classes and, second, because of its partly anti-colonial and quasi-socialist messages. On the stylistic and narrative level, however, it remained faithful to mainstream cinema. No conscious attempts to break the rules on these two levels were made before the 1960s.

It was only after the military defeat in 1967 that new ideas and artistic orientations which departed to a certain degree from the mainstream began to spread. In particular, the members of the New Cinema Society (founded in 1969) were inspired by European 'new wave' cinema and, most significantly, by the ideas of the Oberhausen Manifesto. The society included screenwriters, directors and film critics who intended to produce politically committed films that deviated from the prevailing Egyptian mainstream. The two full-length feature films that were directed by its members are *Ughniyya 'Ala al-Mamar / Song on the Passage* (1972) by 'Ali Abd El-Khalek and *Zilal 'Ala al-Janib al-Akhar / Shadows on the Other Side* (1973) by Ghaleb Chaath. Both films were based on literary works and introduced in the narrative a kind of 'polyphony' that disrupts the omniscient realist discourse to create a variety of subjective voices and perspectives.

Other individual attempts to break from the mainstream were made, such as Husain Kamal's *al-Mustahil / The Impossible* (1965), *al-'Usfur / The Sparrow* (1972) by Youssef Chahine and *Zawjati Wa-l-Kalb / My Wife and the Dog* (1971) by Sa'id Marzuq. The extensive use of flashbacks, daydreams and nightmares gave these films their special character. *Zawjati Wa-l-Kalb* seems particularly successful in leading the spectator astray, as the largest part of the film's action turns out to be a fantasy imagined by its main character, the warden of a lighthouse, who has sent his colleague with a message to his young wife and is tortured by the idea of his wife making love to the messenger.

The most interesting Egyptian art-movie is *al-Mumya'* (1969) by Chadi Abdessalam, primarily because of its stylistic achievements. However, due to neglect by its producer, the General Film Organisation, the film was only released in 1975; thus the immediate impact of this (eventually) highly acclaimed film remained small. The opposite was true of Youssef Chahine's work. He was the first to introduce a radically personal cinema with his semi-autobiographical *Iskandariyya Lih? / Alexandria Why?* (1978). It is not just one of his most accomplished films, but also encouraged young directors across the whole Arab world, including Mohammed Malas and Nouri Bouzid. Chahine supplemented this film, which brought him the Silbener Bär award in the Berlin Film Festival of 1979, with two other films: *Haduta Misriyya / An Egyptian Fairy-Tale* (1982) and *Iskandariyya Kaman Wa Kaman / Alexandria Now and Forever* (1989). This trilogy was characterized by its narrative and stylistic hybridity, mixing genres and film types – Chahine used everything from archival documentary footage to theatre peformances, as well as songs, dances and flashbacks, all adding up to a subjective statement on his family as well as socio-political surroundings.

Other young Egyptian directors made more or less successful attempts to make their autobiographies or at least enrich their films with autobiographical items: Yousri Nasrallah did so in *Sariqat Sayfiyya / Summer Thefts* (1988) and in a strongly transfigured way in the unique *Mercedes* (1993). Stylistically less eccentric but narratively to the point was Khairy Beshara's *al-'Awama 70 / Houseboat 70* (1982), the portrait of a young film-maker who is confronted with a political murder. He turns out to be mentally paralyzed, unable to respond, being caught in emotional and political contradictions and torn between his personal predilections and the ideal of social responsibility.

Exceptional, on both the narrative and thematic levels, are two works by Daoud Abd El-Sayed: *al-Bahth 'An Sayyid Marzuq / The Search for Sayyid Marzuq* (1991) and *Ard al-Khawf / Land of Fear* (1999). Both have plots structured around the motifs of an existential journey through which an individual tries in vain to retrieve their own identity. *Ard al-Khawf* may be considered one of the most accomplished Egyptian films of the last decade on the cinematic level, as well as on the narrative level. It manages to dress up the metaphysical quest for truth in a thrilling gangster film plot, featuring Ahmad Zaki as an undercover agent who becomes an influential drug dealer, loses track of his superiors and finally loses confidence in his real identity.

The major problem hampering the development of an alternative Egyptian art-cinema is the lack of economic facilities. Co-production with Europe has proven to be one way out of the dilemma, dictating other thematic and aesthetic orientations. Otherwise film-makers are entirely dependent on the industry, with all the obstacles and interferences related to it.

Remakes and literary adaptation

The Egyptian film industry from the very beginning sought literary and cinematic sources of inspiration, both regional and international. Some of the first literary adaptations based on local writing were *Zaynab* (1930) by Muhammad Karim and Ahmad Galal's *Shajarat al-Durr* (1935), which were adapted from novels by Muhammad Husain Haikal and Jirji Zaydan respectively. Subsequently the tendency to adapt increased and the list of Egyptian authors whose works were adapted is long: Taufiq al-Hakim in *Rusasa Fi-l-Qalb / A Shot in the Heart* (1944) by Muhammad Karim, Yusuf Idris in *al-Haram / The Sin* by Henri Barakat, Ihsan 'Abd al-Quddus in *al-Banat Wa-l-Saif / Girls and the Summer* (1960) by Salah Abu Seif (among others), Yusuf al-Siba'i in *Nadia* (1969) by Ahmad Badrakhan, Isma'il Wali al-Din in *Hamam al-Malatili / The Malatili Bath* (1973) by Abu Seif, Ibrahim Aslan in *al-Kitkat* (1991) by Daoud Abd El-Sayed and so on. Regional legends, fairy-tales and popular epics and songs (like the *mawal*) were adapted too.

Egyptian literature in particular shaped realism decisively. The realist novelist Naguib Mahfouz became one of the most adapted authors, with thirty-eight of his novels and short stories presented on screen. Two Mahfouz adaptations directed by Abu Seif – *Bidaya Wa Nihaya / Beginning and End* (1960) and *al-Qahira 30 / Cairo 30* (1966), the latter from Mahfouz's *al-Qahira al-Jadida* (*The New Cairo*) – are among the most important films of Egyptian realism.

Other major writers contributed to realism as well. Taufik Salih's *Yawmiyat Na'ib Fi-l-Aryaf / Diary of a Country Prosecutor* (1968) was based on Taufiq al-Hakim's novel. Youssef Chahine adapted the novel *al-Ard* (*The Earth*) by 'Abd al-Rahman al-Sharqawi, to produce one of the most notable examples of Egyptian realism. Other directors owe their few realist films to adaptations of literary texts: Henri Barakat for his *al-Haram* (1965), Kamal El-Cheikh for *al-Liss Wa-l-Kilab / The Thief and the Dogs* (1962) and *Miramar* (1968), and Husain Kamal for *Tharthara Fawq al-Nil / Adrift on the Nile* (1971), the last three all from works by Mahfouz.

Furthermore, Egyptian film-makers 'Egyptianized' many internationally known literary works, primarily by French, British and Russian authors – to name only a few of them, they included Dumas *fils*, Balzac, Gide, Wilde, Emily Brontë and Dostoevsky – as well as a limited number of Americans – such as Mark Twain and Arthur Miller, among others. French realism in particular enjoyed great popularity, mainly during the 1940s and 1950s: *La dame aux camélias* by Alexandre Dumas *fils* was adapted up to six times – the closest adaptation to the original was *Layla* (1942) by Togo Mizrahi

Figure 14 Fajr al-Islam / The Dawn of Islam

– and its main motif (the loyal courtesan and an upper-class son in love) was recycled in numerous other films. *Le Comte de Monte Cristo* by Dumas *père* was also adapted six times – first by Henri Barakat in *Amir al-Intiqam / Prince of Revenge* (1948) – so was Pagnol's *Fanny*. Victor Hugo's *Les misérables* was adapted twice by Kamal Selim in 1942 and then by 'Atif Salim in 1978. Emile Zola's *Thérèse Raquin* was translated into cinema in (among other films) *Lak Yawm Ya Zalim / Your Day is Coming* (1951) by Salah Abu Seif.

Most prominent among non-French writings were *Crime and Punishment* and *The Brothers Karamazov* by Dostoevsky, *Anna Karenina* and *Resurrection* by Tolstoy and Gogol's *The General Inspector*. Classic plays, such as Molière's *The Miser* and Shakespeare's *Romeo and Juliet*, also proved to be popular sources. *Taming of the Shrew* was presented most recently in Inas al-Dighidi's *Istakusa / Lobster* (1996).

Foreign works tended to be Egyptianized to the extent that they were no longer recognisable. Screenwriters often retained only the basic plot of the story, stripping it of of all its temporal and regional specificities – this happened to *Anna Karenina* in *Nahr al-Hubb / Stream of Love* (1958) by 'Izz al-Din zu-l-Fiqar. Placing setting and characters in an entirely local context offered the opportunity to repackage conservative values in a more modern framework. The same applies also to film remakes. In the majority they followed American models, more or less successfully copying the plot and placing it (sometimes but not always convincingly) in an Egyptian context. Between 1942 and 1992, 196 remakes and literary adaptions from American sources were counted. The most adapted directors were Frank Capra, Billy Wilder, George Cukor, William Wyler, Alfred Hitchcock, King Vidor, Brian de Palma and Francis Ford Coppola.

Only a few remakes may be considered milestones in Egyptian film history, contrary to the literary adaptations which were not only more prestigious but managed also to achieve higher cinematic standards. This may be due to the fact that in the main it was less talented directors who tended to remake foreign box-office hits and for primarily commercial reasons. However some of those worth mentioning are *Layla Bint al-Aghniya' / Layla, Daughter of the Rich* (1946) by Anwar Wagdi (based on Capra's *It Happened One Night*), *Imra'a Fi-l-Tariq / A Woman on the Road* (1958) by 'Izz al-Din zu-l-Fiqar (adapted from King Vidor's *Duel in the Sun*) and *Darbit Shams / Sun Stroke* (1980) by Mohamed Khan (a remake of Antonioni's *Blow Up*).

Short films and documentaries

Short films and documentaries in Egyptian cinema are neglected, both in terms of production and distribution opportunities and through a lack of documentation and analysis. As elsewhere, in Egypt the production of shorts preceded the full-length feature. Yet short films and documentaries were soon marginalized by the film industry, despite constant official and unofficial attempts to develop them.

The first Egyptian documentaries presented small items, like De Lagarne's *The Streets of Alexandria*, shot in 1912, or later Bayyumi's recordings of different places and events (including the return of Sa'd Zaghlul from exile in 1923) for his *Amun* newsreel. The first regular newreels, *Jaridat Misr / Egypt Journal*, were issued by Sharikat Misr and directed by Hasan Murad. The following films were either instructional and primarily concerned with development, like Muhammad Karim's *al-Ta'awun / Co-operation* (1931) and Gamal Madkur's *Mashru' al-Qirsh / The Penny Project* (1932), or propagandistic, like *al-Mu'tamar al-Wafdi 'Am 1934 / The Wafdist Congress in 1934* and *Bank Misr Wa Shurakah / Misr Bank & Co.* (1935), both by Niazi Mustafa.

After *Jaridat Misr* was provided with sound in 1938, it was issued on a weekly basis. Studio Misr became the producer of the first carefully structured documentaries, which were already being shot before the end of the 1940s when the pioneer of Egyptian documentary, Sa'd Nadim, set up a short-film section at the studio that produced largely information films. Notwithstanding these efforts, the studio did not secure steady and continuous production, neither did the ministries of health, agriculture and social affairs who had also started producing documentaries relevant to their interests. All in all, forty films of this type were realized between 1924 and 1952.

After 1952, the Ministry of National Guidance created a film production department but failed to achieve its objectives. Several other governmental administrations tried their luck in the production of instructional films and different public film units were created, among them the short-lived Cinema Support Organization (*mu'asassat da'm al-sinima*). In 1962 it produced some interesting films, like Wali al-Din Samih's *Hurub al-'a'ila al-Muqadasa / The Flight of the Holy Family*, Taufiq Salih's *al-Qulla / The Jug* and Sa'd Nadim's series (seven films) on Nubia.

The most productive institution during the Nasserist reign was the Information Administration, with an output of around 120 films between 1954 and 1966. Its production was dominated by developmental, tourist and ethnographic films that documented traditions, crafts, monuments, development programmes and national industrial achievements, notably with Khalil Shauqi's *al-Hadid Wa-l-Sulb / Iron and Steel* (1958) and more importantly through a series shot by Salah al-Tuhami which started in 1961 with four parts called *Zikrayat Muhandis / Memories of an Engineer* and depicted the construction of the High Dam. In 1962 the series was issued monthly under the title *Sibaq Ma'a al-Zaman / Race against Time* and amounted to thirty-seven films.

After the creation of the General Egyptian Film Organization in 1963, the National Documentary Film Centre was set up in 1968 – it operated properly only for one year. It produced, however, one of the few experimental films of Egyptian cinema, *Thawrat al-Makkan / The Revolution of Machines* (1968) by Madkur Thabit. The Film Centre was reorganized in 1971 under the supervision of Sa'd Nadim. It secured a stable continuous production only until 1976, though, with a total output of sixty films. It is noteworthy that the early 1970s were characterized by a new wave in style and, to a certain extent, technique. During this period some of the most critical documentaries appeared, characterized by a deep interest in people's living conditions. Less conformist to the state and more conscious of social problems, *al-Nil Arzaq / Daily Bread on the Nile* (1972) by Hashem El-Nahas (Hashim al-Nahas), Khairy Beshara's *Tabib Fi-l-Aryaf / The Countryside Doctor* (1975), Daoud Abd El-Sayed's *Wasiyyat Rajul Hakim Fi Shu'un al-Qarya Wa-l-Ta'lim / The Advice of a Wise Man in Matters of the Village and Education* (1976) and 'Abd al-Mun'im 'Uthman's *Fi-l-Mishmish / Never* (1977) may be considered closest to the notion of 'direct cinema' on the ideological level, although not in technical terms.

The productions of the Film Centre involved all kinds of short films, including animation and children's films alongside documentaries. However, its output was irregular and inconsistent due to the constant changes of official guidelines, an unclear production policy and the lack of money and facilities. The Film Centre's reliance on old equipment and techniques has been an additional problem. Until the early 1990s, when the Film Centre shifted to include video production, documentaries were mainly shot on 35 mm film. Because of very tight budgets, film-makers usually had to use film stock at a ratio of 1:4, which hampered the development of a real direct cinema in the field of documentaries. Any acceptable film produced under these circumstances must be considered an achievement, notwithstanding its inevitable blemishes.

In spite of the Film Centre's unsteady production policy during the 1980s, there were nonetheless a number of interesting documentaries and short fiction films, such as Ahmad Qasim's *Attiba' Fi-l-Madina* (1981), *Thulathiyyat Rafah / Rafah Trilogy* (1982) and *Suq al-Rijal / Men's Market* (1991) by Husam 'Ali, Asma' al-Bakri's *al-Burtri / The Portrait* (1981), 'Awad Shukri's *al-Tal'a / The Funeral* (1982), Sami al-Salamuni's *al-Sabah / The Morning* (1983), 'Ali Badrakhan's *'Amm 'Abbas al-Mukhtari' / Uncle 'Abbas the Inventor* (1985), *Lu'b 'Iyal / Children's Games* (1990) by Nabiha Lutfi and *Shari' Qasr al-Nil / Qasr al-Nil Street* (1993) by Fu'ad al-Tuhami, among others. Interesting historical documentaries furnished with a multitude of archival material were offered by Muhammad Kamil al-Qalyubi in *Waqa'i' al-Zaman al-Dha'i': Muhammad Bayyumi / Chronicle of the Lost Time: Muhammad Bayyumi* (1991) and Magdi 'Abd al-Rahman in *Wasaya 'Ali Mubarak al-Bahira Fi Ahwal Misr Wa-l-Qahira / 'Ali Mubarak's Splendid Testimonies in Egypt's and Cairo's Conditions* (1993).

Independent documentary film-making was for a long time more or less represented by a single person, 'Attiat al-Abnudi, who directed her first short *Husan al-Tin /*

Horse of Mud in 1971 – a silent observation of women in the brick industry. She is one of the few directors who managed to finance her films either by herself or through co-production but without relying primarily on state institutions. She more-over remained largely faithful to direct cinema, using only 16 mm and video cameras and laying great emphasis on direct observation and spontaneous interviews, as in her remarkable portrait of a farmer's wife *al-Ahlam al-Mumkinna / Permissible Dreams* (1982).

A kind of poetic documentarism was developed during the 1980s by the television director and cameraman 'Ali al-Ghazuli. Unlike al-Abnudi, al-Ghazuli's films were almost entirely staged, but reflected the lifestyle of the different regions he was depicting, such as the Sinai in *Hakim Sant Katrin / The Saint Katherine Doctor* (1987) or the northern salt-lakes in *Sayd al-'Asari / Afternoon Fishing* (1990). National Television had started documentary production in 1966, first through the Surveillance of Cinema Programmes (*muraqabat al-baramij al-sinima'iyya*) department and then, since 1975, through the General Surveillance of Documentary and produced during its first decade an average of ten films per year, largely for tourists.

In general, the Egyptian documentary of the 1990s shifted towards developmental topics, shot on video by an increasing number of women directors, dealing to a large extent with gender issues and financed by funds from development organizations: these include Nabiha Lutfi's *Illa Ayn / Where?* (1991) on female illiteracy and Taghrid al-'Asfuri's beautifully shot *Arzaq / Daily Bread* (1995) on small girls in the labour force. 'Attiat al-Abnudi's *Ayam al-Dimuqratiyya / Days of Democracy* (1998) is the most accomplished and least educational of these films, as it follows the campaigns of female candidates during the 1997 parliamentary elections.

Up until now, one of the most consistent Egyptian documentaries in form and content has been Yousri Nasrallah's full-length *Sibyan Wa Banat / Apropos Boys, Girls and the Veil* (1995), co-produced by French television. Dealing with the highly topical questions of gender relations among Egyptian youth and veiling, this video is characterized by very high technical standards and is visually enriched by the director's experience with the *mise-en-scène* and continuity issues common to fiction films.

Almost no experimental cinema has developed in the Egyptian short film, with a few sporadic exceptions like Madkur Thabit's purely visual *Thawrit al-Makann* (1968) and some films realized at Chadi Abdessalam's Experimental Film Unit (*wahdat al-film al-tajribi*), a section of the National Film Centre founded in 1968. The short films produced by the Unit tended, with a few exceptions, to be documentaries. Their most important innovation was that they did not comment on the images, contrary to what has been considered until then obligatory to the Egyptian documentary. Now the image alone was supposed to be able to carry the crucial information. Therefore, film-makers of the department (to which 'Atif al-Bakri, Samir 'Uf and Ibrahim al-Mugi belonged) were submitted to less restrictions in their consumption of raw stock than usual at the Centre. The most remarkable films from the Unit were *Lu'lu'at al-Nil / Pearl of the Nile* (1972) by Samir 'Uf and *Afaq / Horizons* (1973) by Abdessalam. In contrast, apart from Youssef Chahine's subjective essay on present-day Cairo, *al-Qahira Minawarra Bi-Ahliha / Cairo Seen by Youssef Chahine* (1991), only a few Egyptian narrative experimental films were produced.

The Egyptian short fiction film has remained even more in the shadow of the film industry and bureaucracy than the documentary. Although movie theatres are obliged by law to screen a short film before a full-length film, the distribution of short films is circumvented or neglected. In general short fictions were, if at all, produced by the National Film Centre – like, for example, Abdessalam's fiction *al-Fallah al-Fasih / The Eloquent Peasant* (1970), based on an ancient Egyptian text, or Hala Khalil's remarkable *Tiri Ya Tayara / The Kite* (1996), about the adolescence of a girl.

During the last decades, the production of short fiction film has mainly been confined to graduation projects from the Higher Film Institute, exemplified by numerous promising works, such as Radwan al-Kashif's *al-Janubiyya / Woman from the South* (1984), Sandra Nash'at's *Akhir Shita' / The Last Winter* (1992), Hany Khalifa's *'Arabat al-Sayyidat / Ladies Only* (1993), Sa'd Hindawi's *Yawm al-Ahad al-'Adi / Normal Sunday* (1995) and Rasha al-Kurdi's *Awal Mara / First Time* (1998). Lately the new satellite channels (notably the Nile Thematic Channels) have also helped to revive the short film by airing and producing new works, like *'Alamat Abril / April Signs* (1999) by Ahmad Mahir.

Like the fiction film, animation remained totally underdeveloped and marginalized. Nushi Iskandar, Rida Gibran and Ihab Shakir started their careers in the 1970s and tried to develop animation based on popular artforms. Only a few directors were able to distinguish themselves in that field by creating an individual style, primarily Munna Abu al-Nasr with *al-Muntassir / The Victor* (1989) and the graduation projects *al-Sadd / The Dam* (1990) by Sabir 'Aqid and *Hakadha Tabdu / She Seems Like That* (1993) by Rihab 'Adil Anwar.

Filmography

Ahl al-Qimma / People from the Top

1981, 125 mins, colour, Arabic

Director:	'Ali Badrakhan
Producer:	'Abd al-'Azim al-Zaghabi
Screenwriter:	'Ali Badrakhan, Mustafa Muharram
Cinematographer:	Muhsin Nasr
Editor:	Sa'id al-Shaykh
Music:	Gamal Salama
Designer:	Mahir 'Abd al-Nur
Leading Players:	Su'ad Husni, Nur al-Sharif, 'Izzat al-'Alayli

Adapted from a novel by Naguib Mahfouz, this film is the first 'serious' film about the *infitah* (or 'open-door policy') and the setbacks of this policy. Enriched by an excellent realist *mise-en-scène* by its director 'Ali Badrakhan and the refined (because sensitive) performance of top star Su'ad Husni, the film precedes other so-called 'New Realist' works and in fact deserves more attention from the cinematic point of view than Atef El-Tayeb's *Sawaq al-Utubis / The Bus Driver* (1983), which was commonly considered the starting point for New Realism. Similar to other New Realist works *Ahl al-Qimma* evolves from the problem of social descent as experienced by the old middle class, facing the increasing influence of *arrivistes* and *nouveaux riches* who (in most of these narratives) surface through illegal practices. The first are represented in this work by an upright police officer ('Izzat al-'Alayli) and his younger sister (Su'ad Husni) who suffers from emotional and material deprivation. When she is courted by a successful young entrepreneur she finally gives in and agrees to marry him, although it turns out in the course of her brother's investigations that her admirer was a former pickpocket and has made his money through fraud and corruption.

One of the strongest parts of the narration is the pragmatic and unconciliatory finale, ending with the girl giving up her family and pride – in other words she betrays her class for the sake of a better life. This effect is achieved by the complex depiction of characters and their surroundings, moving the story away from any oversimplifications.

Ard al-Khawf / Land of Fear

1999, 145 mins, colour, Arabic

Director:	Daoud Abd El-Sayed
Producer:	Shu'a'
Screenwriter:	Daoud Abd El-Sayed
Cinematographer:	Samir Bahzan
Editor:	'Adil Munir
Music:	Ragih Dawud
Designer:	Onsi Abou Seif
Leading Players:	Ahmad Zaki, Farah, 'Abd Allah Ghayth

Scripted by the director himself, the story of a secret agent who has lost his identity reflects some of Daoud Abd El-Sayed's recurrent philosophical concerns. Unlike his earlier, much more subtle but also confusing *al-Bahth 'An Sayyid Marzuq / The Search for Sayyid Marzuq* (1991), which was questioning identity against the background of social instability and civil insecurity, *Ard al-Khawf* searches out the very basic metaphysical forces which may affect a human's moral as well as physical existence. This quest is wrapped in an exciting thriller: During the late 1960s, police officer Adam (performed by Ahmad Zaki) is assigned a secret task – to infiltrate the underworld for a very long time period and report on developments, particularly of the drug business. He is asked to commit any crime necessary in order to be convincing and is promised a general amnesty when his mission ends. Indeed, the former agent becomes a successful criminal and finally attains the position of one of the most ruthless drug tycoons. However, he keeps on sending reports and warnings to his superiors, but rarely receives any response from above – particularly after several changes in government and police administration. Eventually he learns through the postman Mussa (Moses), who is as uninformed as he is ominous, that most of his letters had never been delivered. This information leaves him a real culprit with no excuses. Haunted by the police and an increasing insecurity about his real identity, Adam tries in vain to retreat from his dirty business.

Ard al-Khawf does not only intrigue through the doubts it plants about the idea of any ethical and moral guidance and righteousness, but also through the obvious irony with which the storyline leads the protagonist's good moral intentions astray. The film, moreover, stands out through its stunning *mise-en-scène*, expressed not only in the rhythm created by camera movements and editing, but also by the richness and variety of sets and the overall coherence of the visual design in relation to the camerawork.

All this supports the contemplative character of many scenes, to which Ragih Dawud's music and the poetic voice-over (spoken by the protagonist) make a decisive contribution. With this film, Abd El-Sayed proves to be a true Mohsen Makhmalbaf (see the chapter on Iranian film) of Egyptian cinema.

al-Awama 70 / Houseboat No. 70

1982, 129 mins, colour, Arabic

Director:	Khairy Beshara
Producer:	Mima li-l-intaj al-sinima'i
Screenwriter:	Fayiz Ghali
Cinematographer:	Mahmud 'Abd al-Sami'
Editor:	'Adil Munir
Music:	Gihad Dawud
Leading Players:	Ahmad Zaki, Kamal al-Shinawi, Taysir Fahmi, Magda al-Khatib

Based on a strongly autobiograhical original idea from the director, this film may be considered one of the most profound *cinéma d'auteur* works of Egyptian cinema. The documentary film-maker Ahmad (Ahmad Zaki) is preparing a documentary on a cotton mill when he learns through 'Abd al-'Ati, one of the workers, about an incident of severe fraud. A short while later the worker is found dead, while Ahmad decides (together with his fiancée, the journalist Widad) to pursue the case through his film project. However, the film-maker soon gets detained and accused of being responsible for the worker's death. Helpless and disappointed, the director gives up the investigation and likewise the whole project. Although the film articulates some of the typical New Realist concerns (such as corruption and abuse of power), it achieves this by focusing primarily on the internal conflict of the main protagonist and thereby turns into a more personal narrative, depicting his ambiguous and tormented relation to reality in general and people in particular. This is made possible by loosening the basic dramatic structure and inserting numerous more observational scenes that express the protagonist's ambivalence. Although he is in love with his fiancée, he still maintains a secret sexual relationship with an older more mature woman (Magda al-Khatib). His hesitancy and doubts are not only contrasted on the emotional level by his much more self-confident partner Widad, but also on the social and political level by the courage of the worker 'Abd al-'Ati and the pragmatic wisdom of his uncle (performed by Kamal al-Shinawi). The self-criticism expressed in *al-Awama 70* adds to its force and moves it away from any New Realist tendency to portray things as being black or white.

Bab al-Hadid / Cairo Main Station

1958, 98 mins, black and white, Arabic

Director:	Youssef Chahine
Producer:	Gibra'il Talhami
Screenwriter:	'Abd al-Hay Adib, Muhammad Abu Yusuf
Cinematographer:	Alvise Orfanelli

Editor:	Kamal Abu al-'Illa
Music:	Fu'ad al-Zahiri
Designer:	'Abbas Hilmi
Leading Players:	Youssef Chahine, Hind Rustum, Farid Shauqi, Hasan al-Barudi

Bab al-hadid or 'the iron gate' is the colloquial term for Cairo Main Station. There the crippled and ragged peasant Qinawi (brilliantly played by Chahine himself) has been stranded. He lives in the station in a shabby old wagon that is only decorated with a series of pin-up girls and he makes his living by selling newspapers to the travellers. Qinawi is a voyeur *par excellence* who is allowed to participate in life only by watching. The woman, however, for whom his heart beats is not interested in him. The sexy and decisive soft-drink seller Hanuma (charmingly performed by Hind Rustum) only has eyes for the porter, Abu Siri'. After a failed flirtation, Qinawi attempts to kill Hanuma, but injures another girl instead. When Qinawi goes for Hanuma's blood a second time, he ends up in a straitjacket.

The motifs of murder and the chase add considerable suspense to *Bab al-Hadid*. At the same time, several parallel events unfolding within the station break the basic dramatic structure of the background story: there are the porters led by Abu Siri' who try to set up a trade union; a panicked peasant family wander through the crowd; a feminist delivers a speech; a couple in love keep their secret appointments. These inserts are mainly observations made by Qinawi and allow the audience to participate in his voyeurism. Thus the conventions of the thriller are undercut by a certain observational realism that is concerned with the main topics of the time: social injustice, women's liberation and the socialist project of the Nasserist era. Yet what gives this film its special place in Chahine's rich oeuvre is certainly the successful *mélange* of social criticism and entertainment, represented by several hilarious and cheerful moments: for example, Qinawi catches Hanuma dancing with a group of young people in a train but joins in at last to dance with one of her Coke bottles. In addition the film is characterized by an interest in psychology that is rarely expressed in Egyptian cinema. Indeed, the impressive depiction of material and sexual deprivation escalates into a dramatic psychic catharsis. It is, last but not least, Chahine's sympathetic performance as the main character that elucidates Qinawi's relationships without falling prey to superficiality or a false spectacle.

Du'a' al-Karawan | The Cry of the Plover

1959, 105 mins, colour, Arabic

Director:	Henri Barakat
Producer:	Aflam Barakat
Screenwriter:	Yusuf Guhar, Henri Barakat
Cinematographer:	Wahid Farid
Editor:	Muhammad 'Abbas
Designer:	Mahir 'Abd al-Nur
Leading Players:	Fatin Hamama, Ahmad Mazhar, Amina Rizq

Du'a' al-Karawan is one of the most distinguished but also darkest Egyptian melo-dramas. It achieved a high reputation not only because of Henri Barakat's skill in directing this particular genre, but also because of its popular literary model, a novel by Taha Hussein which is characteristic of many works of that period in its modernizing intentions. The film deals with revenge and killing for the sake of honour, which is one of the recurrent motifs linked to any fictional representation of the Egyptian countryside and, in particular, to Upper Egypt; it feeds mostly into the discourse of so-called 'back-wardness'. A peasant mother and her two unmarried daughters, Amna and Hanadi, have to leave their village after the death of the father. Hanadi starts working as a servant for a rich young bachelor (Ahmad Mazhar) who seduces her. When this becomes known, Hanadi's maternal uncle kills her to save the family's honour. Amna (performed by superstar Fatin Hamama) decides to take revenge in her own way and starts to serve the bachelor herself. As she resists his flirtations and even an attempted rape, he finally falls in love with her. At the moment when they realize their mutual love, he gets killed in Amna's arms while trying to protect her from a bullet fired at her by her uncle.

Du'a' al-Karawan is characterized rather by its classic dramatization than by the sentimentality of family drama. This impression is not only supported by the vigour and strength of the heroine, but also by the dark black-and-white photography and the reduced set design that transforms the countryside (as well as the interior of homes) to a cold cypher instead of the opulent host of strong feelings.

Ghazal al-Banat / Girls' Flirtation

1949, 120 mins, black and white, Arabic

Director: Anwar Wagdi
Producer: Sharikat al-aflam al-muttahida (Anwar Wagdi & co.)
Screenwriter: Badi` Khayri, Nagib al-Rihani
Cinematographer: `Abd al-Halim Nasr
Editor: Kamal El-Cheikh
Designer: Antoine Boliseuz
Leading Players: Layla Murad, Nagib al-Rihani, Anwar Wagdi, Yusuf Wahbi

Ghazal al-Banat is not a perfect or coherent work, but it combines all the assets of three great talents of the time: Anwar Wagdis congenial stance of cinematic entertainment, Layla Murads charming acting and beautiful voice and Nagib al-Rihani's warm touching humor and witty dialogues. The story is that of a pasha's daughter (Murad) who has some difficulties with her Arabic lessons. Her father hires poor teacher Hamam (al-Rihani), who does first loose his heart to his pupil, but saves her than from a greedy lover just to watch her fall in love with an attractive officer (Wagdi). The story line is spiced with funny sketches, second rate music hall performances, beautiful songs including a Muhammad `Abd al-Wahhab performance and last not least one of the most charming duettos of Egyptian cinema, sung and spoken by Layla Murad and al-Rihani.

Iskandariyya Lih? / Alexandria, Why?

1978, 133 mins, colour, Arabic

Director: Youssef Chahine
Producer: Misr International, ONCIC
Screenwriter: Muhsin Zayid, Youssef Chahine
Cinematographer: Muhsin Nasr
Editor: Rashida 'Abd al-Salam
Music: Fu'ad al-Zahiri
Designer: Nihad Bahgat
Leading Players: Muhsin Muhi al-Din, Muhsina Taufiq, Mahmud al-Miligi,
                      'Izzat al-'Alayli, Ahmad Mihriz

This film is definitely one of the turning points in its director's cinematic career. It was the first Arab film to receive a Silberner Bär (at the 1979 Berlin Film Festival) and marked a shift in Chahine's orientation towards a more personal *cinéma d'auteur*. Moreover, it was the start of his semi-autobiographical trilogy, which continued with *Haduta Misriyya / An Egyptian Fairy-Tale* (1982) and was completed by *Iskandariyya Kaman Wa Kaman / Alexandria Now and Forever* (1989).

The narration features Yahia, Chahine's *alter ego* (represented by Muhsin Muhi al-Din), but also a range of other partly real and partly fictional characters who add up to a kaleidoscope of cosmopolitan and vibrant Alexandria at the moment when Rommel invaded during World War II. Black marketeers, pashas, nationalists, Islamists, Jews and even homosexuals populate numerous parallel stories, loosely intertwined with the adolescence of the main character Yahia. He is about to graduate from the prestigious Victoria College in Alexandria, but is much more interested in Hollywood films starring Ginger Rogers and Fred Astaire. He dreams of becoming an actor. But the city is living through a difficult time. As the German troops approach, speculation and the black market flourish. Yahia's family is in crisis too. The father, an idealistic lawyer, prefers to go fishing than deal with an unjust jurisdiction, while the mother is desperately trying to make ends meet. Yahia's prosperous fellow students plan their studies abroad, while he is forced to start boring training in a bank. When, against all expectations, he is granted a scholarship to the United States, the family collects its last savings in order to enable him to travel.

In spite of numerous historical inaccuracies at the level of costumes and set design, the film nonetheless has a vibrant charm due on one hand to its rich multiple narrative and on the other to the hybridity of its cinematic style, which resembles a firework of bits and pieces that include clippings from historical newsreels and fiction films, variety dances and theatre performances, as well as different generic elements ranging from comedy to realism.

Lahn al-Khulud / The Eternal Song

1952, 125 mins, black and white, Arabic
Director: Henri Barakat
Producer: sharikat Misr li-l-intaj wa-l-sinima
Screenwriter: Yusuf `Issa
Cinematographer: Julio di Luca
Editor: Fathi Qassim
Designer: Antoine Polizois

Leading Players: Fatin Hamama, Farid al-Attrash, Madiha Kamil, Magda

Lahn al-Khulud is one of the most accomplished Egyptian musicals, combining some beautiful al-Atrash' songs and a heavily melodramatic plot. Its coherence is apart from its smooth mise-en-scène and convincing acting due to the successful integration of the musical performance into the action, achieved through cross cutting and parallel-actions. Petite Fatin Hamama features in this film as a young orphan who is taken into custody by a relative whose capricious daughter (Madiha Kamil) manages to marry the best friend of the orphan's family, a gifted musician. The girl tries in vain to hide her admiration for him. The singer too feels increasingly attracted particularly as his wife is only interested in celebrating parties. In another melodramatic twist the orphan falls ill, is threatened to die but rescued eventually by her lover's decision to repudiate his careless wife.

Lashin

1939, 105 mins, black and white, Arabic
Director: Fritz Kramp
Producer: Sharikat Misr li-l-sinima wa-l-tamthil (Studio Misr)
Screenwriter: Ahmad Badrakhan, Fritz Kramp
Cinematographer: Georges Estello
Editor: Niazi Mustafa
Music: 'Abd al-Hamid 'Abd al-Hay
Designer: Robert Scharfenberg
Leading Players: Hasan 'Izzat, Nadia Nagi, Husain Riyad, Ahmad al-Bey

Being one of the early Studio Misr productions, this is also one of the most challenging historical spectacles of Egyptian cinema, to which the spirit of German director Fritz Kramp seems to have added a good deal of social explosiveness. It is centred around Commander-in-Chief Lashin. He serves a weak tyrant king, who is manipulated by a minister who, in turn, distinguishes himself by exploiting the impoverished people. When eventually the popular Lashin is jailed, a mutiny is sparked off among the people who seek to secure his release.

In the original film version, the unjust king was overthrown; however, after interference from the censor, Fritz Kramp was asked to save the king's head at the end of the film by turning him into a good ruler who assists Lashin's just causes. All in all a quite coherent work, *Lashin* convinces by its aesthetic qualities, which combine historicism with a relatively realist and simple representation. This becomes primarily visible in costume and set, both designed by the leftist and former colleague of Bertholt Brecht, Robert Scharfenberg. It is likewise visible in the acting style of two otherwise marginal actors: Hasan 'Izzat and Nadia Nagi (who plays Lashin's lover).

Layla al-Badawiyya / Layla the Bedouin

1937 (not released until 1944), 140 mins, black and white, Arabic
Director: Bahiga Hafiz
Producer: Fanar Film (Bahiga Hafiz)

Screenwriter:	Bahiga Hafiz, Ibrahim al-'Aqqad
Cinematographer:	Muhammad 'Abd al-'Azim, Hasan Murad
Editor:	Fahi Bujidian
Music:	Bahiga Hafiz
Designer:	Wali al-Din Samih
Leading Players:	Bahiga Hafiz, Husain Riyad, Raqya Ibrahim, Zaki Rustum

Layla is the beautiful daughter of the leader of an Arab tribe. She is in love with one of her cousins, but gets captured by the troops of the Persian king and delivered to his harem. After she refuses to marry the king and makes a failed attempt to escape, she is tortured and almost raped. Soon, however, her tribe – led by her beloved cousin – manage to rescue her. The film manifests its political subtext during the finale: Layla – the Arab virgin liberated from a foreign tyrant – is carried on the shoulders of her kin as a symbol of liberty and cultural resurrection. Apart from these subtle nationalist connotations, the work astonishes through its lavish sets and costumes. The latter were designed by the director herself, who also composed the music and performed the main part. Although the *mise-en-scène* and acting style were still influenced by the expressiveness and gesturing of silent cinema, the film is certainly one of the real (if, for a long time, unacknowledged) classics of Egyptian cinema. The film music, however, is the strongest part, as it merges the songs and the background music to one whole impressing composition.

Layla Sakhina / A Hot Night

1995, 120 mins, colour, Arabic

Director:	Atef El-Tayeb
Producer:	Aflam Misr al-'Arabiyya (Wasif Fayiz)
Screenwriter:	Rafiq al-Sabban, Muhammad Ashraf
Cinematographer:	Hisham Sirri
Editor:	Ahmad Mitwalli
Music:	Moody Imam
Leading Players:	Nur al-Sharif, Libliba

Layla Sakhina was one of the last works of the late New Realist Atef El-Tayeb. It stars Nur al-Sharif in a plot similar to their first film collaboration, *Sawaq al-Utubis / The Bus Driver* (1983), that has commonly been considered the starting point of New Realism. It features a taxi driver on a hot nocturnal pursuit through the city. His mother is in hospital, waiting for urgent surgery, but money for the operation is missing and her son needs to collect it immediately. One of his customers (played by Libliba) turns out to be a prostitute who was just robbed by her clients. She is also in search of money, as her landlord wants to throw her and her little sister out of their home the next day. The taxi driver feels pity for her and helps to find her runaway clients. On their way, they pick up a black marketeer who sells foreign visas and work permits. After a subsequent gunfight, the couple is left with an attaché case full of money. The driver decides to hand it in at the police station, but is taken into custody himself. When the policemen arrive in search of the case, the prostitute proves to be more pragmatic. She has hidden the money and will, it is suggested (the film has an open ending), hire a lawyer and take care of the driver's family.

The conflicts of this narrative do not spring from an extremely powerful antagonist, but from different social groups and institutions, such as the hospital, the police force and landlords. This anti-capitalist orientation is underpinned by various references to traditional moral codes and intersects with current gender concepts. The female prostitute is an absolutely positive heroine. Her immorality is placed in a social context, which encourages sympathy rather than repulsion, for she finances the education of her younger sister who does not know about her sibling's profession. When the prostitute learns about the taxi driver's sick mother, she offers to give him her last piece of jewellery. The driver is, likewise, chivalrous. He helps her to pursue her clients and even gets himself involved in a brawl for her sake.

Layla Sakhina is not only a thrilling road movie, but also displays the most appreciated characteristics of El-Tayeb's directing: sympathetic and informed depictions of the urban lower class milieu, along with an appropriate degree of action-film elements (including physical violence and chase scenes).

al-Mumya' / The Mummy: The Night of Counting the Years

1969, 103 mins, colour, Arabic

Director:	Chadi Abdessalam
Producer:	General Film Organization
Screenwriter:	Chadi Abdessalam
Cinematographer:	'Abd al-'Aziz Fahmi
Editor:	Kamal Abu al-'Illa
Music:	Mario Nachimbini
Designer:	Salah Marei
Sound:	Nasri 'Abd al-Nur
Leading Players:	Ahmad Mar'i, Nadia Lutfi, Zuzu Hamdi al-Hakim, Shafiq Nur al-Din, Muhammad Khayri

This film is considered the major masterpiece of Egyptian cinema, addressing the quest for a cultural identity and the adequate appropriation of history. Set at the time of the archeological discovery of the royal tombs near Thebes in 1881, it circles around the quest for cultural identity *vis-à-vis* a stolen and exploited past. Wanis, son of the chief of the Hurrabat tribe, learns (after the death of his father) that his tribe is living on tomb robbery. He thinks it ignominious to participate in defiling tombs and starts asking questions about those who have been laid to rest. Are they his own ancestors? What is the meaning of those signs that they have left on the walls of the tombs and temples? Wanis' older brother refuses to take part in the violation and is murdered a little while later on the orders of the tribe's elders. He leaves his younger brother helpless, torn between feeling shame on one hand and responsibility towards his relations on the other. Soon Wanis discovers that the archeologists who come from far away know how to decipher these hieroglyphs. His decision to betray to them the location of the tombs marks the often difficult process of becoming aware of one's own history.

Al-Mumya' treats the relation between contemporary Egyptians and their ancient culture allegorically. The protagonist's wish to take up the challenge of his past is met at the level of visual representation, as well as through all the other stylistic means applied to the film. The clear and strict composition of images refers to the monumental stasis of Old Egyptian sculptures and paintings. The same effect is achieved by the sparing and dignified movements of the actors, their relief-like arrangement in front of the rocks, the desert or in buildings. The use of classical Arabic, in general not common in Egyptian cinema, further reinforces the impression of monumentalism at the linguistic level. However, the visual allusion to past magnitude does not feed on a shallow glorification, since it is heavily contradicted at the level of the narration by the experience of painful loss of that same past.

Qandil Umm Hashim / Umm Hashim's Lamp

1968, 115 mins, black and white, Arabic

Director:	Kamal 'Attiyya
Producer:	General Film Organization
Screenwriter:	Sabri Musa
Cinematographer:	'Adil 'Abd al-'Azim
Editor:	Husain 'Afifi
Music:	Fu'ad al-Zahiri
Designer:	Hilmi 'Azab
Leading Players:	Shukri Sarhan, Samira Ahmad, Salah Mansur, 'Abd al-Warith A'sarr, Amina Rizq

Adapted from a story written by Yahia Haqqi, *Qandil Umm Hashim* is an unfolding of a deeply modernist concern, focusing on the so-called 'conflict of cultures'. After finishing his medical studies in Europe and having had an inspiring romance with a European woman, Isma'il returns to his traditional neighbourhood in a provincial town. His cousin and fiancée is very kindhearted, but far too simple-minded for him. The conflict escalates the moment that Isma'il discovers she has fallen prey to an eye-disease and his mother has tried to treat it by dripping the oil of the venerated Umm Hashim in the girl's eyes. Isma'il – an eye-specialist himself – is outraged by their ignorance and destroys the lamp which holds the oil, much to the distress of his neighbourhood and family. However, the protagonist soon understands that he has to reconcile himself to tradition without denying his modern education. At the end he treats his cousin successfully, while pretending to her that he is using the holy oil for the treatment.

The film sets up cultural development as a conflict between local tradition and modern Western education, and successfully visualizes the problems that may arise for an individual in that context. Even though one may disagree with such a binary view, Kamal 'Attiyya's sensitive and sympathetic *mise-en-scène* (including the section shot in Europe) adds a lot to the credibility of the depiction and at the same time reflects the intellectual concerns of the film's literary model.

Sariqat Sayfiyya / Summer Thefts

1988, 97 mins, colour, Arabic

Director / Screenwriter: Yousri Nasrallah
Cinematographer: Ramsis Marzuq
Editor: Rahma Muntassir
Sound: Gasir Gabr
Music: 'Amr Khayrat
Set Design: Onsi Abou Seif
Leading Players: Menha al-Batrawi, Saif 'Abd al-Rahman, Mona Zakariyya, 'Abla Kamil

This semi-autobiography by Chahine's most important disciple is a socially committed film that avoids drawing political allegories, although allusions to the country's political conditions during the 1960s are laid over the images of painful personal memories almost like a superstructure. From the perspective of a little boy, the film depicts the social and private tensions that arise in an upper-middle-class family during a summer holiday spent on their estate. The family is in a state of unrest for several reasons: on the personal level, much to everyone's distress the boy's parents decide to divorce; on the political level, the clan's standing among the peasant workers is threatened by the Nasserist state's attempts to nationalize their property. This again results in conflicts within the family, with some siding with the family and others with the peasants.

Sariqat Sayfiyya is one of the few Egyptian films that avoids schematizing the haute bourgeoisie by means of its personal depiction of situations and characters. It describes the parents' broken marriage, the extravagance and egocentrism of some of their relatives, as well as depicting the fear of the servants and workers, all in a realist and observational style.

Ta'ir 'Ala al-Tariq / *A Bird on the Road*

1981, 110 mins, colour, Arabic
Director: Mohamed Khan
Producer: al-Misriyya li-l-Sinima
Screenwriter: Bashir al-Dik
Cinematographer: Sa'id Shimi
Editor: Nadia Shukri
Music: Kamal Bakir
Leading Players: Ahmad Zaki, Fardus 'Abd al-Hamid, Farid Shauqi, Athar al-Hakim

Ta'ir 'Ala al-Tariq is based on an idea by director Mohamed Khan and includes one of his recurrent motifs: being on the move, which is explicitly represented not only in this film but also in *Mishwar 'Umar* / *'Umar's Errand* (1986) and *Kharaj Wa Lamm Ya' udd* / *Missing* (1985). The main character here is a taxi driver called, tellingly enough, Faris ('the knight'). He works on the road between Cairo and the provinces. There he meets Fawziya and her elderly husband Gad, whom he starts to drive regularly to their farm in Fayid. However, he finds himself attracted to Fawziya and finds out that she had been forced into her marriage with Gad. Eventually she asks for a divorce, a request that her husband rejects. He even mistreats her violently the moment he finds out about her secret love for Faris. In spite of the seemingly trivial story, the film unfolds its strength in its beautiful photography, the accurate depiction of the milieu and, most importantly, the intensity of the human relationships on display – it is them that carry the real drama of the story. The complex depiction of character is – last but not least – supported by Ahmad Zaki's impressive performance in one of his earliest main parts and Fardus 'Abd al-Hamid's silent and sensitive performance in what is nonetheless a strong role.

Za'ir al-Fajr / Visitor at Dawn

1973 (released 1975), colour, Arabic
Director: Mamduh Shukri
Producer: Aflam 656 (Magda al-Khatib)
Screenwriter: Mamduh Shukri, Rafiq al-Sabban
Cinematographer: Ramsis Marzuq
Editor: Ahmad Mitwalli
Music: Ibrahim Hagag
Designer: Nihad Bahgat
Leading Players: Magda al-Khatib, 'Izzat al-'Alayli, Zizi Mustafa, Shukri Sarhan, Tahia Carioca, Yusuf Sha'ban

Za'ir al-Fajr is one of the most sophisticated political thrillers to deal with Nasserist abuses, made in Egypt by a young director who died shortly after the completion of this film. The work was moreover banned for a while by the censors and finally released in 1975. It is interesting to note that Shukri does not concentrate on the spectacular physical abuse, but rather explores the psychological terror exerted by a totalitarian regime.

   State prosecutor Hasan ('Izzat al-'Alayli) starts investigating the death of the journalist Nadia (Magda al-Khatib), who seems to have died from natural causes. However, she belonged to a politically active group and had been imprisoned for her outspoken and bold articles. In the middle of his investigations, Hasan is ordered to drop the case. Pursuing it nonetheless, he is eventually confronted by a web of guilt that involves state security, as well as the dead journalist's fellow activists. What marks this film out is not only its intelligent and exciting screenplay, but also a well mastered *mise-en-scène* that avoids any spectacular effects to dwell rather on the interplay of human relationships.

List of directors

'Abd al-'Aziz, Muhammad (b. 1940, Cairo)

'Abd al-'Aziz, who graduated in 1964 from the Higher Film Institute, directed forty-eight feature films between 1972 and 1992. He assisted Salah Abu Seif and Hilmi Halim, among others, and started directing with an episode of *Suwwar Mamnu'a / Forbidden Images* (1972), along with Ashraf Fahmi and Madkur Thabit. Muhammad 'Abd al-'Aziz became known for his comedies, but later directed social dramas too, like his *Intabihu Ayuha al-Sada / Attention, Gentlemen!* (1980) which marked – along with other works – the beginning of *infitah*-criticism in Egyptian cinema. Many of his comedies drew their humour from the social contradictions displayed, such as in his *Fi-l-Sayf Lazzim Tuhhib / In Summer You Must Love* (1974). He directed one of the first 'Adil Imam films, *al-Mahfaza Ma'aya / The Wallet Is With Me* (1978) – considered one of the director's best films. 'Abd al-'Aziz's next comedy to star 'Adil Imam, *Rajab Fawq Sath Safih Sakhin / Rajab on a Hot Tin Roof* (1979), became a major box-office hit. During the 1980s the director turned towards social drama with, among other films, *Ajras al-Khatar / The Alarm Bells* (1986) and *Lu'bat al-Intiqam / The Revenge Game* (1992). In spite of his commercial success, in general 'Abd al-'Aziz has attracted little attention because of the predominantly mediocre cinematic quality of his films.

'Abd al-Wahhab, Fatin (b. 1913, Damietta; d. 1972)

The director of fifty-seven full-length feature films, 'Abd al-Wahhab is considered the master of Egyptian comedy. He graduated from the Military Academy in 1939 and started his cinema career during the 1940s as an assisting director at Studio Misr. His first directing job was in 1948 on *Nadia*, a tear-jerking melodrama starring 'Aziza Amir that was released the following year. 'Abd al-Wahhab soon shifted to farce and comedy with films like *Isha'it Hubb / Love Rumour* (1960), for example. He realized five of the Isma'il Yasin film series, including *Isma'il Yasin Fi-l-Jaysh / Isma'il Yasin in the Army* (1956) and *Isma'il Yasin Fi-l-Bulis / Isma'il Yasin in the Police* (1957). His most accomplished Yasin film, *al-Anissa Hanafi / Miss Hanafi* (1954), was not part of the series and the story revolved around a sex-change. Some of the comedies he filmed during the 1960s attained a very high degree of sophistication because of well-structured plots that often focused on gender roles and male/female conflicts. He tended to use dramatic actors and actresses who had no reputation for comedy, instead of established comedians. Hence he had Lubna 'Abd al-'Aziz appear in one of her few comic roles in *Ihtaris Min Hawwa / Beware of Eve* (1962), Shadia and Rushdi Abaza in their hilarious *al-Zawja Raqam 13 / Wife No. 13* (1962) and Fatin Hamama in *al-Ustadha Fatima / Professor Fatima* (1952).

Abd el-Khalek, 'Ali ('Abd al-Khaliq) (b. 1944, Egypt)

The director of twenty-six full-length films, Abd El-Khalek graduated from the Higher Film Institute in 1966. He directed documentaries before making his first feature film in 1972: *Ughniyya 'Ala al-Mamar / Song on the Passage*. Co-produced by the Young Cinema Society and the General Film Organization, the film dealt with Egypt's defeat by Israel in 1967. It was an adaptation of a play by 'Ali Salim, which defined the film's largely verbal character. Abd El-Khalek did not remain a politically committed director though, soon shifting to the mainstream, but some of his films still showed a certain socio-political inclination, including his acclaimed *al-'Ar / Shame* (1982) and *Arba'a Fi Muhimma Rasmiyya / Four on an Official Mission* (1987). The first dwelled on a typical New Realism and *infitah* topic, about a rich and respected businessman whose children find out after his death that he had secured the family's wealth by dealing drugs. In contrast, the second was an ironic social comedy, starring Ahmad Zaki, that depicted the difficulties of a rural civil servant who has the task of accompanying some public property (including a donkey) to the capital. Some of Abd El-Khalek's successful films were also characterized by an interest in suspense, like his fairly thrilling espionage film *I'dam Mayyit / Execution of a Dead Man* (1985). He experimented moreover with the (uncommon in Egypt) science fiction genre, directing *al-Bayda Wa-l-Hajara / Eyewash* (literally 'The Egg and the Stone', 1990), which is characterized by the evident lack of technical facilities.

Abd el-Sayed, Daoud (Dawud 'Abd al-Sayyid) (b. 1946, Cairo)

Abd El-Sayed graduated in directing from the Higher Film Institute in 1967. He directed only five shorts and six full-length feature films, making him one of the least prolific, yet artistically and intellectually unconventional, contemporary Egyptian directors. He assisted Youssef Chahine and Kamal El-Cheikh, among others, and directed shorts starting from 1972. Through them he developed his own poetic style of film-making, as seen in his portrait of the painter Hasan Sulayman: *al-'Amal Fi-l-Haql / Working in the Field* (1979). His first fiction, *al-Sa'alik / The Vagabonds* (1985), was considered one of the best New Realist films. It tried to dismantle the setbacks of the *infitah* policy through the portrait of two nobodies who gain an incredible fortune only to turn against each other in the end. In contrast to other *infitah* films, El-Sayed's work was characterized by its deep psychological understanding of his characters, avoiding any conventional moral dichotomies. The director's first and only box-office hit was *al-Kitkat* (1991). The humorous story of a blind old man (interpreted by Mahmud 'Abd al-'Aziz) who lives in a popular neighbourhood, and sees through and tricks everybody around him, was adapted from Aslan's novel *al-Malik al-Hazin*. Another contribution to New Realism was Abd El-Sayed's *Sariq al-Farah / Wedding Thief* (1995), which experimented with the musical genre in the setting of a Cairo shantytown. Otherwise, most of Abd El-Sayed's scripts evolve from disturbing existential experiences. In *al-Bahth 'An Sayyid Marzuq / The Search for Sayyid Marzuq* (1991), an average employee is haunted for no obvious reason by state security. In contrast, the elderly heroine (Fatin Hamama) of *Ard al-Ahlam / Land of Dreams* (1993) loses her passport the night of her deadline to emigrate to the United States. In *Ard al-Khawf / Land of Fear* (1999), Ahamd Zaki features as a disguised police officer who is told to change his identity and to become one of the largest drug dealers in the country. However, as governments and administrations change and his life is increasingly endangered, he discovers that he has lost track of his superiors and is left with a totally confused identity.

Abdessalam, Chadi (Shadi 'Abd al-Salam) (b. 1930, Alexandria; d. 1986)

A production-designer and director, Abdessalam made one full-length feature and six short films or documentaries. He graduated in architecture in 1955, a pupil of production-designer and director Wali al-Din Samih. He not only designed native historical spectacles, like *al-Nasir Salah al-Din / The Victorious Saladin* (1963) by Youssef Chahine and *Wa Islamah / Oh Islam!* (1961) by Andrew Marton, but also designed costumes for the Polish film *Pharao* (1965) by Jerzy Kawalerovicz and an episode of Rossellini's serial *Mankind's Fight for Survival* (1967). He contributed moreover in the design of those parts of Manciewicz's Hollywood spectacle *Cleopatra* (1963) that were shot in Egypt. Abdessalam was appointed head of the department of experimental film (*wahdat al-film al-tajribi*) in 1968, which constituted a section of the National Film Centre. He tried to foster a more visually oriented way of film-making. Abdessalam's short film, *Afaq / Horizons* (1974), which unfolds (with no voice-over commentary) a panorama of artistic activities in the country at that time, is an example of his 'experimental' production mode. Apart from *Jiyush al-Shams / Armies of the Sun* (1975), which depicts the experiences of soldiers during the October or Yom Kippur War in 1973, all his other shorts were deeply concerned with ancient Egyptian culture, such as the short fiction *al-Falah al-Fasih / The Eloquent Peasant* (1970) (based on an old Egyptian text), *Kursi Ikhnatun al-Dhahabi / Akhenaten's Golden Throne* (1982), *al-Ahram Wa Ma Qabliha / Before the Pyramids* (1984) and *'An Ramsis al-Thani / Apropos Ramses II* (1986). The same applies to Abdessalam's first and only full-length feature, *al-Mumya' / The Mummy: The Night of Counting the Years* (1969), which tried to apply the principles of ancient Egyptian representation in cinema. Although the film was awarded the Georges Sadoul prize in 1970, it was only released by the General Film Organization in 1975 and was screened in just one cinema. Today, *al-Mumya'* is considered the most outstanding work and art-film of Egyptian cinema. Abdessalam's following project on the Pharaonic heretic and philosopher Akhenaten, did not find an Egyptian producer, despite many years of intensive preparation and research terminated by the director's death in 1986. One of Abdessalam's multiple legacies is his disciples, notably the two set designers Salah Marei (Mar'i) and Onsi Abou Seif (Abu Saif), who have enriched Egyptian cinema with their qualitatively high standard of work.

al-Abnudi, 'Attiyat (b. 1939)

A documentary film-maker, al-Abnudi directed twenty-two documentaries on film and video, of all lengths. She studied first law and then directing, graduating from the Higher Film Institute in 1971, and was further trained at the London Film School. Her first short, *Husan al-Tin / Horse of Mud* (1971), signalled (together with the work of others like Hashim al-Nahas) a new orientation in the Egyptian documentary towards direct cinema that was most visible in al-Abnudi's ZDF co-production *Iqa' al-Haya / Rhythm of Life* (1989) – a symphony of observations on traditional work and handicrafts in Upper Egypt, juxtaposing the quasi-cyclical movements of traditional tools and handicrafts with the rituals of life and death. Al-Abnudi remained one of Egypt's few independent film-makers, relying for financing on various sources, including co-productions. *Illi-ba' Wa Illi-ishtara / Vendors and Buyer* (1992), which is her only publicly produced film, dealt with the problems of fishermen at the Suez Canal caused by the increasing privatization of public property, including shores and fishing grounds. Many of her films were concerned with women, such as *Bihar al-'Attash / Seas of Thirst* (1981) and the brilliant and intimate portrait of a clever peasant woman *al-Ahlam al-Mumkinna / Permissible Dreams* (1982), as well as *Rawya* (1994), *Nisa' Mas'ulat / Responsible Women* (1995) and the full-length documentary *Ayam al-Dimuqratiyya / Days of Democracy* (1996), which is an impressive chronicle of the problematic female participation in Egyptian parliamentary elections. Her only staged film is *Sandwich* (1977), which is in its observational style close to documentary.

Abu Seif (Saif), Salah (b. 1915, Cairo; d. 1996)

Abu Seif was the director of some shorts and forty full-length feature films. He started working at Studio Misr in 1934 and became Kamal Selim's assistant during the shooting of *al-'Azima / Determination* in 1939. He shot several short films, before directing his first fiction film: the romance *Da'iman Fi Qalbi / Always in My Heart* (1946). His early phase included the mainstream costume drama *Mughamarat 'Antar Wa 'Abla / The Adventures of 'Antar and 'Abla* (1948), based on a popular Arab legend, and the likewise quasi-historical Italo-Egyptian co-production *al-Saqr / The Falcon* (1950). Salah Abu Seif was considered Egypt's major realist director for making the films that followed, although only about a third of his work showed a realist inclination. His first works in that direction were his adaptation of *Thérèse Raquin*, *Lak Yawm Ya Zalim / Your Day is Coming* (1951), and *al-Usta Hasan / Master Hasan* (1952). Most of Abu Seif's acclaimed so-called 'realist' works were scripted by the novelist Naguib Mahfouz or adapted from Mahfouz's novels; these included *Bidaya Wa Nihaya / Beginning and End* (1960) and *al-Qahira 30 / Cairo 30* (1966) from *al-Qahira al-Jadida* (*The New Cairo*). The collaborations between the two started with the film *al-Muntaqqim / The Avenger* (1947) and amounted to a total of nine joint scripts, among others the realist but nonetheless crime- and suspense-oriented *al-Futuwa / The Thug* (1957), *Raya Wa Sakina / Raya and Sakina* (1953), *al-Wahsh / The Beast* (1954), *Shabab Imra'a / Youth of a Woman* (1956) and the entertaining and partly comic *Bayn al-Sama' Wa-l-Ard / Between Sky and Earth* (1959), about a group of people stuck in a lift. Thus spectacular stories set in popular surroundings, often addressing male criminality and / or female immorality, became Abu Seif's trademark. Notably in *Shabab Imra'a*, he presented a middle-aged woman from a popular neighbourhood seducing a young male student and spoiling his career. The film was criticized for its overt misogyny. Yet Abu Seif's diverse oeuvre also includes some of the successful Ihsan 'Abd al-Quddus adaptations, such as *al-Wisada al-Khaliyya / The Empty Cushion* (1957), *La Anam / I Do Not Sleep* (1957), *al-Tariq al-Masdud / The Closed Way* (1958), *Anna Hurra / I Am Free* (1959) and *La Tutfi' al-Shams / Don't Extinguish the Sun* (1960), which all discuss issues of female liberation. After the nationalizations of the 1960s, between 1963 and 1965 Abu Seif became supervisor of the public production company Film Intag and at the same time founded the short-lived Institute for Scriptwriting. From the 1970s onward, Abu Seif directed mostly mediocre films. The few exceptions were praised more for their thematic indulgence in the spectacular than for their cinematic qualities: these included *Hamam al-Malatili / The Malatili Bath* (1973), which was characterized by its sexual libertinage, and the adaptation of Yusuf al-Siba'i's novel *al-Saqqa Mat / The Water Carrier Died* (1977), which tackled the rarely discussed question of mortality. Salah Abu Seif contributed moreover to the historical and religious genre: his *Fajr al-Islam / Dawn of Islam* (1971), featuring the plight of early Muslim believers, although considered one of the best religious films is characterized by its outright moralism, its exaggerated characters and its artificial settings. The same applies to his expensive Iraqi-produced costume drama *al-Qadisiyya* (1982), which staged the historic battle fought in 636 CE that led to the fall of pagan Persia. This film too attempted to dismiss and ridicule the enemies of Islam to the point of losing all credibility itself, in particular because of the amazingly weak script, inappropriate performances and a deficient *mise-en-scène*. Abu Seif's very last and insignificant film was *al-Sayyid Kaf / Mister K.*, released in 1994.

'Arafa, Sherif (Sharif) (b. 1960, Cairo)

The son of the director Sa'd 'Arafa, Sherif 'Arafa graduated from the Higher Film Institute in 1983 and directed a total of eleven films between 1987 and 1999. 'Arafa is one of the most talented mainstream directors of the 1990s. He was one of those who revived Egyptian music-hall in *Sama' Huss / Silence!* (1991) and *Ya Mahalabiyya Ya / Oh that Pudding, Oh!* (1991). Furthermore, he directed some of the comic action films starring 'Adil Imam, among others *al-Mansi / The Forgotten* (1993) and *Tuyur al-Zalam / Birds of Darkness* (1995). His social comedy *al-Irhab Wa-l-Kabab / Terrorism and Kebabs* (1992) is considered one of the most successful films of the decade.

Badrakhan (Badr Khan), Ahmad (b. 1909, Cairo; d. 1969)

The director of forty-one full-length films, an actor and father of 'Ali Badrakhan, Ahmad Badrakhan trained at Studio Misr and was sent by the studio on a scholarship to France. In 1934 he published his book *Al-Sinima*, in which he spoke in favour of a spectacular and glamorous mainstream cinema, and wrote the screenplay for Fritz Kramp's *Widad* (1936). He presided at times over the Film Union and the Artists' Union, along with his work as an adviser for the General Film Organization during the 1960s. He was only a fairly gifted director, though he created some accomplished melodramatic musicals like the *La dame aux camélias* adaptation *'Ahd al-Hawa / Promise of Love* (1954). His first film was *Nashid al-Amal / Hymn of Hope* (1937), starring the singer Umm Kulthum. Apart from this work, he directed three other Umm Kulthum musicals: *Dananir* (1940), *Aida* (1942) and *Fatima* (1947). He more-over introduced the singers Farid al-Atrash and Asmahan to the screen in their cinematic breakthrough *Intissar al-Shabab / The Victory of Youth* (1941). Later, Badrakhan showed a certain patriotic and anti-colonial inclination in *Allahu Ma'na / God is with Us* (1955) and *Mustafa Kamil* (1952). The latter, a biography of one of Egypt's nationalist thinkers, was echoed in another cinematic biography by Badrakhan: *Sayyid Darwish* (1966) – Darwish, apart from being a great musician, composed what later became the Egyptian national anthem.

Badrakhan (Badr Khan), 'Ali (b. 1946, Cairo)

The talented son of Ahmad Badrakhan, 'Ali Badrakhan graduated in directing from the Higher Film Institute in 1967. He was the director of some shorts – such as the documentary *'Amm 'Abbas al-Mukhtari' / Uncle 'Abbas the Inventor* (1985) – and nine largely interesting full-length fiction films. He adapted two Naguib Mahfouz novels, one his political film *al-Karnak* (1975) and the other his social drama *Ahl al-Qimma / People from the Top* (1981). The first was criticized for its undifferentiated anti-Nasserism, whereas the second was praised for being one of the first and best New Realist works of the 1980s. In any case, Badrakhan's neat *mise-en-scène* increased the value of both works. He directed, moreover, two historical works: *Shafiqa Wa Mitwalli / Shafiqa and Mitwalli* (1978) and *al-Gu' / Hunger* (1986), both equipped with an essence of social and political critique. His major success with the audience was his well-made gangster film *al-Rajul al-Thalith / The Third Man* (1995). Badrakan's films are characterized by a variety of genres and subjects, a good *mise-en-scène* and remarkable direction of performers – notably Su'ad Husni (temporarily also his wife) who starred in most of his films, including some of her best roles.

Barakat, Henri (b. 1914, Cairo; d. 1997)

Barakat studied law and stayed for a while in France to improve his directing abilities, before directing eighty-five full-length fiction films between 1942 and 1993. He worked as an editor and director's assistant before making his first film, *al-Sharid | The Drifter*, in 1942. Barakat was not only one of the most productive Egyptian film-makers, but also one of the most talented. He displayed his abilities mainly in the two mainstream genres: musical and melodrama. Barakat directed some light musical comedies, such as '*Afrita Hanim | Lady Ghost* (1949), a charming remake of Alfred Green's *One Thousand and One Nights* (1946). He signed for numerous other musicals starring Farid al-Atrash, including moving melodramas, such as *Lahn al-Khulud | Song of Eternity* (1952) and *Risalat Gharam | Love Letter* (1954). In fact, Egyptian cinema owes to Barakat some very sophisticated and classical melodramas: *Hasan Wa Na'ima | Hasan and Na'ima* (1959), *Du'a' al-Karawan | The Cry of the Plover* (1959) and the realist *al-Haram | The Sin* (1965), to name just a few. The latter was adapted from a Yusuf Idris novel. Some of Barakat's highly praised films were literary adaptations, such as the patriotic *Fi Baytinna Rajul | A Man in our House* (1961) and the quasi-feminist *al-Bab al-Maftuh | The Open Door* (1963). Barakat discovered, moreover, the Lebanese singer Sabah and presented her for the first time in *al-Qalb Lahu Wahid | The Heart Loves Only One* in 1945. He directed in Lebanon two of the most successful musicals, starring the Rahbani Brothers and the singer Fayruz: *Safar Barlak* (1967) and *Bint al-Haris | Daughter of the Guardian* (1968). The quality of Barakat's films declined after the 1960s, although some of his films which showed social interest – like the family-planing film *Afwah Wa Aranib | Mouths and Rabbits* (1977) and the *infitah*-critique *Laylat al-Qabd 'Ala Fatima | The Night of Fatima's Arrest* (1985) still raised interest. His last film, *Tahqiq Ma'a Muwatinna | Investigating with a Female Citizen* (1993) was, however, a mediocre social drama.

Bayyumi, Muhammad (b. 1894, Tanta, Egypt; d. 1963)

A cameraman and director of newsreels, several short fictions and one full-length film, Bayyumi is considered one of the pioneers of Egyptian cinema. He left Egypt in 1920 for film training in Germany, came back in 1923 with his own equipment and in the same year shot Victor Rosito's full-length fiction, *Fi Bilad Tut 'Ankh Amun | In the Country of Tutankhamun*. He moreover founded his own newsreel (entitled *Amun*) also in 1923, shot numerous documentary items and directed a first short fiction of his own: *Barsum Yabhath 'An Wazifa | Barsum is Looking for a Job*, starring Beshara Wakim. In 1924 Bayyumi adapted the popular play, *al-Bash Katib | The Chief Secretary* (1924) for the screen. In 1925 he sold his equipment to Talaat Harb's *Sharikat Misr li-l-sinima wa-l-tamthil*, after being hired by the same company. After shooting some documentaries, he quit the job and moved to Alexandria, where in 1932 he founded the Egyptian Film Institute, through which he offered courses free of charge in zincography, photography and film-making. The major cinematic product of the Institute was Bayyumi's only full-length fiction: *al-Khatib Nimra 13 | Fiancé No. 13*

(1933), which was not a great success. One year later, Bayyumi closed the school and terminated his cinematic career.

Beshara, Khairy (Khayri Bishara) (b. 1947, Tanta, Egypt)

Beshara graduated in directing from the Higher Film Institute, obtained a scholarship for further training in Poland and went on to direct thirteen short documentaries, twelve full-length feature films and Christian devotionals like: *Asrar al-Qalb* / *Secrets of the Heart* (1997). Between 1974 and 1981, he contributed decisively to the artistic and thematic revival of Egyptian documentary with several distinguished shorts, among others *Sa'id al-Dababat* / *The Hunter* (1974) and *Tabib Fi-l-Aryaf* / *The Countryside Doctor* (1975). During the 1980s he shifted to directing only fiction. He kept some of the documentary's characteristics in his fiction films, visible in the inclusion of purely descriptive shots of places and surroundings that are often missing in Egyptian mainstream cinema, as well as in his preference for a mobile and even partly hidden camera – of which he made excessive use in his realist melodrama *Yawm Murr Yawm Hulw* / *Bitter Day, Sweet Day* (1988) and his congenial musical *Ays Krim Fi Glim* / *Ice Cream in Glim* (1992). Beshara, who started as a New Realist during the 1980s, directed two accomplished films of the new wave: *al-Tawq Wa-l-Iswirra* / *The Collar and the Bracelet* (1986) and *Yawm Murr Yawm Hulw*, although both demonstrated an inclination towards the melodramatic. Then Beshara switched to social drama and musicals, trying to revive the latter, starting with his box-office hit *Kaburya* / *Crabs* (1990), in which he infused a class conflict-based plot featuring a young boxer with refreshing trival songs and dances. He pursued this orientation further in *Ays Krim Fi Glim*, which (despite a weak screenplay) is persuasive because of its rich visuals and an even richer soundtrack that mixes all kinds of music. The recurrent theme of Beshara's films is conflictual class differences, which are expressed in almost all his mainstream works. Yet his characters, plots and settings became increasingly odd, as in the comic *Harb al-Farawla* / *Strawberry War* (1994) which features a bored millionaire who hires a deprived couple to entertain him by committing crimes. They subsequently involve him in a kidnapping and bank raids. In *Qishr al-Bunduq* / *Nutshells* (1995), an eating contest held in a luxurious hotel was taken to exemplify social conflicts along class and gender lines. The exceptional work in Beshara's filmography is *al-'Awama Raqam 70* / *Houseboat No. 70* (1982). It is his only production which may be considered a genuine *auteur*-film, characterized (contrary to the rest of his oeuvre) by a coherent screenplay and individualized acting. Furthermore, it convinces by a smooth *mise-en-scène* and a personal atmosphere reflected in its settings and characters.

Chahine, Youssef (Yusuf Shahin) (b. 1926, Alexandria, Egypt)

Director, actor and one of the most important film-makers in Egypt, Chahine has produced thirty-one feature films and six shorts. Initially trained at the Pasadena Playhouse, California, he appeared in several of his own films, sometimes in leading roles. His first film was *Baba Amin* / *Papa Amin* (1950), a folk comedy, followed by rural dramas like *Ibn al-Nil* / *Son of the Nile* (1951) and *Sira 'Fi-l-Wadi* / *Mortal Revenge* (1954), and the comedies *al-Muharrij al-Kabir* / *The Big Buffoon* (1952), *Nisa*

Figure 15   Yaumiyat Na'ib Fil-aryaf / Diary of a Country Prosecutor

Billa Rijal / Women without Men (1953). His costume dramas include *Shaytan al-Sahra' / Demon of the Desert* (1954) and his musicals are *Wadda'tu Hubbak / Goodbye to Your Love* (1957) and *Inta Habibi / You are My Love* (1957). *Sira 'Fi-l-Mina' / Dark Waters* (1956) was his first attempt at social realism, which was to be an important theme in his work. His best-known film of the 1950s is *Bab al-Hadid / Cairo Main Station* (1958), a study in the *film noir* genre, with the lighter *Hubb Li-l-Abad / Yours Forever* (1959) following closely in time but to less critical acclaim. *Bab al-Hadid* is a blend of social realism, political protest, sentimental comedy and tragedy, and is the first of many films that Chahine was to produce which combined a large variety of themes and techniques, where the director places contradictions in the film to prevent the audience from an easy identification with one character or another. Although *Bab al-Hadid* was initially commercially unsuccessful, it was to be seen later as a highly significant film, reflecting the deep changes that were taking place in Egyptian society. There is also *Jamila al-Jaza'iriyya / Jamila the Algerian* (1958), a political thriller about the war of independence which was heavily criticized in Algeria itself. Some of his films are quite closely based on other films, such as his *Sayyidat al-Qitar / The Lady on the Train* (1952) which is closely modelled on *Citizen Kane*.

While the 1950s saw Chahine trying out a variety of techniques and tones, in the next decade he moved more certainly into larger-scale films. *Bayna Aydik / In Your Hands* (1960) is no more than a marriage farce and yet it involves a highly skilful application of shot and sequence. This results in a film which, despite the slimness of its content, is effective in impressing its audience with its sensuality. *Rajul Fi Hayati / A Man in My Life* (1961) is high-bourgeois melodrama, while *Nida' al-'Ushshaq / Call of the Lovers* (1961) is darker in tone. A major film is *al-Nasir Salah al-Din / The Victorious Saladin* (1963), Chahine's first attempt at an epic. The comparison between Saladin, the great leader who unites the Arabs to defeat their foes while at the same time displaying magnanimity and religious toleration, and President Nasser is persuasively made through the skill of the main actor, Ahmad Mansur, and reveals Chahine's skill with large-scale productions. *Fajr Yawm Jadid / Dawn of a New Day* (1964) appears to be derivative of both Antonioni and Douglas Sirk, yet presents an interesting drawing out of tension and romantic suspense. Chahine explored a variety of less ambitious styles in *Bayya' al-Khawatim / The Seller of Rings* (1965) and *Rimal Min Dhahab / Golden Sands* (1966), before directing *al-Nas Wa-l-Nil / People of the Nile* (1968) and *al-Ard / The Earth* (1969). These combine social realism with an associative montage that moves back and forth in time, attempting to establish a feeling of the synthesis of the past and present. Water is an important image in both films, representing human sexuality and violence as a theme running through social and economic change.

Al-Ikhtiyar / The Choice (1970) was the start of his work in the 1970s and continues the themes of the two-sided nature of reality and of human personality. *al-'Usfur / The Sparrow* (1973) maintains the theme of social protest, as does *'Awdat al-Bin al-Dall / Return of the Prodigal Son* (1976), which repeats the allegorical theme of Egypt as a highly divided society. In this film, a provincial family is characterized by one brother's socialist ideals and another's commercialism, and the production is illustrated with jaunty musical numbers of an optimism and naïvety entirely out of place with the dysfunctionality of the theme. The fact that Chahine comes from Alexandria is a vital aspect of his background and is represented self-consciously in his autobiographical trilogy *Iskandariyya, Lih? / Alexandria, Why?* (1978), *Haduta Misriyya / An Egyptian Fairy-Tale* (1982) and *Iskandariyya Kaman Wa Kaman / Alexandria Now and Forever* (1990). *Wada'a Bonaparte / Adieu Bonaparte* (1985) should be linked with the trilogy also, since it too involves the use of the notion of homosexuality as integral to colonialism and in a surprisingly favourable light, as a mixture of exploitation and affection. The Chahine-figure in *Iskandariyya Kaman Wa Kaman*, this time played by Chahine himself, is seen to transcend his love for a young man and replace it with love for a young woman, but the trilogy is faithful to his technique of regarding the past, present and future as part of a seamless web, since there is no notion of a final development towards a perfect end, just a constant renewal of a fascination with beauty and sensuality. His *al-Yawm al-Sadis / The Sixth Day* (1987) returns to the traditional themes of Egyptian cinema, but does not do much to challenge the idea that Chahine's work had become increasingly introspective and expressionistic in the 1980s.

Several of Chahine's films were collaborations with major writers such as Naguib Mahfouz (*Jamila*, *Salah al-Din* and *al-Ikhtiyar*) and Abd al-Rahman Sharqawi (*The Land*), both writers who were committed to representing the lives of ordinary Egyptians in a realist manner. Some of Chahine's work was criticized in just the same way as these writers were accused of exaggerating the sordid aspects of Egyptian life, and there were periods during which political events restricted his work in Egypt. He plays major roles in *Bab al-Hadid* and *Iskandariyya Kaman Wa Kaman*, and many minor roles in some of his other films. He was responsible for starting Omar Charif on his film career, including him in three of his films. Although some critics accuse Chahine of eclecticism and self-indulgence, he often manages to combine the different cinematic genres which he employs successfully into an artistic whole.

Chahine's last three co-productions were two historical films – *al-Muhajir / The Emigrant* (1994) and *al-Masir / The Destiny* (1997) – and one trivial, yet in Egypt astonishingly successful, social drama – *al-Akhar / The Other* (1999).

Figure 16 al-Tawq Wa-l-Iswirra / The Collar and the Bracelet

al-Dighidi, Inas (b. 1954, Cairo)

Graduating in 1975 from the Higher Film Institute, al-Dighidi directed eleven full-length feature films. Former assistant of Henri Barakat and Salah Abu Seif, she became the most successful woman director of mainstream cinema, combining largely female-oriented topics with a spectacular plot and *mise-en-scène*. She was criticized for her vulgarity because she felt at ease depicting sex and violence. Her first film '*Afwan Ayuha al-Qanun / Excuse Me Law!* (1985) dealt with gender inequality by pointing out how the judiciary differentiates between men and women in the case of the same crime. Other films by al-Dighidi stress the active role of women less than their traditional moral vulnerability. In spite of being victims at times, her heroines commit violent acts including killing, as in *al-Qatilla / The Murderess* (1992) and *Disco Disco* (1994), or at least struggle successfully against social discrimination and sexual exploitation, for instance in *Lahm Rakhis / Cheap Flesh* (1995). In *Imra'a Wahida La-Takfi / One Woman is Not Enough* (1990), *Istakusa / Lobster* (1996) and *Dantilla / Lace* (1998) she focused instead on the funny side of gender relations by mocking both sides.

El-Cheikh (al-Shaykh), Kamal (b. 1919, Cairo)

An editor and director, El-Cheikh directed thirty-five full-length fiction films between 1952 and 1987. He was first trained as an editor at Studio Misr. In 1952 he made a successful début with *al-Manzil Raqam 13 / House No. 13*, which installed him immediately in the Egyptian context as an extraordinary thriller director. During the 1950s he directed some of Egypt's best psychological thrillers, including *Tujjar al-Mawt / Death Traders* (1957), *Sayyidat al-Qasr / Lady of the Palace* (1958) and *al-Layla al-Akhira / The Last Night* (1963). One of his most impressive works was *Hayat Aw Mawt / Life or Death* (1954) which was, unprecedented in the Egyptian film industry of the time, almost entirely shot in the streets. It focused on a little girl who is sent out to buy medication for one of her parents but is given a wrong and deadly mixture. She then gets lost in the streets on her way home. The suspense of the whole film derives from the question of who will reach the parents earlier: the girl or the representative of the pharmacy. During the 1960s El-Cheikh's work showed increasing political and social interest, as he proved in his literary adaptations, the realist gangster film *al-Liss Wa-l-Kilab / The Thief and the Dogs* (1962) and his two political films *Miramar* (1969) and *al-Rajul Aladhi Faqad Zilah / The Man Who Lost His Shadow* (1968), adapted from a novel by Fathi Ghanim. His *'Ala Man Nutliq al-Rasas? / At Whom Do We Shoot?* (1975) became one of the most acclaimed political films of the decade. El-Cheikh's latest film, *Qahir al-Zamman / Vanquisher of Time* (1987), was one of the few successful attempts to introduce the science-fiction genre to Egyptian cinema.

El-Tayeb, Atef ('Atif al-Tayyib) (b. 1947, Cairo; d. 1995)

The director of two short documentaries and eighteen feature films (completed between 1982 and 1995), El-Tayeb graduated in directing from the Higher Film Institute in 1970 but had to serve in the army after graduation until the Yom Kippur (October) War in 1973. He worked as an assistant to Youssef Chahine and Chadi Abdessalam, among others. When he turned to directing he became the most prolific New Realist director, with many of his films scripted by the writer and director Bashir al-Dik. His second feature, *Sawaq al-Utubis / The Bus-Driver* (1983), was already written by al-Dik; it was enthusiastically praised as the starting point of New Realism, although in form and content it had had predecessors. In fact, set in an urban working-class surrounding which is threatened by social disintegration and dissent because of the *infitah*, the film was replete with the moral certainties of the era and embodied all that New Realism came to stand for. El-Tayeb's own moral affiliations seemed contradictory, as he was torn between tradition and secularism. In *Abna' Wa Qattala / Sons and Murderers* (1987), for instance, a Muslim fundamentalist student falls prey to his father's unscrupulous materialism. In general, the director became the fiercest attacker of nepotism and official abuse, with a preference for violent showdowns and endings. In *al-Takhshiba / The Arrest* (1984), *Malaf Fi-l-Adab / A Vice Squad File* (1986), *Hubb Fawq Hadabit al-Harram / Love at the Pyramids* (1986) and *al-Bari' / The Innocent* (1986), the average citizen becomes a victim of executive forces, either the police or the state security service. In spite of his ideology, El-Tayeb was a good *metteur-en-scène* with a good sense for working-class environments. He made only a few less-accomplished films, such as *al-Badrun / The Cellar* (1987) and the portrait of the Palestinian cartoonist *Naji al-'Ali* (1992). By accurately depicting original settings and fast editing, he knew how to create action and suspense – for example in his relatively trivial gangster films *Katibat al-'Idam / The Execution Squad* (1989) and *Did al-Hukuma / Against the Government* (1992). His temporary loss of realist focus and cinematic quality during the 1990s was overcome in his last movie, *Layla Sakhina / A Hot Night* (1996), a thrilling road movie centred around the frightening trip of a taxi driver and a prostitute through nocturnal Cairo.

Fadil, Muhammad (b. 1938, Egypt)

Graduating in agriculture in 1960, Fadil mainly directed television films. The most spectacular among them, *Nasir 56* (1994), a biography of the former Egyptian nationalist leader Nasser, was also released in cinemas. His films are characterized by sophisticated character-traits and a heavy interest in the accurate description of milieu, as in *Tali' al-Nakhl / The Palm Tree Climber* (1987) which featured a young man infected with bilharzia. His only two films for cinema are *Shaqqa Fi-Wassat al-Balad / A Downtown Apartment* (1977) and *Hubb Fi-l-Zinzana / Love in a Prison Cell* (1983), starring Su'ad Husni and 'Adil Imam in a delicate love story set in prison.

Fahmi, Ashraf (b. 1936, Cairo)

Fahmi was the director of forty-two full-length films, as well as a few documentaries, between 1971 and 1998. He studied first history, then graduated in 1963 from the Higher Film Institute in Cairo and left for California, where he studied cinema at UCLA. He specialized in gangster films that mainly centred around adultery and treason. His early works seemed promising – such as his contribution to the compilation film *Suwwar Mamnu'a / Forbidden Images* (1972). His most acclaimed films were *Layl Wa Qudban / Night and Prison Bars* (1973), *Ma'a Sibq al-Israr / Premeditated* (1979) and *Wa La Yazal al-Tahqiq Mustamirran / The Investigation is Still Going On* (1979). Both feature murders initiated by adultery. Up to the present time he has adhered to the typical gangster film format. His *Layl Wa Khawana / Night and Traitors* (1990) shows a gangster who was betrayed to the police by his companions and tries to avenge himself for their treason after his release from prison. During the 1980s Fahmi contributed to the wave of *infitah* criticism by combining the gangster film with social drama in *al-Khadima / The Servant* (1984), starring Nadia al-Gindi, which features the struggle of a servant to become a mistress herself and is spiced with a good deal of violence and criminality.

Galal, Ahmad (b. 1897, Port-Said; d. 1947)

Ahmad Galal was a director, actor, film critic, screenwriter and producer, as well as the father of Nadir Galal. Between 1929 and 1947 he directed seventeen full-length films. He started as a journalist, but then shifted to screenwriting. He re-scripted the screenplays for 'Aziza Amir's production *Layla* (1927) and *Wakhz al-Damir / Pangs of Remorse* (1931), directed by Ibrahim Lama and produced by Assia Daghir, in which he also played the main part. He acted in several of the films he directed himself, as in one of the first Egyptian historical movies *Shajarat al-Durr* in 1935. He married Assia

Daghir's niece, the actress Mary Queeny, in 1940. Together they founded the Studio Galal after World War II. Galal's first directing work was *Ghadat al-Sahra' / The Young Lady from the Desert*, co-directed with the Turkish director Wedad Orfi in 1929. In general, Galal preferred melodramatic plots dealing with marital problems, for example in *Fattish 'An al-Mar'a / Look for the Woman* (1939), or partly combined with seduction and murder, as in *'Indama Tuhibb al-Mar'a / When a Woman Loves* (1933). In comparison to other pioneers of Egyptian cinema, his films seem cinematically unsophisticated.

Galal, Nadir (b. 1941, Cairo)

The director of forty-seven full-length feature films between 1972 and 1998, Nadir Galal is the son of director Ahmad Galal and actress / producer Mary Queeny. He studied commerce and graduated in 1964 in directing from the Higher Film Institute. Assisting Salah Abu Seif, Taufiq Salih and Youssef Chahine, among others, Galal became one of the most successful directors of mainstream cinema. His début, *Ghadan Ya'ud al-Hubb / Tomorrow Love Will Return* (1972), produced by his mother, was a typical melodrama featuring a seduced woman. This was echoed in *La Waqt Li-l-dumu' / No Time for Tears* (1976) and *Aqwa Min al-Ayam / Stronger than Time* (1979). During the 1980s the element of crime became increasingly important to his narratives. Although he had already made his first gangster film in 1974 – *Budur*, which was set in a working-class surrounding – he only started specializing in that genre with *Khamsa Bab / Gate Five* (1983), which dealt with drug-dealing. His collaboration with the two current top-stars (Nadia al-Gindi and 'Adil Imam) was of major importance in leading him to develop in that direction. Up to 1994 he directed eight films starring al-Gindi, among others *Gabarut Imra'a / The Power of a Woman* (1984) and *Malaf Samia Sha'rawi / The Samia Sha'rawi File* (1988), and six films with Imam, such as the political film *al-Irhabi / The Terrorist* (1994) and the comic historical *Risala Illa al-Wali / Message to the Ruler* (1997). He became a good technician of the action movie and knew how to create suspense in his different works, whether they were gangster or espionage films – for instance in *Muhimma Fi Tall-Abib / Mission in Tel Aviv* (1992), starring Nadia al-Gindi once again.

al-Imam, Hasan (b. 1919, Mansura, Egypt; d. 1988)

al-Imam started his career by acting in Yusuf Wahbi's troupe Ramsis in 1936. He is one of the most productive Egyptian directors, making a total of ninety full-length feature films between 1947 and 1986. Dismissed as trivial, al-Imam focused on melodramatic plots that relied mainly on female seduction and moral vulnerability. His films featured dozens of fallen women and belly dancers. Hence he discovered and subsequently presented two of Egypt's major vamps – Hind Rustum during the 1960s and Nadia al-Gindi in the 1970s – in melodramatic roles. Al-Imam realized one of the biggest box-office hits in Egypt with his musical *Khalli Balak Min Zuzu / Take Care of Zuzu* (1972), starring Su'ad Husni. His choice of stories and his cinematic style led eventually to a kind of melodramatic style fostered partly by his use of lavish sets, as in his famous *Shafiqa al-Qibtiyya / Shafiqa the Copt* (1963), which presented the life of a well-known nineteenth-century belly dancer.

Kamal, Husain (b. 1932, Cairo)

An active director in both the theatre and films, Kamal directed thirty full-length features between 1965 and 1997. He graduated from the French IDHEC in directing in 1956, assisted Youssef Chahine and made short television films, before he became one of the artistically promising and committed directors of the 1960s. His *al-Mustahil / The Impossible* (1965) was characterized by its innovative style which included some surrealist elements in the story of an impossible love. However, he soon adopted realism with *al-Bustaji / The Postman* (1968), adapted from a novel by Yahia Haqqi, which is considered one of the most accomplished works of the new wave, sharing the observations of a lonely postman in the countryside who passes his time by reading people's letters. The following year he directed a crime-oriented social drama: *Shay'un Min al-Khawf / Something Frightful* (1969). In 1971 he raised attention again with his Naguib Mahfouz adaptation *Tharthara Fawq al-Nil / Adrift on the Nile* (1971), which dealt with the inner social crisis. His largest box-office hit was the musical *Abbi Fawq al-Shajara / My Father Up the Tree* (1969), starring Nadia Lutfi and the singer 'Abd al-Halim Hafiz. Its melodramatic plot was outweighed by lively youthful music-hall dances and fast-paced pop music, staged in original settings. His *Imbiraturiyat M / Empire of M* (1972) became one of the most successful comedies of the 1970s, featuring Fatin Hamama as a strict mother and teacher whose six children decide to run family elections against her. Although she is re-elected as the chief of the household, she promises to become more democratic. Starting from the 1970s, Kamal's work became increasingly mainstream, while the originality of his *mise-en-scène* vanished. For example, he directed the melodrama *Hubb Taht al-Matar* (1975), circling around love and revenge, and one of the first 'Adil Imam comedies, *Ihna Bitu' al-Utubis / Us, From the Bus* (1979). During the 1980s there were not many Kamal films worth mentioning, except for *Qaffas al-Harim / Harem's Cage* (1986), starring Sharihan and 'Izzat al-'Alayli, whose cinematic qualities were misapplied on a trival story discussing female liberation. Concentrating lately on theatre directing, Kamal's comedy *Dik al-Barabir / The Cock of the Walk* (released in 1992) is little more than a burlesque theatrical play.

Karim, Muhammad (b. 1896, Cairo; d. 1972)

One of the major Egyptian film pioneers, Karim directed seventeen full-length feature films between 1930 and 1959. He acted in two of the SITICA productions in 1918 (*Sharaf al-Badawi / The Bedouin's Honour* and *al-Azhar al-Mumita / Mortal Flowers*), before leaving for Rome in 1921 and later for Berlin to enlarge his knowledge of cinema – in Berlin he was allowed to assist during the shooting of Fritz Lang's *Metropolis*. He directed one short fiction film, *Hadiqat al-Hayawan / The Zoo*, in 1927 and one of the first Egyptian full-length feature films, *Zaynab* (a literary adaptation produced by Yusuf Wahbi), in 1930. He remade this film under the same title, although with little success, in 1952. Karim directed the first Egyptian talkie, *Awlad al-Dhawat / Sons of Aristocrats* – another Wahbi production, released in 1932. He became one of the founders of early Egyptian melodrama and directed all seven musicals that star 'Abd al-Wahhab. The first one, *al-Warda al-Bayda' / The White Rose* (1933–4), was the first Egyptian movie to be distributed on a large-scale abroad. The film is characterized by its slow pace and romanticism, expressed in beautiful images of nature, but set the tone in plot and *mise-en-scène* for further melodramas. Karim moreover introduced Fatin Hamama to the screen for the first time at the age of nine and also presented the singer Layla Murad in her first musical (co-starring 'Abd al-Wahhab), called *Yahya al-Hubb / Long Live Love!* (1938). Karim abandoned directing in 1959 to work as the first supervisor of the Higher Film Institute, a position which he held until 1967.

Khan, Mohamed (b. 1942, Cairo)

Between 1980 and 1993 Khan directed sixteen full-length features. He is of Italian and Pakistani origin, graduated at the London School of Film Technique and assisted in directing in Lebanon from 1964 to 1965. The gangster film *Darbit Shams / Sun Stroke* (1980), a remake of Antonioni's *Blow Up*, was his first work in directing and characterized by its excessive use of existing locales. This has remained a characteristic of Khan's work to the present day, along with a highly polished *mise-en-scène* that is primarily expressed through aesthetic settings. The majority of his films have been classified as New Realist, as he took interest in some of the wave's prevalent topics – notably the *arrivisme*, emigration and political abuses of the Sadat era in *Nisf Arnab / Half a Million* (1983), *'Awdat Muwatin / Return of a Citizen* (1985), *Zawjat Rajul Muhimm / Wife of an Important Man* (1988), *Supermarket* (1990) and *Faris al-Madina / City Knight* (1992). Yet Khan's realist work is, in comparison to others, the least melodramatic and less dominated by the prevalent moral certainties. He showed moreover a preference for displaced and alienated personalities, which led him to develop several road movies. *Al-Harrif / The Champion* (1984), starring 'Adil Imam in one of his best roles, was a nuanced portrait of a man who does not come to terms with his family but becomes a street soccer champion. In *Ta'ir 'Ala al-Tariq / A Bird on the Road* (1981), *Kharj Wa Lam Ya'ud / Missing* (1985) and *Mishwar 'Umar / 'Umar's Errand* (1986), some of the best road movies of Egyptian cinema, the main characters

Figure 17 Youssef Chahine and Yusra

undertake decisive journeys which change their lives completely. In general, Khan's films develop unusual and sophisticated character traits. *Ahlam Hind Wa Kamilyya / Dreams of Hind and Camelia* (1988), for instance, is centred around two female servants who have to cope with a multitude of problems and abuses, but whose friendship compensates for many troubles. During the 1990s Khan, along with other New Realists, faced a crisis in form and content. He tried to approach mainstream cinema by directing the musical *Mister Karate* and the melodramatic *al-Gharqana / The Drowning Woman* in 1993. Since then he has not directed a single feature film but he is currently preparing a historical movie on Sadat's life.

Lama, Ibrahim (b. 1904, Chile; d. 1953)

A producer and director of thirty-three full-length feature films, one of Egypt's film pioneers, probably of Druze origins. Together with his brother Badr (their real names were Pietro and Abraham Lama), Lama arrived in Alexandria in 1926 from South America and decided to stay. Their first film, a silent directed by Ibrahim and starring Badr, was *Qubla Fi-l-Sahra' / A Kiss in the Desert* (1928), which is said to have been inspired by the American film *Son of the Sheikh*. Badr starred in around twenty of his brother's films. Most of Lama's films were Bedouin films or historical productions of a largely mediocre cinematic quality. He stopped directing in 1951.

Marzuq, Sa'id (b. 1940, Cairo)

Marzuq directed eleven full-length feature films between 1971 and 1987. He worked first for television, directing two patriotic shorts. His first feature film, *Zawjati Wa-l-Kalb / My Wife and the Dog* (1971), was characterized by its expressiveness and innovative style, focusing on a lonely lighthouseman who imagines his far-away wife committing adultery. Similarly, several of Marzuq's works focused on sexual deprivation. His second film, a bit more mainstream, portrayed two financiers fantasizing about sexual love while searching for an apartment. However, one of Marzuq's late films, *al-Mughtasibun / The Rapists* (1989), featuring Layla 'Ilwi as a raped girl, transformed the topic rather cheaply. During the 1970s and 1980s, Marzuq showed some social interest too in his acclaimed *Uridu Hallan / I Want a Solution* (1975), starring Fatin Hamama and Rushdi Abaza, which depicted the hopeless efforts of a wife to obtain a divorce. This film came at the height of a general discussion on Egyptian personal status law. In *al-Muznibun / The Culprits* (1976) he dealt with corruption and nepotism, and in *Inqaz Ma Yumkin Inqazuh / Save Whatever is Possible* (1985) he tackled the *infitah* by discussing the situation of an unscrupulous businessman and a careless pasha's son opposed by a courageous female teacher. Lately Marzuq's works have developed an increasing thematic triviality and lack cinematic quality as well: examples are the melodramatic *al-Duktura Manal … Tarquss / Doctor Manal … Dances* (1991), a kind of *Khalli Balak Min Zuzu* remake, and *Huda Wa Ma'ali al-Wazir / Huda and His Excellency the Minister* (1995) and the aesthetically exceptional *al-Mar'a Wa-l-Satur / The Woman and the Cleaver* (1997), which both focused mainly on moral aberrations and / or crime.

al-Mihi, Ra'fat (b. 1940, Egypt)

A screenwriter and director of ten full-length features between 1981 and 1998, al-Mihi graduated in 1961 in English literature and in 1964 from the Institute for Scriptwriting. He wrote the script for (among others) Sa'd 'Arafa's *Ghuraba' / Strangers* (1973). His first, but also most accomplished and sensitive work may be categorized as New Realist – it was called '*Uyun La Tanam / Eyes Which Do Not Sleep* (1981), set in a Cairo working-class surrounding, and dealt with the fierce and dramatic struggle of two brothers around their common workshop, sparked off by the older brother's marriage to a young poor girl. She in turn falls in love with the younger brother and initiates a disastrous finale. Al-Mihi soon developed his own original style and thematic orientation, scripting and directing mostly absurd black comedies. His first work in that direction, *al-Afukatu / The Advocate* (1984), starred 'Adil Imam and resulted in a trial initiated by the lawyers' syndicate. In his following films, al-Mihi concentrated on gender relations, ironically playing around with traditional gender roles first in *al-Sada al-Rijal / Men, the Gentlemen* (1987) and then in *Sayyidati Anisati / Dear Ladies!* (1990). The latter became one of his most coherent films, thematically as well as stylistically, with a clear anti-authoritarian stance. During the 1990s his narratives and his style increasingly deteriorated, with loose plots and a deficient *mise-en-scène*, starting with his similarly absurd and surreal *Samak Laban Tamr Hindi / Hotchpotch* (1988) and ending with his trival *Tifaha* (1997). Al-Mihi's most extraordinary work is *Li-l-Hubb Qissa Akhira / Love's Last Story* (1986) – a wild love story that discusses religious beliefs from the perspective of human mortality. This film does not only stand out through its moving, slightly melodramatic, story about the love of a young wife for her dying husband, but also by its setting – a rural island on the Nile – which is used to display in passing the traditional and partly superstitious ways of dealing with disease and eventual death.

Mizrahi, Togo (b. 1905, Alexandria; d. 1986)

A director and producer, Mizrahi was the offspring of a Jewish family and studied commerce. Between 1931 and 1946 he directed thirty-three full-length feature films, and produced and shot his first film *Cocaine* (a silent production) in 1931 in Alexandria, in which he starred himself under the pseudonym Ahmad al-Mashriqi. Mizrahi constructed two small film studios, one in Alexandria and another in Giza. He became the most prolific and successful director of his time, mainly directing farce and comedy, but also some melodramatic musicals. In five of his early films (all shot in Alexandria between 1933 and 1937) he presented the Jewish actor Shalom, who always used his own name in these films and played a poor, naïve but nevertheless lucky native of Alexandria. These works were of a relatively poor cinematic as well as dramatic character, dominated by a variety of funny sketches and bound together by a loose storyline. The most coherent of his Shalom series is *al-'Izz Bahdala / Mistreated by Affluence* (1937), which features a working-class Jew and his Muslim friend, who gain a fortune by luck, move with their families to a rich neighbourhood, but soon find that they prefer their traditional surroundings. Mizrahi shot the majority of 'Ali al-Kassar's most successful farces, such as *al-Sa'a Sab'a / Seven O'Clock* (1937), *al-Tilighraf / Telegram* (1938), *Salifni Talata Gini / Lend Me Three Pounds* (1939) and *Alf Layla Wa Layla / One Thousand and One Nights* (1941). During the 1940s and after he had moved to Cairo, Mizrahi developed a more coherent cinematic style, which he displayed in musicals and melodramas, and he directed Umm Kulthum in one of her best historical films: *Sallama* (1945). More sophisticated yet was his Layla Murad series, comprising *Layla Bint al-Rif / Layla from the Countryside* (1941), *Layla Bint al-Madaris / Layla the Schoolgirl* (1941) and *Layla Fi-l-Zalam / Layla in the Darkness* (1944), thus contributing decisively to the development of the melodramatic Egyptian musical. In particular, his musical *Layla* (1942), through which he adapted Dumas *fils' La dame aux camélias*, may be considered his masterpiece in terms of plot, coherence and *mise-en-scène*. Mizrahi left Egypt for Italy in 1946 and remained there until his death.

Mustafa, Husam al-Din (b. 1926, Egypt)

Husam al-Din Mustafa studied cinema in the United States before directing eighty-eight feature films between 1956 and 1994, twenty-eight of them literary adaptations from books by different Egyptian writers and three from works by Dostoevsky. Mustafa largely directed gangster films and social dramas, such as the thriller *al-Tariq / The Road* (1964), one of the first espionage films *Jarima Fi-l-Hay al-Hadi' / A Crime in the Calm Neighbourhood* (1967), the mafia melodrama *al-Batniyya* (1980) and the thug film *al-Harafish / The Racketeers* (1986), which was adapted from a Naguib Mahfouz novel. Mustafa's few less action-oriented films include the acclaimed *al-Nazara al-Sawda' / The Black Glasses* (1963), after a typical novel by Ihsan Quddus in which a young girl starts taking responsibility, the political film *al-Siman Wa-l-Kharif / Autumn Quails* (1968), an adaptation from a Mahfouz novel about the bigotry of a young political activist, and the religious film *al-Shayma'* (1972). The war film *al-Rasasa La Tazal Fi Jaybi / The Bullet is Still in My Pocket* (1974) was one of Mustafa's few films to be praised for its social commitment. Its plot is based on the classical melodramatic motif of rape used to represent society's corruption.

Mustafa, Niazi (b. 1910, Assiut, Egypt; d. 1986)

An editor and the most prolific Egyptian mainstream director so far, between 1937 and 1987 Niazi Mustafa directed a total of 107 features and a few documentaries. He was sent on a scholarship by Studio Misr and so received some training at the Munich Film Institute and the UFA Studios in Berlin. At Studio Misr he directed several documentaries and supervised the editing department. He edited *Widad* and *Lashin*, among others. His first film, the comedy *Salama Fi Khayr / Salama is Doing Fine* (1937), is considered one of the Egyptian film classics. It enjoyed a great success not just because of Nagib al-Rihani performing the role of the errand boy who is mistaken for the sultan, but also because of the coherence of its plot and *mise-en-scène*. In the course of his long career, Niazi Mustafa contributed to almost every film genre, be it comedy, melodrama, musical, Bedouin film, costume drama or gangster film. Many classics appear in his filmography. Most of his Bedouin films and costume dramas were interpreted by his wife, the actress Koka – these include *'Antar Wa 'Abla / 'Antar and 'Abla* (1945), *Sultanat al-Sahra' / Sultana from the Desert* (1947), *Layla al-'Amriyya* (1948), *al-Faris al-Aswad / The Black Knight* (1954), *Samra' Sayna' / The Dark Sinai-Woman* (1959) and *'Antar Ibn Shaddad* (1961). Mustafa also directed numerous successful light musicals, such as *al-Hawa Wa-l-Shabab / Love and Youth* (1948), featuring Layla Murad and Anwar Wagdi, and *Taxi al-Gharam / Love Taxi* (1954), starring Huda Sultan as a rich girl who disguises herself as a poor singer in order to convince a taxi-driver to marry her, despite the class difference between them. Mustafa also contributed some film farces, such as *Isma'il Yasin Tarzan* (1958) or *al'Ataba Gazaz / Glass Threshold* (1969), starring Fu'ad al-Muhandis', as well as *Bint Ismaha Mahmud / A Girl Called Mahmud* (1975), about a girl who circumvents her father's prohibition against studying by wearing men's clothes. In general, Mustafa showed little social or political interest: his *Ard al-Abtal / Land of Heroes* (1953), touching on the Palestine War in 1948 and starring Koka, is little else but a melodrama, similar to the family dramas *Sijara Wa Ka's / Cigarette and Wineglass* (1955) and *al-Sahira al-Saghira / The Little Magician* (1963), which rely on romantic love and treason. Mustafa contributed also to the gangster film genre, particularly the thug film. He was one of the first to introduce this character to the screen with *Futuwat al-Husainiyya / Husainiyya Thugs* (1954), but up to the 1980s he also directed numerous regular gangster films, like one of his last films *Wuhush al-Mina' / Harbour Beasts* (1983), about a drug-dealing gang. One of his most thrilling action films was *Dima' Fawq al-Nil / Blood on the Nile* (1961), featuring Hind Rustum as a seductive peasant woman who avenges the death of her husband.

Figure 18 Layla Murad

Nasrallah, Yousri (b. 1952, Cairo)

The director of three feature films and two documentaries, Nasrallah graduated in economics and political science from Cairo University, worked as film critic and directing assistant in Beirut between 1978 and 1982, and became the friend and assistant of Youssef Chahine. All his films were produced by Chahine's company Misr International and funded by French institutions (including television companies). His first film, the semi-autobiographical *Sariqat Sayfiyya / Summer Thefts* (1988), reflected his own painful experience as a child witnessing his parents' divorce set against the backdrop of Nasser's nationalization policies, by which Nasrallah's affluent family was also affected. This beautifully shot film is one of the few *cinéma d'auteur* works of Egyptian cinema. His unique black comedy *Mercedes* (1993) stands out for its original *mise-en-scène*, mixing black-and-white with coloured stock material. It tells the fantastic story of a young leftist who has been declared insane by his mother, but falls in love with a girl who looks exactly like her. The film's infernal end is initiated by Muslim fundamentalists, whose subterranean depots filled with explosives rip the city apart. Nasrallah's latest film, *al-Madina / The City* (1999), features a young working-class Egyptian who dreams of going to France. His trip, however, proves to be a complete failure. In spite of its mannerist touches, the *mise-en-scène* relies heavily on the dynamic between the performers – the film was shot on digital video before being blown up on to 35 mm. The experience for this film was drawn from Nasrallah's powerful full-length documentary *Sibyan Wa Banat / Boys, Girls and the Veil* (1995), in which he portrays a group of young working-class Egyptians.

Saif, Samir (b. 1947, Cairo)

Director (up to 1997) of twenty-two full-length films, a short television film and several religious videos for the Coptic church, Saif graduated in 1969 from the Higher Film Institute. He started his career with first an adaptation of the *Comte de Monte Cristo* as *Da'irat al-Intiqam / The Circle of Revenge* (1976) and then of Tennessee Williams' play *Cat on a Hot Tin Roof* as *Qitta 'Alla Nar / Cat on Fire* (1977). Fascinated by American action films, Saif remade five US productions, among others *Shawari' Min Nar / Burning Streets* (1983) which was modelled on Billy Wilder's *Irma la Douce* and *al-Halal Wa-l-Haram / The Allowed and the Forbidden* (1984) which remade Charles Jarrott's *The Other Side of Midnight*. Saif's films were always quite popular. He directed numerous action comedies featuring top star 'Adil Imam: for instance, *al-Ghul / The Cannibal* (1983) and *al-Halfut / The Trivial* (1985). In spite of often exaggerated performances and limited means to stage car chases or to use special effects and so forth, Saif's films manage to position the viewer either in a breathless stream of trivialities – notably in the tired farce-like *Seven Samurai*-adaptation *Shams al-Zinati* (1991) – or in an endless chain of chases – as in *al-Nimr Wa-l-Untha / The Tiger and the Woman* (1987).

Salih, Taufiq (b. 1926, Alexandria)

The director of seven shorts and seven full-length featue films, Salih graduated in 1949 in English literature and was trained in cinema in Paris until 1951. Taufiq Salih's oeuvre is the only one in Egyptian cinema which may be considered purely 'Third

Worldist'. All his films deal with social injustice, underdevelopment, political abuse and the class struggle. His first film, *Darb al-Mahabil / Fools' Alley* (1955), co-written by Naguib Mahfouz, was set in a popular neighbourhood but represented a kind of allegory of greed and materialism, dismantling the opportunism of the alley's inhabitants who chase a mentally retarded homeless person after they learn that he has won the lottery. It took Salih another seven years to direct his *Sira' al-Abtal / Struggle of the Heroes* (1962), set during the cholera epidemic of the 1930s. It featured Shukri Sarhan as a leftist country doctor who battles not only against the disease, but also against the peasants' ignorance, the midwife's intrigues and the egocentric interests of the feudal landowner. Salih's next films were produced by the General Film Organization. His *Yaumiyat Na'ib Fi-l-Aryaf / Diary of a Country Prosecutor* (1968), taken from Taufiq al-Hakim's novel, counts among the best adaptations. Yet he often came up against censorship and bureaucracy. *Al-Mutamarridun / The Rebels* (1966) and *al-Sayyid Bulti / Mister Fish* (1967) both had to wait two years until their release. In the case of *al-Sayyid Bulti*, which deals with the struggle of working fishermen against a monopolist, the censor used a scene of two young women occupied with removing the hair from their legs to postpone the release of the film. Finally, in the early 1970s, Salih left the country. His *al-Makhdu'un / The Duped* (1974), produced by the Syrian National Film Organization and adapted from Ghassan Kanafani's novel *Rijal Taht al-Shams / Men under the Sun*, was one of the first Arab films to move away from a melodramatic approach to the Palestinian question and to express scepticism regarding pan-Arab solidarity. Salih's last film *al-Ayam al-Tawila / The Long Days* (1980) was produced by the Iraqi Theatre and Film Organization, and presented Saddam Hussein as a patriotic guerilla. Salih, who had moved to Iraq in 1973 in order to teach cinema, returned to Egypt in the mid-1980s and teaches at the Higher Film Institute.

Salim, 'Atif (b. 1927, Sudan)

The director of fifty-six feature films between 1953 and 1994, and assistant of Ahmad Galal and Ahmad Badrakahan, Salim succeeded with his second film, *Ja'alu Minni Mujriman / They Turned Me into a Criminal* (1954), which was based on a screenplay by Naguib Mahfouz. This kind of social orientation was echoed in another well-made work, *Ihna al-Talamdha / We Pupils* (1959), which portrayed three students who – because of a lack of guidance – become responsible for the death of a young girl. In some of Salim's films he took an interest in the problems of the middle class, as in the family drama *Umm al-'Arusa / The Mother of the Bride* (1963), in which an employee is almost ruined because of the planned marriage of his daughter, or *Ayn 'Aqli / Where is My Mind?* (1974), featuring Su'ad Husni as a young woman whose husband suffers from schizophrenia. In spite of a few acceptable mainstream films, most of Salim's later oeuvre is characterized by weak plots or mediocre *mise-en-scène*, as in the political costume drama *Thawrat al-Yaman / The Yemen Revolution* (1966), which attempted to dismiss the former Yemeni ruler as an ignorant and vicious tyrant through its stereotypical and unreal character traits and settings. His boxing film *al-Nimr al-Aswad / Black Panther* (1984), featuring Ahmad Zaki as a black Egyptian boxer who tries his luck in Europe and is supported by his European lover, is also characterized by its artificiality.

Selim (Salim), Kamal (b. 1913, Cairo; d. 1945)

Selim was a screenwriter who, between 1937 and 1945, directed eleven full-length features. *Al-'Azima / Determination* (1939), produced by Studio Misr, was his second film, for which he was highly praised after national independence as it was considered the first realist Egyptian film – in spite of its partly melodramatic structure. As producers were not yet interested in that genre, Selim turned to the prevalent melo-drama and to literary adaptations. He was the first to adapt Victor Hugo's novel *Les misérables* (as *al-Bu'asa'* in 1943), Shakespeare's *Romeo and Juliet* (as *Shuhada' al-Gharam / Martyrs of Love* in 1944) and, last but not least, modelled *Qissat Gharam / Love Story* (1945) on Emily Brontë's *Wuthering Heights*.

Wagdi, Anwar (b. 1904, Egypt; d. 1955)

Wagdi acted in around seventy films and directed thirteen full-length features between 1947 and 1954, mostly light musical comedies and music-hall films. He joined Yusuf Wahbi's Ramsis troupe, before he started acting in secondary roles. His first directing work was *Layla Bint al-Fuqara' / Layla, Daughter of the Poor* in 1947, which he followed with other musicals starring the singer Layla Murad, who had become his wife in 1945. Wagdi films were typically musicals that mixed all kinds of elements: the Egyptian song, music-hall dances, a basically melodramatic plot neutralized by funny characters and a happy ending. He presented this cheerful and entertaining mixture in *'Anbar / Ward* (1947), *Ghazal al-Banat / Girls' Flirtation* (1949) and *Habib al-Ruh / The Soul's Beloved* (1951), among others. He moreover discovered Fayruz when she was a little girl and made her perform in the same type of film, creating *Yasemine* (1950) and *Dhahab / Gold* (1953). Similarly he presented the singer Shadya in *Qatr al-Nada / Dew Train* (1951). In spite of often weak and trival plots which he partly scripted himself, Wagdi's films were highly dynamic and charming, especially because they did not care about presenting their stories seriously. The same applies to Wagdi's acting style. He did not present any torn or tortured personalities, instead preferring clear-cut personae like the police officer in Salah Abu Seif's *al-Wahsh / The Beast* (1954) and *Raya Wa Sakina / Raya and Sakina* (1953), as well as in his own last film *Arba' Banat Wa Dabit / Four Girls and an Officer* (1954). Some of his most distinguished roles were those of a merry entertainer (which he actually was), such as in *Dhahab* and *'Anbar / Ward*.

Wahbi, Yusuf (b. 1898, Fayum; d. 1982)

Wahbi was a producer and actor, and between 1935 and 1963 directed thirty full-length features. He left for Italy in 1920 in order to become an actor and returned in 1922 to found and direct the popular theatre troupe Ramsis, which offered mainly melodramatic plays, often mixed with music. In the 1950s Wahbi became the head of the actors' syndicate and he directed the national theatre during the same decade. Wahbi produced the early melodrama *Zaynab* (1930), by Muhammad Karim, for which he equipped the very small and poor studio Ramsis. He also scripted Karim's *Awlad al-Dhawat / Sons of Aristocrats* (1932), in which he played the main role. Wahbi became known for his theatrical and melodramatic performances, expressed likewise through his way of directing his films, for which he partly adapted plays from the

Figure 19 Isma'il Yasin (right) with Sulayman Nagib

theatre. Wahbi's prefered topics were purely melodramatic: seduction in *Awlad al-Fuqara' / Sons of the Poor* (1942), class difference in *Bint Zawat / Daughter of Aristocrats* (1942), disease in *Shadiyat al-Wadi / Singer of the Valley* (1947), a musical starring Layla Murad, and arranged marriage in *al-Afukatu Madiha / Madiha the Advocate* (1950). His most interesting work is the musical *Gharam Wa Intiqam / Love and Revenge* (1944), starring Asmahan, which mixes a multitude of motifs: crime, death and deceived love. Although his own works are not considered landmarks in Egyptian cinema because of their exaggerated melodramatic orientation, Wahbi left his mark as an actor. He formed a whole school of melodramatic performers, notably 'Aziza Amir, Amina Rizq and Yahia Shahin, while raising his fame through many important films from the 1930s until the 1970s. In fact Wahbi's performances became increasingly realist, starting with *Layla Bint al-Rif / Layla from the Countryside* (1941) and *Gharam Wa Intiqam* and ending with *Miramar* (1969) by Kamal El-Cheikh and *Iskandariyya, Lih? / Alexandria, Why?* (1978) by Youssef Chahine.

zu-l-Fiqar, 'Izz al-Din (b. 1919, Egypt; d. 1963)

An actor and the director of thirty-three full-length films between 1947 and 1962, zu-l-Fiqar started a military career but then turned to directing. He mainly produced melodramas and gangster movies, but there were certain exceptions: *Abu Zaid al-Hilali* (1947), in which he adapted the famous Arab legend, the war and espionage film *Port Said* (1957), which presented the struggle of the civil resistance against military occupation and a female British spy, and the patriotic melodrama *Rudd Qalbi / Give My Heart Back* (1957), which is his most famous (although not necessarily his best) film. Zu-l-Fiqar was primarily praised for his melodramas and a small number of gangster films, notably the thrilling *al-Rajul al-Thani / The Second Man* (1959) which features an undercover agent on the verge of being discovered. One of his first melo-dramas was *Khulud* (1948), starring Fatin Hamama, who became his wife at the end of the shooting. This film introduced the recurrent motifs of zu-l-Fiqar's melodramas – death and disability – with a sick hero who convinces his beloved that he betrayed her in order to make her stop loving him. Hamama featured also in several other works of his, among others *Maw'id Ma'a al-Hayat / Rendezvous with Life* (1953), *Inni Rahilla / I Am Departing* (1955) and the family drama *Nahr al-Hubb / Stream of Love* (1960), in which a woman is forced to marry a rich old man, but falls in love with a young officer, who dies. Accused of adultery she is deprived of her only child and commits suicide. One of zu-l-Fiqar's most stunning melodramas is *Imra'a Fi-l-Tariq / A Woman on the Road* (1958), starring Huda Sultan and Rushdi Abaza – a remake of *Duel in the Sun* which, of course, changes the setting and even gives a slightly different ending. The place is not a ranch but a car workshop and the heroine, married to her lover's brother, kills her husband at the end and is strangled to death by her lover.

List of actors

Abaza, Rushdi (b. 1927; d. 1980)

Abaza appeared first in 1948 in *al-Millyunira al-Saghira / The Little Millionaire* by Kamal Barakat. Between the late 1950s and the early 1970s, he was considered one of the most important male stars, with top billing in almost fifty films. Handsome, but with an air of tough, aggressive masculinity that was supported by his athletic appear-ance, he was often cast as macho man or seducer, as in *al-Zawja Raqam 13 / Wife No. 13* (1962) by Fatin 'Abd al-Wahhab. He also played roles as a gangster, for example in *al-Rajul al-Thani / The Second Man* (1959) by 'Izz al-Din zu-l-Fiqar, as a patriotic resistance fighter in *La Waqt Li-l-Hubb / No Time for Love* (1963) by Salah Abu Seif or as the unjust and vengeful husband in one of his late roles (together with Fatin Hamama) in Sa'id Marzuq's *Uridu Hallan / I Want a Solution* (1975).

'Abd al-'Aziz, Mahmud (b. 1950)

'Abd al-'Aziz appeared first in Ashraf Fahmi's melodramatic *Hatta Akhir al-'Umr / Until the End of Life* in 1975, but soon became a performer of gangster and mafia films, mostly as the good guy – as in 'Ali Abd El-Khalek's *al-'Ar / Shame* (1982), in which he featured as the son of a drug dealer who is shocked to learn about his father's dirty business but agrees to support him. Subsequently he became one of the 'stars in blue jeans', performing in New Realist films predominantly as a working-class man: in *al-Sa'alik / The Vagabonds* (1983) by Daoud Abd El-Sayed, he develops from a homeless person into a rich businessman. More than his colleagues Ahmad Zaki and Nur al-Sharif, who had a similar repertoire, 'Abd al-'Aziz was also chosen for comic roles, playing a character who was a bit clumsy but had a heart of gold, notably in Ra'fat al-Mihi's black comedies *al-Sada al-Rijal / Men, the Gentlemen* (1987) and *Sayyidati Anisati / Wives and Single Women* (1990), as Ma'ali Zayid's counterpart. This persona was echoed more recently in Muhammad Kamil Qalyubi's comedy *al-Bahr Biyidhak Lih? / Why Does the Sea Laugh?* (1995), in which he marries four women (including prostitutes) with the objective of protecting them. During the 1990s he also allowed his persona to age. His performance in *al-Kitkat* (1993) by Daoud Abd El-Sayed as a witty and clever blind musician, father of a grown-up son, seems exaggerated but raised his popularity immensely.

'Abd al-Wahhab, Muhammad (b. 1897; d. 1991)

'Abd al-Wahhab was a singer, composer, actor and producer. He was inspired by all the great singers of his time, like Salama Higazi, and became the pupil of Sayyid Darwish, whose songs he first performed in theatres. 'Abd al-Wahahb is considered responsible for the success of the Egyptian musical in the inter-war period, after he provided compositions short enough to be integrated into cinematic action. He himself starred in only seven films, most of them directed by Muhammad Karim: *al-Warda al-Bayda' / The White Rose* (1933), *Dumu' al-Hubb / Tears of Love* (1935), *Yahya al-Hubb / Long Live Love!* (1938), *Yawm Sa'id / A Happy Day* (1940), *Mamnu' al-Hubb / Forbidden Love* (1942), *Rusasa Fi-l-Qalb / A Shot in the Heart* (1944) and *Lastu Malakan / I Am Not an Angel* (1946). He stopped acting in 1946, possibly due to his age and weak eyesight. These were all obstacles to representing his favourite persona: the unlucky romantic lover. He continued to work off screen, however, composing the music and songs for scores of Egyptian musicals.

'Akif, Na'ima (b. 1932; d. 1966)

'Akif, Na'ima was a circus artist, dancer and actress who played the main character in twenty-two films. Born into a family of circus artists, she was one of the most talented film dancers of her time with the largest repertoire of dance styles and rhythms. Because of her physical and acrobatic capabilities, her beautiful face and her charming acting, she performed mostly the light musical comedies that were typical of that era, many of which were directed by her husband Husain Fawzi. In spite of their weak plots and trivial stories, the films were held together by 'Akif's charm and excellent performances, as well as their varied choreography. Her most successful films were *Lahalibo* (1949), *Baba 'Aris / Daddy as a Bridegroom* (1950) and *Fatat al-Sirk / Circus Girl* (1951) by Fawzi, *Tamr Hinna / Tamarind* (1957) by Hasan al-Saifi and *Baya'it al-Gara'id / The Newspaper Vendor* (1963) by Hasan al-Imam. In the majority of her films, she played a poor but talented singer and dancer who aspired to fame and was caught in a romantic relationship.

al-'Alayli, 'Izzat (b. 1934)

Al-'Alayli graduated from the Higher Theatre Institute in 1959. Slim and with a face that gave him an air of solemn authority, he became associated with roles as police or army officers, starting with the political thriller *Za'ir al-Fajr / Visitors in the Dawn* (1973) by Mamduh Shukri, continuing through *Ahl al-Qimma / People from the Top* (1981) by 'Ali Badrakahn, and ending with *al-Tariq Illa Aylat / The Way to Eilat* (1995) by An'am Muhammad 'Ali. He starred moreover in the Algerian film *Tahunat al-Sayyid Fabre / Monsieur Fabre's Mill* (1982) by Ahmed Rachedi (Ahmad Rashidi) as the politically cornered mayor of a little town. Al-'Alayli also embodied the courageous and outraged peasant in *al-Ard / The Earth* (1968) by Youssef Chahine, a role which he later echoed in Khairy Beshara's *al-Tawq Wa-l-Iswirra / The Collar and the Bracelet* (1986). Two of his most unconventional personae were the mourning water carrier in *al-Saqqa Mat / The Water Carrier Died* (1977) by Salah Abu Seif and the schizophrenic writer who turns out to have killed his twin brother in Youssef Chahine's thriller *al-Ikhtiyar / The Choice* (1970).

Al-Atrash, Farid (b. 1910, Lebanon; d. 1974)

A singer, composer and actor, al-Atrash was born to a Lebanese Druze family who had settled in Cairo. He started his career in Badi'a Masabni's troupe as a singer. His first film, *Intisar al-Shabab / The Victory of Youth* (1941) by Ahmad Badrakhan, in which he performed together with his sister Asmahan, became a great success and was followed by *Ahlam al-Shabab / Dreams of the Youth* (1942) by Kamal Selim, in which he appeared alone. After Asmahan's demise in 1944, al-Atrash developed his favourite character: a young, talented and lonely musician called Wahid (literally 'the lonely'), who was always struggling with love and fate. One of his notable performances as Wahid is in the melodrama *'Ahd al-Hawa / Promise of Love* (1954) by Ahmad Badrakhan. Yet al-Atrash's repertoire also comprises a number of light musical comedies, for instance *'Afrita Hanim / Lady Ghost* (1949) by Henri Barakat, co-starring the dancer Samia Gamal. With Gamal he formed a charming duo in several music-hall films, including *Akhir Kidba / The Last Lie* (1950) by Ahmad Badrakhan and *Ma Ti'ulsh Li-Hadd / Don't Tell Anyone* (1952) by Barakat. He used to compose his own music, which was even more syncretic than 'Abd al-Wahhab's, particularly his dance music. He also experimented with operetta in some of his films, starting with *Intisar al-Shabab* and ending with *Lahn Hubbi / Melody of My Love* (1953) by Ahmad Badrakhan, which co-starred Sabah.

Carioca, Tahiyya (b. 1915, Manzala, Egypt; d. 1999)

An actress and belly dancer, Carioca's real name was Badawiyya Muhammad Karim. She trained in belly dancing at Badia Masabni's variety theatre. She was one of the best dancers of her time, beautiful and talented. She peformed her first dramatic role in *Dr Farhat* (1935) by Togo Mizrahi and was given her first main part in *Uhib al-Ghalat / I Love the Wrong* (1942) by Husain Fawzi. However it was *Lu'bat al-Sitt / The Lady's Game* (1946) that established her fame. In this film she formed an unforgettable duo with Nagib al-Rihani, as a couple who first fall in love but become alienated by the wife's increasing success. Carioca's persona was initially related to the seductive dancer, as in the previously cited film, yet she was soon able to detach herself from that image and establish herself as an actress in purely dramatic roles, first of all creating the persona of the *mu'alima*, the popular mistress – a courageous, clever, independent yet virtuous, traditionally oriented woman, the typical incarnation of an Egyptian *bint al-balad*. She represented this persona most convincingly in Salah Abu Seif's *al-Futuwa / The Thug* (1957). It was echoed, albeit with an evil twist, in *Shabab Imra'a / Youth of a Woman* (1956), in which she enacted a middle-aged woman luring a poor student from the countryside away from his studies. Starting from the 1960s, Carioca increasingly gained weight; she still played the attractive Egyptian Mameluk Queen, Shajarat al-Durr in *Wa Islamah / Oh Islam!* (1961) by Andrew Marton, but then moved on to playing mothers, notably a touching peformance as a retired belly dancer in *Khalli Balak Min Zuzu / Take Care of Zuzu* (1972) by Hasan al-Imam. Some of her last mother roles were in *Li-l-Hubb Qissa Akhira / Love's Last Story* (1986) by Ra'fat al-Mihi and *Mercedes* (1993) by Yousri Nasrallah.

Al-Fakharani, Yahia (b. 1945)

Al-Fakharani studied medicine, before he started acting in television series and films. Since the 1980s he has appeared now and then in cinema. Although corpulent and friendly faced, he is not classified as a funny character but performs highly nuanced humane characters, often representing a regular average citizen. He was therefore a favourite of committed directors and his few main parts were praised for their quality, primarily his roles in '*Awdat Muwatin / Return of a Citizen* (1986) and *Kharaj Wa Lam Ya'ud / Missing* (1985), both by Mohamed Khan, but also in *Li-l-Hubb Qissa Akhira / Love's Last Story* (1986) by Ra'fat al-Mihi, as a loving husband struggling with a terminal disease, and *Ard al-Ahlam / Land of Dreams* (1993) by Daoud Abd El-Sayed, in which he was Fatin Hamama's counterpart – charmingly helping and, at the same time, preventing her from looking for her lost passport.

Figure 20 Anwar Wagdi (right) with Husain Riad

Gamal, Samia (b. 1924; d. 1994)

A dancer and actress, Gamal's real name was Zaynab Khalil Ibrahim. She introduced herself at Badia Masabni's variety theatre and was given her first secondary role in Muhammad Karim's *Mamnu' al-Hubb / Forbidden Love* (1942). She developed her own dancing style, enriching the oriental dance with some expressive modern elements, and was moreover a charming actress, as her first main role proved: she co-starred with Nagib al-Rihani in *Ahmar Shafayif / Red Lipstick* (1946), playing a seductive servant who alienates a husband from his wife and family. The *femme fatale* did not become her prevalent persona, however. In spite of being a dancer, she soon developed into the character of a beautiful yet innocent woman. She formed a charming and often hilarious double act with the singer Farid al-Atrash in a whole series of films, comprising among others Henri Barakat's Thousand and One Nights fantasy *'Afrita Hanim / Lady Ghost* (1949), *Akhir Kidba / The Last Lie* (1950) by Ahmad Badrakhan and Barakat's *Ma Ti'ulsh Li-Hadd / Don't Tell Anybody* (1952), in which he sang and she danced in some rather sophisticated music-hall choreographies. Gamal's bright and joyful smile enabled her to fit into slightly comic roles, as performed in *Nashala Hanim / Lady Pickpocket* (1953) by Hassan al-Saifi and *Sukkar Hanim / Mrs Sugar* (1960) by Sayyid Bidir. Gamal retired in 1972.

Al-Gindi, Nadia (b. 1940)

Al-Gindi gained her first role in *Jamila al-Jaza'iriyya / Jamila the Algerian* (1958) by Youssef Chahine. Her first main part was that of a belly dancer in a typical Hasan al-Imam melodrama, *Bamba Kashar* (1974), which is the biography of a dancer of the 1920s. Today al-Gindi is Egypt's best-paid female star, although not the best actress. She mainly relies on belly dancing, seductive gestures and tight clothes to present her favourite persona of the often mistreated but nonetheless powerful *femme fatale*. She did, however, feature in *al-Batniyya* (1980) by Husam al-Din Mustafa as a victim of male-dominated society, while in *al-Khadima / The Servant* (1984) by Ashraf Fahmi she developed her persona to play an *arriviste* who sought higher social status by any means possible, including mean intrigues and violence. Al-Gindi was considered a top star by producers during the 1990s, but dismissed as vulgar by the critics. She shifted role again to play several courageous, patriotic and seductive women, such as in the espionage film *Muhimma Fi Tall-Abib / Mission in Tel Aviv* (1992) by Nadir Galal. In *al-Jasusa Hikmat Fahmi / The Spy Hikmat Fahmi* (1994) by Husam al-Din Mustafa and *Imra'a Hazat 'Arsh Misr / A Woman Shook Egypt's Throne* (1995) by Nadir Galal, both set in pre-revolutionary Egypt, she serves as a link to the nationalist Free Officers and helps them to overthrow the throne and the colonialists.

Hafiz, 'Abd al-Halim (b. 1929; d. 1977)

A singer and actor in fifteen movies, Hafiz graduated from the Conservatoire of Arab Music in 1948 and worked as a music teacher before becoming a famous singer. He was particularly close to the hearts of post-revolutionary youth, less because of his famous patriotic songs than for his lively music and numerous love songs, which he also presented on the screen. His first two films, *Dalila* (1956) and *Maw'id Gharam / Love Rendezvous* (1956), were directed by masters of the melodramatic musical:

Muhammad Karim and Henri Barakat. Hafiz's pleasant appearance and improving performances made him the perfect young romantic and unhappy lover – he first played the role in *al-Wisada al-Khaliyya* / *The Empty Cushion* (1957) by Salah Abu Seif and last played it in Husain Kamal's box-office hit *Abbi Fawq al-Shajara* / *My Father Up the Tree* (1969), which co-starred Nadia Lutfi as a sympathetic but unhappy courtesan. Apart from the works mentioned above, the majority of Hafiz's films were directed by Hilmi Halim and presented Hafiz's dominant melodramatic persona of a poor working-class singer, aspiring to fame while being involved with a rich girl. Examples of films in which he plays this role include *Ayamina al-Hulwa* / *Our Good Days* (1955) and *Hikayat Hubb* / *Love Story* (1959). The latter, featuring a sick young man, was seen as paralleling Hafiz's real life, as he suffered from a deteriorating health condition. He died of acute bilharzia at the age of 48.

Hamama, Fatin (b. 1931)

Hamama was dubbed the 'First Lady of Arab Cinema'. She starred in dozens of films and is still popular, in spite of her increasing age. Her name seems to be associated with Egyptian melodrama more than any other performer, although in reality she starred in a huge variety of works, including comedies and realist films. Hamama acted for the first time at the age of nine, in Muhammad Karim's *Yawm Sa'id* / *Happy Day* (1940). Among her first works as a grown-up were *al-Yatimatayn* / *Two Orphans* (1948), a melodrama by Hasan al-Imam, the quasi-realist *Ibn al-Nil* / *Son of the Nile*

Figure 21 Tahiyya Carioca (centre)

Figure 22 Ibn al-Nil / Son of the Nile

(1951) and the comedy *Baba Amin / Daddy Amin* (1950), both by Youssef Chahine and in which she played innocent young girls and daughters. Because of her expressive baby-face and her always delicate figure, she seemed the ideal embodiment of a help-less and vulnerable (yet constantly virtuous) middle- or upper-class girl thrown into or throwing others into emotional turmoil, as in *Lahn al-Khulud / Song of Eternity* (1952) by Barakat, for example, or *Sira' Fi-l-Wadi / Mortal Revenge* (1954) by Youssef Chahine. Yet she also succeeded in representing working-class and rural personalities: a simple girl in *Lak Yawm Ya Zalim / Your Day is Coming* (1951) by Salah Abu Seif, a servant in *Du'a' al-Karawan / The Cry of the Plover* (1959) by Henri Barakat, an urban lower-class mother in *Yawm Murr Yawm Hulw / Bitter Day, Sweet Day* (1988) by Khairy Beshara and the peasant in Barakat's *al-Haram / The Sin* (1965). The latter was perhaps her most impressive role, playing a raped woman who had unintention-ally killed her newborn child and then fallen ill – first arousing the community's anger and then their pity. Since the late 1960s Hamama has also participated in (not always original) socially committed modernist works, like Barakat's *al-Bab al-Maftuh / The Open Door* (1963), *Afwah Wa Aranib / Mouths and Rabbits* (1977), *Laylat al-Qabd 'Ala Fatima / The Night of Fatima's Arrest* (1985) and *Uridu Hallan / I Want a Solution* (1975) by Sa'id Marzuq. Her last appearance to date was in *Ard al-Ahlam / Land of Dreams* (1993) as an upper middle-class mother who is asked by her children to emigrate to the United States in order to help them obtain their own visas.

Hamdi, 'Imad (b. 1909; d. 1984)

Hamdi graduated in commerce and worked in the administration of Studio Misr before he was asked to perform his first main part in Kamil al-Tilmissani's *al-Suq al-Sawda' / The Black Market* (1945) as a responsible employee fighting the corruption in his neighbourhood. In spite of his aggresive first role, Hamdi (perhaps due to his calm aura and shy expression) became one of the main romantic lovers in Egyptian cinema and was rarely associated with the working class. He acted in many sentimental films, such as *Saji al-Layl / Night Fell* (1948) by Henri Barakat (he played a doctor), *Wada'a Ya Gharami / Farewell My Love* (1951) and, the most acclaimed of his performances, *Bayn al-Atlal / Among the Ruins* (1959) by 'Izz al-Din zu-l-Fiqar. With the retreat of melodrama, Hamdi's importance diminished. He appeared now and then in secondary roles, the last and highly acclaimed one was the touching role of a father whose work-shop is threatened by expropriation in *Sawaq al-Utubis / The Bus-Driver* (1983) by Atef El-Tayeb.

Husni, Su'ad (b. 1941)

Husni is probably the most talented Egyptian actress so far – able to sing, dance and act. She started her career with the melodrama *Hasan Wa Na'ima / Hasan and Na'ima* (1959) by Henri Barakat. In spite of her aura of overt sensuality and emotionality, she was too good an actress to be confined just to the role of female victim or *femme fatale*. She performed in a huge variety of mainstream films, a highlight being her role as the student daughter of a belly dancer in *Khalli Balak Min Zuzu / Take Care of Zuzu* (1972) by Hasan al-Imam, in which she delightfully sings and dances and loves the blonde beau Husain Fahmi. At the same time Husni was able to represent disturbingly complex characters in such films as Sa'id Marzuq's *Zawjatti Wa-l-Kalb / My Wife and the Dog* (1971) and *al-Khawf / Fear* (1972), and Mohamed Khan's *Maw'id 'Ala al-'Asha' / Rendezvous for Dinner* (1981), in which she played a lonely and emotionally deprived woman. She presented painfully disillusioned characters, such as the working-class girl in *al-Qahira 30 / Cairo 30* (1966) by Salah Abu Seif, the political activist and student in *al-Karnak* (1975) and the deprived middle-class employee in *Ahl al-Qimma / People from the Top* (1981) by 'Ali Badrakahn, which is one of her most touching roles. She appeared for the last time in 'Ali Badrakhan's *al-Ra'i Wa-l-Nisa' / The Shepherd and the Women* (1991).

Imam, 'Adil (b. 1940)

Egypt's current top star and comedian, Imam acts in both theatre and cinema, attracting interest for the first time in 1972 with the play *Madrassit al-Mushaghibin / School of Rebels*. After his first main part in *Ihna Bitu' al-Utubis / Us, From the Bus* (1979) by Husain Kamal, he adopted the figure of the working-class, subversive yet almost nihilist, average citizen trying in vain to cope with a disintegrating post-*infitah* society. In *Ihna Bitu' al-Utubis*, set during the Nasserist period, the main character is caught, although he is innocent, placed in police custody and tortured as a rebel. The film ends with an armed revolt. One of Imam's following films, Muhammad 'Abd al-'Aziz's *Rajab Fawq Sath Safih Sakhin / Rajab on a Hot Tin Roof* (1979) became a major box-office hit and featured a peasant who goes to town only to end up in prison while experiencing all kinds of absurdity. During the late 1980s Imam developed his persona from the rebel-despite-himself to a stronger and cleverer character, starring in several police and gangster films, like Samir Saif's *al-Nimr Wa-l-Untha* / *The Tiger and the Woman* (1987) and Nadir Galal's *Jazirat al-Shaytan* / *Devil's Island* (1990). However, Imam's speciality remained the enactment of comic characters against an often socially or politically dramatized background, notably in *al-Afukatu* / *The Advocate* (1984) by Ra'fat al-Mihi or *al-Irhabi* / *The Terrorist* (1994) by Nadir Galal. Nonetheless, Imam was dismissed as vulgar during the his first decade of appearances because of, on one hand, his burlesque acting and, on the other, his nihilist characters. However, *al-Irhabi* brought him closer to the establishment, as he helped with that work to dismiss the Muslim fundamentalists as crooks and infidels. Apart from his comic desperados, Imam performed a few realist and psychologically sophisticated characters, notably a prisoner involved in a difficult love story in *Hubb Fi-l-Zinzana* / *Love in a Prison Cell* (1983) and an unhappy *arriviste* in *Hatta La Yatir al-Dukhan* / *So that the Smoke Does Not Vanish* (1984) by Ahmad Yahia, and most distinguished in Mohamed Khan's *al-Harif* / *The Champion* (1984) he played a young father and husband who tries, in spite of economic and family restraints, to realize his dream of becoming a street soccer champion.

Al-Kassar, 'Ali (b. 1887; d. 1957, Cairo)

Al-Kassar's real name was 'Ali Khalil Salim, and he worked as a cook and waiter before joining a small theatre group in the Sayyida Zaynab neighbourhood. More than other comedians his performances were rooted in the activities of the farce performers and nineteenth-century *fasl mudhik* (funny sketch) enactors. Unlike Yusuf Wahbi and Nagib al-Rihani, al-Kassar had no regular theatre of his own, but wandered instead. In cinema al-Kassar performed first in Bonvelli's short film *al-Khala al-Amirikaniyya* / *The American Aunt*, shot in 1920, and found cinematic success through his popular role as the black Nubian (*barbari*) 'Uthman 'Abd al-Basit, a real *Karagöz* – a notoriously unlucky character who finally gets off lightly at the very end of the film. Often suspected to be one, al-Kassar was not Nubian himself, yet for decades he was called 'Egypt's *barbari*'. Originally developing his Nubian mask for the theatre, al-Kassar brought it to the screen for the first time in Alexander Warkash's 1935 film *al-Bawab* / *The Doorkeeper* and later developed a whole serial comprising, among others, *Ma'at Alf Junaih* / *Hundred Thousand Pounds* (1936), *al-Sa'a Sab'a* / *Seven O'Clock* (1937), *al-Tilighraf* / *Telegram* (1938), *Salifni Talata Gini* / *Lend Me Three Pounds* (1939) and *Alf Layla Wa Layla* / *One Thousand and One Nights* (1941), mostly directed by Togo Mizrahi. During the 1940s his popularity gradually vanished. His last film was *Nur al-Din Wa-l-Bahhara al-Thalatha* / *Nur al-Din and the Three Sailors* (1944).

Mazhar, Ahmad (b. 1918)

After pursuing a military career Mazhar started acting in 1955 and became one of the gentlemen of Egyptian cinema, supported by his slim elegant appearance, his clean-cut face (embellished with a small moustache) and his restrained acting. He primarily represented educated and refined personalities, like the doctor in *al-Layla al-Akhira* /

The Last Night (1963) who helps the married heroine to uncover the lies in which she had been living for years. His rational aura also enabled him convincingly to enact patriots and resistance fighters in *Jamila al-Jaza'iriyya / Jamila the Algerian* (1958) by Youssef Chahine and *Nur al-Layl / Light of the Night* (1959) by Raymond Nassur. One of his most successful roles so far was as the medieval warlord Saladin in *al-Nasir Salah al-Din / The Victorious Saladin* (1963) by Youssef Chahine; this was preceded by a similar role as a noble Arab knight in *Wa Islamah / Oh Islam!* (1961) by Andrew Marton, in which he fought the Mongol invasion instead of the Crusaders. Some of the few films in which he went against his usual character-type were *Du'a' al-Karawan / The Cry of the Plover* (1959), in which he played the rich seducer, and *Shafiqa al-Qibtiyya / Shafiqa the Copt* (1963) by Hasan al-Imam, as well as *al-Qahira 30 / Cairo 30* (1966) by Salah Abu Seif. In the latter two films, he embodied sly aristocrats. Since the 1970s he has rarely appeared on screen.

al-Miligi, Mahmud (b. 1910; d. 1983)

Al-Miligi was trained in Fatima Rushdi's theatre troupe before performing for the first time in 1933 in Rushdi's film *al-Zawaj / The Marriage*. With strong facial features and a sharp look he became the major gangster type of Egyptian cinema, embodying unscrupulous personalities in dozens of stories and contexts, from vicious nightclub owners (as in *Ghazal al-Banat / Girls' Flirtation*, 1949) to evil doctors (*al-Manzil Raqam 13 / House No. 13*, 1952) and violent gang leaders (*al-Wahsh / The Beast*, 1954). In spite of his acceptance of these stereotypical roles, al-Miligi was an excellent actor who became even more expressive when he was not typecast. Youssef Chahine was the first director to make extensive use of al-Miligi's full capabilities. His courageous and uncompromising peasant in the anti-colonialist epic *al-Ard / The Earth* (1968) is one of the unforgettable characters of Egyptian cinema. Chahine collaborated with Miligi for the first time in *Jamila al-Jaza'iriyya / Jamila the Algerian* (1958), in which the latter played a French lawyer fighting in vain to save the convicted heroine's life. By contrast, in *al-'Usfur / The Sparrow* (1972) al-Miligi presented a completely disillusioned and lethargic character, quite opposite to the dynamic 'evil' of his mainstream characters. He moreover acted one of his most touching roles in *Iskandariyya Lih? / Alexandria Why?* (1978), as a painfully disillusioned lawyer and the father of Chahine's alter ego.

Murad, Layla (b. 1918; d. 1995)

A singer and actress, Murad was born into a Jewish family of musicians but converted to Islam in 1946, together with her brother Munir (a singer, composer and actor). Between 1938 and 1955 Murad starred in twenty-seven musicals, mostly light comedies and some melodramas. Murad's voice was first heard in *al-Dahaya / The Victims* (1933) by Bahiga Hafiz, dubbing the heroine's singing. She was chosen for her first actual film role by Muhammad 'Abd al-Wahhab, playing his partner in *Yahya al-Hubb / Long Live Love!* (1938) by Muhammad Karim. In the films that followed, she often appeared as a sensitive, delicate yet charming, aristocratic girl – she was nicknamed the 'Cinderella of cinema'. Some of her major melodramatic roles were in Togo Mizrahi's extraordinary *Dame aux camélias* adaptation *Layla* (1942), Henri Barakat's

Figure 23 Du'a' al-Karawan | The Cry of the Plover

Shati' al-Gharam | Beach of Love (1950) and Youssef Chahine's *Sayyidat al-Qitar | The Lady from the Train* (1952). She also formed a happy film partnership with her husband Anwar Wagdi: he directed and produced seven of her musicals, among others *Ghazal al-Banat | Girls' Flirtation* (1949) and *Habib al-Ruh | The Soul's Beloved* (1951), and performed opposite her in a few other films, including *'Anbar | Ward* (1947). In 1955, after her last divorce from Wagdi and having been falsely accused of supporting Israel, Murad married director Fatin 'Abd al-Wahhab, withdrew from cinema and, a few years later, also stopped singing.

al-Rihani, Nagib (b. 1887; d. 1949)

The star of eight feature films, al-Rihani was son of an Iraqi father and an Egyptian mother. He had some training in France before working as an entertainer in variety theatres, performing in (among other places) Franco-Arabe. In 1918 he founded his own troupe with its own theatre. One of his most famous vaudevilles was *Hasan, Murqus Wa Kuhin | Hasan, Murqus and Cohen*, which was adapted to the screen after his death. Together with Badi' Khayri, he scripted many plays, first for theatre and then for cinema. His first full-length feature, *Sahib al-Sa'ada Kish Kish Bey | His Excellency Kish Kish Bey* (1931) by Stéphane Rosti and al-Rihani, was centred around a popular Rihani character. The film was largely improvised during shooting and dealt with a naïve countryman who leaves his village in order to enjoy himself in the city but is deceived and robbed. Al-Rihani subsequently adapted Pagnol's *Topaze* in 1934 as *Yaqut Afandi | Yaqut Effendi* (produced by the French company Gaumont and directed by Rosié). Later in his comedies Rihani specialised in playing the poor working-class good guy who has disastrous encounters with either women, as in *Lu'bat al-Sitt | The Lady's Game* (1946) and *Ahmar Shafayif | Lipstick* (1946), or upper-class people, as in *Salama Fi Khayr* / *Salama is Fine* (1937) and *Si 'Umar* / *Mr 'Umar* (1941) by Niazi Mustafa, as well as *Ghazal al-Banat* / *Girls' Flirtation* (1949) by Anwar Wagdi. He presented his character usually with a good deal of self-irony and empathy.

Rizq, Amina (b. 1910)

The oldest living Egyptian film and theatre actress, Rizq acted in around one hundred films. She joined Wahbi's Ramsis troupe in 1924 and acted for the first time on screen in Jacques Schutz's *Su'ad al-Ghajariyya* / *Su'ad the Gypsy* (1928). She also starred in the first Egyptian talkie, *Awlad al-Dhawat* / *Sons of Aristocrats* (1932) by Yusuf Wahbi. Faithful to Wahbi's school, her acting remained confined to the exaggerated gestures of melodrama for decades. For this reason (and also her lack of attractiveness) she mostly appeared as a supporting actress and rarely presented complex or ambiguous characters, although through the course of the years her acting style became more natural. One of her few main roles was in *al-Duktur* / *The Doctor* (1939) by Niazi Mustafa, a melodrama in which she falls in love with a doctor from a rural background but is opposed by her family. Nonetheless, Rizq appeared so often in Egyptian cinema that it seems almost unthinkable without her – to cite only a few films out of her long filmography, she acted in *al-Bu'asa'* / *Les Misérables* (1942) by Kamal Selim, *Ba'i'at al-Khubz* / *Bread Vendor* (1953) by Hasan al-Imam and *Fajr al-Islam* / *The Dawn of Islam* (1971) by Salah Abu Seif. Later, she became the incarnation of the Egyptian working-class mother, as portrayed in Abu Seif's *Bidaya Wa Nihaya* / *Beginning and End* (1960) and the comedy *Umhahat Fi-l-Manfa* / *Mothers in Exile* (1980) by Muhammad Radi. During the 1990s she also presented some charming and convincing mothers – in *Harb al-Farawla* / *The Strawberry War* (1994) by Khairy Beshara, for example – and grandmothers – such as in two films by Daoud Abd El-Sayed, *al-Kitkat* (1991) and *Ard al-Ahlam* / *Land of Dreams* (1993).

Rosti, Stéphane (b. 1891, Egypt; d. 1964)

An actor, director and one of Egypt's film pioneers, Rosti was born in Egypt to an Italian mother and an Austrian father. He started acting in theatre in 1917. His first work in directing was the completion of 'Aziza Amir's production *Layla* in 1927. In 1928 he adapted Amin 'Atallah's popular play *al-Bahr Biyidhak Leh?* / *Why Does the Sea Laugh?* (1928), in which he also acted. In 1931 he co-directed *Sahib al-Sa'ada Kish Kish Bey* / *His Excellency Kish Kish Bey* with Nagib al-Rihani. In his next films, Rosti focused on performing, creating one of the early villain personae of Egyptian cinema – a character whose viciousness is thoroughly cloaked behind friendly politeness. He played some of his most remarkable roles in *Qitar al-Layl* / *Night Train* (1953) by 'Izz al-Din zu-l-Fiqar, *Hasan Murqus Wa Kuhin* / *Hasan, Murqus and Cohen* (1954) by Fu'ad al-Gaza'irli and *Sayyidat al-Qasr* / *Lady of the Palace* (1958) by Kamal El-Cheikh.

Rushdi, Fatima (b. 1908, Alexandria)

An actress, producer and director, Rushdi is one of the pioneers of Egyptian cinema. She started her career in theatre and was trained by her husband, theatre director 'Aziz 'Id. Rushdi was called the 'Sarah Bernhardt of the Orient' because she performed many of the classical Bernhardt roles – in *Tosca* or *La dame aux camélias*, for example. She moreover founded a theatre troupe of her own. She appeared on screen for the first time in 1928 in Ibrahim Lama's second film, *Faji'a Fawq al-Haram / Disaster on the Pyramids*. Her most famous role was that of a young working-class girl falling in love with the neigbour's son (performed by Husain Sidqi) in one of the first 'realist' works: *al-'Azima / Determination* (1939) by Kamal Selim. She also acted in several other films by Selim, such as *Illa al-Abad / Forever* (1941), and in Ahmad Kamil Mursi's film *al-'Amil / The Worker* (1943), among others, and produced works for other directors, such as Ibrahim 'Imara's *al-Ta'isha / The Heedless* (1946) in which she herself starred. She appeared for the last time on screen in 1955, albeit in a secondary role, in Ahmad Diya' al-Din's *Da'uni A'ish / Let Me Live*. In 1933 Rushdi directed her first and only film, *al-Zawaj / The Marriage*, which featured her as an unhappy woman who has been forced into an unfavourable marriage by her father and finds a tragic death at the end of the film.

Rustum, Hind (b. 1931)

Rustum started acting in secondary roles in 1947 and retired during the mid-1970s. It was Hasan al-Imam who associated her persona with sexuality and seduction in two telling titles released in 1955: *al-Jasad / The Body* and *Banat al-Layl / Girls of the Night*. Thus she became the major vamp of the 1960s – a voluptuous blonde, she carried an air of Rita Hayworth and Marilyn Monroe, with appropriate dress and matching sex appeal. Yet she did not embody the silly attractive girl, rather using her aura for dramatic entanglements – to cite only her most acclaimed characters, she played the avenging angel in *Dima' Fawq al-Nil / Blood on the Nile* (1961) by 'Atif Salim and, above all, the unlucky nineteenth-century belly dancer in *Shafiqa al-Qibtiyya / Shafiqa the Copt* (1963) by Hasan al-Imam. Her most unconventional roles were the cheerful soft-drink seller Hanuma whom a maniac threatens to stab in Youssef Chahine's *Bab al-Hadid / Cairo Main Station* (1958) and the attractive lady stuck in an elevator in Salah Abu Seif's *Bayn al-Sama' Wa-l-Ard / Between Sky and Earth* (1959).

Sarhan, Shukri (b. 1924)

Sarhan was one of the first graduates of the Higher Theatre Institute. In spite of a successful mainstream career as an actor, his image was bound to a certain extent to the first wave of Egyptian realism. He was introduced to the screen by Youssef Chahine in *Ibn al-Nil / Son of the Nile* (1951), in which he plays a young peasant who leaves home and family for the town only to be lured into immorality. He played a similar role in *Shabab Imra'a / Youth of a Woman* (1956) by Salah Abu Seif. Close to these weak characters was the persona of the criminal-despite-himself, as in *Ihna al-Talamdha / We Pupils* (1959) by 'Atif Salim and, first and foremost, *al-Liss Wa-l-Kilab / The Thief and the Dogs* (1962) by Kamal El-Cheikh. Some of his most complex and at times ambiguous characters were the lonely rural postman in Husain Kamal's *al-Bustaji / The Postman* (1968), the idealistic doctor in *Sira' al-Abtal / Struggle of the Heroes* (1962) and the leader of a failed rebellion in *al-Mutamarridun / The Rebels* (1966), both of the latter directed by Taufiq Salih.

Shadia (b. 1931, Cairo)

A singer and actress in 110 films, Shadia's real name was Fatima Ahmad Kamal. She was not only gifted with a beautiful voice, but also a charming and friendly appearance. Shadia first starred in *al-'Aql Fi Ajaza / The Mind on Vacation* (1947) by Hilmi Rafla, who discovered Shadia when she was dubbing songs for another actress. Shadia played an innocent young girl in love in *Qatr al-Nada / Dew Train* (1951) by Anwar Wagdi. During the 1960s her characters gained more complexity. She starred in many light comedies, among others *Karamat Zawjatti / My Wife's Honour* (1967) by Fatin 'Abd al-Wahhab and *'Afrit Mirati / My Wife's Ghost* (1968) by Ahmad Dia' al-Din. Her most acclaimed films were *al-Zawja Raqam 13 / Wife No. 13* (1962) and *Mirati Mudir 'Am / My Wife is a General Director* (1966), both by 'Abd al-Wahhab, through which she created the image of a beautiful and tender yet clever woman, more than able to be a powerful opponent for her male partners. At the same time she was able to star in melodramatic and even realist roles, such as in the tear-jerking *al-Mar'a al-Majhula / The Unknown Woman* (1959) by Mahmud zu-l-Fiqar, or convincingly playing the role of a kindhearted prostitute in the realist *al-Liss Wa-l-Kilab / The Thief and the Dogs* (1962) or a servant in the political film *Miramar* (1968), both by Kamal El-Cheikh. Her last film was *La Tas'alni Man Ana / Don't Ask Me Who I Am* (1984) by Ashraf Fahmi. In 1987 Shadia stopped performing in public and veiled herself.

al-Sharif, Nur (b. 1946)

Graduating from the Higher Theatre Institute in 1967, al-Sharif started his career immediately with films like Sa'id Marzuq's *Zawjati Wa-l-Kalb / My Wife and the Dog* (1971) and *al-Khawf / Fear* (1972). One of his first remarkable roles was that of a young student opposed to the authorities in *al-Karnak* (1975) by 'Ali Badrakhan. The role of the outraged young working-class 'man in blue jeans', either righteous or crooked, became part of his persona throughout the 1980s: he starred in some extraordinary films like *Ahl al-Qimma / People from the Top* (1981) by 'Ali Badrakahn, *Sawaq al-Utubis / The Bus-Driver* (1983) by Atef El-Tayeb and *al-Sa'alik / The Vagabonds* (1983) by Daoud Abd El-Sayed, through which his image became bound to New Realism. Even in the 1990s he continued to represent underdogs, as in El-Tayeb's road movie *Layla Sakhina / A Hot Night* (1994), yet he was also able to embody the unscrupulous businessman, for instance in *Zamman Hatim Zahran / Hatim Zahran's Times* (1988) by Muhammad Naggar. His most unconventional roles were as a tormented director representing Youssef Chahine's *alter ego* in *Haduta Misriyya / An Egyptian Fairy-Tale* (1982), as an average employee caught in a traumatic nocturnal odyssey in Daoud Abd El-Sayed's *al-Bahth 'An Sayyid Marzuq / The Search for Sayyid Marzuq* (1991) and, last but not least, as the philosopher Ibn Rushd (Averroës) in Chahine's historical *al-Masir / The Destiny* (1997).

Sharif, Omar ('Umar) (b. 1932, Alexandria)

Sharif's real name was Michel Shalhub. His first acting role (already a main part) was offered to him by Youssef Chahine for *Sira' Fi-l-Wadi / Mortal Revenge* (1954), which co-starred Fatin Hamama who became Sharif's wife after the shooting. With his large expressive eyes and an overall handsome appearance he convinced more through his appearance than by his acting, and seemed the perfect manifestation of adolescent girls' dreams. He subsequently starred as a deprived lover in *Nahr al-Hubb / Stream of Love* (1960) by 'Izz al-Din zu-l-Fiqar and as a duped husband in *Fadiha Fi-l-Zamalik / A Scandal in Zamalek* (1959) by Niazi Mustafa. In fact, Sharif played numerous different personae, ranging from the couragous *ibn balad* (ordinary Egyptian) to the patriot and resistance fighter, as in Chahine's *Sira' Fi-l-Mina / Struggle in the Harbour* (1956), El-Cheikh's *Ard al-Salam / Land of Peace* (1957) and Barakat's *Fi Baytinna Rajul / A Man in Our House* (1961). He also enacted the morally confused young men in *Sayyidat al-Qasr / Lady of the Palace* (1958) by Kamal El-Cheikh and *Ihna al-Talamdha / We Pupils* (1959) by 'Atif Salim, and the egocentric *arriviste* in *Bidaya Wa Nihaya / Beginning and End* (1960) by Salah Abu Seif. One of his few comic roles was playing a clumsy young lover in Fatin 'Abd al-Wahhab's farce *Isha'it Hubb / Love Rumour* (1960). Sharif is the only Egyptian actor who made a real international career, first starring in the French orientalist film *Goha* (1958) by Jacques Baratier, then in *Lawrence of Arabia* (1962) and *Doctor Zhivago* (1965) by David Lean. The latter laid the foundations of his international reputation. In the following two decades he performed in numerous American and European productions. After his return to Egypt in the late 1980s he revived his Egyptian career with a few mediocre films: *al-Arajuz / The Puppeteer* (literally *Karagöz*, 1989) by Hani Lashin and *al-Muwatin Misri / The Citizen Misri* (1991) by Salah Abu Seif, among others.

Shawqi, Farid (b. 1925; d. 1998)

The most prolific actor of Egyptian cinema, Shawqi appeared in a total of 293 films, as well as producing twenty-six. He graduated from the Theatre Institute in 1946 and appeared in the same year in Yusuf Wahbi's *Malak al-Rahma / Angel of Mercy*. During the first decades of his work he was mainly asked to perform roles as malicious gangsters, drug dealers, smugglers or violent racketeers, largely because of his heavy build and coarse-looking face. As a supporting actor he often played the role of the hero's vicious opponent, as in *Sira' Fi-l-Wadi / Mortal Revenge* (1954) by Youssef Chahine or the historical *Wa Islamah / Oh Islam!* (1961) by Andrew Marton. He starred in many gangster films, such as *Tujjar al-Mawt / Death Traders* (1957) by Kamal El-Cheikh and *Abu Hadid* (1958) by Niazi Mustafa. His impressive appearance also made him ideal for enacting the role of the warrior, as in *al-Saqr / The Hawk* (1950) by Salah Abu Seif and Niazi Mustafa's *'Antar Ibn Shaddad* (1961). Shawqi starred in the majority of the thug films. He was introduced to this genre in the highly acclaimed *al-Futuwa / The Thug* (1957) by Abu Seif, in which Shawqi mutates from a naïve peasant to a sly monopolist. This is one of his best-remembered roles. In realist-oriented films he was made to play workers, as in *al-Usta Hasan / Master Hasan* (1952) again by Abu Seif or Chahine's *Bab al-Hadid / Cairo Main Station* (1958). One of his unique and complex roles was the tender older brother, morally committed in spite of himself, in Abu Seif's *Bidaya Wa Nihaya / Beginning and End* (1960). Since the late 1970s he has increasingly been given father roles, as in Samir Saif's *Qitta 'Ala Nar / Cat on Fire* (1977), or parts playing elderly, possessive and even aggressive husbands, for instance in *Ta'ir 'Ala al-Tariq / A Bird on the Road* (1981) by Mohamed Khan and *'Uyun La Tanam / Eyes Which Do Not Sleep* (1981) by Ra'fat al-Mihi.

al-Shinawi, Kamal (b. 1925)

Having acted in some 150 films, al-Shinawi is still active today. He first appeared in Niazi Mustafa's *Ghanni Harb / Nouveau Riche* (1947). At the beginning he was type-cast and confined to the role of the young sympathetic beau who falls in love. Even in the stylistically innovative *al-Mustahil / The Impossible* (1965) by Husain Kamal, he represented a bourgeois academic who falls in love with a neighbour's wife. Al-Shinawi, who was rarely seen in a working-class role, did however succeed in now and then breaking away from his traditional persona: he played an evil gangster in *al-Mar'a al-Majhula / The Unknown Woman* (1959) by Mahmud zu-l-Fiqar and an opportunistic journalist in *al-Rajul Aladhi Faqad Zilah / The Man Who Lost His Shadow* (1968) by Kamal El-Cheikh. With increasing age he was not given main parts any more, but instead played some extraordinary secondary roles – such as the leftist uncle in Khairy Beshara's *al-'Awama Raqam 70 / Houseboat No. 70* (1982) and the extremely serious and concerned (though helpless) minister of the interior in *al-Irhab Wa-l-Kabab / Terrorism and Kebabs* (1992) by Sherif 'Arafa.

Umm Kulthum (b. 1904; d. 1974)

Both singer and actress, Umm Kulthum appeared in six movies. Called the *kawkab al-sharq* ('Star of the Orient') or on a more local and popular level *al-sitt* ('the mistress'), she is considered the most extraordinary and popular Egyptian vocal interpreter of the twentieth century and was also adored in many other Arab countries. In 1936 she was persuaded by Tal'at Harb to appear in the first Studio Misr production, *Widad* (1936), by Fritz Kramp. Four of her following melodramatic films were directed by Ahmad Badrakhan: *Nashid al-Amal / Song of Hope* (1937), *Dananir* (1940), *'Aida* (1942), a slightly unsuccessful attempt to modernize the opera, and *Fatima* (1947). Probably her best film is *Sallama* (1945) by Togo Mizrahi, in which she appeared (as she did in *Widad* and *Dananir*) as a faithful and talented slave. Umm Kulthum was a less than gifted actress and suffered, just like 'Abd al-Wahhab, from weak eyesight; she did not pursue her cinematic career further, which did not affect her musical fame.

Yusra (b. 1955)

Yusra was introduced to the screen by 'Abd al-Halim Nasr in his film *Qasr Fi-l-Hawa'/ A Palace in the Air* (1975) and became the best actress of modern times. Her earlier delicate build and elegant aura enabled her in the beginning to fit into the role of academic or middle-class women. Since the 1980s she has presented a variety of female characters, ranging from queens to workers, from doctors to prostitutes. She was one of Youssef Chahine's preferred actresses, appearing in *Haduta Misriyya / An Egyptian Fairy-Tale* (1982) as his *alter ego*'s wife, and continued performing for him in the role of a student in *Iskandariyya Kaman Wa Kaman / Alexandria Now and Forever*

Figure 24 al-Ard / The Earth

(1989) and as an ancient Egyptian queen in *al-Muhajir / The Emigrant* (1994). Her most complex and touching roles were in *Al-Sa'alik / The Vagabonds* (1983), by Daoud Abd El-Sayed, as the poor tea-vendor who falls in love with her husband's best friend and in *Mercedes* (1993), by Yousri Nasrallah, as both the unscrupulous mother and inhibited girlfriend of the film's main protagonist – she played these two different characters at once. During the 1990s, having gained some weight, Yusra became the partner of the comedian 'Adil Imam in, among other films, *Jazirat al-Shaytan / Devil's Island* (1990), *Risala Illa al-Wali / Message to the Ruler* (1997) by Nadir Galal and, above all, in Sherif 'Arafa's *al-Irhab Wa-l-Kabab / Terrorism and Kebabs* (1992), in which she presented one of her most hilarious roles as a clever prostitute who becomes the ally of a putative terrorist.

Zaki, Ahmad (b. 1949)

Zaki graduated from the Higher Theatre Institute in 1973 and made his first appearance one year later. He is considered one of the best actors of his generation, although his dark complexion is usually not considered favourable for actors. Nonetheless Zaki became one of the so-called 'heroes in blue jeans' that were closely linked to New Realism: he knew how to give his deprived characters emotional and psychological credibility without any exaggeration. His roles as a young economically and emotionally deprived car mechanic in *'Uyun La Tanam / Eyes Which Do Not Sleep* (1981) and as a lonely taxi driver who falls in love with someone else's wife in *Ta'ir 'Ala al-Tariq / A Bird on the Road* (1981) set the tone for his early persona. The working-class underdog in confrontation with society remained his trademark in *Hubb Fawq Hadabit al-Harram / Love at the Pyramids* (1986) by Atef El-Tayeb, *Ahlam Hind Wa Kamilyya / Dreams of Hind and Camelia* (1988) by Mohammed Khan or the more

Figure 25 Ahmad Zaki

recent *Idhak al-Sura Titla' Hilwa / Smile, Please!* (1998) by Sherif 'Arafa, as well as in the two musicals *Kaburya / Crabs* (1990) by Khairy Beshara and *Mister Karate* (1993) by Mohamed Khan. Some of Zaki's most stunning achievements were, apart from these examples, the performance of a naïve and uneducated soldier, victim of a merciless political system, in El-Tayeb's *al-Bari' / The Innocent* (1986) and, the exact opposite character, the complex personality of a fascist officer in *Zawjat Rajul Muhimm / Wife of an Important Man* (1988) by Khan. Zaki also worked in more mainstream films, representing employees, lawyers, gangsters and policemen – a highlight being the television production *Nasir 56* (1994) by Muhammad Fadil, in which he played the former Egyptian national leader Nasser.

Acknowledgements

Many thanks to Oliver Leaman for contributing Youssef Chahine's biography and to Magdi 'Abd al-Rahman for providing film lengths and titles of the Higher Film Institute's graduation projects.

References and further reading

'Abd al-Rahman, M. (1996a) 'Film Layla al-badawiyya', *al-mihrajan al-qawmi al-thani li-l-sinima al-misriyya*, Cairo: Sunduq al-tanmiyya al-thaqafiyya, pp. 17–38.

——— (1996b) 'Qamus al-mukhrijat al-sinima'iyyat al-misriyyat', *al-mihrajan al-qawmi al-thani li-l-sinima al-misriyya*, Cairo: Sunduq al-tanmiyya al-thaqafiyya, pp. 45–57.

'Abd al-Rahman, M., Mar'i, S. and Shukri, G. (eds) (1994) 'Shadi 'Abd al-Salam … shu'a' min Misr', special issue, *al-Qahira* 145 (December).

Abu-Lughod, L. (1995) 'Movie Stars and Islamic Moralism in Egypt', *Social Text* 42 (spring): 53–67.

Abu Shadi, A. (1997) *Kamal al-Shinawi: shams la taghib*, Cairo: Cultural Development Fund.

Acrame, E. (1978) 'Denationaliser le cinéma', *Les 2 écrans* 7: 37–42.

Arasoughly, A. (ed.) (1996) *Screens of Life: Critical Film Writing from the Arab World*, St Hyacinthe: World Heritage Press.

al-'Ariss, I. (1979) *rihla fi-l-sinima al-'arabiyya*, Beirut.

al-'Ariss, I., Berrah, M., Cluny, C.-M., Lévy, J. and Thoraval, Y. (1987) 'Dictionnaire de 80 cinéastes arabes', in M. Berrah (ed.) *Les cinémas Arabes et Grand Maghreb*, CinémAction 43, Paris; 172–185.

Armbrust, W. (1996) *Mass Culture and Modernism in Egypt*, Cambridge: Cambridge University Press.

Armes, R. (1987a) *Third World Film-Making and the West*, Berkeley: University of California Press.

——— (1987b) 'Youssef Chahine', *Third World Film-Making and the West*, Berkeley: University of California Press, pp. 243–54.

Aswad, F. (1993) *Kamal al-Shinawi: al-fatta al-dhahabi fi-l-sinima al-misriyya*, Cairo: Mihrajan al-Qahira al-sinima'i al-dawli.

al-Bandari, M., Qasim, M. and Wahbi, Y. (1994) *mawsu'at al-aflam al-'arabiyya*, Cairo: Bait al-ma'rifa.

Bayumi, H. (1994) *Farid Shawqi*, Cairo: 18th International Cairo Film Festival.

Bergmann, K. (1993) *Filmkultur und Filmindustrie in Ägypten*, Darmstadt: Wissenschaftliche Buchgesellschaft.

Bernard, M.-C. (ed.) (1989) *Le Caire et le cinéma égyptien des années 80*, Cairo: CEDEJ.

Berrah, M., Lévy, J. and Cluny, C.-M. (eds) (1987) *Les cinémas Arabes et Grand Maghreb*, CinémAction 43, Paris: CERF / Institut du Monde Arabe.

Bosseno, C. (ed.) (1985) *Youssef Chahine l'Alexandrin*, Paris: CinémAction.

Chahine, Y. (1971) 'D'où vient et où va Youssef Chahine' (interview with G. Hennebelle), *L'Afrique litteraire et artistique*, 15 (February): 72–84.

Cluny, C.-M. (1978) *Dictionnaire des nouveaux cinémas arabes*, Paris: Sindbad, esp. pp. 161–72 (article on Chahine).

Darwish, M. (1998) , *Dream Makers on the Nile*, Cairo: AUC Press.

Dawud, A. (1997) *Min ajindat al-sinima al-misriyya: al-rahilun fi mi'at sana*, Cairo: al-markaz al-qawmi li-l-sinima.

El-Sabban, R. (1992) *Tribute to Layla Mourad*, Cairo: 16th Cairo International Film Festival.

Elsaesser, T. (1985) 'Tales of Sound and Fury: Observations on Family Melodrama', in B. Nichols (ed.) *Movies and Methods: An Anthology*, vol. 2, Berkeley and London: University of California Press.

Farid, S. (1973) 'nahw manhaj 'ilmi li-kitabat tarikhuna al-sinima'i', *al-tali'a* 3: 149–65.

——— (1984) 'surat al-mar'a fi-l-sinima al-'arabiyya', *al-hayat al-sinima'iyya* 21 (spring): 4–15.

——— (1987a) *al-binyya al-asassiyya li-l-sinima fi Misr*, unpublished study for the 5th Damascus Film Festival.

——— (1987b) 'al-fidiyu', *sinima* 84–86.

——— (1992) *Adwa' 'ala sinima Yusuf Shahin*, Cairo: al-Hay'a al-misriyya al-'ama li-l-kitab.

——— (ed.) (1994) 'tarikh al-sinima al-'arabiyya al-samitta', *al-ittihad al-'am li-l-fananin al-'arab*.

——— (ed.) (1998) *Farid Shawqi. akhir muluk Misr*, Cairo: al-hay'a al-'ama li-qusur al-thaqafa.

Gaffney, J. (1987) 'The Egyptian Cinema: Industry and Art in a Changing Society', *Arab Studies Quaterly* 9 (1): 53–75.

al-Hadari, A. (1989) *tarikh al-sinima fi Misr*, Cairo: Nadi al-Sinima bi-l-Qahira.

al-Hadidi, M. (ed.) (1983) *al-sinima al-tasjiliyya al-watha'iqqiyya fi Misr wa-l-'alam al-'arabi*, Cairo: dar al-fikr al-'arabi.

Hasan, I. and Tal'at Harb, M. (1986) *ra'id sina'at al-sinima al-misriyya*, Cairo: al-hay'a al-misriyya al-'ama li-l-kitab.

Hasanain, L. (1993) *Layla Murad* Cairo: Amadu.

Jonassaint, J. (ed.) (1984) 'Chahine et le cinéma égyptien', special issue, *Dérives* 43.

Khayati, K. (1990) *Salah Abou Seif Cinéaste Egyptien*, Cairo: Sindbad.

Landau, J. (1958) *Studies in the Arab Theater and Cinema*, Philadelphia: University of Pennsylvania Press.

Lashin, H. (1994) *Shadia*, Cairo: 18th International Cairo Film Festival.

Lüders, M. (1986) *Film und Kino in Ägypten. Eine historische Bestandsaufnahme 1896–1952*, unpublished M.A. thesis, Freie Universität Berlin.

—— (1989) *Gesellschaftliche Realität im ägyptischen Kinofilm. Von Nasser zu Sadat (1952–1981)*, Frankfurt am Main: Peter Lang.

Malkmus, L. and Armes, R. (1991) *Arab & African Film-Making*, London : Zed.

Mursi, S. (1995) 'Layla Murad', special issue, *Dar al-Hilal* 54 (December).

al-Nahas, H. (1975) *Nagib Mahfuz 'ala al-shasha*, Cairo: al-hay'a al-misriyya al-'ama li-l-kitab.

—— (1990) *mustaqbal al-sinima al-tasjiliyya fi Misr*, Cairo: al-Markaz al-Qawmi li-l-sinima.

Rakha, Y. (1999) 'Dancing to the Rhythm of Time', *al-Ahram Weekly* 23–9 September.

Ramzi, K. (1992) *Amina Rizq*, Cairo: Cultural Development Fund.

—— (1994) 'Les sources littéraires dans le cinéma égyptien', in M. Wassef (ed.) *2e Biennale des cinémas arabes à Paris*, Paris: Institut du Monde Arabe, pp. 111–20.

Richter, E. (1974) *Realistischer Film in Ägypten*, Berlin: Henschel Verlag.

Rizkallah, Y. (1995) 'Répertoire des réalisateurs', in M. Wassef (ed.) *Egypte. 100 ans de cinéma*, Paris: Institut du Monde Arabe, pp. 250–83.

Sa'd, 'A.al-M. (1975) *al-mukhrij Ahmad Badr Khan*, Cairo: al-hay'a al-misriyya al-'ama li-l-kitab.

Sadoul, G. (1966) *The Cinema in the Arab Countries*, Beirut: Interarab Centre of Cinema & Television.

al-Sayyid Shusha, M. (1978) *Ruwad wa ra'idat al-sinima al-misriyya fi-l-yubil al-dhahabi 1927–1977*, Cairo.

Shafik, V. (1988) *Realität und Film im Ägypten der 80er Jahre*, unpublished M.A. thesis, Universität Hamburg.

—— (1989) *Youssef Chahine*, Kinemathek 74, Berlin: Freunde der Deutschen Kinemathek.

—— (1990) 'In the Shadow of Culture Industry: The Egyptian Short Film', *Internationale Westdeutsche Kurzfilmtage* 36 (19–25 April): 116–24.

—— (1998a) *Arab Cinema. History and Cultural Identity*, Cairo: AUC Press.

—— (1998b) 'Variety or Unity? Minorities in Egyptian Cinema', *Orient* 4 (December): 627–48.

—— (2000) 'Der Zweck heiligt die Mittel: Stars, Genre und Publikum in Ägypten', in I. Schenk (ed.) *Erlebnisort Kino*, Marburg: Schüren, pp. 200–13.

al-Sharqawi, G. (1970) *risala fi tarikh al-sinima al-'arabiyya*, Cairo: al-hay'a al-misriyya al-'ama lil-kitab.

Thoraval, Y. (1975) *Regards sur le cinéma égyptien*, Beirut: Dar El-Machreq Editeurs.

Wassef, M. (ed.) (1995) *Egypte. 100 ans de cinéma*, Paris: Institut du Monde Arabe.

Wassef, M. and Marei, S. (eds) (1996) *Chadi Abdel Salam. Le Pharaon du cinéma égytpien*, Paris: Institut du Monde Arabe.

Wifi, M. (1999) *Sinima Taufiq Salih*, Cairo: Cultural Development Fund.

Yusuf, A. and al-Abnudi, A. (1999) Attiyat al-Abnudi: *wasf Misr bayn al-waqi' wa-l-hilm*, Cairo: Cultural Development Fund.

Zuhur, S. (ed.) (1998) *Images of Enchantment*, Cairo: AUC Press.

Iranian cinema

Hamid Naficy

Beginning at the start of the twentieth century, Iranian cinema is one of the oldest and most prolific in the Middle East and the Third World. Because of its long and tumultuous history, this analysis is divided into three main historical periods, each with its own industrial, socio-political and textual practices.

Qajar Era cinema (1900–25)

Thanks to the travel diary of Muzaffared-Din Shah Qajar to Europe, the circumstances of the first Iranian non-fiction footage can be pinpointed with rare accuracy. The date is 18 August 1900; the location is the city of Ostend, Belgium; the occasion is Muzaffared-Din Shah's review of a 'flower parade', during which some fifty floats laden with women pass by the Shah – they are throwing bouquets of flowers at him which he joyously returns; the cinematographer is Mirza Ebrahim Khan Akkasbashi, the official court photographer (Qajar 1982: 160), and the camera he uses is a Gaumont which he had purchased on order of the Shah a few weeks earlier in Paris (Omid 1984: 42). He also filmed other scenes of the Shah: in a carriage, on a train and in a park. On his return to Iran with the Shah, Akkasbashi filmed various religious ceremonies and processions, as well as royal court actualities and performances staged for the camera. These films were thought lost, but in the 1980s some of the footage shot by Akkasbashi and other early photographers (including apparently Muzaffared-Din Shah himself) were discovered in the Golestan Palace in Tehran and compiled into a film by Mohsen Makhmalbaf, entitled *Gozideh-ye Tasavir-e Doran-e Qajar / Selected Images of the Qajar Era* (1992). Among the actualities which the film contained are Muzaffared-Din Shah on a hunt in the hills, the Shah with his entourage practising firing a gun and looking through a telescope, riders on donkeys fighting with sticks, riders exiting a Tehran city gate, a tram entering the station, and women veiled in black chador and white face-veil walking by in slow motion and getting on the tram. The performance films included two seated dwarves clowning around and several people beating up a man dressed in Arab garb. About a dozen of these were shot by Akkasbashi (Rahimian 1993: 102, Mehrabi 1996: 7–8).

Textually, these films followed the style of Western actualities and early performance films. They were short, each lasting less than thirty seconds. They were shot with a stationary camera that did not pan or tilt. Some of the subjects were filmed from middle distance, but the majority were filmed from afar. Each film was a single shot. Although there is no evidence of any intentional editing, there is at least one place where an apparently in-camera edit occurs.[1]

During the 1900s, these films (along with French and Russian newsreels) were shown in the royal court and in the homes of the elite during wedding, birth and circumcision ceremonies (Gaffary 1991: 567). To accommodate the rules governing Muslim gender segregation, they were usually screened twice: once for the men alone and a second time for the women alone (Omid 1995: 22). With Akkasbashi's film production and exhibition practice, the model for a private, state-sponsored cinema was created, one that differed from the public commercial cinema model dominant in Europe and North America.

An important consideration in the historiography of cinemas of the Third World is the manner in which class, family relations, court connections, religious and ethnic affiliation, national origin and foreign education of the early pioneers helped to create what Michel Foucault called 'dispositions, maneuvers, tactics, techniques, functionings … a network of relations, constantly in tension, in activity, rather than a privilege that one might possess … ' (Foucault 1979: 26) that overdetermined the emergence of such Western imports as film and cinema (Naficy 2000). Professionally, the majority of the Iranian pioneer cameramen / projectionists were educated in Russia or France. Several of them were from Iranian ethno-religious minorities (Baha'i, Jew and Armenian), were immigrants themselves or were of mixed nationality. Ideologically, they were secular and desired Western-style modernization. In terms of political and class affiliation, the majority were middle class and several were attached to the Qajar court either by marriage or by sponsorship. While their background reveals great diversity in ethnicity, national origin, religious association and politics, they all seemed to have shared the desire for professional training, higher class affiliation and Westernized reforms.

Akkasbashi, for example, was both well-connected and well-educated. His father was Naser-al-Din Shah's chief photographer and he was a freemason who had converted to Baha'ism. Both freemasons and Baha'is were generally pro-Western reformers and were regarded with suspicion by most Muslims. Like his father, Akkasbashi was appointed the court photographer, serving Muzaffared-Din Shah. His integration into the court was solidified when he married into the royal family (Gaffary 1985: 719). In addition to these familial and royal connections, Akkasbashi was part of an emerging crop of foreign educated intelligentsia who favoured Western-style reforms. He had spent some ten years of his life, from the age of fourteen onwards, with his father in Europe, where he had studied photography and engraving (Zoka 1997: 113–16).

Probably the first public cinema in Iran was the non-commercial Cinéma Soleil (Sun), set up in 1900 by Roman Catholic missionaries in the city of Tabriz (Malekpur 1984: 61). Its manager was an Armenian named Alek Sakinian, who worked for the telegraph office and whose nephew was a member of the parliament. Cinéma Soleil was apparently highly popular with reformists and young people, and since seating was limited, the manager would periodically have to close the doors early, causing commotion among those who could not get in (Zoka 1997: 111). As in the case of Akkasbashi, religiosity (in this case, Christianity), ethnicity (Armenian), foreign connection (with the French) and class affiliation (with the upper classes) provided a rhizomatic web of connections that facilitated the introduction of this first public cinema. There is no information as to what Cinéma Soleil showed.

The overdetermination of cinema in such varied social strata did not ensure its monolithic institutionalization, however; for the same sociopolitical factors that favoured cinema also caused tension and haggling in the discourses and practices of cinema. As long as it was a largely private enterprise, cinema was protected. The moment it went public, however, the full force of these and larger socio-political conflicts were unleashed upon it. The religious traditionalists regarded cinema with suspicion and rejected it for corrupting traditional values and eroding their monopoly on shaping the minds of the people, while the secular elite generally regarded it as a sign of progress and modernity to be embraced. This debate would haunt the Iranian cinema throughout its existence, both off and on the screen.

It was Ebrahim Khan Sahhafbashi-e Tehrani, an entrepreneurial businessman and an antique dealer, who first created the model of a public commercial cinema, although his efforts were short-lived. He was a constitutionalist who favoured parliamentary monarchy over the Qajar despotic monarchy. He had seen film for the first time in 1897 in the Palace Theatre in London. Initially, he began showing films (which he had purchased in Europe) in the backyard of his shop and, later (in November–December 1904) he opened the first public commercial cinema in Tehran on Cheragh Gaz Street. However, his cinema, begun during the holy month of Ramadan when piety takes precedence over pleasure, was shut down after only one month, due either to religious proscription by the powerful Shiʻi leader Shaikh Fazlolah Nuri or to royal displeasure with Sahhafbashi's pro-constitution activities. By 1906, the pro-constitution movement, manned by a coalition of secular reformists, bazaar merchants and enlightened clergies, had become a full-fledged revolution, which ushered in a parliamentary monarchy. This Constitutional Revolution (1906–11) and the later Islamic Revolution (1979–80) bracket the tumultuous history both of Iran and of Iranian cinema in the twentieth century.

Another early exhibitor, Mehdi Rusi Khan, had a mixed English and Russian background and was also an ardent supporter of the reactionary Mohammad Ali Shah Qajar, who defied the new constitution by bombing the parliament. Rusi Khan showed Pathé newsreels and comedies, first in the Shah's harem and in the homes of the notables and, beginning in 1908, on a regular basis in two public cinemas in Tehran. However, his theatre and photography shop were both ransacked in 1909 when his sponsor, the Shah, was forced into European exile, where Rusi Khan soon joined him. Another silent-era pioneer was Khan Baba Moʻtazedi who was trained at the Gaumont cinematographic factory in Paris. In 1916 he established the first public cinema for women in Iran (called Cinema Korshid, also meaning 'sun') and made principally newsreel films that were screened in public theatres before feature films.

Factors that hampered the emergence of a coherent and robust local film industry during this period included the persistence of the private, non-commercial model, a lack of necessary economic and technical infrastructures (such as bank loans, film labs, acting and technical schools, and supportive regulations), and the general social conditions and cultural attitudes about cinema. This latter included not only the aforementioned socio-political factors related to the film pioneers themselves but also these additional factors which affected cinema spectatorship: a high rate of illiteracy, a belief that film viewing would lead to moral corruption and the religious taboos against cinema-going and acting, especially for women. Calls for strict censorship of imports were not uncommon.

In 1925, the parliament dissolved the Qajar dynasty, replacing it with the Pahlavi dynasty, which was headed by an illiterate but forceful and pro-modernization officer named Reza Shah Pahlavi. During the Qajar era, no feature-length fiction films had been produced. The first such film, *Abi Va Rabi / Abi and Rabi* was directed in 1930 by Avanes Ohanian, an Armenian-Iranian, and it was filmed by Mo'tazedi. This silent black-and-white comedy depicted the adventures of two men, one tall and one short. No copy of it exists. Ohanian's next work, *Haji Aqa, Aktor-e Sinema / Haji the Movie Actor* (1932), is a technically sophisticated and delightful film which, in a self-reflective manner, deals head-on with the moral corruption charge against cinema. In it, a traditional religious man (Haji) is transformed from one who hates cinema to one who proclaims its values in improving the lot of Iranians. A defensive reviewer in the daily *Ettela'at* commented that the film had 'many shortcomings. It was dark, the faces were dark and, from a technical standpoint, the film was not satisfactory' (Tahaminezhad n.d.: 116). Apparently, he did not consider it sufficiently important to comment on the fact that the film for the first time had set up a conflict between religious tradition and modernity – a conflict that would intensify in the Pahlavi period, both in society and on the screen.

Pahlavi Era cinema (1926–78)

The early sound period's fiction films (1930s–50s)

Iranian cinema not only benefited from the inter-ethnicity, migration and Western education of the film-makers, but also from transnational interchanges between Iran and its neighbouring countries. The first Persian-language sound feature, *Dokhtar-e Lor / The Lor Girl* (1933) was directed in India by Ardeshir Irani and written by the Iranian expatriate poet Abdolhosain Sepenta. The film, a melodramatic love story that also extolled Iranian nationalism and modernization under Reza Shah, was highly successful with Iranians, causing Sepenta to make for export a succession of talking pictures based on Iranian folktales and epics. He wrote, directed and acted in a number of them.

Reza Shah established an authoritarian rule that centralized all meaningful powers in the hands of the Shah and his bureaucracy. This entailed consolidation not only of military and repressive means but also of ideological apparatuses. An interesting example of consolidation in the ideological realm is the formation of the Intellectual Development Organization (*Sazman-e Parvaresh-e Afkar*), which operated a nation-wide network of cultural activities between 1938 and Reza Shah's abdication in 1941 (in favour of his son, Mohammad Reza). The primary aim of IDO was to inculcate Reza Shah's ideology which included Iranian nationalism (the origin of which was located in pre-Islamic times), devotion to the country and to the Shah (*mihanparasti va shahparasti*), and Westernization, including unveiling of women. To carry out these aims, IDO established six commissions, with branches in major cities, concerned with organizing conferences, developing radio programming and audiences, preparing school and general interest textbooks, teaching drama and performing plays, organizing orchestras and musical performances, and improving the production and editing of a pro-government press. The budget for these diverse activities came from the Education Ministry, local municipalities, physical education societies, contributions from the private industry (textile factories in Isfahan province, for example), and a 2 per cent tax on movie theatre tickets. Although there was no separate cinema commission, IDO's activities intersected with cinema at several points, helping to integrate film with the other arts. The movie theatres helped support the organization financially through the box-office tax. In towns where there were no modern auditoriums, movie theatres were used to stage the IDO events. The IDO constitution considered film as one of the apparatuses of 'intellectual development' (Delfani 1996: 1) and IDO chapters resorted to films, plays and musical performances to spice up otherwise dull lectures, some of which failed to attract non-coerced audiences (government officials strongly urged the civil servants not only to attend these events themselves but also to take along their wives without the veil). Finally, IDO activities created a network of relations and dispositions among academics, writers, musicians, dramatists, film-makers and radio producers – members of the various commissions – who favoured cinema.

World War II brought a halt to local film production, but it did not stop the flow of foreign films. The *Annual Survey of Motion Pictures* conducted by the United States Department of Commerce for the year 1941 categorically stated that 'Iran has no film production' (United States Department of Commerce 1941: 6,212). Indeed, the local film industry at the time was limited to the commercial exhibition of foreign films, primarily from the United States and Europe. According to the Department of Commerce report, about 250 feature films were sufficient to supply the Iranian market for one year. United States productions provided 60 per cent of the films shown in that market, Germany provided 20 per cent, and France and Russia provided 5 per cent each (op. cit.). However, an authoritarian and moralistic government heavily censored these films. In 1940, for example, nearly 253 films were censored, 159 of which came from the United States, 32 from Germany, 31 from France and 19 from England. The government censored films showing revolutions, riots and internal disorder, as well as indecency, pacifism and anti-Islamic attitudes (Naficy 1979: 450). Over a decade later, despite censorship, American fiction films continued to dominate the screens, although (according to the weekly *Variety*) 'Russian pictures were muscling in' in 1952. Referring to the nationalistic, anti-British movement in Iran, the paper noted that 'naturally, British films are not so popular any more, but German and French films are getting a foothold in the country' (*Variety*, 29 October 1952: n.p.).

The 'absolute quiet' that had reigned over the local industry for over a decade was broken by Esmail Kushan, who, working in Turkey, had helped dub several foreign films (Russian and French) into Persian. The successful distribution of these films encouraged Kushan to embark on making the first sound feature inside Iran. To accomplish that, he established Mitra Film Company in 1948 and within a period of three years, in spite of technical problems, produced four films. His first film, *Tufan-e Zendegi / The Tempest of Life* (1948), directed by Mohammed Ali Daryabeigi, was not very well received by audiences who were still unaccustomed to Persian talkies and to their low quality. However his second film, *Zendani-e Amir / Prisoner of the Emir* (1949), was of higher quality and more successful, as were the films that followed. In its review of *Zendani-e Amir*, while conceding that the film suffered from technical flaws, a United States government report stated that 'considerable improvement … had been made in sound, lighting, photography and direction, and the story and acting are superior' (United States Department of Commerce 1949: n.p.). Kushan, whom French historian Georges Sadoul named 'the father of the Iranian film industry' (Sadoul 1949: 485), soon established another more extensive film company called Parsfilm Studio, which continued to make popular formula features for the local market, surviving the revolution of 1978–9.

His success caused a swift change in the film industry. Many new film production companies were formed and numerous films were produced. The great majority of these films, however, were patterned on the model of silent-film genres – that is, melodramas, situation comedies and adventure films. A quick survey of about 290 Iranian feature films produced between 1938 and 1965, which I conducted, showed that nearly 52 per cent were categorized as drama or melodrama by film producers themselves, approximately 28 per cent were listed as comedies and 12 per cent were labelled adventure / crime films. Strict censorship (which applied to locally made films as well) combined with competition from foreign imports and the prevailing social and economic conditions (outlined earlier) were partly responsible for driving Iranian filmmakers to make low-quality, formulaic and escapist material.

Institutionalization of the documentary cinema (1950s–70s)

By the early 1930s, theatres played documentaries and newsreels before the feature films. Among these were, in addition to occasional Iranian works, newsreels released by Paramount, Metro, Movietone, UFA and Pathé. The first Persian-language sound newsreel, shown in 1932, was apparently filmed by a Turkish photographer in Turkey, showing the Iranian prime minister, Mohammad Ali Foroughi, conferring with the Turkish leader, Kemal Atatürk, and delivering a brief speech in Persian. The film astonished audiences unaccustomed to hearing Persian spoken in the movies. During the 1940s, foreign newsreels about World War II dominated, especially *Movietone News* and a German newsreel, both of which were provided free to exhibitors by the British and German embassies, respectively. The armed forces of both the Allies and the Axis Powers extensively documented their war activities in Iran, either through official military photographers or through commercial newsreel companies. Much of this material appeared in Western newsreels, sometimes spiced with scenes of native life. The German newsreel showing the Allies' invasion of Iran in 1941, contained not only scenes filmed in Iran but also a Persian language narration, both of which made the newsreel very popular with Iranian audiences (Issari 1979: vol. 1, p. 242). The Allied newsreels also sometimes featured Iranian segments, and one (the American *News of the Day*) carried a Persian language narration after the war.[2] Apparently, at this time many Iranians went to the movies just to see Persian-language newsreels showing Iranian scenes.

With the consolidation of Mohammad Reza Shah's power and the rise of the United States as a world power in the 1950s, an Iranian documentary cinema also emerged and consolidated. Similar to many Third World countries in the throes of anti-colonial liberation fever in the 1950s and the 1960s, cinema – particularly documentary cinema – became an instrument of national identity and nation-building in Iran, even though Iran had not been colonized directly.

The USIA factor | USIA newsreels

The global ascendancy of the United States had a profound impact on the institution-alization of the documentary cinema in Iran. By 1954, foreign newsreels had lost their appeal, at least to Iranian exhibitors, chiefly because both *Movietone News* and *News of the Day* began charging a fee for their products. On 8 July 1954, into the newsreel void stepped a new product, which soon became a weekly newsreel in Persian language and containing in each episode scenes filmed in Iran. It was called *Akhbar-e Iran* (*Iran News*) and it was produced by the United States Information Agency (USIA). USIA supplied copies of the newsreel free of charge to cinemas nationwide, and screened them to villages and schools by means of its own network of forty mobile cinemas (in 16 mm format). By the time *Akbar-e Iran* ceased in 1964, 402 episodes of it had been shown in Iran. Subsequently, USIA produced other sporadic newsreels targeted for Iran and the Near East.[3]

Akhbar-e Iran usually consisted of four to five stories, half of which dealt with Iran. The newsreel was heavily narrated and in general focused on the following topics: American Point IV development projects in Iran, the Shah's activities and travels, important Iranian news events, important news events and foreign-policy items from the United States, and human-interest features. Because the newsreel was consid-ered an official US government product, an American officer oversaw the USIA unit that produced it. However Iranians, who gained a great deal of experience in the process, carried out the main task of putting the films together. This sort of experience locked them into an 'official' style of documentary.

The official documentary style

The real contribution of USIA to the local documentary movement started a few years earlier, coinciding with the rise of Iranian nationalism and the nationalization of the British-controlled oil industry under the popularly elected prime minister, Mohammad Mossadeq. As part of its programme of winning the hearts and minds of non-communist nations, in 1951 the United States Information Service (USIA's arm in Iran) began a programme of showing newsreels and other educational films through its network of mobile film units. At first, American films dubbed into Persian were shown, but soon a Syracuse University team of film-makers and audiovisual special-ists was contracted. The team came to Iran and produced some twenty-two films on geography, sanitation, nutrition and agricultural methods. Foremost among these was a series of five documentary travelogues on northern Iran, Tehran, Isfahan, Persepolis and the oil city of Abadan. Distributed to Iranian schools for their geography lessons, these were perhaps 'the first educational films to be made locally and tailored to Iranian needs' (Issari 1989: 172). These and other USIS films reached a massive audi-ence. According to Mohammad Ali Issari, who was Assistant Film Officer during the entire time that USIS operated in Iran, 'USIS presented an average of 800 separate film shows a month (225 of them in Tehran and vicinity alone) to a total monthly audience of about 350,000 people' (ibid.: 173).[4]

More importantly, from 1951 until 1959 when the Syracuse team left Iran, the team under the auspices of the Point IV programme trained a large number of Iranians in documentary film production and it set up 35 mm and 16 mm production facilities, film-processing plants, sound-recording studios and other allied departments at the

Fine Arts Administration (FAA) in Tehran. It also produced (with the help of newly trained Iranians) some seventy-nine documentaries, which appeared in cinemas before feature films and were distributed to outlying areas via mobile units.

That the USIS had succeeded in establishing a viable institutional basis for documentary production is borne out by the fact that between the departure of the Syracuse team in 1959 and 1965, FAA produced an average of fifteen to twenty-five documentaries and propaganda films a year, some of which were distributed abroad by Iranian embassies (ibid.: 183). In 1959 FAA also began producing a biweekly propaganda newsreel, *Akhbar* (*News*), whose magazine style and pro-Shah contents duplicated USIA's *Akhbar-e Iran*. However, the American impact was deeper than institutionalizing documentary film production, as it extended to the cognitive mapping of Iranians, including the way they conceived of film genres and film style. Specifically, the collaboration of USIS and FAA led to the establishment of an official documentary style, which would prove to be a very resilient model long after the demise of both USIS and FAA.

Politically, official documentaries tended to idealize the person of the Shah, supported the state ideology, politics and policies, and endorsed the US involvement in Iran; ideologically, they showed benefits instead of criticizing and they tended to revive the glories of the Iranian past. In the early 1950s, various political, social and religious laws and taboos made filming of current social conditions in Iran difficult. A report prepared by Society for Applied Anthropology (dated 22 February 1951) for the International Moving Picture Division of the US Department of State helped guide the USIS film-making effort. In it, the Society made a number of recommendations that are worth noting here, for they provide a veritable blueprint for the generic attributes of the official style.

The report recommended that the following situations be avoided: filming of women, particularly if they are unveiled; religious ceremonies, especially official ones; anything that might 'suggest that the people of Iran are second-rate', and arousing Iranians' fond feeling for their past practices, which might result in rejection of the new Western procedures. On the other hand, the report recommended the following practices: make the films interesting and lively; show real individuals in realistic situations, instead of focusing on an isolated individual filmed in close-ups that show an isolated part of their behaviour; make technical procedures understandable by placing them in the context of human relations; emphasize the benefits obtained by following the recommended procedures; use humour and humorous situations, not humorous commentary or sarcasm; incorporate the kind of objections that conservatives have to the new ways, then refute them; use a very slow and careful build-up of transitions, go from the general (long shot) to the particular (close-up), use a slow pace and avoid sudden transitions; show instead of tell, and, finally, for voice-overs use a 'person with a recognizable high-class or good Persian accent', not a person with a minority accent. Noting that 'Iranians have a very strong sense of national pride and pride in the achievements of their civilization', the report recommended that, where possible, in connection with technical assistance films, materials should be used which 'reflect the achievement of Iran' (quoted in Issari 1979: vol. 2, pp. 577–91).

As a result of incorporating these recommendations, the official films used humour, dramatization and re-enactment to enliven their subjects for the audience, the majority of whom were illiterate. To facilitate comprehension, their pace was slow and their narratives simple and linear. Sometimes these films were sensitive to the cultural orientation of Iranians, employing such indigenized aesthetic features as panning from right to left to match the direction in which Persian language is written (Issari and Paul 1977: 233–34). Finally, a voice-of-God off-camera narration, which gave information and cued viewers to particular aspects of each scene, was the norm.

The ideological imbrication of pro-Shah and pro-US politics was not only guranteed by the structural relationship between USIA and FAA, and evident in the Society for Applied Anthropology's recommendations and the text of USIS films, but also encouraged by the key role of Mohammad Ali Issari, who functioned simultaneously as Assistant Film Officer to the USIS and as the official cinematographer of the Shah. In his capacity at USIS, he supervised the exhibition of films by the mobile film units throughout the country and the making of local documentaries. In his capacity as the official court photographer, he accompanied the Shah on his travels at home and abroad, and filed film reports for inclusion in *Akbar-e Iran* and *Akhbar* newsreels, which were shown in theatres. Portions of these newsreels were also reprinted on 16 mm stock for distribution via mobile film units to villages and towns nationwide. In addition, from 1958 to 1962, he simultaneously worked on a freelance basis with many American and European commercial newsreel companies and television networks, feeding them items on Iran. In this task, he was very industrious and prolific, filming between 300 and 400 newsreel items. As he noted,

> In this way I was able to spread throughout the world news of developments in Iran and of the activities of the Shah, the government and the people in laying the foundation for the 'Great Civilization' [the Shah's ambitious social project in the late 1970s].
>
> (Issari and Paul 1977: 182)

Because of his pivotal position at the intersection of various film institutions, his political conservatism, his pro-Shah politics and his professionalism in film production, Issari contributed greatly to the development of the official style of film journalism during the 1950s and the 1960s – a contribution that continued abroad into the 1970s, when as a film professor at Michigan State University he was involved in producing a multi-part film series extolling Iranian dynastic history.

This official style was taking form during a period of tremendous social turmoil, involving not only Iranian nationalism (which led to the nationalization of British oil concerns) but also the rise of communism as a serious political alternative. As Premier Mossadeq's popularity increased and his power-struggle with the Shah intensified, the Truman Administration began fearing his susceptibility to communism. In 1953 the American CIA (with aid from the British MI6) toppled Mossadeq in a coup, reinstating the Shah – an intervention that would mar Iranian–American relations and indirectly help consolidate the official style as the reigning model of documentary film-making.

Controlled proliferation

This official style and the official cinema that it spawned were institutionalized in two ways. First, USIA-educated film-makers who had been trained in the style, gradually fanned out and took positions throughout the blossoming film industry. By making widely distributed official films themselves, they set the standards for the documentary form; as managers of film production in government agencies and elsewhere, they enforced those standards; as teachers in film schools, they set a powerful model for the style and they trained the new practitioners of the style. Second, institutionalization was achieved by the mid-1960s by means of consolidating the production of documentaries in two major state agencies. One was the Ministry of Culture and Arts (MCA) (formed when Fine Arts Administration was reorganized) and the other was the National Radio and Television (NIRT), both of which were headed by relatives of the Shah and his wife Queen Farah. Other state agencies, as well as some non-governmental agencies, also sponsored occasional documentaries, using the style. The institutionalization of the official style suited government policy of using communication media to serve its developmental and propaganda projects. The enormous budgets at the disposal of MCA and NIRT encouraged the proliferation of documentaries; on the other hand, the control exerted by these agencies tended to discourage experimentation and diversity of form and content. Both of these factors encouraged the official style, which, despite its hegemony, was not homogeneous, as it was practised to varying degrees of faithfulness, resulting in diverse genres.

In what follows, documentaries of this period are classified under generic categories and exemplars of each are briefly sketched.[5] While some key made-for-television documentaries are discussed, television news and news documentaries are not.

Institutional documentaries These films tended to bolster, directly or indirectly, the prestige of the institutions that sponsored them. Sometimes they accomplished this by documenting and explaining the activities and operation of the sponsoring institutions, and sometimes by associating the sponsor's name with a prestigious documentary project that was unrelated to the institution. The direct form dominated in Iran, although the most notable institutional documentary – *Khaneh Siah Ast / The House is Black* (1961) – was not a direct propaganda film. Under the aegis of the Society for Assistance to Lepers, the celebrated poet Forugh Farrokhzad directed this powerful and lyrical documentary about the lives of lepers in the Baba Baghi colony near Tabriz. She made the film in collaboration with Golestan Film Studio, headed by writer / film-maker Ebrahim Golestan – a collaboration that would lead to a number of joint institutional documentaries for the oil industry. *Khaneh Siah Ast* was filmed over a twelve-day period and it was deftly edited by Farrokhzad herself. In a poetic off-camera voice-over by Farrokhzad, accompanied by touchingly filmed shots and sequences – a woman putting on make-up in front of a mirror, children deformed by leprosy in a classroom thanking God for their various God-given abilities, preparation for a wedding, a man walking the yard back and forth, with each step counting the days of the week – the film emphasized the desolate humanity of the lepers and their commonality with others.

On its release, the film became a powerful plea for understanding and for raising funds for the leper colony (Issari 1989: 191) and it won the top award at the 1963 Oberhausen Film Festival. However, in the heatedly politicized 1970s, driven by the twin engines of official culture and official censorship, all films tended to be read politically or symbolically, even if they were not so coded by the film-makers. The desolate leper colony could thus be read as representing Iranian society in the throes of the revolution brought about by the Shah. The 'black' or the 'dark house' of the title could be read as referring to the house of Iran and thus a criticism of official culture. This symbolic reading was encouraged by the film's refusal to identify the location of the leper colony and the date of filming, which tended to universalize its enclosed society. Such subversive and symbolic interpretations may have been responsible for the limited distribution of the film during the mid-1970s, although both Farrokhzad and Golestan claimed that 'In making this work we had absolutely no intention to criticize [our] society and circumstances' (quoted in Haidari 1998: 202). Nonetheless, *Khaneh Siah Ast* became a *cause célèbre* among Iranian intellectuals, a celebrity that was intensified by Farrokhzad's own great poetic leaps before her tragic and untimely death in a car accident in 1966.[6]

The National Iranian Oil Company produced a large number of institutional films, the majority of which were technical films on oil and petrochemical subjects. However, it also sponsored general documentaries that, while depicting the importance of the oil industry, extolled the Western-style modernization of Iran.[7] Among these were the many films made by Golestan Film Studio, the most famous of which was *Mowj, Marjan Va Khara / Wave, Coral and Rock* (1965). This acclaimed feature-length documentary, which is a highly visual but somewhat verbose propaganda film for the oil industry, documented the installation of underwater oil pipelines to Khark Island in the Persian Gulf and the construction of a major port for loading the oil into supertankers.

In 1971 the Iranian government celebrated the 2,500th anniversary of the founding of the Persian Empire by sponsoring or providing 'assistance' to a number of films about the grandiose affair or related topics. Among these was Farrokh Golestan's *Forugh-e Javidan / Flames of Persia* (1972), about the celebrations, in which Orson Welles' voice-over narration claimed the event was 'one of the most historic cultural gatherings that the world has seen'. *Tales from a Book of Kings* (1974), produced by Time-Life Inc., was based on Ferdowsi's epic *Shahnameh / Book of Kings* and it showed some of the 258 exquisite miniature paintings that the Houghton version of the book contains. By using music, narration and excellent photography and editing, the film recreated some of the stories related in the book. In the process, it emphasized the regal position of the Shahs, their kindness, sense of justice and the wisdom of obedience. Although some of these motifs were present in the original poems, the undue emphasis placed on them here and the timing of the release of the film suggested more than mere coincidence. The caption at the film's end underscored the linkage. It thanked the Iranian ambassador to Washington for his 'generous assistance and co-operation' for making possible the production of the film 'in commemoration of the 2,500th Anniversary of the Founding of the Persian Empire by Cyrus the Great and the First Declaration of Human Rights'.

In the 1970s the Iranian government, seeking to improve its image abroad as a supporter of humanitarian and artistic projects – part of the 'culture of spectacle' project which will be discussed later – embarked on several co-production projects with foreign companies to make feature and documentary films.[8] Two prestigious multi-part non-fiction projects that resulted are briefly noted. One was the eight-part series *Crossroads of Civilization* (1977), co-produced by British journalist David Frost (Paradine Films) and the Iranian Ministry of Culture and Arts. The film's US$2.5 million budget was underwritten by Bank Melli Iran, but this excluded the money spent on equipment, manpower, materials and the logistical services provided by the Iranian armed forces. Modelling itself on such acclaimed British television series as *Civilisation* and *The Ascent of Man*, in seven episodes *Crossroads of Civilization* covered Iranian history from the early Medes to the present. The eighth programme, a lengthy interview with the Shah Mohammad Reza Pahlavi, was not released, perhaps due to the growing anti-Shah social climate. Overall, the series dealt with many issues of Iranian history, including external threats, methods of dealing with internal and external pressures, the roles of various kings and religions, and the Constitutional Revolution of 1906–11, using recreations, paintings, historical photos and films, and interviews with experts. The second project was a US$250,000 contract between National Iranian Radio and Television and Michigan State University (MSU) for a number of films on Iranian history called *Ancient Iran* (1977). Produced by Mohammad Ali Issari, veteran USIS film-maker and professor of film at MSU, these films were designed for use in American high schools and colleges. The series caused controversy among the students and faculty of MSU on account of its attempt to 'legitimize the Shah's regime', which resulted in the cancellation of the contract after the completion of only three episodes (Naficy 1984: 4). While technically well made and historically valuable, these two series were compromised by their sponsorship by and association with an increasingly discredited Iranian government.

The year 1975 was the fiftieth anniversary of the Pahlavi dynasty. The government celebrated the year-long festivities by requiring all kinds of agencies to produce official documentary films heralding their achievements under the Pahlavi rule. These films are noted here because they recounted not only the achievements of the individual institutions, but also those of the institution of monarchy. As such they are exemplars of the official style. NIRT's broadcast of one such film almost every week reflected the enormity of the project, which strained the resources of the industry and caused an unprecedented inflationary rise in the cost of film services and equipment in the country.

Fine-art documentaries   The MCA (successor to Fine Arts Administration) sponsored many documentaries about Iranian history, arts and crafts. Mohammad Qoli Sattar directed *Esfahan / Isfahan* (1957), which showed the historical monuments of this ancient capital city in great detail. Mostafa Farzaneh directed three films, including the award-winning *Miniatorha-ye Irani / Persian Miniatures* (1958). Fereydoun Rahnema, a gifted poet and writer, directed *Takht-e Jamshid / Persepolis* (1961), a lyrical film whose dynamic editing of the shots of stone engravings in Persepolis recreated the rise, grandeur and fall of the famous Achamenid palace and dynasty. Throughout the 1960s and the 1970s, Manuchehr Tayyab made a number of highly visual documentaries on the ancient crafts and architectural monuments of Iran, including *Seramic / Ceramics* (1964), *Masjed-e Jame' / Jame' Mosque* (1970) and *Me'mari-ye Safaviyeh / Safavid Architecture* (1974). Ebrahim Golestan, too, directed *Tapehha-ye Marlik / Marlik Hills* (1964) on archeological discoveries.

These films indirectly fed the government-supported nationalist ideology by linking the present-day, rapidly modernizing Iran to either its pre-Islamic roots or to its post-Islamic Iranian manifestations. At the same time, by grounding Iran in a prehistoric and antiquarian past, they inadvertently countered the destabilizing effects of Westernization.

Ethnographic documentaries   Many films dealt with Persian and Muslim religious institutions and rituals. The majority were straightforward and descriptive, although several experimented with music and editing innovations. Abolqasem Reza'i directed an intimate film on pilgrimage to Mecca, called *Kaneh-ye Koda / The House of God* (1968). In *Adian / Religions* (1971), Tayyab focused on the co-existence of a multiplicity of religions in Iran. Sponsored by NIRT, Naser Taqvai directed two well-assembled films that explored religious themes visually. *Bad-e Jen / The Jinn's Wind* (1970), narrated by the raspy voice of the famous poet Ahmad Shamlu, dealt with possession and exorcism rituals practised on the coast of the Persian Gulf, particularly in Bandar Langeh. As the film reports, the source of these beliefs and rituals were the African slaves who in ancient times were brought to the southern shores of Persia. The exorcism, which involved mixed gender dancing and chanting to the incessant and rhythmic drumbeats until trance was achieved, was filmed with both hidden camera and direct cinema techniques. Taqvai's *Arba'in* (1971), shot in the port city of Bushehr by the Persian Gulf, was a highly visual documentary on the religious processions and mourning rituals that commemorate the fortieth day of martyrdom of Imam Hosain. This film, too, emphasized rhythmic action and rhythmic editing, and it used no voice-over narration.

Manuchehr Tabari, an NIRT film-maker, made a shocking short film, *Lahazati Chand Ba Daravish-e Qaderi / A Few Moments with Qaderi Dervishes* (1973), in which using an invasive *cinéma verité* camera, he documented the extraordinary acts of faith of dervishes under trance conditions in Iranian Kurdistan. This included their swallowing large stones and a handful of razor blades, eating live snakes, puncturing their own bodies with long skewers and ending with the attempt by one of them to swallow the camera lens. While very powerful, the film was a mere document of a trance session, offering no context and no historical or ethnographic understanding. Another noted NIRT film-maker, Parviz Kimiavi, directed *Ya Zamen-e Ahu / Oh Dear Saviour* (1971), an uncanny and intimate document of pilgrimage to the shrine of Imam Reza in Mashhad, which contrasted the grandeur of the shrine with the desperation of the assembled supplicants. Finally, Ali Asgar Asgarian made *Shabih-e Shahadat / The Taziyeh of Martyrdom* (1976), an ambitious five-camera coverage of the famous Horr and Abbas Taziyeh (passion play) performances.

Iranian tribes, their way of life and their migration patterns had long fascinated not only foreigners but also Iranians. An American film served as a model and inspiration for Iranian film-makers. This was the seminal 1925 documentary *Grass*, made by Merian C. Cooper, Ernst Schoedsack and Marguerite Harrison, which movingly and warmly documented the annual migration of the Bakhtiari tribes – whom the film called 'The Forgotten People' – through turbulent rivers and treacherous snow-clad mountain peaks. Part of the reason for its impact on Iranians must be sought in the way it was distributed in Iran. In the 1940s, the British Ministry of Information acquired the film, added a Persian narration to it (written and read by well-known writer Mojtaba Monovi) and distributed it widely, via the British Council mobile film units and commercial cinemas throughout Iran. The voice-over narration, which removed the original ethnocentric intertitles, and which extolled Iranian culture and antiquity, indigenized the film and made it accessible and popular with Iranians, including with the tribal elders who praised it in their correspondence with me. Despite its many flaws – offensive titles, condescending attitudes towards the tribes, faked scenes of a storm and hunting, lack of social context and representation of the tribes as a mass of indistinguishable people and animals – *Grass* was a valuable ethnographic film that provided the most extensive and the earliest document of migration in Iran.[9]

In the late 1950s, Cooper and Schoedsack attempted to remake *Grass* as a more coherent, plot-driven, colour film, and they filmed much footage in Iran; but, as demonstrated by the rough cut that they put together and which I have viewed, the film never cohered and it was abandoned.[10] Iranian film-makers, too, attempted to remake the film from a local point of view. One notable attempt was by Hushang Shafti, an USIA-trained film-maker, who in 1962 at the head of a large crew of cameramen and soundmen filmed the Bakhtiaris' migration in south-western Iran. The resulting film, *Shaqayeq-e Suzan / The Flaming Poppies* (1962), was technically well made and superior to its foreign predecessor in terms of colour, sound and multiple camera viewpoints. However, it lacked the grandeur, drama and scale of *Grass*.[11] It was widely distributed in Iran and abroad, and was popular. This type of exchange of filmic self-representation and representation by the other is a feature of Iranian relations with the West.[12]

Anthropologist Nader Afshar Naderi and film-maker Gholam Hosain Taheridust each made a film called *Balut / Acorn* (in 1966 and 1973 respectively). Both were made in the Kuhgilu-ye region of the Zagros Mountains. Naderi's film documented the preparation of bread from acorns, a process that he placed in the context of the daily activities of the tribal nomads over a period of one year. Taheridust's film, on the other hand, showed the preparation of acorns as recreated by one family and filmed in just two days. Their different approaches to the same subject reflected their different training as anthropologist and film-maker.

Like the fine-art documentaries, these ethnographic films began the modern project of documenting and understanding the present-day Iran in the light of the past. However many of them, made by film-makers not subject specialists (ethnographers, anthropologists and ethnomusicologists), were analytically and scientifically weak. At best, they were either descriptive or provided only visual documentation. In retrospect, it appears that their task was primarily to explore and establish the diversity and antiquity of the peoples who formed 'Persia' before it became contaminated by modernity and transformed into 'Iran'.

Social issues documentaries   From the mid-1960s onward several socially conscious films were made. These may have been a response to the brief uprising of 1963, which was brutally suppressed. They were also a result of the dislocating consequences of the Shah's various top-down Westernization and developmental projects – the White Revolution, Shah–People Revolution and Great Civilization – and the increasing social inequality, officially sanctioned corruption and political suppression. Because they dealt with current affairs and social conditions often in a somewhat critical manner, these films suffered from censorship and limited public exhibition much more than those of other documentary genres. For example, Kamran Shirdel's many documentaries for MCA were rarely shown, among them *Zendan-e Zanan / Women's Prison* (1965) and *Qaleh / The Castle* (1966), the latter about prostitution in Tehran's red light district. A number of films which dared to criticize social-service institutions received little or no exhibition. Among them were the following three: Khosrow Sinai's

Ansu-ye Hayahu / Beyond the Barrier of Sound (1968) was about a school for the deaf and mute; Reza Allamehzadeh's *Shab-e Momtad / Eternal Night* (1972) centred on a school for the blind, and Mohammad Hosain Mahini Hasanabadi's *Ordu-ye Kar / Work Camp* (1974), which was partly filmed clandestinely, focused on inmates of a government work camp who boldly expressed their dissatisfaction not only with the camp but also with the whole social system.

Avant-garde documentaries   Both social issues and avant-garde documentaries broke some of the codes of the official style. The chief contribution of social documentaries to that end was to reverse the mode of discourse of the official films from praise to criticism. Their social criticism was itself a critique of the official style. In addition, they tore apart the straitjacket of 'voice of God' voice-over narration by experimenting with different, subjective modes of address. The avant-garde films extended these subversions a step further by bolder experiments with form and structure, often as a way to camouflage the content and to escape censorship.

Among these strategies of formal and ultimately political subversion was experimentation with a hybrid form, consisting of both fictional and documentary elements. Ahmad Faruqi's *Tolu'-e Fajr / Dawn of the Capricorn* (1964) mixed documentary footage of Isfahan with the story of a budding relationship between two children. Kimiavi's short film *P-e Mesl-e Pelikan / P as in Pelican* (1972) and his feature-length hybrid film *Bagh-e Sangi / Stone Garden* (1976) each centred on a different old man who, despite living in ruins or desolated deserts, has a rich imagination which suffuses and transforms his barren physical environment. By mixing documentary and recreated scenes Kimiavi not only evoked the lives of these men but also problematized and destabilized the official style – and he escaped censorship because the films could be interpreted as flight of fancy not straight documentation. This innovative hybridization of the documentary, which would in a few years become emblematic of post-modern film-making, would in due course (particularly under the Islamic Republic) come to pose a serious ethnical dilemma for both non-fiction and fiction film-makers.

Experiments with editing, which resulted in breaking the authority of the often-verbose narration, was another strategy. Taqvai's *Arba'in*, Hagir Daryoush's *Gowd-e Moqqadas / The Sacred Pit* (1964) and Tayyab's *Ritm / Rhythm* (1971) are examples. Formal experiments of an impressionist nature were also tried, such as in Kiumars Derambakhsh's *Sarebanan / Desert Caravans* (1974) and in *Bazar Migeryad / The Bazaar Weeps* (1976) made by two students, Abbas Baqerian and Reza Gharavi.

Shirdel's path-breaking *Unshab Keh Barun Umad / The Night It Rained* (1967) cleverly problematized the notions of 'documentation' and 'reality' through irony and parody, by offering multiple and often conflicting views on the heroic action of a boy who had stopped a train before its derailment. This film was also one of the few Iranian documentaries that deconstructed itself by self-referentially foregrounding its own production. These avant-garde films were few and far between and, like the social issues films, they suffered from censorship, delayed exhibition and no exhibition. For example, *Unshab Keh Barun Umad* was only exhibited publicly eight years after its completion and only then in a film festival.

The institutionalization of the official documentary by the state was a double-edged sword. On one hand, it meant steady support for documentary production that was otherwise difficult to obtain in Iran. On the other hand, it meant that, even if at times non-traditional, non-official films escaped prior censorship (during script approval phase), there was no guarantee that they would be exhibited once they were made. This is because both MCA and NIRT, which sponsored the bulk of the documentaries, were also in charge of censoring, exhibition and broadcast of these films. They could produce the films; they could also withhold or hamper their exhibition. The documentary cinema was thus caught in the contradictions of the system that supported it. In this era, contradictions and compromise beset not only individual film-makers but also state institutions concerned with cinema.

Emergence of new fiction cinemas (1960–78)

The decade of the 1960s was as tumultuous for Iran as for many other countries in the world, bringing with it both the freedoms which petrodollars and globalization of capital promised and the inequalities that they actually produced in non-Western countries. A public protest in 1963, spearheaded by Ayatollah Ruhollah Khomeini, was violently crushed by the security forces and Khomeini was exiled to Turkey and Iraq – a move that would backfire badly against the Shah years later. For the time being, this forceful action consolidated the Shah's power further – a process that had begun after his 1953 reinstatement and continued as he expanded the state-security apparatuses and the state's control of the consciousness-producing industries. Not only socially relevant documentaries but also fictional films met with official disapproval and confiscation. For example, *Jonub-e Shahr / South of the City* (1958), made by the French-educated film-maker Farrokh Gaffary, which realistically and critically depicted life in the poverty-stricken southern district of Tehran, was banned and its negative mutilated (Gaffary 1970: 91). A few years later, *Reqabat Dar Shahr / Rivalry in the City* was released, which was nothing but a re-edited version of Gaffary's film without director attribution. Gaffary's next film *Shab-e Quzi / The Night of the Hunchback* (1964) and Ebrahim Golestan's first fiction film *Khesht Va Ayeneh / Mud-Brick and Mirror* (1966), an intriguing urban melodrama, were subjected to censorship and to public apathy, as the public's taste had been conditioned by glossy foreign films and formulaic local productions.

The Iranian government's need for political control of culture and art matched the interests of the US media companies for economic control of the world markets. Global interests thus overshadowed the regional media influences (from India, Turkey and Egypt) which had previously been significant in shaping Iranian cinema. American companies began selling all kinds of products and services, from feature films to television programmes, from television receivers to television studios, from communications expertise to personnel training; in short, they sold not only consumer products but also their consumer ideology. As a result, although NIRT became a vast institution, producing thousands of hours of sophisticated programming annually, 40 per cent of its schedule in 1974 was taken up by Western products, which were primarily American (Naficy 1981: 358).

However, two films jolted the complacent local film industry, which had generally been producing low-quality, formulaic melodramas, comedies and 'tough guy' films, setting in motion new film genres and movements. One important genre and one key movement are treated below.

*The tough guy (*luti*) film genre*

One of these pioneering films was Masud Kimiai's *Qaisar* (1969), which updated and rejuvenated the 'tough guy' genre, making the *luti* films about tough guys and their lifestyle immensely popular during the next decade. This genre had begun with Majid Mohseni's *Lat-e Javanmard / The Generous Tough* (1958), which he wrote, directed and in which he acted as the protagonist, a well-meaning tough guy who is charged with protecting the daughter of a friend. The popularity and profitability of the genre after *Qaisar* is demonstrated by the doubling in number of such films (from twenty-one in 1971 to forty in 1972) and by the number of movie theatres which simultaneously showed these films in Tehran and the provinces.[13] For example, *Aqa Mehdy Va Shalvarak-e Dagh / Mr Mehdy and the Hot Pants* (1973) was shown simultaneously in thirteen theatres in Tehran, *Aqa Mehdy Vared Mishavad / Mr Mehdy Arrives* (1974) was screened simultaneously in eleven theatres in Tehran and in seventeen theatres in twelve other cities, and *Pashneh Tala / The Golden Heel* (1975) was exhibited simultaneously in eleven Tehran theatres and in twenty-two provincial theatres in eighteen cities.

Public popularity notwithstanding, these films were then considered (and continue to be considered) by critics and intellectuals – religious and secular alike – as entirely frivolous, empty of meaning and demeaning. Their bias against this genre was so pervasive and naturalized that the social scientists who studied audience reactions to films, failed to include the tough guy genre in their questionnaires, while they found a place for two popular foreign genres: the western and the martial arts film. The few serious studies of the tough guy genre regarded these films as symptoms of the social pathology, cultural aberration and falsehood characteristic of the late Pahlavi era (Akbari 1973, Mehrabi 1984: 87, Tahaminezhad 1986, Karimi 1990). This pathological formulation was possible because these studies assumed an imaginary, originary, stable culture of purity and authenticity for Iran, which they rarely questioned and which they believed was defiled by the tough guy films. It was also because they considered cinema primarily a means for realistic presentation of life, instead of a social institution engaged in representation and signification. The tropes of disease and pathology were so dominant that critics failed to fully understand that *luti* film-making was a rule-bound activity of meaning production, collective expression and cultural negotiation. Generic approaches can shed light not only on the way social and ideological forces are inscribed in the films of a particular genre but also on the manner in which genres influence social and ideological discourses (Altman 1981, Schatz 1981, Neal 1983, Naficy 1996a, Altman 1999). By examining the dynamics of generic conventions and codes and by tracking their evolution, we can learn much about the deep structures and preoccupations of society. This is because these conventions tap into deeply held values and concerns, which have become naturalized as taken-for-granted common senses of that society, requiring no examination. Thus generic studies can go far beyond the mere question of realism and realistic portrayal of the tough guys and their lifestyle. Generic conventions, of course, are not permanent: they change in correlation with political formations, social tensions, film industry production and marketing practices, and the spectators' reactions.

The popularity of the tough guy genre in the 1960s and the early 1970s, its decline in the late 1970s, its brief demise after the revolution of 1979 and its resurfacing (albeit in a different guise) under the Islamic Republic and in exile, all suggest the manner in which meaning-production and generic conventions are evolutionary and involved in larger social formations and cultural negotiations. Indeed, this genre provides a site where the tensions of Western-style modernization and its impact on traditional social structures can be studied. Finally, the pleasure involved in watching the *luti* films stems not so much from the 'shock of the new' but, as with narratives that belong to an oral tradition, from the recognition of the familiar, the pull of the permanent or, in the words of Umberto Eco, from the 'return of the identical' (Eco 1985: 168, 179).

The *luti*-film tough guys and the *luti* ideology are ancient, pre-Islamic institutions whose origin is traced back to the Mithraic myths (Bahar 1976: 18). They are complex and in them are found co-mingled many seemingly contradictory tendencies – themselves having evolved over time (Mahjub 1969: 873–4). Here I will concentrate on one set of binary tendencies. Historically, the tough guys formed a social grouping that was fundamentally urban (Hanaway 1970: 142, Bahar 1976: 16) and, in nineteenth-century Iran, it included two basic types: entertainers and urban social bandits (Floor 1981: 86). As entertainers, they played music, danced, performed comic acts and organized Shi'i passion plays (called Taziyeh) and other religious ceremonies. As social bandits, they bore two contradictory tendencies. As a *luti* (meaning 'generous and brave'), they acted heroically in a sort of Robin Hood fashion. They obtained justice for the underdog, showed respect for the elders and kindness to women and children, and exhibited self-sacrifice, bravery, truthfulness, loyalty and piety (Mostowfi 1945: 409, Khanlari 1969a: 1,073–7, Khanlari 1985). The central quality that ideal *luti*s were (and are) expected to possess (and which is the ideal of Iranians in general) is inner purity (*safa-ye baten*), which has been defined as 'consistency of feeling and behavior' or 'harmony between interior and exterior' (Bateson *et al.* 1977: 268–9). In their villainous *lat* role (meaning 'ruffian'), on the other hand, they worked as middlemen between rival clerics, landowners and government officials. Hired by them, they helped settle scores, collect taxes and in general obtain social control through violence. Each type was both feared and respected within his neighbourhood for different reasons. This respect was evident in movie theatres. In the early days of cinema if the tough guys arrived late at the neighbourhood movie theatre, the projectionist would stop the movie in their honour, resuming it only after they were seated (Mehrabi 1984: 420). Politically, both *luti* and *lat* types were in the main conservative, or even reactionary, as they often showed allegiance to social causes based less on patriotism than on their rivalry with opposing groups (Khanlari 1969d: 265, Floor 1981: 91).

The culture which was inflected in the tough guy films was derived not only from the life of the contemporary tough guys but also in part from the Iranian oral tradition and popular romances, such as *Samak Ayyar*, *Darab Nameh*, *Firuz Shah Nameh*, *Eskandar Nameh*, *Hosain-e Kord* and *Amir Arsalan-e Namdar*. According to William Hanaway, these romances had three functions: (1) to entertain; (2) to teach, preserve and transmit values, and (3) to re-evaluate the present in the light of the past (Hanaway 1970: 7–8, 1971b: 60). I apply the term 'tough guy film' or '*luti* film' to the films that deal with both the *luti* and the *lat* characters. Significantly, these films, as exemplified by Masud Kimiai's *Qaisar* (1969) and *Dash Akol* (1971), are informed by not only the contents of the oral epics and popular romances, but also by their formal attributes. Consequently *luti* film-making (like popular romance story-telling) may be viewed as one way in which Iranians entertained, reworked, reinterpreted, preserved and transmitted their deep values and reactions to the world. Thus these films were not only representations of a society and representatives of its artistic traditions, but also compilations of that society's evolving inherited lore.

Although the tough guy genre evolved over the years, its basic components remained rather stable. These include: formulaic plots involving male rivalry, jealousy and revenge, often over women and turf; a presentational acting style that emphasizes destiny and the presentation of ideal types, particularly of manhood; strong binary characters of *luti* and *lat*, with subsidiary characters of holy or whorish women; pleasurable depiction of the tough guy lifestyle and exploits in their favourite hangouts, such as in tea-houses, nightclubs, bars and the streets, involving their favourite dances, musical numbers, songs and brawls; adherence to specific codes of dress, language and behaviour (chivalric and violent) that set the good guys apart from the bad guys, and repeated casting of familiar and beloved actors in heroic and villainous roles, including their female counterparts (Naficy 1985a, 1992b). A veritable star system developed for the tough guys, whereby a limited number of actors who repeatedly played recognizable types became very popular with audiences, and their pictures were widely circulated in the mass media. Mohammad Ali Fardin, for example, acted in at least forty *luti*-type films before 1970 (Bahrami 1972) and in many more thereafter. Women actors and dancers of the tough guy films, too, were very popular, particularly in pushing products in print and television advertising (for these reasons the *luti* films' lead actors and actresses were banned from cinema after the revolution).

Kimiai's *Qaisar* polished the existing tough guy genre by developing a strong binary opposition between good guy (*luti*) and bad guy (*lat*), and by linking the good with Iranian tradition and the bad with its violations. In some circles these violations were read as referring to encroaching Westernization and secularization. Thus the genre's revenge plot, usually involving defending a kinswoman, was re-coded to mean the defence of Iranian authenticity as well. Such coding and interpretations made *Qaisar* (named after its forceful *luti* protagonist, played by Behrouz Vossoughi) very popular with audiences who were predominantly male. Kimiai also intensified the pacing of the genre by using an action-oriented filming style, dramatic camera angles and hand-held cameras, and stirring music – many of which were borrowed from the American westerns.

When Qaisar discovers that his brother has been murdered by a rival tough and his sister raped, causing her to commit suicide, he launches on a path of personal revenge which destroys his rivals and results in his own murder in a shoot-out with the police. The film caused a great controversy among film critics, who either blasted it as retrogressive and pandering to baser instincts of violence and revenge, or praised it for filmic innovations and for its subtextual oppositional politics (Mehrabi 1984: 127–31). However, the film's unprecedented box-office revenues of 2 million tumans demonstrated that audiences had loved a locally produced film and commercial producers turned to young directors, opening the way for the emergence of the New Wave films, which awaited the jolt from the second pioneering film: *Gav | The Cow* (1969).

In the meantime, Kimiai's next film *Dash Akol* (1972), based on a short story by renowned novelist Sadeq Hedayat, consolidated the tough guy genre and the director's high status.[14] In it, a respected *luti* named Dash Akol (played by Behrouz Vossoughi) accepts the dying wish of his wealthy friend to take care of his wife and beautiful daughter. However, by accepting that responsibility and by falling in love with his friend's daughter Dash Akol violates the *luti* ideal of independence and freedom from material and carnal desires. These violations make him vulnerable to the challenge of a younger bully: a *lat* named Kaka Rostam (played by Bahman Mofid), whom Dash Akol does not kill in deference to yet another *luti* code, that of showing generosity to an underling – a generosity which Kaka Rostam fully exploits by stabbing Dash Akol to death. In the social context of the 1970s, the venal rivalry of newcomer Kaka Rostam with old-timer Dash Akol, his amoral behaviour towards women and children, and his unfair killing of Dash Akol could be interpreted as symbolizing the trouncing of the Iranian traditions and culture by the rapacious Western culture that the petrodollars and the Shah's White Revolution were ushering in.

These disruptive social changes must have stirred deep anxieties, which surfaced in this and many other tough guy movies of the time. In them, the age-old Iranian ideal character (the *luti*) was made to grapple with a modern world filled with instability and temptations, which the films devalued by coding them as excessively unethical, sexual, violent, materialistic and exploitative. Of course, such coding did not always have the intended effect; at times they made modernization even more alluring instead. In the course of the evolution of the genre over the years, the tough guy characters also underwent changes. If in the 1950s they were generally portrayed as helpful, self-less and inclined to protect the weak, in the 1970s they emerged more as hooligans prone to drinking, rabble-rousing, and verbally and physically abusing the weak. As the men became more violent, women's representation in tough guy films grew more sexualized, particularly in the obligatory song-and-dance numbers which were staged for the pleasure of diegetic male toughs. These transformations in male and female representation, often coded as betrayals of authentic values, turned the toughs (even the modern anti-social ones) into powerful nostalgic figures, for each *luti* has a recondite potentiality to embody the Iranian ideal – through them the audience could long for a centre that no longer held: that ever-elusive inner purity.

Westernized movie critics disdained both the type of static traditional values embedded in the tough guy films and the films' sometimes low technical quality and apparent improvisational style (an indication of their oral origin). The government for its part neither wanted to encourage the tough guys' take-charge-by-means-of-violence attitude (which could be read subversively and politically as anti-authoritarian), nor the damning of modernization as corrupt, nor the portrayal of poverty and marginality as the norm in a modernizing Iran.[15] The tough guy audiences, on the other hand, which were largely comprised of recent rural male migrants and urban poor living in the stifling society of 1970s Iran, seemed to have found in the *luti* characters authority figures worth identifying with – however distorted their portrayal and that of the Iranian society that contained them may have been. They often cheered on the tough guys as they redressed a wrong or took violent revenge. One might speculate that the increased male violence and female sexuality on the screens in some way represented the return of the politically and sexually repressed.

At the height of their popularity, in 1972, the government passed an edict against the tough guy films. Significantly, it did not ban the films outright, but banned certain components of the genre, such as personal revenge, knife-wielding, playing at being a tough guy, producing shameless sounds, uttering indecent and meaningless words, gambling with knuckle-bones, pigeon-flying and displaying of details of sexual relations designed to satisfy prurient desires and attract customers. Within three years of the edict, the output of the tough guy genre declined from forty to twenty-four films and by 1978 (the year of the revolution) it dropped to a mere five. However, the genre did not disappear with the Pahlavi regime's demise.

From its establishment in early 1979, the new Islamic government distrusted the un-Islamic leanings of the late Pahlavi-era tough guys, whom it associated with that era's corrupting Western influences. This is ironic, for the tough guy films' coding of Westernization as corrupt, which was previously engaged in partly as a politically oppositional strategy and partly as an economic measure to attract audiences, was now being interpreted as propagating that very corruption. In 1979 the revolutionary court, in an announcement that appeared in a major national daily, summoned ten actors before the court for 'preliminary investigation' (this indicates that the actors were perhaps in hiding). Among these were famous actors of the tough guy films, including Mohammad Ali Fardin, Naser Malek Motii, Behrouz Vossoughi, Simin Ghafari, Puri Banani, Reza Paik Imanverdi and Iraj Qaderi. As if to reassure them that nothing severe awaited them, the announcement noted that other actors who had voluntarily appeared before the court had been released after promising to change their ways and to abstain from doing anything that was against Islamic values.[16] Regardless of whether they appeared before the court or not, Pahlavi-era tough guy films and tough guy stars (male and female) were soon banned. However, the tough guy genre's characters, stories, codes and themes did not entirely disappear from the screens. Instead, they were reworked. Genres, especially those with heavy cultural and ideological investments, do not die – they just evolve. They change in order to stay the same. Three forms of reworking are discussed below.

First, immediately after the revolution certain films, such as Iraj Qaderi's *Barzakhiha / Hell-Dwellers* (1982), starring well-known *luti* character actors Malek Motii, Fardin and Qaderi, tried to recycle the Pahlavi-era tough guy types and formulas by updating them to fit the revolutionary era's ethos. The film was apparently popular, but the tough's death in defence of the country in the war with Iraq was not sufficient to redeem him. One reviewer condemned the film for insulting the 'martyrs' and the 'sacred beliefs' of the people (quoted in Naficy 1987: 453). Another complained that post-revolutionary film businessmen had replaced the trappings of the Pahlavi-era tough guys with those of the Islamist guerrillas. Instead of wearing the former tough guy's fedora hat and dark suit, and brandishing a knife, the post-revolutionary tough guys wore a beret and a guerrilla jacket, and carried a gun (Ebrahimian 1979: 5). Second, if the Pahlavi-era tough guys were shown in the post-revolutionary films, they were generally coded as corrupt and unethical: that is, as ruffian *lat*s not *luti*s. For example, in Mehdi Sabbaghzadeh's *Parvandeh / Dossier* (1983), an imprisoned tough guy acts as a stool pigeon for the authorities, an action that violates the tough guys' ideal code of conduct. Third, a new Islamic tough guy surfaced, who subscribed to an altered (but nevertheless recognizable) version of the code of dress, postures and mannerisms of the pre-revolution tough guys, and whose aims were now strictly and selflessly to help the Islamic community (*ummah*).

Unlike the Pahlavi-era tough guys, these Islamicized toughs were not idealized; as a result, they were more susceptible to transformation, as in the case of the illiterate hero of the television series *Hamsayeh-ha / The Neighbours*, who learned to read and write from a boy, obtain a decent job and carry out his missionary tasks of serving the community. Even though formulaic, deviant toughs were in this manner reformed, redeemed and brought into the fold. In Khosrow Malekan's feature film, *Shab Shekan / Night Breaker* (1985), a tough guy addict was reformed by an ex-tough guy war veteran who had redeemed himself by fighting in the Iran–Iraq war. In Kimiai's post-revolutionary films, such as in *Dandan-e Mar / The Snake Fang* (1989), tough guys resurface in different ways and guises, sometimes almost unrecognizable to the untrained eye. Many of the post-revolutionary tough guy films, including *Dandan-e Mar*, had the toughs involved in anti-social and illegal activities such as addiction and the smuggling of a variety of contraband.

By being involved in the process of cultural negotiation and social change, through continually coding and re-coding its contents and conventions, the tough guy genre managed to survive. The most daring and entertaining re-coding occurred in Davud Mirbaqeri's *Adam Barfi / The Snowman* (1994), which was partly filmed in Turkey. The film was banned in Iran for several years and released only after the election as president of reformist former Minister of Culture and Islamic Guidance, Mohammad Khatami. Immediately it became very controversial as Islamist hardliners, including the militant Supporters of the Party of God (*Ansar-e Hezbollah*), attacked the theatres that showed the film in major cities, including in Tehran and Isfahan (Peterson 1997). However, government officials (including the president) voiced support for the film and audiences flocked to the movie theatres. The film was so popular that the Isfahan theatre, which had been attacked, continued to show the film for over a month there-after. Ostensibly the reason for the attack was the film's theme of transvestitism. The film's protagonist (played by Ali Abdi) dreams of going to the United States, but as there is no American embassy in Iran, he travels to Turkey to obtain a visa. After his various disguises fail to get him a visa there, he gets involved in a scheme (hatched by expatriate Iranian tough guys) to disguise himself as a woman and to marry a willing American for US$6,000. The lead actor, Abdi, dons women's clothes, hair and make-up; thus dressed, he appears unveiled in public (which is unlawful in Iran) and he skilfully performs a camp masquerade as a woman. Whether intended or not, this masquerade may evoke in the minds of the viewing public the camp masquerading as women by gay men (representation of gays is also unlawful). A more serious reason for the protest, therefore, may have been not just transvestitism but also the film's treatment of such important taboo subjects as unveiled women, homosexuality and gender crossing, all of which are severely punished in Islamist Iran where the boundaries segregating genders, inside and outside, and self and other are so strictly patrolled and enforced.

A yet more subtle, but no less serious, reason both for the attack on *Adam Barfi* and for its popularity, may have been the rather open display of the transplanted Iranian toughs in Turkey, who were involved in shady smuggling operations and sang their favourite songs from pre-revolution days, sprinkling their conversations with colourful *luti* phrases and gestures, and wearing some of their coded clothing.[17] They were also shown to frequent a bar, a favourite hangout of the tough guys in pre-revolution cinema, where they drank amber drinks that strongly suggested beer (outlawed in Iran). These scenes (and others involving unveiled women) could not have been staged so openly in Iran. It is as though the tough guy film had to cross the national borders in order for it to remain true to its generic codes – like many Iranians who left the Islamic Republic instead of putting up with unacceptable compromises. *Adam Barfi*'s audiences recognized these transgressions with appreciation, clapping to the beat of the tough guy singing and cheering the actors on. The film not only revived the tough guy's lifestyle, but also reworked the genre's revenge theme, so that the *luti*s ended up defending not so much their own personal honour as their national honour, particularly as refugees and immigrants in Turkey.

That the tough guy films were enduringly fascinating to Iranians and served to express and interpret their changing identity was again illustrated by the resurgence of these films among Iranian exiles in the United States. This resurgence involved exhibiting previously made tough guy films and producing new ones in exile. Since 1982, over two dozen feature films produced prior to the 1979 revolution were screened in public cinemas, principally in New York and Los Angeles. Many of these were also available on video cassettes, including a compilation tape called *Rangarang / Colourful* (Episode 123), which contained favourite song-and-dance numbers from pre-revolution films, including ones from tough guy films.

More significant, however, was the role of television and video, which in the 1980s and 1990s offered a home for the production and exhibition of tough guy films in exile. In fact, these films were made on video, shown in serial form on exile television, and distributed for sale and rental on video cassette. Several are discussed. One is *Balatar Az Khandeh / Beyond Laughter* (1985), which starred well-known tough guy character actors of the pre-revolution genre who are now in exile, such as Bahman Mofid, Morteza Aqili and Bahram Vatanparast, and was written and directed by Morteza Aqili. It began as a television serial that chronicled the *luti* lifestyle in Iran before the Islamic revolution, after the revolution and in exile in the United States. It was aired on a weekly basis on the *Jam-e Jam* television programme in Los Angeles in 1985 and was later released as a ninety-minute video. *Gharibeh-ha / The Strangers* was also first serialized in the 1980s (on the *Jomeh* television programme) and was subsequently released as a feature-length comedy. Starring Morteza Aqili, the film focused on the humorous exploits of the tough guys in the United States. *Sherkat-e Jahelan Dar Los Angeles / The Tough Guys' Company in Los Angeles* was another feature-length tough guy video film produced in the 1980s in Los Angeles. There were also a number of music videos, interestingly enough by women, which deployed tough guy characters or made fun of them; among them were Jaklin's mafia video and Leila Foruhar's *Helhelleh / Cry of Exultation* video.[18]

Significantly the exile-produced serials, films and videos were all comedies, which had fun with and made fun of the *luti* characters and the *luti* filmic codes at the same time as they banked on audience familiarity with and enjoyment of these characters and codes. One reason may be sought in the ameliorative effects of humour in assuaging the pain of exilic loss and deterritorialization. Another may be sought in the distance of exile, which creates the objectivity and scope that are also necessary for self-criticism. These films also helped preserve what many displaced Iranians believed to be their core 'authentic' national values. As Manuchehr Bibian, producer of *Balatar Az Khandeh*, told me:

> *Luti*s are representatives of Iranian culture and tradition. The Islamic regime is destroying all that. But by doing this series, we help preserve that culture and tradition.

> (Naficy 1993a: 185)

By means of these narratives, the deterritorialized Iranians could thus be reterritorialized, at least temporarily. But, as I have shown elsewhere, the production of authenticity in exile is always accompanied and contaminated by its nemesis: inappropriateness and impurity. As a result, despite the desire and dream of many exiles for purity, the texts they produced (including the tough guy films and videos) tended to be hybridized and mulatto, suffused with destabilizing mimicry and unintended excess (ibid.: 178–88).

The New Wave film movement

The spark that the social realist film-makers Gaffary and Golestan had ignited with their *Jonub-e Shahr* / *South of the City* (1958), *Shab-e Quzi* / *The Night of the Hunchback* (1964) and *Khesht Va Ayeneh* / *Mud-Brick and Mirror* (1966) was fanned by Fereydoun Rahnema's *Siavash Dar Takht-e Jamdhid* / *Siavash in Persepolis* (1965) and Davud Mowlapur's *Showhar-e Ahu Khanom* / *Ahu's Husband* (1966), before finally bursting into flame with not only Kimiai's *Qaisar* (1969) but also Dariush Mehrjui's second film *Gav* / *The Cow* (1969). If *Qaisar* gave rise to a modernized tough guy genre, *Gav* led to what was later called the New Wave film movement. *Gav*, which was both funded and banned for one year by the MCA, was about a farmer (played by Ezzatollah Entezami) who upon losing his cow, which is the sole source of his livelihood, begins to embody the animal in spirit and body. Its focus on villagers was regarded as a return to the roots, echoing in a different genre the tough guy films' return to the authentic bedrock of Iranian society and psychology. Its honest treatment and truthful portrayal of village life, using a sparse (if somewhat primitive) style was regarded as a breath of fresh air, linking it to the Italian neo-realist cinema. Finally, its adaptation of a story by a leading dissident writer, Gholamhosain Saedi, was a harbinger of a new alliance between educated film-makers (Mehrjui received his B.A. in philosophy from UCLA) and oppositional contemporary writers. At this point, a bit of contextualization is in order.

In the 1970s, the Shah's government, sensing a threat from both leftist and Islamist forces and from dislocation caused by Westernization, intensified its attempt at constructing and administering a type of official culture, which depended on revitalizing a partly fabricated monarchic, chauvinistic ideology and history that pre-dated Islam. This revivalism took the form of a series of state-sponsored grandiose national spectacles and rituals, such as the Shah's own coronation, staged lavishly in 1967 and celebrated for a week nationwide, and the grand pageantry in 1971 that honoured the 2,500th anniversary of the Persian Empire, which cost some US$300 million dollars (Mottahedeh 1985: 327) and, as noted earlier, led to the production of many documentaries.[19] Then there were the year-long festivities in 1975, celebrating the fiftieth anniversary of the Pahlavi rule, which prompted an unprecedented flurry of commissioned film and television productions. Finally the Shiraz Festival of Art and Culture, a ten-day annual extravaganza sponsored by NIRT, became a key showcase for the Shah's revitalization project. In this dynamic festival were placed in syncretic tension the most modern world-class theatrical productions (of Growtowski and Peter Brook) and European ballet troupes (of Maurice Béjart) side-by-side with the most ancient indigenous productions (Taziyeh passion plays, Siahbazi comic performances,

Ruhowzi traditional theatre and classical Persian music) – all performed at Persepolis, in other ancient sites and in the streets of Shiraz.

Spectacle was clearly part of the ruling ideological and modernization projects, whose overarching labels evolved over the years from 'The Shah–People Revolution' to 'The White Revolution' to 'The Great Civilization'. The core aim of these projects was for the Shah to push Iran into the pantheon of industrial superpowers in less than a decade, while simultaneously and syncretically reviving a symbolic construction of a glorious monarchy in the past to which he claimed a direct (but in fact ersatz) lineage. The Shah now called himself Shahanshah Aryamehr (King of Kings, the Light of the Aryans). What Jeremy Tunstall wrote about his use of television was also true of his support for all the other arts. According to him, the Shah was using television as:

> a weapon to consolidate power, confer prestige, divide the bureaucracy, to project a single national culture, and generally to identify his personality and office with national plans and prestige. The television conception of Iranian tradition appears to resemble a Cecil B. DeMille movie in which the part of the Shah is played by the Shah.
>
> (Tunstall 1977: 247)

In order to press cinema into such service, it was important to harness its powers. This was attempted by means of sponsorship – that is, by attenuating the flow of seemingly limitless financial resources of the state, flush with the newly quadrupled oil prices, to various governmental agencies, festivals, museums and film-makers. It was also attempted by wide-ranging censorship of all the arts and by suppression of dissenting voices by intimidation, imprisonment and co-optation. Control was attempted in yet another way, by superimposing a network of royal relatives and confidants in key power positions within broadcasting, culture, arts and censorship organizations. Examples were those heading NIRT (Reza Qotbi, Queen Farah's cousin), the MCA (Mehrdad Pahlbod, Princess Shams' husband), the Film Industry Development Company of Iran (Mehdi Boushehri, Princess Ashraf's husband) and the Institute for Intellectual Development of Children and Young Adults (Lili Amir-Arjomand, close friend of the queen).

However, it is important to point out that these organizations' support of cinema and the film industry was only partly driven by the ideological imperatives of the culture of spectacle. It was also driven by a genuine desire in their technocratic strata to promote and professionalize the Iranian cinema. Certain non-governmental and professional formations also were engaged in this process. Ironically many of the state-sponsored film-makers were dissidents whose films were far from being panegyric odes to the regime; instead they were implicitly critical of the social conditions – for which they paid a price and by which they gained prestige. The confluence of these forces led to the emergence of a vast rhizomatic web of relations, dispositions and formations that overdetermined the rise of the Iranian New Wave cinema in the 1970s. Among them, were the following formations.

Institutions   NIRT and MCA rapidly became the twin key engines of culture and arts, supporting cinema, theatre, television, radio, music and many other arts by means of sponsoring individual artists, as well as numerous festivals, publications, theatres, film companies, orchestras and training schools. The establishment of university and college degree programmes in film production and history (affiliated with MCA, NIRT and Tehran University), a nationwide Super 8 film-training network called Free Cinema (Cinema-ye Azad) and the Institute for Intellectual Development of Children and Young Adults, with its nationwide network of libraries and live-action and animated film production centres, helped to decentralize and systematize the education and training of new talent for cinema and the production of new films. Free Cinema and the Institute for Intellectual Development of Children and Young Adults went further, by sponsoring the production, distribution, exhibition and archiving of young film-makers' works.[20] Many of these films were praised in international film festivals.

Film festivals   In the meantime, numerous film festivals emerged in Iran, among them the Educational Film Festival (begun in 1963), the International Festival of Films for Children and Young Adults (1967), Sepass Film Festival (1969), Cinema-ye Azad Film Festival (1970), the National Film Festival (1970), Tehran International Film Festival (1972), the Asian Youth Film Festival (1974) and the Festival of Super 8 Films (1974). These festivals provided Iranian film-makers with an opportunity to see foreign films, which they would otherwise have been unable to see, and to exchange ideas with their foreign counterparts. In addition, film clubs (such as Kanun-e Film, Farabi Film Club, the Cinémathèque of the Tehran Museum of Contemporary Arts and the various university film societies), as well as the cultural arms of foreign embassies (primarily the Iran–America Society, Göethe Institut, British Council, Alliance Française and Iran–Russia Cultural Society), screened foreign films in their original language on a regular basis for the public. In this manner, film festivals, film clubs and cultural attachés of foreign embassies became instrumental in increasing the public's exposure to quality foreign films and in raising the general level of film culture in the country.

Periodicals   Periodicals that seriously examined the art of film-making and film criticism – some of them underwritten by state institutions such as NIRT and MCA – took advantage of the plethora of film venues and the avid new readership, augmenting the quality of cinematic discourse. These included *Vizhe-ye Sinema va Te'atre*, *Sinema 52*, *Farhang va Zendegi*, *Sinema-ye Azad*, *Rudaki*, *Tamasha* and *Sorush*.

Production companies   Powerful film production companies, such as Telfilm and the Film Industry Development Company of Iran, were established in co-operation with the government to invest in films directed by Iranians and to channel co-production deals with international companies. Although co-production arrangements consisted primarily of using Iranian petrodollar financing and little use was made of local technical or on-camera talent, a certain amount of prestige and experience was gained from this arrangement.

Such a multi-dimensional infrastructure would not have come into being were it not for the quality and quantity of products that the film industry in general and the energetic, young and educated New Wave film-makers in particular were producing. A number of these film-makers were foreign-trained and, like those in the earlier Qajar period, had a significant collective impact on cinema; among them were Fereydoun Rahnema, Farrokh Gaffary, Bahman Farmanara, Dariush Mehrjui, Kamran Shirdel, Parviz Kimiavi, Sohrab Shahid Saless, Khosrow Haritash and Hajir Daryoush. These, together with other self-taught or locally trained directors like Bahram Baizai, Abbas Kiarostami, Masud Kimiai, Naser Taqvai, Parviz Sayyad and Amir Naderi, formed a formidable (but an all-male) cinematic force. The almost simultaneous emergence of a new generation of socially conscious leftist writers, such as Gholamhosain Saedi, Sadegh Chubak, Hushang Golshiri and Mahmood Dolat Abadi, whose works these film-makers adapted or with whom they collaborated on original screenplays, resulted in abandoning the traditional formulaic film genres and forms and their replacement with increasing realism and criticism, introduction of interiority and character psychology, and improved technical quality. It is the collaborative synergy of these directors and writers and the resultant narrative innovations, as well as the profession-alization of the film industry and the aforementioned infrastructural support from the state, that paved the way for a new film movement.

On the heels of Kimiai's *Qaisar*, Mehrjui's *Gav* delivered a second blow that shat-tered film industry complacency, ushering in what became known as the New Wave movement in Iran. Mehrjui's film embodied the contradictions that became the hall-mark of this movement: its sponsorship by the state and its censorship and banning by the state. The film's release was withheld because the government feared that it might contradict 'the official image of Iran as a modern nation of promise and plenty'.[21] However, when the film was unofficially entered in the Venice International Film Festival in 1969 and garnered a top award, the ministry lifted the ban. From then on, international festivals became players in the Iranian politics of cinema. On release, the film was greeted with great critical and public enthusiasm, generating high box-office revenues.[22] The international and national success of *Gav* opened the way for govern-ment support of the New Wave, hoping to create a positive international profile at the time as it was under criticism from an increasingly vociferous population of Iranian students abroad. In this way, the culture of the spectacle widened its horizons to reach over national borders. However, the New Wave was essentially a 'cinema of discon-tent', whose realistic and often critical assessment of contemporary social conditions, expressed through allegory and symbolism, contradicted the aims of its sponsors, causing tensions in the relationship and the censorship or confiscation of the works. These, in turn, both compromised the films and heightened audience interest in them, putting the film-makers in a double bind. Their acclaim at international festivals raised the profile of film-making as an art, a form of intellectual labour and a commercial enterprise. Foreign film festivals and film-goers thus became alternative audiences which these film-makers began to address. This bifurcated local and inter-national audience would prove to be a mixed blessing. For, on one hand, the New Wave film-makers' success abroad generally guaranteed them more political or commercial freedom at home, while, on the other hand, the foreign audiences and their expectations distorted their work somewhat, earning them criticism at home on the ground of peddling Third World misery to outsiders, instead of paying attention to native film-goers by glorifying their achievements. These were the sort of criticisms that other successful Third World film-makers also encountered.

Nonetheless, the success of *Gav* and the uneasy alliance of state and art-cinema encouraged other film-makers and producers, and a surge of original films, some of the best made in Iran, began appearing, as though a dam had been broken. The New Wave had begun. For example, the Institute for Intellectual Development of Children and Young Adults produced such important shorts as Amir Naderi's *Saz-e Dahani / Harmonica* (1973) and Abbas Kiarostami's *Mosafer / Traveller* (1973), and most of the finest animation films in Iran. Telfilm produced or co-produced such features as Hajir Daryoush's *Bita* (1972), Arbi Avanesian's *Cheshmeh / The Spring* (1972), Naser Taqvai's *Aramesh Dar Hozur-e Digaran / Tranquillity in the Presence of Others* (1971), Masud Kimiavi's *Mogholha / The Mongols* (1973), Bahman Farmanara's *Shazdeh Ehtejab / Prince Ehtejab* (1974), Sohrab Shahid Saless' *In der Fremde / Far From Home* (1975), Kimiai's *Ghazal* (1976), Kimiavi's *Bagh-e Sangi / Stone Garden* (1976), Mehrjui's *Dayereh-ye Mina / The Cycle* (1978) and Farmanara's *Sayehha-ye Boland-e Bad / Tall Shadows of the Wind* (1979). Likewise, the Film Industry Development Company produced Khosrow Haritash's *Malakut / Kingdom of Heaven* (1976), Mohammad Reza Aslani's *Shatranj-e Bad / Chess of the Wind* (1976), Baizai's *Kalagh / The Crow* (1977) and Kiarostami's *Gozaresh / Report* (1977).

Several New Wave films were also produced independently or commercially, such as Naderi's stirring *Tangsir* (1973) and Baizai's allegorical film about intolerance, *Gharibeh Va Meh / The Stranger and the Fog* (1975), and Golestan's biting satire *Asrar-e Ganj-e Darreh-ye Jenni / The Secrets of the Valley of the Jinn's Treasure-Trove* (1974), but these were outnumbered by those supported by governmental and semi-governmental agencies.

It must be noted that the New Wave film-makers did not form a cohesive film movement, as they were not driven by a monolithic ideology or by a programmatic style, undergirded by a singular financial infrastructure and film industry practice. They were a group of ambitious film-makers with diverse class background and ethno-religious affiliations, and they maintained individualistic – sometimes even antagonistic – tastes, aspirations and styles. These factors and the divisive politics of the government and the commercial stranglehold of major distributors discouraged these and other members of the film industry from forming sustained independent civil-society organizations, such as professional unions and pressure groups, through which they could represent themselves and exert collective influence. The majority of the New Wave film-makers were probably leftist in their political outlook and opposed to the Shah's government, but a majority of them also benefited from its largess, even if they bit the hand that fed them – like many great East European film-makers of the same era. Thus they remained largely atomized and compromised. As a result, the New Wave cinema was not so much a film-making movement as a film-making moment.

In this regard, it is worth taking note of one important exception: an effort to create an independent film collective in 1973. It began with the mass resignation of nineteen well-known producers, directors, cinematographers, composers and actors (almost all of them from the New Wave) from the National Union of Film Workers, an organization to which, according to an unwritten law, every person working in cinema had to belong (Daryoush 1975: 222). The resignations were driven by the signatories' desire to create a film industry 'worthy of our culture and nationality', since (according to them) all that the current films possessed of the rich Iranian culture was their Persian-language dialogue. The dissenters announced that they would use every legal means possible, including accepting financial aid from 'his excellency, Satan' to make films and to circumvent the 'distribution monopoly'. Their ultimate aims were to satisfy both the needs of consumers nationwide and their own desire to make films that 'while representing our culture, national characteristics and artistic growth, could also earn the country some foreign exchange' (all quotations are from Sho'ai 1975: 382–3).

To achieve that end, they created a film co-operative called the Progressive Film-makers' Union (PFU; Kanun-e Sinemagaran-e Pishro). Some of the film-makers invested their own money in their films, but ironically a great portion of the funding came from governmental and semi-governmental agencies, such as NIRT and its film subsidiary Telfilm, the Ministry of Economy, and the Film Industry Development Company of Iran.[23]

Nonetheless, the first films produced under the aegis of PFU were most impressive: Sohrab Shahid Saless' *Tabi'at-e Bijan / Still Life* (1975), Parviz Sayyad's *Bonbast / Dead End* (1979) and Dariush Mehrjui's *Dayereh-ye Mina / The Cycle* (1974). Shahid Saless had already made a name for himself nationally with his seminal first film *Yek Etefaq-e Sadeh / A Simple Event* (1973); his *Tabi'at-e Bijan* catapulted him to the inter-national arena. For this was a breakthrough film both in style and in its sensitive portrayal of the life of an old railway guard at an isolated rural junction. Its attention to daily details and to the nuances of feelings and relationships, combined with the depiction – at once harsh and poetic – of the life of the guard and his family and of his approaching retirement, filmed at a slow deliberate pace, made a powerful impact on audiences at home and abroad. However, when the government stopped the production of his next film, *Qarantineh / Quarantine*, Shahid Saless chose to go into exile in Germany, where he lived for some twenty-three years and made more than a dozen difficult films, before moving to yet another painful exile in the United States, where he died in 1997 (Naficy 2001).

Sayyad's *Bonbast* became a proto-exilic film for him, as it was completed a year before his own exile. It posited the Iranian society under the Shah as a prison, whose inhabitants were under constant police surveillance. It centred on the story of a young woman (played by Mary Apik) who is pursued by a man she thinks is a suitor but who turns out to be a security agent tailing her brother. Looking out of her window over-looking a cul-de-sac, she (mis)reads with disastrous consequences the surveying gaze of the state police as the desirous look of a potential suitor. *Bonbast*, which won a top award from the Moscow Film Festival, was Sayyad's most serious and politically nuanced work, and both the Pahlavi and the Islamist regimes apparently banned it.

On completion, Mehrjui's *Dayereh-ye Mina* (co-produced by PFU and Telfilm) became entangled in a web of special interest pressure exerted by the Iranian Medical Association and government censorship imposed by MCA, which kept the film out of distribution. It would take more than three years of negotiations and appeals to the ruling powers (including the queen, who supported the film) to finally obtain clear-ance. Furthermore, this came about only after the film had already been shown and critically well received abroad. *Dayereh-ye Mina*, based on a story by Saedi and adapted by him and Mehrjui, centred on the story of an old man (played by Esmail Mohammadi) and his teenage son Ali (Said Kangarani), who come to the capital city of Tehran to seek treatment for the old man's terminal gastrointestinal problems. It graphically related Ali's metamorphosis as a result of his involvement with corrupt and ruthless blood-banks that procure tainted blood from down-and-outs and addicts to sell it to hospitals whose staff, from cooks to physicians, seem to be driven by self-interest alone. By the film's end Ali is fully initiated in the art of unethical exploitation of others. In spite of its humour, colourful language and lively characters *Dayereh-ye Mina* is a darkly pessimistic and critical film about the cost of unbridled modernization in a society in transition. The film ingeniously embodies the dark side of this national transition and personal metamorphosis (of Ali), by staging much of the action at night or during the daily transition periods of dawn and dusk (Naficy 1985b: 704).

Some of the PFU signatories made films independently. Among them was playwright, theatre scholar and theatre director Bahram Baizai – his first feature *Ragbar / Downpour* (1972) had placed him among the New Wave film-makers – who made the enigmatic and richly textured *Gharibeh Va Meh / The Stranger and the Fog* (1975). With this film, he introduced into cinema certain thematic and narrative elements of ancient Iranian passion plays (Taziyeh) which would mark his individual style henceforward. Among these elements were an epic scale, claustrophobic atmosphere, archetypal characters, the passionate display of emotions, circular structures and themes of intolerance, injustice and martyrdom. Like his previous *Ragbar* and several of his later films, in *Gharibeh Va Meh* the harmonious life of a closed diegetic community is disturbed by the arrival of a stranger, whose presence throws into question the established order and relations, threatening the community's existence. The reaction of the community, a remote seaside village, to the newcomer named Ayat (Khosrow Shojazadeh) evolves from excitement to suspicion, fear to rejection, antagonism to marriage, and finally to separation. Filmed with sophisticated elegance, Ayat arrives and departs by the sea mysteriously, leaving the community off balance. His brief sojourn represents the journey of life and humans' search for identity, his departure a return to some mystical origin. *Gharibeh Va Meh*'s religious and philosophical musings made it unique (Naficy 1985c), but it shared the theme and the structure of return with other key New Wave films, among them Kimiai's *Dash Akol* and Mehrjui's *Gav*. Return to the origin is one of the characteristics of Frantz Fanon's second phase of creating a 'national culture', and of its cinematic elaboration by Teshome Gabriel (Fanon 1968: 206–48, Gabriel 1989). It is significant that the return to the past, or to some originary moment, that these New Wave films seemed to long for, was also a key feature of the Shah's attempts to create an official national culture, to which the New Wave film-makers were opposed. The coincidence in the official and oppositional cultures of the paradigm of return, among others, demonstrates that the oppositional film-makers had more in common with the official culture than they either realized or admitted.

While PFU's products were highly promising, this effort at creating an alternative mode of production did not produce many films and it did not last long. In fact, despite their remarkable output in terms of quality, the New Wave films as a whole represented only a small fraction of the forty-five to eighty feature films that were annually produced in the 1970s, a majority of which were escapist works, including tough guy films. These popular films were entertaining and they did deal with the disruptions of modernization and Westernization, albeit at an unconscious level and by means of repetitive formulaic themes and narrative structures. They did so, like many Third World films, through a binary structure that contrasted country with city, poor with rich, traditional with modern, religious with secular, self with other and native with foreign in such a way that the nativist term in the binary structure was favoured (Naficy 1981). The New Wave films' treatment of these same issues, however, was much more deliberate, realistic and original. There was another uncanny relationship between the popular films, particularly the tough guy genre, and the New Wave films. While the popular films often looked to the West, their narrative system – based on Persian story-telling and characterization – was deeply Iranian. On the other hand, the New Wave films often looked back to the roots while their narrative system, based on realism and the classical Hollywood style, was highly Western.

By mid-1970s, the film industry's socio-economic bases had begun to crumble, driving producers into bankruptcy. Several factors stood out. Import laws made it more lucrative to import films than to produce them locally. Nearly a quarter of the films' box-office receipts were taken away in taxes, for which little service was rendered. Inflation was pushing the cost of raw stock, equipment, services and salaries very high, while an imperial decree kept the ticket prices for this most popular form of entertainment deliberately low (Naficy 1979: 459). Low budgets for films procured at high interest-rates created so much instability that even a short lag between a film's completion and its release could drive producers into bankruptcy. Widespread censorship of political themes lengthened the lag, as completed films waited for months or even years to obtain exhibition permits (Mehrjui's *Dayereh-ye Mina / The Cycle* waited for three years). This jeopardized the producers financially and forced the directors into either timidity or obfuscation. Ironically the New Wave films adversely affected local film production by fragmenting the audience. Tired of formula tough guy, song-and-dance and family melodrama films, a portion of the audience sought relief in New Wave films, which – because of pervasive censorship – were unable to meet their heightened expectations. Unsatisfied by the heavily compromised films or by the abstruse filmic language that some of them used to evade censorship, the audience turned once again to foreign films. But many of the imports were considered softcore. For example, in February 1978 (a year before the fall of the Shah) the daily *Kayhan* reported that of 120 movie theatres in Tehran, 67 were showing 'sexy' films – a majority of which came from Italy and the United States (Naficy 1981: 351). The Ministry of Culture and Art announced that it would ban the production, import and exhibition of sexploitation films. These intentions, however, were highly suspect in so far as they had been voiced previously with little effect and in the light of the flouting of the existing laws against exhibiting such films, which had gone unpunished. Thus, while government involvement in film production contributed to the emergence of the New Wave films, its involvement in regulating the industry and censoring the films ultimately weakened both the industry and the cinema.

Faced with dismay and disarray, and a dearth of prestigious films, as well as the threat of a boycott by American film distributors who demanded a higher rate of return, the government decided in 1976 to increase admission prices by 35 per cent, allocate a sizeable credit to film-making, create the Film Import Association to streamline imports and invest in co-production projects with European and American companies. The changes created a short-lived resurgence in output but resulted in insignificant co-production returns. By 1978 the social turmoil that would lead to a revolution was underway, a turmoil in which movie theatres were heavily implicated. Many New Wave film-makers stayed in Iran during the revolution and, after a period of forced hiatus, began to make films under the Islamic Republic, gaining international fame and sometimes fortune: among them were Mehrjui, Kiarostami, Kimiai, Baizai and Taqvai. In fact, they were instrumental in reviving the Iranian cinema after an initial period of chaos and transition, putting it on the map of world cinema in the 1990s. Others went into exile (some before the revolution) where they made films, with mixed results: among them were Naderi, Shahid Saless, Sayyad, Tayyab, Allamehzadeh, Aslani and Marva Nabili. A number of these, particularly Naderi and Shahid Saless, contributed to the independent cinemas of Europe and the United States. All of them, and many more newcomers who turned to film-making abroad, served to collectively create an Iranian diaspora and exile cinema.

Islamic Republic Era cinema (1979–99)

In the early days of the anti-Shah revolution, later renamed the 'Islamic Revolution', cinema was condemned for what was widely perceived to be its support of the Shah's Westernization projects. Indeed traditionalists accused cinema of becoming an agent of cultural colonization of Iran by the West. As a result, movie theatres became a favourite target of revolutionary wrath, expressed most savagely in the August 1978 fiery inferno in Abadan's Rex Theatre, which killed nearly 400 spectators.[24] After this event, burning or destroying cinemas became an integral part of the dismantling of the Shah's regime. By the time the Islamic government was installed less than a year later, 180 cinemas nationwide had been destroyed, leaving only 256 extant. This created a shortage of exhibition sites from which the current cinema still suffers. However, unlike the Qajar Era clerical leader Shaikh Fazlollah Nuri, the clerical leaders of the 1979 revolution were not opposed to cinema *per se*. They were against what Ayatollah Ruhollah Khomeini called the 'misuse' of cinema by the Pahlavi regime to morally corrupt and politically subjugate the Iranians (Naficy 1992a: 181). Consequently, instead of proscribing it, they advocated its adoption as an ideological apparatus with the goal of using it to transform the Pahlavi culture into an Islamic culture. The major concepts the authorities frequently pronounced when speaking of 'Islamic culture' can be classified under the following categories: nativism (return to traditional values and mores), populism (justice), defence of the disinherited (*mostaz'afan*), monotheism (*towhid*), anti-idolatry (*anti-taqut*), theocracy (*velayat-e faqih*, rule of the supreme jurisprudent), ethicalism and puritanism (*Amr-e beh Ma'ruf va Nah-ye az Monkar*), political and economic independence (*esteqlal*) and combating arrogant world imperialism (*estekbar-e jahani*, a coded term for the United States). The last two concepts were condensed in the oft-repeated slogan 'neither East nor West'.

Nearly twenty years later, the Toronto International Film Festival and New York Film Festival respectively called the Iranian cinema of the 1990s one of the 'pre-eminent national cinemas' and one of the 'most exciting' cinemas in the world.[25] This was a new vital cinema with its own special industrial and financial structure and unique ideological, thematic, generic and production values. And it was part of a more general transformation in the political culture of the country since the revolution. Significantly there were some similarities and continuities with the Pahlavi Era film industry, which will be noted. But this was not an 'Islamic' cinema, a monolithic, propagandistic cinema that upheld the ruling ideology; in fact, at least three major types of cinema evolved.

The first to emerge was the state-sponsored 'Official Cinema', which explicitly supported the government's ideological projects and policies. Financial returns were not a major factor, while ideological earnestness was. Much of this cinema was non-fictional, dealing with and glorifying the revolutionary movement against the Shah and the savage eight-year war with Iraq. Many of the Official Cinema films were broadcast on television. The 'Populist Cinema', funded by the private sector, was a commercial cinema which nonetheless affirmed the post-revolutionary Islamic values – not as manifestly as the Official Cinema, but embedded in the plot, theme, character, portrayal of women and *mise-en-scène*. The 'Art Cinema' or 'Quality Cinema', on the other hand, engaged with those values and tended to critique, often implicitly, the social conditions under the Islamic government. The Populist Cinema and the Art Cinema evolved almost simultaneously, gaining prominence as the Official Cinema waned. The struggle over the Art Cinema was the most intense, for Art Cinema film-makers (at least in the first dozen years after the Islamic Republic was established) were largely dependent on state financing and support at the same time as they wished to remain ideologically and aesthetically independent, even critical, of their sponsors.

In terms of quantity, the Art Cinema was the smallest of the three forms (accounting for perhaps 10 to 15 per cent of the national output), but in terms of local / international prestige and foreign market revenues, it was the most significant. Because of this impact and the light that it sheds on the cultural complexity of the Iranian cinema, the Art Cinema is emphasized here. A documentary film movement, first centring on the revolution, then on the eight-year war with Iraq and, finally, on social issues, also emerged, which had its own Official, Populist and Art Cinema attributes. The chief public venues for them were the varied revolutionary and war-related organs and national television networks – almost all of them state-run.

In what follows, the historical and aesthetic evolution of cinema and the film industry under the new regime are examined.

Purging the Pahlavi cinema (1978–82)

The first stage in transforming the Pahlavi cinema (dubbed by religious hardliners the 'cinema of idolatry') into an Islamicized cinema was the cleansing of the Pahlavi-era movie theatres, which began with their fiery destruction. Fortunately, with the exception of Rex Theatre, no casualties were reported since most of the theatres were apparently empty when they were attacked. Those theatres that remained had their names changed, usually from Western names popular during the Pahlavi period to Islamic, Third World ones.[26] Some theatres were converted for other purposes and the stage of the Rudaki Hall theatre apparently underwent a ceremonial Muslim ablution (*ghosl*) in order to transform it from an 'unclean' stage into a religiously clean one (Saedi 1984: 7).

The next step in this transformation was the curbing of the foreign imports that had flooded the market, a market in which neither local businessmen nor the government were investing due to volatile and uncertain economic and political conditions. Russian and Eastern bloc films – inexpensive to import – surpassed the American, Italian and Japanese films. For example, 74 (or more than a third) of the 213 foreign films licensed by the Ministry of Culture and Islamic Guidance (MCIG) for 1981 came from the Soviet bloc. Sixty-nine of these were produced in the Soviet Union alone. Italy ranked second with thirty-eight films and, surprisingly, the United States came in third with twenty-seven movies.[27] Of the new imports, those that catered to the revolutionary spirit clearly dominated. The best known of these, banned during the Shah's era, included Constantine Costa Gavras' *Z* and *Etat de siège / State of Siege*, Patricio Guzman's *Batalla de Chile / Battle of Chile*, Moustapha Akkad's *al-Risalah / The Message* and Gillo Pontecorvo's *La Battaglia di Algeri / The Battle of Algiers*.

The clerical establishment was concerned but divided about film imports. Some praised these so-called 'revolutionary films' because they showed 'the struggle of people oppressed by colonialism and imperialism'.[28] Others condemned them as made-in-Hollywood films with only a 'revolutionary mask'.[29] The secular intellectuals, too, worried about the influx of cheap revolutionary foreign films, but for different reasons. For example, playwright Gholamhosain Saedi charged that those films were 'full of cannons, tanks, rifles, weapons and corpses, without regards to quality or artistic merit' (Saedi 1982: 7).

As early as July 1979, efforts to purify the imports by reducing their in-flow began. First, importing B-grade Turkish, Indian and Japanese films was curtailed, followed closely by a ban on all 'imperialist' and 'anti-revolutionary' films (Naficy 1992a: 209, n. 29). As the political relationship between the United States and Iran deteriorated, American films were the next group to be excluded. In fact, because of the belief that Western films cause moral corruption, a larger percentage of Western films were denied exhibition permit than films from any other region. In the first three years of the post-revolutionary regime, 898 foreign films were reviewed, 531 of which were denied exhibition permit. Of these, 317 came from the Western bloc, 140 from the Eastern bloc and 17 from the Third World (ibid.: 185). The curbing of Western imports was, however, not uniform or hermetic, as American films that had been imported prior to the cut-off (such as *Airport 79* and *High Noon*) continued to appear on the screens even during the 'hostage crisis' period.

Local films also underwent this transitional purification which, like everything else in this period, was by turns chaotic, *ad hoc*, expedient and ingenuous. Film producers engaged in a cat-and-mouse game with the government. They re-titled, edited or re-edited their films. For example, Amir Shervan's film *Bi Harekat, Tekun Nakhor / Freeze, Don't Move* was re-titled *Jahel Va Mohassel / The Tough Guy and the Student* during the revolution and, after the revolution, it was re-titled again, to become *Hero'in / Heroin*. None of these changes improved the film's box office! Sensing the inevitability of Islamization, film exhibitors attempted to control the damage by voluntarily keeping sex off the screens and by 'replacing dirty films with entertainment of an educational caliber'.[30] One method was censorship by magic marker, which involved painting over the naked legs and exposed body parts of women in every frame. When this method failed, the exhibitors simply cut off the offending scenes.[31] At times, the cutting was so drastic that films became incomprehensible.

Dissatisfied with the limited changes made by the producers and exhibitors, the government mandated an exhibition permit for films. This meant that all the already-made films had to be reviewed, with the result that a remarkable number of Iranian films were banned. Of the 2,208 features made before and immediately after the revolution (up to 1982), only 252 were granted exhibition permits (Naficy 1992a: 187). Since very few post-revolutionary films had been made, such a high rate of denial represented both a decisive rejection of the Pahlavi Era cinema and an effective end to the post-revolutionary *laissez-faire* atmosphere. Low-quality films were not the only type to receive the axe; many films of the New Wave directors were also banned, among them Khosrow Haritash's *Malakut / The Divine One* (1976), Mohammad Reza Aslani's *Shatranj-e Bad / Chess of the Wind* (1976), Parviz Kimiavi's *O.K. Mister* (1979), Bahram Baizai's *Cherikeh-ye Tara / Tara's Ballad* (1978) and *Marg-e Yazdgerd / Yazdgerd's Death* (1980), Dariush Mehrjui's *Hayat-e Poshti-ye Madreseh-ye Adl-e Afaq / The Yard Behind Adl-E Afaq School* (1980) and Ali Erfan's *Aqa-ye Hiroglif / Mr Hieroglyphic* (1980).

The purification process was applied not only to the theatres and the films, but also to the people who worked in the industry. A general charge against many entertainers and film-makers at this time was that they were associated with the Shah's Westernized excesses, corruption, amorality and security agency Savak. As a result, they were subjected to the Islamically inspired cleansing, which involved legal charges against them, incarceration, confiscation of their property, banning of their faces, voices and bodies from the screen, censoring of their products and, on rare occasions, even execution (Naficy 1987: 452). Some theatre owners were arrested and charged with crimes, ranging from smuggling narcotics to peddling pornography, and from prostitution to being an agent of Israel. Uncertainty about what was allowed led to a general purging of women from the screens.

These draconian purification measures were only one set of reasons for the slow revival of cinema. Islamization was not pro forma by any means, as many other socio-political and economic factors contributed to creating a very fluid and contentious atmosphere within the film industry. These included the massive financial damage that the film industry suffered during the revolution, a lack of government interest in cinema during the transitional period, a vacuum of centralized authority, antagonistic rivalry over cinema among various institutions, the absence of an appropriate cinematic model (no 'Islamic film' genre existed), heavy competition from imports, a drastic deterioration of the public image of cinema, haphazard censorship of films and the flight into exile of many in the industry.

It was under these circumstances that, in January 1980, the Society of Cinema Owners rightly criticized the government for its inaction regarding cinema. Significantly, however, it urged the government to refrain from unplanned 'spontaneous reform'.[32] The film producers, who shared the theatre owners' concerns, wanted to reduce government interference in the film industry. In a 1981 open letter, they urged it to apply the constitution 'organically and comprehensively' to prevent Iranian cinema from becoming a caricature of the Eastern bloc cinema (Naficy 1987: 188). A few films of quality were made: among them Naderi's *Jostoju / Search* (1980) and Baizai's two films *Cherikeh-ye Tara* and *Marg-e Yazdgerd*, both of which were banned. The Pahlavi Era tough guy genre was suppressed completely, to emerge in disguised forms later.

Documenting the revolutionary period and the compilation genre

In this feverish period, a movement to document the anti-Shah activities emerged, in which both fiction and documentary film-makers participated. Freed from censorship and organized repression and fired by revolutionary ardour, film groups and individuals used equipment and raw stock 'liberated' from MCA, NIRT and other agencies to record the ever-growing pace of demonstrations. After the departure of the Shah and the establishment of the Islamic Republic in early 1979, much of this footage was compiled into raw sound-and-vision pieces and broadcast by NIRT. Indeed, the revolutionary events, the taking of American hostages and the recently begun war with Iraq created a situation ripe for the emergence of a new documentary style: namely, the compilation-newsreel genre. Many of these were amateur films, for novices or political groups without film experience made them. *Azadi / Freedom* (1979) was an example – like many films of this genre, it was shot on 16 mm format and broadcast by television networks (many were also filmed on Super 8 format or on video). It was not an analytical film; rather, it was given to the cursory but emotional presentation of raw sounds and pictures of revolutionary events from the points of view of the Muslim factions. It had a 'you are there' quality, with its well-integrated slogans, chants and songs, and with its images which were sometimes out of focus and its dialogue which at times was cut off mid-sentence by editing.

Experienced film-makers also made many compilation-newsreel films, among them was Barbod Taheri's feature-length *Soqut-e '57 / The Fall of '57* (1979). But even these pro-revolution films were soon subjected to censorship as the fast-changing pace of events redefined previously accepted history and facts. Taheri, who had filmed Baizai's first feature film *Ragbar / Downpour*, contended that *Soqut-e '57*, about the coming revolution, was widely shown in Iran until it was banned in 1984. The reason he was given for the banning was this: 'there are moments in the life of a nation when people no longer need to know what has actually happened'. He was told that to obtain a new exhibition permit, he would have to remove documentary footage of actual events showing wide participation of secular and leftist groups in the revolution, armed forces' attacks on demonstrators and even Khomeini's first speech, delivered in a Tehran cemetery in which he had condemned the Shah for making cemeteries prosperous. Thus the process of rewriting of history entered the documentary cinema as well. Complaining that 'Islamic censorship' had gripped cinema 'like an octopus', Taheri chose life in exile, leaving the country in mid-1985.[33]

Some of the compilation films went beyond the documentation and reportage of immediate events and took a longer historical view, using archival footage and photographs culled from foreign archives or liberated from Iranian archives. During the revolution, these archives were ransacked and their contents were often burned and destroyed. The black burn-marks on the pavements outside many archive buildings and television stations testified to this fiery destruction. With these actions, many historically valuable news films, documentaries and fictional films of the Pahlavi Era were forever lost.[34] The soundtrack of the compilation films generally consisted of live sounds of chants, demonstrations, gunfire and speeches, often accompanied by highly partisan and rhetorical off-camera voice-overs.

Beside individuals who filmed the revolutionary events independently, many government agencies sponsored film-makers to document the revolution, its roots and its aftermath. The Ministry of Culture and Art, now called the Ministry of Culture and Islamic Guidance (MCIG), supported Hosain Torabi's *Bara-ye Azadi / For Revolution* (1979); national television networks supported Naderi's *Jostoju / Search*, Manuchehr Moshiri's *Az Khak Ta Khak / From Dust to Dust* (1981) and Asadollah Niknejad's *Dard-e Hamsangaram / The Pain of My Fellow Trench Man* (1981); the

Centre for the Intellectual Development of Children and Young Adults sponsored Abbas Kiarostami's *Qaziyyeh: Shekl-e Avval, Shekl-e Dovvom / Problem: Alternative One, Alternative Two* (1978), Mohammad Reza Moqqadasin's *Kurehpaz Khaneh / Brick Factory* (1981) and Mohammad Reza Aslani's *Kudak Va Este'mar / Child and Imperialism* (1981).

A new development in this period, was the emergence of non-governmental nation-wide video and film exhibition networks managed by radical oppositional groups. The two major groups of the time, Sazman-e Mojahedin-e Khalq and Sazman-e Cherikha-ye Fada'i-ye Khalq, established these networks to disseminate information and to agitate. The Mojahedin opted for a video distribution system, by means of which they showed their own products to their supporters throughout the country. The Fada'ian, on the other hand, chose the more expensive film distribution system, which relied on making multiple copies of films that were exhibited in universities and colleges nationally. Unlike the Mojahedin's, this latter network was a commercial enterprise.

The Mojahedin's programming was almost entirely documentary in nature. It consisted of lightly edited footage of events and rallies or of speeches given by its leaders, such as the *Tazahorat-e Madaran-e Mosalman / Demonstration of Muslim Mothers* (1979?), *Mosahebeh ba Khanevadeh-ha-ye Khoshdel va Zolanvar / Interview with Families of Khoshdel and Zolanvar* (1979), *Sokhanrani-ye Masud Rajavi / Masud Rajavi's Speech* (1979) and *Sokhanrani-ye Baradaran Masud Rajavi va Musa Khiabani / Speeches of Brothers Masud Rajavi and Musa Khiabani* (1980).

The Fada'ian's programming, spearheaded by film-maker Reza Allamehzadeh, was more versatile, consisting of re-edited documentaries from Vietnam, the Soviet Union and Eastern Europe dubbed into Persian, as well as indigenous documentaries which Fada'ian members or sympathizers put together. Allamehzadeh himself directed *Harf Bezan Torkaman / Speak Up Turkmen* (1979), fifty copies of which were circulated. He also made *Mahi-ye Siah-e Kuchulu-ye Dana / The Wise Little Black Fish* (1980), about Samad Behrangi, a famous leftist schoolteacher. Another Fada'ian product was *Marg Bar Amperialism / Death to Imperialism* (1979), which was a filmed record of Said Soltanpur's polemical play that had been staged in the Tehran streets. These films were shown in mosques, colleges, universities and other educational institutions throughout the country. However, an official censor who according to Allamehzadeh was actually blind, banned Allamehzadeh's *Mahi-ye Siah-e Kuchulu-ye Dana*![35]

The Kurdish resistance movement, too, created documentaries about its various military battles with the Islamic government, most of which were shown abroad. Among them were *Dargiriha-ye Mahabad / Altercations in Mahabad* (1980?) and *Jang-e Sanandaj / Battle of Sanandaj* (1980).

The operation of these oppositional video and film networks gradually came to a halt when, in 1980, the government launched its Cultural Revolution project, which closed down all universities, thus robbing the groups (especially the Fada'ian) of their major film exhibition assets – halls, projectors and student audiences. By mid-1981, when the government began systematically to suppress all opponents, no above-ground oppositional film practice remained and Allamehzadeh went into exile in the Netherlands. In its place, another official documentary cinema emerged that was supported by the television networks, the Ministry of Culture and Islamic Guidance, the Foundation for the Dispossessed, the Reconstruction Crusade, the Basij Corps and the Farabi Cinema Foundation.

Some of the footage shot during and immediately after the revolution found its way abroad, where it was put together into compilation documentaries by Iranian exiles. All were anti-Shah and pro-revolution, many were made by leftist student film-makers and a majority attempted with various degrees of rhetorical bombast to recount the political history of Iran in the twentieth century, leading up to the anti-Shah revolution. Among those made in the United States were Rafigh Pooya and Marcia Goodman's *Jom'eh-ye Khunin / Bloody Friday* (1979), *Iran Dar Bohbuheh-ye Enqelab / Iran in the Throes of Revolution* (1979) made by the Iranian Students Association, *Sho'lehha-ye Azadi / Flames of Freedom* (1979) by the Confederation of Iranian Students, and Mohammad Tehrani's *Ta Azadi / Till Revolution* (1980). Tehrani's two-hour M.F.A. thesis film (at UCLA) attempted to present an impartial view of Iranian history from the early Pahlavi period to the revolution. It noted the contribution of various factions to the revolution, but its length, uneven pacing and unwieldy structure worked against it. Bigan Saliani's feature-length film *Iran: Inside the Islamic Revolution* (1980) was the only one aired by the Public Broadcasting System. It was based on his six-month stay in Iran in 1978–9, during which he focused on life in the village of Abgir to document the impact of the revolution. It also provided a historical analysis of Iran since Mossadeq's overthrow in the 1950s, using interviews with participants. This was technically the most polished of all Iranian documentaries. However, it was flawed by its one-sided view of the revolutionary potential of the clerics in Iranian history. Rafigh Pooya's *Dar Defa' Az Mardom / In Defence of the People* (1981) was also a sophisticated product. It used the footage of a Shah Era televised military trial of a group of leftist intellectuals, among them Khosrow Golsorkhi, Keramat Daneshian and film-maker Allamehzadeh, to frame Pooya's analysis of the rise and fall of the Shah and the subsequent political developments in Iran, including the failed military attempt to rescue the American hostages (Golsorkhi and Daneshian, who boldly confessed to and defended their communist beliefs, were subsequently executed). The film's chief drawback was insufficient explanation of both the frame of the film and the circumstances surrounding the defendants' imprisonment, trial and death.[36]

Institutionalizing a new 'committed' cinema (1982–99)

Early in this phase, the Islamic hardliners took charge of all major institutions and – with the waging of the long and devastating war with Iraq, the resolution of the American hostage crisis and the routing of all major organized opposition – consolidated their grip on the country. Like the Pahlavi Era, political consolidation entailed a takeover of culture and the arts, including cinema and broadcasting. If the purging and purifying of the old film industry was chaotic, destructive and rapid, the institutionalization of the new cinema necessitated planning and constructive effort. However, this involved a restructuring not only of the industry but also of public taste.[37]

If the Shah ensured his control of the culture industry by appointing royal relatives and loyal confidants to head the various key institutions, cronyism based on shared Islamic values became a primary early factor in facilitating this new restructuring. A group of Islamically committed young men who had formed Ayat Film company prior to the revolution supplied some of the key figures for this purpose, as they took up key positions within the new government, the film industry and allied institutions immediately after the revolution. For example, Mir Hosain Musavi became prime minister, Fakhred-Din Anvar took a number of high posts both within MCIG and Voice and Vision of the Islamic Republic (the broadcasting network), Mohammad Ali Najafi became the first supervisor of cinema within MCIG, Mostafa Hashemi was appointed to a high position in Ayatollah Khomeini's Propaganda Office and Mohammad Beheshti became the director of the new and powerful Farabi Cinema Foundation. Initially after the revolution, Ayat Film members were among the few people whom the new government trusted because of both their arts / architecture background and their Islamic commitment. Their impact on restructuring the film industry was wide and deep because of their dispersion in the consciousness-shaping industries, their managerial competence and their longevity in office throughout the first dozen years of the Islamic regime, during which time Hojjatolestalm Mohammad Khatami was the Minister of Culture and Islamic Guidance. However, these key figures, including Khatami (who would be elected to the country's president in a landslide victory in 1997), had been brought down by the mid-1990s as a result of a major national debate, fanned by hardliners who claimed that an organized, multi-faceted 'cultural invasion' of the country by 'Western imperialism' was underway.[38] With their removal, a new post-Khomeini era began.

Regulating the industry

Early on, MCIG was charged with overseeing the film industry. In June 1982, the cabinet approved landmark regulations governing movies and videos and charged MCIG with their implementation. The concentration at MCIG of power to set policies and to regulate and enforce them, both reduced the confusion of the previous period and enhanced the government's control. These regulations codified many of the 'Islamic values' noted earlier and they were instrumental in facilitating the shift away from Pahlavi cinema. They stipulated that all films and videos shown publicly must bear an exhibition permit. Furthermore, they banned films and videos that:

- Weaken monotheism and other Islamic principles or insult them in any manner
- Insult directly or indirectly the prophets, imams, the velyat faqih (supreme jurisprudent), the ruling council or the mojtaheds (jurisprudents)
- Blaspheme the values and personalities held sacred by Islam and by other religions mentioned in the constitution
- Encourage wickedness, corruption and prostitution
- Encourage or teach dangerous addictions and unsavoury professions such as smuggling
- Negate the equality of all people regardless of colour, race, language, ethnicity and belief
- Encourage foreign cultural, economic and political influence contrary to the government's 'neither West nor East' policy
- Express or disclose information that can hurt the country and which might be exploited by foreigners
- Show details of scenes of violence and torture in such a way as to disturb or mislead viewers

- Misrepresent historical and geographical facts
- Lower audience taste by low production and artistic values
- Negate the values of self-sufficiency and economic and social independence

These ambiguous regulations[39] were the new government's attempt at codifying Islamic values that, during the transition period, had been largely undefined and subject to local and expedient interpretations. Over the years, they were enforced with varying degree of zeal, but they continually evolved towards a liberal interpretation.

Initially, MCIG developed a tripartite policy that involved providing 'guidance', 'sponsorship' and 'supervision' to the film industry (Dadgu 1991: 63–5). The guidance and supervision functions were implemented during the multi-step review process in which the regulations classifying 'Islamic values' were applied in great detail to every film. MCIG reviewed each synopsis, screenplay and completed film, suggesting or demanding alteration. If the synopsis were approved, permission to write the screenplay would be granted. If the screenplay were approved, a production permit – approving cast and crew by name – would be issued. On approval of the completed film, an exhibition permit would be issued, specifying the cinemas in which the film would be shown. Until mid-1989, all film ideas were subjected to this process, undergoing many changes prior to their release as films. Statistics bear out the effectiveness of the review process (and perhaps the low quality of the submitted scripts): of 202 screenplays reviewed between 1980 and 1982, only 25 per cent were approved (Naficy 1992a: 183–94). However, many films that received a production permit and got completed, were refused an exhibition permit (Omid 1987: 697–713). Some of those that did receive exhibition permits were subjected to what might be called 'vigilante censorship', whereby official or unofficial vigilante religious groups harassed the filmgoers or damaged the movie theatres. For example, Baizai's *Mosaferan / Travellers* (1991), which had an exhibition permit, was not screened in four cities because motorcycle-riding vigilantes threatened the theatres and their patrons. Likewise, as noted earlier, the supporters of the Party of God attacked the theatres that were showing Mirbaqeri's *Adam Barfi / The Snowman*. But this form of censorship was localized and rather limited, as both of these films were shown in other theatres and cities, supported by appreciative audiences.

The various components of censorship did not remain static, however. In April 1989, the government loosened its grip by allowing previously censored films to be screened. Barely a month later, for the first time in Iranian cinema, the requirement for screenplay approval for quality film-makers was removed. While laudable, the removal of the script-approval phase ironically made the film producers, concerned with their heavy investment in films, more cautious and prone to self-censorship. In this manner, the guidance and supervision functions were internalized by those who were subjected to them.

But since such internalization was not complete and was resisted by many filmmakers (internalization was never panoptic), external government censorship and intimidation continued. As a result, a number of films by veteran and new filmmakers were banned, even those made by Grade A film-makers. Two films by the New Wave film-maker Baizai (*Cherikeh-ye Tara / Tara's Ballad* and *Marg-e Yazdgerd / Yazdgerd's Death*) remained permanently banned. *Hayat-e Poshti-ye Madreseh-ye Adl-e Afaq / The Yard Behind Adl-E Afaq School*, which had been completed by New Wave film-maker Mehrjui in 1980, continued to be banned until its release in 1989 under the new title *Madreseh'i Keh Miraftim / The School We Went To*. Mehrjui's *Banu / Lady* (1991) was also banned for some time. Two years after its completion, the authorities ruled that it could be released if the close-up shots of the female lead were removed.[40] Three films of the rising star of post-revolutionary cinema, Mohsen Makhmalbaf, proved to be controversial and were confiscated. They were *Nowbat-e Asheqi / A Time to Love* (1991), *Shabha-ye Zayandehrud / Zayandehrud Nights* (1991) and *Nun Va Goldun / The Bread and the Vase* (1995). Censorship was so harsh and arbitrary that in mid-1995, a group of 214 film-workers in an open letter to MCIG demanded a thorough re-evaluation of the complex rules and procedures governing film production and exhibition; without such a re-evaluation they predicted that the 'national film industry' would fall prey to foreign films. To prevent that situation, the signatories demanded that independent professional guilds that could supervise the industry be strengthened.[41] In essence, they were demanding that the industry be allowed to move out of the political into the professional sphere, that self-regulation replace government regulation. As will be seen, these efforts bore fruit.

Like many authoritarian regimes, such as those of communist Poland and Hungary and of Pahlavi Era Iran, by limiting the explicit expression of ideas by official censorship, the Islamist regime forced Iranian film-makers to develop creative and subversive alternatives for indirect expression, resulting in hermeneutically rich but sometimes contradictory, convoluted and unrealistic films.[42] Lack of realism was particularly glaring in the representation of male / female relationships (discussed later) and in the representation of the clergy. Although indirect political and social criticism was not uncommon in Art Cinema films, care was taken not to offend the clerical establishment or the religious doctrines and saints. This was partly accomplished by the almost total erasure of official Islam and of the clerics from the bulk of high-quality films – an anomaly and a lie given the dominant presence of official Islam and Islamic officials in the society at large.

However, the significant and signifying contribution of political, social and economic censorship to the rise of Art Cinema cannot be discounted, despite its already recounted ill effects. For these limitations did not just hamper expression, they also sharpened it. When the boundaries of what is permissible are as clearly defined and as deeply internalized as under the Islamic Republic, these boundaries become a challenge for critical artists against which they can test their creativity and develop their *auteur* style. Kiarostami has, without condoning it, repeatedly pointed to this unexpectedly positive outcome of censorship.

Encouraging local production

The liberalizing measures were not limited to the guidance and supervisory functions; they extended to the financial sponsorship of cinema. The state involvement in film production, a feature of Pahlavi Era cinema, not only continued but also intensified to the point of a *de facto* takeover of all means of production for a period of time. In 1983, MCIG created Farabi Cinema Foundation (FCF) to centralize and control the import and export of films, raw stock and film equipment, and to encourage local production – a task that it accomplished with much success. The monopolization of many aspects of the industry meant that the government had to render some services in return, such as facilitating bank loans, rationalizing cumbersome rules and regulation, and expediting the production and exhibition of films. In the first six months of 1984, for example, the following measures were taken: the municipal tax for local films was reduced from 20 per cent to 5 per cent, while it increased from 20 per cent to 25 per cent for imported films. Ticket prices were increased by 25 per cent. FCF was exempted from paying customs duty for its imports. And changes in the composition of the 'screen committee' that was responsible for assigning films to theatres allowed representatives of producers and exhibitors to take part in the proceedings. By 1999, the government reduced its direct involvement in film exhibition by turning over the task of assigning films to theatres for exhibition to the industry itself.

To generate funds for health, social security and workers' compensation provision for entertainers and film-makers, the Majles (parliament) passed a resolution late in 1985 that imposed a 2 per cent tax on the box-office receipts of all theatres. To further bolster local production, the 1987 national budget passed by the Majles contained a provision for banks to offer long-term loans for film production. In May 1989, MCIG announced further measures: allocation of foreign-exchange funds for importing chronically scarce technical equipment and supplies, availability of interest-free credits and long-term loans, sponsorship of local films in international film festivals and, finally, the inauguration of a social security system for film-workers were approved by the parliament.

The attempts by the Rafsanjani administration in the mid-1990s to privatize major industries was extended to cinema, resulting in a partial removal of government subsidies to the film industry and in a more forceful emergence of the private commercial sector in film-making. The Populist Cinema began to surface more widely from this period. The progressive film-rating system put into place in the late 1980s encouraged the production of Art Cinema films, but it also extended government's control over the films. It awarded Grade A films the best exhibition sites, opening dates and longer runs, and it awarded the makers of such films higher budgets, loans at lower interest and increased television publicity. FCF's director Mohammad Beheshti told me in an interview (Tehran, August 1991) that because of these measures a new and unprecedented situation had developed in post-revolutionary Iran, whereby 'the best-quality films are also often the most popular films'. However, this was not true in the case of all Art Cinema films, some of which gained more acceptance abroad than at home.

Another rating system based on the age of the film-goers, which had been tried ineffectively before the revolution, was tried again, most prominently in 1999 for the popular film *Masa'eb-e Shirin / Sweet Agony* (1999). Children under the age of eighteen were not allowed to enter the theatre, causing much controversy since (like all others) this film had already undergone the rigorous multi-phased review process and had received an exhibition permit. The revival of this age-based rating system threatened to become an additional phase in that process. However, public and industry pressure forced a change in the film's rating to PG-17, allowing children under seventeen to attend the film if accompanied by a parent. The influential *Mahnameh-ye Sinemai-ye Film* noted in an editorial that since the review process eradicated sex, obscenity and bad words from cinema, unbridled violence had become a key permissible attraction. It supported the age-based rating system as a viable method for curbing this type of violence on television and cinema screens, and in domestic and imported films alike. How this rating system is to be prevented from becoming another form of censorship remains to be seen.[43]

At the same time that it encouraged local film-making, the government restricted the import of foreign films, thus removing a key obstacle to the development of the local film industry. While competition from foreign films can help to improve local productions, the qualitative discrepancy in the Third World between European and American films and indigenous products is so great that competition is generally more stifling than stimulating for the local industry. Thus protectionism was at this point, when the local film industry was so weak, an enlightened and necessary policy. The result was that Iranian cinema found a captive audience, who gradually got to like what was made for them, and in turn influenced the film-makers to make films for them. The doubling of the population since the revolution extended the potential spectatorial base. Foreign films found their way to the audience through pirated videos that were widely, but often clandestinely, available.

The positive impact of these measures was reflected in the steady rise in the quantity of films produced (see Table 1). The feature-film output, which stood at a high figure of twenty-eight films in 1979–80 (the year of the revolution) due to the pre-revolution films that were in the pipeline, declined precipitously to fifteen in 1981–2. However, it increased steadily thereafter, during the consolidation period, to reach sixty-four in 1997–8. This made Iranian cinema one of the most productive in the

Table 1 Number of feature films produced after the Revolution

Year of production	Number of features produced
1980	28
1981	31
1982	15
1983	24
1984	30
1985	41
1986	43
1987	52
1988	42
1989	48
1990	56
1991	45
1992	52
1993	56
1994	45
1995	62
1996	63
1997	54
1998	64
Total sum	851

Source: Farabi Cinema Foundation 1997: 75, 1998: 12. [44]

world. According to Attola Mohajerani, Minister of Culture and Islamic Guidance, in 1998 Iranian cinema ranked tenth in the world in terms of output, surpassing Germany, Brazil, South Korea, Canada and Australia, and far exceeding the high-volume traditional Middle Eastern film producers, Egypt and Turkey.[45]

Despite high inflation, the production cost of Iranian films was very low, hovering between US$100,000 and US$200,000. Such relatively low investment could be recovered and profits made given the size and the captivity of the primary audience. But without foreign competition at home and foreign-exchange money from audiences abroad, the Iranian film industry's capacity for sustained innovation and increased income will be limited.

Exhibition bottleneck and alternative venues

The increased production revealed a glaring shortage in film exhibition venues – the most underdeveloped aspect of the industry. Although incomplete and inconsistent, statistics show that the number of theatres and film-goers increased rapidly during the first post-revolution decade. For example, the number of commercial theatres nation-wide grew from 198 in 1979 to 277 in 1984, and the seating capacity increased from 141,399 to 170,265. Likewise, attendance at Tehran movie theatres rose from some 24 million in 1984 to nearly 28 million in 1986. However, film-going in the first decade did not reach the peak of the Shah's era, although curtailment of previously allowed forms of entertainment and cheap tickets made cinema one of the few affordable forms of mass entertainment. Some of the reasons for the apparent audience disinterest may be found in the decreased number of movie theatres nationwide compared to the Shah's time, the undesirability of theatre locations, the bad condition of the halls and the projection systems, the low quality of many of the films and the audience demography, which consisted primarily of young, unmarried and unemployed males who sometimes heckled women. The aggressive and male-oriented genres and themes of the Official and some of the Populist Cinema films, which further discouraged family and women spectators, compounded these factors. During the 1980s, movie theatres were classified into four categories, but few of them ranked high. Although the condition of the halls and projection equipment and the quality of the films improved considerably in the 1990s, the increase in the number of cinemas was negligible (increasing by only 6 between 1984 and 1997, reaching 283 theatres nation-wide, with 76 theatres in Tehran alone). The doubling of the population since the revolution, from some 30 million to nearly 60 million, deepened the crisis of exhibition space nationwide. The government repeatedly announced plans to expedite and encourage the building of new commercial cinemas, including multiplexes, but the pace remained much too slow. Part of the reason was the takeover of more than 100 of the country's theatres by government-supported Islamist organizations such as the Foundation of the Disinherited in the 1980s and the Centre for Islamic Thought and Art in the 1990s. The latter organization was also involved in the production and distribution of films. The private sector found it difficult to compete with such a powerful vertically integrated organization. The number of national television networks was increased from two to five, with the aim of serving two of the largest and most disaffected population segments: young adults and urban residents.[46] These extra television channels opened up new venues for film viewing.

The general poor quality of the Official and Populist Cinema movies, and the overall lack of variety on television, helped to make the new medium of video a popular alternative. By 1998 some 15 million television sets and 7 million video-cassette recorders (VCRs) were operating in the country (Farabi Cinema Foundation 1997: 8). Since watching television and videos was a communal activity in Iran, the audience size is much larger than these figures suggest. Nevertheless this alternative, like other aspects of society, was subjected to continuous negotiation, often involving the cultural invasion debate.

From the beginning, the government had a love–hate relationship with video – the main means of showing foreign films – fearing that it would undermine the 'Islamic culture' that it was propagating. As a result, it frequently flip-flopped, alternately banning, curtailing, ignoring or begrudgingly permitting video cassettes and VCRs. Government oscillation encouraged a burgeoning black market in major cities. To combat the illegal videos and increasingly popular global satellite television, in the mid-1990s the government itself became a promoter and distributor of feature and television films on video. To accomplish this, it created the Institute of Visual Media. However, the quantity, quality and variety of the officially approved videos came up short both of expectation and competition. People's gravitation towards satellite tele-vision continued, causing the Grand Ayatollah Mohammad Ali Araki's to ban it in 1994 in a *fatwa*. Recycling previous clerical leaders' metaphors of cinema as disease, the *fatwa* declared: 'Installing satellite antennae, which opens Islamic society to the inroads of decadent foreign culture and the spread of ruinous Western diseases to Moslems is *haram* [forbidden]'.[47] The government urged the owners of satellite receivers to voluntarily remove their dishes, threatening them with high fines (up to US$750) and confiscation of equipment. It also declared a prison term and the incred-ibly steep sum of US$25,000 fine for importing, selling or installing the dishes.[48] Despite some arrests and fines, the ban was not very successful – equipment owners found creative ways to camouflage or to miniaturize their satellite dishes. This failure and the regulatory loopholes that exempted government officials and foreign legations from the ban created a fluid cultural space.

By 1999, however, the government hit on a more enlightened policy to deal with the unauthorized use of videos and satellite television. It drew up a plan according to which it would relinquish video distribution to the private sector, by licensing local film producers and video distributors to import foreign films on video. To prevent unfair competition from Western imports, a perennial problem in much of the world, it tied the importing of foreign films on video to the production of local films. For example, local film producers could import four foreign films (fictional, non-fictional or short subject) for every feature film they produced in Iran.[49] This was designed to encourage both production and importation of film, raising the level and choice of films available.

Film export and international film festivals

With the formation of Farabi Cinema Foundation, the marketing of Iranian Art Cinema films abroad became a serious and ultimately profitable endeavour. In 1986 only two post-revolutionary films were shown in foreign festivals, while 230 films were screened in 1990 in some seventy-eight international festivals, winning eleven prizes

(Khosrowshahi 1991: 28–31). This international presence, which has seen a manifold increase since then, not only garnered prestige for the film-makers and for Iranian cinema, but also generated the needed hard currency that could potentially rescue the Art Cinema film-makers from dependence both on state sponsorship (with its strings attached) and on the local audience (with its taste culture). Although commercial producers, too, marketed their films abroad independently, FCF remained the key representative of Iranian cinema worldwide until the mid-1990s.

Some exiled opponents of the Islamist government, particularly entertainers and film-makers (including Parviz Sayyad), vehemently objected to the screening of films from Iran in foreign film festivals because, they claimed, these events would lend legitimacy to the government (Sayyad 1996). They called for the boycott of Iranian film festivals abroad and campaigned against the films, film-makers and festival organizers. Despite their efforts, however, the quality of the films was so high that both these festivals and the participating films and film-makers grew in number and popularity, placing Iranian Art Cinema on the map of world cinema.

The Pahlavi Era New Wave film-makers, including Sayyad, had accomplished a similar feat in the 1970s (on a much smaller scale) without gaining legitimacy for the Shah's government. In fact, their films had tended to undermine the regime. Likewise, instead of whitewashing the Islamist government's harsh treatment of dissidents, minorities, intellectuals, women and cinema, the participation of Art Cinema films in international festivals provided important fora not only for the understanding of but also for the criticism of such treatment. Most film viewers and reviewers made a distinction between Iranian film-makers and the government, for many Art Cinema directors either ignored or criticized the government and its official culture in their films, for which they paid dearly by having their works censored, delayed or banned. Unlike the bitter exiles, who focused solely on political issues and on governmental control and manipulation to either belittle or explain away the success of the Iranian cinema, these viewers and reviewers gave credit to the film-makers' political knowledge and professional skills, the high quality of the films and the criticism embedded in them.

Emergence of an auteur *cinema*

So it was that, in 1992, Toronto International Film Festival called Iranian cinema 'one of the pre-eminent national cinemas in the world today' (p.8 of the festival catalogue), a verdict that was echoed years later by a *New York Times* reviewer who called it 'one of the world's most vital national cinemas' (Holden 1999). The cinema to which it referred was the Art Cinema, particularly that segment of it that was peopled by *auteur* directors. No film-maker received more critical and popular acclaim in the West than Kiarostami, whose picture appeared on the cover of the July–August 1995 issue of *Cahiers du cinéma* (no. 493) above a caption that simply declared: 'Kiarostami le magnifique'. Inside, nearly fifty pages were devoted to discussing his work. Other *auteur* film-makers who received wide international recognition were Mohsen Makhmalbaf, Dariush Mehrjui, Rakhshan Banietemad, Bahram Baizai, Majid Majidi, Jafar Panahi, Abolfazl Jalili and Tahmineh Milani.[50]

These were *auteurs* because their vision and personality dominated the entire film-making process, from inception to completion, and because certain common thematic, narrative and stylistic features recurred in their films. In addition, several of them wrote their own screenplays (Kiarostami, Mehrjui, Baizai and Makhmalbaf) or collab-orated with others in their writing (Mehrjui), thereby consolidating their authorship. A few directors edited their own films, further ensuring their control over their film's parentage – Kiarostami edited *Khaneh-ye Doust Kojast? / Where's the Friend's Home?* (1989), Makhmalbaf *Arus-ye Khuban / The Marriage of the Blessed* (1989) and Baizai *Shayad Vaqti Digar / May Be Some Other Time* (1988). Several of them also collab-orated intimately and significantly with their spouses or children (Mehrjui's wife supervised his films' production design and sets, Banietemad's husband produced her films and Samira Makhmalbaf's father helped her with the screenplay of her first feature film, *Sib / The Apple* (1997). A study of the films' ending credits reveals the important contribution of a web of familial and familiar associations to authorship in a film industry and society that were both fraught with uncertainty and anxiety.

The many awards that the *auteur* cinema film-makers regularly garnered from inter-national film festivals did more than open up these festivals as potential sources for audiences for Iranian cinema – they also offered access to foreign television networks, art-house and commercial cinemas, and mainstream video chainstores (such as Blockbuster). For the first time, the income from these sources was significant enough to begin to change the hitherto dual basis of film-making in Iran (state sponsored and commercially financed). This third source of financing (foreign-currency earnings) was economically important for the film industry as a whole and for individual film-makers, who thereby gained a relative measure of independence – a new phenomenon in Iranian cinema. The foreign earnings were not small, considering the lopsided exchange rate in 1999 of up to 10,000 Iranian rials to one US$1 and the low budgets of most films (less than US$200,000). Some films did very well in their commercial release abroad. For example, Majid Majidi's Oscar-nominated film *Bachehha-ye Aseman / The Children of Heaven* (1997, distributed in the US by Miramax) earned over US$1 million dollars in four months in ten Hong Kong cinemas alone, taking a position among the top ten box-office earners of the summer.[51] Kiarostami, Makhmalbaf, Mehrjui, Panahi and Jalili were among the newly semi-independent *auteurs*, whose mode of production and multiple transnational audiences freed them somewhat from the tyranny of both local taste and local money (both governmental and commercial). This led to a curious situation: independently produced Art Cinema films which were banned in Iran, such as Makhmalbaf's *Sokut / Silence* (1998), could make money abroad – money he did not have to share with anyone, as he had financed the film himself. Such a transnational reach helped these semi-independent film-makers to come into their own both stylistically and financially. However, this transformation made them vulnerable to the charge of being elitist, xenophilic, unpa-triotic and even un-Islamic.

The on-going ascendance of the Pahlavi Era New Wave film-makers in the Islamic Republic pointed to the continuity in Iranian cinema and to the key contribution of these film-makers to the rise of the cinema from the ashes of revolutionary fires. At the same time, the emergence of nearly a dozen women directors of feature films indi-cated the ruptures and new developments in the hitherto male-dominated cinema.

Due to their serious tone and subject matter, their sometimes obtuse symbolism and their slow pacing, these *auteur* films were not always the most popular, although some were very popular and their film-makers were treated with a great deal of respect as public intellectuals. In the West, the names that are most prominently displayed on the theatre marquees are usually those of the stars and most popular films are star vehicles. In pre-revolution Iran, too, mainstream films were keyed to the drawing power of the stars. However, the reverse is true in the post-revolutionary period. The purification and purging processes, discussed earlier, not only swept aside the Pahlavi Era film stars but also the star system itself, which was considered to be integral to the culture of spectacle and idolatry that circulated images and icons of the Shah himself, foreign consumer products, and local and Western pop stars. The post-revolutionary media (particularly television and periodicals) incessantly displayed the icons and images of key religious figures, but they never became 'stars'. However, in the late 1990s there emerged an inchoate star system involving movie actors.[52] The real stars of the post-revolutionary cinema were the *auteur* film-makers whose movies were known by their names and whose vision, creativity and personality, at once uncompromising and wily, suffused and distinguished their works. As authors, they made thought-provoking films with the same ease and mastery with which writers write. From this perspective, they came as close in Iranian cinema as has ever been the case to Alexander Astruc's visionary notion of 'camera-pen' film-making (Astruc 1968).

However popular some of the films were inside Iran, cinema will not flourish there as a viable, non-governmental, commercial industry without freedom and foreign markets. The aggressive entry of Iranian films in international festivals was a step in the right direction, because it led to the commercial distribution and exhibition for the first time of an increasing number of these films by American and European companies. Foreign audiences are likely to provide another source of pressure for freedom of expression in Iranian cinema.

The wide application of Islamic regulations and censorship rules, and the political exigencies of the time, resulted in the dominance of certain themes. Masud Purmohammad's study of the themes in screenplays for films from 1987 is summarized in Table 2. These themes clearly showed the preoccupations of Iranian society caught in the transition of political regimes and the trauma of a lengthy war. The censorship regulations and political exigencies also engendered certain genres, among them war, action–adventure, comedy and family melodrama. While war films were

Table 2 Themes of feature films made in 1987

Themes	Number of films
Amnesia as a result of shock of war	5
Psychological disorders	9
Emigration or escape from the country	11
Problems and disputes within families	14
War as a primary and ancillary theme	12
Wealth does not bring happiness (Islamic values)	20
Exposing the Pahlavi regime	11
Exposing anti-government groups (*goruhakha*)	4
Total number of films	86

Source: Purmohammad 1987: 8.

more dominant in the Official Cinema, action–adventure, comedy and family melo-dramas generally dominated the Populist Cinema. Art Cinema film-makers dealt with similar themes, but in the manner of *auteurs* they avoided genre cinema's formulaic structures and conventions. But this cinema, too, generated its own regularities and patterns of signification, which can loosely be designated as genre and movement. The genres of humanist films and war films, and the women's film movement are discussed below.

Humanist genre

One characteristic that surprised audiences, particularly those outside Iran, was the quiet humanism of Iranian Art Cinema – a humanism that stood in sharp contrast to the belligerent rhetoric and violent politics of the Islamist government. Perhaps the very fact that Iranians had undergone a desired but cataclysmic revolution, a devastating lengthy war with Iraq, a humiliating hostage-taking episode that placed Iran among the 'pariah' nations and resulted in its economic, political and diplomatic isolation, and massive and violent suppression of their human rights at the hands of their government, made them appreciate and long for an ideal, harmonious community in which humanistic values ruled – values that emphasized the commonality of all humans and their basic goodness.

Humanism was a key characteristic of Iranian Art Cinema and it manifested itself in a range of themes and stylistic features. Fatemeh Motamed Aria, a prominent female actor, characterized it as 'a compassionate cinema', adding that

> it is our plea for compassion that is capturing the world, not our advanced technique or our high technology. Our cinema is being presented to the world because of the kindness of a child towards his sister, or the compassion of a mother towards her child.[53]

This concern for others was tied to an optimistic worldview. Accordingly, in this cinema individual efforts for the collective good were rewarded, for people were not thought of as autonomous and selfish individuals, but as interdependent beings whose fate and well-being were inextricably bound together. There was also the sense that humanistic and ethical values made for a better life here and now, as well as in the hereafter. Some films pushed these ideas to the point of moralism. Manifest moralism was strongest in the Populist Cinema which, instead of concentrating on deeper Persian and Islamic mystical values, tended to cater to superficial morality, characterized by easily attainable hopes, cheap emotions and inexpensive good deeds (Karimi 1988). Moralism was also present in the Art Cinema films, but in submerged and subtle forms, as 'ethicalism'. In the best of these films, 'ethicalism' meant aversion to materialism and desire for a spiritual centre.

The optimism and ethicalism of the Art Cinema films had a messianic source, which made the contemporary bad times tolerable because of the hope that a messiah will one day make them better. But this messianism was not strictly speaking religious or Islamic, for its agent was not a religious figure, a Mahdi or (for the Shi'is) the twelfth imam who is in occlusion, but often a surprising secular figure: a child. The purported innocence of children allowed revelation to be channelled through them and the messianic structure permitted hope of redemption and salvation to come through their individual actions. This is why Kiarostami is able to call children the embodiment of 'the ideal mystic', about whom one hears much but whose living examples are few and far between (quoted in Akrami 1991b). It is the irrepressible, almost messianic, hope represented by children that drives the narratives of Kiarostami's *Khaneh-ye Doust Kojast? / Where's the Friend's Home?* (1989), Jafar Panahi's *Badkonak-e Sepid / The White Balloon* (1995) and *Ayeneh / The Mirror* (1997), Majidi's *Bachehha-ye Aseman / The Children of Heaven*, and Naderi's *Davandeh / The Runner* (1985) and *Ab, Bad, Khak / Water, Wind, Dust* (1985), films in which dogged children relentlessly and single-mindedly forge ahead towards small but ultimately significant victories.

In the messianic structure, there is always a link to the past and a return to the 'good old days'. Significantly, again, in the Art Cinema films this return is not coded as religious, one that takes us back to an Islamic originary moment; rather it is coded as humanistic, one that returns us to the fundamental and spiritual core-values of all humans – kindness, empathy, selflessness, self-sacrifice. The radicalism of these films lies in their secular hope for the future and in their secular but ethical construction of life's fundamentals.

However, while these films did not advocate the official religious culture and ideology directly, their emphasis on humanism, optimism, ethicalism and spiritualism implicated them to some extent in the dominant ideology in so far as these values were similar to the Islamic values that the regime regularly professed but only occasionally practised. As a result, the government tolerated – even welcomed – whatever implicit or explicit criticism that these films offered, for the films neither fundamentally opposed the ruling doctrine nor the ruling power-structure. It must be borne in mind, however, that not all humanist films (among them Baizai's works) carried moralist, ethical or quasi-religious undertones.

Figure 26 Khaneh-ye Doust Kojast? / Where's the Friend's Home?

There was more that set these humanist films apart from the Populist Cinema films than the aforementioned themes and perspectives. Instead of relying on violence, action-driven plots, larger-than-life characters and emotions, and special-effects wizardry, the humanist films focused on small ordinary people, particularly children, engaged in the seemingly insignificant events of daily existence: returning a copybook to a friend in Kiarostami's *Khaneh-ye Doust Kojast?*; a latch-key kid (played by Amir Mohammad Purhasan) taking care of his infant brother in Ebrahim Foruzesh's *Kelid / The Key* (1986); schoolchildren attempting to replace a broken water jar in Foruzesh's *Khomreh / The Jar* (1992); a young girl (Samaneh Jafar Jalali) sharing her red boots which she loves with another child in Mohammad Ali Talebi's *Chakmeh / The Boots* (1992); a young girl (Aida Mohammadkhani) attempting to buy a goldfish for the Noruz New Year celebration in Jafar Panahi's *Badkonak-e Sepid*; a twelve-year-old boy (Reza Moqqadam) helping an elderly woman recover her lost money and health in Parviz Shahbazi's *Mosaferi Az Jonub / The Traveller from the South* (1996); a schoolgirl (Mina Mohammad Khani) attempting to find her way home from school in Panahi's *Ayeneh*; a brother and sister from a poor family (Mohammad Amir Naji and Bahareh Sediqqi) sharing one pair of shoes to go to school in Majidi's *Bachehha-ye Aseman.*

The neo-realist treatment of these subjects (location filming, use of non-actors in principal parts, children as key protagonists, concern with everyday events and people, and naturalistic lighting, acting, *mise-en-scène*, filming and editing) focused attention on both the reality of post-revolutionary Iranian society, which established that society's exotic difference and specificity, and on the moral and ethical dimensions of daily existence there, which tapped into universal human values. The wisdom of these films was this: to be universal it was necessary first and foremost to become local. In addition, it was essential to treat these ordinary people and small events realistically, for realism reinforced at the level of style the thematic humanism of the films. One reason for the wide praise and success of the Iranian cinema abroad is to be found in precisely this marriage of humanism and realism, for together they tended to counter the corrosive effects of both the official culture of violence at home and the post-modernist culture of irony and cynicism abroad.

The manner in which Art Cinema directors themselves characterized their films corroborates this theorization of the humanist genre. Mehrjui linked the post-revolutionary Art Cinema to its predecessor the New Wave movement, calling it a 'truthful cinema' whose 'starting hypothesis is that human beings are essentially good'; Baizai labelled it 'a naïve, decent, innocent and "boring" cinema', and Kiumars Purahmad characterized it as a 'humanistic cinema', that is 'tiny, bashful and modest' (all quoted in Akrami 1991a). These attributes of smallness, decency and truthfulness were most emphatically promulgated in Kiarostami's films. His *Khaneh-ye Doust Kojast?* was a key early film in this genre. Characterized as 'agonizingly slow' but ultimately 'rewarding' (*Variety*, 16 August 1989: n.p.), it depicted the relentless efforts of an honest elementary schoolboy named Ali (Babak Ahmadpur) to find the house of his friend Mohammad Reza (Ahmad Ahmadpur) in an adjoining village in order to return Reza's copybook which he had taken by mistake, despite a wilful lack of understanding from his parents. Ali's efforts are driven not only by his desire to correct his own mistake, but also by the realization that if Reza does not turn in his homework in his own copybook he will be expelled from school. Ali's defiance of familial authority, his fear of his authoritarian teacher and his dogged insistence on doing the morally correct thing are reminders of similar themes that Kiarostami examined in his devastating documentary critique of the Iranian educational system in *Mashq-e Shab / Homework* (1989).

Such ethicalism, optimism and humanism became hallmarks of Kiarostami's style and that of his protégés, among them Ebrahim Foruzesh and Jafar Panahi. But as he evolved into a semi-independent *auteur* whose films garnered wide international acclaim and revenue, he increasingly began to subvert or nuance these humanistic values by self-reflexive and deconstructive narrative strategies in such films as *Kelosup, Nama-ye Nazdik / Close-Up* (1989) and *Ta'm-e Gilas / Taste of Cherry* (1997). *Kelosup, Nama-ye Nazdik* dealt with the real-life story of a man named Hosain Sabzian (playing himself) who is so infatuated with cinema and with film-maker Mohsen Makhmalbaf (playing himself) that he impersonates Makhmalbaf. He passes as Makhmalbaf until a disenchanted family sues him. *Ta'm-e Gilas*, which is ostensibly about suicide, ends with a scene in which Kiarostami is directing the film. These strategies, which cast doubt on the certainty of reality and on the realness of filmic realism, endeared him to intellectuals abroad and made him the object of intellectuals' envy at home.[54] While *Ta'm-e Gilas*'s manifest theme is suicide and the moral and philosophical questions that suicide raises, a fiction that the film perpetrates, deep down it is about male companionship. However realist in filming style, the deconstructive ploys of self-reflexivity and irony are so overwhelming within the text and in its ending that the film's homosexual subtext is ignored – so much the better, for in a society in which homosexuality is considered deviant and taboo (even though it is common) and is severely punished, the explicit expression of such a topic would indeed have been suicidal for the director.[55] Mehrjui, too, in several of his films – among them *Hamoon* (1990) and *Derakht-e Golabi / The Pear Tree* (1998) – dealt with the spiritual and philosophical crises of humanism in a style that was at once fantastic and realistic.

Many religiously inspired film-makers also wrestled with ethical, moral and humanistic dilemmas, including Makhmalbaf, who began as an ideologue for and paradigmatic practitioner of the Official Cinema in such films as *Tobeh-ye Nasuh / Nasuh's Repentance* (1982), *Do Cheshm-e Bisu / Two Sightless Eyes* (1984) and *Baikot / Boycott* (1986). However, Makhmalbaf proved to be a moving target as he evolved with every film, making each of them unique, while Kiarostami's preoccupations and style remained remarkably constant in his last several films. Makhmalbaf's most radical transformation occurred with his *Arus-ye Khuban / The Marriage of the Blessed* (1989), which focused on a shell-shocked photographer named Haji (Mahmud Bigham) as a metaphor for a nation that was itself in shock. Haji is released from hospital to the family of his wealthy fiancée (Roya Nonahali) for recuperation. He cannot rest easy, however, as flashbacks of the scenes he has witnessed in the war with Iraq or images of poverty and drought in Africa that he has seen on television haunt him and disturb his peace of mind. He is hired back as a photojournalist for a newspaper, but the paper refuses to print the grim scenes of poverty, prostitution and drug abuse that he and his fiancée document in the Tehran streets. On his wedding night, Haji relapses and, in a sequence that provides a cyclical closure, he finds himself back in the hospital. The film uses sophisticated flashbacks and elements of surrealism to weave a complex narrative that takes the audience deeper into both the inner world of the photographer and the decaying social milieu in which he operates. It criticizes the Iranian society for its failure to live up to the high ideals of an Islamic society.

With this film, Makhmalbaf began a new independent path for himself, which led to his increasing critique of doctrinaire religious beliefs and of Official Cinema's tenets. He accomplished this by casting serious doubt on the Iranian reality and on the realist film style with his use of humour in *Nassered-Din Shah, Aktor-e Sinema / Once Upon a Time Cinema* (1992), of self-reflexivity and self-inscription in *Salam Sinema / Salaam Cinema* (a.k.a. *Cinema, Cinema,* 1994) and *Nun Va Goldun / The Bread and the Vase* (1995), and of multiple perspectives in *Nowbat-e Asheqi / A Time to Love* (1991) and *Gabbeh* (1995).[56]

The transcendent and transgressive qualities of Kiarostami and Makhmalbaf films are to be found in the combination of secular humanism and realism, and in their quiet questioning of both. As a result, realism in their films is not uniform or simple; rather it is a hybridized form that weaves documentary and fictional elements to create texts that are highly post-modern at the same time as being ethical (this hybridized form is the continuation of a similar oppositional practice that New Wave film-makers, particularly Kamran Shirdel and Parviz Kimiavi, had initiated over two dozen years earlier). Their post-modernism is to be differentiated from that of most Western film-makers by its gentle irony, not the neo-nasty cynical irony so endemic to American television talkshows and series and to popular films. This sort of irony adds to their humanistic ethos, instead of undermining it. Nonetheless, such narrative strategies, which generated uncertainty, were deeply counter-hegemonic, for nothing is as subversive as doubt for a regime that insists on an official version of reality and on doctrinaire certainty, and which patrols all boundaries of gender and genre assiduously.

In the 1980s, leading clerics – including Hojjatolestalm Mohammad Khatami, then Minister of Culture and Islamic Guidance – urged film-makers to propagate the notions of 'self-sacrifice, martyrdom and revolutionary patience'.[57] These concepts were overdetermined in Iranian cinema, but they found their most natural expression in the Official Cinema films, particularly in those that dealt with the war with Iraq (1980–8).

War film genre

Soon after Iraq invaded Iran in September 1980, the supreme jurisprudent Ayatollah Khomeini ordered a mobilization of all sectors. Because of the twin problems of shortage of raw stock and funds, however, it took the Ministry of Culture and Islamic Guidance and the private sector some time to mobilize the film industry in support of the war effort. Although the first film about the war, *Border / Marz* (1981) directed by Jamshid Haidari, was made by the private sector, the public (government) sector produced the lion's share of war films, whose official label was 'sacred defence cinema' (*sinema-ye defa-e moqaddas*).

During the war, fifty-six fiction feature-films were made, most of which concentrated primarily on military operations, while a few concerned themselves with the war's social and psychological toll. By 1990, two years after the ceasefire, this number had increased to seventy-four (Dorri Akhavi 1992: 13), demonstrating the continued significance of the war to both society and the regime. However, the increased quantity of the films that celebrated Islamic martyrdom, self-sacrifice and revolutionary patience was not matched by improved quality. Nonetheless, the war films received encouragement not only in their production and distribution but also in their exhibition, including their screening in the annual Film Festival of the 'Imposed War'. Table 3 lists the organizations whose films were screened at the 1983 festival and the number and types of film shown. They ranged from features to short subject films and from fiction films to documentaries, although the documentary form clearly dominated.

As is evident, these war films were made by a variety of governmental and private-sector organizations, demonstrating the overdetermination of the official war culture in the country. But, since the government produced an overwhelming majority of the films (thirty-three of the thirty-five films listed), the table also demonstrates the significant role of the government in propagating that culture as a result of its almost total control of Iranian society's major institutions during the war.

The winners of best film awards (feature and short subject respectively) were *Kilometr-e Panj / The Fifth Kilometre* and *Abadan, Shahr-e Bigonah / Abadan: The*

Table 3 Organizations contributing to the 1983 War Film Festival

Producing organization	Documentary	Fiction
Voice & Vision (television networks)	14	2
Armed Forces' Ideological–Political Bureau	1	0
Islamic Propaganda Organization	2	0
Centre for Intellectual Development of Children & Young Adults	3	1
Ministry of Culture & Islamic Guidance	0	2
Islamic Centre for Artistic & Cinematic Studies	0	2
Islamic Centre for Amateur Film-making	0	2
Revolutionary Guards Television Unit	2	0
War Propaganda Organization	1	0
Islamic Art and Thought Bureau	1	0
Private sector	0	2
Total	24	11

Source: Nuri and Ashuri 1983.

Innocent City. At the conclusion of the festival, the board of juries announced its pleasure with the local productions by declaring that, unlike documentarists elsewhere who focused on the materialistic and militaristic aspects of wars, Iranian film-makers had chosen to reveal the 'love, sacrifice and resistance' of the war.[58]

However, this appeared to reflect only the official view, for neither film-industry professionals and critics nor audiences shared it. The authoritative film journal *Mahnameh-ye Sinemai-ye Film*, for example, noted that while Italian film-makers had created the neo-realist school under similar war conditions, the Iranian cineastes had 'concentrated on phony war adventures, sensationalism and superficial sloganeering designed to encourage the war effort'.[59] That audiences, too, were turned off by these films' low quality and strident rhetoric was evident from the low turnout at the 1982 Imposed War Film Festival, during which many viewers left the theatres during the screenings. Likewise the jury of the 1984 festival refused to select a best film or to grant a prize to any film, due to the low quality of the entries.[60] A major complaint against all films made in the 1980s, including the war genre, was their low quality and their ideological earnestness. Of 115 films that *Mahnameh-ye Sinemai-ye Film* studied, it rated thirty-five of them as sleazy, fifty-seven as bad, twenty-two as mediocre, one as good and none excellent.[61] However, the official culture was far from homogenous and monolithic, as indicated by the remarks of then powerful speaker of parliament Hojjatoleslam Ali Akbar Hashemi Rafsanjani, who urged a lighter and more entertaining treatment of serious subjects in cinema. He said:

> It is true that a film must have a message, but this does not mean that we must deny its entertaining aspects. Society needs entertainment; lack of joy reduces one's effectiveness and involvement.[62]

The heterogeneity of the war genre is also evident in several novel developments in the war film genre, which elevated the quality of the genre's products and the discourses about them. One was the formation in early 1982 of the Forty Witnesses (*chehel shahed* – it began with forty cameramen) Film Unit within the volunteer Basij Corps, spearheaded by Akbar Ureh'i, who had a degree in sociology. Unit members were male high-school students, some of whom had never seen a film camera. After a brief training period, however, they were sent to the front to film the war using Super 8 equipment (some 16 mm and video footage was also shot). If they were short on film education, they were supercharged with faith, idealism and the belief that their cameras were more effective than weapons.[63] According to Asadollah Niknejad and Mehrdad Kashani, who worked with the Forty Witnesses Film Unit for a while and instructed them in film-making, the cameramen-witnesses had a tendency to focus primarily on scenes of action, killing and dying.

> We asked them not to limit themselves to these scenes, for the primary aim of war films is a historical one. After the end of the war, history will want to know what happened, where it happened, who was involved and when it happened. We taught them to cover the contextual issues and to take notes and identify what they were filming. We wanted them not to deal with the war emotionally, but rationally; instead of filming the jets bombing, we wanted them to concentrate on the victims and on the consequences. Other war units were operating at this time, but what

made this group's work valuable was their amateur status, the fact that they had not been indoctrinated.[64]

Accompanied by an assistant, who carried both a machine gun and film supplies, each cameramen-witness showed great individual initiative and bravery in covering the front. The footage was sent to the Basij Militia headquarters for processing, and it is unlikely that any of them saw the rushes during the war. Both the cameramen and their accompanying militia were volunteers and they volunteered for each specific mission. Their object was less to make films than to cover the war. Perhaps for this reason (and to ensure the security and secrecy of war missions) not much of the vast amount of their footage was turned into completed films or shown publicly.

Apparently, the archival condition under which this footage is stored is so dismal that this valuable historical record is fast deteriorating (Sadri 1995: 44). The war took its toll on the young film-makers as well: by mid-1984, eight boys had been killed in action, with one declared missing in action.

One film that was assembled from the Forty Witnesses' output was *Moharram Dar Moharram / Moharram in Moharram* (1983), about an operation in 1982 called Moharram, which took place during the religiously sacred month of Moharram. Niknejad and Kashani directed the film, whose editing took an inordinate amount of time (some eight months) as the footage was not shot with the intention of putting a film together. *Moharram Dar Moharram*, which begins with pictures of the Forty Witnesses' 'martyrs', linked the Iran–Iraq war with the paradigmatic Shi'i war event in which imam Hussein was martyred in Iraq on the plains of Karbala in 61 AH by the Ummayid Caliphate, an event whose anniversary is celebrated and mourned elaborately during the month of Moharram. The film emphasized this link by intercutting scenes from the current war with Iraq with the Taziyeh passion play re-enactments of the events of Karbala. Another film was *Chehel Shahed, Ravayat-e Dovvom: Azadi-ye Khorramshahr / Forty Witnesses – The Second Narrative: Liberation of Khorramshahr* (1984?), which documented the Baitolmoqqadas operation that led to the liberation of this Persian Gulf city from Iraqi hands.

The other development was the rise of two Islamically committed film-makers who produced a range of films related to the war that were of high quality, both in style and thought, and who proved to be politically and cinematically influential. These were the most prominent Official Cinema film-makers, one a documentarist and the other a fiction film-maker. Seyyed Morteza Avini headed a documentary film unit, called Jihad Television Unit, that was co-sponsored by both Channel 1 television network and the Reconstruction Crusade. Taking advantage of this in-between status, in the course of a decade Jihad TV produced for national broadcast a massive and long-running series of films collectively called *Ravayat-e Fath / Narrative of Victory*. In turn, each series consisted of many individual films, most of which were about the war; however, other urgent socio-political issues in Iran, as well as the plight of Palestinians and Lebanese Shi'ites, were also serialized (Avini 1997). The treatment of these latter topics indicates the extent to which *Ravayat-e Fath* was an Official Cinema film series, for support of Palestinian independence and opposition to Israel were two foreign policy pillars of the Iranian government.

While realistic, many of these films were also idealistic: they portrayed real events through the filter of both Shi'i ideology and Islamist rhetorical devices. Avini himself was not only involved in the making of films, travelling to the war front – where he was eventually killed – but he also trained the film crews ideologically and technically, and wrote extensively about cinema from a religious and philosophical point of view. After his death, *Ravayat-e Fath* became a cultural institution (under his brother's leadership), enshrining Avini as a martyr, publishing his posthumous works, teaching film and the other arts, and distributing films and books about the war.

The other influential 'Islamically committed' film-maker was Ebrahim Hatamikia, whose early war-related films *Didehban / Sentry* (1988) and *Mohajer / The Emigrant* (1990) explored the psychological and sociological impact of the war front on the home front. With the success of these films, which one critic called 'the most important fruit of the Iranian war films', he became a highly influential director (Seif 1998: 349). In his subsequent glossy film *Az Karkheh Ta Rhine / From Karkheh to Rhine* (1992), he explored the psychology of a disabled veteran on a medical trip to Germany, adding to the war theme the tension of direct contact with the West and of displacement to foreign lands. In *Azhans-e Shisheh'i / The Glass Agency* (1997), Hatamikia dealt with the crisis of re-integrating war veterans into society almost a decade after the war's end. It centred on a war veteran who takes people hostage in a travel agency to obtain free plane tickets to take his friend, a wounded war veteran, to London for emergency surgery. One of the most popular and controversial films of post-revolutionary cinema (it swept eight of the top awards at the 16th International Fajr Film Festival), *Azhans-e Shisheh'i* was an ambivalent and, as some charged, expedient film – on one hand, it seemed to call for an end to the war mobilization era with its preferential treatment for veterans and, on the other hand, it severely and unfairly criticized those who questioned the war, its conduct and its deleterious effect on society. Perhaps with this film Hatamikia was attempting to distance himself somewhat from the Official Cinema ideology. Despite his ambivalence about the continued preferential treatment of war veterans, he found room in his film (however briefly and implicitly) to criticize film-maker Abbas Kiarostami, who was represented by a Westernized intellectual among the hostages in the agency, wearing dark glasses indoors and more concerned about leaving the country than saving the lives of the hostages.

The private-sector producers, too, contributed to the war cinema genre by turning their attention by the mid-1980s on the dynamics of the ideological and psychological dimensions of the war. Hasan Karbakhsh's *Diar-e Asheqan / The Lovers' Domain* (1983) examined the psychology of a young reserve soldier and the meaning of self-sacrifice and duty, while Manuchehr Asgarinasab's *Khaneh-ye Dar Entezar / Expectant House* (1987) portrayed wartime society with technical polish.

Thematically, waiting and searching for the dead, the missing in action and the disappeared drove many of the best war films, such as those of Hatamikia. The inability to locate the bodies to bury them turned the dead and the disappeared into powerful presences that haunted the living, disrupting their lives. Thus possessed, they were unable to properly mourn for the dead, which intensified their trauma. Sometimes these absent figures were made present by the agency of video within film. Finally, the living were not only haunted by the dead or by the disappeared, but also by doubt about who was alive and who was dead.

While the war encouraged the production of war films, it actually had a dampening effect on the film industry because, during the most heated periods of fighting (in 1980 for example), government blackouts reduced the number of film showings to two or less per night. In addition, the many air-raid warnings in major cities caused the evacuation of theatres, sometimes without compensation to the patrons. These factors caused a drastic reduction in the audience base, damaged the economic health of the industry, reduced the production of new films and increased the recycling of old films.

As time wore on and the war, culture of war and memories of war receded, the production of war films decreased. The high cost of war films – which required a huge theatre of operations and massive amount of equipment, materials and personnel – also discouraged the production of realistic war films that dealt with the fighting front. This ushered in a genre of cheap war films. Threatened with the twin problems of mediocre products and the possible disappearance of war films, the government created the Society for the Sacred Defence Cinema, whose mission was to facilitate the production and exhibition of quality war movies.[65] Despite this effort, the war film has had its day; however, war is likely to remain a productive theme, since unresolved issues relating to its causes, management, long-term consequences and the assignment of blame will continue to surface.

It must be noted in the end that not all of the films dealing with the war that were made during the war were pro-war. As early as 1985, Baizai made his deeply humanist *Bashu, Gharibeh-ye Kuchak / Bashu, the Little Stranger*. By highlighting the importance of Persian as the national language among the diegetic characters who spoke diverse regional and ethnic languages, such as Arabic, Gilaki and Persian, the film favoured nationalism. On the other hand, by stressing the reconciliation of the diverse minorities that form the Iranian society it advocated humanistic values. The film centred on an Arab–Iranian boy named Bashu (Adnan Afravian), who escapes the Iraqi attacks in the south to take refuge in the north. There a single mother (Susan Taslimi), whose husband is on the war front, takes him in against the advice of her family and fellow villagers. Like many war-struck people, Bashu is safe but haunted by the war, particularly by the image of his dead mother who seems to inhabit not only his memory but also, as the film unfolds, the diegesis. War and division are the film's ever-present subtext, but it is the evolving and deepening bonding of the little exiled man with the lively but lonely woman that carries the day.

Although made in Iran, this is a paradigmatic film of exile by an accomplished film-maker operating in a type of unofficial internal semi-exile. Baizai's uncompromising and literate works from the early 1970s did not only bring high-culture status to Iranian cinema but also landed their director in trouble with government censors (during both the Pahlavi and the Islamist regimes). He therefore single-handedly developed a genre of unproduced drama literature, consisting of some two dozen published plays and screenplays that were never produced. According to Baizai, *Bashu*'s release was delayed by several years due to his refusal to make some eighty changes demanded by the official censors.[66] Almost a decade after his *Mosaferan*, Baizai is yet to receive permission (from the government) or funding (from the private sector) to make his next feature film, despite repeated attempts.

Women and cinema

The themes of shock and psychological disorders, broken families, and dislocation were explored with particular emphasis in family melodramas, which centrally involved women. It is in the on-screen representation and behind-the-scenes treatment of women that the tensions surrounding the Islamization of cinema crystallize.

The aforementioned film and video regulations stipulated that Muslim women on the screen must be chaste and play an important role both in society and at home, particularly in raising God-fearing and responsible children. In addition, they were not to be treated like a commodity or used to arouse sexual desires. These general and ambiguous guidelines profoundly affected the filmic representation of women. The most significant early effect was self-censorship, which led to avoiding all stories that involved women. In this way, film-makers evaded entanglement with the censors. Masud Purmohammad's study pointed out the very low presence of women as 'heroes' in films made as late as 1987: of thirty-seven films he reviewed, the protagonists were men in twenty-five films, women in three films, and both men and women were equally heroic in seven films (Purmohammad 1987: 8). Women's representation did not remain static, however – it evolved from almost total absence (in the early 1980s) to pale presence (in the late 1980s) to powerful presence (in the late 1990s).

In the movies women wore modest clothing and donned a long tunic and headscarf, or wore a chador (a head-to-toe cloth), and they behaved decorously. This resulted in an unrealistic and distorted representation of women, for they were shown veiling themselves from their next of kin and treating them in a formal manner as though they were strangers, something they would not do in real life. This made the realistic representation of women and of male–female relations, even friendship, almost impossible. This curious situation arose because in the movies all private spaces were considered to be public spaces, and men and women were expected to behave accordingly. As a result, female characters had to veil themselves not from their diegetic next of kin but from the male actors who played their parts and from the male audience-members who, by definition, were considered to be unrelated (or *namahram*) to them.[67] Some film-makers staged their entire films in exterior locations to avoid the unrealism that filming indoors would force on them. It is for this reason that Makhmalbaf filmed all the scenes of *Gabbeh* (1995), his lyrical film about love, outdoors.

To portray women, an aesthetics of veiling and an averted look, instead of the direct gaze, developed that was unique to the Iranian cinema, but this evolved toward liberal interpretation, in tandem with the women's increasingly assertive social roles. If women were portrayed at all early on, they were given limited parts: reflecting the regulations, they were usually housewives or mothers. They were generally filmed in long-shot and any physical contact between men and women was prohibited – even between those who were intimately related – as was any eye contact between them, particularly that expressing 'desire'. In response, film-makers developed clever methods of using framing, composition and lighting to both mask and reveal, very much like the way women strategically used their own chador or veil. In Mehrjui's *Leila* (1996), the dressing and undressing of the lead female named Leila (Leila Hatami) is shown in a series of close-ups of her body parts, instead of in medium- or long-shots that would have exposed her unveiled body. In a bedroom scene, perhaps the first such scene in the post-revolutionary cinema, Leila is shown reclining in bed while her husband is undressing to join her. However, both of them are masked by a lighting scheme that strategically covers her supposedly unveiled hair and arms and his undressed body.

The veiling aesthetics also ruled out non-verbal intimacy from the screens, as men and women could not touch each other or hold hands. This resulted in the ingenious use of a variety of substitutes, third parties, doubles, objects or even animals that mediated between the principals, passing on their charged intimacy. In *Gabbeh*, for example, a goat mediates an intimate scene between the young Gabbeh and her suitor. In a long-shot, we see Gabbeh seated behind the goat and milking it vigorously, when the man approaches and positions himself in front of the goat. He then looks at Gabbeh and clearly establishes eye contact with her and begins to gently caress the goat's horns. Then, in a close-up, we see her looking up at him as her hands move to and fro. In another close-up, he is seen standing, looking at her with pleasure, and reciting poetry to her. The suggestion of intimacy, even fellatio, is clear – but the two principals never touch each other. In a scene in Hatamikia's *Az Karkheh Ta Rhine / From Karkheh to Rhine*, where an injured war veteran has to hug his sister, a male double is used for the sister and the scene is filmed in long-shot, with the double's back to the audience. In the final scene of Banietemad's *Nargess* (1991), a struggle between a thief named Adel (Abolfazl Purarab) and his young wife Nargess (Atefeh Razavi) over love and money is staged so that they wrestle with the bag of money that is between them, without ever touching each other. Likewise, in Banietemad's *Banu-ye Ordibehesht / The May Lady* (1997), a concerned single mother named Forugh (Minoo Farshchi), who wants to comfort her rebellious teenage son (Mani Kasraian), expresses her love and intimacy toward him by means of mediating objects: in one scene a towel with which she dries his wet hair and in another a blanket through which she caresses him.

In Mohsen Makhmalbaf's poetic *Sokut / Silence*, filmed in Tajikistan, eroticism is encoded in the budding relationship of two pre-pubescent children (one a blind boy and another a girl). Perhaps for the first time in post-revolution cinema a pubescent girl dances on camera, but the film-maker cleverly defuses the sexual charge of the dance by turning it into a dance ritual. (Despite this strategy, the censors made the release of the film dependent on the removal of this fifty-second sequence. Due to Makhmalbaf's refusal, the film remains banned in Iran.) However, his filming and editing strategies, which highlight in extreme close-ups the beauty and luminescence of the girl's face, lips, cheeks, ears and skin, turn her into, if not a sexual, at least a sensual object. Ostensibly, the extreme close-up photography is designed to impart the way the blind boy sees the world by touching the texture of things, but in doing so the girl's isolated body parts are turned into fetish objects for the male scopophilic pleasure. This creates a complex spectatorial situation: to enjoy themselves, male spectators will either have to assume the deviant position of a child molester or assume that the little girl is an adult, thus avoiding the first position. The situation becomes more complex if we take into consideration the fact that a girl actor is playing the boy's part. This introduces homoerotic dimensions as well as the feeling that the director has cheated the viewer by the masquerade. All these considerations make for an ambivalent spectatorial experience. The substitution of children for adults was one of the favorite ploys of post-revolution film-makers, but none used it so boldly and yet so ambivalently.

Another ploy for expressing intimacy was the use of poetry, whereby characters expressed their feelings towards one other not by direct address, but by quoting poems. In Banietemad's *Kharej Az Mahdudeh / Off the Limit* (1987), for example, the husband (Mehdi Hashemi) declaims a love poem to his wife (Parvaneh Masumi) during their meal, and in her film *Banu-ye Ordibehesht*, Forugh quotes poetry to her unseen lover. These sorts of substitution and staging were so well done and so seamlessly integrated into the rest of the film that audiences did not generally notice them.

Some directors employed different, even reverse, strategies. In *Banu-ye Ordibehesht*, Banietemad created a deliciously expressive, even erotic, film about heterosexual love at the expense of absenting the male love object from the diegesis. He is only present as a disembodied voice on the phone or in letters. This absenting of the man from the diegesis is a radical feminist reworking of the rules of veiling that had excised women from the screen, turning the rules on their head. Because one side of this amorous relationship is absent, the verbal address by means of poetry, letters and telephone conversations can be, and is, unusually direct and open. In *Mosaferan / Travellers*, Baizai chose elaborate *mise-en-scène* and filming in order to avoid showing men and women in the same diegetic space or even in the same shot. Kiarostami circumvented the problem of representing women altogether by avoiding them in most of his films. In this manner, these film-makers sidestepped or subverted the lie that the veiling ideology and aesthetics forced on them. However, these avoidance strategies created their own potential problems: complexity, obtuseness and elaborateness where simplicity and directness would have been best. Another negative side-effect of cinematic veiling was that certain historical periods (such as the Pahlavi Era) and certain geographical regions (such as the West) were for quite some time closed to Iranian cinema. Limiting the repertoire of roles for female characters was yet another undesirable consequence. Since they had to act properly at all times, female 'bad guys' were unthinkable. One exception was Banietemad's *Nargess*, in which a key protagonist (Farimah Farjami) was a thief; a transgression for which she paid with her life. The veiling aesthetics also affected the on-screen relationships of the men, resulting in fascinating gender reconfigurations – such as suggesting male homoeroticism, as does Mohammad Reza A'alami in his *Noqteh Za'f / The Weak Point* (1983) – that were inimical to the ruling ideology, requiring severe punishment.

In short, during the second post-revolutionary decade the film-makers pushed the envelope in terms of the portrayal of women, at the same time as the constraints on women's representation gradually lessened and the regulations governing them were either loosened or interpreted more liberally. In addition, not all directors fully or equally abided by the regulations. Some fought them by indirection and implication, others head-on. While through ingenuity and guile they expanded the permissible vocabulary of women's representations and gendered relations, something was lost in the process – that is, love. The representation of love, even within the confines of religiously legal definitions, was very limited and underdeveloped, although Banietemad's *Nargess* and *Banu-ye Ordibehesht*, Makhmalbaf's *Gabbeh* and *Nowbat-e Asheqi / A Time to Love*, and Mehrjui's *Leila* offered some instances of love on the screen.

If women faced many difficulties appearing in front of the cameras, they encountered fewer obstacles attending film schools and working behind the cameras in both cinema and television – as long as they abided by the 'Islamic' codes of conduct, dress, acting and the gaze. 'Purified' and disengaged from its association with corruption, vice and amorality, cinema became a legitimate profession, open to women more than ever, causing a remarkable rise both in the number of women directors and in the quality of films by them – a veritable women's cinema. More female feature-film directors emerged in the first decade after the revolution than in the preceding eight decades combined. They include the following directors: Tahmineh Ardekani, Mahasti Badii, Rakhshan Banietemad, Faryal Behzad, Marziyeh Borumand, Puran Derakhshandeh, Samira Makhmalbaf, Yasamin Maleknasr, Marzieh Meshkim, Tahmineh Milani and Kobra Saidi. Their films dealt with a range of topics – from family and housing problems to physical and mental disability to love and film-making – and a variety of genres – from social comedies to psychological dramas. Banietemad and Milani were the most productive and accomplished. Banietemad, whose earlier films (such as *Kharej Az Mahdudeh*) had represented women conservatively, grew bolder with each film. Her confident *Banu-ye Ordibehesht* dealt with issues unprecedented in post-revolutionary cinema: a divorced single mother and film director who wants to both raise her Westernized teenage son and maintain a romantic relationship with a male friend. Milani's *Do Zan / Two Women* (1998), called an Iranian 'feminist' film, centred on friendship between two women, who represented the actual and the potential situation of women. The film critiqued the way marriage and home-making, while offering some security to women, can become their prisons. The men, who promise women all kinds of freedom to gain their hands in marriage, turn into jealous bullies once married and become in essence the women's prison guards. While her critique of the unfair structure of gendered relations was germane, her binary treatment of women and men was highly reductive.

Samira Makhmalbaf's *Sib / The Apple* critiqued a real-life father who, for eleven years, had kept his two real-life daughters imprisoned in his house (all playing themselves), until a television programme broadcast a report about them, creating a sensation. In the process, Makhmalbaf turned the veil and the *hejab* (system of modesty) into a panoptic technology by inscribing them at many levels and in many domains: the girls are veiled by their imprisonment in the dark and dank rooms; an iron gate prevents their access to the yard all day while their father is out; the mother, who is similarly imprisoned, is completely covered from head to toe by her chador, with barely a small hole open for her sightless eyes, and the high walls surrounding the house veil it from the outside. However, the outside world intrudes: the neighbours keep an eye on the house, the social-work system intervenes on behalf of the girls and the media sensationalizes their story. *Sib* itself contributed both to the inscription of the veil and to its critique. It is the friendship of the girls with a neighbouring boy, who tempts them with an apple, that breaks both their imprisonment and the panoptic control over them, and liberates not only the girls but also the film itself.

Clearly the veil, its ideology and its aesthetics were a serious imposition and a constraint on women, but it served to politicize them by heightening their awareness of other forms of social, religious and patriarchal repression. This added to their earlier politicization, which their significant participation in the revolution had brought about. Thus there was a trade-off for the imposition of the veil, which is that once veiled, women could appear in the public sphere legitimately and forcefully, where they could demand their rights and assert themselves.[68] Cinema became the beneficiary of this double-edged sword.

A major change gradually occurred in official and public attitudes toward cinema and working in the film industry. Cinema, rejected in the past as part of a frivolous superstructure, was adopted as a necessary part of Islamic Republic's infrastructure.

Fakhred-Din Anvar, Undersecretary of Culture and Islamic Guidance in charge of the Film Affairs Department, explained how this was attempted:

> Believing culture to be the structure undergirding all aspects of running a society ... the Department has directed all its efforts towards ensuring that cinematic activities and film-making are included in all legislation, laws, systems and regulations.[69]

Likewise working in the film industry, once disdained and disparaged, became acceptable and respectable, making possible the entry of women. Hojjatoleslam Ali Akbar Hashemi Rafsanjani, then speaker of the Majles, publicly put his stamp on this shift when he declared in March 1987 that:

> Our entertainers, male or female, did not enjoy the same esteem that today they enjoy from the lay and the religious people. ... This is a real revolution.[70]

Films, judged solely on their ideological purity and their usefulness to official policies immediately after the revolution, began to be evaluated on the basis of their ability to enlighten and entertain. As early as 1984, Hojjatoleslam Mohammad Khatami, Minister of Culture and Islamic Guidance, had declared this repositioning of cinema in no uncertain terms:

> I believe that cinema is not the mosque. ... If we remove cinema from its natural place, we will no longer have cinema.[71]

The immense popularity and the high revenues of Mehrjui's social satire *Ejarehneshinha / The Tenants* (1986) – the highest in Iranian cinema up to that time – was a testimony that the public, too, wanted films to be both well made and entertaining. This sort of widely dispersed repositioning of cinema continued apace into the 1990s.

Exilic and diaspora films

No study of Iranian cinema is complete without a discussion of the output of the Iranian film-makers in their Western exile and diaspora since the revolution. According to one study, which I conducted, they made over 300 fiction, non-fiction, animated and avant-garde films in two decades of displacement in nearly a dozen European and North American countries. This made them by far the most productive film-making group (in terms of quantity) among the Middle Eastern exiles in the West. Although these film-makers were diverse in terms of politics and religion, the majority of them were united in their opposition to the Islamist regime, and while they worked in different countries, making films in various languages, their films shared certain features that accented their films exilically and diasporically. Theirs is part of an emerging global 'accented cinema' that I have been writing about, which is centrally concerned with expressing the pain and the pleasures of displacement and the problematic of multiple locations and identities (Naficy 1993a, 1996a, 1999, 2001).

Many of the older generation of directors, such as Parviz Sayyad and Reza

Allamehzadeh, were preoccupied with Iranian politics and their films were highly political and polemical, limiting their appeal. Other accomplished film-makers, such as Sohrab Shahid Saless, Amir Naderi and Houshang Allahyari, were less focused on Iran or Iranian politics and they achieved an *auteur* style and a measure of universal appeal (Naficy 1998b). A younger generation who were born or bred outside Iran, such as Caveh Zahedi, Mitra Tabrizian, Shirin Etessam, Shirin Neshat, Mehrnaz Saeedvafa, Ghazel and Persheng Vaziri, increasingly made their presence felt in the Iranian exilic and diaspora cinema, as well as in the independent and art-cinema film sectors in their countries of residence.

The most accomplished feature films made in exile include the following: Shahid Saless' *Utopia* (1983) and *Rosen für Afrika / Roses for Africa* (1991), Parviz Sayyad's *The Mission* (1983), Marva Nabili's *Nightsongs* (1984), Ghasem Ebrahimian's *The Suitors* (1989), Reza Allamehzadeh's *Mehmanan-e Hotel-e Astoria / The Guests of Hotel Astoria* (1989), Jalal Fatemi's *The Nuclear Baby* (1990), Caveh Zahedi's *A Little Stiff* (1992) (with Greg Watkins) and *I Don't Hate Las Vegas Anymore* (1994), Amir Naderi's *Manhattan by Numbers* (1993) and *Avenue A.B.C. ... Manhattan* (1997), Shirin Etessam and Erica Jordan's *Walls of Sand* (1994), and Houshang Allahyari's *Höhenangst / Fear of Heights* (1994).

Like the individual film-makers, the Iranian diasporized cinema evolved in several phases, from disavowing dislocation to engaging with it, with location and with locationality. Its form also evolved, from feature fiction to documentary to avant-garde. Of interest was also the emergence of the 'music video' genre that flourished in the United States, particularly in Los Angeles, which was dubbed a 'Persian Motown'! The videos were aired frequently by Iranian exile television in Europe and North America, and they were also available in ethnic grocery stores (and as bootlegs in Iran). These videos offered the exiles a new form of both self-expression and collective identity formation, and they provide researchers of transnational media with fascinating textual materials (Naficy 1998a).

Significantly, women and feminism became major influences both in films and in music videos. Together, these forms of Iranian exilic and diaspora cinema are contributing not only to the national cinemas of the countries in which the film-makers reside, but also to the emerging global cinema of diaspora that is accented by our era's profound sense of displacement, fragmentation and globalization.

Filmography

Aramesh Dar Hozur-e Digaran / Tranquillity in the Presence of Others

1971, 88 mins, black and white

Director:	Naser Taqvai
Producer:	Telfilm
Screenwriter:	Naser Taqvai
Cinematographer:	Mansur Yazdi
Music:	Hormoz Farhat
Leading Players:	Akbar Meshkin, Soraya Qasemi, Manuchehr Atashi, Mohammad Ali Sepanlu, Leila Baharan, Masud Asadollahi, Mehri Mehrnia

Based on Gholamhossein Saedi's eponymous novel. An elderly colonel moves to a small town to spend his retirement in tranquillity. His wife had passed away years earlier but he has two daughters, who work as nurses in Tehran. In time, the colonel marries a younger wife and moves to Tehran, where he discovers that his daughters have changed for the worse. His older daughter eventually commits suicide and her younger sibling enters into an unsuitable marriage. Deeply disturbed by these events, he goes insane and is taken to a mental institution. His only hope and joy is his young wife.

Arus-ye Khuban / *Marriage of the Blessed*

1989, 95 mins, colour

Director:	Mohsen Makhmalbaf
Producer:	Institute for Cinematic Affairs of the Foundation of the Disinherited and Veterans
Screenwriter:	Mohsen Makhmalbaf
Cinematographer:	Alireza Zarrindast
Editor:	Mohsen Makhmalbaf
Music:	Babak Bayat
Leading Players:	Mahmud Bigham, Roya Nonahali, Hossein Moslemi, Mohsen Zehtab, Ameneh Kholbarin

Haji (Mahmud Bigham), a shell-shocked photographer, returns to Tehran from the Iraq–Iran war front. He struggles to reconcile himself with both his memories of the violent war, the television images of starving African children and the downside of post-revolutionary Islamic society that does not appear to follow the moral and compassionate codes of idealized Islam. He is hired back by a newspaper as a photo-journalist, but the editor refuses to print some of the grim pictures of poverty, prostitution and drug abuse that he and his fiancée have taken in the streets of Tehran. On their wedding night, Haji has another flashback to the war, which takes him back to the hospital, where the film had begun.

Azhans-e Shisheh'i / *The Glass Agency*

1997, 100 mins, colour

Director:	Ebrahim Hatamikia
Producer:	Varahonar, Farabi Cinema Foundation
Screenwriter:	Ebrahim Hatamikia
Cinematographer:	Aziz Sa'ati
Editor:	Hayedeh Safiari
Music:	Majid Entezami
Sound:	Mahmud Samakbashi, Mohsen Roshan
Leading Players:	Parviz Parastui, Habib Rezai, Reza Kiyanian, Qasem Zare, Mohammad Hatami, Asghar Naqizadeh, Sadeq Safai

Abbas (Habib Rezai) is a veteran of the war with Iraq who must go abroad for a delicate surgical operation to remove shrapnel that is lodged near his jugular vein. His wartime commander, Haji Kazem (Parviz Parastui), comes to his aid to expedite his hasty departure. Everything is arranged except the plane tickets, which are hard to obtain as a result of the Noruz (Iranian New Year) travel log-jam. Desperate for a ticket, Haji holds up a travel agency and takes all its customers hostage, creating a massive security problem and an intense personal re-evaluation of the war and its enduring legacy for post-war society.

Bachehha-ye Aseman / *The Children of Heaven*

1997, 90 mins, colour

Director:	Majid Majidi
Producer:	Centre for the Intellectual Development of Children and Young Adults
Screenwriter:	Majid Majidi
Cinematographer:	Parviz Malekzadeh
Editor:	Hasan Hasandust
Sound:	Yadollah Najafi, Mohammadreza Delpak
Leading Players:	Mohammadamir Naji, Mirfarrokh Hashemian, Bahareh Seddiqi

When Zohreh loses her shoe, she and her brother Ali face a problem that is born of poverty. However, the two youngsters come up with an ingenious solution. Unbeknownst to their parents, they develop a scheme for sharing Ali's only pair of shoes everyday that they go to school. In the process, they have to surmount many obstacles.

Badkonak-e Sepid / *The White Balloon*

1995, 85 mins, colour

Director:	Jafar Panahi
Producer:	Voice and Vision of Islamic Republic (Iranian Television), Channel 2
Screenwriter:	Abbas Kiarostami
Cinematographer:	Farzad Judat
Editor:	Jafar Panahi
Sound:	Mojtaba Mortazavi, Said Ahmadi, Mehdi Dezhbodi
Leading Players:	Aida Mohammadkhani, Mohsen Kafili, Fereshteh Sadr Orfai, Anna, Borkowska, Mohammad Bakhtiari

A short time before the start of the Noruz (Iranian New Year which is celebrated in late March), a little girl named Raziyeh (Aida Mohammadkhani) goes out to buy a goldfish to decorate the traditional new year table. She loses her money, but she doggedly searches for it, enlisting the help of various children to retrieve it.

Banu-ye Ordibehesht / *The May Lady*

1997, 88 mins, colour

Director:	Rakhshan Banietemad
Producer:	Alireza Raisian, Jahangir Kosari
Screenwriter:	Rakhshan Banietemad
Cinematographer:	Hossein Jafarian
Editor:	Masumeh Shahnazari, Mostafa Kherqehpush
Sound:	Parviz Abnar
Leading Players:	Minu Farshchi, Mani Kasraian, Golab Adineh, Atefeh Razavi, Baran Kosari

Forugh Kia (Minu Farshchi) is a middle-aged documentary film-maker, making a film about successful women as role models. In her private life, she is a divorced single mother raising her teenage son (Mani Kasraian), who is interested in photography and Western pop music. She is also in love with a man who does not appear in the film, but with whom she communicates at length throughout the film via letters and the telephone. As she goes about making her film, interviewing prominent and ordinary women, she struggles to reconcile her professional life with her own desires and with those of the two important men in her life.

Bashu, Gharibeh-ye Kuchak / Bashu, the Little Stranger

1985, 122 mins, colour

Director:	Bahram Baizai
Producer:	Centre for the Intellectual Development of Children and Young Adults
Screenwriter:	Bahram Baizai
Cinematographer:	Firuz Malekzaseh
Editor:	Bahram Baizai
Music:	Firuz Malekzadeh
Sound:	Jahangir Mirshekari, Asghar Shahvardi, Behruz Moavenian
Leading Players:	Susan Taslimi, Adnan Ghafravian, Parviz Purhosseini, Akbar Dudkar

A young boy named Bashu (Adnan Ghafravian), who lives on the coast of the Persian Gulf, loses his family to Iraqi bombing during the eight-year war between Iran and Iraq. He stows himself away in a truck that takes him far north to the verdant shores of the Caspian Sea. He seeks refuge in the fields of a mother of two children named Nai (Susan Taslimi), whose husband is away seeking employment in some town. After much struggle over cultural, linguistic and racial differences, Nai adopts the exiled boy and they form a deepening bond. In time, Nai's husband returns with one arm missing. But the nuclear family is once again reconstituted, this time with Bashu as a new member.

Cheshmeh / The Spring

1972, black and white

Director:	Arbi Avanesian
Producer:	Arbi Avanesian, Telfilm

Screenwriter: Arbi Avanesian
Cinematographer: Nemat Haqiqi
Leading Players: Arman, Mahtaj Nojumi, Jamshid Mashayekhi, Parviz Purhosseini

A man falls in love with his friend's wife (Mahtaj Nojumi), a love he does not divulge out of respect for his friend. Meanwhile the woman takes a young lover and meets with him in an abandoned house. Caught in the vice of this moral dilemma, her husband's friend commits suicide and the women of the village reveal her love affair with the young man. Publicly shamed, the woman also commits suicide. Her husband buries her body in the dry pond of the abandoned house.

Davandeh / The Runner

1985, 94 mins, colour
Director: Amir Naderi
Producer: Centre for the Intellectual Development of Children and Young Adults
Screenwriter: Amir Naderi, Behruz Gharib
Cinematographer: Firuz Malekzadeh
Editor: Bahram Baizai
Sound: Nezamodin Kiai
Leading Players: Majid Nirumand, Abbas Nazarnik, Musa Torkizadeh

Amiro (Majid Nirumand) is a young boy, who like many other boys of this unnamed Persian Gulf port city, ekes out a living by shining shoes, selling water and ice, and collecting discarded bottles from the sea for resale. His relationship with the foreign (Western) sailors, magazines, films, music, aeroplanes and ships is complex. He is attracted to the West, particularly to the flight magazines that the street vendors sell, and to the planes and ships that frequent the port. At the same time he is repelled by sailors, particularly by one who accuses him of robbery. Amiro and his cohorts engage in various games of competition and supremacy, racing against each other, against a moving train, against the ocean waves and, in an exciting final scene, against an ice block that is being rapidly melted by oil fires.

Dayereh-ye Mina / The Cycle

1978, 95 mins, colour
Director: Dariush Mehrjui
Producer: Telfilm (Maleksasan Veisi), MCA, Iran Film Service and Cinematography Company, Film-maker's Cooperative of Iran
Screenwriter: Gholamhosain Saedi and Dariush Mehrjui
Cinematographer: Hushang Baharlu
Editor: Talat Mirfenderski
Leading Players: Said Kangarani, Ezzatollah Entezami, Ali Nasirian, Foruzan, Bahman Forsi, Esmail Mohammadi

Based on the story 'Ashghalduni' by Gholamhosain Saedi. An old man (Esmail Mohammadi) and his teenage son Ali (Said Kangarani) arrive in Tehran from the country to seek a cure for the old man's terminal gastrointestinal ailment. The film centres on the development of these two men, one at the end and the other at the beginning of their adult lives. In the process of seeking help, the father and son are exposed to the underbelly of Shah Era public health and medical care establishments, which are found to be utterly corrupt and amoral. The most disturbing aspect is the procuring of contaminated blood from addicts, its sale to hospitals and blood-banks, and its injection into needy patients.

Do Zan / Two Women

1998, 96 mins, colour

Director:	Tahmineh Milani
Producer:	Arta Film, Arman Film
Screenwriter:	Tahmineh Milani
Cinematographer:	Hossein Jafarian
Editor:	Mostafa Kherqehpush
Sound:	Parviz Abnar
Leading Players:	Niki Karimi, Atila Pesiani, Mohammad Reza Forutan, Merila Zarei, Reza Khandan

Two close friends, studying architecture at Tehran University, drift apart with the onset of the 1979 revolution and the ensuing cultural revolution that closed the universities in order to 'Islamicize' them. Now, fifteen years later, they meet again and review what has happened to them personally and professionally in the ensuing years. Told from the women's point of view, the film offers a critique of men and of patriarchy.

Gabbeh

1995, 75 mins, colour

Director:	Mohsen Makhmalbaf
Producer:	Khalil Dorudchi, Khalil Mahmudi
Screenwriter:	Mohsen Makhmalbaf
Cinematographer:	Mahmud Kalari
Editor:	Mohsen Makhmalbaf
Sound:	Mojtaa Mirtahmaseb
Leading Players:	Seyyed Abbas Sayachi, Shqayeq Jowdat, Aqa Hossein Moharrami, Roqiyyeh Moharrami, Parvaneh Qalandari

A *gabbeh* is an ancient type of knotted rug made by Iranian tribes. A tribal girl named Gabbeh weaves a *gabbeh* during her migration, knotting her impossible love for a young horseman into the carpet's design. Decades pass and the lovers grow old, but the love remains; so does the *gabbeh* that commemorates the love. The film itself is Makhmalbaf's intricately woven tapestry of enduring love, elusive time and the vibrant colours of life.

Gav / The Cow

1969, 104 mins, black and white

Director:	Dariush Mehrjui
Producer:	Dariush Mehrjui, MCA
Screenwriter:	Dariush Mehrjui, Gholamhosain Saedi
Cinematographer:	Feraidun Qavanlu
Editor:	Zari Khalaj
Music:	Hormoz Farhat
Sound:	Bahram Darai
Leading Players:	Ezzattolah Entezami, Ali Nasirian, Jafar Vali, Jamshid Mashayekhi, Esmat Safavi

Based on a story by Gholamhosain Saedi. Mash Hassan (Ezzattolah Entezami) has a cow which is his only source of livelihood. When the cow dies in Hassan's absence, the villagers (who fear being blamed for the animal's death) bury the cow and pretend that it has escaped the village. Grief-stricken, Mash Hassan so profoundly identifies with the absent animal that he becomes it. The villagers herd him like a cow towards town to visit a physician, but he stumbles and dies.

Gharibeh Va Meh / The Stranger and the Fog

1975, 140 mins, colour

Director:	Bahram Baizai
Producer:	Rex Cinema Theatre Company, Mohammad Taqi Shokrai
Screenwriter:	Bahram Baizai
Cinematographer:	Mehrdad Fakhimi
Editor:	Bahram Baizai
Music:	Bahram Baizai
Sound:	Mohsen Kohlar
Leading Players:	Khosrow Shojazadeh, Parvaneh Masumi, Emsat Safavi, Manuchehr Farid

The more or less harmonious life of a Caspian Sea fishing village is disturbed by the mysterious arrival by sea of a wounded stranger, named Ayat (Khosrow Shojazadeh). The villagers' reactions to the newcomer evolve throughout the film, from excitement to suspicion, rejection to fear, antagonism to acceptance. A young widow named Rana (Parvaneh Masumi), whose fisherman husband – a heroic figure to the villagers – is thought to have been devoured by the sea, becomes the primary centre of Ayat's attention. However, mysterious and ominous signs (such as a bloodied sickle) point to possible pursuers of Ayat, frightening the villagers. Ayat is made to undergo a number of tests to gain the community's trust and to qualify to become Rana's husband: in any case, they come to need him for their own defence. In turn, when the mysterious attackers finally arrive by the sea, the community defends Ayat. At the end, fearing further persecution by his pursuers and lured by the attraction of what is beyond, Ayat leaves Rana and his new-found community in the same way that he had arrived, alone in a boat.

Haji Aqa, Aktor-e Sinema | Mr Haji, the Movie Actor

1932, black and white

Director:	Avanes Ohanian (Oganians)
Producer:	Maqasedzadeh Foruzin, Habiollah Morad, Avanes Ohanian (Oganians)
Screenwriter:	Avanes Ohanian (Oganians)
Cinematographer:	Paolo Potemkin, Ebrahim Moradi
Editor:	Avanes Ohanian (Oganians)
Leading Players:	Habiollah Morad, Asia Qostanian, Abbasqoli Edalatpur, Zema Oganians, Abbas Tahbaz, Avanes Ohanian

A film director is looking for a subject for his latest film. He decides to clandestinely film a traditional man named Haji (Habiollah Morad), who is opposed to cinema on moral grounds. His daughter (Asia Qostanian), her fiancé (Abbas Tahbaz) and Haji's manservant (Abbasqoli Edalatpur) all conspire with the director in a series of comic escapades to film Haji. When the film is completed and is shown publicly, Haji is transformed by seeing himself on the screen and by the enthusiastic audience response he receives. Accordingly, he declares that cinema is one of the best tools for educating the public.

Kelosup, Nama-ye Nazdik | Close-Up

1989, 90 mins, colour

Director:	Abbas Kiarostami
Producer:	Centre for the Intellectual Development of Children and Young Adults
Screenwriter:	Abbas Kiarostami
Cinematographer:	Alireza Zarrindast
Leading Players:	Hossein Sabzian, Hasan Farazmand, Abolfazl Ahankhah, Hushang Shomai, Mehrdad Ahankhah, Mrs Ahankhah, Mohsen Makhmalbaf

This film is based on a real-life news story. A young man (Hossein Sabzian) who looks somewhat like the well-known film director Mohsen Makhmalbaf is so enamoured of the director that he takes on his identity. He enters the life and the household of the Ahankhah family by pretending to be Makhmalbaf scouting for a film location. When the scouting lasts too long and no film crew appears, the family suspects Sabzian and takes him to court for having falsified his identity. All the participants re-enact their real-life roles and the court proceedings are filmed in a documentary fashion. The director and his fan are united in a touching sequence.

Leila

1996, 110 mins, colour

Director:	Dariush Mehrjui
Producer:	Dariush Mehrjui, Faramarz Farazmand
Screenwriter:	Dariush Mehrjui

Cinematographer:	Mahmud Kalari
Editor:	Mostafa Kherqehpush
Music:	Keivan Jahanshahi
Sound:	Asghar Shahverdi, Jahangir Mirshekari
Leading Players:	Leila Hatami, Ali Mosaffa, Jamileh Sheikhi, Mohammdreza Sharifnia, Turan Mehrzad, Amir Paivar, Vahideh Mohammadi, Shaqayeq Farahani, Parisa Zarei, Faraj Balafkan

Based on a story by Mahnaz Ansarin. Leila (Leila Hatami) and Reza (Ali Mosaffa) are in love and happily married, but when they discover that Leila cannot conceive a child their world is turned upside down. Neither Reza nor Leila are concerned with the issue because they love each other, but Reza's strong-willed, autocratic and meddling mother (Jamileh Sheikhi) insists that her only son must produce a child. She forces her will on her indecisive son and whittles down the resistance of Leila, who is tortured by guilt due to her infertility. Finally, the young couple agree that Reza should find a second wife – a humiliating and painful process in which Leila herself participates. This process destroys their once happy union and leads Leila into a deep psychological depression and crisis.

Mogholha | The Mongols

1973, 92 mins, colour

Director:	Masud Kimiavi
Producer:	Telfilm
Screenwriter:	Masud Kimiavi
Cinematographer:	Michel Terrier
Music:	Folk music from Khorasan and Turkoman regions
Leading Players:	Fahimeh Rastegar, Parviz Kimiavi, Aqa Seyyed Ali Mirza, Edris Chamani, Darvish Abbas

A director of a television series on the history of cinema (Parviz Kimiavi), who has been grappling with the screenplay of his first feature film, receives an assignment to oversee the installation of a television relay station in a remote region of Zahedan province, near the Afghanistan border. He has already hired Turkoman tribespeople for his film and selected his filming locations. Meanwhile his wife (Fahimeh Rastegar), who is working on her Ph.D. dissertation about the Mongol invasion of Iran, attempts to dissuade him from accepting the assignment. One night, while working on his history of cinema series, the director fantasizes a diegetic world that consists of clever juxtapositions of his different worlds: the history of cinema, the history of the Mongol invasion, his own film idea and his imminent assignment to the desert.

Nar 'O Nay | Pomegranate and the Reed

1988, 100 mins, colour

Director:	Said Ebrahimfar
Producer:	Farabi Cinema Foundation, Said Ebrahimifar, Hossein Iri

Screenwriter: Said Ebrahimfar
Cinematographer: Homayun Paivar
Music: Fariborz Lachini
Leading Players: Jahangir Almassi, Ghazal Elmi, Ali Asghar Garmsiri, Rasul
                       Najafian, Pari Assari

A photographer in search of pictures for a play on atomic scientist Robert
Oppenheimer comes across an old man fallen in the street. He rushes the man to the
hospital and, while waiting to hear about his condition, he reads the man's diary. In
beautifully and sensitively photographed flashbacks, the film reveals in loving detail
the man's childhood and growing-up in Kashan, accompanied by a lyrical narration
written by poet Ahmadreza Ahmadi. The film is principally a rumination on loss – of
parents, childhood innocence and rooted rural traditions.

Qaisar

1969, 108 mins, black and white
Director: Masud Kimiai
Producer: Abbas Shabaviz
Screenwriter: Masud Kimiai
Cinematographer: Mazyar Partow
Editor: Mazyar Partow
Music: Esfandiar Monfaredzadeh
Sound: Mohammad Mohammadi
Leading Players: Behruz Vosuqi, Puri Banai, Naser Malekmotii, Jamshid
                       Mashayekhi, Iran Daftari, Bahman Mofid

While the neighborhood tough guy Qaisar is away, a member of a rival gang rapes his
sister. Unable to endure the shame, she commits suicide. A rival gang member kills her
elder brother (Naser Malekmotii) when he attempts to take revenge. On his return,
Qaisar is stunned by the news and sets out to avenge both deaths. He kills one of the
culprits in a dramatic bathhouse scene and murders the other in the slaughterhouse.
Later, he is himself gunned down in an altercation with the police.

Shazdeh Ehtejab / Prince Ehtejab

1974, black and white
Director: Bahman Farmanara
Producer: Telfilm (Maleksasan Veisi), Bahman Farmanara
Screenwriter: Hushang Golshiri and Bahman Farmanara
Cinematographer: Nemat Haqiqi
Music: Ahmad Pezhman
Leading Players: Jamshid Mashayekhi, Fakhri Khorvash, Nuri Kasrai, Vali
                       Tirandami, Hossein Kasbian, Parvin Soleimani, Firuz
                       Behjatmohammadi

Based on Hushang Golshiri's eponymous novel. Prince Ehtejab (Jamshid Mashayekhi), one of the last remaining heirs of the Qajar royal family, is suffering from tuberculosis, which he knows is fatal. He spends his last days alone in the magnificent rooms of his wintry palace, from where he recollects the glory days of his ancestors as well as days of degradation. Among the latter are the gruesome manner in which his cruel grandfather murdered his mother and brother, and the way that he himself caused the death of his wife.

Tabiat-e Bijan | Still Life

1975, 93 mins, colour

Director:	Sohrab Shahid Saless
Producer:	Telfilm (Maleksasan Veisi), Progressive Film Union (Parviz Sayyad)
Screenwriter:	Sohrab Shahid Saless
Cinematographer:	Hushang Baharlu
Editor:	Ruhollah Emami
Sound:	Mohammd Sadeq Alami, Ahmad Khanzadi, M. Farshian
Leading Players:	Z. Boniadi, Zahra Yazdani, Habib Safarian, Mohammad Kani

An old railwayman lives at a remote junction point with his wife, who weaves rugs in their humble home. Their stoic solitude is broken by occasional visitors, particularly by the one-night visit of their son, an army draftee. In time, the old man receives his retirement notice, followed by the arrival of his young replacement. These events so upset his quiet equilibrium that he goes to the railway headquarters in town, where he lodges a vociferous protest in vain. Disappointed he gets drunk in a café. The next day, he and his wife evacuate their premises and leave for an unknown destination.

Ta'm-e Gilas | Taste of Cherry

1997, colour

Director:	Abbas Kiarostami
Producer:	Abbas Kiarostami
Screenwriter:	Abbas Kiarostami
Cinematographer:	Homayun Paivar
Editor:	Abbas Kiarostami
Leading Players:	Homayun Ershad, Mohammad Hosseini Baqeri, Hossein Nuri

On an autumn afternoon, a well-to-do middle-aged man (Homayun Ershad) who has decided to commit suicide, is looking for a partner in crime – a man who would promise for a sum of money to bury him should he succeed in his attempt. He drives around the streets of Tehran in his sports utility vehicle looking for such a partner. He stops, asks questions of passersby and invites them into his car without result. Disappointed, he treks into the nearby hills and dales, driving up and down the sinewy roads, where he encounters an assortment of young men, who are by turn suspicious, fearful or angry at his plan and all refuse to co-operate. At last an old dermatologist, who has had a near-death experience of his own, promises to help, but not before making a touching and passionate plea for the sacredness and beauty of life. The film ends with a self-reflexive tag, in which the director wraps up the shoot.

List of directors

Baizai, Bahram (b. 1938, Tehran)

Baizai is a multi-faceted, independent author, screenplay writer, theatre director, film director, university professor and film editor. He did not finish his university education and studied cinema on his own. He published two books on theatre: *Namayesh dar Iran / Theatre in Iran* and *Namayesh dar Chin / Theatre in China*, the former being an authoritative source. In the course of his long career, he has written over two dozen screenplays and plays; some of the latter he directed himself. Although his screenplays were published, many of them were never produced, particularly under the Islamic Republic. In general, these plays and screenplays critically re-examined and re-evaluated Iranian history and culture, using both ancient Iranian theatrical forms (such as the Taziyeh), Asian theatrical forms (such as the Japanese Nō theatre) and European forms. In the 1970s, he was a member of the New Wave film movement and of the Progressive Film Union, from which he resigned within a year. In 1973 he began teaching at Tehran University's Fine Arts College, where he was popular with students but not with the administration, which apparently expelled him after the revolution. When he could not get his films made under the Islamic Republic, he edited other directors' works, among them Varuzh Karim Masihi's short film *Salander* (1980) and Amir Naderi's *Jostoju-ye Do / Second Search* (1981) and *Davandeh / The Runner* (1984).

He directed two short films: *Amu Sibilu / Mustachioed Uncle* (1970) and *Safar / Journey* (1972). His feature-film output is small due to problems he encountered financing his uncompromising films, and the difficulties he faced in getting his screenplays and completed films cleared by the official censors. His feature films are *Ragbar / Downpour* (1972), *Gharibeh Va Meh / The Stranger and the Fog* (1975), *Cherikeh-ye Tara / Tara's Ballad* (1978), *Marg-e Yazdgerd / Yazdgerd's Death* (1980), *Bashu, the Little Stranger / Bashu, Gharibeh-ye Kuchak* (1985), *Shayad Vaqti Digar / Perhaps Some Other Time* (1987), *Mosaferan / Travellers* (1990) and *Sagkoshi / Killing Rabid Dogs*. His films have received high praise nationally and internationally (see Qukasian 1992).

Women are strong presences and narrative agents in his films, even though the gaze remains male.

Banietemad, Rakhshan (b. 1954, Tehran)

In 1979, Banietemad received her B.A. in film-making from Tehran University's Dramatic Arts College. From 1973 until her graduation, she also worked as a set designer for Vision & Voice of the Islamic Republic (television networks). Before entering feature film-making, between 1979 and 1986 Banietemad made several short films: *Sazmanha-ye Mali-ye Yahud / Jewish Financial Institutions*, *Tadabir-e Eqtesadi-ye Jang / Economic Planning of the War*, *Farhang-e Masraf / Culture of Consumerism*,

Esteqlal-e Mohajerin-e Rustai Dar Shahrha / *The Independence of Rural Immigrants in the Cities* and *Tamarkoz* / *Concentration*. She also worked as planning manager and assistant director on a number of features, among them *Aftabneshinha* / *Sun-Dwellers* (1982) and *Golha-ye Davudi* / *Chrysanthemums* (1984).

Her feature films are *Kharej Az Mahdudeh* / *Off the Limit* (1987), *Zard-e Qanari* / *Canary Yellow* (1989), *Pul-e Khareji* / *Foreign Exchange* (1989), *Nargess* (1991), *Rusari-ye Abi* / *The Blue Veiled* (1994) and *Banu-ye Ordibehesht* / *The May Lady* (1997). The most prolific and accomplished of the Iranian female directors, Banietemad gained national presence with *Nargess*, before achieving international stature with *Rusari-ye Abi*. Her representation of women in her early films was quite conservative, but it grew in boldness until *Banu-ye Ordibehesht*, her most progressive and experimental work. Documentary, however, remained a passion for her and she continued to make socially critical films including *Akharin Didar Ba Iran-e Daftari* / *Last Visit with Iran Daftari* (1995), an affectionate portrait of a famous actress, and *In Filmharo Beh Ki Neshun Midin?* / *Who Will You Show These Films To?* (1992–4), a searing documentary about the homeless people and shantytown dwellers of Tehran that has not been shown publicly. Her latest work is *Baran Va Boomi* / *Baran and Boomi* (1998), a short fictional film about love that was shot on the Island of Kish in the Persian Gulf.

Hatamikia, Ebrahim (b. 1961, Tehran)

Hatamikia was raised in a family so religious that it shunned television at home and forbade the movies outside the home. Nevertheless, as a junior high-school student Hatamikia sneaked into cinemas to see Indian song-and-dance films. In 1980 he began to study cinema and film-making at the Islamic Centre for Amateur Film Production (Markaz-e Islami-ye Filmsazi-ye Amator), where he made several short Super 8 films, including *Kurdelan* / *The Inwardly Blind* (1982), an anti-Mojahedin Khalq film. With the onset of war with Iraq, he joined the Revolutionary Guards and was sent to the front to make documentaries. Deeply moved by what he saw, however, he gravitated towards fictional treatment of the war with his *Torbat* / *Sacred Earth* (1983), another Super 8 film. His next film, *Serat* / *The Road* (1985), this time shot on 16 mm, won an award at Fajr International Film Festival, opening the way for his entry into professional cinema. The making of *Serat* brought together Hatamikia and another important war-film director, Mortaza Avini. He made one more 16 mm film, *Towq-e Sorkh* / *The Red Yoke* (1985), before his full entry into the world of 35 mm feature films, starting with *Hovviat* / *Identity* (1986).

His subsequent features – almost all of them dealing with the war, its psychological dimensions and the ethical issues of loyalty, treason, sacrifice, waiting, loss and longing – are *Didehban* / *The Sentry* (1988), *Mohajer* / *Immigrant* (1989), *Vasl-e Nikan* / *The Union of the Benevolent* (1991), *Az Karkheh Ta Rhine* / *From Karkheh to Rhine* (1992), *Khakestar-e Sabz* / *The Green Ash* (1994), *Bu-ye Pirahan-e Yusof* / *The Smell of Joseph's Shirt* (1995), *Borj-e Minu* / *The Heavenly Tower* (1995) and *Azhans-e Shisheh'i* / *The Glass Agency* (1997) (see Mo'azezinia 1998). These films made Hatamikia the most celebrated war-film director, who with each work deepened and widened his treatment of war-related subjects, even years after the war with Iraq was over.

Kiarostami, Abbas (b. 1940, Tehran)

Kiarostami received his B.A. in art from the Fine Arts College, Tehran University, and in 1970 began making short films for the Centre for the Intellectual Development of Children and Young Adults, an organization for which he made most of his films. His short films, all but the last made for the Centre, are *Zang-e Tafrih / Recess* (1972), *Tajrobeh / Experience* (1973), *Do Rah-e Hal Bara-ye Yek Mas'aleh / Two Solutions for One Problem* (1975), *Manam Mitunam / I, Too, Can* (1975), *Rangha / Colours* (1976), *Lebasi Bara-ye Arusi / Wedding Clothes* (1976), *Rah-e Hall-e Yek / The First Solution* (1978), *Qaziyyeh: Shekl-e Avval, Shekl-e Dovvom / Problem: Alternative One, Alternative Two* (1979), *Behdasht-e Dandan / Dental Hygiene* (1980), *Beh Tartib Ya Bi Tartib / With Discipline or Without Discipline* (1981), *Hamsoraya / Choral Singers* (1982), *Hamshahri / Fellow Citizen* (1983) and *Film-e Sad Saniyeh-i ba Durbin-e Lumier / A Hundred-Second Film with the Lumières' Camera* (1995).

From time to time Kiarostami wrote screenplays for other directors, such as for Ebrahim Foruzesh's *Kelid / The Key* (1986). Unlike many film-makers who use the short-film format as a jumping board for their professional feature career, Kiarostami continued to make short films while making features. Because of his self-reflexive and interventionist style, some of his films, shorts and features cannot readily be classified because they blur the boundary of fictional and non-fictional film typology. Indeed, almost all of his recent films problematize not only the nature of reality but also that of film ontology.

Kiarostami's feature-length films are *Mosafer / Traveller* (1974), *Gozaresh / Report* (1977), *Avvaliha / The Firsts* (1984), *Khaneh-ye Doust Kojast? / Where's the Friend's Home?* (1986), *Mashq-e Shab / Homework* (1988), *Kelosup, Nama-ye Nazdik / Close-Up* (1989), *Zendegi Va Digar Hich / Life and Nothing More* (a.k.a. *And Life Goes On*, 1991), *Zir-e Darakhtan-e Zaitun / Under the Olive Trees* (1993), *Ta'm-e Gilas / Taste of Cherry* (1996) and *Bad Ma Ra Khahad Bord / The Wind Will Carry Us* (1999) (see Qukasian 1997). Many of his features since *Khaneh-ye Doust Kojast?* garnered lavish praise and prestigious prizes at international film festivals, making Kiarostami the most famous and influential Iranian director. He wrote the screenplays for most of his own features, and edited and designed the production for a number of them. In this manner, he became truly the author of his own films and the progenitor of the humanist genre.

Kimiai, Masud (b. 1944, Tehran)

Kimiai learned film-making by experience, beginning as assistant director to the action director Samuel Khachikian on *Khodahafez Tehran / Goodbye Tehran* (1966). Subsequently, Kimiai made a few short films, among them *Pesar-e Sharqi / Eastern Boy* (1975) and *Asb / Horse* (1976).

The feature films he directed, several of which were titled with the protagonist's name, are *Biganeh Bia / Come Stranger* (1966), *Qaisar* (1969), *Reza Motori / Reza the Driver* (1970), *Dash Akol* (1971), *Baluch* (1972), *Khak / Earth* (1973), *Gavaznha / The Deer* (1975), *Ghazal* (1976), *Safar-e Sang / The Travel of the Stone* (1978), *Khat-e Qermez / The Red Line* (1982), *Tiq Va Abrisham / Blade and Silk* (1986), *Sorb / Lead* (1988), *Dandan-e Mar / Snake's Fang* (1989), *Goruhban / Sergeant* (1991), *Radd-e Pay-*

Figure 27 Zendegi Va Digar Hich / Life and Nothing More

e Gorg / Wolf Tracks (1993), *Tejarat / Commerce* (1994), *Ziafat / Feast* (1995), *Soltan / Sultan* (1996) and *Mersedes* (1997) (see Qukasian 1990).

Kimiai's early films *Qaisar* and *Dash Akol* shook Iranian cinema, helping to bring about the emergence of both the New Wave movement and the tough guy genre. He was highly productive under the Islamic Republic, but less influential than during the previous era. Although women are present in his films, sometimes prominently as in *Ghazal* (named after the female protagonist), they tend to be subsidiary characters, as they generally serve to define the men who form the core of Kimiai's films. As such, his is a male cinema.

Kimiavi, Parviz (b. 1939, Tehran)

Kimiavi received his film production degree in 1966 from the famed Parisian school IDEC, where he began working as assistant director for the state-run ORTF television network. On his return to Iran in 1969, he made his short documentary *Tappehha-ye Qaitari-yeh / Qaitari-yeh Hills* (1969), followed in quick succession by further documentaries: *Ya Zamen-e Ahu / Oh Deer Saviour* (1970), *Bojnurd Ta Quchan / From Bojnurd to Quchan* (1970), *Bazar-e Mashhad / Mashhad's Bazaar* (1970), *Shiraz-e 70 / Shiraz 70* (1970), *Masjed-e Gowharshad / Gowharshad Mosque* (1971) and *P Mesl-e Pelikan / P as in Pelican* (1971). The best of these, such as *Ya Zamen-e Ahu* and *P Mesl-e Pelikan*, were impressionistic documentaries that mixed fact, fantasy and desire in uncanny and ironic ways to expose and to comment on Iranian culture, art and society.

His pre-revolution feature films, too, were stylistically experimental and fresh as they blurred the boundaries separating fictional and non-fictional films, often with insightful humour. They are *Mogholha / The Mongols* (1973), in which he equated the entry of television into Iran to the devastating Mongol invasion; *Bagh-e Sangi / Stone Garden* (1975), which centred on an idiosyncratic old man who had turned an isolated spot of the desert near Kerman into a stone garden, and *O.K. Mister* (1979), which poked savage (if sometimes overwrought) fun at the coming of oil and industrialization to Iran under the Pahlavi regime.

He made most of his films (shorts and feature films) for the national television network (NIRT) or for its film subsidiary, Telfilm. He was working for NIRT when the revolution took place, an event in which he participated by extensively filming the demonstrations and by joining the television-workers' strike against the Shah. The latter landed him in jail. However, according to Kimiai in an interview with me, subsequent pleas by well-known European artists (such as Constantine Costa Gavras, Yves Montand and Simone Signoret) were helpful in gaining his freedom (Naficy 1989). In 1981, Kimiavi left the country for a lengthy exile in Paris, where he directed numerous documentaries for television, among them *La tranche / The Trench* (1981), *Portrait d'un jeune Tunisien / Portrait of a Tunisian Boy* (1982), *Oswaldo Rodriguez* (1983), *Le blue jean / Blue Jeans* (1984), *Simone Weil* (1988) and *Zourkhaneh: La maison de force / Zurkhaneh: The House of Strength* (1988).

In the mid-1990s Kimiavi returned to Iran where, after much difficulty, he made his impressive feature-length film *Sarzamin-e Man Iran Ast / My Country is Iran* (1998).

Makhmalbaf, Mohsen (b. 1957, Tehran)

He was raised in an Islamist family, which shaped his worldview and his early artistic works. While in high school, he wrote religiously inspired plays and was recruited into an underground Islamist group called Balal Habashi (named after an Ethiopian called Bilal who was Prophet Mohammad's first muezzin). In 1974, when he was seventeen, Makhmalbaf was arrested during his group's clumsy attempt to disarm a policeman (recreated in *Nun Va Goldun / The Bread and the Vase*). He was condemned to five years in prison, but was released with the onset of the 1979 revolution. After his release, he worked in radio for a while, but soon joined an Islamist arts centre (Howzeh-ye Honari-ye Sazman-e Tabliqat-e Eslami). He rapidly became the leading member of this organization, under whose auspices he made many of his early films (up to *Bysikelran / The Cyclist*). Through his films and writings, he became the regime's ideologue of Islamization of cinema and the most prominent of the post-revolutionary generation of film-makers.

Makhmalbaf proved to be a prolific film-maker, releasing a feature film almost every year (and sometimes more). This was partly a result of the official sanction that he received early on due to his support for the Islamic government and its Islamization ideology. However, what is remarkable is the divergence of styles and concerns in his works and his constant search for the novel and for the truth. As a result, despite his fundamentalist beginning and his constant change, there is a certain trajectory to his works, which reflects the gradual transformation of Makhmalbaf's own thinking. If the early films were driven by fundamentalist, doctrinaire beliefs, his later films (beginning with *Arusi-ye Khuban / The Marriage of the Blessed*) are characterized by fundamental doubt and by a multiplicity of perspectives. This did not sit well with the authorities, particularly the hardliners, who debated and condemned several of his films in parliament and the press, causing them to be banned.

Unlike most Art Cinema film-makers, Makhmalbaf began his career making feature-length fictional films and moved towards the short form and the documentary only later. His features are *Towbeh-ye Nasuh / Nasuh's Repentance* (1982), *Este'azeh /*

Taking Refuge (1983), *Do Cheshm-e Bisu / Two Sightless Eyes* (1984), *Baikot / Boycott* (1986), *Dastforush / Peddler* (1987), *Bysikelran / The Cyclist* (1988), *Arusi-ye Khuban / The Marriage of the Blessed* (1988), *Nowbat-e Asheqi / A Time to Love* (1990), *Shabha-ye Zayandehrud / Zayandehrud's Nights* (1990), *Nassered-Din Shah, Aktor-e Sinema / Nassered-Din Shah, the Movie Actor* (1991), *Honarpisheh / The Actor* (1992), *Salam Sinema / Salaam Cinema* (a.k.a. *Cinema, Cinema*, 1994), *Gabbeh* (1995), *Nun Va Goldun / The Bread and the Vase* (1995), *Sokut / Silence* (1997) (see Haidari 1997).

To date, Makhmalbaf has made only two short documentaries, both of which are stylistically inferior to his features. One is *Gozideh-ye Tasvir Dar Dowran-e Qajar / Selected Images of the Qajar Era* (1992), which is about the artwork in the Golestan Palace in Tehran – including the first actuality films, dating to the Qajar Era, that were discovered there. While the actualities are highly valuable historical and cinematic documents, his use of insistent barking dogs on the soundtrack to demonstrate his antipathy toward the monarchy, mars the film. Likewise, his *Sang Va Shisheh / Rock and Glass* (1993), about glass-making and glass-breaking, suffers from its political rhetoric and the politicized use of fictional films, including those of Charlie Chaplin. Makhmalbaf has written screenplays for other directors and edited other directors' films. He has also extensively published his own stories and non-fiction commentaries.

Mehrjui, Dariush (b. 1939, Tehran)

Mehrjui received his B.A. in philosophy from UCLA in 1959, but he was drawn to cinema. He began by directing feature films, but in between features he made two short films: *Isar / Munificence* (1976) and *Infaq / Nourishment* (1977), both commissioned by Iran's Blood Transfusion Centre. He also made two major documentaries about historical movements and figures: *Alamut* (1976) and *Voyage au pays de Rimbaud / Journey to the Land of Rimbaud* (1983). The first was about the Assassins' fort Alamut, near Qazvin, and about their way of life and belief system. This was never shown on Iranian television for which he had made it. In the 1970s, Mehrjui was a member of the New Wave film movement and of the Progressive Film Union. Soon after the revolution of 1979, he moved to France for a few years, where he made the second of his long-form documentaries, *Voyage au pays de Rimbaud*, about the French poet Arthur Rimbaud. This film was commissioned and aired by the French television channel FR3. Mehrjui found France inhospitable to his film-making projects and returned to Iran to spearhead, with other New Wave film-makers, the renaissance of the Iranian cinema.

Like several veteran film-makers, his long film-career spans both the Pahlavi and Islamic Republic Eras. He directed many feature films, whose screenplays he either wrote himself or collaborated on with well-known writers. Many of the films were adaptations of Iranian, European and American literary works. This collaborative mode of production was a contributory factor to the emergence of the New Wave film movement. Many of Mehrjui's films suffered from official censorship, causing short or long delays in their release. (In one case, there was a delay of nearly a decade. These delays are noted in parentheses below.)

The features he directed are *Almas 33 / Diamond 33* (1967), *Gav / The Cow* (1969, released in 1970), considered to be one of Iranian cinema's seminal works, *Aqa-ye Halu / Mr Gullible* (1970, released in 1971), *Postchi / The Postman* (1970, released in

1972), *Dayereh-ye Mina* / *The Cycle* (1974, released in 1977), *Madresseh'i Keh Miraftim* / *The School We Went To* (1980, re-titled and released in 1989), *Ejarehneshinha* / *The Tenants* (1987), *Shirak* (1998), *Hamun* (1990), *Banu* / *Lady* (1992, released in 1998), *Sara* (1993), *Pari* (1995), *Leila* (1997) and *Darakht-e Golabi* / *The Pear Tree* (1998). His fame began with *Gav* and continued apace in the subsequent decades, winning him numerous international awards (see Zera'ati 1996). *Banu*, *Sara*, *Pari* and *Leila* all centrally dealt with female protagonists, named in the title; however, they were not feminist films. While during the Pahlavi Era, Mehrjui's films were marked by their socially conscious criticism, many of his post-revolution films were characterized by their philosophical and mystical ruminations. Significantly, his Pahlavi Era films focused on the lives of people on the social margins, while his post-revolution films centred on male and female middle-class intellectuals, a class that Iranian film-makers generally avoided and the official Islamist culture generally disdained. As such, these shifts may be interpreted as embodying both accommodation and resistance to the culture of the Islamic Republic.

Milani, Tahmineh (b. 1960, Tabriz)

Milani graduated in architectural design from the Science and Industry University. She soon became involved in film, joining the Free Cinema centre in Tabriz in 1979. This involvement became professional when she began working as assistant director, set designer and screenwriter for feature directors.

Milani's own feature films are *Bachehha-ye Talaq* / *The Children of Divorce* (1989), *Afsaneh-ye Ah* / *The Legend of the Ah* (1990), *Digeh Cheh Khabar?* / *What Else is New?* (1991), *Kakado* (1994) and *Do Zan* / *Two Women* (1999). Because of her outspoken defence of women and her bold representation of them in her films, particularly in *Kakado* and *Do Zan*, she has had run-ins with the authorities. Her *Kakado* was already being shown when it was banned. The ban was apparently because its protagonist, an eight-year-old girl, was unveiled, but since the banning took place only after Milani had made a speech in which she criticized the Ministry of Culture and Islamic Guidance's policies, it is likely that the speech and her critical views were the real cause. That she thereafter encountered numerous difficulties in getting her screenplays approved and gaining permission to film them corroborates this point. On its release during Mohammad Khatami's reformist presidency, Milani's *Do Zan* became at once immensely popular and highly controversial – it was labelled the first Iranian feminist film.

Naderi, Amir (b. 1945, Abadan)

Naderi entered cinema as a photographer and assistant director. His first films were shorts: *Entezar* / *Waiting* (1974), *Marsi-yeh* / *Elegy* (1975–7) and *Barandeh* / *The Winner* (1984). *Barandeh* was later reworked and expanded into his impressive visual feature *Davandeh* / *The Runner* (1985). A number of his films, including the shorts, were made under the aegis of the Centre for the Intellectual Development of Children and Young Adults.

Naderi made two primary types of feature-length films: socially conscious action–adventure films and visually lyrical films. The former predominated in his early career (*Tangna*, *Tangsir*), while the latter characterized his later works (*Davandeh*, *Manhattan by Numbers*). His feature films are *Khodahafez Rafiq* / *Goodbye Friend* (1971), *Tangna* / *Strait* (1972), *Tangsir* / *Tight Spot* (1973), *Saz-e Dahani* / *Harmonica* (1974), *Sakht-e Iran* / *Made in Iran* (filmed in the United States, 1978), *Jostoju-ye Yek* / *Search 1* (1980), *Jostoju-ye Dovvom* / *Search 2* (1981), *Davandeh* / *The Runner* (1985) and *Ab, Bad, Khak* / *Water, Wind, Dust* (1987) (see Haidari 1991).

After his *Ab, Bad, Khak*, Naderi went into voluntary exile in the United States, where he established himself in New York. There, after years of earning a living as a fashion photographer and film editor, he directed two feature films: *Manhattan by Numbers* (1993) and *Avenue A.B.C. … Manhattan* (1997). Both are visually stunning but essentially dystopic films of angst in the New World. Many of Naderi's films, of both action and lyrical genres, centre on single males whose single-minded personal or social obsession drives the plot. Several of these, such as *Davandeh* and *Manhattan by Numbers*, are semi-autobiographical, but the director's personal stake and self-inscription are disguised. Like Shahid Saless, Naderi denies that he is in exile or that his exile films are Iranian.

Shahid Saless, Sohrab (b. 1944, Tehran; d. 1998, Chicago, Illinois)

Shahid Saless received his training in film production in Austria and France and began making films in Iran in the late 1960s. While employed by the Ministry of Culture and Arts, he made numerous documentaries and short films: *Qafas* / *Cage* (1969), *Mahabad* (1969), *Raqs-e Daravish* / *Dance of the Dervishes* (1969), *Rastakhiz: Ta'mir-e Asar-e Bastani-ye Takht-e Jamshid* / *Renaissance: The Repair of Historical Monuments of Persepolis* (1969), *Dovvomin Namayeshgah-e Asiai* / *The Second Asian Exhibition* (1969), *Raqsha-ye Torbat-e Jam* / *Torbat-e Jam's Dances* (1970), *Raqsha-ye Mahhali-ye Turkaman* / *Turkoman Indigenous Dances* (1970), *Raqs-e Bojnurd* / *Bojnurd Dance* (1970) and *Aya?* / *Whether?* (1971). He made a short film on colour and power relations, *Siah Va Sefid* / *Black and White* (1972), for the Centre for the Intellectual Development of Children and Young Adults.

Shahid Saless directed his first feature, *Yek Ettefaq-e Sadeh* / *A Simple Event* (1973), under the guise of working on a short film. It brought him to national attention. His compelling, award-winning *Tabi'at-e Bijan* / *Still Life* (1974) put him on the international map of cineastes, garnering high praise and the top directing award, the Silver Bear, from the Berlin Film Festival. He left Iran in 1974 for Germany because of the stifling conditions governing the film industry, which stopped his production of *Qarantin-eh* / *Quarantine* (a film he never completed). In the course of his twenty-three years of German exile, he made thirteen uncompromising, lengthy films for cinema and television. Many of his features are over two hours in length and have won international recognition. They are *Dar Ghorbat* / *In der Fremde* / *In Exile* (1974–5), *Reifezeit* / *Time of Maturity* (1975), *Tagebuch eines Liebenden* / *Diary of a Lover* (1976), *Die Langen Ferien der Lotte H. Eisner* / *Lotte H. Eisner's Long Vacation* (1979), *Ordnung* / *Order* (1979–80), *Grabbes Letzter Sommer* / *Grabbe's Last Summer* (1980), *Ein Leben: Chekov* / *A Life: Chekhov* (1981), *Empfänger Unbekannt* / *Recipient Unknown* (1982), *Utopia* (1982), *Hans – Ein Junge in Deutschland* / *Hans – A Boy from Germany* (1983), *Der Weidenbaum* / *The Willow Tree* (1984), *Wechselbalg* / *Changeling* (1985) and *Rosen für Afrika* / *Roses for Africa* (1991).

After several fallow years, during which he unsuccessfully attempted to find producers in Europe, he terminated his German exile by relocating first to Canada and then to the United States in the mid-1990s, where he died at the age of fifty-four. In a series of conversations with me, Shahid Saless disputed his characterization as an exilic film-maker. Instead, he preferred to think of his exile as a kind of 'long vacation' – a reference to *Die Langen Ferien der Lotte H. Eisner*, his affectionate film about a Jewish-German film scholar who, on leaving Nazi Germany by train for permanent exile in France, declared that she was going on a long vacation. Yet Shahid Saless's critically dystopic films, his successful but marginalized career as a film-maker in Germany and his inability to finance his films in a globalized and commercialized economy in which profitability reigns supreme (which drove him finally to leave his adopted homeland for yet another exile) all point to a deep undercurrent of exilism in his life and oeuvre (Naficy 1998b, Dehbashi 1999, Naficy 1999).

Taqvai, Naser (b. 1940, Abadan)

Taqvai graduated with a B.A. from Tehran University's Literature College and his first creative efforts were impressionistic short stories (in sensibility and style resembling Ernest Hemingway's writing) about his native Persian Gulf region. He was pulled into cinema by his involvement with Ebrahim Golestan's *Khesht Va Ayeneh / Mud-Brick and Mirror*. However, before directing feature films, he distinguished himself as an accomplished documentarist, whose many films (similar to his short stories) were informed by his subtle ethnographic understanding of his subjects.

Taqvai made his many documentaries under the auspices of NIRT and the Centre for the Intellectual Development of Children and Young Adults. All of them were filmed on 16 mm format. They are *Taximetr / Taxi Meter* (1967), *Arayeshgah-e Aftab / The Sunny Barbershop* (1967), *Nankhorha-ye Bisavadi / Dependents of Illiteracy* (1967), *Telefon / Telephone* (1967), *Raqs-e Shemshir / Sword Dance* (1967), *Forugh Farrokhzad* (1967), *Panjshanbeh Bazar-e Minab / Minab's Thursday Bazaar* (1969), *Nakhl / Palm Tree* (1969), *Bad-e Jen / The Jinn's Wind* (1969), *Arbain* (1970), *Rahai / Liberation* (1971), *Musiqi-ye Jonub: Zar / Southern Music: Zar* (1971), *Mashhad-e Qali* (1971) and *Panjomin Jashn-e Honar-e Shiraz / The Fifth Shiraz Festival of the Arts* (1971).

While making short documentaries and feature films, Taqvai made a multi-part television series based on Iraj Pezeshgzad's humorous novel *Daijon Napeleon / Uncle Napoleon* (1975), which became very popular nationwide and received very good critical reviews as well. The series created a collection of memorable characters and lines of dialogue that became part of Iranian popular culture.

Taqvai made relatively few feature films, given that his long career dates back to the Pahlavi Era. They are *Aramesh Dar Hozu-re Digaran / Tranquillity in the Presence of Others* (1969), *Sadeq Kordeh / Sadeq the Kurd* (1972), *Nefrin / The Curse* (1973), *Nakhoda Khorshid / Captain Khorshid* (1986) and *Ay Iran / Oh Iran* (1989). He wrote the screenplay of his first film in collaboration with the opposition writer Gholamhosain Saedi, but wrote the scripts for all the others by himself. *Aramesh Dar Hozu-re Digaran*, which dealt in unsparingly realist style with the waning days of a former military general under the Shah, was interpreted politically as criticizing the government, causing the film to be cut. It was an important film in the emergence of

New Wave cinema. *Nakhoda Khorshid* is a very free adaptation of Hemingway's novel *To Have and Have Not*. For this film Taqvai returned to his native Persian Gulf roots: the action unfolded in an unnamed port city, which had become an exile colony peopled with an assortment of criminals and lepers. It is a no-man's land in which lawlessness, avarice and human dignity intertwine. Taqvai deftly fashioned a fascinating story, richly textured with colourful characters and a local culture that he clearly knows and loves (see Haidari 1990).

List of actors

Aghdashloo, Shohreh (Tabar, Vaziri) (b. 1951, Tehran)

Aghdashloo started her acting career with the Namayesh Academy on the stage. Her first film was *Suteh Delan*, and she played the role of the prostitute with the heart of gold who falls in love with a simpleton, played by Behrooz Vossoughi. She also appeared in the more banal *Gozaresh / The Report*. She emigrated initially to Britain, where she returned to the stage, before appearing in the United States with her husband Hooshang Toozie in the very successful *Booyeh Khosh-e Eshg / Sweet Smell of Love*, in which she played her actual role as an immigrant with all the attendant family problems that involves. She plays the mother in *Maryam*, a coming-of-age film dealing with an Iranian–American teenager, providing a subtle nuanced performance.

Apick, Mary

Apick has had a long career in films, starting at the age of ten in films with her mother Apick Youssefian and Parviz Sayyad. Her most important films are *Dash Akol*, *Asrar-e Ganje Dareye Jenni / Secret of the Treasure of the Strange Valley* and *Bonbast / Dead End*, the latter a creation of Parviz Sayyad for which she won the Best Actress Award at the 1977 Moscow Film Festival. She plays a girl in love with a young man who turns out to be a Savak agent intent on arresting her brother. Now living in the United States, she has recently worked producing children's films.

Fardin, Mohammad-Ali (b. 1930, Tehran; d. 2000, Tehran)

Fardin died at the age of seventy, having abandoned the cinema after the 1979 revolution and gone into the bakery business instead. Originally a wrestling champion, he earned great respect in Iran for staying in the country. His career in the cinema started in 1959 with *Cheshmeh-ye Ab-e Hayat / Spring of Life*, directed by Siamak Yasami, but it was not until his second film, *Ensanha / Human Beings*, that he became popular, reaching a height of success with *Soltan-e Qalba / Sultan of Hearts*. It was perhaps the music and singing in films like this which caused such disapproval among the religious authorities in the new austere revolutionary society. Despite the ban, his videos were popular, despite being illegal in Iran. He represented a man of the people, the ordinary man who was capable of standing up to the elite and the powerful. Although his acting may be criticized for naïvete and the films tend to rely on stereotypes, Fardin played an important part in helping to create a national form of film. At the height of his popularity he was earning comparatively huge sums for his work and his picture could be seen all over the country.

Googoosh (Fa'egeh Atashin) (b. 1950, Azerbaijan)

Googoosh is not primarily an actor, but rather a singer of immense popularity, but she played a very important part in films. Born Fa'egeh Atashin, she was brought up by an inadequate father and from the age of five was forced to earn a living in Tehran by singing. When she was ten, she had a successful role in the film *Fereshteye Farari / Runaway Angel*, which was her second film, the first being *Bim Va Omid / Fear and Hope* (1958). It was her singing more than her acting ability which led to her great popularity in the film industry; her ability to remain at the cutting edge of fashion also helped. Many of the people with whom she associated had a shady background, especially her husbands, and this increased the romanticism of her public image, along with her physical delicacy and air of vulnerability. She appeared in many popular films, including *Bita*, *Mah-e Asal / Honeymoon*, *Hamsafar*, *Mamal Amrikaie / Mamal the American*, *3 Divaneh / Three Lunatics* and the risqué *Dar Emtedad-e Shab / Through the Night*. The latter had a considerable impact in the Middle East.

Although the onset of the revolution made it necessary for her to leave the public stage, she has in the year 2000 been allowed to tour abroad and sing in public, although her films are still not allowed to be shown in Iran itself.

Sayyad, Parviz (b. 1939, Lahijan)

Like so many involved in the Iranian film industry, Sayyad moved between acting and film-making. He started off as a stage actor, then moved into television in 1960 with the founding of Iranian National Television. His career really took off with the mini-series *Amir Arsalan*, in which he starred with Mary Apick and her mother Apick Youssefian. He went on to develop a popular character called Samad – this character underpinned his further work on national television. If there is anything that his different roles have in common, it is his portrayal of the individual caught up in wider social and political events which are beyond their control. Often he was the country bumpkin trying to come to terms with life in the big city. After the revolution he moved to the United States, where he has directed and produced anti-Islamic Republic plays and films.

Acknowledgements

Many thanks to Oliver Leaman for supplying the *List of actors*.

Notes

1 As Tom Gunning and André Gaudreault demonstrated at the 1999 Society for Cinema Studies conference in Palm Beach Florida (Panel D1, April 16), in-camera edits occurred frequently in early cinema.
2 For titles and descriptions of all Western newsreels about Iran, including military footage filmed during World War II, see Naficy 1984.
3 For a full list of *Akhbar-e Iran* and other USIA newsreels and films, see Issari 1979, Naficy 1984, Issari 1989.

4 For Issari's eyewitness account of film screenings in Iranian villages and audience reactions, see Issari and Paul 1977: ch. 5.

5 For details, see Naficy 1978–9, Naficy 1991a.

6 For extensive readings on Farrokhzad's cinematic career, including the screenplay of *Khaneh Siah Ast*, see Haidari 1998.

7 Its predecessor, the Anglo-Persian Oil Company, also had a long history of sponsoring documentaries. Among them were *The Persian Oil Industry* (1925), about the operations of the company and the good life it was bringing to its workers and to Iranians. In 1928, it was shortened to fifteen minutes and retitled *In the Land of the Shah* for exhibition in British cinemas. The change was prompted by the feeling that the original title would have 'at once branded it an advertising film'. The film in its various versions was widely shown in England. Likewise, *Oil for the Twentieth Century* (1951) presented fascinating pictures of the company's operation and of Iran, but the frequent references to the social amenities provided by the company gave the impression that it was a philanthropic organization (Naficy 1984).

8 Among the completed features were Orson Welles' *F for Fake* (1976), Patrice Chereau's *La chair de l'orchidée / Flesh and the Orchid* (1974), Junya Sato's *Gogol 13* (1976), Valerio Zurlini's *The Desert of Tartars* (1977) and Leslie Matinson's *Missile X* (1978).

9 The original silent film *Grass* was reissued in the 1990s by Milestone Films and Video, which added a Persian music soundtrack to it.

10 The rough cut, which may have been put together to raise funds to complete the filming, contains shots of migration interspersed with painted tableaux which were fillers for the missing scenes that the film-makers planned to film on a future trip. This never materialized due to lack of funding.

11 A later and more successful English remake is Anthony Howarth's visually beautiful and evocative *People of the Wind* (1978). It presented the daily activities of the Babadi subtribe showing women, men and children cooking, milking, herding, migrating, participating in a wedding, shopping and trading. Ja'far Qoli, the tribal chief, decrying the government's efforts to settle the migrating tribes, declares that 'migration is what we are'. The film's soundtrack contains folkloric songs sung by Shusha.

12 For a detailed discussion of films that Western film-makers and television networks have made about Iran and Iranians, see Naficy 1984 (including the introduction), Naficy 1995.

13 According to a magazine report, some fifty tough guy films were in production in 1972 alone. See 'Hafteh-ye Gozashteh Nagahan Sinema-ye Iran Motovaqef Shod!', *Film va Honar* 389 (27 June 1972 / 7 Tir 1351).

14 For more on Kimiai's films and long career, see Qukasian 1990.

15 Indeed Kimiai's next film, *Gavaznha / The Deer* (1975), about the friendship of a thief and a dope addict, was coded by him and decoded by his audiences as a politically anti-government film. It was during the screening of this film in August 1978 in the Rex Theatre in Abadan that a fire deliberately set by anti-Shah arsonists burned nearly 400 people to their death, fanning the fire of the revolution that would bring the Shah down (Naficy 1992a). It is not known if the targeting of the theatre had anything to do with the film it was showing.

16 'Honarpishegan-e Sinema beh Dadgah-e Enqelab Ehzar Shodand', *Ettela'at* (11 March 1980 / 22 Esfand 1358): 4.

17 Cleverly, the film uses only brief excerpts of these songs, long enough to be recognized and appreciated, but short enough to not arouse the censors' ire.

18 On the function of music videos, including that of tough guy videos, see Naficy 1998a: 60–2.

19 For the 2,500th anniversary occasion, many valuable as well as propagandistic literary, artistic, historical, ethnographic, archeological and linguistic projects supporting this revitalized ideology were also commissioned, and dissident voices were suppressed.

20 According to Basir Nasibi, head of Free Cinema, some 300 film-makers, aged from thirteen to forty, were members of his organization nationwide (Nasibi 1994: 42). Over the years, the film production centres of the Institute for Intellectual Development of Children and Young Adults trained hundreds of young 'amateur' film-makers, who made hundreds of films under its aegis. The Institute also commissioned some of the most accomplished film-makers to make films, among them Bahram Baizai, Abbas Kiarostami, Masud Kimiai,

Amir Naderi, Kiumars Purahmad and Arsalan-e Sasani. It also commissioned some of the best animated films in Iran, by such film-makers as Farshid Mesqali, Morteza Mommayez, Nafiseh Riahi and Nurreddin Zarrinkelk (Mehrabi 1984: 352–76).

21 'Persian Film-Makers Map Expansion into International Market; Eye Co-Productions', *Variety* (12 November 1969): n.p.

22 For an extensive collection of reviews of Mehrjui's films and interviews with him, see Zera'ati 1996.

23 'Film Cooperative Emerges as Key Unit in Tehran Production', *Variety* (14 August 1974): n.p.

24 Although official sources attempted to place the blame for the incident on religious factions, the overwhelming public consensus held the (by then discredited) government responsible. Testimonies and documents compiled after the fall of the Shah, however, established a clear link between the arsonists and the anti-Shah clerical leaders (Naficy 1992a).

25 See p. 8 of the Toronto International Festival of Festivals Catalog (4 September 1992) and Miller 1992.

26 For example, in Tehran, Atlantic was changed to Efriqa (Africa), Empire to Esteqlal (Independence), Royal to Enqelab (Revolution), Panorama to Azadi (Freedom), Taj (Crown) to Shahr-e Honar (City of Art), Golden City to Felestin (Palestine), Polidor to Qods (Jerusalem) and Ciné Monde to Qiam (Uprising).

27 'Moscow Gets Tehran's Oscar', *Iran Times* (4 February 1982): 16.

28 'Sokhani Kutah dar Bareh-ye Namayesh-e Filmha-ye Khareji', *Enqelab-e Eslami* (2 June 1980 / 3 Khordad 1359): 6.

29 'Yaddashtha'i bar Mas'aleh-ye Sinemaha-ye Darbasteh dar Iran', *Enqelab-e Eslami* (2 July 1980 / 10 Tir 1359): 5.

30 'Iran Theaters to Ban Sex on their Own', *Variety* (23 May 1979): 7.

31 'Magic Marker Cinema Censor', *Iran Times* (29 June 1979): 16.

32 *Ettela'at* (30 January 1980 / 11 Bahman 1358): 20.

33 Author's interview with Barbod Taheri, Los Angeles, 10 September 1985.

34 Based on author's interview with Mohammad Hasan Khoshnevis, director of Iran's National Film Archive, Tehran, 28 July 1998.

35 The information on the Fada'ian's film programme is based on the author's interview with Reza Allamehzadeh, Los Angeles, 7 October 1988.

36 For a comprehensive filmography of Revolutionary Era documentaries, see Naficy 1984.

37 On restructuring the television system, see Sreberny-Mohammadi and Mohammadi 1994.

38 For more on Ayat Film and the cultural invasion debates, see Naficy (forthcoming).

39 All the regulations discussed here are from an unpublished internal document obtained by the author from MCIG: 'Marahel-e Mokhtalef-e Nezarat bar Sakht va Namayesh-e Film', pp. 40–9. (For their full Persian text, see Naficy 1996b.)

40 *Gozaresh Film 95* (September 1997): 44–6.

41 *Mahnameh-ye Sinema'i-ye Film* 13 (June 1995 / Khordad 1374): 24–5.

42 Contradictions surfaced not only in the film texts but also in the lively film-culture context, including in film periodicals. On the evolution of film periodicals, see Naficy 1993b.

43 'Sanat-e Khoshunat, va Darajehbandi-ye Film', *Mahnameh-ye Sinemai-ye Film* 240 (September 1999 / Shahrivar 1378): 6.

44 The statistics about feature-film output vary depending on the sources consulted. The figures for the years immediately following the revolution are particularly unreliable. Those cited here are from official government sources.

45 'Iran Dahomin Keshvar-e Donia', *Mahnameh-ye Sinemai-ye Film* 239 (August 1999 / Shahrivar 1378): 38.

46 *Kayhan Havai* (19 July 1995): 15, *Kayhan Havai* (26 July 1995): 15.

47 *Iran Times* (25 May 1994): 1.

48 *Kayhan Havai* (26 April 1995), p. 23.

49 'Sakht-e Sad Sinema ta Payan-e Emsal', *Mahnameh-ye Sinemai-ye Film* 239 (August 1999 / Shahrivar 1378), p. 27.

50 There are other important *auteur* film-makers of note, among them the New Wave veterans Masud Kimiai, Parviz Kimiavi and Naser Taqvai.

51 How much of these foreign earnings was channelled to the directors depended on contractual arrangements – see '*Bachehha-ye Aseman* yek Million Dollar Forukht', *Iran Daily* (13 September 1999), carried by *The Iranian* webzine at:
http://www.iranian.com/News/ 1999/September/hk.html

52 The stars of the Iranian media in the late 1990s were major Iranian sports figures (particularly soccer players), local movie stars (such as Niki Karimi and Fatemeh Motamed Aria) and international movie stars (such as Leonardo DeCaprio). In the summer of 1998, when the mega-hit *Titanic* was released, Iranian newspapers and magazines – as well as T-shirts that young people wore in the streets – bore the pictures of DeCaprio, even though wearing such T-shirts was illegal.

53 Quoted in 'Jashn-e Sinema Avay-e Mehrabani-ye Mast … ', *Hamshahri* (15 September 1999) on the internet edition of Tehran's Persian language daily at:
http://www.neda.net/ hamshahri/780624/adabh.htm

54 For extensive materials on Kiarostami's films and career, see Qukasian 1997.

55 Bahram Baizai and Dariush Mehrjui also used self-referential techniques in their films. In Baizai's *Mosaferan / Travellers*, the lead actor announces to the camera that she and her family, who are about to take off for a wedding in another city, will never get there, as they will all die in a car accident. In Mehrjui's *Leila*, a lead character breaks the fourth wall several times by speaking to the camera.

56 For extensive materials on Makhmalbaf's films and career, see Haidari 1997.

57 'Sarmaqaleh', *Fashnameh-ye Honar* 3 (spring–summer 1983 / 1362): 16.

58 'Etelaiyeh-ye Hey'at-e Davaran', *Mahnameh-ye Sinema'i-ye Film* 7 (September–October 1983 / Mehr 1362): 11.

59 'Sinema-ye Iran va Hafteh-ye Jang', *Mahnameh-ye Sinema'i-ye Film* 5 (August–September 1983 / Shahrivar 1362): 4–5.

60 'Sinema Dar Hafteh-ye Jang', *Mahnameh-ye Sinema'i-ye Film* 18 (October–November 1984 / Aban 1363): 12.

61 'Movafaqiyatha-ye Eqtesadi va Natayej-e Kaifi', *Mahnameh-ye Sinema'i-ye Film* 3 (November–December 1985 / Azar 1364): 9.

62 'Khameneh'i ba Sinema Mokhalef ast va Rafsanjani ba an Movafeq', *Kayhan* (30 May 1985): 2.

63 'Ba Durbin, Dar Sangar … ', *Mahnameh-ye Sinema'i-ye Film* 17 (September–October 1984 / Mehr 1363): 12–13, 48.

64 Based on my interviews with Niknejad and Kashani, Los Angeles, 15 August 1987.

65 'Sinema dar Hafteh', *Tous* (21 August 1998), from website at:
http://www.neda.net/tous /210577/arts14.htm

66 From my interview with Bahram Baizai, Houston, 5 November 1993.

67 For a full discussion of veiling and unveiling aesthetics both in society and on cinema screens, see Naficy 1991b, 1994.

68 A film that demonstrates the way that ordinary women demanded their rights and asserted themselves is the fascinating documentary feature *Divorce Iranian Style* (1998), made by two women: a film-maker (Kim Longinoto) and an anthropologist (Ziba Mir-Husseini). The film was shot over a six-week period in a Tehran family court and it documents the forceful efforts of several women to divorce their husbands.

69 'Sinema-ye Pass az Enqelab, dar Aghaz-e Dahe-ye Dovvom', *Mahnameh-ye Sinemai-ye Film* 75 (March–April 1989 / Noruz 1368): 73.

70 'Sinema Jozv-e Zendegi-ye Mardom Shodeh ast', *Mahnameh-ye Sinemai-ye Film* 48 (March–April 1987 / Noruz 1366): 73.

71 'Ma Agar Sinema ra az Ja-ye Khodash Kharej Konim Digar Sinema Nakhahim Dasht', *Kayhan Havai* (24 October 1984): 15.

References and further reading

Akbari, A. (1973 / 1352) *Lompanism*, Tehran: Nashr-e Sepehr.

Akrami, J. (1991a) 'Cinema II: Feature Films', in Ehsan Yarshater (ed.) *Encyclopaedia Iranica*, Costa Mesa, CA: Mazda Publishers, vol. 5, pp. 572–57.

—— (1991b) 'Cinema in Persia IV: Film Censorship', in Ehsan Yarshater (ed.) *Encyclopaedia Iranica*, Costa Mesa, CA: Mazda Publishers, vol. 5, pp. 585–6.

—— (1999) 'Friendly Persuasion: Iranian Cinema After The Revolution', feature-length documentary.

Altman, R. (1981) *Genre: The Musical*, London: Routledge & Kegan Paul.

—— (1999) *Film / Genre*, London: British Film Institute.

Astruc, A. (1968) 'The Birth of a New Avant-Garde: La Caméra Stylo', in P. Graham (ed.) *The New Wave: Critical Landmarks*, New York: Doubleday & Co., pp. 17–23.

Avini, S. (1997 / 1375) *Ravayat-e Fath beh Ravayat-e Shahid Seyyed Morteza Avini*, Tehran: Moasesseh-ye Farhangi-ye Ravayat-e Fath.

Bahar, M. (1976 / 2535) *Barresy-e Farhangi-Ejtemai-ye Zurkhanehha-ye Tehran*, Tehran: High Council of Culture and Art.

Bahrami, M. (1972 / 1351) 'Varshekastegi-ye Fekri', *Film* (winter): n.p.

Bateson, C., Clinton, J., Kassarjian, J., Safavi, H. and Soraya, M. (1977) 'Safay-i Batin: A Study of the Interrelations of a Set of Iranian Ideal Character Types', in L. Brown and N. Itzkowitz (eds) *Psychological Dimensions of Near Eastern Studies*, Princeton: Darwin Press, pp. 257–74.

Dadgu, M. (1991 / 1370) *Nokati Piramun-e Eqtesad-e Sinema-ye Iran*, Tehran: Filmkhaneh-ye Melli-ye Iran.

Daryoush, H. (1975) 'Iran', in P. Cowie (ed.) *International Film Guide*, London: Tantivy Press.

Dehbashi, A. (ed.) (1999) *Yadnameh-ye Sohrab Shahid Saless*, Tehran: Entesharat-e Shahab-e Saqeb and Entesharat-e Sokhan.

Delfani, M. (1996 / 1375) *Farhangsetizi dar Dowreh-ye Reza Shah (Asnad-e Montashernashodeh-ye Sazman-e Parvaresh-e Afkar)*, Tehran: Sazman Asnad-e Melli-ye Iran.

Dorri Akhavi, B. (1992 / 1371) *Filmshenasi-ye Defa-e Moqaddas (1360–1370)*, Tehran: Moavenat-e Tabliqat va Entesharat, Sepah Pasdaran.

Ebrahimian, M. (1979 / 1358) 'Aqayan! Motma'en Bashid Mardom Shoma ra Qaichi Mikonand!', *Ettela'at* (2 Ordibehesht): n.p.

Eco, U. (1985) 'Innovation and Repetition: Between Modern and Post-Modern Aesthetics', *Daedalus* (fall): 161–84.

Fanon, F. (1968) *The Wretched of the Earth*, trans. Constance Farrington, New York: Grove Press.

Farabi Cinema Foundation (1997) *A Selection of Iranian Films*, Tehran: Farabi Cinema Foundation.

—— (1998) *A Selection of Iranian Films*, Tehran: Farabi Cinema Foundation.

Floor, W. (1981) 'The Political Role of the *Lutis*', in M. Bonine and N. Keddie (eds) *Modern Iran: The Dialectics of Change and Continuity*, Albany: State University of New York Press.

Foucault, M. (1979) *Discipline and Punish: The Birth of the Prison*, trans. A. Sheridan, New York: Vintage Books.

Gabriel, T. (1989) 'Towards a Critical Theory of Third World Films', in J. Pines and P. Willemen (eds) *Questions of Third Cinema*, London: British Film Institute, pp. 30–53.

Gaffary, F. (1970) 'From Magic Lantern to Modern Cinema', *Variety* (10 May): 91.

—— (1973) *Le Cinéma en Iran*, Tehran: Le Conseil de la Culture et des Arts, Centre d'Étude et de la Coordination Culturelle (November).

—— (1985) 'Akkas-Basi', in E. Yarshater (ed.) *Encyclopaedia Iranica*, vol. 1, London: Routledge Kegan & Paul, p. 719.

—— (1991) 'Cinema I: History of Cinema in Persia', in E. Yarshater (ed.) *Encyclopaedia Iranica*, vol. 5, Costa Mesa, CA: Mazda Publishers, pp. 567–72.

Haidari, G. (ed.) (1990 / 1369) *Moarefi va Naqd-e Filmha-ye Naser Taqvai*, Tehran: Entesharat-e Behnegar.

—— (1991 / 1370) *Moarefi va Naqd-e Filmha-ye Amir Naderi*, Tehran: Nashr-e Soheil.

—— (1997 / 1376) *Moarefi va Naqd-e Filmha-ye Mohsen Makhmalbaf*, Tehran: Entesharat-e Agah.

—— (1998 / 1377) *Forugh Farrokhzad va Sinema*, Tehran: Nashr-e Elm.

Hanaway, W., Jr (1970) *Persian Popular Romances Before the Safavid Period*, Ph.D. dissertation, Columbia University.

—— (1971a) 'Formal Elements in the Persian Popular Romances', in J. Haidari (ed.) *Review of Nationalities: Iran*, New York: St John's University, pp. 139–60.

—— (1971b) 'Popular Literature in Iran', *Iran: Continuity and Variety*, Fourth Annual New York University Near Eastern Round Table (1970–1), New York: New York University Press, pp. 59–75.

Holden, S. (1999) 'A Spiritual Vision Imbues the Trials of a Blind Boy', *New York Times* (September 25): A17.

Issari, M. (1979) *A Historical and Analytic Study of the Advent and Development of Cinema and Motion Picture Production in Iran (1900–1965)*, Ph.D. dissertation, Los Angeles: University of Southern California, 2 vols.

—— (1989) *Cinema in Iran, 1900–1979*, Metuchen: Scarecrow.

Issari, M. and Paul, D. (1977) *A Picture of Persia*, New York: Exposition Press.

Karimi, I. (1988 / 1367) 'In Nakoja Abad Kojast?', *Mahnameh-ye Sinemai-ye Film* 72 (December / Dey): 52–4.

—— (1990 / 1369) 'Qahreman ya Qorbani', *Mahnameh-ye Sinema'i-ye Film* 92 (July / Tir): 17–20.

Khanlari, P.N. (1969a / 1348) 'A'in-e Ayyari', *Sokhan* 18, 11–12 (March–April / Farvardin): 1,071–7.

—— (1969b / 1348) 'A'in-e Ayyari', *Sokhan* 19, 1 (May–June / Khordad): 19–26.

—— (1969c / 1348) 'A'in-e Ayyari', *Sokhan* 19, 2 (June–July / Tir): 113–22.

—— (1969d / 1348) 'A'in-e Ayyari', *Sokhan* 19, 3 (July–August / Mordad): 263–7.

—— (1985 / 1364) *Shahr-e Samak*, Tehran: Agah.

Khosrowshahi, J. (ed.) (1991 / 1370) *Baztab-e Sinema-ye Novin-e Iran dar Jahan*, Tehran: Entesharate Ghazal.

Mahjub, M. (1969 / 1348) 'A'in-e Ayyari', *Sokhan* 19, 9 (January / Bahman): 869–83.

Malekpur, J. (1984 / 1363) *Adabiyat-e Namayeshi dar Iran: Dowran-e Enqelab-e Mashruteh*, vol. 2, Tehran: Entesharat-e Tus.

Mehrabi, M. (1984 / 1363) *Tarikh-e Sinema-ye Iran az Aghaz ta Sal-e 1357*, Tehran: Entesharat-e Film.

—— (1996 / 1375) *Farhang-e Filmha-ye Mostanad-e Sinema-ye Iran, az Aghaz ta Sal-e 1375*, Tehran: Daftar-e Pazhuheshha-ye Farhangi.

Miller, J. (1992) 'Movies of Iran Struggle for Acceptance', *The New York Times* (19 July 19): H9, H14.

Mo'azezinia, H. (ed.) (1998 / 1376) *Majmueh-ye Maqalat dar Naqd va Mo'arefi-ye Asar-e Ebrahim Hatamikia*, Tehran: Kanun-e Farhangi-Honari-ye Isargaran.

Mostowfi, A. (1945 / 1324) *Sharh-e Zendegani-ye Man*, vol. 1, Tehran: Mohammad Ali Elmi.

Mottahedeh, R. (1985) *The Mantle of the Prophet: Religion and Politics in Iran*, New York: Pantheon.

Naficy, H. (1978–9) *Film-e Mostanad*, Tehran: Free University of Iran Press, 2 vols.

—— (1979) 'Iranian Feature Films: A Brief Critical History', *Quarterly Review of Film Studies* 4: 443–64.

—— (1981) 'Cinema as a Political Instrument', in N. Keddie and M. Bonine (eds) *Modern Iran: The Dialectic of Continuity and Change*, New York: State University of New York Press, pp. 341–59.

—— (1984) *Iran Media Index*, Westport: Greenwood.

—— (1985a) 'Iranian Writers, the Iranian Cinema and the Case of Dash Akol', *Iranian Studies* (spring–autumn): 231–51.

—— (1985b) 'The Cycle (Dayereh-ye Mina)', in F. Magill (ed.) *Magill's Survey of Cinema: Foreign Language Films*, Los Angeles: Salem Press, pp. 700–5.

—— (1985c) 'The Stranger and the Fog (Gharibeh va Meh)', in F. Magill (ed.) *Magill's Survey of Cinema: Foreign Language Films*, Los Angeles: Salem Press, pp. 2,949–55.

—— (1987) 'The Development of an Islamic Cinema in Iran', *Third World Affairs*, London: Third World Foundation, pp. 447–63.

—— (1989) 'Sabk-e Pishtaz-e Sinema-ye Kimiavi', *Simorgh* 1, 2 (March): 92–5.

—— (1991a) 'Cinema in Persia III: Documentary Films', in E. Yarshater (ed.) *Encyclopaedia Iranica*, vol. 5, Costa Mesa, CA: Mazda Publishers, pp. 579–85.

—— (1991b) 'Zan va "Masaleh-ye Zan" dar Sinema-ye Iran-e Ba'd az Enqelab', *Nimeye Digar* 14 (spring): 123–69.

—— (1992a) 'Islamizing Cinema in Iran', in S. Farsoun and M. Mashayekhi (eds) *Iran: Political Culture in the Islamic Republic*, London: Routledge, pp. 173–208.

—— (1992b) 'Guneh-ye Film-e Jaheli dar Sinema-ye Iran: Barressi-ye Sakhtari-ye Film-e Dash Akol', *Iran Nameh* 10, 3 (summer): 537–52.

—— (1993a) *The Making of Exile Cultures: Iranian Television in Los Angeles*, Minneapolis: University of Minnesota Press.

—— (1993b) 'Iran', *CinémAction numéro spécial: Les revues de cinéma dans le monde* 69: 209–13 (also published in 1992 as 'Cultural Dynamics of Iranian Post-Revolutionary Film Periodicals', *Iranian Studies* 25, 3–4: 67–73).

—— (1994) 'Veiled Visions / Powerful Presences: Women in Post-revolutionary Iranian Cinema', in M. Afkhami and E. Friedl (eds) *In the Eye of the Storm: Women in Post-revolutionary Iran*, London and New York: I.B. Tauris with Syracuse University Press, pp. 131–50.

—— (1995) 'Mediating the Other: American Pop Culture Representation of Post-revolutionary Iran', in Y. Kamalipour (ed.) *The US Media and the Middle East: Image and Perception*, Westport: Greenwood, pp. 73–90.

—— (1996a) 'Phobic Spaces and Liminal Panics: Independent Transnational Film Genre', in R. Wilson and W. Dissanayake (eds) *Global / Local: Cultural Productions and the Transnational Imaginary*, Durham: Duke University Press, pp. 119–44.

—— (1996b) 'Taneshha-ye Farhang-e Sinemai dar Jomhuri-ye Eslami', *Iran Nameh* 14, 3 (summer): 383–416.

—— (1998a) 'Identity Politics and Iranian Exile Music Videos', *Iranian Studies* 31, 1 (winter): 52–64.

—— (1998b) 'Sohrab Shahid Saless's Accented Films and Claustrophobic Spaces', *Film International* 6, 1 (summer): 53–8.

—— (1999) 'Between Rocks and Hard Places: The Interstitial Mode of Production in Exilic Cinema', in H. Naficy (ed.) *Home, Exile, Homeland: Film, Media and the Politics of Place*, London and New York: Routledge, pp. 125–47.

—— (2000) 'Self-Othering: A Postcolonial Discourse on Cinematic First Contact', in F. Afzal-Khan and K. Seshadri-Crooks (eds) *The Pre-Occupation of Post-Colonial Studies*, Durham: Duke University Press, pp. 292–310.

—— (2001) *An Accented Cinema: Diasporic and Exilic Filmmaking*, Princeton: Princeton University Press.

—— (forthcoming) 'Film Culture and Cinema in Postrevolutionary Persia', in E. Yarshater (ed.) *Encyclopaedia Iranica: Supplement*, New York: Bibliotheca Persica Press.

Nasibi, B. (1994) *Dah Sal Sinema-ye Azad dar Iran*, Saarbrücken: Cinema-ye Azad.

Neal, S. (1983) *Genre*, London: British Film Institute.

Nichols, W. (1994) 'Discovering Form, Inferring Meaning: New Cinemas and the Film Festival Circuit', *Film Quarterly* 47, 3 (spring): 16–30.

Nuri, T. and Ashuri, D. (1983 / 1362) 'Durbinha beh Su-ye Jebheh', *Mahnameh-ye Sinemayieh Film* 7 (Mehr): 10.

Omid, J. (1984 / 1363) *Paydayesh va Bahrehbardari, Tarikh-e Sinema-ye Iran*, vol. 1, Tehran: Radiab.

—— (1987 / 1366) *Farhang-e Filmha-ye Sinemai-ye Iran, az 1351 ta 1366*, vol. 2, Tehran: Entesharat-e Negah.

—— (1988 / 1367) *Farhang-e Sinema-ye Iran*, Tehran: Entesharat-e Agah.

—— (1992 / 1371) *Farhang-e Filmha-ye Sinemai-ye Iran, az 1358–1371*, vol. 3, Tehran: Entesharat-e Tasvir.

—— (1995 / 1374) *Tarikh-e Sinema-ye Iran (1279–1375)*, Tehran: Entesharat-e Rowzaneh.

Peterson, S. (1997) 'Reluctant Nod to Cultural Shift: Iran Eases Ban on Its Own Films', *Christian Science Monitor: International Edition*, http://www.csmonitor.com/durable/1997/12 /23/intl.

Purmohammad, M. (1987 / 1366) 'Ebteda Sangha-ye Kuchak', *Mahnameh-ye Sinemai-ye Film* 64 (May–June / Khordad): 4–8, 64.

Qajar, M. (1982 / 1361) *Safarnameh-ye Mobarakeh-ye Muzaffared-Din Shah Beh Farang*, transcribed by Mirza Mehdi Khan Kashani, 2nd edn, Tehran: Ketab-e Foruzan.

Qukasian, Z. (ed.) (1990 / 1369) *Majmueh-ye Maqalat dar Naqd va Mo'arefi-ye Asar-e Masud Kimiai*, 2nd ed. Tehran: Entesharat-e Agah.

—— (1992 / 1371) *Majmueh-ye Maqalat dar Naqd va Mo'arefi-ye Asar-e Bahram Baizai*, Tehran: Entesharat-e Agah.

—— (1997 / 1375) *Majmueh-ye Maqalat dar Naqd va Mo'arefi-ye Asar-e Abbas Kiarostami*, Tehran: Nashr-e Didar.

Rahimian, B. (1993 / 1372) 'Savaneh-e Tarikh-e Sinema-ye Iran', *Mahnameh-ye Sinema'i-ye Film* 100 (December / Dey): 100–5.

Rosen, M. (1992) 'The Camera of Art: An Interview with Abbas Kiarostami', *Cinéaste* 19, 2–3: 38–40.

Sadoul, G. (1949) *Histoire du cinéma mondial des origines à nous jours*, Paris: Flamarion.

Sadri, M. (1995 / 1374) *Filmbardari-ye Mostanad-e Jangi*, Tehran: Howzeh-ye Honari-ye Sazman-e Tabliqat-e Eslami.

Saedi, G. (1982 / 1361) 'Farhang Koshi va Farhang Zadai dar Jomhurey-ye Eslami', *Alefba*, n.s. (winter); trans. as 'Iran Under the Party of God', *Index on Censorship* (January 1984): 16–20.

—— (1984 / 1363) 'Namayesh dar Hokumat-e Namayeshi', *Alefba* 5, n.s. (winter): 1–9.

Sayyad, P. (1996) *Rah-e Doshvar-e Sinema-ye dar Tab'id*, Los Angeles: Parsian.

Schatz, T. (1981) *Hollywood Genres: Formulas, Film-making and the Studio System*, New York: Random House.

Seif, M. (1998 / 1377) *Kargardanan-e Sinema-ye Iran*, vols 1 and 2, Tehran: Kanun-e Farhangi-ye Isargaran.

Sho'ai, H. (1975 / 1354) *Farhang-e Cinema-ye Iran*, Tehran: Chapkhaneh Sherkat Herminco.

Siavoshi, S, (1997) 'Cultural Politics and the Islamic Republic: Cinema and Book Publication', *International Journal of Middle Eastern Studies* 29, 4 (November): 509–30.

Sreberny-Mohammadi, A. and Mohammadi, A. (1994) *Small Media, Big Revolution: Communication, Culture and the Iranian Revolution*, Minneapolis: University of Minnesota Press.

Tahaminezhad, M. (1986 / 1365) *Sinema-ye Royapardaz-e Iran*, Tehran: Aks-e Moaser.

—— (n.d.) 'Rishehyabi-ye Ya's dar Sinema-ye 1308 ta 1315 Iran', *Vizheh-ye Sinema va Te'atr* 2–3.

Tunstall, J. (1977) *The Media are American*, New York: Oxford University Press.

United States Department of Commerce (1941) 'Annual Survey of Motion Picture Industry in Iran', *Industrial Reference Service: Part 8 – Motion Pictures and Equipment* 32 (March): 6,212.

—— (1949) Office of International Trade, *World Trade in Commodities – Iran* (February): n.p.

Zera'ati, N. (1996 / 1375) *Majmueh-ye Maqalat dar Moarefi va Naqd-e Asar-e Dariush Mehrjui*, Tehran: Entesharat-e Nahid.

Zoka, Y. (1997 / 1376) *Tarikhe Akkasi va Akkasan-e Pishgam dar Iran*, Tehran: Entesharat-e Elmi va Farhangi.

Israeli cinema

Judd Ne'eman

The beginning of Israeli cinema corresponds to the beginning of the Zionist enterprise in Palestine. This confluence of the national cinema with the nation-building process itself makes any historiography of Israeli cinema irremediably entangled with the history of Zionism. At the turn of the nineteenth century Jewish settlers in Palestine were forging a utopian venture: a new Jewish society founded on secular values totally divorced from traditional Jewish society in Eastern and Central Europe where the settlers originated. The local cinema emerged during World War I when the first film-maker in Jewish Palestine, Ya'akov Ben-Dov, began turning his camera, for several years recording on film the realization of the Zionist project in Palestine. Ben-Dov's silent films were targeted at Jewish audiences in Europe and North America. Quite often institutions of the Zionist movement, such as Jewish National Fund (JNF) and the Palestine Foundation Fund (PFF), financed and otherwise assisted the production of such films and newsreels. The films were widely used as propaganda promoting Jewish immigration to Palestine, for fund-raising among Jewish communities and for political lobbying in Europe and America.

An overall corpus of hundreds of films and newsreels dedicated to the Zionist project in Palestine includes several filmic genres: newsreels, documentary films, structured short films and several feature films. Zionist cinema can be divided into three historical periods: agricultural pioneering (1918–36), Holocaust-related cinema (1945–8) and heroic–nationalist films (1948–67). The Zionist cinema prevailed until in the early 1960s when two new models of 1960s cinema emerged concurrently: popular cinema and modernistic cinema. Following the 1967 Six-Day War, Israel abandoned its utopian Zionist discourse, a so-called 'humanitarian civilizing mission', and became involved in a colonialist project in the Occupied Territories. At the same time, when it became evident that films were no longer an effective tool for political indoctrination, the Israeli government finally took the long overdue decision to start up the first national television channel. As of January 1970, government television was on air, and it broadcast on a regular basis every day of the week. This date marks the end of the cinema era for local media, when moving images were expertly produced and disseminated for propaganda purposes. The first channel dominated the broadcast scene until the early 1990s when cable and commercial channels challenged its hegemony.

Zionist realism (1920s–50s)

Following Ben-Dov's pioneering endeavours in the years after World War I, other film-makers arrived in Palestine and developed the new medium: starting in 1927, Nathan

Axelrod turned out newsreels and commercials for movie theatres, while Baruch Agadati produced newsreels intermittently in the early 1930s. Movie theatres opened in the big cities, in particular in Tel Aviv, newspapers began to publish film reviews and the British government of Palestine issued censorship regulations controlling the theatrical release of films, most of which were imported from Europe and the United States. Not until the early to mid-1930s, following the shippment of film equipment belonging to Jewish refugees from Nazi Germany who were then arriving in Palestine, did conditions mature for the production of local films for theatrical exhibition. Among the many newsreels and short documentaries that Jewish film-makers produced in 1930s Palestine, there were several long documentaries and dramas, such as *Lecha'im Hadashim / Land of Promise* (Juda Leman, 1934), *Zot Hi Ha'aretz / This is the Land* (Baruch Agadati, 1934) and *Awoda* (Helmar Lerski, 1935). The first fiction films produced for theatrical release were also made in the 1930s, including *Oded Hanoded / Oded the Wanderer* (Haim Halachmi and Nathan Axelrod, 1933), *Tzabar / Sabra* (Alexander Ford, 1933) and *Me'al Hachoravot / On the Ruins* (Nathan Axelrod, 1938), which were successfully exhibited in the big towns.

While differing from their predecessors in genre and cinematic rhetoric, the 1920s and 1930s films repeated the same narrative of national redemption: the realization of the Zionist enterprise in Palestine. Dedicated to the ideal of reviving the land of Palestine, the films emphasized agricultural props and objects, such as ploughs, tractors, horse-drawn wagons, and abundant fruit and vegetables. Traditional Jewish symbols, such as the Star of David and the Menorah, were also used and along with agricultural activities, house- and road-construction, and the tools and objects associated with them, were often shown. Retrospectively these films constitute a comprehensive cinematic iconography of Zionism's pioneering period. Little film time was dedicated to individual and family life. Instead the films focused mostly on groups of pioneers tilling the land, building houses and roads, and drilling water wells, with many long shots and wide-angle shots to include as much of the physical reality as possible. When occasionally the camera did capture someone in close-up, they never conveyed emotion or different modes of behaviour. Instead, pioneers posed for the camera with blank expressions or a smile that delivered a collective message, the personification of an idea (Burstein 1990). Films employed a realist style, with abundant long shots and panoramic camera-movement, showing an expanse of land represented first as desert and then, following the pioneers' tilling of the soil, as flourishing paradise. In recent years the similarities between these films and Soviet socialist realist films have led the genre to be called 'Zionist realism' (Gross and Gross 1991).

The 1936–9 Arab uprising in Palestine and, more importantly, the outbreak of World War II, severed the country's connections with Europe and the US. Difficulties in importing raw-stock and film equipment to Palestine caused Jewish film-making to falter until the end of World War II. Post-war documentaries and dramas focused on the plight of Holocaust survivors arriving in Palestine to join ranks in the Jewish settlements with the pioneers. These films portrayed the process by which emotionally broken survivors were made well again through agricultural training in a kibbutz or, for young immigrants, special boarding school. The training of the newcomers often concludes with an initiation rite and the admission of the survivors into the pioneering group. Films such as *Adama / Tomorrow is a Wonderful Day* (Helmar Lerski, 1947), *Beit Avi / My Father's House* (Herbert Kline, 1947) and *Dim'at Hanechama Hagedola /*

The Great Promise (Joseph Leytes, 1947) showed Holocaust survivors that underwent Zionist transformation. As if resurrected from the ashes, the survivors are reborn to become pioneers in the Zionist enterprise. This short-term 'therapy' in films reflects the Zionist leadership's determination to mobilize as many Holocaust survivors as they could, viewing them as the last human reservoir of settlers and soldiers to put to the service of the future Jewish state. Since the only compensation for the evil of the Holocaust acceptable to Zionism was the establishment of a Jewish state in Palestine, films produced during the period after the end of World War II and following the declaration of the Jewish state in 1948 focused on this linkage. *Klala Lebracha / Out of Evil* (Joseph Krumgold, 1950), for example, opens and ends with the image of film's principal narrator, a Holocaust survivor, standing in a fortified bunker overlooking 1948 Jerusalem under Arab siege, aiming his rifle at the enemy. 'The use of arms in self-defence' was how this Zionist remedy for Holocaust trauma was articulated in many late 1940s and 1950s films.

The Israeli film industry made its first steps towards the production of feature films for theatrical exhibition on a commercial basis in the 1950s. While the government continued to adhere to the Zionist movement's policy of using films for propaganda only, many entrepreneurs, film-makers and film technicians – recently emigrated from well-established film industries in Europe, the US and Arab countries – initiated the independent production of feature films. Two film studios, Geva Films and Hertzelia Motion Pictures Studios, opened in Israel, selling laboratory services and renting state-of-the-art film equipment to independent producers. Very soon the studios themselves became producers of newsreels and documentaries, as well as of feature films. In the Knesset in 1954, the Bill for Encouragement of Israeli Films encouraged the government to increase its spending on the development of a local film industry.

More than ten feature films were produced at irregular intervals during the 1950s, including *Giv'a 24 Eina Ona / Hill 24 Doesn't Answer* (Thorold Dickinson, 1955), *Be'ein Moledet / Lacking a Homeland* (Nuri Habib, 1956), *Amud Ha'esh / Pillar of Fire* (Lary Friesch, 1959) and *Hem Hayu Asara / They Were Ten* (Baruch Dienar, 1959). While the scripts, dialogue, acting and visual design were far behind the highest world standards, the very making of these films was an achievement. While these feature films did not differ thematically from the earlier Zionist realist films that had been made under commission, the shift of focus was quite remarkable. Most films left out the 1940s Holocaust survivors and instead highlighted 'mythic Israeli heroes: sabras, kibbutzniks and soldiers, often within the context of the Israeli–Arab conflict, … [and] within the confines of the war genre' (Shohat 1989: 57). This corpus of post-1948 war films was retrospectively called 'the heroic–nationalist genre'. The production in Israel of a major Hollywood film – *Exodus* (Otto Preminger, 1959), which made a worldwide box-office success of the definitive story of Zionism – cleared the way for further large-scale foreign and domestic productions in country. The most significant domestic offspring of *Exodus* was an Israeli version of *Birth of a Nation*: Baruch Dienar's *Hem Hayu Asara / They Were Ten*, which was a remake of the 1930s Zionist realist feature-film *Tzabar / Sabra*.

While *Tzabar* was a characteristic example of Zionist realist cinema, *Hem Hayu Asara*, created in the 1950s during a decade of military conflict, became the prototype film of the heroic–nationalist genre. Like the original film, the remake tells the story of a group of pioneers at the beginning of the Zionist enterprise in Palestine who build a communal settlement on a barren hill in Galilee. The film interweaves the cultivation of the land with struggle against the Palestinians over territory and water resources. *Hem Hayu Asara* highlights the theme of the group versus the individual. Feature films in the 1950s complied ideologically with the constraints of the Zionist master-narrative, but at the same time they enjoyed a certain artistic freedom to go beyond the aesthetics of Zionist realism. A similar approach characterized heroic–nationalist films of later years, such as *Hu Halach Basadot / He Walked Through the Fields* (Yosseph Milo, 1967), *Kol Mamzer Melech / Every Bastard a King* (Uri Zohar, 1968), *Matzor / Siege* (Gilberto Tofano, 1969) and *Shtey Etzba'ot MiTzidon / Ricochets* (Eli Cohen, 1986). Later heroic–nationalist films (*Matzor* for example) may use avant-garde techniques but, like the earlier *Hem Hayu Asara* which was cinematically both articulate and well made, they still openly comply with Zionist ideology.

The Bourekas films (1960s–70s)

The 1960s were the formative years of Israeli cinema. Following decades of direct Zionist indoctrination in the cinema, for the first time a new genre of cinema emerged, formally liberated from the Zionist master-narrative. The scope of themes broadened to include inter-ethnic tensions, urban life, crime and class struggle. A new method of government financing (a tax rebate was offered that depended on the number of tickets sold) gave rise to the production of an unprecedented plethora of local films, through which a new generation of film-makers and technicians became prominent. A decade after its inauguration, heroic–nationalist cinema was no longer representative of the socio-political transformations that had taken place in Israel and had to give way to new modes of cinema.

The violent demonstrations that exploded in the working-class Wadi-Salib neighbourhood in Haifa in 1959 foreshadowed the emergence of an ethnic and political consciousness among Mizrakhi (mainly Jews originating in Arab countries) who had previously been acquiescent to the Zionist policy of racial discrimination. While the Ashkenazi (Eastern and Central European Jewish) majority in Israel identified with the idea of a modern secular state, the Mizrakhi immigrants, most of them arriving in the 1950s, perceived Israel as the land of the Biblical fathers where Jewish messianic hope was to come to fruition. Confrontation between the two worldviews (Zionist utopian and the Jewish messianic), as well as class and ethnic differences, deepened the divide between the Ashkenazi and Mizrakhi Jewish communities in Israel. The new dynamics of conflict in what had been until then a consensual society became the background for the creation of two innovative models of cinema that repudiated both the heroic–nationalist and the earlier Zionist realist cinematic genres: the popular 'Bourekas' and the modernist 'new sensibility' cinemas.

Sallah Shabbati (Ephraim Kishon, 1964), which gained unprecedented success at the box office with over a million tickets sold and was nominated for an Academy Award in the US, became the cornerstone of a new local genre of popular cinema: Bourekas films.[1] Sallah, the 'all-Eastern' protagonist of this film (Shohat 1989: 138–55), looks at the pioneering myth of the kibbutz with irony and sarcasm, providing sceptical reflections on one of the most sacred values of socialist Zionism: the 'religion of labour'. The term 'religion of labour' was coined and developed by the

Jewish philosopher A.D. Gordon. A Zionist who was also a fervent Zionist ideologue, he wrote extensively of physical work as the liberating ethos of the Jews:

> From now on our principal ideal should be – work. ... If we will turn work in itself into an ideal – we shall be healed.

(Gordon 1970 [1911]: 28)

Images of such an ideology of healing through physical labour dominated Zionist realist films. The concluding scene of *Sallah Shabbati* suggests, in an oblique way, a possible alternative to this Zionist socialist dogma. Sallah and his Ashkenazi friend sit together in a truck, driving Sallah's family and their belongings from the immigrants' camp to an apartment in a new housing project that they have been given. Sallah motions to his son to hand over the backgammon board. When he invites his Ashkenazi friend, who has played backgammon with him throughout the film, to join in a final game, he says to him: 'Let's get back to work!' In many other scenes in the film, physical work is replaced by alternative activities such as wheeling-and-dealing, playing games or practical jokes, doing business and even sabotaging one's own work. These activities – portrayed as part of a dichotomy with physical work – colour the film with a distinct subversive tone that undermines the Zionist ethos of the 'religion of labour'.

Catz VeCarasso / *Katz and Carasso* (Menachem Golan, 1971), another well-known Bourekas film, puts across on screen the domestic lives of a Mizrakhi and an Ashkenazi family who are competing with each other in business. Produced in 1971, the film was exhibited in the very year when the Israeli Labour government prescribed severe and often violent measures to break up demonstrations by the Black Panthers, a protest movement of Mizrakhi Jews from poverty-stricken neighbourhoods. While *Catz Vecarasso* ignored the emerging class awareness of Mizrakhi Jews, the film candidly suggested that, unlike the unbridgeable generation gap, the differences between Mizrakhi and Ashkenazi that were basically ethnic could and should be over-come by means of inter-ethnic marriage. By representing both families as middle class, the film removed any signs of class difference between Ashkenazi and Mizrakhi, promoting the melting-pot ideology as a remedy for ethnic cultural differences. However, despite its social illusionism, the film's subtext subverted its own melting-pot discourse through redeeming images and sounds of Mizrakhi traditional society that had been suppressed by the Askenazi Zionist ideology. Many Bourekas films, such as *Nurith* (George Ovadia, 1972), *Salomonico* (Alfred Steinhardt, 1972) and *Charlie Vachetzi* / *Charlie and a Half* (Boaz Davidson, 1974), adopted the mixed-marriage formula, while at the same time nurturing the suppressed ethnic music, cuisine and Arabic and Spanish dialects of Mizrakhi Jews.

Marginalized in Zionist realist and heroic–nationalist films, the image of the Mizrakhi family came exuberantly to the fore in the Bourekas cinema of the 1960s and 1970s. While the Ashkenazi cultural elite publicly discussed these films in a conde-scending manner, the films did respond to a deep-seated yearning among both Mizrakhi Jews and Ashkenazi Holocaust survivors. These communities strove to re-establish family values at the heart of Israeli society, where collective values have been *bon ton* ever since the heyday of socialist Zionism in the 1920s and 1930s. The centrality of the family in many Bourekas films points to a revocation of utopian

Zionism and to its replacement with the values of traditional Jewish society – both East and West. The considerable use by film-makers of the narrative conventions of comedy and melodrama helped camouflage this popular genre's subversive subtext. Despite its sometimes awkward style, simplistic narratives and, more importantly, advocacy of political illusions, the Bourekas cinema cemented class and ethnic aware- ness among Mizrakhi Jews and forecasted future social changes. Interestingly, for a new generation of filmgoers in the 1990s, many of these films became cult movies.

The new sensibility (1960s–70s)

Another film genre emerged in the mid-1960s that differed in its values and codes from heroic–nationalist cinema, but at the same time it conflicted with the popular model of the Bourekas films. During the war-free years between the 1956 Suez War and the 1967 Six-Day War, Israel enjoyed an atmosphere of political and existential stability. In the mid-1950s a new urban identity began to crystallize and a new generation of poets, novelists, painters, sculptors and musicians, later known as the 'state genera- tion', emerged and immediately became a mouthpiece for modernism and contemporary art in the country. Local films of a new school appeared on the screens and film critics called this new cinema, with its evident inclination towards modernism, the 'Israeli new wave', associating it with its European counterparts – particularly the French new wave. Being myself a film-maker who participated in this movement, I prefer to draw attention the domestic aspects of the change by calling this new school the 'new sensibility'.

Two innovative film-makers announced the rise of this modernistic cinema: David Perlov with his lyrical documentary *B'Yerushalayim / In Jerusalem* (1963) and Uri Zohar with an anarchist / avant-garde film *Hor Balevana / Hole in the Moon* (1965). These two films undermined both the canonical realism of Israeli cinema and the deep-seated trend of emulating American genres and modes of production. A fore- runner of the 'new sensibility' cinema, in retrospect *Hor Balevana* appears an idiosyncratic film that is not at all representative of its school, deconstructing the genres of classical cinema, moving between parody and satire, and questioning the very idea of genre in cinema. Much like the source of its inspiration, the non- Hollywood American film *Hallelujah the Hills* (Adolfas Mekas, 1962), *Hor Balevana* is full of anarchistic caprice and the magic of youth. Employing a two-fold narrative strategy it parodies the abandoned Zionist pioneering ideals: it is a satire on the real- ization of the Zionist vision, on one hand, and a story about cinematic endeavour itself being a realization of utopia, on the other. Merging two utopian endeavours, Zionism and cinema, the film raises the question of the relationship between the polit- ical and cinematic avant-gardes in the history of Israeli cinema: new sensibility films combined an outright radical critique of Zionism with an attempt to put an end to cinema's servitude to the dominant politics of the time.

The socio-political torrents that eroded the hegemony of the Zionist left after Israel was nearly defeated in the 1973 Yom Kippur War, culminated in 1977 with the first ever national election victory for the right-wing Likud Party. Regarded by many as a watershed in Israeli history, this political upheaval became the turning point of Israeli cinema as well. Existing models of film-making began to recede, while new ones appeared. Of the couple of hundred feature-films produced in the 1960s and 1970s,

Figure 28 Hor Balevana / Hole in the Moon

around fifty are associated with the new sensibility cinema. Many of them were scripted and produced by their directors and therefore had many things in common. New sensibility films were characterized by low-budget production, black-and-white film, shoots done on location using live urban scenery, debutant actors and non-actors playing principal roles, improvised scripts, fragmentary plots with open endings, the use of vernacular language and slang, experimental cinema rhetoric, existential malaise and so on. The unwritten manifesto of the new sensibility film-makers included two main issues: on one hand, disengaging cinema from the political hegemony and, on the other, gaining public recognition for the social role of the autonomous film-maker.

The economic boom that followed the June 1967 war and the increase in government funding for the film industry helped the new generation of film-makers to pursue their artistic ambitions. At the same time, the beginning of broadcasting by Israeli public television provided the audience with an overabundance of everyday images, social themes, authentic characters and natural colloquial language, thus creating for the film-makers a new frame of reference in the domain of the Real. The television broadcast liberated documentary film-making from the ideological constraints of the

Israeli Film Service – until then the major public organization commissioning documentary films. Three cinematheques were established in the 1970s – in Tel Aviv, Jerusalem and Haifa – as well as the first film department at Tel Aviv University and the Israeli Film Institute. Cinema was at last incorporated into the system and recognized as a significant art-form that deserved public funding and attention.

The new sensibility films, which revolutionized the cinema scene and made a lasting impact on the next generation of film-makers, had a rough look and tackled marginal themes. In *Shlosha Yamim Veyeled / Three Days and a Child* (Uri Zohar, 1967), a native Israeli is transformed from heroic soldier into introverted neurotic. *Hasimla / The Dress* (Judd Ne'eman, 1969) sketches three love stories of immature youths in Tel Aviv – the last one pays homage to Truffaut's *Jules et Jim*. Like the short film *Le'at Yoter / Slow Down* (Avraham Heffner, 1968), *The Dreamer* (Dan Wolman, 1970) focuses on the lives of the old – a subject considered taboo in a society that venerated the myth of youth. *Mikreh Isha / A Woman's Case* (Jacques Katmor, 1969) used sophisticated montage techniques to critique sexual obsession and misogyny. *Shablul / Snail* (Boaz Davidson, 1970) transformed the camaraderie of the pioneering group into the mundane friendship of youth in a bohemian milieu. *Haglula / The Pill* (David Perlov, 1972) parodied the Zionist fantasy of eternal youth. *Or Min Hahefker / Light Out of Nowhere* (Nissim Dayan, 1973) is a neo-realistic film that engaged with class issues that had previously been silenced. *Le'an Ne'elam Daniel Vax? / But Where is Daniel Wax?* (Avraham Heffner, 1972) mercilessly dissected the native Israeli stereotype. *Metzitzim / Peeping Toms* (Uri Zohar, 1972) is a pitiless self-obituary for the declining myth of urban youth. *Hagiga La'einayim / Saint Cohen* (Assi Dayan, 1975) satirized Israel's cult of poets. In *Habanana Hashchora / The Black Banana* (Benjamin Hayeem, 1976), film-maker Hayeem evoked the style of American underground cinema. Other films, such as *Belfer* (Igal Bursztyn, 1978), *Sus Etz / Rockinghorse* (Yaki Yosha, 1978), *Shraga Katan / Little Man* (Ze'ev Revah, 1978), *Transit* (Dan Waxmann, 1979), *Noa Bat Sheva-Esrey / Noa at Seventeen* (Yitzhak Yeshurun, 1982) and *Al Hevel Dak / A Thin Line* (Michal Bat-Adam, 1981), share the attributes of the new sensibility cinema but at the same time manifest a social and political awareness characteristic of the political cinema of the 1980s.

The political cinema (1980s)

The new trends in cinema in the 1980s can be traced back to the social and political changes in Israel following the 1973 Yom Kippur War that resulted in the political upheaval of 1977. Labour's loss of power to a nationalist right-wing government alienated the Ashkenazi cultural elite. The political mobilization of the cultural elite against the right-wing government and its nationalist agenda brought about a new school of cinema – the political cinema. These films protested against 'the political reality in Israel but, more importantly, articulat[ed] the question of Israeli identity' (Gertz 1993: 76). The political cinema of the late 1970s and the 1980s articulated a radical critique of Zionism that exceeded in rigour and degree of dissent the protest discourse of the political left. This new awareness of politics at large went hand in hand with a style of political activism modelled on the trade unions. The new sensibility activists organized and, for the first time in the history of Israeli cinema, convinced the establishment that cinema is an art-form. Following tenacious political lobbying by the Kayitz group[2] of film-makers, the Ministry of Education and Culture established the Fund for the Promotion of Israeli Quality Films in 1979. Public finance was to be invested directly in the production of local feature films, thus liberating the film-makers from their dependency on private finance and the box office. In a short time 'The Fund', as it was called, became the main means of production for feature films and many young film-makers were able to make their debuts. From the 1980s more space in newspapers was dedicated to film reviewing. A new generation of film critics, such as Nachman Ingber, Meir Schnitzer and Uri Klein, has gained much influence and popularity, becoming leaders of opinion in the domestic cultural scene. Israeli cinema had finally reached a point where it held the coveted status of an art-form – discussed in the media by well-informed, theoretically skilled film-critics and funded from the public coffers.

Three films produced in the late 1970s were precursors to the wave of 1980s political films, covering three thematic areas. *Khirbet Hiz'ah* (Ram Loevy, 1978), dealing with the Palestinian Nakba[3] and the roots of the Israeli–Palestinian conflict, was the first in a series of 'conflict films'. *Massa Alunkot / Paratroopers* (Judd Ne'eman, 1977), the first anti-heroic army film, set the stage for several 1980s and early 1990s army and war films that critiqued Israeli militarism. *Roveh Chuliot / Wooden Gun* (Ilan Moshenson, 1978), set in early 1950s Tel Aviv, portrayed the complex relationship between Holocaust survivors and native Israeli Jews, becoming the forerunner of a number of Holocaust-related films that I have called 'shadow cinema'.

The conflict films drafted a revised Zionist master-narrative, the original form of which appeared in such films as *Tzabar / Sabra* and *Hem Hayu Asara / They Were Ten*. The 1980s films drew a more realistic picture of the Israeli–Palestinian conflict, stripping the Zionist project of its 'humanitarian civilizing mission' and unveiling its colonialist nature. *Hamsin* (Daniel Wachsmann, 1982) deals with the Israeli–Palestinian conflict inside Israel, addressing the primary sin of Zionist colonialism – the confiscation of land from Israeli Palestinians. *Gesher Tsar Me'od / On a Narrow Bridge* (Nissim Dayan, 1985) tells the story of an impossible love in the Occupied Territories between an Israeli officer and a Palestinian teacher, both torn apart by conflicting loyalties. *Me'achorei Hasoragim / Beyond the Walls* (Uri Barabash, 1984) transforms the Palestinians from terrorists to freedom fighters when Israeli and Palestinian prisoners are caught in a common struggle against the prison management. *Chyuch Hagdi / Smile of the Lamb* (Shimon Dotan, 1986) condemns the practices of the Israeli military government in the occupied West Bank. *Avanti Popolo* (Rafi Bukai, 1986) rewrites the conflict as an absurd play. The play takes place in a 1967 Sinai battlefield where Israeli soldiers befriend Egyptian POWs, played by Palestinian actors. *Sadot Yerukim / Green Fields* (Yitzhak Yeshurun, 1989) questions the validity of Zionism in view of the murderous aggression that it perpetrates against the Palestinians. The visual rendering in this cinema combined, on one hand, images of Palestinian traditional society with, on the other, Israeli urban industrial society. The juxtaposition of these contrasting images, not reconciled by the cinematic sequences in which they appear, created a critique sometimes stronger than that expressed by the dramatic plot. Finally, the radical critique of the Israeli occupation articulated by these films unsettled the Israeli audience, since it touched on the *raison d'être* of the entire Zionist project.

Produced in 1978 after three decades of silence, *Roveh Chuliot* marked Israeli

Figure 29 Rove Chuliot / Wooden Gun

cinema's return to the suppressed theme of the Holocaust. The 1980s and 1990s cycle of shadow cinema includes *Machvo'im / Hide and Seek* (Dan Wolman, 1980), *Tel Aviv Berlin* (Tzipi Trope, 1986), *Biglal Hamilchama Hahee / Because of that War* (Orna Ben-Dor, 1988), *Hakaitz Shel Aviya / The Summer of Aviya* (Eli Cohen, 1988) and *Eretz Hadasha / New Land* (Orna Ben-Dor, 1994). In the last scene of *Roveh Chuliot* a young native Israeli boy is sure that, in a war game the boys were playing, he has just killed another boy – a Holocaust survivor. As he is running away along the beach, he meets a female survivor who lost her children in the Holocaust. She invites him in and, on the walls of her shack, he is suddenly faced with the famous picture of the young Jewish boy with his hands raised in front of a Nazi soldier. The situation in the picture comes to life on the screen and the boy hears the voices of his friends as they pressured him in the war game to shoot his rival, the Holocaust survivor, with his wooden gun. He realizes, in much the same way as the audience does, that in the war game he was standing in the same position as the Nazi soldier in the picture. Having realized this, the boy's empathy for the sufferings of the Holocaust survivor he had previously resented distances him from his native Israeli friends and their militaristic game. *Rove Chuliot* (and *Machvo'im* as well) demonstrates how the Israeli taboo on 'dangerous' feelings of empathy with the weak is communicated to youngsters through the process of socialization.

The 1980s war films re-examine the national ideal of self-sacrifice for the homeland that was at the core of the 1950s–60s heroic–nationalist cinema. Films produced following the 1973 Yom Kippur War, and the national trauma associated with it, refute the death ethos deep-seated in the Israeli mind. The films explore the moment of death in combat by manipulating cinematic time. The scene portraying the moment of death is repeated many times in these films – in both soundtrack effects and dialogue (*Massa Alunkot / Paratroopers*, *Betzilo Shel Helem Krav / Shell Shock*). The characters in such films are obsessed with the memory of the fallen soldier (*Ha'ayit / The Vulture*, *Tzlila Chozeret / Repeat Dive*, *Echad Mishelanu / One of Us*). A dying soldier becomes a metaphor for society as a whole (*Himmo Melech Yerushalayim / Himmo, King of Jerusalem*). The memory of a dead soldier is represented by a fetishistic object – a tape recording, a poster or a home movie – that plays a meaningful role in the plot of the film (*Tzlila Chozeret*, *Echad Mishelanu*, *Blues Lachofesh Hagadol / Late Summer Blues*).

Chayal Haleila / Soldier of the Night (Dan Wolman, 1984) increased the scale of military nihilism, with killing in combat replaced by simple murder – the young civilian protagonist, having been rejected by the army, takes revenge by murdering soldiers. *Za'am Vetehila / Rage and Glory* (Avi Nesher, 1984) is a retrospective film, focusing on the Jewish underground in the 1940s, that transforms the notion of self-sacrifice for the homeland into self-sacrifice for its own sake. *Ressissim / Burning Memory* (Yossi Zomer, 1989) depicted shell-shocked soldiers, pointing to the decline of heroes from self-sacrifice in combat to suicide. *Echad Mishelanu* (Uri Barabash, 1989) dealt with the cover-up of the murder of a Palestinian detainee in an Israeli army base in the Occupied Territories. In *Onat Haduvdevanim / Time of the Cherries* (Haim Bouzaglo, 1991) the protagonist, an army reserve soldier who is called to the war in Lebanon, is a copywriter in his civilian life who is launching a publicity campaign for a popular cigarette brand called 'Time'. The film ends with him being killed in Lebanon and his picture appearing on huge roadside billboard posters with the slogan: 'Have a Good Time'.

Apocalypse and inner-exile cinema (the 1990s)

'End' notions in Israeli cinema are related to the shattering of the Zionist utopian ideals and their replacement by the dystopia of military rule in the Occupied Territories. While representations of dystopia first appeared in 1980s films such as *Atalia* (Akiva Tevet, 1984), *Himmo Melekh Yerushalayim* (Amos Gutmann, 1987) and *Nisuyim Fictivyim / Marriage of Convenience* (Haim Bouzaglo, 1988), only *Hacholmim / Unsettled Land* (Uri Barbash, 1987) put a fully fledged dystopian portrayal of the Zionist enterprise on screen. Films of the 1980s and 1990s manifested a clear dystopian propensity that emanated from the suppressed historical events – the Holocaust and the Palestinian Nakba – that gradually appeared on the public agenda and in the cinema. *Haderech LeEin Harod / The Voice of Ein Harod* (1990) inverts the Zionist master-narrative by turning it into an end representation of Zionism. Set in the not-so-distant future, Israel is under military rule and permanent curfew. Two men – a Jewish political dissident and an Arab prisoner – are on the run. They try to break through roadblocks on their way to reach a free radio station at a kibbutz. Ruins, catacombs and *film noir* lighting create a bleak doomsday ambience for the final scene, in which the utopian 'beacon of light' kibbutz is revealed to be deserted and dilapidated, with a solitary old man broadcasting from a small radio transmitter.

A picture of 'a perpetual civil war between rival minorities' (Eco 1992) in Israeli society is drawn in *Hachaim Al Pi Agfa / Life According to Agfa*. A trendy café-bar, a

Figure 30 Hachaim Al Pi Agfa / Life According to Agfa

microcosm of Tel Aviv nightlife, sets the stage for rival factions to meet: rich and the poor, Ashkenazi and Mizrakhi, Jews and Arabs, police and criminals, kibbutz members and urbanites, civilians and the military. As morning breaks, army officers who were earlier thrown out of the bar by the police return, arms in hand, and massacre everybody in cold blood. Zionist utopians sought to create a full integration of the many Jewish ethnic groups on their return to the homeland. The film negotiates the failure of such utopian thinking and its consequent evolution to a cataclysm of self-annihilation.

Side by side with the apocalyptic orientation, the 1990s saw the emergence of films that demonstrated an indifference to apocalyptic notions, instead celebrating the fantastic and surreal. These films shun realism, the most common mode of Israeli cinema, and use post-modernist strategies to express their post-ideological worldview.

In the late 1990s the focus shifts from national problems to everyday life. Unlike the alienated and dissident new sensibility films of the 1960s and 1970s, the new quest in the 1990s was rooted in a sense of 'homelessness'. A new form of identity – neither here nor there, associated with both the difficulties of immigration and a sense of inner exile – came to the fore in different films.

The forerunners of this inner-exile cinema were such films as *Shuru* (Savi Gavison, 1990) and *Sipurei Tel Aviv / Tel Aviv Stories* (Ayelet Menachemi, Nirit Yaron, 1992), which ignore national issues and are somewhat indifferent to politics. *Sh'khur* (Shmuel Hasfari, 1994) is a plea for ethnicity, an attempt at legitimizing the notion of inner exile and allowing the unified collective identity to disintegrate for the sake of searching for roots – a search that the film admits is futile. Unlike the 1960s new sensibility cinema, which clearly had an ideological agenda, such films as *Clara Hakdosha / Saint Clara*, *Osher Lelo Gvul / Everlasting Joy* and *Holeh Ahava Meshikun Gimmel / Lovesick on Nana Street* avoid dealing directly with social or political issues, focusing instead on the fantasies and obsessions of the individual.

Clara Hakdosha (Ori Sivan and Ari Fulman, 1995) takes place in a small developing town in the Negev desert in southern Israel at the end of the millennium. The protagonist is an adolescent girl, a new immigrant from Russia and therefore by definition 'rootless'. She uses supernatural powers to revolutionize the life of the town's people, themselves immigrants of another era. The film combines an apocalyptic vision with a strong sense of self-exile, reaching its climax when the townspeople leave, fearing an earthquake foreseen by Clara. Clara and several youths are now the only residents in a ghost town and they are free to celebrate in an anarchistic mood. *Zichron Devarim / Devarim* (Amos Gitai, 1996), based on the highly esteemed novel *Past Continuous* by the late Ya'kov Shabtai, sketches a bleak picture of Tel Aviv in the 1970s, developing the theme of inner exile to its inevitable conclusion: suicide, both personal and national. The three main characters in the film, men in their forties, fool around in the urban set-up as if at a moveable feast, able to connect neither to their past nor to their life in the present.

A post-modern approach is dominant in many 1990s films. These include *Onat Haduvdevanim*, which deals with the war in Lebanon; *Leneged Einayim Maraviyot / Under Western Eyes* (Yossef Pitchhadze, 1996), a surreal road movie featuring an emigré father-figure; and *Osher Lelo Gvul / Everlasting Joy* (Yigal Burstein, 1996), a meta-cinematic text. Other films can be traced back to Zohar's *Hor Balevana / Hole in the Moon*. Such films as *Holeh Ahava Meshikun Gimmel / Lovesick on Nana Street* (Savi Gavison, 1995), which opts for the psychiatrist asylum as being the best of all existing worlds, and *Hachaverim Shel Yana / Yana's Friends* (Arik Kaplun, 1999), which shapes the experience of recent Russian immigrants as a frenzied inner-exile farce, subverting both ethnicity and the dominant collectivity. These films associated with the anarchist trope of 1960s new sensibility cinema, but at the same time reflect the 1990s inner-exile mood. They allude to both popular notions about the end of the millennium and to the idea of a 'global village' in which the nation-state, along with its oppressive ideologies, has become obsolete.

Several hundred feature films were produced in the 1980s and 1990s, many supported by the Israeli Film Fund. The launch of both commercial and cable television in the early 1990s created new opportunities for the younger generation of scriptwriters, directors and producers. From then on, commercial broadcasters had the most significant role in the development of Israeli cinema. They commissioned and financed many television dramas, documentaries and mini-series like *Mishpat Kastner / Kastner Trial*, *Bat Yam – New York* and *Florentine*. The production of many drama series and other locally produced television programmes enabled the industry to compete successfully with more lavish foreign programmes. In 1993 the New Fund for Israeli Cinema and Television was founded and supported the production of many documentaries that have gone on to win international awards. In 1996 the Israeli Film Fund suffered a major setback, however, when the Ministry of Industry withdrew its financial support. As a result the number of feature films produced diminished significantly. Further cuts to the Fund in the 1998 budget and a sense of instability in the industry led film-makers to organize and take militant action to improve conditions for film-making in the country. Following extensive lobbying of the government and in the Knesset, supported by street demonstrations the film-makers' lobby, they were successful in bringing about new legislation: the Bill for the Cinema. The Bill secures government finance on a regular annual basis for the various film production funds and related activities, such as festivals, cinematheques, film archives, film conservation, research and publication.

At the very end of 1999 a bitter conflict developed between the Forum of Film-makers (the broadest coalition of trade unions for film and television professionals ever formed in Israel), on one hand, and the broadcasters, private owners and public authorities, on the other. The central issues at stake were, first, the percentage of local productions transmitted nationally on both commercial and public channels and, second, the content question: ratings and journalism versus other quality-content genres. While in the past film-makers have seldom been supported by the cultural elite, it would seem that the current struggle is going to mobilize other producers of art and culture, and many concerned NGOs that have become involved in the politics of broadcasting. It is a commonplace that the future of any small national cinema is under the control of broadcasters. Fortunately, the creative energy is not entirely in their hands. By forming a broad coalition of organizations with social and political agendas, the film-makers can radicalize their struggle. It may be that the film-makers and their allies will finally have a real say about the quality and content of televised broadcasting, and eventually about Israeli culture at large.

Filmography

Ad Sof Haleila (literally 'Into the Night') / When Night Falls

1985, 90 mins, colour, Hebrew
Director / Screenwriter: Eitan Green
Producer: Micha Sharfstein
Cinematographer: Amnon Salomon
Editor: Era Lapid
Music: Yitzhak Klepter
Leading Players: Assi Dayan, Yoseph Millo, Orna Porat, Danny Roth, Haya Pik-Pardo

Giora, an officer suspended from the army and the owner of a Tel Aviv pub, works out his frustration on his estranged wife and his casual dates. The pressure on him increases with demands from the criminal underworld for protection money and the sudden appearance of his alienated father. This dystopian drama foregrounds the tragic disruption between fathers and sons, as well as the shattered myth of the Sabra, once a builder and fighter, a delegate of the Zionist utopia, but here a self-destructive drunk estranged from his family and from society at large. The lamenting of the past is reinforced by the casting of Millo and Dayan as father and son, a reprise of the roles they performed in the heroic–nationalist film *Hu Halach Basadot* / *He Walked Through the Fields* (1967). The many scenes shot at night convey a dark and morbid mood – the characters burdened with disillusionment, guilt and despair. The film received good reviews, but poor box office (approximately 11,000 tickets).

Adama (literally 'Earth') / *Tomorrow is a Wonderful Day*

1947, 46 mins, black and white, Hebrew (English narration)
Director: Helmar Lerski
Producer: Otto Sonnenfeld, Hadassah Women's Organization
Cinematographer: Sasha Alexander, Robert Schiller
Editor: Harry Komer
Music: Paul Dessau
Narration: Sam Balter

A docu-drama of a young Holocaust survivor, who suffers post-traumatic stress and is unable to adjust to the society of Sabra children in a youth village in Palestine. Dr Lehmann, who wrote the storyline, was the founder and head of the youth village which absorbed many young refugees from Europe. This Zionist realist film joins other films of that period in attempting to explore the complex guilt-ridden relationship between the Jewish community in Palestine and the Holocaust survivors; as in other narratives, its protagonists are rehabilitated and find their place in the Zionist project. The film was processed in Israel but completed in the United States, and the Zionist organization Hadassah, which distributed the film, re-cut it, renamed it and added an English narration without Lerski's consent. Unfortunately the original print and the negatives were lost in a fire. The film was an entry in the Lucarno and Cannes Film Festivals.

Afula Express / *Pick a Card*

1997, 95 mins, colour, Hebrew
Director: Julie Shles
Producer: Assaf Amir
Screenwriter: Amit Lior, Julie Shles
Cinematographer: Yitzhak Portal
Editor: Maor Keshet
Music: Yuval Shafrir
Leading Players: Tzvika Hadar, Esti Zackheim, Arye Moskona, Orli Perl, Natan Zehavi

Batia and David move from the provincial town of Afula to Tel Aviv, where David hopes to develop a career as a magician. When he fails to attain his dream, Batia leaves him and returns to her hometown. This debut feature, which focuses on love and disillusionment, brings the social fringe to the centre of attention, thus challenging both Israel's social hierarchy and the bias in Israeli cinema towards the upper-class Tel Aviv Sabra. The film received favourable reviews and did well at the box office. It won the Wolgin Award at the 1997 Jerusalem Film Festival, as well as Israel Film Academy Best Film Award.

Ahava Rishona | First Love

1982, 90 mins, colour, Hebrew
Director / Screenwriter: Uzi Peres
Producer: Ruth Peres
Cinematographer: Avraham Karpik
Editor: Ilana Ben-Ari
Music: Francis Levon
Leading Players: Gila Almagor, Yiftach Katzur, Hanan Goldblatt, Uri Levi, Debby Hess

On the eve of her fortieth birthday, Ziva, a married woman, reunites with her first lover from days back on a kibbutz. Her son, who wishes to keep the family intact, thrusts his sister into the stranger's arms. This is the second film in a series entitled *Human Errors* by the director. The film aims to create a local version of the classic Hollywood melodrama, focusing on incest and sexual repression. It received mixed reviews and modest box office (around 45,000 tickets were sold).

Ahavata Hahachrona Shel Laura Adler | Laura Adler's Last Love Affair

1990, 96 mins, colour, Hebrew and Yiddish
Director / Screenwriter: Avraham Heffner
Producer: Marek Rosenbaum
Cinematographer: David Gurfinkel
Editor: Lena Kadish
Music: Shem-Tov Levi
Leading Players: Rita Zohar, Menashe Warshavsky, Avraham Mor, Shulamit Adar

Laura, an old-time star of a Tel Aviv-based Yiddish theatre, receives an offer to star in a Hollywood film. This offer rejuvenates Laura, who is aware of her ever-declining audience. She even conducts a love affair with a younger man, but then discovers that she has cancer. This self-reflexive melodrama, which integrates staged scenes from an Yiddish play, underscores the oppositions between reality / stage and life / art through a minimalism that does not allow pathos. Heffner's fascination with the past serves as a subtle critique of Zionism's assault on the Yiddish language in order to make place for Hebrew. The film received favourable reviews but poor box office. It won the

Wolgin Award at the Jerusalem Film Festival and was an entrant in the Venice Film Festival.

Al Hevel Dak / A Thin Line

1981, 90 mins, colour, Hebrew
Director / Screenwriter: Michal Bat-Adam
Producer: Gideon Amir, Avi Kleinberger, Michal Bat-Adam
Cinematographer: Nurit Aviv
Editor: Tal Shoval
Music: Yoni Rechter
Leading Players: Gila Almagor, Alex Peleg, Liat Pansky, Avner Hizkiyahu,
                           Miri Fabian

Nili, an eleven-year-old girl, is sent to spend the summer with her aunt in a kibbutz, while her mother is hospitalized in a psychiatric ward. When the girl returns home to Tel Aviv, she has to support her mother and take care of the household. Bat-Adam's second feature is an autobiographical psychological drama, told from the perspective of a child, and deals with recurrent motifs in the director's work: mother–daughter relationships, the painful drama of growing up and society's attitude to mental disorders. As in her other films, the emphasis is on the moods and emotions presented by the actors. The film received mixed reviews and poor box office, but won the Israel Best Film Award.

Al Tig'u Li BaSho'a / Don't Touch My Holocaust

1994, 140 mins, Hebrew / German / Arabic

Figure 31   Al Hevel Dak / A Thin Line

Figure 32 Al Tig'u Li Basho'a / Don't Touch My Holocaust

Director / Screenwriter: Asher Tlalim
Producer: Dani Siton, Daniel Faran
Cinematographer: Yoram Milo
Editor: Gil Balshai
Music: Tom Tlalim

Al Tig'u Li Basho'a shows the staging of *Arbeit Macht Frei*, a theatre production focusing on the Holocaust by an Israeli avant-garde group based in Acre and headed by Dudi Ma'ayan, and the group's tour of Berlin, Dachau, Prague and Theresenstadt. The film, integrating staged and documentary scenes, follows the reactions of the German audiences, as well as the voyage of the director to his hometown of Casablanca. It also examines the significance of the ethos of the Holocaust as manipulated by the Zionist elite. The film won the Israel Film Academy Best Documentary Award.

Amud Ha'esh / Pillar of Fire

1959, 75 mins, black and white, English
Director: Larry Friesch
Producer: Yitzhak Agadati, Mordechi Navon, Larry Friesh
Screenwriter: Hugh Nissenson, Larry Friesh
Cinematographer: Haim Shreiber
Editor: Nellie Gilad

Music: Moshe Wilensky
Leading Players: Yitzhak Shilo, Nehama Hendel, Lawrence Montaigne, Amos
                          Mokadi, Uri Zohar

Set during the 1948 War of Independence, *Amud Ha'esh* focuses on an outpost in the
Negev desert, where five men and one woman stand against a battalion of Egyptian
tanks on its way to Tel Aviv. When trying to break through the siege, four soldiers are
killed; only the American Zionist, David, and the Sabra, Rachel, are left in the outpost.
This low-budget film in the heroic–nationalist genre, one of the few made about the
1948 war, highlights the motif of sacrifice of the individual for the sake of the homeland and the ethos of the few against the many. The film failed at the box office, partly
due to its English dialogue. It was the first film to be produced in Geva studios.

Amud Ha'esh / *Pillar of Fire*

1979, 19 hrs, colour, Hebrew
Series editor: Yigal Lossin
Producer: Ya'akov Eisenman
Researcher: Neomi Kaplansky
Narration: Yossi Banai

This huge television documentary series, comprising nineteen hour-long segments,
recounts the return of the Jews to the land of Israel in the years 1896–1948, showing
the important events of the period: the birth of Zionism at the end of the nineteenth
century; the Balfour Declaration; the birth of the Palestinian movement; the 1920s
pioneers; the 1929 pogrom by Arabs against Jews; the immigration of Jews to
Palestine at the eve of World War II; the Arab Uprising of 1936; the partition plan
and its rejection by the Arabs; the Holocaust. At the time it was the largest production
by Israeli television, projecting and asserting Zionist ideology. The documentary was
based on footage retrieved from more than thirty archives and private collections all
over the world, as well as interviews with more than 250 people. The series attracted
great public interest, with accompanying chat-shows and vast press coverage, as well
as protests from different groups claiming that they had not been privileged enough in
the series. It was re-edited into a series of seven segments, with an English narration,
for screening in England, Denmark and other countries.

Ani Akhmed / *My Name is Akhmed*

1966, 13 mins, black and white
Director: Avshalom Katz
Producer: Dany Schik
Screenwriter: Ram Loevy
Music: Tzvi Ben-Porat

In this docu-drama, feelings of alienation characterize the experience of an Israeli
Arab youth who arrives in Tel Aviv from his village in the north to seek his fortune as
a construction worker. In Tel Aviv the Arab workers try to camouflage their identity in

order to avoid physical and verbal abuse. In this first attempt by a Jewish film-maker to explore the life of Israeli Arabs, the protagonist's voice accompanies the film and thus intensifies the perspective of the 'other'. Akhmed Yussuf Mashraweh, on whom the film centres, was first a subject of a radio programme by Ram Loevy.

Ani Ohev Otach Rosa / I Love You Rosa

1972, 100 mins, colour, Hebrew
Director:	Moshe Mizrachi
Producer:	Menachem Golan, Noah Films
Screenwriter:	Moshe Mizrachi
Cinematographer:	Adam Greenberg
Editor:	Dov Hoenig
Music:	Dov Seltzer
Leading Players:	Michal Bat-Adam, Gabi Oterman, Yosef Shiloah, Levana Finkelstein

Set at the end of nineteenth century and introduced as a flashback, the narrative unfolds the life story of Rosa, a young Sephardi Jewish widow in Jerusalem. According to Jewish law she cannot remarry unless her husband's brother either marries her or frees her. The brother is only eleven years old and Rosa raises him in her house but later refuses to marry him. This unique love story is embedded in an

Figure 33 Ani Ohev Otach Rosa / I Love You Rosa

oriental Jewish community that lives in harmony with its Arab neighbours and focuses on a female character who could be perceived as a feminist of her time. Mizrachi's feelings for the community lend the film a dignity rare in Israeli cinema, which is usually prejudiced against oriental Jews. The film received mixed reviews but good box office (selling some 280,000 tickets) and won Israel Best Film Award, as well as a nomination for an Oscar in the Foreign Language Film category.

Atalia

1984, 90 mins, colour, Hebrew

Director:	Akiva Tevet
Producer:	Omri Maron, Nathan Hakeini, Dani Schik
Screenwriter:	Tzvi Kerzner
Cinematographer:	Nurit Aviv
Editor:	Reuven Korenfeld
Music:	Nahum Heiman
Leading Players:	Michal Bat-Adam, Yiftach Katzur, Dan Toren, Gali Ben-Ner

A drama based on a story by Yitzhak Ben-Ner that describes Atalia, a forty-year-old war widow who lost her husband in the 1956 Israel–Egypt war. Atalia, an eccentric living in a kibbutz on the eve of the 1973 Yom Kippur War, takes as a lover a young man who is twenty years her junior. Group pressures drive them to move to the city. The film's dystopian critique of kibbutz ideology focuses on the conformity and group pressures within the kibbutz, and underscores the conflict between the individual and the collective, as well as women's marginality. The film received poor reviews and poor box office (only 80,000 tickets were sold).

Avanti Popolo

1986, 84 mins, colour, Hebrew and Arabic

Director / Producer / Screenwriter:	Rafi Bukaee, Kastel Films
Cinematographer:	Yoav Kosh
Editor:	Zohar Sela
Music:	Uri Ophir
Leading Players:	Salim Dau, Suheil Haddad, Danny Roth, Tuvia Gelber, Dani Segev

A drama set in the last hours of the 1967 war. Two Egyptian soldiers, an actor and a peasant, are trying to reach the Suez Canal on their way home. An Israeli patrol opens fire on them and the actor saves their lives by pleading, like Shylock, 'Hath not a Jew eyes?'. Finally the two reach the canal only to be shot dead by bullets coming from both banks. This low-budget surreal tragi-comedy, its aesthetic shaped by lack of means, stands out among the 1980s Israeli–Palestinian conflict films in its universalist pacifism and leanings towards the absurd. Even though its protagonists are not Palestinians (significantly, the actors portraying them are Israeli Palestinians) and the narrative goes back two decades, it joins other films of the period in advocating the subjectivity of the 'other' and in deconstructing the heroic–nationalist narrative. The film received favourable reviews and modest box office (around 110,000 tickets). It was chosen as Best Israeli Film by Israeli film critics and won the Golden Leopard at the Lucarno Film Festival.

Aviv BeEretz Yisrael / Springtime in Palestine

1928, black and white, silent
Director: Yosef Gal-Ezer
Producer: Jewish National Fund (JNF), Palestine Foundation Fund (PFF)
Screenwriter: Ernst Mechner, Max Kolpe
Cinematographer: Ya'akov Ben-Dov
Editor: Yosef Gal-Ezer, Willi Prager
Music: Max Lampel

Perhaps the most successful Zionist realist documentary, rendering images of Judea in the springtime, the Jordan river, archeological excavations and the festivities of Jewish communities of different ethnic origins. It was the first film to be distributed by the two major Zionist funds and the first documentary to have an original music score. In order to produce the film, Ben-Dov established a new and more sophisticated film laboratory in Jerusalem. Additional editing was done in Berlin by Yosef Gal-Ezer, the head of the Information Department of PFF, and German film-maker Willi Prager. The film premiered in Berlin and was shown in fifty-six countries, including the Far East, remaining JNF's flagship film for several more years. *Aviv Be'eretz Yisrael* was Ben-Dov's last major project, for which he did not even receive a director's credit. The prints are now lost and only a few scenes have survived.

Awoda / Work

1935, 48 mins, black and white, silent
Director / Cinematographer: Helmar Lerski
Producer: Paul Boroshek, Palestine Pictures
Music: Paul Dessau

An example *par excellence* of the Zionist realist genre, this unique documentary glorifies the achievements of the pioneers and the Zionist movement in Palestine. The main body of the film illustrates the *tour de force* of the Jewish pioneers – paving roads, planting, harvesting, building new communes and drilling for water – and culminates in the water gushing out of the well and restoring the land to fruitfulness, a basic theme of Zionism. Lerski's work, achieved with a small mobile camera and natural light, is memorable for its photography, which follows the spirit of German expressionism, and for its creative montage of juxtaposed images, such as machinery and sweating muscles. The negative was developed in Jerusalem but the editing and the soundtrack were done in Budapest. The film was entered for the 1935 Venice Biennial but, despite local and the international acclaim, its distribution was limited – probably because the PFF wanted to promote *Le'khayim Khadashim / Land of Promise* (made at the same time). *Awoda* was lost for many years and only in 1978 was a print recovered in England and brought to the Israel Film Archive in the Jerusalem Cinematheque.

Aya: Autobiographia Dimyonit / Imagined Autobiography

1994, 94 mins, colour, Hebrew

Director / Screenwriter:	Michal Bat-Adam
Producer:	Marek Rosenbaum
Cinematographer:	Yoav Kosh
Editor:	Boaz Leon
Music:	Amos Hadani
Leading Players:	Michal Bat-Adam, Michal Zuaretz, Liat Goren, Gedalia Besser

Aya, a film-maker, is married and a mother, and takes care of her aging father. She makes a film about her childhood, focusing on her mentally unstable mother and on her own experiences at a kibbutz school, as well as on her current difficulties as mother, wife and professional. This self-reflexive drama employs a fragmented narrative, moving between present to past, often playing the past twice, in dramatized scenes from the film-within-a-film and in Aya's tortured memories. Bat-Adam's seventh film consolidates motifs from two other autobiographical films: *Al Hevel Dak / A Thin Line* (1981) and *Ben Loke'ach Bat / Boy Meets Girl* (1983), whose protagonist is young Aya. The film highlights an obsession with the past and plays with the opposition between art / life. It received favourable reviews.

Bar 51 (a.k.a. 'Orphans of the Storm')

1985, 110 mins, colour, Hebrew

Director:	Amos Gutman
Producer:	Enrique Rottenberg
Screenwriter:	Edna Mazia, Amos Gutman
Cinematographer:	Yossi Wein
Editor:	Tova Asher
Music:	Arik Rudich
Leading Players:	Guilano Mer, Smadar Klachinski, Ada Valeri-Tal, Alon Aboutboul

A drama in which Thomas and Mariana leave their small town after their mother dies. In Tel Aviv they find shelter in the home of a bar hostess who gives them bed and board for the favours granted to her by Thomas. Mariana succeeds as a dancer, but her brother falls into drugs and despair. This nihilistic film, a decadent portrayal of night-time Tel Aviv that is overshadowed by the doomed love between the two siblings, deals with life on the fringes where the outcasts seek solace from their feverish solitude. The film treats issues such as homosexuality, incest and other sexual taboos through the format of the melodrama, thus echoing Fassbinder's cinematic choices. It won mixed reviews and modest box office (some 32,000 tickets).

Bat Yam – New York

1995, television series, colour, Hebrew
Director / Screenwriter: David Ofek, Yossi Madmoni
Producer: Micha Shagrir (for Channel 2)

The Zlayit family of Jewish-Iraqi origins lives in Bat Yam, a suburb of Tel Aviv. Of five children, two live in New York. This series' dramatic and (sometimes outrageously) comic situations are based on the tension between the younger generation, striving to disengage from traditional values, and parents' attempts to preserve those same values. These tensions are mirrored in and distorted by videotaped messages that the New York-based son and daughter send to their family. Video, the obsession of another brother who makes video recordings of weddings, plays a major role in the structure of this series, underscoring the 1990s post-modernistic conviction that the only access to reality is via an artifact – in this case, video footage. Nevertheless, the series' use of non-actors, its unfinished look and its stylistic similarities to the documentary subvert this message and allow access to authentic aspects of Israeli life. The narrative deconstructs the Bourekas genre and promotes the 1990s inner-exile solution to the question of the melting pot. *Bat Yam – New York* received favourable reviews.

Bayit / House

1980, 90 mins, black and white, Hebrew and Arabic
Director / Screenwriter: Amos Gitai
Producer: Israeli Television
Cinematographer: Emmanuel Aldema

Bayit tells the story of one house in Jerusalem. Its owner, a Palestinian physician, left it during the 1948 war; it was first inhabited by a family of Jewish immigrants from Algeria and later by an Israeli professor of economics who hired Palestinians from the Occupied Territories to convert it into a posh three-level villa. The various incarnations of the house reflect ideological transformations and class metamorphoses in Israeli society, and at the same time it serves as a microcosm of the Israeli–Palestinian conflict. Israeli Television refused to broadcast this documentary and Gitai consequently left Israel to work in France.

Be'ein Moledet / Lacking a Homeland

1956, 90 mins, colour, Hebrew
Director / Screenwriter / Producer: Nuri Habib
Cinematographer: Nuri Koukou
Editor: Nuri Habib, Nuri Koukou
Music: Moshe Wilensky
Leading Players: Shoshana Damari, Shaike Ophir, Sa'adia Damari, Eitan Freiber

In Yemen in 1926 Naomi, a singer in a coffeehouse who was orphaned as a child and raised by Arabs, takes a young Jewish boy into her home. The two join a band of Jews on their way to the land of Israel, led by a Zionist emissary. When border guards are about to shoot the exhausted Jews, a rescue force of Jews from Palestine saves the day. This period drama, which dramatizes the Zionist credo of returning to the homeland, was the first to deal with the immigration of Jews from an Islamic country and also the first colour film to be shot in Israel. Habib, who previously made films in Iraq and Iran, borrows strategies that typify Arabic films, including exaggerated acting, a static camera and an overbearing musical score. The film received favourable reviews and was also distributed in the United States.

Beit Avi / My Father's House

1947, 85 mins, black and white, English
Director: Herbert Klein
Producer: Meyer Levin, Herbert Klein
Screenwriter: Meyer Levin
Cinematographer: Floyd Crosby, R. Ziller
Music: Henry Brandt
Leading Players: Irene Broza, Itzhak Danziger

An eleven-year-old Holocaust survivor wanders on his own across Palestine, looking for his father from whom he was separated during the war. In Jerusalem he is confronted by the traumatic news of his father's fate and goes back to the kibbutz that adopted him. This Zionist propaganda film was meant primarily for Jewry of the diaspora, displaying a panoramic view of the scenery and people of the land of Israel and utilizing the Holocaust as the moral justification for the soon-to-be-born state of Israel. Bitter arguments on the set between director Klein (who tried to bring a more realistic attitude to the screen) and screenwriter Levin (who insisted on portraying Palestine in a romantic light) resulted in a film idealizing the hardships typical of those years and portraying the Arabs as pro-Zionist. The film was shown for eighteen consecutive weeks in New York. Later, Levin published a novel by the same name.

Beit She'an – Seret Milchama / Beit She'an – A War Movie

1996, 60 mins, colour, Hebrew
Director: Doron Tsabari, Rino Tzror
Producer: Avi Armoza, Gabi Rosenberg
Screenwriters: Rino Tsror and Doron Tsabari
Photographer: Dror Moreh
Editor: Noam Veisman
Music: Shushan

A film documentary that traces the lives of players and supporters of a football team in a small development town in the Galilee over six weeks. The game is the focus not only of the team, but also of all the town's residents – a metaphor for their dream of a better life. Their acute local patriotism, symptomatic of their isolation and despair, becomes a political statement about the ruptures in Israeli society in the 1990s.

BeNahalal / In Nahalal

1961, 15 mins, black and white, Hebrew
Director: Emil (Millek) Knebel
Producer: Yigal Effrati (IFS)
Cinematographer: Adam Greenberg

This film, made on the occasion of the fortieth anniversary of Nahalal (a village in the Jezreel valley), diverges from the Zionist realist codes of documentary film-making of that period and chooses as an alternative the realistic portrayal of everyday life in a village. Scenes of work and family life are represented here not as the epitome of an ideology but as plain human endeavour. This is the first film to offer such an alternative and it paved the way for later films to depart from Zionist realist dogma.

Betzilo Shel Helem Krav (literally 'In the Shade of Shell Shock') / Shell Shock

1988, 96 mins, colour, Hebrew
Director / Screenwriter: Yoel Sharon
Producer: Yehiel Yogev, Meir Amshalom, Yoel Sharon
Cinematographer: Yoav Kosh
Editor: Zohar Sela, Arik Rudich
Leading Players: Dan Turgeman, Asher Tzarfati, Anat Atzmon, Gili Ben-Uzilio

Dan Turgeman (Micha) and Babay Jihad (Sumchi) in the morning after the attack, the crucial moment in SHELL SHOCK, a film directed by Yoel Sharon. An Angelika Films release.

Figure 34 Betzilo Shel Helem Krav / Shell Shock

Micha, a fashion photographer and lieutenant in the reserves, saw his tank crew burned in the 1973 Yom Kippur War. He suffers shell shock and is treated in a psychiatric hospital. There he befriends a colonel whose unit was mistakenly wiped out by Israeli jets. This nihilistic drama deals with post-traumatic situations, focusing on two tortured Sabras: one who cannot forget, the other who cannot remember. The director, himself badly wounded in the war, focuses on guilt and self-reproach, rejecting the ethos of heroic self-sacrifice. The film received mixed reviews and poor box office (selling only 23,000 tickets).

Biba

1977, 58 mins, colour, Hebrew
Director / Screenwriter: David Perlov
Producer: Yigal Efrati, David Schitz (IFS)
Cinematographer: Dany Shneur, Avino'am Levy, Yachin Hirsch
Editor: Era Lapid
Music: Eden Partosh

In 1973 Perlov arrived at a village in the Jezreel valley 'to photograph beautiful people'. One of them was Uzi Israeli. Several months later Israeli was killed in the 1973 Yom Kippur War. On the village's fiftieth anniversary in 1977, Perlov returned, this time to visit Biba, the widow of Uzi. This documentary focuses on the way that the absent figure of Uzi, the 'beautiful Israeli', continues to be present in the lives of his family and friends, and questions the personal sacrifice embedded in the heroic ethos.

Biglal Hamilchama Hahee / Because of that War

1988, 93 mins, colour, Hebrew
Director / Screenwriter: Orna Ben-Dor
Producer: David Schutz, Shmuel Altman (IFS)
Cinematographer: Oren Shmukler
Editor: Rahel Yagil
Music: Yehuda Poliker

The protagonists of this shadow-genre documentary film are popular rock singer Yehuda Poliker and lyricist Ya'akov Gilad. Set against the success of their record and show *Efer Veavak* ('Ashes and Dust'), which consist of texts relating to the Holocaust, Poliker and Gilad discuss the trauma of childhood in the shadow of parents who had survived the Holocaust but did not share the horrors of the past with their offspring. The return of repressed memories and consequently a feeling of relief and deep sorrow mark the interviews. This debut full-length film, made by the daughter of Holocaust survivors, reinstates the notion that the Holocaust is the *raison d'être* for the state of Israel. The film received good reviews and surprisingly good box office for a documentary (selling some 100,000 tickets). It won the Critics' Award at the Berlin Film Festival and a mention in the Leningrad Film Festival.

Blues Lachofesh Hagadol (literally 'Summer Holiday Blues') / Late Summer Blues

1987, 101 mins, colour, Hebrew
Director: Renen Schorr
Producer: Ilan de Vries, Renen Schorr, Doron Nesher
Screenwriter: Doron Nesher
Cinematographer: Eitan Harris
Editor: Shlomo Hazan
Music: Rafi Kadishzon
Leading Players: Dor Zweigenbom, Yoav Tzafir, Shahar Segal, Noa Goldberg

A group of Tel Aviv high-school students celebrate their last days of innocence prior to joining the army during the 1970s Israel–Egypt war of attrition with its daily death toll. The protagonist, Margo, documents the group's frolics with his Super 8 camera, as well as a protest sparked off by the death of their friend in combat. This group portrait comes to grips with Israeli militarism and the spirit of the period, associated with the international student protests, the Vietnam War and the hippy movement. The film also covers subjects (such as sex, drugs and music) that are typical of films about youth. It received good reviews and fair box office (around 280,000 tickets were sold), and won the Israel Best Film Award. It participated in (among others) the Montreal, Hong Kong and Chicago Film Festivals.

Boquito

1983, 28 mins, black and white, Hebrew
Director: Reuven Hecker

This docu-drama was a graduation film, made in the Film Department of TAU. It focuses on the Lebanon War. The film-maker returns as a reserve soldier to a site south of Sidon where two of his friends were killed and documents the routine activities of the Israeli soldiers, mainly checking the cars of locals at roadblocks. The soldiers live in a deserted villa, from which they can see the Lebanese children play with bomb shrapnel. This was one of the first films to openly criticize Israel's policies in Lebanon. 'Boquito' is the name of the coastal highway leading from Beirut to Tel Aviv.

Bouba / On the Fringe

1987, 88 mins, colour, Hebrew
Director: Ze'ev Revach
Producer: Ya'akov Kotzky
Screenwriter: Hillel Mitelpunkt, Ze'ev Revah, Ya'akov Kotzky
Cinematographer: Ilan Rosenberg
Editor: Zion Avrahamian
Music: Dov Seltzer
Leading Players: Ze'ev Revah, Hanni Nachmias, Yossi Graber, Asher Tzarfati

Bouba is a drama based on a play by Hillel Mitelpunkt. Bouba, who was badly wounded in the Yom Kippur War and consequently lost his ability to speak, finds refuge in the Negev desert, where he runs a gasoline station. The arrival of a young woman and soon afterwards his brother, a criminal on the run from the underworld, causes upheavals in Bouba's world. This melodrama, focusing on the traumas that followed the Yom Kippur War, features characters who live on the fringe of society. Bouba, the only character in the film to be part of the dominant ethos by the merit of his war sacrifice, also pays dearly for his disassociation from the other outcasts. The film received poor reviews and modest box office (around 42,000 tickets were sold). *Bouba* won the Critics' Award at the Rio de Janeiro Film Festival.

Bi'ur Haba'arut / Eradicating Illiteracy

1965, 15 mins, black and white, Hebrew
Director / Screenwriter: Yitzhak Tzepel Yeshurun
Producer: Yigal Efrati (IFS)
Cinematographer: Yachin Hirsh
Editor: Tova Biran
Music: Mel Keler

In a village in the Galilee, Sabra women soldiers teach Hebrew to illiterate new Jewish immigrants from Iran. Step by step the young soldiers revolutionize the world of the older immigrants. This is one of the first films to make little use of authoritative narration, allowing the immigrants to express in non-Sabra Hebrew their social and existential problems, a mode of representation considered taboo in commissioned documentaries of that period.

B'Yerushalayim / In Jerusalem

1963, 31 mins, colour, Hebrew
Director / Screenwriter: David Perlov
Producer: Yigal Efrati (IFS)
Cinematographer: Adam Greenberg
Editor: Anna Gurit
Narration: Ya'akov Malkin, David Perlov
Music: Eden Partosh

This portrait of Jerusalem ignores the 'holy city' notion and instead focuses on mundane Jerusalem: stonecutters, beggars, children playing hide-and-seek, peddlers, old people, ultra-orthodox Jews and faces peeping through the cracks in the wall of the old city, along the borderline. Perlov's suggestive camerawork achieves an artistic freedom unprecedented in Israeli documentaries of that period. The film includes a rare interview with Maury Rosenberg, who in 1911 made the first film in Palestine. The documentary stirred controversy due to the images of beggars and only the intervention of then Prime Minister Levi Eshkol made the screening possible.

Casablan

1973, 122 mins, colour, Hebrew
Director / producer: Menachem Golan
Screenwriter: Menachem Golan, Haim Hefer
Cinematographer: David Gurfinkel
Editor: Dov Hoenig
Music: Dov Seltzer
Choreographer: Shimon Braun
Leading Players: Yehoram Gaon, Efrat Lavie, Yossi Graber, Yehuda Efroni, Arie Elias, Etti Grottes

Casablan, a young man from a Jewish Moroccan family who won a medal for his bravery in the Six Day War, heads a street gang in Jaffa. The municipality intends to demolish their rundown neighbourhood and the residents gather money to finance their legal defence. When the money is stolen, the police arrest Casablan. This first Israeli musical, an expensive production with dozens of actors, dancers and extras, emulated the American musical *West Side Story*. The film focused on ethnic / class tensions and, in particular, on the paternalism of the Ashkenazi establishment. As is customary in the Bourekas genre, the reconciliation between Sephardi and Ashkenazi Jews is celebrated in a mixed marriage. *Casablan* received favourable reviews and was Golan's most profitable film (selling over 1,200,000 tickets). Based on a play by Yigal Mossinzon, it originated in a successful 1960s musical show by Haim Hefer, Amos Etinger, Dan Almagor and Yoel Zilberg, that also starred Yehoram Gaon. The film was screened in about sixty countries and was a big hit in South America and South Africa.

Catz VeCarasso / Katz and Carasso

1971, 100 mins, colour, Hebrew
Director: Menachem Golan
Producer: Yoram Globus
Screenwriter: Menachem Golan, Yossef Gross
Cinematographer: David Gurfinkel
Editor: David Troyhertz
Music: Nurit Hirsch
Leading Players: Yossef Shilo'ah, Shmuel Rodensky, Yehuda Barkan, Gadi Yagil, Nitza Shaul, Efrat Lavie

Katz and Carasso are owners of competing insurance companies; one is Ashkenazi and the other Sephardi. Katz has two sons and his rival has two daughters. By the end of the film the sons and daughters have fallen in love and the two families are brought together. This prototype film of the Bourekas genre ignores class differences and prefers to highlight the ethnic-cultural gap, which can be easily bridged by mixed marriage. *Catz Vecarasso* laid the groundwork for later Bourekas films, subverting its own melting-pot discourse by underscoring ethnic customs. It received mixed reviews but did well at the box office.

Charlie Vachetzi / *Charlie and a Half*

1974, 105 mins, colour, Hebrew
Director: Boaz Davidson
Producer: Simcha Zvuloni
Screenwriter: Eli Tavor
Cinematographer: Amnon Salomon
Editor: Alain Yakobovich
Music: Yair Rosenblum
Leading Players: Yehuda Barkan, Ze'ev Revah, Arie Elias, Haya Katzir, Geula Noni, David Shoshan

Charlie, a charming tramp from an Jewish Iraqi family, and Miko, a boy who dropped out of school, survive through petty fraud. When Charlie marries Gila, an Ashkenazi daughter of a bourgeois family, Miko leaves for America. This Bourekas melodrama, focusing on Sephardi–Ashkenazi tensions and class gaps, uses humour and gags to cover up the socially and politically oppressive system. Miko's departure at the end implies giving up on the idea of integration within Israel. The film received poor reviews but excellent box office (selling around 700,000 tickets), in time becoming a cult movie.

Chavura Shekazot / *What a Gang*

1962, 80 mins, black and white, Hebrew
Director: Ze'ev Havatzelet
Producer: Mordechai Navon, Yitzhak Agadati (Geva Films)
Screenwriter: Yisrael Wissler, Shaul Biber, Bomba Tzur
Cinematographer: Nissim Leon
Editor: Anna Gurit
Music: Alexander Argov
Leading Players: Yossi Banai, Bomba Tzur, Oded Teomi, Gila Almagor, Avner Hyzkyahu

Chavura Shekazot is based on a novel by Wissler. In the film Yosinyu, a naive youth joins a training unit of the *Palmach* (Jewish military troops in pre-state years) on a kibbutz in the 1940s, the days of the British Mandate and illegal immigration. He goes through a series of tests until he is accepted as an equal member. This light coming-of-age situation comedy discloses the ambivalent mood of the early 1960s by paying tribute to the *Palmach* and its heroic–nationalist ideals, while at the same time mocking its values. The film received good reviews and good box office (around 390,000 tickets sold).

Chayal Haleila / *Soldier of the Night*

1984, 86 mins, colour, Hebrew
Director / Producer / Screenwriter: Dan Wolman
Cinematographer: Yossi Wein
Editor: Shosh Wolman

Music:	Alex Cagan
Leading Players:	Ze'ev Shimshoni, Iris Kaner, Yiftach Katzur, Yehuda Efroni

Ze'ev is a young man in love with Iris, a student who works part-time as a waitress. He spends his nights on mysterious expeditions dressed in military uniform and carrying a weapon. When the radio reports a series of nightly murders, the victims of which are soldiers, Iris suspects her boyfriend. This low-budget drama, the most radical film about the impact of militarism on society ever to be made in Israel, not only parodies the ideals of the heroic–nationalist genre, but rejects 'soldiering' itself – the protagonist tears himself out of his peer group and chooses his own nihilistic perspective. The narrative also refers to homophobia and narcissism, and Wolman utilizes expressionistic and *film noir* strategies to construct a dark picture, quivering with angst and repressed violence. The production took three years to complete and failed to attract a large audience (only 9,000 tickets were bought). The film initially polarized reviewers but later won new appreciation.

Cholot Lohatim / *Blazing Sands*

1960, 90 mins, colour, Hebrew

Director / Producer / Screenwriter:	Rephael Nussbaum (Israeli–German co-production)
Cinematographer:	Ytzhak Herbst
Editor:	Erika Shtegman
Music:	Ziegfried Wegener
Leading Players:	Dalia Lavie, Uri Zohar, Hillel Ne'eman, Oded Kotler

Dina, a young dancer, organizes a rescue team to save her boyfriend, wounded in Petra in Jordan. She and four men, disguised as Bedouins, cross the border; only one returns. This heroic–nationalist drama, based on real accounts, reflects the romantic aspirations of many young Israelis in the 1950s, who saw in the journey to the site of the ancient Nabatean town a trial of courage in the spirit of the War of Independence. The film employed strategies taken from the Western, with panoramic shots of the desert and the Bedouins portrayed as Indians. It provoked a public scandal, its makers were blamed for encouraging Israeli youth to sacrifice their lives in vain. A further sensation was caused by the use of Lavie's half-naked body for Hollywood-style promotion of the film. Reviews were poor as well, due to unsatisfactory dubbing into Hebrew.

Chyuch Hagdi / *Smile of the Lamb*

1986, 95 mins, colour, Hebrew and Arabic

Director:	Shimon Dotan
Producer:	Yonatan Aroch
Screenwriter:	Shimon Dotan, Shimon Riklin, Anat Levi-Bar
Cinematographer:	Dani Shneur

Editor:	Netaya Inbar
Music:	Ilan Wurtzburg
Leading Players:	Tuncel Curtiz, Rami Danon, Makram Khuri, Danny Muggia, Iris Hoffman

Chyuch Hagdi is based on a novel by David Grossman. The newly appointed Israeli governor of the West Bank carries out a harsh policy towards the Palestinians, thus alienating his friend who is a liberal army physician. The physician is captivated by the tales of Hilmi, a wise old Arab villager. When the old man learns that his son was killed by Israeli troops, he holds the doctor hostage. This Israeli–Palestinian conflict drama elaborates the evils of the occupation, while portraying it as a dead-end situation. The moral triumph of Hilmi, who practises the *Tzumud* (clinging to one's land), as well as the tragic fate of the peace-activist protagonist, punished for his enlightened fantasy, is typical of the guilt-laden conflict films. This film stands out through its lyrical, poetic treatment, demonstrating the influence of films by the Tavianyi in its cinematography and music. Shooting took place on location in a West Bank Arab village, whose residents were hostile to the crew – especially to Khuri, an Israeli-Palestinian who played the role of the governor. The film provoked considerable interest at the Cannes Film Festival but failed critically and commercially in Israel (selling only 9,000 tickets). It won the Israel Best Film Award and Curtiz won the Silver Bear at the 1986 Berlin Film Festival.

Clara Hakdosha / Saint Clara

1995, 75 mins, colour, Hebrew

Director / Screenwriter:	Ori Sivan, Ari Fulman
Producer:	Marek Rosenbaum, Uri Sabag
Cinematographer:	Valentin Blonogov
Editor:	Dov Stoyer
Music:	Barry Saharov
Leading Players:	Lucy Dubincheck, Halil Elohev, Yigal Naor, Maya Maron, Johnny Piterson

Clara Hakdosha is based on a novel by Pawel Kohut. At the end of the millennium, life in a remote industrial town is changed by the supernatural powers of thirteen-year-old Clara, a new immigrant from Russia. When the townspeople flee after she predicts an earthquake, she stays, giving up her special gift for the sake of first love. This apocalyptic and inner-exile debut feature integrates various social and cultural elements into a magical fantasy that privileges the fringe and suggests, through its hyper-realistic imagery, that perspectives can be altered only by breaking the limits of reality. The film received good reviews and won the Israeli Film Academy Best Film Award and the Jury Prize at the Czech Karlovy Vary Film Festival.

Dim'at Hanechama Hagedola (literally 'Tears of Consolation') / The Great Promise

1947, 48 mins, black and white, English

Director: Joseph Leytes
Producer: Margot Klausner (JNF)
Screenwriter: Shulamit Bat-Dori
Cinematographer: Stanislave Lipensky
Leading Players: Shafrira Zakai

A Jewish soldier of the British Palestine Brigade in Europe arrives at a camp of Holocaust survivors and, in an attempt to convince the youngsters to emigrate to Palestine, tells them about the wonders of the kibbutz settlements in the Galilee. Consequently some survivors go to Israel, but cannot adjust to kibbutz life. In accordance with Zionist realism, this film highlights the success of one girl's attempts to integrate herself into the Zionist project, suggesting that Zionism is the ultimate shelter. The first post-war film to be produced in Palestine, this docu-drama was made by a director already noted in his Polish homeland. The film was distributed in the United States with a filmed introduction by the wife of Colonel Mickey Marcus, one of the heroes of the War of Independence. In 1952 Leytes made *Kirya Ne'emana / Faithful City*, recounting the experiences of young Holocaust survivors during the 1948 War of Independence.

Echad Mishelanu / One of Us

1989, 110 mins, colour, Hebrew
Director: Uri Barabash
Producer: Tzvi Spielman, Shlomo Mugrabi (Israfilm)
Screenwriter: Benny Barabash
Cinematographer: Amnon Salomon
Editor: Tova Asher
Music: Ilan Wurtzberg
Leading Players: Alon Aboutboul, Sharon Alexander, Dalia Shimko, Dan Toren, Arnon Tzadok

Rafa, a military investigator, arrives at an army base in the Occupied Territories to investigate the death of a Palestinian prisoner. There he confronts the commander, a friend from training days in the paratroops, who tries to cover up the affair. In the end the truth comes out, hurting all parties involved. This nihilistic allegory, which draws on similar accounts in the Israeli press, explored the evils of occupation and the outer edges of the army ethos, deconstructing its motto 'one for all and all for one' and asserting the moral stance of the individual over the collective. The film received mixed reviews, but did quite well at the box office and won the Israel Best Film Award.

Eddie King

1992, 92 mins, colour, Hebrew
Director: Gidi Dar
Producer: Rafi Bukaee, Gidi Dar
Screenwriter: Gidi Dar
Cinematographer: Ariel Semel

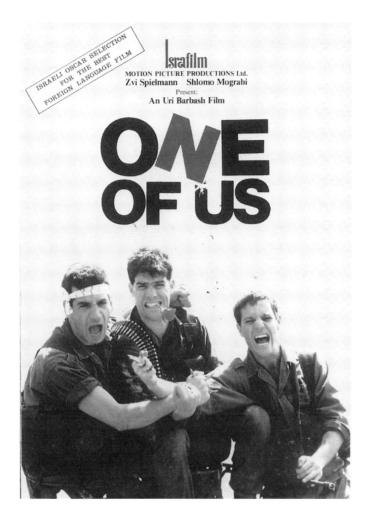

Figure 35 Echad Mishelanu / One of Us

Editor:	Dani Yitzhaki
Music:	Chen Harpaz
Leading Players:	Eitan Bloom, Shuli Rand, Ronit Elkabetz, Albert Iluz

Eddie, an out-of-work actor searching for a meaning in life, finds himself on a train going from Haifa to Tel Aviv in the company of two petty crooks and a *femme fatale* who are scheming to con a media tycoon. The police join in the game, but get no answers from Eddie. This post-modern discourse, joining other similar efforts of the 1990s, employs quotations from other films and cross-cuts between genres to form a pastiche that prevents direct access to either the crime plot or the life of the characters. The film-maker's definition echoes Godard: 'A gangster film without gangsters'. *Eddie King* received favourable reviews but poor box office (selling only 5,000 tickets), and won the Bronze Leopard in the Lucarno Film Festival.

Eduyot / Testimonies

1993, 55 mins, colour, Hebrew
Director / Screenwriter: Ido Sela
Producer: Amit Breuer
Cinematographer: Eitan Harris
Editor: Tamar Yaron

This documentary comprises a series of interviews with Israeli soldiers who served in the Occupied Territories during the *intifada* and raises the moral dilemmas involved in warfare against a civilian population. The soldiers, of various ethnic, cultural and economic backgrounds, recount brutal incidents in which they beat, shot at and tortured the Palestinian population. Their reflections and ambivalence, sometimes to the point of extreme self-reproach, draw a bleak picture of Israel's occupying practices *vis-à-vis* the Palestinians. This impression is accentuated by the black background against which the interviews are conducted, reminiscent of a prisoner's cell. This is one of the most unsettling films made on this issue and it was never broadcast in Israel.

83

1983, 87 mins, colour, Hebrew
Director: Ram Loevy, Shimo Dotan, Yigal Burstein, Judd Ne'eman
Producer: Nissim Zion
Screenwriter: Shimon Dotan, Yehusua Sobol, Yigal Burstein, Amnon Dankner, Ruhama Marton
Cinematographer: Yossi Wein, Daniel Shneur, Mossi Armon, Yachin Hirsh, Nurit Aviv, Arie Shlezinger, Emil Knebel
Editor: Netaya Inbar, Anat Lubarsky, Rahel Yagil, Tova Asher, Nelli Gilad
Leading Players: Misha Asherov, Yair Rubin, Dalik Volinitz, Moti Shirin, Ezra Kafri, Aviva Ger

A compilation of six short films, both documentaries and fiction, which focuses on the Israeli–Palestinian conflict. In 'Hisardut' / 'Survival' (Ram Loevy) an army officer gives a lecture on the advantage of nuclear weapons to the members of a deaf-mute association; 'Mazkarot Mi'Chevron / 'Memories from Hebron' (Shimon Dotan) exposes the helplessness and humiliation of an Israeli patrol in the Casbah of Hebron; 'Yisurav Shel Dr Vider' / 'The Suffering of Dr Vider' (Yigal Burstein) narrates the story of a Jewish physician who contracts Palestinian workers to reconstruct his apartment and is left with their excrement; in 'Ha'Layla Bo Nolad Ha'melech'/ 'The Night the King was Born' (Judd Ne'eman) two army officers and one Jewish real estate agent force a Palestinian peasant to give up his land; 'Villa' (Yigal Burstein) focuses on the massive building of Jewish settlements in the West Bank; 'Mazkarot Mi 'Tel-Aviv' / 'Memories from Tel Aviv' (Shimon Dotan) recounts the end of a major demonstration protesting against the Sabra–Shatilla massacre during the war with Lebanon. The films deal with the impact of occupation on Israeli society from different angles, employing different cinematic strategies and moving from documentary to absurd fiction. Some of the films privileged the

Palestinian characters, but most privileged the Israeli perspective, expressing the guilt felt by the liberal left. The censor banned the episode 'The Night the King was Born', claiming it was offensive to the Israeli army and would incite the Palestinians. Later a ruling by the supreme court allowed it to be screened.

Eldorado

1963, 88 mins, black and white, Hebrew
Director: Menachem Golan
Producer: Mordechai Navon
Screenwriter: Menachem Golan, Amatzia Hiuni, Leo Filler
Cinematographer: Nissim Leon
Editor: Nellie Gilad
Music: Yochanan Zarai
Leading Players: Haim Topol, Gila Almagor, Tikva Mor, Shaike Ophir, Yosef Yadin

Figure 36   Eldorado

Eldorado is a melodrama based on a play by Yigal Mossinson. An ex-convict finds a legitimate job and meets a young woman, the daughter of a lawyer, but his past pursues him in the form of his former girlfriend Margo, who is a prostitute, and his ex-partner, who tries to force him to return to his life of crime. This debut feature by Golan manifested an interest in genre film for the first time in Israeli cinema. The narrative follows the gangster-film formula and employs conventions from *film noir* to create a doomy atmosphere. At the same time Golan underscores ethnic tensions and thus foreshadows the Bourekas genre. *Eldorado* won the Israel Best Film Award and was a major box-office success, with audiences numbering some 600,000 people.

Emile Habibi: Nish'arti be'Haifa / Emile Habibi: I Stayed in Haifa

1997, 60 mins, colour, Hebrew and Arabic
Director / Screenwriter: Dalia Karpel
Producer: Marek Rosenbaum, Dalia Karpel
Cinematographer: Noam Tayech
Editor: Anat Lubarsky

A portrait of a Palestinian-Israeli author – prominent in modern Arabic literature – during the last weeks of his life. Habibi, a resident of Nazareth, was an MP for the Israel Communist Party for nineteen years and an Israel Prize for Literature laureate. This travelogue confronts Habibi at significant places in his life: Haifa, Jerusalem and Acre (important for his homecoming after 1948). The title echoes the memorial words on his tombstone in Haifa.

Eskimo Limone / Lemon Popsicle

1978, 95 mins, colour, Hebrew
Director: Boaz Davidson
Producer: Menachem Golan, Yoram Globus (Noah Films)
Screenwriter: Boaz Davidson, Eli Tavor
Cinematographer: Adam Greenberg
Editor: Alain Yakubowitch
Musical Adviser: Uri Aloni
Leading Players: Yiftach Katzur, Yonathan Segal, Tzachi Noy, Anat Atzmon, Ophelia Shtruhl

At the end of the 1950s, three high-school students in Tel Aviv are enjoying themselves having sex and listening to music. Sensitive Bentsi falls in love with Nili, but she is seduced by Momo and gets pregnant by him. This comedy about youth and growing up broke all box-office records in Israel (over 1,100,000 tickets were sold). This was the ninth feature film by Davidson, who had previously made Bourekas films. The success of the film – due also to its nostalgic soundtrack and the young cast, several of whom later became major film stars – bred seven sequels, all extremely popular in Israel, as well as in Germany, Japan and South Africa. It also started the careers of Golan and Globus in Hollywood. *Eskimo Limone* won the Israel Best Film Award.

Etz o Palestine (literally 'Tree or Palestine', meaning 'Heads or Tails') | The True Story of Palestine

1962, 80 mins, black and white, Hebrew
Director: Nathan Axelrod, Yoel Zilberg, Uri Zohar
Producer: Nathan Axelrod, Avraham Deshe
Screenwriter: Haim Hefer
Cinematographer: Nathan Axelrod
Editor: Lea Axelrod
Music: Yitzhak Graciani
Narration: Haim Topol, Ori Levi

This is a compilation of episodes from Carmel newsreels made by Nathan Axelrod from the beginning of the 1930s until the establishment of the state of Israel. This humorous and nostalgic anthology shows classic images of Zionist realism, such as draining the swamps, establishing the kibbutzim, protesting against the British, bringing illegal immigrants into the country, building Tel Aviv harbour, entertainment and sporting events, and various public figures (including prominent statesmen like David Ben Gurion). The re-editing and modern narration make this an ironic look at the spirit of the 1960s. *Etz o Palestine* won critical and commercial success, with sales of 351,000 tickets.

Ezrach Amerikayi | American Citizen

1992, 100 mins, colour, Hebrew and English
Director / Screenwriter: Eitan Green
Producer: Marek Rosenbaum
Cinematographer: Daniel Shneur
Editor: Era Lapid
Music: Adi Renart
Leading Players: Guy Garner, Yicho Avital, Eva Hadad, Baruch David

A drama in which Yoel, an epileptic sports reporter for a local newspaper in the small coastal town of Ashdod, befriends Michael, a new player for the local basketball team. The narrative unfolds the relationship between the young Israeli who worships the NBA and the older American who has known better times, and offers a portrayal of male bonding unlike the usual Israeli bonding based on the battlefield or sexual escapades. As in his other films, Green is interested in the human aspect and the basketball is employed only as a backdrop. The film received favourable reviews but disappointing box office (only 25,000 tickets were sold). It was entered for the Los Angeles and Shanghai Film Festivals.

Florentine

1997, television series, colour, Hebrew
Series creator: Udi Zamberg, Eitan Fuchs
Director (first season): Eitan Fuchs
Series producer: Udi Zamberg, Michael Tapuach

Supervising screenwriter: Ido Bornstein

This television drama series paints a group portrait of young urbanites who live in Florentine, a Soho-like neighbourhood of Tel Aviv, in the months prior to the assassination of Yitzhak Rabin. The series follows the dramas in their lives, coloured by 'me generation' indifference to political and social problems and the pursuit of love, sex and artistic ambitions. Nevertheless, some general topics do engage the characters, since they have direct impact on their lives: homosexuality, gender issues, the generation gap and, of course, anything to do with culture (particularly music and cinema). The polished look of the series, keeping up with current trends in fashion and design, draws a neat picture of contemporary Israeli society. Here the inner-exile theme is almost caricatured, suggesting that, after all, there is more that unifies than divides in a multimedia culture.

Fortuna

1966, 115 mins, black and white, Hebrew
Director:	Menachem Golan
Producer:	Micha Cagan, Meir Dagan, Menachem Golan
Screenwriter:	Yoseph Gross, Menachem Golan, Alexander Ramati, Volodia Smitiov
Cinematographer:	Yitzhak Herbst
Editor:	Dani Shick
Music:	Dov Seltzer
Leading Players:	Pierre Brasseur, Ahuva Goren, Shmuel Kraus, Mike Marshall, Yossi Banai

Fortuna, a daughter of a patriarchal Jewish Algerian family who live in a development town in the Negev desert, is in love with a young French engineer. Her father insists on her marrying an old man to whom she was promised in the old country. Her attempt to escape the arranged marriage ends in tragedy. This Bourekas melodrama, based on a short story by Menachem Talmi, foregrounds ethnic and class tensions, portraying the North African Jews as largely violent and backward, a stereotype typical of Golan's films that reflects the bias of the Sabras and European Jews against the massive 1950s immigration from North Africa. As in Golan's other films, the woman is objectified and fetishized: this was the first Israeli film to show nudity in abundance. The film received good reviews and excellent box office (some 630,000 tickets were sold).

Gemar Gavia / Cup Final

1991, 107 mins, colour, Hebrew and Arabic
Director:	Eran Riklis
Producer:	Micha Sharfstein
Screenwriter:	Eyal Halfon (from an idea by Eran Riklis)
Cinematographer:	Amnon Salomon
Editor:	Anat Lubarsky

| Music: | Raviv Gazit |
| Leading Players: | Moshe Ivgi, Muhammed Bakri, Salim Dau, Yousuf Abu-Varda, Suheil Hadad |

Cohen, an owner of a fashion shop, is about to fly to Spain for the soccer cup match when he receives a reserve duty call to Lebanon. His patrol encounters a Palestinian ambush and he is taken prisoner by PLO fighters. This war drama employs the Lebanon War as a topic as well as a backdrop for exploring the relationship between Israelis and Palestinians, here turning from open hostility to familiarity and even comradeship born of a common enthusiasm for soccer. The film's portrayal of the PLO fighters (played by Israeli–Palestinian actors), although stereotypical, is still in accordance with the Israeli-Palestinian conflict films, granting identity and space to the 'other' and negotiating a dialogue. By reversing roles the narrative questions the supremacy of Israel and its policies, and the film's images of smoky alleys of refugee camps and uninhabited ruins help put across its dead-end pessimism. *Gemar Gavia* received mixed reviews but did very well at the box office (selling 600,000 tickets) and earned the Silver Palm in the Valencia Film Festival and the Grand Prix in the Salerno Film Festival.

Gesher Tsar Me'od (literally 'A Very Narrow Bridge') / On a Narrow Bridge

1985, 100 mins, colour, Hebrew
Director:	Nissim Dayan
Producer:	Micha Sharfstein
Screenwriter:	Haim Hefer, Nissim Dayan
Cinematographer:	Amnon Salomon
Editor:	Dani Shik
Music:	Poldi Shetzman
Leading Players:	Aharon Ipale, Salwa Nakara-Haddad, Markam Khoury, Uri Gavriel

Gesher Tsar Me'od is based on a story by Haim Hefer. Benny, a reserve military prosecutor for the administration in the occupied West Bank, falls in love with Leila, the school librarian from a prominent Christian Palestinian family in Ramallah. Due to fierce opposition they are forced to separate. This political melodrama, focusing on Israeli–Palestinian conflict and re-establishing Dayan's interest in doomed relationships, as well as the affinity between oriental Jews and Arab culture, was the first Israeli feature to be shot in the Occupied Territories. The film joins other political films of the 1980s in condemning the occupation and attempting to construct a dialogue, its story of doomed love objectifying the impossibility of co-existence. The film's design emphasizes the Byzantine architecture of Ramallah, foregrounding pre-Muslim Christianity. The production, amid stone throwing and threats of terrorist action, was discussed widely in the media, but the film received mixed reviews and poor box office (only some 23,000 tickets were sold).

Giv'a 24 Eina Ona / Hill 24 Doesn't Answer

1954, 101 mins, black and white, English
Director: Thorold Dickinson
Producer: Thorold Dickinson, Peter Frye, Zvi Kolitz
Screenwriter: Tzvi Kolitz, Peter Frye
Cinematographer: Gerald Gibbs
Editor: Joanna Dickinson, Thorold Dickinson
Music: Paul Ben Haim
Leading Players: Yitzhak Shilo, Edward Mulhare, Michael Wager, Zalman
                                       Levioush, Margalit Oved, Haya Hararit

Giv'a 24 Eina Ona is based on stories by Zvi Kolitz. Several hours before the ceasefire
in the 1948 War of Independence, a group of four soldiers sets out to secure a hill on
the road to Jerusalem. The film opens with the image of the dead soldiers and unfolds
as a flashback, recounting their experiences as the basis for their commitment to the
Zionist cause. This heroic–nationalist master-narrative underscores the central theme
of this genre: the glorification of self-sacrifice for the homeland. The narrative underscores themes of 'the few against the many' and 'good versus evil' as a broad
ideological basis for the exhausting 1948 war with its heavy casualties. This US–Israeli
big-budget co-production originated with Margot Klausner and was backed by WIZO
(Women's International Zionist Organization). One of the first to focus on the War of
Independence, the film was given a warm reception and was shown in many European
capitals.

Givat Halfon Eina Ona / Halfon Hill Doesn't Answer

1976, 92 mins, colour, Hebrew
Director: Assi Dayan
Producer: Naftali Alter, Yitzhak Shani
Screenwriter: Assi Dayan, Naftali Alter
Cinematographer: Ya'akov Kallach
Editor: David Tour
Music: Naftali Alter
Leading Players: Yisrael Poliakov, Shaike Levy, Gavri Banai, Tuvia Tzafir,
                                       Nitza Shaul

Gingy, who serves on an army base in the Sinai desert, is ordered to bring back a
defector. On his way back, his girlfriend sneaks into the luggage compartment of the
car. Her father follows her and is taken hostage by the Egyptians, only to be released
by Israeli soldiers disguised in UN uniforms. This outright farce mocks the absurdities
of military discipline, the traditional values of family, Biblical myths and Israeli
machismo. The anarchistic narrative employs slapstick and caricature to camouflage
its subversive text. The film's huge success (selling some 670,000 tickets) was also due
to the participation of Hagashah Hahiver ('The Pale Tracker'), a successful entertainment trio. *Givat Halfon Eina Ona* received mixed reviews but, in time, became a cult
movie.

Golem Bama'agal / Blind Man's Bluff

1993, 95 mins, colour, Hebrew

Director:	Aner Preminger
Producer:	Haim Sharir
Screenwriter:	Tal Zilberstein, Aner Preminger
Cinematographer:	Ya'akov Eisenman
Editor:	Tova Asher
Music:	Haim Permont
Leading Players:	Hagit Dasberg, Nicole Castel, Gedalia Besser, Anat Waxman, Dani Litani

Miki, a gifted pianist, prepares for her graduation recital at the music academy, while at the same time having to cope with her Holocaust-survivor mother, her former boyfriend and her new lover, a pub singer. This rites of passage drama, which pays homage to Truffaut, focuses on the emotional tribulations of love, but also brings to the surface the wound of the Holocaust and examines its consequences for the second generation. *Golem Bama'agal* won the Wolgin Prize at the Jerusalem Film Festival and Best Film at the Montpellier Film Festival.

Ha'ayit / The Vulture

1981, 95 mins, colour, Hebrew

Director / Producer / Screenwriter:	Yaki Yosha
Cinematographer:	Ilan Rosenberg
Editor:	Yaki Yosha, Anat Lubarsky
Music:	Doron Salomon
Leading Players:	Shraga Harpaz, Shimon Finkel, Ami Weinberg, Nitza Shaul

Ha'ayit is based on a story by Yoram Kaniuk. Boaz, an army officer fighting in the Yom Kippur War, sees his friend fall in battle. When he returns to Tel Aviv he produces forged poems to please the friend's father and consequently becomes involved in the commemoration of war heroes through a mini-industry of memorial albums. This nihilistic drama, the first to deal with the traumas of the Yom Kippur War, refutes the patriotic ethos and self-sacrifice ideology, and the film's rhetoric, by repeatedly displaying the moment of death in combat and employing documentary footage, constructs a post-traumatic picture in the spirit of other 1980s films. Yet it stands out through its outraged iconoclasm over the memorialization of the fallen and in its portrayal of a cynical, promiscuous and sometimes brutal protagonist – a caricature of the heroic Sabra. The film stirred up a bitter dispute among the Israeli public and government officials pressurized the censor to ban it. Later, the producers had difficulties finding theatres that would show the film and, when it was finally screened, there were further protests and attempts to stop it being shown. Reviews were mixed and the film did poorly at the box office, with only 17,000 tickets sold.

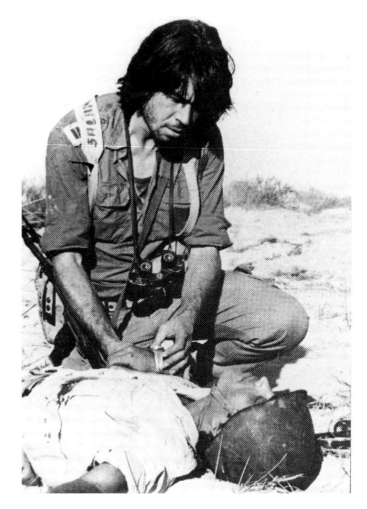

Figure 37 Ha'ayit / The Vulture

Habanana Hashchora / The Black Banana

1976, 90 mins, colour, Hebrew / Yiddish / Arabic / English
Director: Benjamin Hayeem
Producer: Benjamin Hayeem, Ellis Hayeem
Screenwriter: Benjamin Hayeem, Alexander Klein
Cinematographer: Emil Knebel
Editor: Benjamin Hayeem
Music: Moritz Osherovich
Leading Players: Danny Kinrot, Orna Orshan, Erik Menkin, Pnina Menkin,
                       Jesse Nachiesi

Habanana Hashchora is a slapstick comedy in which a hippy Yeshiva boy is smuggled by Hassidic Jews from the United States back to Israel in a coffin so that he can wed a woman who claims he impregnated her. In Israel he gets involved in a series of wild encounters with Arabs, kibbutz members and Texan millionaires, all of whom keep bumping into each other until the happy ending. This new sensibility avant-garde farce conjugates the various components of Israeli society into an absurd narrative that parodies the melting-pot ideal of Zionism, but at the same time admits to an almost childish enthusiasm for the same ideal. The scandalous mixture of nudity, cannabis and orthodox Jews caused the censorship board to ban the film, but the ban was lifted after the director made minor changes. The production itself was also unusual, with the director establishing a board of trustees and distributing shares to the public. The film received mixed reviews and fared poorly at the box office. Hayeem subsequently made several short films and then returned to the United States.

Habayit Berehov Shelush / *The House on Shelush Street*

1973, 110 mins, colour, Hebrew
Director: Moshe Mizrachi
Producer: Menachem Golan
Screenwriter: Moshe Mizrachi, Yerach Guber, Rachel Fabian
Cinematographer: Adam Greenberg
Editor: Dov Hoenig
Music: Dov Seltzer
Leading Players: Gila Almagor, Ofer Shalhin, Michal Bat-Adam, Yosef Shiloah, Shaike Ophir

Clara is a widow with four children in late 1940s Tel Aviv. During a period of curfew and underground activities against the British, she strives to maintain the integrity of her family. Her fifteen-year-old son is having an affair with a young kibbutz divorcee and, in attempt to sabotage this relationship, she sends him to work in a factory where he is politicized. This story, based on Mizrachi's youth, focuses on the disintegration of old traditions in the face of modern Sabra values and mourns the rupture between Jews and Arabs through hostile acts that foreshadow the 1948 War of Independence. Mizrachi employs new sensibility practices, drawing on Italian neo-realism. The film received favourable reviews and a relatively good box office (approximately 270,000 tickets). It won the Israel Best Film Award and was nominated for an Oscar in the Foreign Language Film category.

Habchira Ve'hagoral / *Choice and Destiny*

1993, 118 mins, colour, Yiddish
Director / Producer / Screenwriter: Tzipi Reibenbach
Cinematographer: Avi Koren, David Gurfinkel
Editor: Ziva Postek

The parents of the female director – eighty-year-old Itzhak and seventy-two-year-old Fruma, both Holocaust survivors – are the subjects of this documentary. The father, who was a forced labourer in the crematorium and gas chambers at the Matthausen death camp, recounts his experiences there while the mother sits silently next to him. The director follows her parents through their daily routine, a good deal of which has to do with food preparation and eating, rituals that intensify the subtext of hunger in the camps. The film's slow pace and repeated rituals, along with its intimate shots, creates a full-blown picture of two tortured individuals, thus transcending its time and place. *Habchira Ve'hagoral* won the Grand Prix at the Yamagata Film Festival in Japan, the Jury Award in Amsterdam, as well as mentions in the Lyon and Jerusalem Film Festivals. It is also on the curriculum of film schools in various countries.

Hachaim Al Pi Agfa / Life According to Agfa

1992, 100 mins, black and white, Hebrew

Director / Screenwriter:	Assi Dayan
Producer:	Yoram Kislev, Rafi Bukaee
Cinematographer:	Yoav Kosh
Editor:	Zohar Sela
Music:	Naftali Alter
Leading Players:	Gila Almagor, Shuli Rand, Irit Frank, Avital Dicker, Dani Litani

This drama narrates the story of one night in a Tel Aviv pub, where the middle-aged owner lives for borrowed moments with her married lover, while the barwoman documents the events with her camera and the waitress retreats to cocaine. Two Palestinians work in the kitchen and a pianist sings pacifist blues. The appearance of an aggressive group of army soldiers disturbs the balance and, after they are kicked out of the pub, they return and spray the place with bullets. Dayan's stylized nightmare of self-annihilation, moulded after *Casablanca*, is at the same time the negation and conclusion of the Zionist utopia. The bloody closing scene neutralizes the intolerable tensions between men and women, Sephardi and Ashkenazi, Jews and Arabs. The doomsday missionaries are Israeli army officers, once delegates of the heroic–nationalist ethos, here dislocated and maimed, the murderous horsemen of the apocalypse. The anarchistic mood stands out as a philosophical credo, reflecting the bleak political mood of 1990s Israel. The film was received with almost unanimous acclaim and did moderately well at the box office (selling 200,000 tickets). Subsequently Dayan completed two more films to form a trilogy. *Hachaim Al Pi Agfa* won the Israel Film Academy Best Film Award, as well as receiving mentions in the Jerusalem and Berlin Film Festivals, and was entered for the film festivals in Toronto, Montpellier, Calcutta and Singapore.

Hachaverim Shel Yana / Yana's Friends

1999, 90 mins, colour, Hebrew and Russian

Director:	Arik Kaplun
Producer:	Uri Sabag, Einat Bikel, Marek Rosenbaum, Moshe Levinson
Screenwriter:	Arik Kaplun, Simeon Vinokur
Cinematographer:	Valentin Belanogov

Editor: Tali Halter, Einat Glazer-Zarhin
Music: Avi Binyamin
Leading Players: Nir Levy, Evlyn Kaplun, Smil Ben-Ari, Moscu Alcalay,
                           Dalia Fridland

Yana, a young Russian Jew who lands in Tel Aviv during the 1991 Gulf War, soon finds herself pregnant and alone, sharing a cramped apartment with Eli, a wedding photographer, who secretly videotapes her during intimate moments. The ensuing terrible fight between them is interrupted by a missile attack which forces the two back to the sealed room and a passionate reconciliation. This surreal drama turned romantic comedy, affiliated with the inner-exile films, was made by an immigrant from Russia and privileges the massive Russian immigration of the early 1990s. It goes beyond that, however, to deal with universal dreams of home and love in the face of war, dislocation and the barriers of language / culture. The film makes use of Tel Aviv's specific locality and relates to Israel cinematic genres, but also employs the conventions of popular situation comedy and the metacinematic use of photography. *Hachaverim Shel Yana* won the Israel Film Academy Best Film Award, the Wolgin Award at the Jerusalem Film Festival and the Grand Prize at the Czech Karlovy Vary Film Festival.

Hacholmim (a.k.a. 'The Dreamers', literal translation) / Unsettled Land

1987, 109 mins, colour, English
Director: Uri Barabash
Producer: Ben Elkerbout, Ludi Boeken, Katriel Shehori
Screenwriter: Benny Barabash, Eran Preis
Cinematographer: Amnon Salomon

Figure 38   Hacholmim / Unsettled Land

Editor:	Tova Asher
Music:	Misha Segal
Leading Players:	John Shea, Arnon Tzadok, Kelly McGillis, Cristine Boisson, Ohad Shachar

A group of pioneers who have settled in the Galilee aspire to build a new society, but see their dream shattered in the face of sexual and ideological tensions within the group and hostility from nearby Arab villagers. An attempt to build trust with their neighbours fails and the drama ends in bloodshed. This Israeli–Dutch big-budget co-production (US$2 million) with Hollywood stars is a contemporary dissident remake of two Zionist classic master-narrative films: *Tzabar / Sabra* (1933) and *Hem Hayu Asara / They Were Ten* (1960). The narrative substitutes the Zionist utopia of the earlier films with a dystopic vision, as its protagonists fail to execute the Zionist project and either leave or die. Unlike the earlier films, the land here is inhabited, the Arab Sheikh is accorded authority and a sense of moderation, and the plight of the individual rather than the collective is made explicit. The film received poor reviews and poor box office (only selling some 5,000 tickets), but gained worldwide distribution.

Haderech LeEin Harod (literally 'The Road to Ein Harod') / *The Voice of Ein Harod*

1990, 91 mins, colour, English

Director:	Doron Eran
Producer:	Doron Eran, Yoram Kislev
Screenwriter:	Rami Na'aman
Cinematographer:	Avi Karpic
Editor:	Irit Raz
Music:	Ilan Wurtzburg
Leading Players:	Tony Peck, Alessandra Mussolini, Arnon Tzadok, Rami Danon, Shlomo Tarshis

This drama was based on a novel by Amos Keinan. A young journalist flees Tel Aviv and makes his way to the Ein Harod kibbutz in the north of the country – the last resort of the underground forces fighting the ruling junta. After forcing an escaped Palestinian prisoner to be his guide, he arrives at his destination to find the place deserted. This bleak narrative joins a series of dystopian apocalyptic narratives which called for the abolition of the Zionist project. Its thematics are reinforced by cold, bluish lighting and *film noir* compositions. 'The voice' of the English title refers to the last of the pioneers, an old radioman broadcasting humanistic messages from the ruins of Zionism. This big-budget production (US$800,000) suffered a bitter critical and commercial failure.

Hagamal Hame'ofef / *The Flying Camel*

1994, 93 mins, colour, Hebrew

Director / Screenwriter:	Rami Na'aman
Producer:	Marek Rosenbaum

Cinematographer:	Yoav Kosh
Editor:	Tova Asher
Music:	Shem-Tov Levy
Leading Players:	Gideon Zinger, Salim Dau, Laurence Bouvard, Gilat Ankori

This fable focuses on two friends – Bauman, a Jew and former history professor who lives in a shack in a junkyard and collects Bauhaus artifacts, and Phares, an Arab garbage collector who dreams of replanting his father's orange grove – and their joint mission of restoring a statue from the 1930s of a flying camel – a symbol of Tel Aviv. This typically post-political film of the 1990s entangles the Israeli–Palestinian conflict with a fantastic angel and reunites the rivals in a reconstruction of the past, using the nostalgic statue of the flying camel as an icon of hope for the future.

Hagiga La'einayim (literally 'What a Sight') / Saint Cohen

1975, 86 mins, colour, Hebrew

Director:	Assi Dayan
Producer:	Naftali Alter
Music:	Naftali Alter
Screenwriter:	Assi Dayan, Naftali Alter
Cinematographer:	Ya'akov Kallach
Editor:	David Tour
Leading Players:	Yoseph Shiloah, Talia Shapira, Avner Hizkiyahu, Miriam Gavrieli

Shaul, a young poet, retreats to a small town in the Galilee where he attempts to commit suicide, but the residents of the town save his life. When they find out that he is a national figure they scheme over how to kill him, but in the meantime he finds his *raison d'être* in the arms of a local girl. This satire employs the absurd in order to high-light the pettiness and greediness of the provinces, which emerge as a microcosm of an Israeli society that is obsessed with their passion for national icons. The film's new sensibility practices are atypical of Dayan's work in this period – he was mostly devoted to popular comedies. Despite favourable reviews, its screening was postponed for two years due to the onset of the Yom Kippur War and it then failed at the box office, selling only 5,000 tickets.

Haglula / The Pill

1972, 93 mins, black and white, Hebrew

Director:	David Perlov
Producer:	Joseph Hershenzon
Screenwriter:	Nissim Aloni
Cinematographer:	Adam Greenberg
Editor:	Jean-Claude Zarbiv, Dov Hoenig, Jacques Erlich
Music:	Yochanan Zarai
Leading Players:	Yossi Banai, Avner Hizkiyahu, Gideon Zinger, Germain Unikovsky

Ganz, an easy-going entertainer, swallows a pill of youth and instantly becomes a mass idol. When he feels the effect of the pill wearing off, he swallows an entire jar and starts to fly. This new sensibility satire, the only fiction film by noted documentarist David Perlov, integrates modernistic aesthetics with a fantastic narrative. The cold, calculated direction acts against the vaudeville elements and the outcome is a peculiar farce that pokes fun at the idolization of youth. Production took four years and the film received polarized reviews and poor box office (only 22,000 tickets were sold).

Hakaitz Shel Aviya / The Summer of Aviya

1988, 95 mins, colour, Hebrew
Director:	Eli Cohen
Producer:	Eitan Evan, Gila Almagor
Screenwriter:	Gila Almagor, Haim Buzaglo, Elli Cohen
Cinematographer:	David Gurfinkel
Editor:	Tova Ne'eman
Music:	Shem-Tov Levy
Leading Players:	Gila Almagor, Kaipo Cohen, Marina Rosetti, Elli Cohen, Avital Dicker

Hakaitz Shel Aviya is based on a autobiographical novel and a play by Gila Almagor. Aviya, a ten-year-old girl, returns from her boarding school to spend the summer holiday of 1951 with her mother (played by Almagor), a mentally unstable Holocaust survivor. The other children avoid Aviya and she clings to a stranger, who is new to the neighbourhood, imagining that he is her father. The film focuses on the shadow of the repressed horrors of the Holocaust and on the patronizing attitudes of Israeli society, suggesting that mother and daughter reflect the inadequacies of society rather then their own. *Hakaitz Shel Aviya* did moderately well at the box office (selling approximately 200,000 tickets) and won critical acclaim in Israel, as well as the Silver Bear at the Berlin Film Festival and the Grand Prix at the Belgrade Film Festival. In 1995 Almagor and Cohen joined up again to make the sequel *Etz Hadomim Tafus / Under the Domim Tree*, which portrayed Aviya when she was older.

Hakochav Hakahol / Planet Blue

1995, 86 mins, colour, Hebrew
Director:	Gur Bentwich
Producer:	Gur Bentwich, Zohar Dinar, Alon Aboutboul
Screenwriter:	Zohar Dinar, Orli Liberman, Gur Bentwich
Cinematographer:	Alon Eilat
Editor:	Ayelet Ofarim, Sacha Franklyn
Music:	Hajs Vroom, Gong
Leading Players:	Alon Aboutboul, Zohar Dienar, Nirit Katzenstein, Ilan Pathi

On his way to Cairo, Muly leaves his backpack with one of the pedlars in the central bus station of Tel Aviv. When the pedlar disappears, Muly adopts his identity and embarks on a fantastic voyage in which he encounters various eccentrics, all hoping to reach Planet Blue. This fantastic road movie, which employs underground strategies and focuses on the quest for meaning by young Israelis in a world devoid of ideologies, signifies the new inner-exile cinema of the 1990s, weary of politics and seeking answers in New Age philosophy. The film took three years to produce and was screened in small theatres without publicity. In time it became a cult movie.

Hakomediantim / Komediant / The Comedians

1999, 80 mins, colour, Hebrew / English / Yiddish
Director: Arnon Goldifinger
Producer: Amir Harel
Screenwriter: Oshra Schwartz
Cinematographer: Yoram Milo
Editor: Einat Glazer-Zarhin

This documentary narrates the story of Yiddish theatre from the beginning of the century, as reflected through the Burstein family: father Pessach and the mother Lillian, stars of the Yiddish theatre on Broadway during the hey-day of Yiddish theatre during the 1920s and 1930s, and their twin children Mike and Susan, who joined their parents on stage. At times, the Bursteins look like heroes of a Jewish melodrama, one of many that they had played on stage. The film won Best Documentary Award from the Israel Film Academy.

Halahaka (a.k.a. 'The Troupe', literal translation) / Sing Your Heart Out

1978, 110 mins, colour, Hebrew
Director: Avi Nesher
Producer: Yitzhak Kol
Screenwriter: Avi Nesher, Sharon Harel
Cinematographer: Ya'akov Kelach
Editor: Yitzhak Tzchayek
Music: Yair Rosenblum
Leading Players: Gidi Gov, Liron Nirgad, Meir Suissa, Dafna Armoni, Gali Atari

This musical comedy unfolds the intrigues within a military entertainment troupe during the 1970s war of attrition between Israel and Egypt. Three newcomers confront the hostility of the older members and, between shows, the members of the group go through a series of crises due to intense competition and sexual and personal frictions. This debut feature, saturated with nostalgia for the popular songs of the army entertainment troupes, is a group portrait coloured with narcissism, male chauvinism and cynicism, all of which cover up naïvety and vulnerability. The new Sabra emerges as an Israeli variant of the 'me generation'. *Halahaka* received favourable reviews and huge box office (some 570,000 tickets), in time becoming a cult movie. It won several prestigious awards and was distributed widely in the United States.

Hamilchama Le'achar Hamilchama / The War After the War

1969, 85 mins, black and white, Hebrew
Director: Micha Shagrir
Producer: David Goldstein
Screenwriter: Moshe Hadar
Cinematographer: Amnon Salomon, Yechiel Ne'eman
Editor: Nira Omri
Music: Nahum Heiman
Narration: Yaron London, Elimelech Ram, Rivka Michaeli, Daniel
                             Pe'er

This heroic–nationalist documentary was shot during the euphoria following the 1967
Six Day War. While Israeli soldiers fight a war of attrition on the Suez Canal and
chase PLO fighters along the Jordanian border, the UN mediator Gounar Yaring
jumps from one country to another, in Tel Aviv people celebrate in discotheques and
in Jerusalem they invade the eastern city with its restaurants and markets. Two
wounded men, an Israeli paratrooper and a PLO fighter, are treated in an Israeli
hospital, lying next to each other. This epic account of war and peace supports Israel's
post-war policies, sometimes with explicit propaganda. It received good reviews and
relatively good box office (150,000 tickets).

Hamsin (a.k.a. 'Eastern Wind', English for 'Hamsin')

1982, 90 mins, colour, Hebrew
Director: Daniel Wachsmann
Producer: Ya'akov Lifshin
Screenwriter: Daniel Wachsmann, Dan Verte, Ya'akov Lifshin
Cinematographer: David Gurfinkel
Editor: Levi Zini
Music: Raviv Gazit
Leading Players: Shlomo Tarshish, Yasin Shawap, Hemda Levy, Ruth Geller,
                             Shmuel Shilo

Gedalya, a Jewish farmer who raises cattle in the Galilee, offers to purchase a piece of
barren land from his Arab neighbours. This incites a violent reaction from Arab
youths and eventually the land is confiscated by the state. In the meantime the
farmer's sister is having an affair with his Palestinian-Israeli farmhand and the
outraged farmer sets a stud bull on him. This was the first feature film to focus on the
Jewish–Arabic conflict within Israel, a topic usually underplayed in Israeli cinema.
The drama highlights the primary sin of Zionism: the colonial appropriation of Arab
land by Jews. It thus cracks the smooth surface of the relationship between the two
nations, foregrounding nationalistic zeal and exploring prejudice and sexual taboos.
The film's suffocating mood and its tragic denouement do not allow for any hope.
Hamsin received favourable reviews but only modest box office (some 100,000 tickets),
and the censor limited the audience to eighteen years or older due to the violent
scenes. The film won the Israel Best Film Award, the Silver Leopard at the Lucarno
Film Festival and a human rights prize at the Strasbourg Film Festival. While it was

screened in the Israeli Film Festival in New York, the Israeli consul did not attend the screening, claiming that it damaged Israel's image.

Hanashim Mimul / *The Women Next Door*

1992, 84 mins, colour, Hebrew and Arabic
Director / Screenwriter / Producer: Michal Aviad
Cinematographer: Yvonne Miklosh
Editor: Era Lapid
Music: Shlomo Mizrachi

The director, her female cameraperson and a female Palestinian assistant director set out to shoot a series of encounters with women from both sides of the Israeli–Palestinian conflict. This documentary discloses how Palestinian women cope with military occupation carried out by men and how the implications of a militaristic chauvinistic society affect Israeli women. Two memorable scenes are a dialogue with a Palestinian activist, disrupted by Israeli soldiers, and the monologue of a young Israeli woman, who as a soldier was in charge of stripping and searching Palestinian women at a border crossing. The film won mentions at the film festivals in Chicago and Berlin, and at the International Women's Film Festival in Barcelona.

Hasimla / *The Dress*

1969, 80 mins, black and white, Hebrew
Director / Producer: Judd Ne'eman (Israfilm)
Screenwriter: Orna Spector, Rachel Ne'eman, Judd Ne'eman
Cinematographer: Yachin Hirsch
Editor: Tova Biran, Nellie Gilad
Music: The Churchills (Israeli rock band)
Leading Players: Assi Dayan, Liora Rivlin, Motti Barkan, Yair Rubin, Gabi Eldor Amir Urian

This film comprises three separate episodes that portray the lives of young people in 1960s Tel Aviv. 'Hasimla' / 'The Dress' describes a day in the life of a young librarian who buys an expensive dress to impress an acquaintance who prefers her roommate. 'Hamikhtav' / 'The Letter' narrates the story of a bored young clerk who places a lonely hearts ad but fails to win the love of the woman he selects. In 'Thomas Khozer' / 'Thomas Returns' a young actor, thrown out of his apartment, joins his estranged wife and her boyfriend in a *ménage à trois* – an homage to *Jules et Jim*. These three vignettes focus on the quest for love and the need for self-exploration, underscoring the personal and favouring mood over drama. The film employs typical French new wave strategies such as using hand-held cameras, shooting on location and improvisation. This European sensibility, later entitled the 'new sensibility' by Ne'eman (a term applied to all personal films made in Israel during that period), won the film favourable press but poor box office (the film sold some 24,000 tickets). The film was entered in the Cannes, Berlin and San Francisco Film Festivals.

Hayam Ha'acharon / *The Last Sea*

1980, 100 mins, black and white, Yiddish / English / French
Director / Screenwriter: Haim Gouri, Jacques Ehrlich, David Bergman
Producer: Beit Lohamei Haghettaot (Ghetto Fighters' Museum)
Editor: Jacques Ehrlich
Music: Yossi Mar-Haim

Edited from authentic footage, this documentary narrates the story of illegal Jewish immigration from Europe after World War II. It follows in the footsteps of Holocaust survivors gathered from all over Europe, who embark on rundown ships on their way to Palestine where they try to break the British blockade. The film illustrates the atmosphere and living conditions on the crowded ships, and shows the immigrants' emotional responses on arriving in Palestine. It employs interviews with the survivors and the Zionist emissaries that guided them, as well as with British policemen, integrating the illegal immigration into the heroic–nationalist ethos and reassessing the Zionist ideology for the 1970s. This is a second film in a trilogy based entirely on documentary footage retrieved from archives and newsreels in Israel, Europe and the United States. The press welcomed the film.

Hayei HaYehudim Be'Eretz Yisrael / *Life of the Jews in Palestine*

1914, 77 mins, black and white, silent
Director / Producer: Noah Sokolowsky (Mizrach Co.)
Cinematographer: Miron Osip Grossman

The first documentary shot in Ottoman Palestine that portrayed scenes of the everyday life of the Zionist colonies and communes. Russian Zionist Sokolowsky began shooting on board his ship *en route* from Odessa to Palestine. The left-wing Hebrew press claimed that the film falsified reality because it showed Jewish colonists posing as workers when they in fact employed Arab and Jewish labourers. The film premiered at the 11th Zionist Congress in 1914, was shown at Zionist gatherings and cinema houses in Eastern Europe, and even reached New York. The original nitrate negative, lost after World War I, was found in 1997 in France and restored at the Israeli Film Archive.

Hedva Veshlomik / *Hedva and Shlomik*

1971, television mini-series, black and white, Hebrew
Director: Shmuel Imberman
Producer: Israeli Television
Screenwriter: Orna Spector, Yehonatan Gefen
Leading Players: Menachem Zilberman, Yael Aviv, Tuvia Tzafir, Yossi Greber,
                   Lea Keonig

This satire, based on a novel by Aharon Meged, was the first Israeli television series to be produced in Israel. It narrates the story of a young couple who leave the kibbutz and arrive in Tel Aviv – at a time when leaving a kibbutz was considered a betrayal of

Zionist ideology. The naïve, clumsy protagonist tries his luck at all kinds of work, only to find himself again and again in conflict with his wife's bourgeois parents. The series, produced just three years after the launch of Israeli television, was very popular but received poor reviews. In 1991 a sequel series was produced, narrating the lives of the protagonists twenty years later.

Hem Hayu Asara | They Were Ten

1960, 108 mins, black and white, Hebrew

Director:	Baruch Dienar
Producer:	Baruch Dienar (Orav Films)
Screenwriter:	Gabriel Dagan, Baruch Dienar, Menachem Shuval
Cinematographer:	Lionel Banes
Editor:	Helga Cranston
Music:	Gary Bertini
Leading Players:	Leo Filler, Yisrael Rubinshik, Amnon Kahanovich, Ninet Dienar, Oded Teomi

In the 1890s, a group of pioneers (nine men and one woman) settles in the Galilee, where they attempt to plow the hard land and at the same time cope with the hostility of their Arab neighbours, who refuse to share the well. The woman gives birth but dies shortly afterwards, and at her funeral the drought comes to an end. This drama, based on the authentic diaries of nineteenth-century pioneers, was the first Israeli feature to gain recognition abroad. It focuses on the central theme of the Zionist master-narrative – the redemption of the land and its restoration to fertility – and draws on the earlier *Tzabar | Sabra* (1933), as well as on the American Western. Although the Arabs are portrayed as primitive natives, the film treatment of the Jewish–Arab conflict is more complex than in earlier films and even allows Arabic dialogue. The narrative also allows for ambivalence regarding the commune and the Zionist project in general. The film received mixed reviews and moderate box office (approximately 180,000 tickets) but was distributed by Twentieth-Century Fox in twenty-four countries. This was the first local film to benefit from a tax refund per ticket, a government decision that brought about a regular sequence of film-making. *Hem Hayu Asara* won the Best Film Award at the Mannheim Film Festival and mentions in other film festivals.

Himmo Melekh Yerushalayim (a.k.a. 'Bell Room') | Himmo, King of Jerusalem

1987, 84 mins, colour, Hebrew

Director:	Amos Gutmann
Producer:	Enrique Rottenberg, Ehud Bleiberg
Screenwriter:	Edna Mazia
Cinematographer:	Jorge Gurevitch
Editor:	Ziva Postek
Music:	Ilan Wurtzburg
Leading Players:	Alona Kimchi, Dov Navon, Amiram Gavriel, Amos Lavie

Himmo, once the Don Juan of Jerusalem but now blind and maimed, is nursed by young, beautiful Hamutal. When the war is over and the men are about to leave the hospital, Himmo receives the *coup de grâce* from Hamutal. This melodrama (based on a novel by Yoram Kaniuk) is set against 1948 War of Independence, when Jerusalem was under siege and wounded Israeli soldiers were evacuated to an abandoned monastery. Kaniuk's allegory about the sacrifice of the Messiah for the new-born state becomes in Gutmann's adaptation a meditation on eros and thanatos. Gutmann rejects heroic values and his interests are aesthetic: the décor and lighting underscore this preference. His film received mixed reviews and poor box office (selling only 21,000 tickets). It was an entrant in the Chicago and San Francisco Film Festivals, among others.

Holeh Ahava Meshikun Gimmel (literally 'Lovesick from Project C') / Lovesick on Nana Street

1995, 94 mins, colour, Hebrew
Director / Screenwriter: Savi Gavison
Producer: Anat Asulin, Savi Gavison
Cinematographer: Yoav Kosh
Editor: Tali Halter-Shenkar
Music: Ehud Banai
Leading Players: Moshe Ivgi, Avigail Arieli, Hana Azoulai-Hasfari, Menashe Noi

Victor, the 'village idiot' of a shabby urban neighbourhood who broadcasts Turkish melodramas via a pirate television cable station, falls desperately in love with attractive drama instructor Michaela. When she rejects him, he collapses and is confined in a psychiatric clinic. This absurd portrayal of frustrated love fuses reality and fantasy in its attempt to examine the borders of sanity, using the asylum as an inner-exile habitat – a surreal a point of reference. Gavison repeats the zany mood of *Shuru*, here coloured with bleak overtones, and subverts the Bourekas genre in its ironic portrayal of social stereotypes. The film received mixed reviews but won the Israel Film Academy Best Film Award, as well as the Wolgin Award at the Jerusalem Film Festival.

Hor Balevana / Hole in the Moon

1965, 90 mins, black and white, Hebrew
Director: Uri Zohar
Producer: Mordechai Navon
Screenwriter: Amos Keinan
Cinematographer: David Gurfinkel
Editor: Anna Gurit
Music: Michael Columbie
Leading Players: Uri Zohar, Avraham Heffner, Shoshik Shani, Ze'ev Berlinski, Shmuel Kraus, Arik Lavie, Dan Ben-Amotz

In this satire a Jewish immigrant opens a kiosk in the Negev desert. Another kiosk soon pops up opposite. Since they have no customers, the two decide to enter show business and make a film. They conduct auditions which attract a mob of young girls and furnish a Wild West town made of cardboard with Indians, Samurai, Arabs, King Kong, Charlie Chaplin and Tarzan. Eventually all the residents of the town direct their outrage at the film-makers. Zohar's first feature, a landmark in the history of Israeli cinema, is an avant-garde hallucinatory farce that parodies all of the sacred ideals of Zionism. The narrative satirizes the blooming of the desert, dedication to physical work, placing the needs of the commune above those of the individual and the whole concept of the Zionist realist films, as in the scene of a woman in a lace dress holding a gun in one hand and a plough in the other. Zohar also subverts basic conventions of generic cinema, exposing the production apparatus of the film and introducing the film director as the new pioneer. In choosing a cinematic over a Zionist utopia, the film paved the way for the new sensibility films. Zohar went on to make ten further films, but none of them matches the radical mood of this first feature. *Hor Balevana* was the critics' choice at the Cannes Film Festival but in Israel it received poor reviews and disappointing box office (only some 48,000 tickets). In time it became a classic and was a subject of tribute in the 1988 Jerusalem Film Festival.

Hu Halach Basadot / *He Walked Through the Fields*

1967, 96 mins, black and white, Hebrew

Director:	Yoseph Millo
Producer:	Yitzhak Agadati, Ya'akov Shteiner
Screenwriter:	Charles Heldman, Moshe Shamir, Yoseph Millo
Cinematographer:	James Allen
Editor:	Nira Omri
Music:	Alexander Argov
Leading Players:	Assi Dayan, Iris Yotvat, Shraga Friedman, Yoseph Millo, Gideon Zinger

An Israeli soldier returning from the battlefields of the 1967 Six Day War visits the agricultural school where his father Uri was a student in the 1940s. Constructed as a flashback, the film goes back to 1946 when Uri, a young kibbutz member just out of school, falls in love with Mikka, a Holocaust survivor. He volunteers for a bridge-bombing mission, a *Palmach* (pre-state Jewish underground militia) operation against the British, and is killed in action, while his girlfriend is pregnant with their child – the young protagonist of the framing narrative. This heroic–nationalist drama, based on a popular novel and play by Moshe Shamir which glorifies the mythological Sabra, became a dominant Israeli fiction. The film departs from the novel not only in its employment of a framing story but also in highlighting Uri's concerns with private life rather then with national issues, thus reflecting the 1960s bias towards individualism. As a transition film, it still advocates self-sacrifice for the homeland but at the same time projects the norms of the state, demystifying the utopian ideals of the kibbutz and the *Palmach*'s partisan spirit. The film received mixed reviews but a good box office (selling some 320,000 tickets) and had vast cultural impact. Assi Dayan's role in this film made him an Israeli icon.

I Like Mike

1962, 120 mins, black and white, Hebrew

Director:	Peter Frye
Producer:	Yitzhak Agadati, Mordechai Navon, Yakov Steiner (Geva / IFA Films)
Screenwriter:	Peter Frye, Edna Shavit, Shlomo Bendkover, Yakov Steiner
Cinematographer:	Nissim Leon
Editor:	Nellie Gilad
Music:	Arie Levanon
Leading Players:	Batya Lancet, Haim Topol, Ilana Rovina, Ze'ev Berlinski, Sy Gitin

Tamara is in love with a kibbutz-born army officer, but her mother wants her to marry Mike, the Texan son of a millionaire who is in love with an female Israeli soldier whose photo he spotted in a newspaper. The film, an adaptation of a very successful play by Aaron Meged, was a huge commercial success (selling approximately 660,00 tickets), the first film in Hebrew to become a hit. The rejection of the Zionist–socialist ethos, identified with the pioneering years, enabled the growth of comedies that turned their back on heroic values. Nevertheless, Frye's comedy-satire integrates the American Jew into the Zionist vision via a cattle ranch in the Negev desert, Ben Gurion's utopian locus, where Jews and Arabs are able to co-exist in harmony.

Jenny VeJenny / Jenny and Jenny

1997, 60 mins, colour, Hebrew

Director / screenwriter / producer:	Michal Aviad
Cinematographer:	Eitan Harris
Editor:	Tali Halter-Shenkar
Music:	Doron Shenkar

This documentary follows the summer holiday of two seventeen-year-old cousins, both third-generation children of Jewish immigrants from North Africa, in the Bat Yam suburb of Tel Aviv. Their everyday experiences, including trivial matters such as quarrels and partying, and more tragic aspects such as an estranged father, serve to expose the undercurrent of tensions within Israeli culture, torn between Eastern and Western traditions. It won Best Documentary from the Israel Film Institute (IFI) and was an entrant in the Denver and Boston Film Festivals, among others.

Kadosh (literally 'Sacred')

1999, 110 mins, colour, Hebrew

Director:	Amos Gitai
Producer:	Amos Gitai, Michel Proper
Screenwriter:	Amos Gitai , Eliat Abecsis
Cinematographer:	Reneto Berta
Editor:	Kobi Netanel, Monica Colman
Music:	Luis Squalvis

Leading Players: Yoram Hatav, Ya'el Abecsis, Uri Klausner, Meital Barda

Rivka and Malka, two sisters who live in an ultra-religious community in Jerusalem, face personal crises: Rivka is forced to divorce her beloved husband after ten years of childless marriage and Malka is forced to marry a man she does not love. One of the rare occasions in Israeli cinema that a fiction film touches on the intimate life of orthodox Jews, the film unveils sexual desire as a powerful force in a community that represses it. As in his other films, Gitai refuses to revert to pathos and applies distancing techniques to create a restrained passion play. *Kadosh* was entered for the Cannes Film Festival and won praise from European reviewers, but did not do well critically or commercially in Israel.

Khirbet Hiz'a

1978, 53 mins, colour, Hebrew
Director: Ram Loevy
Producer: Israel Television
Screenwriter: Daniella Carmi
Cinematographer: Meir Diskin
Editor: Tova Asher
Leading Players: Dalik Volinitz, Shraga Harpaz, Gidi Gov, Amira Polin

In the 1948 War of Independence, a squad of soldiers await the order to take an Arab village (the title is the name of this fictional village). When the order is given, the soldiers burst into the village, rounding up the population and herding them onto trucks that will take them across the border to Jordan. One soldier tries to give a jerry can of water to the villagers, but is too late and the trucks leave without water. This drama, which initiated the Israeli–Palestinian conflict films and was based on a story by Izhar (who took part in the war), touches on one of the crucial topics in Israeli history: the expulsion of Palestinian villagers from their homes as part of a policy from above. It also focuses on a central Israeli ethos – the 'purity of arms' – showing Israeli troops shooting at civilians, deporting them and blowing up their houses. This was the first film to deconstruct the Zionist master-narrative and to demystify heroic–nationalist values to such an extent. Today it can be judged as a pioneering work in the revisionist historiography of Zionism. Its thematics are reinforced by Loevy's cinematic approach, privileging the terrified villagers staring silently at the soldiers from windows and doorways, and using the only conscientious soldier as narrator. The film stirred a major public reaction, including discussions in the Israeli parliament; its first screening was postponed for several months.

Kirkas Palestina / Circus Palestine

1998, 88 mins, colour, Hebrew
Director / Screenwriter: Eyal Halfon
Producer: Uri Sabag, Einat Bikel, Mark Rosenbaum, Haim Sharir
Cinematographer: Valentin Belangov
Editor: Tova Asher

Music:	Shlomo Gronich
Leading Players:	Yoram Hatav, Yevgenia Davidina, Amos Lavie, Basam Zuamut

Old lion Shweik, the main attraction of a Russian circus performing in the West Bank in the midst of the *intifada*, disappears during the opening night. An Israeli NCO falls in love with the beautiful lion trainer and together they set out to find the lion. This comic fantasy highlights the absurd realities rooted in the Israeli–Palestinian conflict. The Israeli army, the Jewish settlers, the Palestinians and the circus people are all part of a complex human picture that the film attempts to decode. This drama received mixed reviews and poor box office, but won the Israeli Film Academy Best Film Award.

Klala Lebrakha / *Out of Evil*

1950, 85 mins, black and white, English

Director:	Joseph Krumgold
Producer:	Leo Hermann
Cinematographer:	Alphonso Frenguelli, Leroy Phelps
Editor:	Larry Katz, Joseph Kay
Music:	Daniel Zamburski, Mordechai Ze'ira
Leading Players:	Azaria Rappaport, Nachum Buchman, Esther Margalit

This docu-drama, based on a novel by Yehuda Ya'ari, also contains a film within a film (namely, *Balaam's Story* by Helmar Lerski and Paul Levy). This unusual Zionist realist film combines fiction and documentary. It unfolds as a flashback of Yossef, a soldier in the 1948 War of Independence, unveiling the life story of his parents, who were the first lovers in a kibbutz in the 1920s. Group pressures push them to leave and go back to Europe, where they perish in the Holocaust. Their son, the protagonist of the framing narrative, survives and comes back to the kibbutz. A performance by a puppet theatre in the kibbutz narrates the biblical story of Balaam. The three themes – the kibbutz drama, the Balaam story and the epic of the war – resonate with each other, subverting the Zionist utopia and at the same time integrating the Holocaust into its scheme. The puppet of Balaam serves as an overall interpreter of the plot, warning that rigid ideologies might lead to disaster. The puppet play was directed in 1947 as a short musical by Helmar Lerski and puppet-theatre director Paul Levy, and Krumgold integrated it into his film. The film, laden with contradictions, represents changes in the Israel of 1949 and the first doubts about the Zionist utopia and the heroic approach.

Kobi VeMali / *Kobi and Mali*

1978

Director / Screenwriter:	Yitzhak Tzepel Yeshurun
Producer:	Yossi Meshulam (Israeli TV)
Cinematographer:	Ya'akov Eisenman
Editor:	Tova Asher

Music:	Alex Cagan
Leading Players:	Meir Azulai, Dalia Malka, Shalom Shmueli, Uzi Hemda

In this television drama Kobi, a teenage boy, attempts to breaks from life on the streets with his petty thief friends and return to school. His love for Mali, the girl-friend of the gang's leader, brings about a tragic and violent outcome. This account of juvenile delinquents, depicting hopelessness and dead-end situations, is one of the rare films from this period that focuses on Eastern Jews outside the Bourekas genre. Yeshurun's new sensibility practices (such as improvisation, shooting on location and utilizing non-actors) is a subversive political as well as aesthetic statement. The film won the Best Dramatic Feature Award from Israel Television.

Kol Mamzer Melech / *Every Bastard a King*

1968, 120 mins, colour, Hebrew

Director:	Uri Zohar
Producer:	Avraham Deshe, Haim Topol
Screenwriter:	Eli Tavor, Uri Zohar
Cinematographer:	David Gurfinkel
Editor:	Anna Gurit
Music:	Michel Columbie
Leading Players:	Pier Angeli, Yehoram Gaon, Oded Kotler, William Berger, Tami Tzifroni

Roy Cummings, an American journalist who comes to Israel to cover events on the eve of the 1967 Six Day War, befriends two Israelis who act heroically: his driver who is an arrogant philanderer but saves the life of a wounded soldier and a pacifist restaurant owner who makes a solo flight to Egypt in an attempt to bring about a truce. The journalist himself is killed when he steps on a mine. This heroic–nationalist drama underscores the new Sabra values: professionalism, achievement and technological supremacy. At the same time it replaces the pioneers' values with a new hedonism, foreshadowing the post-war materialistic ethos. Zohar employs strategies from Hollywood war films – staging numerous battle scenes and using an international cast – and presents war as the ultimate adventure, in which the enemy is little more than a faceless shadow. His film received favourable reviews and huge box office (approximately 740,000 tickets were sold).

Kufsa Shechora / *Black Box*

1993, 95 mins, colour, Hebrew

Director:	Yeud Levanon
Producer:	Gideon Kolirin
Screenwriter:	Neomi Sharon, Yeud Levanon
Cinematographer:	Avi Koren
Editor:	Tali Halter
Music:	Adi Renart
Leading Players:	Bruria Albek, Ami Traub, Mati Sari, Roni Ayalon

Alex, a professor in a London university, returns to Israel after he learns that he is dying of cancer. When he revisits his ex-wife, their love is rekindled and so is the struggle over the soul of their disturbed teenage son. While the original Amos Oz novel is an allegory of the collapse of the Zionist ethos through the confrontation between an intellectual of the Zionist elite and a delegate of a new proto-fascist Messianic ethos (the future elite), the film drama foregrounds the obsessive love story and an ambivalence towards both past and present that is typical of its dystopian narrative. The film did poorly commercially and critically.

Kurdania

1984, 38 mins, colour, Hebrew
Director / Screenwriter: Dina Zvi-Ricklis
Cinematographer: Eran Ricklis
Editor: Rivka Yogev
Music: Raviv Gazit
Leading Players: Yehudit Milo, Reuven Dayan, Alon Aboutbul, Liat Pansky

Two immigrant families in 1950s Israel, one from Iraq and one from Poland, are about to leave their dwellings in the shantytown Kurdania on their way to government housing. The social and mental transformation is displayed through the eyes of a young immigrant girl, a daughter of the Jewish-Iraqi family. This debut short film subverts the Bourekas conventions and employs neo-realist practices to examine the declining patriarchal system, ethnic tensions and the favouritism that typified the massive immigration of the 1950s.

Le'an Ne'elam Daniel Vax? / But Where is Daniel Wax?

1972, 94 mins, colour, Hebrew
Director / Screenwriter: Avraham Heffner
Producer: William Gross
Cinematographer: Amnon Salomon
Editor: Jacques Ehrlich
Music: Ariel Zilber
Leading Players: Lior Yeini, Yishai Shahar, Esther Zevko, Yael Heffner, Yosef
                          Carmon

Spitz, a singer who built a career in the United States, returns to Israel and revives his relationship with past friends. Only Wax, the idol of the class, is missing and Spitz is determined to find him. When he does, Wax is found to be a balding middle-aged bourgeois, a distorted mirror of the protagonist's own life. This debut feature, one of the prominent examples of the new sensibility, focuses on disillusionment associated with mid-life crises, but also reflects cultural changes in post-1967 Israeli society. Fascination with the past – a recurrent motif in Heffner's further films – serves here to intensify personal insights, but at the same time casts an ironic glance at the Zionist project, questioning its relevance. The slow pace and French-influenced *mise-en-scène* construct a mood of mental suffocation in which the alternatively depressed or ridiculous characters make their banal statements. The critics celebrated the film as part of a new realistic oeuvre, but it was several years before it was shown in a movie-theatre and it then failed at the box office, selling only 9,000 tickets. Over the years the film has become recognized as a masterpiece of Israeli cinema, although some people criticized Heffner for his depoliticizing approach. The film won the Council for Culture and Art Award.

Le'at Yoter / Slow Down

1968, 18 mins, black and white, Hebrew
Director / Producer / Screenwriter: Avraham Heffner
Cinematographer: Adam Greenberg
Editor: Jacques Ehrlich
Leading Players: Fanny Lubitsch, Avraham Ben-Yosef

This drama is based on a story by Simone de Beauvoir about one day in the life of an elderly couple. She is cross and will not talk to him. This 'still life' study of old age is unique in many ways. Heffner employs here for the first time his minimalist approach, highlighting a look or a touch, creating a special tempo that refuses any contrived drama and extends time. The film also does not use dialogue, instead relying on the woman's voice-over, thus reinforcing the intimacy of the framework by use of an inner voice. The grainy shots in black and white give it an impressionistic feel. This debut short film affiliated Heffner with the new sensibility genre, not only because of his cinematic practices but also his subject – normally taboo in the cinema of that period. *Le'at Yoter* gained mentions at the Venice and Melbourne Film Festivals.

Lechem / Bread

1986, 84 mins, black and white, Hebrew and Arabic
Director: Ram Loevy
Producer: Dana Kogan (Israeli Television)
Screenwriter: Meir Doron, Gilad Evron, Ram Loevy
Cinematographer: Meir Diskin
Editor: Rahel Yagil
Music: Ilan Harel
Leading Players: Rami Danon, Rivka Bachar, Moshe Ivgi, Etti Ankri

In the poor development town of Dimona in the Negev dessert, Shlomo (a bakery worker) loses his job when the bakery shuts down. Meanwhile, his son gets in trouble with the police and his daughter returns to washing floors after trying her luck in Tel Aviv. Shlomo, disillusioned and desperate, locks up his wife and four children at home and declares a hunger strike. This television drama by Levy, the in-house director for Israeli Television, dealt for the first time on Israeli television with social alienation, focusing on Jewish immigrants from North Africa who comprise the majority of the population in the development towns, in which economical distress is perpetuated into the second and third generations. The drama displays their hopelessness, condemning both the Zionist ideology and the cynical bureaucracy. The film won high praise, as well as the Prix Italia for television drama.

Leilsede (literally 'Passover Eve') / Passover Fever

1995, 100 mins, colour, Hebrew
Director / Screenwriter: Shemi Zarchin
Producer: Micha Sharfstein, Amitan Manelzon
Cinematographer: Amnon Zlayit
Editor: Einat Glaser-Zarhin
Music: Adi Cohen
Leading Players: Gila Almagor, Yossef Shiloah, Esti Zackheim, Alon Aboutboul, Miki Kam, Anat Waxman

A middle-class family gathers together to celebrate Passover. The mother suspects her husband of being unfaithful; the older son ignores his ex-wife; the daughter disregards her children; the younger son tries to hide his anorexia. Above it all hovers the memory of another son killed in action. This intimate melodrama, punctuated by moments of comedy, presents the family as a microcosm, depicting universal themes as well as specific issues inherent in Israeli society, such as coping with bereavement. The film received mixed reviews.

Lecha'im Hadashim (literally 'To a New Life') / Land of Promise

1934, 56 mins, black and white, English and Hebrew
Director: Juda Leman
Producer: Leo Herman
Screenwriter: Maurice Samuel
Cinematographer: Charles W. Herbert
Music: Boris Morros, Daniel Sambursky
Lyrics: Natan Alterman
Narration: David Ross, Zalman Shazar

This Zionist realist documentary, the first 'talking' documentary to be produced by local talents, is a propaganda film meant to glorify the Zionist project. The film displays images of pioneers singing while they plough the earth and harvest the crops. Some of these images render the ultimate stereotype of the Zionist pioneer. Leo Herman of the PFF (who initiated the project for fund-raising purposes) collaborated in the production with Fox Studios in the United States and with producer Margot Klausner. Jewish audiences outside Palestine were deeply impressed and many said that the film was the trigger for their immigration to Palestine. The PFF distributed the film for fifteen years until the 1950s. In 1935 it won Best Documentary Award at the Venice Biennial. The original negatives were destroyed by a fire at Fox Studios and several prints in English were the only ones to survive.

Leneged Einayim Maraviyot / *Under Western Eyes*

1996, 95 mins, colour, Hebrew
Director / Screenwriter: Yossef Pitchhadze
Producer: Dubi Baruch, Yossef Pitchhadze
Cinematographer: Shai Goldman
Editor: Dov Steuer
Music: Berry Sakharof
Leading Players: Eyal Shechter, Liat Glick, Ezra Kafri, Carmel Betto

Gary, an Israeli architect who lives in Berlin, returns to Israel for his father's funeral only to discover that his father, a scientist who spied for the Soviet Union, is alive. Together with a young actress, he embarks on a voyage to the Negev desert with security agents on his heels. This debut road movie, inspired by Joseph Conrad's novel, focuses on a quest for existential meaning by a rootless *emigré*, a typical protagonist of the inner-exile films – one of a series of uprooted characters in 1990s Israeli cinema, who perceive Israeli reality as an absurd play devoid of any political or ideological significance. The film's post-modern and apocalyptic approach is reinforced by a fragmented narrative that blends present and past, comedy and tragedy. *Leneged Einayim Maraviyot* received favourable reviews, and won the Wolgin Award in the Jerusalem Film Festival and the Jury Award at the Berlin Film Festival.

Lo Sam Zayin / *Don't Give a Damn*

1987, 90 mins, colour, Hebrew
Director: Shmuel Imberman
Producer: Yisrael Ringel, Yair Pradelsky (Roll Films)
Screenwriter: Hanan Peled
Cinematographer: Nissim Leon
Editor: Atara Horenstein
Music: Benny Nagari
Leading Players: Ika Zohar, Anat Waxman, Liora Grossman, Shmuel Vilozhny

Lo Sam Zayin is based on a novel by Dan Ben Amotz. Rafi, a Tel Aviv hunk who gets paralysed from the waist down after being wounded in combat, strikes out at everyone who wants to help him, especially his girlfriend and a good friend who shortly afterwards is killed in action. This nihilistic drama, focusing on post-traumatic experiences and shattered masculinity, is set in the wake of the 1973 war. Courage and self-sacrifice are refuted and subverted here through the rhetoric of an angry and vulnerable post-Yom Kippur War Sabra, obsessed with cripples and prostheses. The film received mixed reviews but very good box office (some 450,000 tickets were sold), and it was distributed in the United States.

Lo Tafhidunu (literally 'You Shall Not Put Fear into Us') / *The Illegals*

1947, 47 mins, black and white, English
Director / Producer: Meyer Levin

Cinematographer:	Jean-Paul Alphen, Bernard Hess
Music:	Walley Karveno-Paquin
Leading Players:	Tereska Torres, Yankel Mikalowitch

This Zionist realist docu-drama deals with the illegal immigration to Palestine following World War II, when thousands of Holocaust survivors tried to break the British blockade, guided by members of *Hagana* (a Jewish militia in pre-state years). Levin documented the refugees crossing borders and embarking on ships, following one group aboard the *Unafraid*, which ended up in Cyprus with its passengers interned in camps. Apart from two actors portraying a young couple, all the other participants were Holocaust survivors actually *en route* to Palestine. Levin hid the negatives at different points along the way and later collected them as he returned to the laboratory in Paris. Pathé issued a five-minute newsreel from this footage that caused a sensation at the time. Excerpts from the film were later incorporated into *Hayam Ha'acharon* / *The Last Sea*.

Lihyot Malka / *To be a Queen*

1977, 50 mins, black and white, Hebrew

Director / Screenwriter:	Gideon Ganani
Producer:	Micha Shagrir, Dan Arazi
Cinematographer:	Dani Shneur
Editor:	Ana Finkelstein

This documentary tells the story of Orly Khida, a twenty-year-old soldier from a poor neighbourhood who challenges for and wins the title of 'Water Queen of Israel'. The story of Orly Khida is not only about the breach between dreams and their actualization, but also a portrait of Israeli society. After winning the title, Khida got a small part in a film, worked as a saleswoman in a boutique and today is a matchmaker in Los Angeles.

Ma'agalim Shel Shishabat (a.k.a. 'Weekend Circles', literal translation) / *Circles*

1980, 86 mins, colour, Hebrew

Director / Screenwriter:	Idit Shechori
Producer:	Yehezkel Alani, Ya'akov Kotzki
Cinematographer:	Nurit Aviv, Gadi Danzig
Editor:	Ludmila Goliath
Music:	Avner Kenner
Leading Players:	Rahel Shein, Hava Ortman, Noa Cohen-Raz, Galit Gil, Yoel Lerner

In this drama, four young women spend a long weekend in Tel Aviv. Dorit is an outgoing swinger; Tamara is a depressed divorcée; Lior is the experimenting type; and Gili, just released from the army, is the innocent one. They move from a party to a pub and end up swimming naked in the Mediterranean. This debut psycho-drama focuses on the politics of gender and discusses the practice of uninhibited sex in an alienated urban setting. Joining other new sensibility films, it highlighted the personal and departed from mainstream cinematic practices. *Ma'agalim Shel Shishabat* received mixed reviews and poor box office, but was an entry in the Cannes Film Festival and in the Festival of the Mediterranean Forum in France.

Ma'asseh Betayar Amerika'i BeEretz Yisrael (literally 'A Tale of an American Tourist in Palestine') / Palestine Awakening

1923, 17 mins, black and white, silent
Director / Screenwriter: William Topkis
Producer: Jewish National Fund (JNF)
Cinematographer: Ya'akov Ben-Dov

This first attempt at narrative film is a Zionist propaganda travelogue featuring a wealthy American who tours the Zionist settlements of Jewish Palestine in the company of a Jewish guide and consequently decides to settle in Palestine. This first production by the JNF was scripted and directed by American Zionist Topkis, who wished to encourage Jewish tourism to Palestine. The character of the American tourist bridges the gap between the western spectator and the oriental 'reality', and this device was later used in other Zionist fiction films. The JNF bureaucrats omitted all the close-ups and some of the scenes not in accordance with its policy. The film premiered at the 13th Zionist Congress in Carlsbad in 1923 and went on to become a vast commercial success.

Machvo'im / Hide and Seek

1980, 90 mins, colour, Hebrew
Director: Dan Wolman
Producer: Dan Wolman, Jeffrey Justin
Screenwriter: Dan Wolman, Avi Cohen
Cinematographer: Ilan Rosenberg
Editor: Shosh Wolman
Music: Amnon Wolman
Leading Players: Doron Tavori, Binyamin Armon, Gila Almagor, Haim Hadaya

Uri, a twelve-year-old boy who lives with his grandfather in Mandatory 1946 Jerusalem while his parents are in Europe smuggling Jewish survivors into Palestine, suspects that his beloved tutor is a spy. One day he is shocked to see him naked in bed with a young Arab boy. This period, low-budget drama of initiation focuses on a plea for tolerance in a community permeated with anti-Arab sentiment and homophobia, and uses its protagonist to link sexual and political taboos. The shadow of the Holocaust underscores the political conflict. The film displays typical new sensibility strategies, such as highlighting mood over drama and the rejection of heroism. *Machvo'im* received good reviews but poor box office (only around 9,000 tickets were sold). It won the Israel Best Film Award and was entered for film festivals in Toronto, San Francisco, Berlin and Los Angeles.

Makom, Avoda / Work, Place

1988, 81 mins, colour, Hebrew / Arabic / Thai
Director / Cinematographer: Nurith Aviv
Producer: Liora Kamenetzky
Editor: Etti Wieseltier

Foreign labour, a phenomenon typical of the 1990s, is examined here in one village in the Jordan valley. Until the *intifada*, Palestinians from a nearby village worked the fields, but after one of the community's members was murdered, the farmers decided to employ Thais. This documentary addresses the question of cheap labour, set against the Israeli–Palestinian conflict.

Mar Manie / Mr Manie

1996, 300 mins, colour, Hebrew / German / English / Yiddish / Ladino
Director: Ram Loevy
Producer: Dana Kogan (Israeli TV)
Screenwriter: Gilad Evron
Cinematographer: Assi Rosack
Editor: Sara Salomon
Leading Players: Yehoram Gaon, Yarden Bar-kochva, Max Digby, Olf Henzel-Kirst, Mark Ivanir

This five-part drama series, based on a novel by A.B. Yehoshua, narrates the story of a Jewish Sephardi family through the testimonies of five narrators, each of whom encounters members of the family at different points in time during a 150-year period starting in the mid-nineteenth century. The dramas are set in different times and countries but are linked by a mystery disclosed only in the end. Each segment is dramatized in a different language and conveys a different mood and different cinematic strategies. This saga, focusing on the puzzle of Jewish identity, highlights Jewish history as the story of the oppressed, the dissident, the rebellious and the insane, thus deconstructing and subverting the Zionist master-narrative. This multi-language series, which employed distancing cinematic strategies thereby departing from mainstream television, earned relatively low ratings and polarized reviews.

Martin

1999, 50 mins, colour, Hebrew
Director / Screenwriter: Ra'anan Alexandrowicz
Producer: Ra'anan Alexandrowicz, Ido Sela
Cinematographer: Christoff Offelein, Martin Farkas
Editor: Ron Goldman
Music: Karni Postel

An eccentric Holocaust survivor who lives in a village adjacent to the Dachau concentration camp, where he was detained during the war, attracts the attention of three young tourists visiting the camp and becomes their source of historical evidence. This documentary addresses questions of memory and how memory construes history. The film won the Wolgin Award at the Jerusalem Film Festival.

Massa Alunkot (literally 'Journey of Stretchers') / Paratroopers

1977, 90 mins, colour, Hebrew

Director / producer:	Judd Ne'eman
Screenwriter:	Daniel Horwitz, Rachel Ne'eman, Kobi Niv
Cinematographer:	Hanania Bar
Editor:	David Tur
Music:	Shem-Tov Levy
Leading Players:	Gidi Gov, Moni Mushonov, Dov Glickman, Michael Warshaviak, Jetta munte

A recruit to the paratroops fails to adjust to the tough discipline and, during training, he throws a hand grenade into a room and follows it too quickly. His commanding officer, suspecting that the death was in fact a suicide, decides to retire from the army. This pioneering nihilistic drama deals for the first time with the devastating impact of the army on the individual and portrays the military system as the fundamental adversity of Israeli society, depicting its oppressiveness as a habitat that nurtures the death ethos. The conflict between the individual and the group reflects, as in many new sensibility films, the decline of the national consensus, as well as the partiality for individualism. Unlike other personal films, Ne'eman employs high production values, using numerous locations, many extras and panoramic scenes. The film was widely discussed in the Israeli media, although it received mixed reviews and modest box office (selling some 95,000 tickets). The military censors eventually approved the film and in the end it was adopted by the army as an instructional film. *Massa Alunkot* was the first Israeli film entered for the London Film Festival and was screened in film festivals in Italy, Canada, Australia and Holland.

Matzor / Siege

1969, 85 mins, black and white, Hebrew

Director:	Gilberto Tofano
Producer:	Ya'akov Agmob
Screenwriter:	Dan Ben-Amotz, Gilberto Tofano
Cinematographer:	David Gurfinkel
Editor:	Dani Schik
Music:	Yohanan Zarai
Leading Players:	Gila Almagor, Yehoram Gaon, Dan Ben-Amotz, Yael Aviv, Amir Urian

Tamar, a war-widow and mother of a young child, lost her husband in the 1967 Six Day War. She now lives in a state of mental siege, which involves mourning rituals and feelings of isolation and despair. The appearance of David, a bulldozer driver, brings new hope, only for it to be crushed when he is called up for reserve duty at the Suez Canal. This modernistic psychological drama, made by an Italian theatre director and based on an idea from Gila Almagor, is an exceptional film of the heroic–nationalist genre. It focuses on a female character rather than a male hero, and on issues such as family and intimacy. The narrative stresses the personal and foregrounds bereavement and loss, thus depicting Israeli society as a whole as being under siege. Tofano merges dramatic scenes with documentary footage, mostly of funerals, and incorporates radio announcements to create a claustrophobic mood. The film did very well critically and commercially, selling 500,000 tickets.

Me'achorei Hasoragim / Beyond the Walls

1984, 97 mins, colour, Hebrew and Arabic
Director: Uri Barabash
Producer: Rudy Cohen
Screenwriter: Benny Barabash
Cinematographer: Amnon Salomon
Editor: Tova Asher
Music: Ilan Wurtzberg
Leading Players: Arnon Tzadok, Muhammed Bakri, Rami Danon, Hillel Ne'eman, Assi Dayan

In a maximum security prison, Uri (leader of Israeli criminal prisoners) and Issam (leader of the Palestinian political prisoners) fight for dominance. The two are sent to solitary confinement and there they form an alliance and declare a general hunger

Figure 39 Me'achorei Hasoragim / Beyond the Walls

strike. This 1980s Israeli–Palestinian conflict film *par excellence*, a prison drama in the Hollywood tradition, won critical and commercial acclaim (selling some 600,000 tickets), partly due to its successful idealized solution to a dead-end situation. The sadistic warden in the film – who condones rapes and murders – is an Ashkenazi Jew and the film seems to suggest that the Ashkenazi establishment oppresses both Sephardi Jews, who comprise the majority in Israeli prisons, and the Palestinians, and that an alliance of the oppressed, rooted in the Orient, would eradicate political and social injustices. On another level, the narrative's larger than life characters (Issam is portrayed as a tormented Jesus) and cathartic plot builds a moral structure that redeems the tortured prisoners by their mere act of rebellion against tyranny. The film won the Israel Best Film Award, was a nominee for Best Foreign-Language Film in the Oscars, won the Critics' Award at the Venice Film Festival, was Best Film at the Lucarno Film Festival and was distributed worldwide by Warner Brothers. A sequel, *Beyond the Walls II*, was produced in 1992 with the same talent involved, but failed to win critical or commercial success.

Me'al Hakhoravoth / Over the Ruins

1938, 70 mins, black and white, Hebrew
Director: Nathan Axelrod, Alfred Wolf
Producer: Nathan Axelrod
Screenwriter: Tzvi Liberman
Cinematographer: Nathan Axelrod
Music: Emanuel Pugatchov
Leading Players: Yehuda Gabai, Dania Levine

Tzvi Liberman's screenplay for this film was based on his own novel. A Jewish counsellor in a Palestine youth village, the children of which are refugees from Nazi Germany, recounts the heroic story of Jewish children in the Galilee, whose village was ruined by the Romans. The first locally made Zionist realist drama with soundtrack and dialogue, this film attempts to create a sequence of Jewish history, ancient and modern, drawing on both the tragedy of Jews in Europe and the hope for the nascent independent state. The low budget and prolonged shooting (due to hostile Arab acts during that period, as well as the lack of experience of both directors) resulted in poor reviews and box office.

Menelik

1999, 56 mins, colour, Hebrew and Amhari
Director / Producer: Daniel Wachsmann
Screenwriter: Daniel Wachsmann, Yigal Tzur
Cinematographer: Micha Livne
Editor: Maor Keshet, Yair Elazar

According to the myth, Menelik was the son of King Solomon and the Queen of Sheba. This documentary follows Gadi Abadja ,a new immigrant to Israel, whose Jewish father was murdered in Ethiopia while his Christian mother was left behind. He sleeps in the Central Bus Station of Tel Aviv and gets by on small thefts. The second part of the film describes his voyage to Ethiopia and to his past, exploring the question of Ethiopian indentity.

Metzitzim / Peeping Toms

1972, 90 mins, colour, Hebrew

Director:	Uri Zohar
Producer:	Yitzhak Kol
Screenwriter:	Uri Zohar, Arik Einstein
Cinematographer:	Adam Greenberg
Editor:	Avi Lifshitz
Music:	Shalom Hanoch
Leading Players:	Uri Zohar, Arik Einstein, Sima Eliyahu, Mona Silberstein, Tzvi Shissel

Guta, an aging beach bum who runs a kiosk on the beach of Tel Aviv, allows his friend Elli, a pop singer, to use his beach house for extramarital affairs. In the meantime Guta himself, together with a young protegé, peeps into the women's dressing rooms and they enjoy the favours of the neighbourhood prostitute. Zohar's ninth film, and the first in a trilogy dedicated to restless Sabras, is considered his masterpiece. Focusing on fringe culture and the lost generation of the 1960s, this comedy celebrates hedonism and idleness to such extent that it stands out as the ultimate antithesis of the heroic–nationalist genre. The self-indulgent protagonist, played by Zohar himself, refuses commitments and yields to passive voyeurism as a reaction to the overachievement of previous generations. Although the film concurs thematically with the new sensibility, it stands out in its different cinematic approach, using an abundance of dialogue, warm and radiant photography and crowded scenes. The film received favourable reviews and moderate box office (around 190,000 tickets were sold) but later became a cult movie.

Miba'ad Lere'alat Hagalut / Through the Veil of Exile

1992, 86 mins, colour, Arabic

Director / Cinematographer:	David Benshetrit
Producer / Screenwriter:	David Benshetrit, Sinai Bar-David
Editor:	Sinai Bar-David
Music:	Elias Tayasir

The protagonists of this documentary are three Palestinian women in a state of internal exile. Dalal, arrested at sixteen for associating with a terrorist organization, returns home after twelve years in an Israeli prison only to face rejection, both because she adopted a male role and because she is a single woman. Um Muhammad, a peasant living in a refugee camp, places her trust in God alone, while Mary Chass, a Christian from Haifa, moved to Gaza only to find herself and her family were strangers there. The film addresses the notion of the 'other' from various perspectives, but privileges the perspective of Palestinian women, removed from the focal point of

Figure 40 Miba'ad Lere'alat Hagalut / Through the Veil of Exile

the Palestinian struggle, isolated behind their veil. *Miba'ad Lere'alat Hagalut* won the Best Documentary Award in the Golden Gate competition at the San Francisco Film Festival and was entered for the New York and Boston Film Festivals, among others.

Michael Sheli / My Michael

1975, 80 mins, colour, Hebrew
Director: Dan Wolman
Producer: David Lipkind, Shlomi Cohen
Screenwriter: Dan Wolman, Esther Mor
Cinematographer: Adam Greenberg
Editor: Dani Schik
Music: Alex Cagan
Leading Players: Oded Kotler, Efrat Lavie, Irit Alter, Moti Mizrachi

This drama is based on a novel by Amos Oz. Hanna, a kindergarten teacher in 1950s Jerusalem and the wife of Michael, a geology professor, gradually withdraws into her fantasies, which consist of an erotic game with Palestinian twin friends from her childhood in Mandatory Jerusalem. The film is a faithful adaptation of Oz's novel, constructing the female protagonist as mentally disturbed (in a similar fashion to other, later Israeli films), but at the same time investing in her the acute political symbolism of reunion with the repressed Arab. *Michael Sheli* employs new sensibility strategies, such as highlighting mood and foregrounding the personal at the expense of the national. It received mixed reviews but did well at the box office (some 190,000 tickets were sold). It was Israel's entry for the Oscars.

Michel Ezra Safra Uvanav / *Michel Ezra Safra and Sons*

1983, television mini-series, colour, Hebrew
Director: Nissim Dayan
Producer: Yossi Meshulam (Israeli TV)
Screenwriter: Nissim Dayan
Cinematographer: Shraga Merhav
Editor: Yair Achi-Ilan, Rina Ben-Melech, Ofra Reisenfeld
Music: Alex Kagan
Leading Players: Makram   Khuri,   Lilith   Nagar,   Amos   Lavie,   David
                        Menachem, Tiki Dayan

This five-segment saga, based on a novel by Amnon Shamosh, illustrates the fate of one Jewish family from Halleb in Syria during the period 1936–76. Its first segments focus on Michel, the respectable patriarch of the family, and his harmonious relations with his Arab neighbours. Hostile activities towards Jews brings about the emigration of the sons and daughters from Syria. This relatively large-scale production, with sixty actors and hundreds of extras, deals with the tragic fate of an old Jewish community, one that sustained good relations with its Arabic neighbours and enjoyed economic prosperity. Dayan portrays their everyday life, cultural and religious rituals, and depicts their tragedy when they dispersed all over the world. Reviewing Zionism as an underlying force in this tragedy places the immigration to Palestine and later to Israel in a subversive context. The series earned excellent reviews and high ratings.

Michtavim MiLevanon / *Letters from Lebanon*

1997, 50 mins, colour / black and white, Hebrew
Director / Screenwriter: Yehuda Kave
Producer: Daphna Kaplanski / Israeli Television
Editor: Ada Fink

This documentary describes the Israeli–Lebanon War (1982–5) as reflected through the eyes of Israeli combat soldiers. The letters and diaries of the soldiers are narrated against newsreel footage from Israeli and foreign television, revealing confusion, rage and fear, and construe an emotional dissonance in the face of the dry reports of the media. This documentary was inspired by an American film that was based on letters from Vietnam and is dedicated to the memory of the 654 soldiers who died in the Middle East war.

Mikreh Isha / *A Woman's Case*

1969, 69 mins, black and white, Hebrew

Director: Jacques Katmor
Producer: Avrham Deshe
Screenwriter: Jacques Katmor, Amnon Salomon
Cinematographer: Amnon Salomon
Editor: Nellie Gilad
Music: The Cherchils
Leading Players: Helit Katmor-Yeshurun, Yossef Spector, Ann Tochmeyer, Aharon Almog

Spector, a successful publicity agent who promotes products using women's bodies, meets a model who avoids his attempt to possess her. As a result he becomes obsessed with wild hallucinations of distorting and corrupting her body, and finally, in an attempt to free himself, he kills her. This fantasy, which deals with masculinity and femininity by projecting them as pure fixations, is one of the first new sensibility films and the only one to use explicit avant-garde strategies. Its radical cinematic approach (applying jump-cuts, extreme close-ups and intertitles) and its treatment of fetishism was unique in the history of Israeli cinema. The film received mixed reviews and poor box office (selling only around 38,000 tickets) but was the first Israeli film to be entered in the International Film Festival in Venice.

Mishpat Kastner / Kastner Trial

1994, 190 mins, colour, Hebrew
Director: Uri Barabash
Producer: Yossi Hasson (Israeli TV Channel 1)
Screenwriter: Moti Lerner
Cinematographer: Muni Shem-Tov
Editor: Rahel Yagil
Leading Players: Sasson Gabai, Yona Elian, Tatiana Olier, Yitzhak Hizkiyahu

This three-part television courtroom drama series is based on one of the most controversial trials in Israel's history. In 1944 Dr Yisrael Kastner, a member of the committee for the rescue of Hungarian Jewry, succeeded in saving the lives of 1,685 Jews by gaining permission for them to leave Budapest. A decade later he was accused of collaborating with the Nazis and was assassinated. Focusing on the courtroom procedures of 1954–5, as well as on the private lives of the protagonists, and drawing on court proceedings and interviews, the drama deconstructs the narrative of the Holocaust, bringing out issues such as the ineffective policy of the Zionist leadership regarding the Holocaust and the morally ambivalent stance of the survivors. The series stirred huge public debate and was acclaimed as the best dramatic series made by Israeli television up to that time.

Mitachat La'af (a.k.a. 'Undernose', literal translation) / Big Shots

1982, 103 mins, colour, Hebrew
Director: Ya'akov Goldwasser
Producer: Ronni Ackerman

Screenwriter:	Haim Marin, Ya'akov Goldwasser
Cinematographer:	Ilan Rosenberg
Editor:	Anat Lubarski
Music:	Shlomo Gronich
Leading Players:	Moshe Ivgi, Uri Gavriel, Juky Arkin, Tzadok Tzarum, Yehudit Milo

In this drama, Herzl and Sammy – two small-time crooks – dream about a major job that will put their lives in order. When Herzl reads in the newspaper that the police have confiscated half a million dollars, they decide to break into police headquarters. This low-budget cops and robbers tragicomedy portrays the milieu of small-time criminals who live on the fringe of society, celebrating the rituals and slang of a usually stereotyped subculture. The film received favourable reviews but modest box office (some 95,000 tickets), though it won the Jury Award at the Cognac Film Festival in France.

Mitrasim / Barricades

1969, 60 mins, black and white, Hebrew and Arabic
Director / Screenwriter:	Ram Loevy
Producer:	Mahmud Abu-Kabir
Cinematographer:	Micha Pen
Editor:	David Milstein

Two families who lost their sons in the 1948 war, Jews from Haifa and Palestinians from a refugee camp in the West Bank, are the protagonists of this early Israeli television documentary, which tries to relate to the issue of the Israeli–Palestinian conflict. The two sons of the Jewish family fell in battle a month apart from each other, while two of the sons of the Arab family died escaping their village in the same war. The film does not bring together the two families, thus underscoring the physical and emotional barricades separating them. Instead Loevy cross-cuts a visit to the graves with a visit to the ruins of the Arabic village, thus stressing the common theme of death and dislocation.

Muhammad Yiktzor / Muhammad Will Reap

1976, 44 mins, black and white, Hebrew and Arabic
Director / Screenwriter:	Yigal Burstein
Producer:	Avshalom Katz, Uzi Peled
Cinematographer:	Ilan Rosenberg
Editor:	Tova Biran

The final collapse of the pioneers' ideology, which advocated working the land, is manifested in this documentary by the phenomenon of employing Palestinians to carry on the physical work in the fields of kibbutzs and other agricultural communes. One interviewee, who still worked the land at an advanced age (close to eighty), declares that this process transforms Israelis into a master race. The director's critique of post-1967 Israel includes a visit to the 'slave market' where Palestinian workers are picked up by local contractors.

Nadia

1986, 90 mins, colour, Hebrew

Director:	Amnon Rubinstein
Producer:	Ehud Ben-Shach
Screenwriter:	Eitan Green, Amnon Rubinstein
Cinematographer:	Ilan Rosenberg
Editor:	David Tour
Music:	Yoni Rechter
Leading Players:	Hanna Azoulai-Hasfari, Youval Banai, Meir Banai, Yosuf Abu-Warda

Nadia, a daughter of an Arab family who studies in a Jewish boarding school, faces a crisis when terrorist action in a nearby city threatens to destroy her fragile relationship with her Jewish fellow students. This drama of initiation (based on a novel by Galila Ron-Feder) deals with the Israeli–Palestinian conflict through a protagonist who projects a double marginality. The closing scene, bringing Jewish youngsters to the Arab village, adheres to the idealized concept of co-existence. The film received mixed reviews and modest box office (around 120,000 tickets).

Nevuchadnetzer BeKaysaria / *Nebuchadnezzar in Caesarea*

1979, 70 mins, colour, Hebrew

Director:	Ram Loevy
Producer:	Micky Laron (Israeli TV)
Cinematographer:	Meir Diskin,Tzadok Prinz, David Yiskuner
Editor:	Tova Asher

This film documents the production of Verdi's *Nabucco* / *Nebuchadnezzar* by the Berlin Opera at the Roman amphitheatre of Caesarea. The mere notion of Germans staging the fall and destruction of independent Judea is a source of acute irony, especially since Israelis play Babylonian troops and Germans play Jewish warriors. This unusual art versus life moment serves in this documentary to examine the burdened German–Jewish past, as well as present local conflicts.

Nisuyim Fictivyim / *Marriage of Convenience*

1988, 90 mins, colour, Hebrew and Arabic

Director:	Haim Bouzaglo
Producer:	Micha Sharfstein
Screenwriter:	Haim Bouzaglo, Yossi Swissa
Cinematographer:	Amnon Salomon
Editor:	Tova Asher
Music:	Yitzhak Klepter

Leading Players: Shlomo Bar-Aba, Irit Sheleg, Eli Yatzpan, Adiv Gihashan, Idit Teperson

Eldad, a teacher from Jerusalem disguised as an American tourist, finds lodging in a cheap Tel Aviv hotel. One day he is picked up by Palestinian construction workers and becomes one of them, pretending to be mute. This dystopian allegory of Israeli–Palestinian conflict focuses on the issue of identity *vis-à-vis* the occupation. The protagonist resigns his identity by assuming muteness, while the Palestinian workers regain their voice which had been appropriated by the Israelis. The film's final statement seems to be that only by crossing the lines and reversing roles can one unveil the mystification of the 'other'. This debut feature was shot in 16 mm and then blown up to 35 mm, rendering the images rough and grainy. The film received mixed reviews and modest box office (selling around 50,000 tickets) but won the Israel Best Film Award (sharing it with *Echad Mishelanu / One of Us*).

Noa Bat Sheva-Esrey / Noa at Seventeen

1982, 86 mins, colour, Hebrew
Director / Producer / Screenwriter: Yitzhak (Tzepel) Yeshurun
Cinematographer: Yitzhak Oren, Ya'akov Saporta
Editor: Tova Asher
Music: Isaac Steiner
Leading Players: Dalia Shimko, Idit Tzur, Shmuel Shilo, Moshe Havatzelet, Adi Ne'eman

Seventeen-year-old Noa, living in Tel Aviv in the early 1950s, experiences the anguish of her torn family and her own coming of age. The split of the kibbutz movement into pro-Soviet and pro-western camps following the Korean War is reflected in the bitter dispute between Noa's mother and her kibbutz-member uncle. Noa's father consequently leaves home and Noa separates from her boyfriend and comrades in the socialist youth movement. This period drama, set against the great social changes of the first years of the state, features a new sensibility protagonist whose pronounced individualism asserts the genre's emphasis on non-conformity and self-realization as a substitute for a shattered socialist or Zionist ethos. Her disillusionment and isolation at the end of the film also reflects the mood of the time that the film was made – a few years after the rise to power of the right-wing Likud party in 1977. This low-budget film, shot over only two weeks, manifests an intentional poverty of cinematic means while highlighting emotions and dialogue. It won high critical praise as well as relative success at the box office, selling some 190,000 tickets.

Nurit

1972, 90 mins, colour, Hebrew
Director / Screenwriter / Producer: George Ovadia
Cinematographer: Yechiel Ne'eman
Editor: Avi Lifshitz
Music: Albert Piamenta

Leading Players: Sassi Keshet, Yona Elian, Jacques Cohen, Tova Pardo, Arie Elias

Rich, beautiful Shoshanna is about to marry poor Moshe in spite of her father's objections. When she hears that he has been killed in an car accident, she attempts to drown herself. Moshe was not killed and goes on to become a successful pop singer, while Shoshanna, saved from drowning, gives birth to their daughter, Nurit. This popular Bourekas musical melodrama utilizes typical Israeli ethnic and class tensions, and celebrates the culture of oriental Jews in customs and music. The film received poor reviews but did very well at the box office (over 700,000 tickets were sold).

Oded Hanoded / Oded the Wanderer

1932, 77 mins, black and white, silent

Director:	Haim Halachmi
Producer:	Haim Halachmi, Natan Axelrod (PAI)
Screenwriter:	Haim Halachmi
Cinematographer / Editor:	Nathan Axelrod
Designer:	Tsvi Goldin
Music:	Emanuel Pugachov
Leading Players:	Shimon Finkel, Shimon Pevsner, Moshe Khurgel, Shifra Ashman

A group of children from a village in the Jezreel valley are on a school outing when one of the boys, Oded, falls behind. He wanders in the mountains until his teacher and his friends bring him back home safely. A subplot narrates the kidnapping of an American tourist by Bedouins. This first dramatic feature film made in Palestine, with professional actors and based on a story by Zvi Liberman, is a Zionist realist adventure film that utilizes the plot to highlight the ancient landscapes of the land of Israel. The film premiered in Tel Aviv, where it was shown to a packed house for eight weeks, a remarkable achievement considering the small Jewish population at the time. Yet it was doomed by the JNF refusal to distribute it because it allegedly presented the country as a barren wilderness. An attempt to produce a soundtrack resulted in the loss of the negatives.

Onat Haduvdevanim / Time of the Cherries

1991, 103 mins, colour, Hebrew

Director:	Haim Bouzaglo
Producer:	Avraham Guedalia, Huguette Elhadad-Azran, Riki Shelach
Screenwriter:	Haim Bouzaglo, Hirsh Goodman
Cinematographer:	Oren Shmukler
Editor:	Era Lapid
Music:	Adi Renart
Leading Players:	Gil Frank, Idit Teperson, Sasson Gabai, Avi Gilor, Eli Yitzpan

Figure 41   Onat Haduvdevanim / Time of the Cherries

When Mickey, a young yuppie copywriter from Tel Aviv, receives orders to serve in the Lebanon War, a premonition of his death in combat moves him to act out his own funeral. A female American scoop-hunting television reporter follows him to Lebanon and becomes romantically involved with him. Just as the Israeli government decides to retreat, Mickey is killed in action. This unsettling post-modern treatment of a topic usually represented in the realist mode, focuses not on the reality of war but on its mediation via advertising or television. Creating a reproduction within a reproduction, with the American television crew taping the dramatized scenes shot by the film's crew, the film denies access to 'reality'. Typically, the war in this nihilistic narrative is fought against mines and bombs, without an enemy, and thus does not make humanistic pleas or anti-war protests. Bouzaglo began writing the script in 1984 but only managed to raise adequate financing after completing his first feature, *Nisuyim Fictivyim / Marriage of Convenience*. Reviews were polarized and the film did not do well at the box office.

119 Kadurim Ve'od 3 / 119 Bullets Plus 3

1996, 62 mins, colour / black and white, Hebrew
Director / Screenwriter: Ye'ud Levanon
Producer: Amit Goren, Ye'ud Levanon
Cinematographer: Ofer Prant, Alon Bernstein
Editor: Tali Shenkar
Music: Doron Shenkar

This film opens in November 1995 at the Tel Aviv square where, an hour earlier, Yitzhak Rabin was assassinated. It goes on to integrate documentary and fictionalized material to create a political statement. The film originated in a documentary that Levanon started to shoot after the 1994 massacre in the mosque at Hebron, in which the murderer, a Jew, fired 119 bullets. *119 Kadurim Ve'od 3* was an entry in film festivals all over the world.

Or Min Hahefker / *Light Out of Nowhere*

1973, 94 mins, black and white, Hebrew
Director:	Nissim Dayan
Producer:	Ya'akov Elkov
Screenwriter:	Nissim Dayan, Ya'akov Elkov
Cinematographer:	Shmuel Calderon
Editor:	Ed Orson
Music:	Albert Piamenta
Leading Players:	Nissim Levi, Shlomo Basan, Abie Saltzberg, Esther Eshed

Seventeen-year-old Shaul is torn between his hard-working father, who wants him to follow in his footsteps, and his criminal brother, who offers easy temptations. He wanders about his poor neighbourhood, which is stricken with drugs, prostitution and violence, and with other bitter and frustrated youths. This low-budget debut feature is the first realistic portrayal of Sabras of oriental Jewish families. The film presents the establishment from their perspective, protesting against the political and economic structure that perpetuates their dead-end situation and underscoring their sense of alienation. *Or Min Hahefker* shuns stereotypes in the fashion of the Bourekas films and allows an open ending in the spirit of the new sensibility films. It applies strategies from Italian neo-realist cinema, such as black and white footage, the use of hand-held cameras and non-professional actors, shooting on location and street language, all contributing to its rough, unpolished look. The film received poor reviews and poor box office (only around 6,000 tickets were sold) but it was 'adopted' by the Black Panther protest movement of the1970s and over the years has won new appreciation.

Osher Lelo Gvul / *Everlasting Joy*

1996, 90 mins, colour, Hebrew
Director / Screenwriter:	Yigal Burstein
Producer:	Haim Sharir
Cinematographer:	Jorge Gurevich
Editor:	Era Lapid
Music:	Scarlatti
Leading Players:	Ariel Zilber, Ya'el Almog, Ofra Weingerten, Ya'ir Rubin

In this film the seventeenth-century philosopher Baruch Spinoza now lives in a middle-class neighbourhood near Tel Aviv, where he attempts to decode the secret of human happiness on his personal computer. His noisy neighbours disturb him and so do two secret-service agents, who are following him. This post-modern fantasy casts a disillusioned and ironical glance over the Israeli bourgeoisie, parodying their material-istic ethos and media addiction, as well as its apolitical and anti-intellectual stance. The film employs modernist distancing strategies and slapstick humour in the spirit of the silent comedies to deconstruct the formula of romantic comedy. It received good reviews but did not do well at the box office.

Pegisha Hozeret (literally 'Reunion') / Four Friends

1999, 61 mins, colour, English / Hebrew / Arabic
Director: Esther Dar
Producer: Neomi Ben-Natan
Screenwriter: Esther Dar, Neomi Ben-Natan
Cinematographer: Ron Rotem
Editor: Era Lapid
Music: Lior Shoshan

Four women meet in 1998 in the American Colony Hotel in East Jerusalem. Salma and Vidad are Palestinians, Olga and Sharona are Jewish. In the 1930s they all shared a dormitory room in an English college in Jerusalem. Salma and Vidad married two cousins and built their homes in Jaffa. In 1948 the two Palestinians and their families fled Jaffa and moved to the West Bank, then under Jordanian rule. The reflection of history through these life stories is poignant in this documentary, which highlights how the realization of someone's dream is another's tragedy.

Ressissim (literally 'Splinters') / Burning Memory

1989, 93 mins, colour, Hebrew
Director: Yossi Sommer
Producer: Ami Amir
Screenwriter: Yossi Sommer, Ami Amir
Cinematographer: Yoav Kosh
Editor: Ya'akov Dagan, Rivka Yogev
Music: Jan Garbarek, Yossi Elefent
Leading Players: Danny Roth, Polly Reshef, Etti Ankri, Alon Oliarchic

Gary, who suffered severe shell shock following a battle in the Lebanon War, is admitted to a rehabilitation centre for a three-week therapy programme. The narrative of this drama unfolds as he and his comrades fight to overcome their traumas. This feature, joining other Israeli films in the 1980s in focusing on post-traumatic experi-ences after combat, foregrounds a strong nihilistic mood and portrays a psychologically wounded Sabra who questions his identity as a man and a soldier. In a series of flashbacks reconstructing the battle, the film makes an explicit anti-military statement, thus echoing the general mood in Israel following the Lebanon War. The film received mixed reviews but was entered for the Berlin Film Festival.

Rimon Be'aza / Hand Grenade in Gaza

1970, 50 mins, black and white, Hebrew
Director / Screenwriter: Mordechai Kirshenbaum
Producer: Israeli TV
Cinematographer: Bnaya Bin-Nun
Editor: Esther Dar

This piece of reportage for Israeli television examines the background of Palestinian terrorism against Israelis in the Gaza Strip. Images of Palestinian workers packed into trucks in a long queue at the Erez Checkpoint, waiting for hours to enter Israel, are followed by images of Palestinian agricultural labourers, locked in an oppressive feudal system and willing to exchange their miniscule salaries for the bonus given for planting bombs. The film was only broadcast in a cut version.

Roveh Chuliot / Wooden Gun

1979, 95 mins, colour, Hebrew
Director / Screenwriter: Ilan Moshenson
Producer: Eitan Even, Richard Sanders, John Hardy
Cinematographer: Gadi Danzig
Editor: Zion Avrahamian
Music: Yossi Mar-Haim
Leading Players: Arik Rosen, Yehudit Sole, Leo Young, Ophelia Strahl, Michael Kfir

Yoni, the leader of a gang of children in 1950s Tel Aviv, aims his wooden gun at his rivals and almost kills one of them. Injured himself, he finds solace at the home of a female Holocaust survivor and this experience changes his perspective on life. This new sensibility low-budget drama of initiation, which draws on autobiographical material, was the first in three decades to focus on the shadow cast by the Holocaust and the ambivalent attitudes held towards the survivors, which comprise elements of guilt and rejection. At the same time it replaced the heroic–nationalist pathos that prevailed after the 1948 War of Independence with the mundanity of existence in times of economical depression and anxiety for relatives left in Europe. The film received favourable reviews but poor box office (around 31,000 tickets were sold), although it was entered for the Berlin and Lucerne Film Festivals.

Ru'hach Hadevarim / The Spirit of Things

1999, 60 mins, colour, Hebrew
Director / Screenwriter: Michael Lev-Tov
Producer: Ya'akov Eisenman (Israeli TV)
Cinematographer: David Yiskuner
Editor: Irit Danon

This film is a dialectical portrait of Israel's most utopian endeavour: the kibbutz. In 1952 a French team shot a documentary on Kibbutz Beit Alfa, focusing on the mythological Sabra and depicting the communal life as heaven on earth. Almost half a century later Lev Tov uses that footage in order to deconstruct the idyllic picture and to examine the contemporary materialistic middle-of-the-road objectives. The narration is executed in ten different languages, from Yiddish to Hungarian, French and Arabic, articulating today's multi-vocal and pluralistic reality and uncovering the various narratives that shaped the evolution of the kibbutz.

Sadot Yerukim / Green Fields

1989, 100 mins, colour, Hebrew
Director / Screenwriter: Yitzhak (Tzepel) Yeshurun
Producer: David Tour
Cinematographer: Gadi Danzig
Editor: Tova Asher
Music: Adi Renart
Leading Players: Sharon Hacohen, Amit Lior, Lia Dultzkaia, Shmuel Shilo, Shmuel Edelman

During the *intifada* a family accompanies its son to a military base in the West Bank. While driving to the base they get involved in a violent confrontation between Israelis and Palestinians, which ends with the father killing a Palestinian. The experience polarizes the family and causes each of them to re-examine their political stance. This dystopian psycho-drama, the first film set against the backdrop of the *intifada*, focuses on the Israeli–Palestinian conflict and challenges the audience to face the tragic outcome of their compliance with the moral corruption instigated by the occupation. The interpretative voice-over accompanying the closing scene undermines the dramatic structure and hints at its limitations. The film received mixed reviews and failed at the box office (with sales of only 3,000 tickets), but won the Wolgin Award at the Jerusalem Film Festival and the Best Film Award at the Rio de Janeiro Film Festival.

Sallah Shabbati

1964, 110 mins, black and white, Hebrew
Director / Screenwriter: Ephraim Kishon
Producer: Menachem Golan
Cinematographer: Floyd Crosby
Editor: Dani Schik
Music: Yohanan Zarai
Leading Players: Haim Topol, Gila Almagor, Arik Einstein, Shraga Friedman, Zaharira Harifai

Sallah, one of the newcomers to Israel in the 1950s mass emigration from Arab countries, is taken with his wife and seven children to an immigration camp. He refuses to work as a day labourer in a nearby kibbutz and passes his time playing backgammon, drinking and selling his vote to politicians. Finally, out of frustration, he initiates a protest demonstration of the new immigrants and gains new lodgings. This highly prized musical comedy, the first feature by the humourist Kishon and the most popular film ever made in Israel (selling 1,300,000 tickets), mocks the socialist values and the 'religion of work' mandatory to Zionist ideology, and underscores the cultural clash between newcomers and Israeli natives, Sephardis and Ashkenazis, thus moulding the stereotypes for a new genre: the Bourekas film. Kishon bluntly satirized sacred cows such as the Sabra, the kibbutz, the Zionist funds and government bureaucracy. The film received mixed reviews but was nominated for an Oscar in the category of Foreign Language Films, despite the protests of Golda Meir, who was shocked by the scene in which plaques with the names of Zionist contributors to forest planting in Israel are replaced by plaques in honour of new contributors. *Sallah Shabbati* won the Golden Globe for Best Foreign Film and opened the Berlin Film Festival. Kishon was later criticized for patronizing his protagonist by presenting him as backward, idle, ignorant and sexist, thereby stereotyping all oriental Jews.

Salomonico

1972, 113 mins, colour, Hebrew

Director:	Alfred Steinhardt
Producer:	Henry Ohana, David Shapira Roni Ya'akov
Screenwriter:	Reuven Bar-Yotam, Eli Tavor
Cinematographer:	Yechiel Ne'eman
Editor:	Anat Lubarsky
Music:	Dov Zeltzer
Leading Players:	Reuven Bar-Yotam, Gabi Amrani, Eti Grottes, Yehuda Efroni, Mosko Alkalai

Salomonico, a proud longshoreman who emigrated to Israel from Salonika in Greece, loses his job when the Tel Aviv port is shut down. He decides to move to a better neighbourhood only to find out that he does not belong there. This Bourekas melodrama deals with topics characteristic of the genre, such as ethnic and class tensions, and advocates mixed marriage as an overall solution to the evils of the system. The film received mixed reviews but huge box office (approximately 690,000 tickets were sold). It initiated a sequel, *The Father*.

Sanjin / Saint Jean

1993, 75 mins, colour, Hebrew

Director:	Julie Shles
Producer:	Amit Breuer
Cinematographer:	Yitzhak Portal
Editor:	Yael Perlov
Music:	Yuval Shafrir, Rami Fortis

The title refers to a large caravan site on the beach near Acre, which houses hundreds of new immigrants from Ethiopia and Russia. They live there, crowded into trailers that stand head to head in the atmosphere of a ghetto. Job-Judah from Ethiopia finds some redemption in long-distance jogs down the nearby seashore. Lena from Russia attempts to commit suicide. This documentary also explores the segregation of the Ethiopians from the Russians and the bias against 'blacks' prevailing among the immigrants. It won the Wolgin Award in the Jerusalem Film Festival.

Scenes in the Holy Land (distributed worldwide as 'Palestine: The Jewish Return from Exile')

1911, 20 mins, black and white, silent
Director / Producer / Screenwriter / Cinematographer: Murray Rosenberg

This travelogue displays images from old and new sites in Palestine, and especially in Jerusalem. Rosenberg started shooting in Egypt *en route* to Palestine. While filming the procession of the Patriarch in Jerusalem, he had to escape an angry mob. An English Zionist, Rosenberg first visited Palestine in 1904, photographing stills that were later to be transformed into a coloured lantern show of the Holy Land. *Scenes in the Holy Land* was shown at the 10th Zionist Congress in Basel in 1911, where it triggered debate over the use of audio-visual devices for Zionist propaganda. It was exhibited in Jewish communities and in theatres all over the world. In 1932 Rosenberg donated the film to the National Library on Mount Scopus, Jerusalem, where it is stored today in the Spielberg Jewish Film Archive. In 1963 David Perlov incorporated footage of the film into his *Byrushalayim / In Jerusalem*. The following year Rosenberg renamed his film *Haseret Harishon Be'eretz Israel / The First Film in the Land of Israel*.

Seret Leila / Night Movie

1986, 34 mins, colour, Hebrew and Arabic
Director / Screenwriter: Gur Heler
Producer: Haim Heler
Cinematographer: Jorge Gurevich
Editor: Yosef Greenfeld
Music: Oded Zehavi
Leading Players: Moshe Ivgi, Akad-Abed El Hai

A Palestinian youth is arrested for staying in Tel Aviv without a permit and is handcuffed to an Israeli soldier. The two are left together for the night, until the army patrol returns. This Israeli–Palestinian conflict short drama employs the limitations of its format to build a concise, almost abstract narrative, which utilizes two protagonists and several locations to create a political allegory. The rapport developing between the two protagonists crosses barriers of nationality and offers a humanistic liberal approach. The sunrise brings back the patrol and brings the film to its tragic denouement, previously alluded to in the depressing urban night scenes, coloured by a *film noir* subtext. This low-budget graduation project, produced in TAU Film Department, won the Best Short Film Award at the Oberhausen and Jerusalem Film Festivals.

Sha'anan Si / Comfortably Numb

1991, 40 mins, colour, Hebrew
Director: Ari Fulman, Uri Sivan
Producer: Avishag Films
Cinematographer: Ari Fulman
Editor: Dov Shtoyer

Set in Tel Aviv during the 1991 Gulf War, this documentary attempts to go beyond news and images of shattered buildings, instead focusing on residents talking about life under the constant terror of missile attacks while they are in sealed rooms, stressing the issues of a state under siege and the shock of a renewed threat of annihilation five decades after the Holocaust. The grandmother of one of the film-makers reminisces about European wars, while a group meeting in a public shelter joins in singing pacifist songs. The film won the Wolgin Award at the Jerusalem Film Festival, as well as the Best Documentary Award from the Israel Film Academy.

Sha'ar Haguy / The Gate to the Valley

1965, 14 mins, black and white, silent (music)
Director / Screenwriter: David Greenberg
Producer: Yigal Efrati (IFS)
Cinematographer: Adam Greenberg
Music: Yehezkel Brown

This poetic collage, the first Israeli documentary to do without narration, focuses on the siege of Jerusalem and the attempts to break through during the 1948 War of Independence. Images of the pastoral woods scarred by skeletons of burned armoured cars are cut into still photographs from the war, making for an almost abstract document, departing from the usual Zionist propaganda of the time.

Shablul / Snail

1970, 80 mins, black and white, Hebrew
Director / Screenwriter: Boaz Davidson
Producer: Tzvi Shissel
Cinematographer: Nurit Aviv
Editor: Anat Lubarsky
Music: Shalom Hanoch
Leading Players: Arik Einstein, Ori Zohar, Tzvi Shissel, Shalom Hanoch, Josi Katz

A series of loosely interwoven episodes, sketches, situations and songs revolving around the life of and an album by popular rock singer Einstein, along with his close friends, among them film directors Davidson and Zohar, and fellow musician Shalom Hanoch. The film shows rehearsals, a divorce ceremony, a karate lesson and a chase by a huge gorilla. This low-budget celebration of nonsense, using new sensibility practices, was shot over fifteen days. It adheres to the revolutionary ethos of the 1960s and the spirit of the hippies and the Beatles, employing experimental cinematic approaches and fusing documentary with fiction. The film received favourable reviews and met with modest box office success (approximately 68,000 tickets were sold). In time it became a cult movie.

Shivrei Tmunot: Yerushalayim / Fragments: Jerusalem

1986–96, 360 mins, colour, Hebrew
Director / Producer / Screenwriter / Cinematographer: Ron Havilio
Editor: Tor Ben-Mayor

This saga in seven segments unfolds the story of the Havilio family, who have lived in Jerusalem since the expulsion of the Jews from Spain in the fifteenth century. The documentary interweaves personal, familial and historical material. It opens with footage reconstructing the director's childhood in a neighbourhood of pre-1967 Jerusalem and goes on to visit the graves of family ancestors in a Jerusalem cemetery. The film offers an abundance of mementoes from the city, among them photos and drawings of Jerusalem from the nineteenth century, as well as documentary footage from the early twentieth century to the present day.

Sh'khur

1994, 94 mins, colour, Hebrew
Director: Shmuel Hasfari
Producer: Yoram Kislev
Screenwriter: Hanna Azoulai-Hasfari
Cinematographer: David Gurfinkel
Editor: Zion Avrahamian
Music: Uri Vidislavsky
Leading Players: Ronit Elkabatz, Gila Almagor, Amos Lavie, Ya'akov Cohen, Hanna Azoulai-Hasfari

Raheli, a television chat-show host from a Jewish Moroccan family, drives from her home in Tel Aviv to a development town in the Negev dessert for the funeral of her father, along with her retarded daughter and her insane sister. During the trip she meditates on her traumatic past: a loving but suffocating mother who practises black magic (*Sh'khur* means 'black magic' in Moroccan Arabic); a blind and fanatical father; authoritarian brothers; and her own struggle to free herself from poverty and an oppressive patriarchal system. The sister and daughter, both locked in their own unintelligible worlds, mirror her psychological distress and force her to integrate the past into her apparently comfortable middle-class present. This dystopian drama, based on autobiographical material from the screenplay writer Azoulai-Hasfari who plays the female protagonist, explores the familiar topics of exploitation of North African Jewish immigrants and the status of women in the traditional family from a fresh, modernist perspective. This is the first film to portray the drama of a North African Sabra without being implicated in the conventions of the Bourekas genre. The film received praise from reviewers and won the Israel Film Academy Best Film Award. It was entered for the Berlin Film Festival.

Shlosha Yamim Veyeled / Three Days and a Child

1967, 90 mins, black and white, Hebrew
Director: Uri Zohar
Producer: Amatzia Hiuni
Screenwriter: Uri Zohar, Dan Ben-Amotz, Amatzia Hiuni
Cinematographer: David Gurfinkel
Editor: Jacques Ehrlich
Music: Dov Seltzer
Leading Players: Oded Kotler, Yehudit Soleh, Jermain Unikovsky, Illy Gorlitzky

Elli, a maths teacher in Jerusalem, agrees to babysit the child of his former girlfriend and her husband for three days. With the girlfriend away, he spends long hours with the child, which brings back memories of betrayed love from his days in a kibbutz. This modernist adaptation of a story by Abraham B. Yehoshua employs new sensibility strategies and draws on the French new wave, mixing present and past, utilizing photography and montage to bring out the subtext of tortured memories, and demystify both the kibbutz and the Holy City. The film highlights nuances at the expense of the dramatic plot and foregrounds the personal perspective, portraying the Sabra as introspective and even neurotic. The film was a great success, critically and commercially, selling some 308,000 tickets.

Shnat 66 Hyta Tova Latayarut / '66 was a Good Year for Tourism

1992, 66 mins, colour, Hebrew and English
Director / Producer / Screenwriter: Amit Goren
Cinematographer: Eitan Harris
Editor: Tali Halter
Music: Yo-Go

In 1966, which was indeed a good year for tourism according to the travel-agent father of the maker of this documentary, the documentarist's family emigrated to the United States. The film-maker spent his youth in New York but at eighteen returned to Israel, while his parents and two brothers stayed behind. His film merges rushes from the editing room with 8 mm home movies and sections depicting a journey to his father's birthplace, Alexandria in Egypt, in search of this roots. Through the story of his family, Goren deals with issues about his own identity and at the same time questions the basic ideology of Zionism. The film won the Wolgin Award at the Jerusalem Film Festival.

Shraga Katan (literally 'Shraga Small') / Little Man

1978, 90 mins, colour, Hebrew

Director: Ze'ev Revah
Producer: Baruch Ella, Ze'ev Revah
Screenwriter: Hillel Mittelfunkt, Ze'ev Revah
Cinematographer: Gadi Danzig
Editor: Zion Avrahamian
Music: Shem-Tov Levy
Leading Players: Ze'ev Revah, Nitza Shaul, Yosef Carmon, Tzachi Noy, Yitzhak Hizkiyahu

Five reserve soldiers sleep with Sophie, a seventeen-year-old and member of a theatre group commissioned to entertain an armoured unit stationed on the Golan Heights. When she realizes that she is pregnant, only Shraga, a factory foreman, takes responsibility. This social drama (based on a play by Hillel Mittelfunkt), foregrounding issues such as ethnic and class tensions, focuses on the relationship between the sexes and suggests through its protagonists, both of Jewish Moroccan families, a new alliance of oriental Jews. The film received mixed reviews and moderate box office success (selling around 210,000 tickets), and was entered for the Miami Film Festival.

Shtey Etzba'ot MiTzidon (literally 'Two Fingers from Tzidon') / Ricochets

1986, 91 mins, colour, Hebrew
Director: Elli Cohen
Producer: Elli Dori (IDF Film Unit)
Screenwriter: Elli Cohen, Tzvi Kretzner, Baruch Nevo
Cinematographer: Yehiel Ne'eman, Ya'akov Saporta
Editor: Avigdor Weil
Music: Benni Nagari
Leading Players: Roni Pinkovich, Alon Aboutboul, Shaul Mizrachi, Ossi Hilele

Gadi, a fresh officer sent to Lebanon during the Lebanon War, consents to the hardline approach taken by his commanding officer against the local population. When the Israeli soldiers track a Palestinian guerrilla leader to the home of a Lebanese villager, Gadi volunteers to storm the house alone. This war film, shot during the last month of Israel's invasion of Lebanon in an occupied Lebanese village by the IDF Film Unit for internal educational purposes, was purchased only later for theatrical distribution. Explicit propaganda, the film uses universal humanistic anti-war messages to consolidate the heroic–nationalist ethos rather than subvert it. In a typical scene the protagonist avoids harming an old man only to find out that the man is hiding explosives, thus reinforcing the moral superiority of the Israeli soldiers. The film's paranoid atmosphere, illustrated by the hostile glances of the Shi'ite villagers and underscored by the shaking hand-held camera, substantiates this apologia for the Lebanon War. Reviews were mixed but the film was a huge box office success, with over 800,000 tickets sold, and won the Israel Best Film Award. It was also entered for Cannes, Berlin and other film festivals.

Shuru

1990, 85 mins, colour, Hebrew

Director:	Savi Gavison
Producer:	Yonatan Aroch
Screenwriter:	Savi Gavison, Yonatan Aroch, Yochanan Raviv
Cinematographer:	Yoav Kosh
Editor:	Tali Halter-Shenkar
Music:	Lior Tevet
Leading Players:	Moshe Ivgi, Sharon Hacohen, Sinai Peter, Keren Mor, Shmuel Edelman

Asher, a small-time Tel Aviv 'operator', acts as a guru for a group of lost souls that includes a woman poet, a vegetable wholesaler abused by his wife, an alcoholic publicist, a sadistic professor of literature and a kind-hearted taxi driver. The encounter between them alters their lives. This low-budget debut feature joins other inner-exile films of this period in rejecting political drama in favour of mundane issues such as urban alienation and the futile quest for identity, which are underplayed in this postmodern hallucinatory situation comedy. The film satirizes marital relationships, feminist activism and homophobia, and pokes fun at American fads. It received favourable reviews and good box office, and won the Israel Film Academy Best Film and Wolgin Awards at the Jerusalem Film Festival.

Sipurei Tel Aviv / *Tel Aviv Stories*

1992, 110 mins, colour, Hebrew

Director:	Ayelet Menachemi, Nirit Yaron
Producer:	Yitzhak Ginsberg, Ehud Bleiberg
Screenwriter:	Shemi Zarchin, Ayelet Menachemi, Nirit Yaron
Cinematographer:	Amnon Zlayeit, Jorge Gurevich
Editor:	Ayelet Menachemi
Music:	Ari Frankel, Shlomo Gronich
Leading Players:	Yael Abecasis, Ruthi Goldberg, Anat Waxman, Sharon Alexander, Sasson Gabai

The three separate short dramas that make up this film all take place in Tel Aviv, all focus on women and are all made by women (who are usually marginalized in Israeli cinema). The first drama, 'Sharona Motek' / 'Sweet Sharon', unfolds a night in the life of a designer who is hunting for the lost key to her apartment and her life. 'Mivtza Khatul' / 'Operation Cat' revolves around the attempts of a local newspaper reporter to save a cat from the sewer. 'Guet' / 'Divorce' is about a policewoman who takes hostages in an attempt to get a divorce from her husband. The dramas focus on personal conflicts and topics common to young people in an urban setting, underscoring characteristic inner-exile themes: love and its frustration; male–female relationships; and the pursuit of self-fulfilment. Feminism is highlighted only by the strong presence of the protagonists, not as an issue in its own right. Nevertheless the film is saturated with feminine sensibilities, reflected also by the open format of the two first stories. The third story utilizes the genre of a chase film and thus adopts male strategies. *Sipurei Tel Aviv* received favourable reviews and did relatively well at the box office (selling around 150,000 tickets). It was an entry at film festivals in Calcutta, Montreal, Shanghai, Toronto and Los Angeles.

Sipurim Ktzarim Al Ahava / Short Stories about Love

1997–8, colour, Hebrew
Director: Gil Lavenberg, Eitan Fuchs, Irit Linur, Uri Rozenvax, Doron Tzabari,
                Ori Sivan, Hagai Levy and others
Producer: Hagai Levi, Sharon Shamir (for Channel 2)

These twelve short television dramas brought young Hebrew writers together with a new generation of film-makers. The prevailing topic is love between young urbanites: a stranger wins the heart of a young girl about to be married in 'Habachur Shel Shuli' / 'Shuli's Man' (44mins); a romance unfolds in a car repair shop in 'Einam Sheli' / 'My Eyes' (44 mins); frustrated love turns out to be the winning card for a ten-pin bowler in 'Chatulot Hara'am' / 'Thunder Cats (38 mins)'. The dramas employ various film practices, but abide by the basic rules of dramatic structure. The project was a breakthrough in television productions, since the producers and directors won artistic freedom and broke the restrictions usually imposed by mainstream commercial television. Following this project, Channel 2 and the Cable TV increased their investment in local television dramas.

Te'alat Blaumilech (literally 'The Blaumilech Dig') / The Big Dig

1969, 89 mins, colour, Hebrew
Director / Screenwriter: Ephraim Kishon
Producer: Ephraim Kishon, Ronni Ya'akov
Cinematographer: Manny Wein
Editor: Peter Masgryev
Music: Noam Sherif
Leading Players: Bomba Tzur, Shraga Friedman, Shaike Ophir, Nissim Azikri

A satire in which a patient escapes from a psychiatric hospital and begins to dig a trench in a central Tel Aviv street. The police assist him, while the mayor uses the trench to promote the city. This satire on bureaucracy and political opportunism, based on Kishon's literary satires, suggests that the root of all evil is the oppression of the 'small man' and parodies Zionist ideals by attributing pioneering zeal to an absurd enterprise. The film received favourable reviews and very good box office (approximately 490,000 tickets were sold), winning the Outstanding Foreign Film Award at the Barcelona Film Festival and a nomination for a Golden Globe.

Tekuma / Resurrection

1998, television series, colour / black and white, Hebrew
Director: Nathan Lifshitz, Tor Ben-Mayor, Ron Rotem, Yehuda Kave, Ayelet
                Heler, Dina Tzvi-ricklis, Ido Sela, Amit Goren, Daniel Wachsmann,
                Asher Telalim and others

Chief Editor: Gideon Drori (Israeli TV / Channel 1)

The biggest and most ambitious documentary project ever produced by Israeli TV. The twenty-two-episode series documents the fifty years of the state of Israel (1948–98) and focuses on the main historical events that shaped this period: the Jewish struggle against the British and the War of Independence, the massive immigration of the 1950s, the 1956 Sinai War, the Eichmann Trial, the 1967 Six Day War, the political upheavals of 1977, the peace agreement with Egypt, the 1982 Lebanon War, the *intifada*, the Oslo Agreements and the assassination of Yitzhak Rabin, as well as secular–religious and Jewish–Arab tensions. Several of the episodes stirred contro-versy due to subversive treatments by some of the film-makers. The series also included rare footage, such as scenes from a Syrian docu-drama produced in the 1960s on the massacre in Kafer Kassem.

Tel Aviv Berlin

1987, 90 mins, colour, Hebrew
Director / Screenwriter: Tzipi Trope
Producer: Smadar Azrielli
Cinematographer: Gadi Danzig
Editor: Rahel Yagil
Music: Shalom Weinstein
Leading Players: Shmuel Vilozhny, Rivka Noiman, Anat Harpazy, Yossef Carmon

Benyamin, a Holocaust survivor living with his wife and daughter in Tel Aviv in 1948, chances on a former *kapo* whom he suspects of having been involved in his father's murder in a concentration camp. Benyamin plans to kill him. This period drama, which deals with the shadow of the Holocaust from a unique angle, reversing the victim–executioner roles, also touches on displacement and its impact on the second generation of Holocaust survivors. This new sensibility film, which draws on autobio-graphical material, received poor reviews and failed at the box office (with only 5,000 tickets sold), but won the Israel Best Film Award and was entered for the Montreal, Berlin and London Film Festivals.

Tipat Mazal / A Bit of Luck

1992, 90 mins, colour, Hebrew
Director: Ze'ev Revah
Producer: Yoram Globus, Boaz Davidson
Screenwriter: Hanan Peled, Ze'ev Revah
Cinematographer: Yoav Kosh
Editor: Zion Avrahamian
Music: Dov Seltzer, Nansi Brandis
Leading Players: Ze'ev Revah, Zehava Ben, Jacques Cohen, Yossi Keinan, Arie Moskona

JoJo, a singer in 1950s Marrakesh, emigrates to Israel with his young daughter, only to face poverty and disillusionment. He turns to alcohol and loses his sight, while his daughter grows up to be a popular singer – an occupation which he condemns. In the end, all their misfortunes are resolved: a rich friend pays for an operation which brings back JoJo's sight and JoJo is reconciled with his daughter. This film (based on Ze'ev Revah's story) uses some of the conventions of Bourekas melodrama, but subverts others in exposing the misfortunes of Moroccan Jews who were forced to the fringe and suffered economic and cultural set-backs on the harsh road to integration. The film received poor reviews but did well at the box office, selling around 250,000 tickets.

Transit

1979, 90 mins, colour, Hebrew
Director: Daniel Wachsmann
Producer: Ya'akov Goldwasser
Screenwriter: Daniel Horowitz, Daniel Wachsmann
Cinematographer: Ilan Rosenberg
Editor: Asher Tlalim, Levi Zini
Leading Players: Gedalya Besser, Liora Rivlin, Yitzhak Ben-Tzur, Yair Elasar, Amnon Meskin

Erich Neusbaum, who escaped Nazi Germany before the war and settled in Palestine, faces another period of rootlessness when he moves to a cheap hotel after his wife has left him, taking their only son with her. He wanders on the fringe of 1960s Tel Aviv, among prostitutes and drug addicts, dreaming of going back to his beloved Berlin. This debut psychological drama deals with the tragic ramifications of displacement and its impact on family life, undermining Zionism's melting-pot ideal. Its low-budget new sensibility practice gives an intimate *mise-en-scène*, wintry cinematography and sparse dialogue. The film received mixed reviews and failed at the box office (selling only around 6,000 tickets), but it was entered for the Cannes, Berlin, London and Los Angeles Film Festivals, among others.

Tzabar / Sabra

1933, 60 mins, black and white, Hebrew (also dubbed into Polish)
Director: Alexander Ford
Producer: Ze'ev Markovitz (Palestine–Poland co-production)
Screenwriter: Alexander Ford, Olga Ford, Mary Sochovolska
Cinematographer: Frank Weinmayer
Music: Shimon Lekes
Editor: Ziegfried Mifflebar
Leading Players: Hannah Robina, Aharon Meskin, Raphael Klatchkin, Shimon Finkel

A group of pioneers settles in an uninhabited part of Palestine and begins to dig a well. They suffer from hunger and contract malaria. After a drought, Arab neighbours attack the Jewish settlement. At the last moment water gushes up from the new well, resolving the violent conflict. Ford, already an established film director in Poland, and his wife Olga wrote a script that would eventually serve as the Zionist master-narrative in the Israeli cinema, consolidating the fundamental elements of the Zionist programme: redeeming the wasteland and restoring it to fertility, constructing a new society and civilizing the 'primitive' native Arabs. The film also features the recurring themes of struggle over water, the Jewish–Arab conflict, power struggles within the commune, malaria and forbidden love. *Tzabar* had a great impact on Israeli cinema in general, as well as on the specific narratives of *Hem Hayu Asara / They Were Ten* (1960) and *Hacholmim / Unsettled Land* (1987). *Tzabar* was a big-budget international production that used sophisticated laboratories in Poland, where the film was dubbed. Ford incorporated documentary footage that was shot before the dramatic scenes, some of which was edited later into newsreels and screened in Poland. At the time of the shooting, the Arabic press protested, calling the film 'hair-raising Zionist propaganda'. *Tzabar* premiered in Poland in 1933, but in Palestine the British government banned it, fearing Arab protests. In 1934 a cut version was shown in Tel Aviv, to poor reviews from the Hebrew press.

Tzlila Chozeret / Repeat Dive

1982, 85 mins, colour, Hebrew
Director / Screenwriter: Shimon Dotan
Producer: Amos Mokadi
Cinematographer: Dani Shneur
Editor: Dani Schik
Music: Zohar Levy
Leading Players: Doron Nesher, Liron Nirgad, Danny Muggia, Ami Traub

Yoav, member of an elite navy commando team, falls in love with Mira. Mira is the widow of Yoav's diving partner who, in a tape-recorded will, 'bequeathed' Mira to Yoav. Mira, obsessed with the memory of her husband, tries in vain to untie her new love's bonds to his commando unit. This nihilistic drama (based on a story by Yehudit Hendel) questions the meaning of bravery and self-sacrifice, cutting through the machismo of the men and exposing their vulnerability. At the same time it questions the status of women, excluded from the allegiances and codes of combat, and presents militarism as a disruptive factor in the social texture. The underplayed dramatic scenes and underwater scenes reflect the mood of the protagonists. *Tzlila Chozeret* received favourable reviews, modest box office (around 160,000 tickets were sold) and the Israel Best Film Award.

Vayhi Biymei / And It Came to Pass in the Days of …

1932, 18 mins, black and white, silent
Director: Haim Halachmi
Producer: PAI
Screenwriter / Cinematographer: Nathan Axelrod
Designer: Tsvi Goldin

| Music: | Gramophone discs and the recorded voice of Moshe Churgal |
| Leading Players: | Moshe Churgal, Yehezkel Fridman, Barouch Hadari |

This film is a comedy in two acts. It portrays three couples (European middle-aged Jews, young American tourists and young Sabra pioneers), who get involved in a series of humorous role-reversals set against the backdrop of the Purim Carnival in Tel Aviv. This first short comedy by local talent draws on Max Sennett as much as on Jewish writer Shalom Aleichem. The budget of £28 came from loans and contributions, and the entire staff was composed of volunteers. The film, dubbed 'a pioneering enterprise' by the Hebrew press, premiered in Tel Aviv and was later shown in theatres in Haifa and Jerusalem prior to the main feature.

Wadi

1981, 45 mins, colour, Hebrew

Director / Screenwriter / Producer:	Amos Gitai
Cinematographer:	Yakov Saporta, Yossi Wein
Editor:	Solvei Nordlond

A documentary about the Roushmeya wadi in Haifa, which was used during the British Mandate as a quarry but since 1948 has been populated by Jewish refugees from Europe, as well as native Arabs who lost their homes in the war. The film focuses on three families: a Palestinian couple, two Romanian brothers and a mixed couple (an Arabic fisherman who is married to a Jewish Holocaust survivor). Their personal stories and tensions reflect the socio-political dilemmas of the region, suggesting that what links Jews and Arabs is a solidarity based on everyday give and take. In 1991 Channel 4 in Britain asked Gitai to revisit the wadi, where he shot *Wadi 81–91*.

Ya Brachen – Mered Hayama'im / The Seamen's Strike

1981, 70 mins, black and white, Hebrew

Director / Screenwriter:	Judd Ne'eman
Producer:	Israeli TV
Cinematographer:	Yechiel Cohen, Ruby Dorot
Editor:	Esther Levine

The circumstances that led to the strike of Israeli seaman 1951 are presented in this documentary as the last stage in the dramatic struggle by the ruling Labour Party, led by Ben Gurion, to eliminate its political opponents. The seamen's demand to disaffiliate their union from the Labour Federation controlled by Ben Gurion was perceived as a subversive act and the government reacted by sending in hundreds of policemen. The film depicts the Ben Gurion regime as having been tainted by despotism, totalitarianism and fear of communism. The seamen's strike was known as the 'Hebrew *Potemkin*'.

Yaldei Stalin / Stalin's Disciples

1987, 90 mins, colour, Hebrew
Director / Screenwriter: Nadav Levitan
Producer: Doron Eran
Cinematographer: Gadi Danzig
Editor: Shimon Tamir
Music: Hava Alberstein
Leading Players: Shmuel Shilo, Yossi Kantz, Hugo Yarden, Rahel Dobson

Three old shoemakers on a kibbutz in the 1950s lose faith in communism in the face of revelations about Stalin's crimes and the manifest anti-Semitism at the Prague Trials. This low-budget period drama, which satirizes the utopian ideology of the kibbutz, unveils the tragedy of people who devoted their whole lives to a questionable ideal and paints the entire Zionist enterprise in a critical revisionist shade. The film failed both critically and commercially (selling only around 4,000 tickets), but was nominated for a Golden Globe and was the first Israeli feature to participate in the Moscow and Warsaw Film Festivals.

Yatzati Lechapes Hahava … Techef Ashuv / Out for Love, Be Back Shortly …

1997, 55 mins, colour, Hebrew
Director / Producer / Screenwriter / Cinematographer: Dan Katzir
Editor: Joel Alexis

The director, a student in the film department of TAU, goes out with his camera to look for love. When he finds Iris, a young woman on the eve of starting her military service, he find it difficult to express his emotions. This love story is set against right-wing protest demonstrations which culminated in the assassination of Yitzhak Rabin. This documentary underscores the impossibility of dissociating the personal from the national, criticizing the role of militarism in Israeli society. The film won the Wolgin Award at the Jerusalem Film Festival.

Yeshayahu Leibowitz in Ma'alot

1981, colour, Hebrew
Director: Yigal Burstein
Producer: David Michalis (Israeli TV)
Cinematographer: Tibi Salomon, Charlie Shitrit
Editor: Ofra Riesenfeld
Participants: Prof. Yeshayahu Leibowitz, Prof. Yisrael Eldad, Dr Menachem Brinker

This documentary features the humanist philosopher Yeshayahu Leibowitz on a trip to the Galilee in the company of his adversary, right-wing historian Yisrael Eldad. During the drive the two conduct a feverish and sometimes violent dispute, and on arrival at the northern border town of Ma'alot they proceed to elaborate, in front of audiences, on Zionist ideology, especially regarding the conflicts between Israelis and

Palestinians and between the state and religion. Leibowitz provokes his audience by declaring that the Israeli army is Judeo-Nazi and that history is the summation of human crimes. For an entire year, the director followed the controversial religious professor of philosophy and science, an idol of the liberal left in Israel. Burstein was asked to edit out some objectionable statements, but the film received unanimous praise.

Yir Ha'ohalim / Tent City

1951, 40 mins, black and white, Hebrew
Director: Aryeh (Leopold) Lahola
Screenwriter / Producer: Baruch Dienar
Cinematographer: Jack Janiloviicz
Editor: Gerald Thomas

Figure 42 Yir Ha'ohalim / Tent City

Music:	Hans May
Leading Players:	Ephraim Pinchas, Uri Edelmann, Nissim Habib, Orna Porat

This film tells the story of two Jewish families, from Germany and from Iraq, who reside in a temporary camp. It is set against backdrop of the massive immigration to Israel of both Holocaust survivors and people from Arabic countries and North Africa. This was the first film to show the newcomers' difficulties and the ethnic tensions caused by cultural differences between Ashkenazi and Sephardi Jews, a topic usually camouflaged in films of that period. Dienar managed to get only private finance for the film, since the Zionist institutions refused to sponsor a film that admitted prejudice among Jews, but his docu-drama won prizes in Boston and New York.

Yizkor, Ha'avadim Shel Hazikaron / *Remember, the Slaves of Memory*

1991, 97 mins, colour, Hebrew

Director / Screenwriter:	Eyal Sivan
Producer:	Reuven Kornfeld, Edgar Tenembaum
Cinematographer:	Roni Katzenelson
Editor:	Jacques Comts

This film examines the reactions of high-school students in Jerusalem to memorial days for the Holocaust and for the fallen in Israel's battles. The documentary suggests that the mechanisms of these rituals, originating in Zionist ideology, construct 'mental slaves', inducing Israelis to adopt the role of eternal victim and refuse to take moral responsibility for their aggressive acts against the Palestinians. The film was shot during the *intifada* and, on its cinematheque screenings, provoked extreme reactions in the Israeli press, who alleged that the Paris-based director had distorted reality in order to please the European left.

Yom Huledet Same'ach Mar Mugrabi / *Happy Birthday, Mr Mugrabi*

1999, 77 mins, colour, Hebrew

Director / Screenwriter:	Avi Mugrabi
Producer:	Avi Mugrabi, Serge Lalu
Cinematographer:	Eithan Haris, Ron Katzenelson
Editor:	Avi Mugrabi
Leading Players:	Avi Mugrabi, Shachar Segal, Doud Kutab

Blurring the distinctions between the personal and the national, fiction and non-fiction, the director of this docu-drama makes an ironic tribute to the fiftieth anniversary of the state of Israel, as well as to his own forty-second birthday. The meta-cinematic narrative unfolds his attempts to make a film about the festivities. In the meantime a Palestinian friend asks him to help with a Palestinian film focused on the Nakba (the Palestinian term for the disastrous outcome of the 1948 war). A third sub-narrative describes Mugrabi's Kafkaesque efforts to build a new home for his family. The film conveys a deep ambivalence about the complex Israeli social, cultural and political realities, simultaneously addressing issues relating to the subject in documentary films. *Yom Huledet Same'ach Mar Mugrabi* won awards and mentions at various film festivals.

Yoman / Diary

1973–83, 330 mins, black and white / colour, Hebrew
Director / Screenwriter: David Perlov
Producer: Mira Perlov, David Perlov (Israeli–UK co-production)
Cinematographer: David Perlov, Gadi Danzig
Editor: Yael Perlov

In *Yoman* film-maker David Perlov documents nearly ten years in his life from the onset of the 1973 Yom Kippur War to the 1981 Lebanon War. The protagonists are Perlov, his wife and his twin daughters. This six-segment monumental diary moves between private and public spheres, between intimate family episodes and political events, and documents (among other things) Perlov's return to his hometown, São Paulo in Brazil. Perlov, a true modernist, uses his camera as if it were a pen, writing down the trivia of his own family life, but also looking out of his window at a political demonstration, narrating the events in his own voice. His unique approach, always privileging the human face and identifying the personal with the political, won him great praise. *Yoman* was broadcast by co-producer Channel 4 in the United Kingdom and screened at the Pompidou Centre in Paris and MOMA in New York, as well as in Israeli cinematheques and on cable television. In 1990, the association of Israeli film critics chose Perlov as the best director of the 1980s for *Yoman*. He is currently making two additional segments for the diary.

Yoman Sadeh / Field Diary

1982, 85 mins, colour, Hebrew
Director / Screenwriter: Amos Gitai
Producer: Richard Copans
Cinematographer: Nurit Aviv
Editor: Scheherazade Saadi

The banality of the occupation in the West Bank is the subtext of this travelogue, which explores the legitimization of violence against Palestinians. Gitai uses his camera as a weapon, confronting Israeli soldiers who forbid his filming and following Israeli settlers on protests against government policy. In a different mood he addresses a Palestinian woman lamenting the uprooting of olive trees by the Israeli authorities and a Palestinian peasant who talks about his links to the land of his ancestors. The film incorporates images of Israeli tanks invading South Lebanon, thus creating an overall statement about aggression.

Za'am Vetehila / Rage and Glory

1984, 118 mins, colour, Hebrew

Director / Screenwriter:	Avi Nesher
Producer:	Avi Nesher, Yitzhak Sehayek
Cinematographer:	David Gurfinkel
Editor:	Yitzhak Sehayek
Music:	Rami Kleinstein, Yizhar Ashdot
Leading Players:	Guiliano Mer, Rona Freed, Roni Pinkovitch, Hanna Azulai, Tuvia Gelber

In Jerusalem in 1942 Yair Stern, the head of the radical anti-British Jewish under-ground, is gunned down by the British CID. Eddy 'the Butcher' is called in to take revenge and plans a series of spectacular terrorist actions that culminate in a massacre. This stylized period drama, drawing on historical accounts that glorify violence for the sake of violence and present self-sacrifice as devoid of ideological significance in the fascist mode, parodies and subverts the heroic–nationalist genre, reinforcing a nihilist view. The big-budget production (US$1 million), employing the form and mannerisms of an American gangster film, received poor reviews and box office (only approxi-mately 48,000 tickets were sold).

Zichron Devarim (literally 'Remembrance of Things') / Devarim

1996, 110 mins, colour, Hebrew

Director:	Amos Gitai
Producer:	Shuki Friedman
Screenwriter:	Amos Gitai, Gilad Evron
Cinematographer:	Renato Berta
Editor:	Zohar Sela
Music:	Uri Ophir
Leading Players:	Assi Dayan, Amos Gitai, Amos Schub, Lea Koenig, Riki Gal

Based on the novel by Ya'akov Shabtai, this drama unfolds nine months in the lives of three friends: Caesar is a photographer in his forties who is estranged from his wife and pursuing the pleasures of the moment; Goldman is a lawyer who lives with his parents; and Israel is a gifted thirty-year-old pianist who lives off Caesar's money. The three move around in a shabby, haunted Tel Aviv, living in a cultural void, antagonized by their Zionist parents and consumed by a death wish. They drown their despair in long conversations, alcohol and promiscuous sex. This dystopian film, an adaptation of one of the most important novels in contemporary Hebrew literature, intellectual-izes topics such as mental impotence and internal exile, also reflecting the post-ideological mood of the 1990s. Gitai employs experimental strategies, including a fragmented narrative that merges past and present, many static shots, extreme close-ups and the unusual application of colour, and creates an associative collage, sometimes intentionally obscure, that challenges the audience to review their own estrangement. The film received mixed reviews but was entered for the Venice Film Festival.

Zot Hi Ha'aretz / This is the Land

1935, 50 mins, black and white, Hebrew

Director:	Barouch Agadati
Producer:	Yitzhak Agadati (Aga Film)
Screenwriter:	Avigdor Hame'iri, Barouch Agadati
Cinematographer:	Hans Lanni, P. Rossi
Music:	Ya'akov Levanon, Mordechai Ze'ira
Lyrics:	Emanuel Harussi, Alexander Penn
Leading Players:	Shmuel Rodenski, Raphael Klatchkin, Moshe Khurgel, Meir Te'omi

Zot Hi Ha'aretz attempts to sum up fifty years of Zionist settlement in Palestine from the foundation of the first Jewish colonies in 1882, offering a thematic conclusion to the Zionist realist genre. It was the first full-length Hebrew film with sound and a private enterprise, merging documentary footage by Ben-Dov (whose archives had been bought by Barouch Agadati in 1934) that dated from the beginning of the century with Agadati's own *AGA* newsreels, as well as dramatized scenes. Agadati interweaves heroic and mundane images from the rural and urban lives of the pioneers with several outstanding historical moments (including Sir Herbert Samuel's arrival in Jaffa in 1920 and Lord Balfour's speech at the 1925 opening of the Hebrew University in Jerusalem). When the film opened in Tel Aviv, it was greeted with great enthusiasm; later it was recognized as a serious historiographic endeavour in pre-state cinema. In 1964 Agadati released (to less acclaim) *Ha'etmol shel Hamakhar / Tomorrow's Yesterday*, a revised version of his docu-drama with different narration and music.

List of film-makers

Agadati, Baruch (b. 1895, Russia; d. 1975, Israel)

Agadati worked variously as a director, producer, choreographer and painter. In 1932 he started, with his brother Yitzhak Agadati (also a producer), the *AGA* newsreel. This was the first Hebrew-language newsreel and Agadati produced it periodically until 1934. After the success of his only feature film *Zot Hi Ha'aretz / This is the Land* (1934), a compilation and docu-drama celebrating fifty years of Zionism, Agadati resumed his career as a painter. In addition to this film and a later revised version called *Ha'etmol Shel Hamachar / Tomorrow's Yesterday* (1964), Agadati made a few short documentaries, among them the short colour film *Tel Aviv* (1950). Agadati, one of Hebrew cinema's unrelenting pioneers, was inspired by Soviet avant-garde cinema; his 1930s footage bears the characteristics of this cinema, which became the prevailing representative form for Zionist utopianism.

Alter, Naftali (b. 1947, Israel)

A director, producer and composer, Alter was a graduate of the London Film School and produced and co-wrote many of Assi Dayan's films, among them *Hagiga La'einayim / Saint Cohen* and *Givat Halfon Eina Ona / Halfon Hill Doesn't Answer*. In 1985 he scripted and directed a comedy, *Irit Irit*, and subsequently directed two more features. He composed music for many films, winning the Best Composer Award for his score for *Hachaim Al Pi Agfa* / *Life According to Agfa*. In 1992–8 he headed the Fund for the Promotion of Israeli Quality Films.

Asher, Tova (b. 1950, Israel)

Asher started as a documentary editor and, since the late 1970s, has edited feature films, television dramas and television series. Among the films she has edited are *Khirbet Hiz'ah*, *Noa Bat Sheva-Esrey* / *Noa at Seventeen*, *Me'achorei Hasoragim* / *Beyond the Walls*, *Bar 51*, *Echad Mishelanu* / *One of Us*, *Golem Bama'agal* / *Blind Man's Bluff*.

Atzmon, Anat (b. Israel)

Atzmon became a star overnight with her role as a teenage beauty in the popular *Eskimo Limone* / *Lemon Popsicle* (1978). She subsequently appeared in *Dizengoff 99*, which became a cult movie. Later she took leading roles in several dramas and melo-dramas, including *Ha'ayit* / *The Vulture* (1981), *Kyish Le'Lo Motzah* / *Dead-End Street* (1982) and *Edut Me'Ones* / *Forced Testimony* (1984).

Aviad, Michal (b. 1955, Israel)

Aviad is a documentary-maker who gained her film degree in San Francisco. In the United States she directed the prized *Acting Our Age* (1987). She has also made several acclaimed documentaries in Israel, among them *Hanashim Mimul* / *The Women Next Door* (1992), *Yarita Pa'am Be'mishehu* / *Ever Shot Anyone?* (1995) and *Jenny VeJenny* / *Jenny and Jenny* (1997). Her films combine documentary and dramatic techniques in a fluent cinematic jargon that discloses her social and political awareness.

Axelrod, Nathan (b. 1905, Russia; d. 1987, Israel)

A photographer, producer, director and editor, Axelrod is considered one of the founding fathers of Israeli cinema. He was also the most prolific film-maker of the pre-state generation. Soon after emigrating to Palestine in 1926, Axelrod filmed news and promotional shorts for Yerushalayim Segal's Moledet company. In 1932 he collaborated with Haim Halachmi on the short comedy *Vayhi Biymei* / *And It Came to Pass in the Days of …* and the first full-length fiction film *Oded Hanoded* / *Oded the Wanderer* (both 1932). In 1935 he started *Yoman Carmel* (Carmel Newsreel), which he produced weekly up until 1941. During World War II he made propaganda and training films for the Jewish Agency and the British Information Office; after the war he resumed production of newsreels until he sold his interests to Israel Motion Picture Studios in late 1950s. During the years of the British Mandate and the first decade of the state of Israel, Axelrod produced up to fifty newsreels a year, documenting important historical events as well as everyday life. He also made documentaries and feature films, such as *Me'al Hachoravot* / *Over the Ruins* (1938), and in 1962 compiled a nostalgic documentary called *Etz o Palestine* / *The True Story of Palestine* (1962) from his newsreels. Some of Axelrod's extensive footage was ruined or lost, but in 1977 his archive was acquired by the Israel State Archives and transferred to safety stock. It is preserved at the Israel Film Archive in the Jerusalem Cinematheque. Axelrod's invaluable heritage has cemented the historical memory of the early years of the nation.

Barabash, Uri (b. 1946, Israel)

Barabash was a graduate of the London Film School. In the 1970s he directed documentaries for Israeli television and foreign networks, as well as television dramas. His debut feature film, *Stigma* (1982), imparts the motifs that would be foregrounded in his later films: male bonds formed in the army, the individual versus the group, and military post-traumatic experience. In other films, *Me'achorei Hasoragim / Beyond the Walls* (1984), *Hacholmim / Unsettled Land* (1987), *Echad Mishelanu / One of Us* (1989) and *Derech Hanesher / Where Eagles Fly* (1990), Barabash criticized Israel's colonialism and militarism. He made a dozen features and television drama series, among them the historical courtroom drama *Mishpat Kastner / Kastner Trial* (1994) and a series recounting the experiences of new recruits in the army. One of Israel's most prolific film-makers and, of his generation, the most closely affiliated with mainstream cinematic strategies, Barbash is noted for his critical approach to Israeli society. His powerfully dramatic films foreground the dilemmas of a militaristic and chauvinistic society, highlighting the conflicts of the male Sabra.

Barkan, Yehuda (b. 1945, Israel)

An actor, director and producer, Barkan starred in many popular comedies by Menachem Golan and Boaz Davidson, among them *Charlie Vachetzi / Charlie and a Half*, *Malkat Hakvish / Queen of the Road* and *Catz VeCarasso / Katz and Carasso*. In the 1980s he found success as the director of several candid-camera films which became box office hits. In 1988 he produced and starred in the popular comedy *Aba Ganuv / The Skipper* (directed by Ya'akov Goldwasser), as well as its two sequels.

Bat-Adam, Michal (b. Israel)

Bat-Adam, a director, actor and scriptwriter, is one of the few female film directors in Israel and the most accomplished. She started as an actress; two of her most memorable roles were in *Ani Ohev Otach Rosa / I Love You Rosa* (1972) and *Atalia* (1984). She also directed three of the films in which she starred. Her directorial debut was *Rega'im / Moments* (1979), a love story about two women. The films that followed also focused on intimate portraits of young women, sometimes in conflict with their mothers, as in *Al Hevel Dak / A Thin Line* (1981) and *Autobiographia Dimyonith / Imaginary Autobiography* (1994). Her latest film, *Ha'ahvah Mi'Mabat Sheni / Love at Second Sight* (1998), unfolds the story of a young female photographer who falls in love with a man whose picture she took by chance. Bat-Adam is the most prolific female director in Israel. She has made nine films to date, and also directed a television drama. Her low-key cinematic style, centring on the actors, enriches her otherwise mainstream films with a touch of melancholy, endowing them with a modernist patina.

Benchetrit, David (b. 1954, Morocco)

A director, cinematographer and producer, Benchetrit was a graduate of Beit Tzvi Film Department. He worked as a cameramen and producer for European and American television networks and made several short documentaries – among them *Nadia* (1983), about a Palestinian girl born in Israeli prison – before directing his first acclaimed documentary feature, *Miba'ad Lere'alat Hagalut / Through the Veil of Exile* (1992), which depicts the lives and tribulations of three Palestinian women. *Samir* (1997) focuses on the life of the Iraqi-born author Sammy Michael. All Benchetrit's films highlight the struggling attempts by the oppressed to redeem their humanity.

Ben-Dor, Orna (b. 1956, Israel)

A graduate of TAU Film Department, Ben-Dor has directed dramas and documentary films for television, such as *Shever Anan / Cloudburst* which comes to grips, for the first time, with the plight of the Holocaust survivors who were sent to fight at the front in the 1948 war. Both her feature films, the full-length documentary *Biglal Hamilchama Hahee / Because of that War* (1988) and the fictional *Eretz Hadasha / New Land* (1994) focused on the predicament of Holocaust survivors in Israel. The highly acclaimed *Biglal Hamilchama Hahee* was a forerunner of a new 1990s documentary genre that focused on second-generation Holocaust survivors. In 1994–9 Ben-Dor was director of the New Fund for Israeli Cinema and Television, expediting the immense development of documentary film-making in the 1990s.

Ben-Dov, Ya'akov (b. 1882, Ukraine; d. 1965, Israel)

Ben-Dov was a pioneering cinematographer who started local documentary film-making in Jewish Palestine. In 1917 he documented the historic entrance into Jerusalem of General Allenby and the British Army. A year later, he made his first documentary focusing on current events and scenes from agricultural Zionist settlements, themes that would recur in all his films. As early as 1918 Ben-Dov was approaching Zionist institutions in Palestine to request support for filming 'whatever is fit and important for us to leave for the memory of the generations to come'. In April 1919, he founded his own company, Menorah (Candelabrum), and shot a second documentary which was distributed all over Europe. *The Return of Zion* (1921), including footage of the arrival of the first British Commissioner, Sir Herbert Samuel, was shown at the 12th Zionist Congress in Karlsbad. This is the only one of Ben-Dov's films that survived almost whole. For the tenth anniversary of the Balfour Declaration in 1927 he prepared the compilation film *A Decade of Building in Palestine* (also known as *The Revival*). In 1923 he shot *Ma'asseh Betayar Amerika'i BeEretz Yisrael / Palestine Awakening* and in 1928 managed to raise money from both Zionist Funds for the production of *Aviv Be'eretz Yisrael / Springtime in Palestine*. In 1934 he sold his films and film rights to Baruch Agadati. Ben-Dov was the first independent reporter-cinematographer of Jewish Palestine to also process and cut his own negatives. Most of his documentaries are structured as compilations and his footage was frequently used in other films. Most of his films were lost, but what was left is invaluable as a historical record.

Bukaee, Rafi (b. 1957, Israel)

A director and producer, Bukaee graduated from the TAU Film Department. After directing a debut feature, the unanimously acclaimed *Avanti Popolo* (1986), he made a drama for television and in 1992 produced the Israeli films *Eddie King* and *Hachaim Al Pi Agfa* / *Life According to Agfa*. In 1997 he made his second feature *Marco Polo*, a fantasy about the adventures in Palestine of the famous Italian traveller. Boukai is noted for his unique fusion of real and surreal.

Bouzaglo, Haim (b. 1953, Israel)

A director and scriptwriter, Bouzaglo was a graduate of the Paris Cinema Academy. He worked as a copywriter and scripted many political campaigns and publicity shorts, as well as the feature *Hakaitz Shel Aviya* / *The Summer of Aviya* (1988). In 1988 he scripted and directed his debut feature, *Nisuyim Fictivyim* / *Marriage of Convenience* to be followed in 1991 by *Onat Haduvdevanim* / *Time of the Cherries* and the Israeli–French co-production *Tzaleket* / *Scar* (1995), a post-modern love story. In the 1990s he also scripted and directed two television drama series, one about police work and the other about prisoners' lives. He teaches film at TAU. All his films are unique in their post-modern approach, which may explain their ambivalent reception in Israel.

Burstein, Yigal (b. 1941, England)

A director and scriptwriter who studied film in London, Burstein was among the founders of TAU Film Department, where he is a professor. Since the 1960s he has directed forty documentaries, dramas and experimental shorts, among them the documentaries *Muhammad Yiktzor* / *Muhammad Will Reap* (1976) and *Yeshayahu Leibowitz in Ma'alot* (1981), and two feature films – a comedy *Belfer* (1978) and a fantasy *Osher Lelo Gvul* / *Everlasting Joy* (1996). He also contributed two episodes to the feature *83*. Burstein published several books on cinema, among them *Panim kisdeh Krav* / *Face as Battlefield* (1990), and contributed essays to newspapers and magazines. His films are politically acute, sometimes with an avant-garde inflection, and tend to counter mainstream values and practices.

Cohen, Elli (b. 1940, Israel)

Cohen was a director, actor and scriptwriter, graduating from the London School of Film. For many years he acted on stage and in films, before indulging in film-making in the 1970s when he started directing documentaries and television dramas. Among his features are *Shtey Etzba'ot MiTzidon* / *Ricochets* (1986), *Hakaitz Shel Aviya* / *The Summer of Aviya* (1988), for which he won the Best Director Award, and *Etz Hadomim Tafus* / *Under the Domim Tree* (1995). In 1999 he directed a dramatic mini-series for Channel 1 about illegal immigration from Morocco in the 1950s. Cohen's refined direction endows his films with rich texture within mainstream cinema.

Danzig, Gadi (b. 1944, Israel; d. 1989, Philippines)

One of the most prominent cameramen of the state generation, Danzig shot dozens of commercials, documentaries and student films, as well as local and international features. In a low-budget film industry, he was often the only alternative for productions that had very little lighting equipment. Among the Israeli features he shot were some renowned films, including *Roveh Chuliot / Wooden Gun*, *Yaldei Stalin / Stalin's Disciples* and *Sadot Yerukim / Green Fields*.

Dar, Esther (b. 1935, Israel; d. 1999, Israel)

A director, producer and editor, Dar was a graduate of the London School of Film Technique. In 1969–72 she headed the editing department of the newly established Israeli Public Television (Channel 1). Later on she became producer-director of documentaries for Channel 1. Among her films are *Beit Shemesh* (1978), a three-part documentary on life in a peripheral run-down town, and *Amos Oz*, a profile of the renowned Israeli writer. Her last documentary was *Four Friends* (1999). Along with other state generation television film-makers, Dar participated in the consolidation of independent documentary film-making in Israel.

Davidson, Boaz (b. 1943, Israel)

Both a director and producer, Davidson studied film in London. He has directed documentaries and television dramas, and his feature films include his debut *Shablul / Snail* (1970), *Charlie Vachetzi / Charlie and a Half* (1974) and *Eskimo Limone / Lemon Popsicle* (1978). In the 1980s he worked in the United States, making films for the Cannon production company. Since then, he has worked in Israel and the United States alternately. Davidson is one of the most prolific film-makers in Israel and several of his films have become cult movies.

Dayan, Assi (b. 1945, Israel)

A director, actor, scriptwriter, producer and writer, Dayan acted in Israeli films, playing the role of the mythical Sabra Uri in *Hu Halach Basadot / He Walked Through the Fields*, as well as in American and European films. Later, he played disillusioned Sabra veterans in films like *Ad Sof Haleila / When Night Falls*. Dayan wrote and directed Bourekas films like *Givat Halfon Eina Ona / Halfon Hill Doesn't Answer* (1976) and social satires like *Hagiga La'einayim / Saint Cohen* (1975), and produced and scripted films for other Israeli directors. He made nine features as a director before directing his most accomplished film, *Hachaim Al Pi Agfa / Life According to Agfa* (1992). *Smicha Hashmalit / An Electric Blanket* (1994) and *Mar Baum / Mr Baum* (1997) followed, forming a trilogy that won awards and much critical acclaim. Dayan, who also published short stories, a book of poetry and a novel, is an outstanding figure in Israeli cinema. His versatile work, encompassing both popular comedies and apocalyptic dramas, and controversial public persona make him the *enfant terrible* of the national film-making scene. Several of his early films became cult movies and his 1990s trilogy stands out as a unique achievement in Israeli cinema.

Dayan, Nissim (b. 1946, Israel)

Dayan is a director, scriptwriter, producer, film reviewer and lecturer. In the late 1960s and early 1970s, he made documentaries and training films, and later did reportage for Israeli television. In 1973 he scripted and directed his first feature, *Or Min Hahefker / Light Out of Nowhere*, the first serious attempt to highlight the class struggle among oriental Jews. In the 1980s he made two more features, *Sofo shel Milton Levy / The End of Milton Levy* (1981) and *Gesher Tsar Me'od / On a Narrow Bridge* (1985), both of which offer critiques of the Zionist ethos. He also made the prestigious television mini-series *Michel Ezra Safra Uvanav / Michel Ezra Safra and Sons* (1983), a family saga about the life of oriental Jews in Syria. He has contributed film reviews to radio and various newspapers, and has lectured extensively on cinema. In his films Dayan brought to the fore the emerging social and political consciousness of oriental Jews, thus creating a new voice in Israeli cinema.

Dienar, Baruch (b. 1923, Germany; d. 1997, Israel)

A director, scriptwriter and producer, Dienar studied scriptwriting at Columbia University in New York and worked as an adviser to Universal Studios in Hollywood. In 1949 he directed the documentary *Hachalutzim Hachadashim / The Pioneers* and went on to produce a dozen films, mostly in association with Israel Motion Picture Studios (IMPS) in Herzlia. In 1951 he scripted and produced Lahola's docu-drama *Yir Ha'ohalim / Tent City*. His first feature, *Hem Hayu Asara / They Were Ten* (1960), about pioneers in the Galilee at the end of nineteenth century, won worldwide acclaim and served as an impetus to the Ministry of Commerce to establish the IFC. In 1972 he made another feature and in 1991 a television drama. From 1979–89 he was the production director of the Fund for Encouragement of Israeli Quality Films. Dienar was a central figure in Israel's young film industry in the 1950s and his experience contributed to the development of a latter generation of film-makers in the 1980s.

Dotan, Shimon (b. 1959, Romania)

Dotan was a graduate of the TAU Film Department. The first film he directed, *Tzlila Chozeret / Repeat Dive* (1982), was followed by two episodes for the political film *83*. His second feature, *Chyuch Hagdi / Smile of the Lamb* (1986), won him the Best Director Award. In 1992 he directed in Israel a Hollywood production set against the backdrop of the Gulf War. Dotan now teaches cinema at Concorde University in Canada and makes films there.

Efrati, Yigal (b. 1930)

Efrati was key figure in the development of documentary film-making in Israel. He was the founder and director of the Israel Film Service for thirty years until his death. During his directorship he encouraged and oversaw the making of over 400 films and, for the first two decades of the state, he was the most important commissioning editor and producer of films in the country. Many Israeli directors started their careers under his patronage.

Eldad, Ilan (b. 1929, Yugoslavia)

Eldad studied film in Belgrade. Since the 1950s Eldad has directed dozens of documentaries and commercials, as well as a dozen dramas for the television and five theatrical features, among them *Sinaia / Clouds Over Israel* (1962), the story of an Israeli pilot and a Bedouin girl set against the 1956 war, and *Shalosh Sha'oth Be Yuni / Three Hours in June*, a documentary made soon after the 1967 war.

Eran, Doron (b. 1955, Israel)

In the 1980s Eran established a production company with Ye'ud Levanon, and the two produced ten feature films. He also directed two features, *Flash* (1987) and the apocalyptic drama *Haderech LeEin Harod / The Voice of Ein Harod* (1990).

Evan, Eitan (b. Israel)

A graduate of London Film School, in the 1970s Evan produced and directed a dozen documentary films, as well as commercials. In the 1980s he moved to producing feature films, among them *Roveh Chuliot / Wooden Gun, Hakaitz Shel Aviya / The Summer of Aviya, Etz Hadomim Tafus / Under the Domim Tree* and, more recently, *Meuskenet / Dangerous Acts* (1998).

Gavison, Savi (b. 1960, Israel)

A director and scriptwriter, Gavison graduated from the TAU Film Department. His two surreal comedies *Shuru* (1990) and *Holeh Ahava Meshikun Gimmel / Lovesick on Nana Street* (1995) both won the Best Film Award, establishing him as one of the most promising directors of the 1990s. Gavison's films adopt neither the utopian themes nor the realistic practices typical of Israeli cinema.

Gilad, Nellie (b. 1919, France; d. 1997, Israel)

One of the pioneers in professional film editing in Israel, Gilad worked in France as assistant editor on films by René Clément and Jean Cocteau. In Israel she started in the 1950s as editor of newsreels for Geva, as well as documentaries and features, among them *Amud Ha'esh / Pillar of Fire, I Like Mike, Eldorado, Mikreh Isha / A Woman's Case, Hasimla / The Dress* and *83*.

Gitai, Amos (b. 1950, Israel)

Gitai is a director, producer and scriptwriter. Since the 1970s he has made numerous documentaries, several focusing on the Israeli–Palestinian conflict. These include *Bayit / House* (1980), *Wadi* (1981) and *Yoman Sadeh / Field Diary* (1982). In 1982 he moved to France, where he continued to make documentaries, as well as several features, shooting in different countries. His films subvert the traditional generic boundaries, fusing fiction and documentary. Examples of his work are *Pineapple* (1983), a documentary about First World–Third World economic and cultural interrelationships; *Esther* (1985), a political adaptation of the biblical narrative; and

Berlin–Jerusalem (1989), a pseudo-docu-drama about poet Elsa Lesker-Schiller and pioneer Mania Shohat. In the 1990s he made a trilogy of feature films focusing on the three big cities of Israel: *Zichron Devarim / Devarim* (1996) in Tel Aviv, *Yom-Yom / Day After Day* (1998) in Haifa and *Kadosh* (1999) in Jerusalem. Gitai, the most renowned abroad of all Israeli film directors, has won many awards at international film festivals. Under European influence his film technique is to adopt a personal mode of address, rich in conflicting tendencies like modern versus post-modern, local versus global, mainstream versus idiosyncratic.

Globus, Yoram *(b. 1943, Israel)*

In 1963 Globus joined Menachem Golan's Noah Films and began distributing Israeli and foreign films. He was also Golan's partner in the Hollywood-based production company Cannon and in the Golan–Globus Israeli group, which owned the Neve Ilan Studios near Jerusalem. In the 1980s Globus turned these studios into one of the most sophisticated media centres in the Middle East. In late 1988 Golan and Globus lost control of Cannon and a year later parted company, Globus buying Golan out and calling his company Globus Group. In 1991 he acted as director of MGM and was the owner of the international distribution company Melrose Entertainment. Today Globus Group is the largest entertainment group in Israel, producing television series and shows at the Neve Ilan centre, in addition to being the proprietor of 140 cinema screens and exclusive distributor for the major Hollywood studios. In 1988 Globus and Golan were reunited and now produce films together once more.

Golan, Menachem *(b. 1929, Israel)*

A director, producer and scriptwriter, Golan is the most prolific producer–director in Israel. In the early 1960s he studied cinema at New York's City College and worked for Roger Corman's production company in Hollywood. On returning to Israel he directed his first feature, *Eldorado* (1963), and at the same time produced Kishon's *Sallah Shabbati*. With producer Yoram Globus, Golan produced and directed popular Bourekas melodramas, including *Fortuna* (1966), *Margo Sheli / My Margo* (1969), *Catz VeCarasso / Katz and Carasso* (1971), the musical *Casablan* (1973), *Operation Thunderbolt* (1977), based on the Entebbe affair, and *Hakosem Melublin / The Magician of Lublin* (1979). Together they produced about forty films, of which Golan scripted and directed more than half. He also produced Mizrachi's *Habayit Berehov Shelush / The House on Shelush Street* and *Ani Ohev Otach Rosa / I Love You Rosa*. Golan won Best Israeli Director for seven of his films. In 1976 Golan and Globus started G.G. Studios (Golan–Globus Studios) near Jerusalem, and in 1979 they purchased a small American company, Cannon, and made it one of the biggest independent Hollywood companies. In Hollywood, Golan produced more than 200 films and directed more than thirty. In 1994 he won an Israel Film Academy lifetime achievement award and in 1999 became an Israel Prize Laureate. In 1998 Golan and Globus were reunited and now produce films and television programmes locally and abroad. A controversial figure, Golan undoubtedly transformed Israeli cinema in the 1960s, his films both altering production methods and introducing new genres, as well as the star system, to the film scene.

Goldwasser, Ya'akov (Yankul) (b. 1950, Israel)

Goldwasser produced and directed hundreds of commercials, as well as four feature films. His directorial debut was *Mitachat La'af | Big Shots* (1982), which was followed in 1988 by the comedy *Aba Ganuv | The Skipper*, produced by and starring Yehuda Barkan. In 1991 he directed *Me'ever Layam | Over the Ocean*, a family drama focusing on Israel in the 1960s, which won the Israel Best Film Award. In 1994 he made the musical *Max Ve-Morris | Max and Morris*, returning to the world of petty thieves which had been the subject of his debut film.

Goren, Amit (b. 1957, Israel)

Goren graduated from the New York University Film Department. Since the mid-1980s he has written and directed documentaries, training films, commercials and videos. His highly praised short drama *Hakluv | The Cage* (1989) focused on Israeli–Palestinian relationships during the *intifada*. In the 1990s he made several prize-winning documentaries: *Shnat 66 Hyta Tova Latayarut | '66 was a Good Year for Tourism* (1992), *Good or Bad, Black and White* (1995), on Russian and Ethiopian immigrants in Israel, and *Eretz Acheret | Another Land* (1998), an introspective personal feature-length documentary. All were recipients of the Wolgin Award at the Jerusalem Film Festival. Goren contributed an episode to the Channel 1 history series *Tekuma | Resurrection* (1998). His innovative approach to film-making was the forerunner of a now widely employed film practice: a local form of the popular 'I-movie'.

Green, Eitan (b. 1951, Israel)

Green is a director, scriptwriter, film reviewer and teacher. He graduated from the TAU Film Department, where he heads the scriptwriting programme. He made an acclaimed short film prior to his debut feature film *Lena* (1980), which portrayed a young immigrant from Russia. This film established the themes and style that dominate his more recent films: everyday urban life, underplayed family drama and a propensity towards minimalism. His second feature, *Ad Sof Haleila | When Night Falls* (1985), allies itself with the dark dystopian mood of the 1980s, whereas he reverts to a lighter mood in *Ezrach Amerikayi | American Citizen* (1992) and *Zolgoth Hadma'oth Me'atzman | As Tears Go By* (1996), a father–son story, as well as in his television drama *Isha Martzipan | Marzipan Woman* (1997). Green has written many film reviews for national newspapers, co-edited a journal for films, edited an anthology about film-makers and is now the script editor for Cable TV. His films display a unique fusion of understatement and pathos.

Greenberg, Adam (b. 1937, Poland)

Greenberg started as a trainee in Geva studios, shooting newsreels and documentaries. Among the features he has filmed are *Operation Thunderbolt*, *Metzitzim | Peeping Toms* and *Haglula | The Pill*. Working as director of photography for Golan's US productions he won recognition and proceeded to become a major cinematographer in Hollywood, where he shot *Total Recall*, *Ghost* and other major productions. He now lives and works in Hollywood. He is considered one of Israel's major cinematographers, noted for his romantic, warm touch.

Greenberg, David (b. 1931, Israel; d. 1990, Israel)

Greenberg was a director, film reviewer and teacher. He started in the 1950s by organizing a network of small cinema clubs at which he screened and discussed the best of European modernism. In 1957–63 he published and edited the monthly *Omanut Hakolnoa* on film art. He produced and directed a few documentary and art films, among them the acclaimed *Sha'ar Haguy / The Gate to the Valley* (1965). In 1968 he made his only feature film *Iris*. In 1965 Greenberg established a private school for film art and laid the foundations for a film archive. He also made the first video-clips for local television. Greenberg was a leading cineaste, a central figure in the cultivation of film art many years before the establishment of the first cinematheque in Israel.

Gross, Nathan (b. 1919, Poland)

In Poland after World War II, Gross directed short films and two feature films in Yiddish. On his emigration to Israel in 1950 he was among the people who started Geva newsreel. In the 1950s and 1960s he directed over 100 short documentaries and training films for the Labour Federation and the IFS, some of which won awards in international film festivals, and one feature film. Between 1962 and 1982 he contributed film reviews to the daily *Al Hamishmar* and published a book about the history of Israeli cinema, *Haseret Hayivri / The Hebrew Film*, with his son Ya'akov Gross.

Gurevitch, Jorge (b. 1957, Argentina)

Gurevitch was a graduate of the TAU Film Department. He directed several shorts and dramas, and shot many short films, as well as features, including *Himmo Melekh Yerushalayim / Himmo, King of Jerusalem*, *Seret Leila / Night Movie*, *Sipurei Tel Aviv / Tel Aviv Stories* (with Amnon Zlayet) and *Osher Lelo Gvul / Everlasting Joy*.

Gurfinkel, David (b. 1939, Israel)

One of the most prolific and valued cameraman in the Israeli film industry, Gurfinkel started in Geva in the 1950s and was soon in great demand in the country. He worked regularly with Uri Zohar, starting at the age of twenty-six with *Hor Balevana / Hole in the Moon*. He worked as chief cameraman for many of Golan's productions and moved to work with him in Hollywood. Gurfinkel won the Israel Best Cinematography Award three times. Among his features are *Matzor / Siege*, *Hamsin*, *Hakaitz Shel Aviya / The Summer of Aviya* and *Sh'khur*. He shot around sixty Israeli feature films, more than twenty foreign films and dozens of short films, documentaries and newsreels. For his work in *Kol Mamzer Melech / Every Bastard a King* he won the Cinematography Award at the Chicago Film Festival. He has cultivated a distinct approach to lighting, taking advantage of the bright natural light typical of Israel.

Gutman, Amos (b. 1954, Hungary; d. 1993, Israel)

A graduate of Beit Tzvi Film Department, Gutman made several prize-winning shorts and four feature films, three of which – *Nagu'a / Drifting* (1983), *Bar 51* (1986) and *Hessed Mufla / Amazing Grace* (1992) – form a trilogy that portrays tortured young homosexuals in conflict with themselves and their surroundings. His penultimate feature, *Himmo Melech Yerushalayim / Himmo, King of Jerusalem* (1987), deals with similar themes but is disguised as a historical drama set in 1948. Gutman's films are noted for a unique cinematic approach that foregrounds aesthetic concerns and expressionistic practices not prevalent in Israeli cinema.

Habib, Nuri (b. 1919, Iraq)

In the 1940s and 1950s Habib produced and directed films in Iran. After emigrating to Israel in 1954 he founded a production company and directed the first colour film in Israel: *Be'ein Moledet / Lacking a Homeland* (1956). In 1958 he made the ethnic melodrama *Rachel*, which failed both critically and commercially, and consequently emigrated to the United States.

Halter, Tali (b. Israel)

Halter graduated from the TAU Film Department. Since the mid-1980s Halter has edited documentaries and feature films, among them: *Shuru, Holeh Ahava Meshikun Ginmel / Lovesick on Nana Street, Shnat 66 Hyta Tova Latayarut / '66 was a Good Year for Tourism, Jenny VeJenny / Jenny and Jenny* and *Hachaverim Shel Yana / Yana's Friends*.

Heffner, Avraham (b. 1935, Israel)

Heffner is a director, scriptwriter, novelist and actor, as well as a professor at the TAU Film Department. In the 1950s he worked as an assistant director in France and later attended film courses at New York University. In 1965 he collaborated with Uri Zohar in writing and acting in *Hor Balevana / Hole in the Moon*. In 1968 he made a short film *Le'at Yoter / Slow Down*, a study of an old couple that has become a classic. He scripted and directed four features: *Le'an Ne'elam Daniel Vax? / But Where is Daniel Wax?* (1972), the comedy *Doda Klara / Aunt Clara* (1977), the thriller *Parashath Winchel / The Winchel Affair* (1979) and the melodrama *Ahavata Hahachrona Shel Laura Adler / Laura Adler's Last Love Affair* (1990). Heffner wrote scripts for films and television, and directed a detective mini-series called *Eretz Ktana, Ish Gadol / Small Country, Big Man* (1998). His first feature, *Le'an Ne'elam Daniel Vax? / But Where is Daniel Wax?*, is regarded as one of the most accomplished films in Israeli cinema. His films manifest a minimalist approach, emphasizing precision in dialogue, acting and *mise-en-scène*. His cinematic austerity endows his films with a subdued musicality that is quite rare among the pronounced and direct voices found in most Israeli films.

Hirsch, Yachin (b. 1934)

Hirsch is a cinematographer, director and film critic. He studied cinematography in New York and started working at Geva Studios in the 1950s. He shot features for new sensibility directors, such as *Isha Bakheder Hasheni / Variations on a Love Theme*, *Hasimla / The Dress* and *Sofo shel Milton Levy / The End of Milton Levy*. Hirsch shot or directed around sixty documentaries, among them a dozen dedicated to Israeli painters.

Imberman, Shmuel (b. 1936, Israel)

Since the 1960s Imberman has made dozens of documentaries, television entertainment shows and dramas. He directed *Hedva Veshlomik / Hedva and Shlomik* (1971), the first drama mini-series on Israeli television, and several features, among them *Tel Aviv–Los Angeles* (1988) and *Menat Yeter / Overdose* (1993). *Lo Sam Zayin / Don't Give a Damn* (1987), which deals with war trauma, is his most critically acclaimed film.

Keller, Helga (b. England)

From the 1940s Keller edited films in the United Kingdom, among them Laurence Olivier's *Hamlet* and *Richard III*. In Israel she edited several documentaries and features, among them *Hem Hayu Asara / They Were Ten* (1960, under her maiden name, Cranston). In the 1970s she taught Screen Education to teachers and developed Film Teaching programmes in the TAU School of Education. She was the editor of the first anthology on cinema ever published in Hebrew (1974).

Kishon, Ephraim (b. 1924, Hungary)

Kishon has been a satirist, playwright, director and producer. Israel's leading humourist in the 1950s and 1960s, he published over fifty books, wrote and directed plays for the stage in Israel and Europe, and made five feature films: *Sallah Shabbati* (1964), which was the forerunner of the new Bourekas genre, *Ervinka* (1967), *Te'alat Blaumilech / The Big Dig* (1969) and *Hashoter Azulai / The Policeman* (1970), satirizing bureaucracy and police incompetence, all of which were big hits. His last film, *Hashu'al Belul Hatarnegoloth / The Fox in the Chicken Coop* (1978), a satire about political corruption, was his only failure, indicating the diminishing public interest in the topics prevalent in his work. Kishon has created protagonists that are unique Israeli archetypes but whose absurd struggle is universal, which might be the reason why his films and novels were acclaimed worldwide. In 1993 he won a Life Achievement Award from the Israel Film Academy. In retrospect, Kishon's carnivalesque films laid the ground for the post-modern mode of 1990s Israeli cinema, which hinges on similar figures of artistic speech.

Klausner, Margot (b. 1905, Germany; d. 1975, Israel)

Klausner was the founder and owner of the Herzlia Film Studios, and promoted many film productions. With her husband she founded a film production company in 1933, which co-produced the Zionist classic *Lecha'im Hadashim / Land of Promise*. The film was invited to the Venice Film Festival. Her struggle to build a modern film studio, Israel Motion Picture Studios (IMPS), in Herzlia began in the late 1940s but only materialized in 1952. In the 1950s–70s the Herzlia Studios had a central role in the development of the Israeli film industry. Klausner produced many films, sometimes in the face of financial losses, and was one of the positive forces that encouraged the struggling film industry of Israel in its first decades.

Knebel, Emil (Milek) (b. Poland)

Knebel worked as a cinematographer, director and professor at TAU. He shot several feature films, among them *Habanana Hashchora / The Black Banana*, as well as over a hundred documentaries, some of which he also directed. In 1978–9 he was an artistic director of the Fund for Quality Films and in 1997–2000 chaired the Film and Television Department at TAU. He made his reputation as a film pedagogue, admired by his many students in film schools in New York, Berlin and Barcelona. His most accomplished film as director was *BeNahalal / In Nahalal* (1961), the first documentary to subvert the Zionist realist tradition, paving the way for other 1960s documentaries that disengaged from this tradition.

Kol, Yitzhak

Kol started as a production manager for *Hem Hayu Asara / They Were Ten* (1960). In 1967 he was appointed general manager of the IMPS in Herzlia, where he set up the satellite broadcasting system for the studios. Under his management the studios became the leading production house for television and cinema in Israel. Between 1983 and 1991 he managed the Golan–Globus Studios and established the communication centre in Neve Ilan near Jerusalem. In 1978 he was chosen as a member of the American Academy of Films and in 1986 was on the board of directors for the international Canon company. Since 1994 he has been a co-director of Roll Films. Kol is one of the most prolific producers in Israel, having been involved in the production of *Ani Ohev Otach Rosa / I Love You Rosa*, *Catz VeCarasso / Katz and Carasso* and *Metzitzim / Peeping Toms*, as well as of numerous television programmes and some twenty foreign films.

Kosh, Yoav (b. Israel)

One of the most prominent of a new generation of Israeli cinematographers, Kosh's first contribution was *Avanti Popolo*. He also shot, among others, *Shuru*, *Hachaim Al Pi Agfa / Life According to Agfa* and *Tipat Mazal / A Bit of Luck*. Kosh is known for his special touch with colour.

Lahola, Areye (Leopold) (b. 1918, Slovakia; d. 1968, Czechoslovakia)

Lahola made short films in his homeland, and in Israel directed training films and the prize-winning docu-drama *Yir Ha'ohalim / Tent City* (1951). In 1955 he made the feature *Even Al Kol Mil / Every Mile a Stone*, the poor reaction to which persuaded him to leave Israel and return to Czechoslovakia.

Lapid, Era (b. Israel)

Lapid has edited feature films, documentaries and dramas since the 1970s, among them *Biba*, *Ad Sof Haleila / When Night Falls*, *Onat Haduvdevanim / Time of the Cherries*, *Hanashim Mimul / The Women Next Door* and *Osher Lelo Gvul / Everlasting Joy*.

Leon, Nissim (Nicho) (b. Bulgaria)

Starting at Geva as a newsreel cameraman, Leon soon became the studio's chief cinematographer. His first feature was *I Like Mike*, followed by *Eldorado*, *Sallah Shabbati* and many others. In 1962 he became a partner in the production company Roll Films and has shot hundreds of commercials, promotional films and documentaries. He also filmed television programmes and has continued to shoot Israeli feature films, among them *Lo Sam Zayin / Don't Give a Damn*.

Lerski, Helmar (b. 1871, Germany; d. 1956, Switzerland)

Lerski was a director, cinematographer and stills photographer. In the 1920s he worked for Ufa Studios in Germany on several films that are now considered masterpieces of German silent film. In 1931 he arrived in Palestine and directed and shot several films, among them *Awoda / Work* (1935) and *Adama / Tomorrow is a Wonderful Day* (1947). In 1948 he made a short puppet film together with Paul Loewy, which was later incorporated into Joseph Krumgold's *Klala Lebracha / Out of Evil*. Soon after Lerski moved to Switzerland, where he was posthumously 'rediscovered' in the 1970s due to a new interest in classic German cinema. His cinematic work in Palestine stands out as a unique achievement among Zionist realist films, both in its modernist-expressive mode and concise structuring.

Levanon, Ye'ud (b. 1952, Israel)

Levanon is a director, producer and scriptwriter. Starting in the 1970s, he directed short films, among them *Kesher Hadvash / The Honey Connection* (1977), a political fiction about a Jewish underground in the Occupied Territories several years before such an underground actually developed. In the 1980s, together with Doron Eran, he produced ten feature films, as well as several foreign films. He directed four features, among them *Lo Leshidur / On the Air* (1980) and *Kufsa Shechora / Black Box* (1993), and several prize-winning documentaries, among them *119 Kadurim Ve'od 3 / 119 Bullets Plus 3* (1996). His most recent documentary, *Moskva al HaYam-HaTichon / Moscow on the Mediterranean* (1999), deals with the life of Jewish immigrants from Russia. In the 1990s he has co-operated with Amit Goren, with each producing the other's films.

Levitan, Nadav (b. 1945, Israel)

Levitan is a director and scriptwriter who graduated from the TAU Film Department. In the 1970s he directed ten documentaries for Israeli TV and since the beginning of the 1980s has made seven features, among them his debut *Sipur Intimi / Intimate Story* (1981), *Yaldei Stalin / Stalin's Disciples* (1987), and *Ein Shemot al Hadlatot / No Names on the Doors* (1997), all unfolding human stories set against the background of a kibbutz. In the 1990s he also made two television dramas. Levitan's work as a director-producer exemplifies that of other film-makers of the state generation, merging their lives into the themes and the zeal of their films, acting much like artisans in their workshops.

Lev-Tov, Michael (b. 1945, Israel)

A director, scriptwriter and teacher, Lev-Tov graduated from the London Film School. Since the 1970s he has made over forty documentary films for Israeli TV, among them segments for the two major documentary series *Amud Ha'esh / Pillar of Fire* and *Tekuma / Resurrection*, a controversial portrait of poet Ya'ir Horwitz in *Words on Way*, a four-segment series on India and his recent *Ru'hach Hadevarim / The Spirit of Things* on Kibbutz Beit Alfa. He teaches cinema in the Sam Spiegel School for Films and Television in Jerusalem.

Loevy, Ram (b. 1940, Israel)

Loevy is a director-producer, scriptwriter and professor at the TAU Film Department. Graduating from the London Film School, Loevy was the house director for Israeli television's Channel 1 from its establishment in 1978 until 1998. He has made over fifty highly acclaimed documentaries and dramas. Among his documentaries are *Mitrasim / Barricades* (1969); *Nevuchadnetzar BeKaysaria / Nebuchadnezzar in Caesarea* (1979), in which the performance at Caesarea of Verdi's opera *Nabucco* by the Berlin Opera House is used to highlight ironic reflections on history and art; and *Ha'seret Shelo Haya / The Film that Wasn't* (1993–4), a two-part documentary about the use of torture in the interrogation of security suspects. Among his television film fictions are *Khirbet His'a* (1978); the prize-winning *Indiani Bashemesh / Indian in the Sun* (1981), a drama about two Israeli soldiers from different ethnic backgrounds; *Lechem / Bread* (1986); and a comedy about the biblical King David called *Keter Barosh / Crowned* (1989). He also directed an episode for *83* and the historical mini-series *Mar Manie / Mr Manie* (1996). In 1993 Loevy was made an Israel Prize Laureate. Loevy's affiliation with television freed him from pursuing finances and enabled him to maintain continuity in his work, a phenomenon usually rare among Israeli film-makers. His clear development, both stylistically and thematically, culminated in his masterpiece *Mar Manie*, unique in its aesthetic and historical approach.

Leytes, Joseph (b. 1901, Poland)

A noted documentarist in his homeland, Leytes came to Palestine in 1943 and made the docu-drama *Dim'at Hanechama Hagedola / The Great Promise* (1947) about Holocaust survivors and the Zionist project in Palestine, as well as a feature film *Kirya*

Ne'emana / *Faithful City* (1952) that focuses on Holocaust survivors during the 1948 War of Independence.

Menachemi, Ayelet (b. 1963, Israel)

A graduate of Beit Tzvi Film Department, Menachemi made three shorts, among them the acclaimed *Crows* (1988), about young people and set against Tel Aviv night scenes. She directed commercials and two feature films, *Aba Ganuv III* / *The Skipper III* (1991) and (together with Nirit Yaron) *Sipurei Tel Aviv* / *Tel Aviv Stories* (1992).

Mizrachi, Moshe (b. 1931, Alexandria, Egypt)

Mizrachi is a director, producer, scriptwriter and teacher. In the 1960s he worked in France as an assistant-director and production manager, and in 1967 produced and co-scripted a mini-series for French television. In 1969 he made his first feature, *The Traveller*, an Israeli–French co-production shot in Eilat which was Israel's official entry in the Berlin Film Festival and a nominee for the Golden Globe. His next feature was shot in France and he continued making films in Israel and France alternately. Menachem Golan produced his next films, shot in Israel, *Ani Ohev Otach Rosa* / *I Love You Rosa* (1972) and *Habayit Berehov Shelush* / *The House on Shelush Street* (1973). Mizrachi's French film *La vie devant soi* (1977) won the Academy Award for Best Foreign Film. His last feature, *Women* (1998), highlights again his interest in Jewish tradition, female characters and Jerusalem. All in all he has made thirteen features and two series for French television. Mizrachi won a tribute for his work at the 1994 Haifa Film Festival. His lyrical realism does not fit into any specific genre and in his treatment of ethnic tensions, family drama and love stories he avoids stereotyping his characters. His cinematic practice creates an introspective and complex atmosphere, drawing on the history of his own family, whose roots are in sixteenth-century Jerusalem, as well as on European film-making.

Navon, Mordechai (b. 1908, Poland; d. 1966, Israel)

One of the main producers of the 1950s and 1960s in Israel, Navon founded Geva studios (with Yitzhak Agadati) and produced the country's first fiction films, among them *I Like Mike* (1962), *Chavura Shekazot* / *What a Gang* (1962), *Eldorado* (1963) and *Hor Balevana* / *Hole in the Moon* (1965). He also produced Geva's newsreels and hundreds of documentaries. Navon can be credited with creating the infrastructure for fiction film-making in Israel.

Ne'eman, Judd (b. 1936, Israel)

Ne'eman is a director, producer, scriptwriter and professor at the TAU Film Department, which he chaired in the 1980s and 1990s. In 1968 and 1969 he compiled three dramatic episodes into the full-length feature *Hasimla* / *The Dress* (1970), one of the first new sensibility films. He directed television dramas, among them *Misaviv Lanekuda* / *Around the Point* (1971), which was the first drama broadcast on the first national television station. Among his documentaries was the controversial historical film *Ya Brachen – Mered Hayama'im / The Seamen's Strike* (1981). His anti-heroic army film *Massa Alunkot / Paratroopers* (1977) heralded a wave of anti-militaristic films that undermined the heroic ethos. In the 1980s Ne'eman made two films for Channel 4 in London – *Fellow Travellers* (1984) and *Streets of Yesterday* (1989) – both of which highlighted the dead-end entanglements of the Israeli–Palestinian conflict. He also contributed an episode to the protest film *83*. Ne'eman has developed the academic research of Israeli cinema and published many papers on this subject. His films reflect a strong bias against totalitarianism and oppression, as well as leanings towards genre cinema and, in particular, *film noir*.

Nesher, Avi (b. 1952, Israel)

Nesher studied cinema at Columbia University in New York. He made two short films that won international awards prior to making of his first feature, *Halahaka / Sing Your Heart Out* (1978), the first Israeli film to celebrate the follies and pain of young people. He made several comedies about the lives of young people in Tel Aviv and the historical drama *Za'am Vetehila / Rage and Glory* (1984), before moving to the United States where he scripted and directed four feature films.

Ovadia, George (b. 1925, Iraq; d. 1993, Israel)

Ovadia was a director, producer and scriptwriter. From the 1950s and until his emigration to Israel in 1964, he lived in Iran, where he was a prominent producer-director with twenty-five fiction films to his credit. In 1967 he directed an Iranian–Israeli co-production and went on to produce and direct popular Israeli Bourekas films on a massive scale, focusing on ethnic and class tensions. He made twelve feature films, both melodramas and comedies, most of them in the 1970s; some became big hits. Among his most successful features were *Ariana* (1971), *Nurit* (1972) and *Sarit* (1974). In the early 1980s he made only two films, both of which failed at the box office. The audiences loved his melodramas, but the critics denounced them as primitive *ciné-romans* and only in his last years was he was recognized as an accomplished director of popular cinema, winning a Life Achievement Award from the Tel Aviv Cinematheque.

Peres, Uzi (b. 1951, Israel; d. 1992, Nepal)

A director, producer and scriptwriter, Peres studied film at TAU and in France. In the 1970s he made several experimental shorts and in 1978 directed his debut feature in Paris: *Pareil pas pareil / Similar Not Similar* a comedy experimenting with montage. Subsequently he directed four melodramas, two in France and two in Israel, among them *Ahava Rishona / First Love* (1982). His work did not conform to Israeli cinema's themes and realistic approach, and was therefore controversial.

Perlov, David (b. 1930, Rio de Janeiro, Brazil)

Perlov is a director, producer, scriptwriter, photographer, painter and professor at the TAU Film Department, of which he was one of the founders. During the 1950s he was assistant to Henri Langlois, the founder of the French *cinémathèque*. In Paris he made an acclaimed animation short and has been making commissioned documentaries in Israel since the 1960s, first for the Jewish Agency and later for the IFS. His films shifted the focus from the collective to the personal, and insisted on a subjective poetic point of view, rejecting Zionist propaganda. Among his numerous documentary films are *B'Yerushalayim / In Jerusalem* (1963), *Tel Katzir* (1965) and *Biba* (1977). He also directed one fiction film, *Haglula / The Pill* (1967), and a docu-drama about the life of Prime Minister David Ben-Gurion. Since 1973 he has been shooting his *Yoman / Diary*, a monumental work now considered one of the finest achievements of Israeli cinema. In 1997 he won a Life Achievement Award at the Jerusalem Film Festival and in 1999 he became Israel Prize Laureate. *Yoman*, the epitome of his work, discloses the social and the private as a unified textual domain. Perlov experiments with modernism without getting lost in an alienating mode and creates a framework that allows him to both sketch and project his art.

Rav-Nof, Ze'ev (b. 1926, Poland; d. 1979, Israel)

Rav-Nof was a director and film critic. He made about forty short documentaries on commissions from the Jewish Agency and the Labour Federation before becoming the most influential film critic of his time. From 1955 he reviewed films in the daily *Davar*, interviewing film-makers and reporting from film festivals. He was chairman of the critics' unit of the Journalists' Association and a member of judging committees at international film festivals. His film essays were compiled in a book (published posthumously) called *Masakh Gadol / Big Screen*.

Reibenbach, Tzipi (b. Israel)

A graduate of the TAU Film Department, Reibenbach has made three feature documentaries since the 1980s: *Almana Plus / Widow Plus* (1981), the award-winning *Habchira Ve'hagoral / Choice and Destiny* (1993) and *Shalosh Achayot / Three Sisters* (1998), the last two films focusing on her family and the Holocaust.

Revah, Ze'ev (b. 1940, Morocco)

Revah is a director, producer, scriptwriter, actor and television presenter. He has played a variety of characters in many films and on the stage, starring in many of the films he himself directed. In his first directorial effort, *Rak Hayom / Only Today* (1976), he portrayed an oriental Jew, underscoring its theme of the pursuit of wealth as a source of conflict. In this film he also established his future interest in situation comedies. Revah made more than fifteen feature films and starred in over twenty. Most of his films are Bourekas comedies and melodramas, such as *Tauth Ba'mispar / Wrong Number* (1979), *Adon Leon / Mr Leon* (1982) and *Tipat Mazal / A Bit of Luck* (1992). He also made several social dramas, including *Shraga Katan / Little Man* (1978) and *Bouba / On the Fringe* (1987). Many of his films were box-office hits, but did not win critical acclaim. In his melodramas he addresses the traditional values of the Eastern Jewish family, largely repressed in Israeli cinema. His exuberant performances and the carnivalesque mode of many of his films give them a rich vitality.

Ricklis, Eran (b. 1954, Israel)

Having studied cinema at TAU and in London, Ricklis directed documentaries for television and hundreds of commercials, some of which won international awards. Among his feature films are *Gemar Gavia / Cup Final* (1991), which won him the Best Director Award; *Zohar* (1993), about a popular pop singer; and *Tzometh Vulcan / Vulcan Junction* (1999), a drama about an early-1970s rock group in Israel. In 1999 he also directed *Gvuloth / Borders*, a documentary following the people who live on the borders of Israel.

Ringel, Israel

In 1962 Ringel founded Roll Films with Yair Pradelski and Nissim Leon. It was one of the first independent production companies in Israel. Over the next two decades he and Pradelski produced about a dozen features, mostly comedies, but also dramas (such as *Lo Sam Zayin / Don't Give a Damn*) and the first national television series (*Hedva VeShlomik / Hedva and Shlomik*). Ringel was also involved in international productions such as *Ashanti* and *Massada*, and today he produces shows and quizzes for Cable TV and Channel 2. For the last five years he has been the chairman of the Israel Film Academy.

Rosenbaum, Marek (b. 1950, Israel)

A graduate of the TAU Film Department, Rosenbaum was one of the most active independent producers in the 1980s and 1990s, and chairman of the Film and Television Producers Association. He has produced dozens of documentaries and commercials, as well as twenty features. Among them are *Ahavata Hahachrona Shel Laura Adler / Laura Adler's Last Love Affair* (1990), *Ezrach Amerikayi / American Citizen* (1992), *Aya: Autobiographia Dimyonit / Imagined Autobiography* (1994), *Clara Hakdosha / Saint Clara* (1995) and *Hachaverim Shel Yana / Yana's Friends* (1999).

Rosenberg, Ilan (b. Israel)

Graduating from the London Film School, Rosenberg has shot many feature films and documentaries since the 1970s, among them *Transit, Machvo'im / Hide and Seek, Ha'ayit / The Vulture, Mitachat La'af / Big Shots* and *Bouba / On the Fringe*.

Rubinstein, Amnon (b. 1948, Israel)

A graduate of the London School of Film Technique, Rubinstein directed a number of dramas and documentaries for Israeli television and has made four feature films: *Nadia* (1986), *Hayanshuf / The Owl* (1988), *Hayeruscha / Heritage* (1993) and *Acharei Hachagim / On the Edge* (1994).

Salomon, Amnon (b. 1940, Israel)

Salomon started at Geva Films as an assistant cameraman. Among his credits are *Mikreh Isha / A Woman's Case, Le'an Ne'elam Daniel Vax? / But Where is Daniel*

Wax?, *Me'achorei Hasoragim* / *Beyond the Walls* and *Ad Sof Haleila* / *When Night Falls*. He has worked with most of Israel's major directors and filmed numerous documentaries and television films. Salomon is known for his aesthetic approach and for his eye for composition and the human face.

Schik, Dani

Since the 1960s Schick has edited dozens of features, dramas and documentaries, among them *Fortuna*, *Hu Halach Basadot* / *He Walked Through the Fields*, *Matzor* / *Siege*, *Michael Sheli* / *My Michael*, *Tzlila Chozeret* / *Repeat Dive* and *Gesher Tsar Me'od* / *On a Narrow Bridge*. He has also trained many of the younger generation of film editors in Israel.

Segal, Yerushalayim (b. 1898, Russia; d. 1993, Israel)

Segal was a producer who pioneered the translation of film intertitles into Hebrew. In the 1920s he founded a translation laboratory and continued translating films and subtitling them for six decades. In 1927 he established the *Moledet* (homeland) company and entered into film production with cameraman Nathan Axelrod. For the following seven years, Segal and Axelrod produced newsreels, documentaries and news, as well as promotional shorts for movie houses. In the 1930s Segal was also a representative for *The Chicago Daily News Universal Newsreel* and sent footage from Palestine to the United States.

Sela, Ido (b. 1955, Israel)

Sela is both a graduate of the TAU Film Department and a teacher there. His graduation short *Kamal Gashash* / *Kamal the Tracker* (1986), which featured a Bedouin tracker, won him Best Film Award at the International Students' Film Festival. Among his other documentaries, *Massa Habchirot shel Meir Ariel* (1989) / *Election Tour of Meir Ariel* went on a tour with a pop singer and *Edooyot* / *Evidences* (1993) focused on Israeli soldiers who were implicated in the *intifada*. There were also three films for a documentary series about Israeli rock culture and a film for *Tekuma* / *Resurrection* (1998). He has also made television dramas.

Shagrir, Micha (b. 1937, Austria)

Shagrir was a producer and director who trained at the BBC in London. With his production company Castel Films, he produced numerous documentaries and training films, as well as the feature film *Avanti Popolo*. He directed documentaries for Israeli TV and made films for theatrical release, an action-drama called *Sayarim* / *Scouting Patrol* (1967) and the full-length documentary *Hamilchama Le'achar Hamilchama* / *The War After the War* (1969), which showed images of Israel following the euphoria of the 1967 war.

Sharfstein, Micha (b. Israel)

Sharfstein was one of the prominent independent film producers of the 1980s. Among the features he produced were *Gesher Tsar Me'od* / *On a Narrow Bridge* (1985), *Ad Sof Haleila* / *When Night Falls* (1985), *Nisuyim Fictivyim* / *Marriage of Convenience* (1988), *Gemar Gavia* / *Cup Final* (1991) and *Zohar* (1993).

Shechori, Idit (b. 1955, Israel)

Shechori graduated from Beit Tzvi Film Department. Following a prize-winning short, she made her debut feature: *Ma'agalim Shel Shishabat* / *Circles* (1980). In 1993 she made a second feature, a psycho-drama called *Beshem Ha'ahvah* / *In the Name of Love* (1993). She is the founder and director of a private school for screenwriting. One of the few female voices in national film-making, her debut feature subverted male-focused cinema and highlighted female interests.

Shehori, Katriel (b. 1947, Israel)

After studying film at the New York University Film School, Shehori started as head of production for Kastel Films before becoming the North America Bureau producer of ZDF for several years. Back in Israel he was associate producer in 1984 of *Me'achorei Hasoragim* / *Beyond the Walls*. The same year he founded his own company, Belfilms, and went on to produce over 200 films, television dramas and shows, among them *Hacholmim* / *Unsettled Land* (1987). Since 1998 he has been the director of the Fund for the Promotion of Israeli Quality Films.

Shissel, Tzvi (b. 1946, Israel)

Shissel worked as a director, actor and producer, and was one of the prominent figures in the Hager production company. During the 1970s the Hager company produced records, shows and films, among them *Shablul* / *Snail* (1970) and the television sketch show *Lul*. Shissel acted in many commercials and films, among them Zohar's *Metzitzim* / *Peeping Toms* and Wachsmann's *Ha'meyu'ad* / *The Appointed*. He has directed several candid-camera films and comedies.

Shles, Julie (b. Israel)

A graduate of Beit Tzvi Film Department, Schles has directed several prize-winning documentaries, among them *Sanjin* / *Saint Jean* (1993) and *Baba Luba* (1995). Her first and only feature to date is *Afula Express* / *Pick a Card* (1997), which won her Best Film Director.

Shneur, Daniel (b. Israel)

Since the 1970s Shneur has shot many feature films, documentaries and shorts, among them *Tzlila Chozeret* / *Repeat Dive*, *83* (with others), *Chyuch Hagdi* / *Smile of the Lamb* and *Ezrach Amerikayi* / *American Citizen*.

Sivan, Eyal (b. 1966, Israel)

Sivan is a director, producer and scriptwriter who resides in France. He made several documentaries in Israel with French finance, including *Akabat Jaber* (1987), about a Palestinian refugee camp near Jericho, *Yizkor, Ha'avadim Shel Hazikaron / Remember, the Slaves of Memory* (1991) and *Ha'spetzialist / The Specialist* (1999), a portrait of Adolph Eichmann drawn from footage taken at the time of his trial. Sivan is a politically committed film-maker who is interested in human rights and historical memory.

Sommer, Yossi (b. 1956, Israel)

A director and art director, Sommer graduated from the London School of Film Technique. He worked as art director on a dozen films before making his directorial debut with *Ressissim / Burning Memory* (1989). In 1997 he made his second feature, *Hadibbuk Be'gan Hatapuchim / The Dybbuk of the Holy Apple Field* (1997), a love story set in an ultra-religious neighbourhood in Jerusalem.

Spielman, Zvi (b. 1925, Poland)

Since the 1960s Israfilm (Spielman and Shlomo Mugrabi's production company) has specialized in providing services, while Spielman himself has acted as production supervisor and line-producer for many foreign productions and co-productions shot in Israel. These have included *A Woman Called Golda* (1982) and *Haben Ha'Oved / The Prodigal Son* (1968). Spielman has produced several local films, among them *Echad Mishelanu / One of Us* (1989).

Steinhardt, Alfred (b. 1923, Poland)

Steinhardt studied film in France and the United States. From the 1960s he directed hundreds of army training films, short documentaries, promotional films and commercials, as well as a full-length documentary about the 1967 war. He also made several Bourekas films and comedies, among them *Salomonico* (1972) and its sequel *Yehiyeh Tor Salmonico / The Father* (1975).

Telalim, Asher (b. 1950, Morocco)

Telalim graduated from Beit Tzvi Film Department. He edited films and reportage for Israeli TV, as well as more than twenty documentaries. These include a 1990 trilogy about rock and emigration that won the Wolgin Award; a 1984 series of fourteen episodes that featured Bedouin life and was broadcast in twenty countries; and *Al Tig'u Li Ba Shoa / Don't touch my Holocaust* (1994). His only feature film, *Z'man Hagamal / The Time of the Camel* (1991), focuses on the lives of the Bedouins in the Negev desert. Telalim teaches cinema at the TAU Film Department.

Trope, Tzipi (b. Israel, 1947)

Trope made several shorts and documentaries before her debut feature, *Miri / Tell Me that You Love Me* (1983), an Israeli–Canadian co-production. In 1987 she scripted and directed *Tel Aviv Berlin* (1987), which won her the Best Director Award. Her most recent feature, *Chronica Shel Ha'ahvah / Chronicle of Love* (1993), focuses on abused women.

Van Lear, Lia (b. 1924, Romania)

Van Lear was founder and director of the Jerusalem Cinematheque and the Israeli Film Archive. In 1955 she and her husband Wim opened a cinema club in Haifa; five years later they opened further clubs in Tel Aviv and Jerusalem. In 1961 she established the Israeli Film Archive, in 1973 the Haifa Cinematheque and in 1974 the Jerusalem Cinematheque, which she has managed since. Van Lear is one of the pioneers of film culture in Israel. She laid the groundwork for cinematheque culture in Israel and put the national cinema on the world map with the Jerusalem International Film Festival. In 1998 she won a Life Achievement Award from the Israel Film Academy.

Wachsmann, Daniel (b. 1946, China)

Wachsmann is a director, producer and scriptwriter who graduated from the London Film School. He made several prize-winning shorts and documentaries, among them *Shirath HaGalil / Song of the Galilee* (1994) and *Menelik* (1999). He also made three award-winning feature films: *Transit* (1980), the political conflict drama *Hamsin* (1981) and the apocalyptic messianic drama *The Appointed* (1990). He was chosen by Israeli film critics as Best Director of the 1980s. His work displays political awareness and cinematic complexity, with his films containing many mythic elements and clandestine quest narratives.

Wolman, Dan (b. 1941, Israel)

Wolman studied cinema in New York, where he directed several prize-winning shorts. Since the 1960s in Israel he has directed a number of documentaries and television dramas, as well as ten feature films, among them *Michael Sheli / My Michael* (1975), *Machvo'im / Hide and Seek* (1980), *Chayal Haleila / Soldier of the Night* (1984) and the prize-winning *Hamerechak / The Distance* (1994). Wolman operates on the fringe of the film industry, usually as an independent producer of his own low-budget films. He is one of the most prominent film-makers of the 1960s–1970s new sensibility wave, and continues its practices to this day. His work focuses on outsiders and misfits, conveying the sensibilities of *cinéma d'art et d'essai*.

Yeshurun, Yitzhak (Tzepel) (b. 1936, Tel Aviv)

Yeshurun is a director, producer and scriptwriter. Since the 1960s he has directed documentaries and training films for the Labour Federation and the IFC, among them *Bi'ur Haba'arut / Eradicating Illiteracy* (1965), which departed from the Zionist realism of the period. In 1976 he scripted and directed his first feature, *Isha Bakheder Hasheni / Variations on a Love Theme*, a fragmented love story that tested the boundaries of the cinematic medium, and in 1978 he directed the television drama *Kobi*

VeMali / Kobi and Mali (1978), which reflected radical social and political concerns. Since the late 1970s he has made a dozen features and television dramas, among them *Noa Bat Sheva-Esrey / Noa at Seventeen* (1982), *Zug Nasuy / A Married Couple* (1983) and *Sadot Yerukim / Green Fields* (1989). In the 1990s he directed a mini-series for cable television, as well as several television dramas – the most recent, *On Air* (1999), focuses again on a family in crisis, torn between personal and national issues. One of the prominent film-makers of the 1960s–70s new sensibility wave, all Yeshurun's films manifest strong leanings towards improvisation and diverge from mainstream practices in both production and film technique.

Yosha, Yaki (b. 1951)

Yosha directed shorts, commercials, features and most recently a television mini-series. Among his features are his directorial debut *Shalom, Tfilath Ha'derekh / Shalom, Prayer of the Road* (1973), a roughly made picture of the counter-culture in 1970s Israel, *Sus Etz / Rockinghorse* (1978) and *Ha'ayit / The Vulture* (1981), both refuting Zionist and heroic values and experimenting with visuals and montage. Some of Yosha's features render radical moods and experimental practices, but in others he reverts to popular entertainment.

Zarchin, Shemi (b. 1961, Israel)

After graduating from the TAU Film Department, Zarchin made several shorts, contributed to the script of *Sipurei Tel Aviv / Tel Aviv Stories* and in 1995 wrote and directed his first feature film, *Leilsede / Passover Fever*. This family drama won the Best Director Award. His second feature, *Dangerous Acts* (1998), was a thriller starring Gila Almagor and Moshe Ivgi that focused on the dramatic relationship between the victim of an car accident and the man who injured her.

Zilberg, Yo'el (b. 1927, Israel)

In 1962 Zilberg compiled *Etz o Palestine / The True Story of Palestine* with Axelrod and Zohar, based on Axelrod's newsreels. He also made more than a dozen popular comedies, among them *Milioner Be'tzaroth / Millionaire in Trouble* (1978) and *Imi Hageneralit / My Mother the General* (1979). In the 1980s he directed films in the United States, among them the hit *Breakdance* (1984). In the 1990s he created and directed the most popular and longest running television series for Israel's Channel 2.

Zohar, Uri (b. 1935, Israel)

Zohar was a director, scriptwriter and actor who started his career as a popular stage comedian. His first feature, *Hor Balevana / Hole in the Moon* (1965), a subversive farce that foreshadowed the making of personal films, established him as an original and outstanding film-maker. Subsequently he made several shorts, a few television programmes and nine features, all in the 1960s and 1970s. Among his features were the modernist drama *Shlosha Yamim Veyeled / Three Days and a Child* (1967), the popular comedy *Hshechuna Shelanu / Fish, Football and Girls* (1968), the war film *Kol Mamzer*

Melech / Every Bastard a King (1968) and in the 1970s a personal trilogy – an elegy to the post-1967 war 'lost generation'. The first film from the trilogy, *Metzitzim / Peeping Toms* (1972), has become a cult movie; the second film, *Einayim Gdoloth / Big Eyes* (1974), is the closest to an autobiographical movie that he ever made, manifesting a deep ambivalence towards his own idiosyncrasies in a melancholic mood that can be detected in some of his other films as well. *Lul*, a series of television spoofs he directed with Boaz Davidson in the 1970s, was compiled in 1988 for theatrical release, reasserting Zohar's originality and unique role in Israeli cinema. The versatility of Zohar's contribution to Israeli cinema is unquestioned, although his artistic road had its ups and downs. He was awarded the Israel Prize, but refused to accept it. In the late 1970s he became orthodox religious and retired from film-making.

Zvi-Ricklis, Dina (b. Iraq)

Zvi-Ricklis directed documentaries, among them *Kurdania* (1984) and *Nekudat Tatspit / Lookout* (1991). *Sipor Sh'Matchil Be'Halvayah Shel Nachash / Dreams of Innocence* (1993) is her only feature. Her bias is towards child protagonists and non-mainstream practices.

List of actors

Aboutboul, Alon

Aboutboul has worked as both an actor and a producer. He achieved meteoric success in the 1980s and by the time he was twenty-one he had seven shorts and one feature film to his name. Among his films were *Shtey Etzba'ot MiTzidon / Ricochets* (1986), *Makom L'Yad Hayam / A Place by the Sea* (1988), *Echad Mishelanu / One of Us* (1989), *The Cage* (1989) and *Streets of Yesterday* (1989). At the age of twenty-four Aboutboul was voted Israel's Best Actor of the 1980s. His roles identified him as a soldier and a macho man, but he escaped this typecasting in his portrayal of a homosexual in *Bar 51* (1985). After spending some time in Los Angeles, he returned to Israel and acted in *Leilsede / Passover Fever* and *Hakochav Hakahol / Planet Blue* (both 1995).

Almagor, Gila (b. 1937, Israel)

Over a period of four decades, Almagor has appeared in more than fifty films, playing Holocaust survivors, war widows, prostitutes, mentally ill women, lovers and mothers. Among her films were *Eldorado* (1963), *Fortuna* (1966), *Matzor / Siege* (1969), *Habayit Berehov Shelush / The House on Shelush Street* (1973), *Al Hevel Dak / A Thin Line* (1981), *Machvo'im / Hide and Seek* (1980), *Hachaim Al Pi Agfa / Life According to Agfa* (1992), *Sh'khur* (1994), *Leilsede / Passover Fever* (1995) and *Dangerous Acts* (1998). In 1988 her autobiographical novel *Hakaitz Shel Aviya / The Summer of Aviya* was adapted for the screen, with her producing and starring in it. She also produced and starred in its sequel, *Etz Hadomim Tafus / Under the Domim Tree* (1995). Almagor, the country's most prolific film actress, has won the Israel Best Actress Award from the Israeli Film Institute ten times (as well as being their Best Actress of the 1990s) and in 1997 collected a Life Achievement Award from the Israel Film Academy. Almagor has created characters that stay in the collective memory, rich in texture and full of vigour.

Atzmon, Anat (b. Israel)

Atzmon became a star overnight due to her role as a teenage beauty in the popular *Eskimo Limone* / *Lemon Popsicle* (1978). Following that, she appeared in *Dizengoff 99*, which became a cult movie. Later she took leading roles in several dramas and melodramas, including *Ha'ayit* / *The Vulture* (1981), *Kvish Le'Lo Motzah* / *Dead-End Street* (1982) and *Edut Me'Ones* / *Forced Testimony* (1984).

Elian, Yona

Elian started acting on stage but became known in the cinema as the tragic heroine of the popular melodrama *Nurit* (1972). Among her other films were *Salomonico* (1972) and *The Last Winter* (1982), in which she played a war widow. Her portrayal of a Holocaust survivor / collaborator in the prestigious television series *Mishpat Kastner* / *Kastner Trial* (1994) won her a very favourable reception.

Gaon, Yehoram (b. 1940, Israel)

A popular singer who made more than forty records over a period of three decades, Gaon simultaneously developed a career as an actor in musicals on stage and in the cinema. He appeared in *Kol Mamzer Melech* / *Every Bastard a King* (1968), *Matzor* / *Siege* (1969), *Ha'Pritza Ha'Gdola* / *The Big Escape* (1970), *Ha'Joker* / *Joker* (1976), *Ha Meaher* / *The Lover* (1986) and *Mivtza Yonatan* / *Operation Thunderbolt* (1977), as well as in several television series, among them *Mar Manie* / *Mr Manie* in 1996. His role in *Casablan* (1973) was his biggest success and the film that made him a star.

Hasfari-Azoulai, Hanna

Hasfari-Azoulai has appeared in international productions, such as *Delta Force 3*. In Israeli films she took leading roles in *Za'am Vetehila* / *Rage and Glory* (1984), *Nadia* (1986), for which she won the Israeli Film Academy Award, *Hamackhtzeva* / *The Query* (1990) and *Holeh Ahava Meshikun Gimmel* / *Lovesick on Nana Street* (1995). She scripted and played the leading role in the acclaimed *Sh'khur* (1994), which won six Israel Film Academy Awards in 1994.

Ivgi, Moshe (b. 1953, Morocco)

The busiest actor in Israeli cinema over the last two decades, Ivgi has starred in many shorts and a dozen of feature films, among them *Mitachat La'af* / *Big Shots*, *Shuru*, *Gemar Gavia* / *Cup Final*, *Holeh Ahava Meshikun Gimmel* / *Lovesick on Nana Street*, *Day after Day* and *Dangerous Acts*. While in the 1980s he was typecast as an underdog, in the 1990s he rose to stardom portraying eccentric heroes in films like *Shuru* and *Holeh Ahava Meshikun Gimmel*. In Gitai's *Day after Day* (1997), Ivgi played the son of a Jewish mother and an Arabic father. In 1998 he played a crippled and paranoid character alongside Gila Almagor's theatrical *grande dame* in *Dangerous Acts*. He also portrayed Menachem Begin in a television drama and himself in a docu-comedy television series in 1999. Ivgi brings to the screen both an uncontestable low-key star quality and a unique capacity for creating a variety of characters from all walks of life.

Khuri, Makram (b. Israel)

After studying in London, Khuri was associated with the Jerusalem Circle Theatre, as well as the Arab Theatre of Haifa. Since 1975 he has been a member of the Municipal Theatre of Haifa troupe and was one of the founders of the Arab stage of this theatre. In cinema he has appeared in *Mitachat La'af / Big Shots* (1982), *Gesher Tsar Me'od / On a Narrow Bridge* (1985), *Chyuch Hagdi / Smile of the Lamb* (1986) and *'Urs al-Galil / Wedding in Galilee* (1987), among others, as well as taking the leading role in the 1983 television series *Michel Ezra Safra Uvanav / Michel Ezra Safra and Sons*. In 1987 he became Israel Prize Laureate for the Theatre. Khuri's most acclaimed roles on screen are those of Jews and thus reflect the polemics of his own position as an Arab in a Jewish dominant culture.

Ophir, Shaike (b. Israel, 1928)

Comedian, impersonator and mime artist. Ophir started his career in a pre-state theatre troupe and then went to France to study mime, later as a member of the troupe of Marcel Marceau. He appeared on American television and on Broadway and upon his return to Israel established a mime company and created popular one-man shows. He acted in more than thirty feature films, mostly in comic roles. In the 1950s he had supporting roles in films such as: *Be'ein Moledet / Lacking a Homeland* (1956), and in the late 1960s gained fame in leading roles in Kishon's *Te'alat Blaumilech / The Big Dig* (1969) and *The Policeman* (1971), for which he won the Golden Globe Award. Among his other films: *Habayit Berehov Shelush / The House on Shelush Street* (1973), *Daughters, Daughters* (1973) and *The Garden* (1977). For several decades Ophir was the most popular and beloved comedian in Israel, both on stage and in the cinema.

Shiloah, Yossef

Shiloah was a graduate of Beit Zvi. Since taking his first cinematic role in the comedy *Mishpakhath Simkhon / The Simchon Family* (1964), he has been cast as Eastern Jews or Arabs in both Israeli films and international productions. He has appeared in over sixty films, mostly in supporting roles: in *Hamatarah Tiram / Sinai Commando* (1968), he portrayed an Egyptian officer; in *Habrikha Hagdolah / The Big Escape* (1970), he appeared as a Syrian prison commander. In the 1970s Shiloah acted in many popular comedies and dramas, among them *Margo Sheli / My Margo* (1969), *Hashoter Azulai / The Policeman* (1971), *Catz VeCarasso / Katz and Carasso* (1971), *Ani Ohev Otach Rosa / I Love You Rosa* (1972), *Habayit Berehov Shelush / The House on Shelush Street* (1973), *Hagiga La'einayim / Saint Cohen* (1975), *Mishpakhath Tzan'ani / The Tsanani*

Family (1976) and *Sofo shel Milton Levy / The End of Milton Levy* (1981). Shiloah was associated with the Bourekas film genre, in which he portrayed Eastern Jews, sometimes as ridiculous caricatures. On other occasions he managed to create characters that transcended stereotypes. He also acted on stage and in the 1990s appeared in a television series. In 1998 he won a special award for his contribution to Israeli cinema.

Shimko, Dahlia

Shimko acted both on stage and in films. Her role as Noa in *Noa Bat Sheva-Esrey / Noa at Seventeen* (1982) brought her a lot of attention and praise. She also appeared in *Magash Hakesef / Fellow Travellers* (1984), *Echad Mishelanu / One of Us* (1989) and *Tzaleketh / Scar* (1995), among others. She also took a major role in the 1995 television series *Bat Yam – New York*. In the 1990s she has devoted her career to the theatre, where she also directs.

Topol, Haim (b. 1935, Israel)

An actor, director and producer, Topol gained international fame with his role in *Fiddler on the Roof* (1971). Among his Israeli features were *I Like Mike* and *Eldorado*, but the role most identified with him was as Sallah in *Sallah Shabbati*, for which he won the Golden Globe. In the 1970s, as well as *Fiddler on the Roof*, Topol produced and directed thirty-five television films based on Bible stories. His credits outside Israel include *The House in Garibaldi Street* and *For Your Eyes Only*. He is the only Israeli actor to have become an international film star and now divides his time between London and Tel Aviv.

Tzadok, Arnon

An actor, director and producer, Tzadok started on stage in Haifa Theatre. His cinematic career is associated with director Uri Barbash's films, starting with the television drama *Chatoon le'Chol Hachayim / Sentenced for Life* (1979). Barbash's debut feature film *Stigma* (1982) and the popular *Me'achorei Hasoragim / Beyond the Walls* (1984) followed, both of which won Tzadok the Israel Best Actor Award. He also appeared in the same director's *Hacholmim / Unsettled Land* (1987) and *Echad Mishelanu / One of Us* (1989). Tzadok co-produced several films and acted in *Haderech LeEin Harod / The Voice of Ein Harod* (1990). His debut feature as a director, *Layla Lavan / White Night* (1995), was a sequel to *Me'achorei Hasoragim / Beyond the Walls* and won him the Young Director's Prize at Cannes Film Festival. On screen Tzadok plays socially underprivileged and tortured men, giving powerful voice to the 'other' Sabra.

List of institutions

Bill for the Promotion of Israeli Films

This was the first bill to support and promote Israeli films and had a great impact on the film industry in the 1960s and 1970s. An Israeli film was specified as one in which at least 80 per cent was photographed, developed and processed in Israel. The bill adapted European models and included tax relief, service preference, loans and direct financial support. The main tool was a government subsidy in the form of a tax payback per purchased ticket, thus supporting mainly commercially successful products with no discrimination as regards quality. In 1954, the government decided to implement this law via the Ministry of Industry and Trade, and appointed Asher Hirshberg as the officer in charge. In this capacity Hirshberg provided an impetus that led to the production of many feature films, among them the first films by Golan, Kishon and Zohar. In 1955 movie theatres were compelled by law to screen Israeli newsreels prior to feature films. In 1962 a fund of US$500,000 was set up in the Ministry of Industry and Trade to support Israeli films.

Camera Obscura

This private Tel Aviv school for the visual arts was established in 1978. In 1984 the school opened an experimental video department that was eventually enlarged and became a permanent department of video art and film. The school offers a four-year study programme in video and film, computer arts, animation and screenwriting. Since 1984 the school has been recognized by the Pratt Institute in New York.

Channel 1

See *Israeli TV (Channel 1)*.

Channel 2

Launched formally in 1993, but actually broadcasting already from 1989, this first commercial television channel in Israel was modelled on ITV in the United Kingdom. It has three separate franchises. The charter for Channel 2 required that at least 50 per cent of its programming be locally produced and its existence has indeed given the local film industry a major boost in the making of series, documentaries and short dramas.

Film and Television Department, Tel Aviv University (TAU)

Opened in 1972, the Film and Television Department combines the history and theory of films with film and television production, direction, photography and scriptwriting, and grants a B.A. Many of Israel's film-makers studied at this school and many teach there. Over 400 students now study in the department, of which 100 are in the production section.

Film Department, Beit Tzvi

In 1971 Beit Tzvi, a school for stage arts that was founded in 1961 by the Ministry of Culture and Education, opened a film department that offered a two-year diploma programme. In 1981 the department changed its vocation from training technicians to training film-makers and several years later began to support the production of features made by graduates. In 1989 the department was shut down.

Film publications

Omanut Hakolno'a   Literally means 'Cinema Art'. The twenty-eight issues of this pioneering quarterly, published and edited by David Greenberg in 1957–63, offered reviews, features and essays, mostly translated from foreign journals such as *Sight and Sound* and *Cahiers de Cinema*.

Closeup   A film journal published from 1973 by the TAU Film Department, the Israeli Film Archive in Jerusalem and students at TAU. This publication, influenced by the French *Cahiers de Cinema*, started as a communal effort, but Uri and Irma Klein soon took over as editors. The five issues of *Closeup* appeared sporadically until 1978.

Kolnoa   Literally means 'cinema'. A film bi-monthly published by the IFI in 1974–82, *Kolnoa* was initiated by Nachman Ingber who was a member of the editorial board and later the periodical's editor. *Kolnoa* offered original as well as translated film reviews, interviews, essays and screenplays. In 1978 the publication changed its editorial board and its form, becoming more political.

Sratim   Literally means 'Films'. Founded in 1985 by Oshra Shwartz and Amir Rotem (graduates of the TAU Film Department) and sponsored by TAU and the IFI, this film and television journal printed six issues in two years. The journal touched on theoretical issues and also applied itself to the local industry.

Cinematheque   The Tel Aviv Cinematheque's bi-monthly magazine, launched in 1988 and edited since then by film writer Edna Feinaru, is the only current film publication in Israel. It offers reviews of festivals around the world, interviews with local and foreign film people, and essays on various aspects of cinema and television.

Fund for the Promotion of Israeli Quality Films

Established in 1979 by the Ministry of Education and Culture after extensive lobbying from the film-makers Levanon, Ne'eman, Schorr and Knebel, the IFI's director Nachman Ingber and the journalist Yossef Priel, this fund marks a watershed in the history of Israeli cinema. Ingber was the first chairman of the fund and Baruch Dienar served as its general manager for the first decade. Although the fund went through many policy changes during its existence, it maintained its main objective of improving the production of quality films in Israel, as well as improving their marketing in Israel and abroad. In 1989 the Ministry of Industry and Trade began sponsorship of the fund, which is now able (on a selective basis) to invest up to US$600,000 in the production of Israeli feature films, as opposed to US$70,000 in its early years. Since 1995 the fund has co-operated with television channels to produce mini-series and films made for television. Over the years the fund has invested in over 200 feature films, about a third of which were first features that their makers could not otherwise have made. The fund reduced the dependency of film-makers on the mass market and encouraged personal, political and controversial films, altering the face of

Israeli cinema. Most of the films produced after 1980 that have been mentioned in this chapter were supported by this fund.

Geva Films

The Geva film studio and laboratory (Sirtei Geva) were founded in 1949 near Tel Aviv by Mordechai Navon and Yitzhak Agadati. In the early 1950s Geva produced news-reels for cinemas and from 1953 to 1966 the studios produced about 100 short films for the Israeli Film Service and the Labour Federation, as well as other institutions. It also produced feature films. One of its main functions was to supply laboratory services. Geva produced several of the first feature films to be made in the state of Israel, among them *I Like Mike*, *Eldorado* and *Chavura Shekazot / A Gang Like Us*. In the 1960s the studio and lab were bought out by the Canadian company Berkey–Pathe Humphries and in 1988 merged with Israel Motion Pictures Studios (IMPS) to become the United Studios of Herzlia.

Haifa Cinematheque

The Haifa Cinematheque evolved in 1975 from a cinema club that had been estab-lished there earlier by Leah and Wim Van Lear. It screens classic and modern films, and hosts an annual film festival.

Haifa International Film Festival

Founded in 1984, since 1993 the Haifa International Film Festival carries the addi-tional title 'Neighbours', signifying its focus on Mediterranean cinema. The festival holds a competition for foreign and Israeli films, and another for Israeli video clips.

International Student Film Festival

Founded in 1986 by students at Tel Aviv University, this biennial event is held in the Tel Aviv Cinematheque with the participation of film schools from over thirty coun-tries. It is considered the largest festival of its kind in the world.

Israel Censorship Board

The Israel Censorship Board was guided from the 1920s by two public notices from the British Mandatory authorities: the Notice for Silent Films and the Notice for Public Exhibitions. The board is an autonomous body, made up of representatives of government and public agencies under the authority of the Ministry of the Interior. In December 1958, for example, the censorship board banned the import of German films, but allowed the screening of German-language films. In 1977, out of 430 films that the board reviewed, twenty-seven were banned. In 1991, the Censorship on Theatre Exhibitions was abolished and censorship of films was limited to rating.

Israel Film Academy

The Israel Film Academy is a public association that was established in 1991 by representatives from the whole spectrum of Israeli film-makers. Since its inception, the Academy has held an annual awards ceremony (based on the Academy Awards in Hollywood) on which its 550 members can vote. The winning film of the year is selected as Israel's entry for the Foreign Film Oscar.

Israel Film Archive

Established in 1961 by Wim and Lea Van Lear, the Israel Film Archive has been a member of the International Federation FIAF (Federation Internationale des Archives du Film) since 1963. The archive, stored and managed in the Jerusalem Cinematheque complex, preserves in celluloid and video over 19,000 films and 50,000 negatives of shorts, newsreels, features, animation and commercials from Israel and the rest of the world, including the invaluable collection of Nathan Axelrod. It holds the world's largest collection of Israeli and Jewish films, as well as having a comprehensive research library.

Israel Film Service (IFS)

A branch of the Ministry of Education and Culture, the Israel Film Service (IFS) was founded in 1960 and serves as a film production and distribution centre. Over the last four decades, the IFS has produced more than 4,000 documentaries, docu-dramas, public information and educational films, spanning a wide range of subjects relating to Israeli history, geography, arts and culture. IFS productions have won more than 260 prizes at international film festivals. In 1965 the IFS became an autonomous section within the ministry and, until the establishment of Israel Television in 1968, was responsible for the production of nearly all documentaries within Israel. IFS's founder and its director for the first three decades was Yigal Efrati, who soon became the largest producer in Israel, in charge of all films commissioned by government offices. The IFS cadre was very small, but the seven or less IFS producers have used hundreds of film-makers, cameramen and editors on a freelance basis. As such, this bureau had an enormous impact on documentary film-making in Israel. In the 1960s the IFS mostly produced government-commissioned films that were, by definition, Zionist propaganda. However, starting in 1970, it began to initiate independent projects, among them co-productions with Israeli TV and even the theatrical release *Biglal Hamilchama Hahee / Due to That War*. The IFS was at its peak in the 1960s and 1970s; its decline thereafter was partly due to the growth of television in Israel.

Israel Film Centre (IFC)

A branch of the Ministry of Industry and Trade, the Israel Film Centre (IFC) was established in 1969. It provided information about Israeli film-making, offered financial incentives and services to foreign productions and co-productions, promoted the marketing of Israeli films at film markets and festivals, and financed Israeli cinema weeks abroad. The IFC's first director, Gad So'en, sought support for Israeli cinema among private factors as well, and as a result the Warner Board established a special fund to promote screenwriting in Israel. Until 1991 the IFC also held the annual awards ceremony for Best Israeli Film that is now held by the Israel Film Academy. The IFC also had a special unit that aimed to support short films, which was headed for many years by Nili Hame'iri. This unit was, prior to the establishment of film schools and the unit's abolishment in 1997, the starting point for many Israeli film-makers. During the 1990s the IFC lost much of its budget and consequently its impact on the industry.

Israel Film Institute (IFI)

This non-profit organization established in 1973, under the sponsorship of the Ministry of Culture and Education, was a central facility for film culture in Israel. The institute organized lectures and symposiums, set up over 150 cinema clubs and published the cinema journal *Kolno'a*. Its original premises also housed an information centre and a library. After its closure in 1998, the library and archives were moved to the Tel Aviv Cinematheque.

Israel Motion Picture Studios (IMPS)

Israel Motion Picture Studios (IMPS) was the first major film studio in Israel. It opened in 1951 in Herzlia, north of Tel Aviv, under the inspiration of Margot Klausner, who was first chairperson and later president. A sound studio opened in 1952 and a laboratory for colour processing opened in 1969. In the early years the studios invested mostly in documentaries, since the foreign feature films produced at that time in Israel were processed in Hollywood. Due to the vast cost of building the studios and because of competition from Geva, the Herzlia studios faced bankruptcy several times. In 1964 the Studios opened a new large studio, in which *Cast a Giant Shadow* was shot a year later. In the first twenty-five years Klausner invested in dozens of Israeli films, among them *Giv'a 24 Eina Ona / Hill 24 Doesn't Answer* and *Metzitzim / Peeping Toms*. During that period the studios' laboratory processed some 1,000 documentaries, 850 advertising films, 400 newsreels, 1,100 television productions and 100 feature films. In 1968, with the establishment of Israeli television, IMPS (under new management headed by Yitzhak Kol) became the regular studio of the only television channel in Israel. In the early 1970s it acquired modern satellite equipment and during the 1973 war provided services for foreign television networks. In 1988 the IMPS merged with Berkey Studios (formerly Geva) into what is now the United Studios of Herzlia.

Israeli Cable TV

Formed in 1990, Cable TV offers primarily topic-oriented channels such as news, sport, cinema, children and culture. There are five licensed cable operators, divided according to geographical regions within the country. Cable TV operators are obliged by law to invest a percentage of their revenues in original local productions and in recent years more films have been made for screening on Cable TV. In 2000 a new consortium of satellite broadcasters started operating in Israel, supplementing Cable TV.

Israeli TV (Channel 1)

Soon after its foundation in 1968, this public body (which was part of the Israeli Broadcast Authority and the only television channel in Israel for two decades) became a creative centre for makers of documentaries, as well as drama. Israeli TV has produced dozens of documentaries and dramas, as well as several major series, giving many film-makers the opportunity to work and develop. With the establishment of the commercial Channel 2 in 1993 (see above), many talents moved to work there and the Channel 1 lost much of its appeal.

Jerusalem Cinematheque

Established in 1974 by Lea and Wim Van Lear, the Jerusalem Cinematheque is still managed by Lea Van Lear. In 1981 it moved to a new complex in Jerusalem which now contains the Israeli Film Archive, a research library with the largest cinema information centre in Israel, and various other educational facilities. Since 1983 the Cinematheque has hosted an annual International Film Festival. The Jerusalem Cinematheque serves as a research centre for academics from all over the world.

Jerusalem International Film Festival

Established in 1983 by Wim and Lea Van Lear, the Film Festival is held annually in the Jerusalem Cinematheque, offering a selection from festivals all over the world, as well as special retrospectives. The festival holds a competition for Israeli films and, since 1989, has presented the prestigious Wolgin Award.

Jewish National Fund (JNF)

Founded in 1901, the fund's primary affiliation with the cinema began with the purchase from 1921 of Ben-Dov's documentaries. Later the JNF sponsored Ben-Dov's films, as well as those of other film-makers, sometimes as sole producer and sometimes in co-production with the Palestine Foundation Fund (PFF) or other factors. Most of the JNF's films were shown outside Palestine and were produced with diaspora Jewry in mind. In the 1920s the JNF supplemented film screenings with printed propaganda, oral addresses prior to the film or mid-screening and, of course, the collection of contributions. The films served as a platform for those collections, making audiences more sympathetic to the idea of buying land in Eretz Israel. Among the JNF's productions were *Ma'asseh Betayar Amerika'i BeEretz Yisrael / Palestine Awakening* (1923) and *Aviv Be'eretz Yisrael / Springtime in Palestine* (1928, co-production with PFF).

Labour Federation

The Labour Federation's film department started in 1945 as a facility for the distribution and screening of 16 mm films in the kibbutzim and villages. In 1953 it had evolved into a production unit that mainly produced documentaries and training films, and was a central production house during the first two decades of the state.

Movie theatres

Entertainment in silent movie theatres was already common in 1900. The first screenings were held privately in the homes of wealthy settlers, as well as in an improvised cinema hall. The projector operator at many of these occasions was the Italian Salvatore Collara, who travelled on a donkey with his projector and films. Only a few movie houses operated in Palestine before World War I. In 1925 seven silent movie theatres were active within Palestine, but in a few years their number had doubled. In the early 1920s the silent movie theatres screened only one film daily, initially accompanied by piano but later by orchestra or even a choir. The first sound film to be screened in Palestine was *Sonny Boy* at the end of 1929. By 1952 Israel had 125 cinemas, housing approximately 80,000 seats. Ten years later the number had doubled again. The 1960s were the height of cinema attendance in Israel: there were 300 cinema houses in 1967, the year before the establishment of Israeli television. The competition with the new medium hurt cinema and, by 1970, 10 per cent of the cinemas had closed. In 1980 there were 180 cinemas but by 1985 only 163. In the 1980s another tendency became apparent: the transition from single cinemas to complex centres containing four to five small- or medium-sized cinemas. In the 1980s and 1990s many cinemas opened in shopping centres, but cinema attendance remained low. This tendency still prevails.

New Cinema Bill

The New Cinema Bill was an initiative made by MP Yona Yahav of the Labour Party and members of the Film Academy in 1998. Its main purpose is to increase total government investment in cinema from around US$1.5 million annually to US$15 million, with the money coming from a percentage of the income generated by commercial broadcasters like the cable and satellite channels or Channel 2. Before the bill was even enacted the government had already revised it, reducing the original level of support by 50 per cent. In 2000 a statutory body was constituted "The National Cinema Board", in which all walks of the cinema art and profession were represented. This body appointed sub-committees that discussed various aspects of the encouragement and governmental financial support of the cinema. A conclusive report and criteria for support were submitted to the Minister of Culture for implementation. Until this very moment (June 2001) not a single recommendation was implemented due to all kinds of bureaucratic and judicial obstacles.

New Fund for Israeli Cinema and Television

Established in 1993 by the Ministry of Culture, this fund promotes Israeli documentaries, television productions and experimental films. It grants up to US$90,000 per film for documentaries or up to US$50,000 for the other types of production, and participates in project development. The New Fund was a breakthrough for documentary cinema in Israel, which had previously been sponsored only by government and other institutional bodies. The New Fund supports films on a selective basis, judged on script and budget proposals, and since its inception has helped many documentaries that won national and international awards. Orna Ben-Dor, who acted as the fund's director from 1994 to 1999, was a key figure in the fund's development.

Palestine Foundation Fund (PFF)

The Palestine Foundation Fund (PFF) was established in 1920 (it became known as the United Israel Appeal after the establishment of the state of Israel). Its first film productions were *Hanoar B'eretz Israel / Young Palestine* (1926), *Aviv Be'eretz Yisrael / Springtime in Palestine* (1928, jointly with the JNF) and *Le'khayim Khadashim / Land of Promise* (1934). The central figure in PFF who contributed to film productions in Palestine was Yosef Gal-Ezer, director of the Information Department, who initiated several film projects and even earned a directing credit for *Aviv BeEretz Yisrael*.

Sam Spiegel Jerusalem Film and Television School

The Sam Spiegel School opened in 1989 with support from the estate of Hollywood producer Sam Spiegel. The school, which is equipped with the most up-to-date facilities, offers a three-year programme in all aspects of film and television production. The head of the school since its inception has been Renen Schorr. To date the school has accumulated dozens of international prizes and a retrospective of the school's graduate films was shown at MOMA, New York, as well as in Hong Kong and Australia.

Steven Spielberg Jewish Film Archive

The Jewish Film Archive was established in 1969 by Hebrew University in Jerusalem and inaugurated formally at the Mount Scopus campus in 1972, with the help of contributor Avraham Ra'ad. Since 1973 it has housed all films produced by the Zionist Federation. In 1977 the archive acquired Baruch Agadati's collection of newsreels, which contains invaluable footage shot by Ya'akov Ben-Dov, now available to the researcher in safety stock. In 1987 the archive took the name of Hollywood director Steven Spielberg, following a generous donation by him.

Tel Aviv Cinematheque

Established by the municipality in cooperation with the TAU Film Department in 1973, Tel Aviv Cinematheque screens classic and modern films, and promotes symposiums, training days and foreign-film weeks, as well as hosting the bi-annual International Student Film Festival. It is an important podium for Israeli film-makers and sometimes the only place their films can be shown. The Cinematheque, headed by Alon Garbuz has a film library and a research centre, and since 1988 it has published a bi-monthly film magazine.

Travelogues and films in Palestine (1896–1917)

The first cameramen came to Palestine in search of exotic locations for the travelogues that were very popular during the first years of cinema. In April 1896 Alexandre Promio from Lumière Brothers in France shot footage in Jaffa, Jerusalem and Bethlehem. In 1899 Oskar Messter filmed the visit of Kaiser Wilhelm II to Palestine. Thomas Peters filmed landscapes in Palestine around 1900. The Edison production company made several 'exotic' films in Jerusalem in 1903: *Arabian–Jewish Dances*,

Jerusalem Busiest Street and *View of Mount Zion*. In 1903 a group of German pilgrims shot a twenty-minute travelogue based on Jesus' life in Nazereth, Bethlehem, the Sea of Galilee and Jerusalem. In 1905 Henry Howse shot the visit of General William Booth, the commander of the Salvation Army, to the grave of Lazarus and the Jordan River. In the same year F. Ormiston-Smith made several travelogues. In 1908 Pathé Company made the film *Jerusalem* and the Frenchman Leo Lefebvre included footage of Christian Holy Land sites in a worldwide travelogue. In 1910 the Eclair Company produced a short drama, *Resurrection of Lazarus*, based on the New Testament. In 1912 the Kalem Company produced *From the Manger to the Cross*, a more ambitious production about the life of Jesus. This film was made by the American Sidney Alcott and shot near the Sea of Galilee and in Jerusalem. Edison cameramen returned to Palestine in 1913 and filmed *Jerusalem and the Holy Land* and *Jaffa, the Seaport of Jerusalem*. Between 1914 and 1917 there is no record of local film-making in Palestine apart from British and Australian military cameramen filming the war.

United Studios of Herzlia

The largest production house in Israel, United Studios produces documentaries, drama, television series, television shows and commercials. The company comprises four large studios with control rooms, computerized sound and lighting systems, laboratory facilities and film archives. The studios house the broadcasting centre for Israel's cable television and most local films, as well as many foreign productions that have been shot in Israel, are processed here. This studio evolved from a merger between IMPS and Geva in 1988.

Zionism

Zionism was the national movement that aimed at establishing a national home for the Jewish people in Palestine. The first Zionist Congress was held in Basel in 1879 and was chaired by Dr Theodor Herzl. The Zionist utopian ethos is manifested in most films made first in Palestine, then Israel, up until the 1960s.

Zionist propaganda

The Zionist movement arose in proximity to the birth of cinema and used the new medium from the outset to promote and distribute its ideas. In 1900 Theodor Herzl sent a *kinematograph* and laboratory equipment to Palestine, but the people in the colonies did not know how to use the new technology. From the 1920s pictures were used as an effective tool for building the image of the New Jew, by which time various Zionist institutions (mainly the JNF) regularly sponsored and produced propaganda films. Most of these films were documentaries screened to diaspora Jews for the purpose of raising funds and encouraging Jewish emigration to Palestine. The IFS continued to finance such documentaries well into the 1970s.

Acknowledgements

The laborious task of collecting and verifying the vast amount of information required for this work necessitated the willingness and cooperation of many parties. I wish to thank the Tel Aviv University Research Grant, and in particular the President of the University, Prof. Yoram Dinstein; the Rector, Prof. Nili Cohen; and the Dean of The Yolanda and David Katz Faculty of the Arts, Prof. Eli Rozik-Rosen, for allocating funds towards the accomplishment of this project. These financial contributions made the project possible. I wish also to thank Lisa Wald of the Tel Aviv University Research Authority, whose advice was vital for obtaining the funding. The staff of the Tel Aviv Cinematheque, in particular Director Alon Garbus; Administrator, Baruch Harpaz; Chief Librarian Tsvia Margalit; and Librarian Dror Izhar were all very welcoming and instrumental in supplying me with many indispensable documents from the Documentation Archive of the Israeli Cinema under their auspices. The Institute for the Study of Jewish Press and Communications at the Tel Aviv University gave us free access to its immense archive. The Steven Spielberg Jewish Film Archive at the Hebrew University of Jerusalem and its Director, Marilyn Koolic, enabled us to access many films as well as to photograph frames from rare films. Many people contributed documents and information. Special thanks go to Asher Hirschberg, the first Director of the Film Industry Department at the Ministry of Industry and Trade, who gave me his historical point of view, and to Rina Rothbart of the Israel Film Center who assisted us with governmental publications.

Credits

Editor and Writer of Introduction: Judd Ne'eman
Text & Translation: Rachel Neeman
Associate Writers: Eldad Kedem and Shmulik Duvdevani
Research: Inbar Shaham

Notes

1   'Bourekas' are small cheese-filled pastries that originated in the Near East and have become a popular fast food in Israel.
2   'Kayitz' is an acronym for 'Kolnoa Israeli Tza'ir' (Young Israeli Cinema) and, at the same time, the Hebrew word for 'summer'. The group was formed in 1978 as a militant ideological group of film-makers that claimed their right to public funding and freedom of speech, and demanded artistic freedom for domestic cinema. The group published a manifesto, the signatories of which included Dan Wolman, Nissim Dayan, Renen Schorr, Nadav Levitan, Ram Levy, Judd Ne'eman, Yaki Yosha and Michal Bat-Adam.
3   *Nakba* is a word in Arabic that means 'catastrophe' or 'disaster'. The national disaster inflicted by the Jews on the Palestinians in the war of 1948, when they lost their land and 800,000 of them became refugees, is called 'The Nakba'.

References and further reading

Be'eri, L. (1980) 'Films and Silent Movie Houses', in A.B. Yaffe (ed.) *The First Twenty Years: Literature and Arts – Tel Aviv 1909–1929*, Tel Aviv: Hakibbutz Hame'uchad.
Ben-Shaul, N. (1997) *Mythical Expressions of Siege in Israeli Films*, New York: Edwin Mellen Press.

Burstein, I. (1990) *Face as Battlefield*, Tel Aviv: Hakibbutz Hame'uchad.

Eco, U. (1992) 'Towards a New Middle Ages', in T. Katz-Freiman (ed.) *Catalogue of Postscripts: 'End'-Representations in Contemporary Israeli Art*, Tel Aviv: Genia Schriber University Art Gallery.

Fainaru, E. and Fainaru, D. (eds) (1999) 'A Hundred Years of Life and Cinema in the Holy Land'; special supplements of *Cinematheque*, 1–7.

Gertz, N. (1993) *Motion Picture: Israeli Fiction in Film*, Tel Aviv: Open University.

Gertz, N., Lubin, O. and Ne'eman, J. (eds) (1998) *Fictive Looks – On Israeli Cinema*, Tel Aviv: Open University.

Gordon, A.D. (1970 [1911]) 'Work', in A. Hertzberg (ed.), *The Zionist Idea – A Historical Analysis and Reader*, Keter Publishing House, Jerusalem, 1970 (Hebrew) pp. 287–9.

Gross, N. and Gross, Y. (1991) *The Hebrew Film*, Jerusalem: privately published.

Halachmi, J. (1995) *No Matter What: Studies in the History of the Jewish Film in Israel*, Jerusalem: Steven Spielberg Jewish Film Archive and The Central Zionist Archives.

Harel, Y. (1956) *Cinema: From the Beginning to Today*, Tel Aviv: Yavne Publishing.

Israeli Film Academy (1990–9) Catalogues.

Israel Film Centre (1972–98) Information bulletins.

Jerusalem Film Festival (1992–9) Catalogues.

Kronish, A. (1996) *World Cinema: Israel*, Madison: Flicks Books.

Lubin, O. (1999) 'Sh'khur', in A. Ophir (ed.) *Fifty to Forty Eight: Critical Moments in the History of the State of Israel*, special issue of *Theory and Criticism* 12–13.

Ne'eman, J. (1995) 'The Empty Tomb in the Postmodern Pyramid: Israeli Cinema in the 1980s and 1990s', in C. Berlin (ed.) *Documenting Israeli Cinema: A Case Study*, Cambridge, MA: Harvard College Library.

—— (1998) 'The Popular Israeli Cinema and Its Social Realism', in G. Ballas (ed.) *Social Realism in the Fifties, Political Art in the Nineties*, Haifa: Haifa Museum exhibition catalogue (September).

—— (1999) 'The Death Mask of the Moderns: A Genealogy of New Sensibility Cinema in Israel', in I. Troen (ed.) *Israel Studies* 4 (1, spring): 100–28.

Schnitzer, M. (1994) *The Israeli Cinema*, Jerusalem: Kineret Publishing House.

Shohat, E. (1989) *Israeli Cinema: East / West and the Politics of Representation*, Austin: University of Texas Press.

Tryster, H. (1995) *Israel Before Israel: Silent Cinema in the Holy Land*, Jerusalem: Steven Spielberg Film Archive.

Cinema in Lebanon, Syria, Iraq and Kuwait

Kiki Kennedy-Day

Censorship

The aims of censorship in Lebanon, Syria and Iraq are not always as transparent as one might think. What is acceptable in a foreign film may not be in a local film, because the censors think it may show their country in a bad light. Thus, although Western films are supposedly censored for sex and 'excessive' violence, in fact the censors do not appear to be overly concerned, as can be seen from the large number of violent and sexy films from the United States that are shown in Lebanon. On the other hand, locally produced films are subject to tighter control, resulting in a marked double standard.

Furthermore, a more subtle form of censorship may take place in the subtitling of foreign films. The Lebanese critic Mohamed Soueid points out that 'Jews' may be translated as 'villains' in the subtitles. Similarly, in the subtitled version intended for Syria of the 1985 film *Rambo: First Blood, Part II* the action was moved from Vietnam to the Philippines to avoid embarrassing Syria's ally Moscow by the portrayal of the Vietcong and by implication the Soviet Union as the villain. Sylvester Stallone (as Rambo) rescues POWs from Japanese captors, rather than the Vietcong, in the Syrian version. The pictures are the same, including obvious red stars on the soldiers' hats, only the words have changed.

In Syria foreign films must be approved by the Censor Board, which is under the supervision of the Ministry of Culture and National Guidance. Although published reports state that the portrayal of sex and violence in imported films is limited, it is hard to believe that such standards are rigorously enforced. For example, *Variety* reported that *Pretty Woman* and *Goodfellas* were screened in Damascus (Cowie 1994). Given that the premise of *Pretty Woman* is that Julia Roberts' character is a prostitute with whom Richard Gere falls in love while on a 'date' and that Martin Scorsese's *Goodfellas*, although it received good reviews, is an extremely graphic depiction of Mafia violence among a group of small-time hoods, it is hard to imagine how their plots could be whitewashed by the censors. In the 1990s Syria's domestic production of films has fallen off to a few films a year from the target production level of fifteen to twenty movies per year. Syrian films appear to be censored for portraying the failure of socialism to pull the country out of poverty during the Assad regime; poverty and the lack of social services in the Dayr al-Zawr region are depicted by Omar Amiralay, for example, and his film *al-Hayat al-Yawmiyya Fi Qaria Suriyya / Daily Life in a Syrian Village* was censored. The film-maker was also forbidden to film civil unrest that occurred during his stay.

Amiralay said in a 1978 interview (Comolli and Daney 1978) that he did not fear the censor but Syria would end up with all its best movies banned and unscreened. Unfortunately for the film-makers this is exactly what has happened. Amiralay's *al-Dijaj / The Chickens* and *al-Hayat al-Yawmiyya Fi Qaria Suriyya*; Mohammad's *Nujum al-Nahar / The Stars in Broad Daylight* and Boutros's *al-Tahaleh / The Greedy Ones* have all languished in the National Film Board's closets, failing to win licences for exhibition. Boutros ran into trouble for daring to show the violence in Syrian society, and Oussama Mohammad's film was closeted for daring to show patriarchal repression and the execution by male relatives of girls who have been accused of having sex. In December 1993 *Le Monde* reported that dialogue considered 'defeatist' was cut by the official censors from Mohammed Malass's film *al-Layl / The Night*.

Samir Zikra, the director of *Haditha al-Nusf Mitr / The Half-Metre Incident*, said in an interview in 1995 that he believed the Syrian censorship committee was beginning to change: the first time they saw his film 'they were in shock', but gradually they became used to it, particularly because they liked the recognition that Syria was gaining at film festivals with this and other films (Bose 1995: 47). The critic Yves Thoraval considers the motivation for censorship in Syrian cinema to be the rulers' view that cinema should be a form of deliberate propaganda. Evidently the people who want to send messages do not feel that the directors – whom the government has funded – are sending the correct messages. The paradox is that the NFO continues to fund intelligent directors with interesting scripts – whether or not the finished films are actually shown at home.

Colonialism

Throughout the Middle East, the cinematic depiction of the struggle against colonialism is perennially popular. This is the case whether the oppressor is historical or contemporary, and whether the colonization is of the cinematographer's own country or abroad. An extreme example of overseas colonization caught on film is the Lebanese film-maker Heiny Srour's *Saat al-Tahrir Dakkat Barra Ya Isti'mar / The Hour of Liberation has Sounded – the Struggle in Oman* (1974), which documents the struggle of the Popular Front for the Liberation of Oman against the imperialist powers and against oil imperialism, particularly by British companies. The position of Palestinians in relation to Israel is seen universally by the Arabs as that of colonized to colonizer. An early depiction of this is the film *Kafr Kassem*.

On the other hand, colonialism has mixed effects in the Middle East. Despite colonial oppression, in countries that were heavily colonized, particularly by the French, an appreciation of cinema has often resulted. A notable case in the region is Lebanon, which had by far the largest number of cinemas and of tickets sold per inhabitant before the civil war left the country in a shambles. The French ruled Lebanon as a mandate territory from 1922 to 1945, following the Ottoman occupation. The French also colonized Syria, although their influence appears to have been less thorough, perhaps because the population was more rural and scattered. Following the official departure of the French, Lebanon was infiltrated by Egyptian directors who came as 'guest workers', many of whom viewed Lebanon as ideal for a working holiday.

Whatever the reason, the Lebanese both made films and were receptive to foreign films from an early date. The tradition of the ciné club (*nadi al-sinima*), originally showing foreign films, continues to the present. In Beirut in 1999 it was still possible to go to a salon, such as the upstairs room of a club, and for a small sum to view a recent film, often meeting the film-maker. In 1999 the films offered by one such club in Beirut included *Il Postino / The Postman* (Italy, 1994), *Majnunak / Crazy of You* by the Lebanese film-maker Akram Zaatari (video, 1999) and *Cry Freedom* (England, 1987).

In 1975 Soubhi Seifeddine directed *al-Rajul al-Samed / The Resister*, the story of the legendary Abu 'Ali Melhem Kassem's struggle against the occupying Ottomans, set in the 1910s. Likewise *al-Fahd / The Leopard* (1972), by the Syrian Nabil al-Maleh, showed a peasant rebellion against the army; although the film is set in post-colonial days, the peasants appear to live in exactly the same feudal condition as they did in colonial times – at the mercy of the army and bureaucrats.

The 1983 Iraqi film *al-Mas'ala al-Kubra / The Big Question* depicted the Iraqi struggle against British occupation in the 1920s. It particularly focused on the leadership of Shaykh Dari Mahmud and was one of the few major movies to to tell its story from the perspective of the colonized. British actors were recruited for the British roles.

In 1998 Samir Zikra was reportedly working on a film about Syria's struggle against the Ottoman occupation, focusing on the life of al-Kawakibi in the last century; its title is *Tourab al-Ghouraba'a / The Sands of Strangers*. al-Kawakibi is an interesting choice of protagonist for a film, as he was an intellectual and a newspaper editor who espoused the idea of pan-Arabism.

Documentaries

The documentary is a popular genre, especially in Syria and Iraq. Some directors have a technical background, for instance the Iraqi Mohammed Shukri Jamil began working as an aide in the film department of the Iraqi oil company, and this early training shows in their films. One of Jamil's early films was *al-Zama'un / The Thirsty* (1971); filmed in an arid region of Iraq, it told the story of semi-nomadic Bedouins who try to dig a well. It is notable for its many documentary elements. From the early 1960s to the mid-1970s Iraqi directors of state-supported films concentrated on documentaries. The General Organization for Cinema sponsored about sixty documentaries before switching to feature films in 1977. However, these were more straightforward – covering the oil industry, rivers, and the spread of medicine in Iraq – than *al-Zama'un*, which began in the documentary mode but added a story.

Film categories do not translate from their Western counterparts, which include feature films, 'fact-based' dramas and documentaries. Omar Amiralay is rather representative in that his documentaries are highly interpretive. Although he is showing pictures from real life, it is reality seen through his eyes and his imagination. Amiralay himself states that his films fall between documentary and fiction. In some scenes he has given *al-Hayat al-Yawmiyya Fi Qariah Suriyah / Daily Life in a Syrian Village* (1974) the same structure as Buñuel's *Las Hurdes / Land without Bread* (Spain, 1937). A mother giving an infant a drink water from a polluted stream is followed by shots of disease-bearing mosquitoes (in *Las Hurdes*) and of disease-causing microbes (*al-Hayat al-Yawmiyya*). In both films children are shown reading in school from textbooks that assume their lives are totally different from the impoverished reality. Amiralay appears to use his films to investigate the nature of reality as lived by the people he films. He says that he is not merely interested in documentary films, as filming then becomes purely 'mechanical'. In 1999 Amiralay said he was working on a film about the relationship between money and power in Lebanon, which he also described as somewhere between documentary and fiction.

Current film-makers in Lebanon have also revisited the documentary, using it to express a point of view. Walid Ra'ad and Jayce Salloum's *Talaeen A Junuub / Up to the South* (video, 1993) uses interviews to explore the experiences of people in the south of Lebanon under Israeli occupation. *Muqaddima Li-Nihayat Jidal / Introduction to the End of an Argument* by Elias Suleiman and Jayce Salloum (video, 1994) manipulates found images from television newscasts, Hollywood movies and early cartoons to demonstrate the portrayal of Arabs in popular culture in the West. It is a documentary in technique in so far as it uses real images, but a definite point of view is expressed by their selection and juxtaposition.

Randa Chahal Sabbagh blended old family snapshots and new filmed interviews with family members to make the semi-documentary *Hurubina al-Ta'isha / Our Heedless Wars* about the effects of the civil war in Lebanon.

Jocelyn Saab's *Ghazal al-Banat 2 / The Razor's Edge* (1985) was filmed during the war and, despite intending to make a feature film, documentary elements invade the film because of the ongoing war. The viewer sees bombed-out buildings, as well as unscripted flares and tracer bullets behind the actors during a night scene.

No matter what type of movie a film-maker intended to make during the war, the war formed a documentary backdrop for all the films made in Beirut at that time. In the final scenes of *Hurub Saghira / Little Wars* (1982), for example, the characters race through bombed-out buildings at the Green Line. Rather than looking like sets, the buildings look like a real war zone (Darraj 1995).

Education

Education has long been a major problem for film-makers and crews in the Middle East (except in Egypt, which has a long tradition of training technical crews). In the early days, getting actors, especially women, was also a problem.

Directors and technicians were thus sent abroad to study. This trend began in the early 1930s when Georges Costi was sent to study cinematography in Paris by Lumnar Film, an early Lebanese film society that was founded by a German patron. By gaining their education abroad, however, many film-makers found themselves at least partly alienated on their return to their own countries. For Syrians, Moscow was the most common choice, at least in the Soviet era when Syria was a client state.

The Syrian directors Abdulatif Abdulhamid, Raymond Butros, Mohammed Malass, Oussama Mohammad, Riyad Shayya, Samir Zikra and Wadi Youssef all studied film-making at VGIK, the Moscow film academy. Omar Amiralay studied at IDHEC in Paris in the turbulent mid-1960s. Moustapha Akkad, who directed *al-Risalah / The Message*, studied at UCLA. Nabil el-Maleh studied at the Film Institute (FAMU) in Prague, perhaps for this reason his early film *al-Fahd / The Leopard* was reviewed in a Czech journal. Burhane Alawiya, who was born in Lebanon but worked in the Syrian film industry, studied at INSAS in Brussels from 1968–73. The famous Iraqi director Mohammed Shukri Jamil trained in the United Kingdom and briefly worked in the British film industry, before returning to Baghdad. Qays al-Zubaidi,

Iraqi director of *al-Yazirly* (1974), studied cinema at Babelsberg in the German Democratic Republic. The Kuwaiti director Khalid al-Siddiq studied cinema in Bombay.

Among the Lebanese, George Nasser (b. 1927) studied film at UCLA from 1951–4 and then studied technique at ORTF in Paris from 1959–60. Jocelyn Saab studied at the Université Saint Joseph, then worked for French television and extensively in Europe. Maroun Baghdadi and Antoine Remy studied at IDHEC in Paris. Samir Habchi was unusual (for Lebanon) in receiving a diploma from the Kiev Institute in Russia; his film *al-E'sar / The Tornado* opens in a Moscow apartment. Gaby Bustros studied cinema in New York and then became the subject, with her family, of Jennifer Fox's *Beirut: The Last Home Movie*. May Masri studied film at San Francisco State University, while her partner Jean Khalil Chamoun studied cinema in Paris. Jean-Claude Codsi studied at the INSAS in Brussels; he also worked as assistant to Burhane Alawiya during the filming of *Kafr Kassem*. Randa Shahal Sabbagh studied in Paris, both through secondary school and at the Université de Vicennes. Heiny Srour studied ethnography at the Sorbonne, with a couple of hours a week studying cinema. Gary Garabédian, the Iranian director of *Garo* (1965), studied film production in the United States. The advantage for the directors is that the country in which they study film will often continue to follow their career, write reviews of their movies and so on.

Since 1988, L'Institut d'Etudes Scéniques, Audiovisuelles et Cinématographiques (IESAV) at the Université Saint Joseph in Beirut has offered a course of study in theatre or film. The audiovisual / cinematic department aims to give students practical knowledge in the technical aspects of film-making. This has been a problem in the Middle East since the earliest days of film-making. In earlier days, after shooting was complete, a film had to be shipped to Europe for processing. Burhane Alawiya has given an interview which bears on two aspects of this problem. First, when filming *Kafr Kassem* in the early 1970s he had to use a half-Belgian, half-Syrian crew, with the important positions filled by the Belgians, because he could not find local technicians to work to the highest standards. Second, he pointed to the degradation of films processed in the Middle East. In technical terms, Alawiya said that Eastman Colour 35 mm processed in the best Lebanese studios (which are the best in the Middle East) would lose 60 per cent of its quality in comparison to processing at Eclair Studios in Paris. At Eclair, he said, one is able to get 85.9 per cent of the real potential from film, while at Baalbek Studios only 25 per cent is realized. In the same interview he also discussed the problem of sound recording, which he also found complicated in the Middle East (*Cahiers du cinéma* 1974–5: 65).

Exile and displacement

Exile and migration is a recurring theme in Middle Eastern cinema, but it has a particular poignancy in Lebanese films. From the first film made in Lebanon, *Moughamarat Elias Mabrouk / The Adventures of Elias Mabrouk* (1929), Lebanese film-makers have been interested in the return of the emigrant after a long sojourn abroad. In this film, director Pidutto followed the return of an emigrant from United States. Pidutti's second movie, *Moughamarat Abu Abed / The Adventures of Abu Abed* (1931), followed the adventures of another Lebanese emigrant, this time returning from Africa. George

Nasser continued the tradition with his 1957 film *Ila Ayn / Toward the Unknown*. This film featured the story of a Lebanese emigrant to Brazil.

While emigrants have always left Lebanon in search of opportunity, the long civil war (1975–90) made many Lebanese internal exiles, forced to leave their homes because of the violence. In Jocelyn Saab's *Ghazal al-Banat 2 / The Razor's Edge* (1985), Samar and her family are displaced from their fishing village in the south of Lebanon. They are internal exiles, living in Beirut. Samar, now fifteen, left seven years earlier when she was too young to remember much about the village. In *al-E'sar / The Tornado* (1992), an art student returns to Beirut from Moscow and discovers he is a displaced person; Akram no longer understands either his city or the tornado of violence that sweeps through the streets. When he was in Moscow, Akram knew who he was – he had a life, an apartment and a girlfriend – in Beirut nothing matters except having a gun. In *An al-Anwan / The Time has Come* (1994) two emigrants return to Lebanon from France, meeting on the Cyprus ferry. In this film, the woman Raya has forgotten her native Arabic language, which is a shorthand way of showing she has lost her Arab identity. In *Ashbah Beirut / Beyrouth fantôme / Beirut Phantoms* (1999) by Ghassan Salhab, Khalil returns to Beirut after ten years in exile, with his friends believing that he is dead. He takes advantage of the confusion to adopt a new identity, but Beirut is too small a city for the trick to work and ultimately leads to failure. Whatever he had hoped his return would bring, he is still displaced and no longer at home in Beirut.

Even those who stayed in Beirut during the war are displaced in Baghdadi's *Hurub Saghira / Little Wars* (1982). The characters stagger through the film looking for their identities: Talal tries to become a local warlord like his kidnapped father; Nabil does not know if he is a war photographer or a drug dealer; and none of the militiamen have any ideals, they are all rowdy drunks.

In Syrian films the idea of displaced persons also becomes important, particularly in the films of Mohammed Malass. In his *Ahlam al-Madina / Dreams of the City* (1984), a young boy, Dib, must leave his home in Quneitra after his father's death and move with his mother to his grandfather's house in Damascus. Dib gets a job and becomes the family breadwinner, as women were not expected to work outside the home in the 1950s. This heart-wrenching film details the failure of one family to adjust to life in the city due to social conditions rather than their own individual failings. *al-Makhdu'un / The Duped* (1974), Taufiq Salih's depiction of men looking for work, is the ultimate portrayal of exile and displacement. The hopelessness of the life of Palestinians in refugee camps leads the men to seek out riches in Kuwait, but only tragedy awaits them there. Even Dureid Lahham's comedy *al-Hudud / Borders* (1984) takes as its premise a man who is displaced, having been exiled to the no-man's-land between borders when he loses his passport by accident. The character is an everyman who could be anyone now that, by a twist of fate, he is outside society.

The Palestinian situation is never far from the consciousness of other Arabs – the official programme in the Iraqi Film Festival of 1978 was comprised entirely of films about Palestinians – so the themes of exile and displacement find great resonance in Arab film-making. A Dutch documentary by Johan van der Keuken called *The Palestinians*, a balanced historical review of the Palestinian situation, received the top prize at the 1978 festival.

Women directors

In the Middle East women directors are numerous and successful at getting films made, especially in Lebanon. Many of them split their time between Paris and Beirut, and some of the best known among them, such as Jocelyn Saab, have indicated they no longer intend to make films about the Middle East. Among such women directors are May Masri, Randa Chahal Sabbagh, Heiny Srour, Jocelyn Saab and Olga Nakkash. However, it should be noted in passing that they make movies, not 'women's movies'.

May Masri is a Palestinian film-maker, living in Lebanon, who directs films in partnership with her husband Jean Chamoun. Their films often focus on issues for Palestinians, such as in *Zahratel el-Kindoul / Wild Flowers: Women of South Lebanon* (1986) and *Children of Shatila* (1989). *Wild Flowers* tells the stories of several women in the south of Lebanon during various actions against the Israeli occupation there. It won a Critics' Award at the Carthage Film Festival and a Special Jury Award at the Damascus Film Festival. *Children of Shatila* follows the lives of several children and young people around the Shatila refugee camp.

Randa Chahal Sabbagh, the daughter of a prominent Lebanese family (her father was one of the founders of the communist party there and her mother was a political journalist), continued the family traditions with *Hurubina al-Ta'isha / Our Heedless Wars* (1995) a political analysis of the war at the personal level.

Heiny Srour, director of *Saat al-Tahrir Dakkat Barra Ya Isti'mar / The Hour of Liberation has Sounded – the Struggle in Oman* (1974) and *Leila Wa al-Zi'ab / Leila and the Wolves* (1985), is one of the more voluble and formal feminists, as well as being a Marxist and anti-imperialist. She decried the treatment of women in society and poor social conditions in general in *Saat al-Tahrir*. Although Srour studied at the Sorbonne in Paris, her course of study was not cinema but ethnology, with only two hours per week of cinema. She considers her choice of cinema to have been a political one, saying that she might otherwise have chosen ballet or painting. She considers that she had many obstacles thrown in her way as an Arab woman, many more than she would have found in the West but far fewer than other Arab women (from other countries or even from rural Lebanon). Srour says: 'Is there a [male] Arab director who has been obliged to hide from his family [because] he wishes to make films?'

Jocelyn Saab began her career as a journalist and documentary film-maker, then made two feature films: *Ghazal al-Banat 2 / The Razor's Edge* (1985) is a girl's coming-of-age story and *Kan Ya Makan Bayrut / Once Upon a Time Beirut* (1994) is a pastiche of film clips from movies made in Beirut, showing views of the city in its glory days before the civil war. Saab, who is now a French citizen, said in a 1994 interview (Thoraval 1994–5) that her future projects would not be set in the Middle East; she was looking to Asia, in particular Vietnam, for her next films.

Olga Nakkash made *Lubnan Qita, Qita / Lebanon: Bits and Pieces* (1994), which was very well reviewed at the Carthage Film Festival. The critic for *Le Monde Diplomatique* considered her film to be remarkable in sensibility and intelligence. In addition to showing the reactions of a range of women to the civil war, *Lubnan Qita, Qita* raises philosophical questions about identity.

The American film-maker Jennifer Fox made *Beirut: The Last Home Movie* (1991), a film that has become famous on the festival circuit. It details the influence of the war on the daily routines of a prosperous Christian family, living in a formerly imposing mansion in the neighbourhood of Ashrafiyah. Although *Beirut: The Last*

Home Movie chronicles domestic moments for a prominent family during the war, its effects are felt everywhere and no one has been spared the consequences. This movie was filmed in 1981, before the Israeli shelling of 1982.

From the summer of 1999 May Kassem, a young Lebanese film-maker, was working on a script about a family that lived locked away in their home for the sixteen years of civil war. Kassem said she had the funding lined up. She had already made a video on Syrian workers in Lebanon who were working on the reconstruction projects.

In Syria and Iraq women participate much less in film-making than they do in Lebanon. Wa'hah El-Raahib is currently the only Syrian woman known to have directed a feature film. El-Raahib, who is also a television actor, studied in France. Her film, *Giddatona / Four Grandmothers*, won a trophy at the Damascus Film Festival in 1997. The Iraqi woman director Khayriya 'Abbas filmed *Sitta 6* in 1987. The Iraqi film industry has been decimated by the embargo following the Gulf War, and no other long film by her is known.

LEBANON

The geopolitical division of Lebanon and Syria into two separate countries is to some extent artificial, especially when it comes to analyzing and classifying directors and actors. Regardless of the government situation, those making films move back and forth between Lebanon and Syria in a very fluid manner. For example, in the summer of 1999 the Syrian film-maker Omar Amiralay was working on projects in Lebanon. Furthermore, many Lebanese film-makers moved to Paris during the Lebanese civil war and may continue to move back and forth between Paris and Beirut. For instance, Maroun Baghdadi's 1991 film *Kharij al-Hayat / Outside Life*, about a French jour-nalist taken hostage in Beirut, is not available on videotape in Lebanon, only in Paris. Whether this is because of the uncomfortable subject matter or because the financial backing was European is uncertain, but given that Baghdadi is perhaps the most famous Lebanese film-maker, it remains strange that his films are not available in his own country.

The major themes addressed by this section are the role of the city Beirut in Lebanese movies, a brief history of Lebanese films, European influences on the devel-opment of Lebanese films, and the influence of the civil war and recent films.

Lebanon occupies a unique place in Arab / Middle Eastern film-making. Lebanese directors have demonstrated their comfort with graphic storytelling, with European references and with full participation in world cinema, despite sixteen years of civil war. Ruined cityscapes and sheet-draped furniture have become part of the director's landscape in many Lebanese films and, although the civil war ended in 1991, its reality continues in the consciousness even of younger film-makers, such as Samir Habchi and Ziad Doueiri. However, the question that perplexes many Lebanese is identity – that is, whether they are Arabs or Europeans – and from this question flow others about language, religion and ethnicity. Whether it is the young mother in *Lubnan Qita, Qita / Lebanon: Bits and Pieces* stating that she is liberal herself, but uncertain whether to raise her children in a free atmosphere because they live in the Middle East; the militiamen in Baghdadi's *Hurub Saghira / Little Wars* who behave like they are living in a gangster flick set in Al Capone's Chicago; or Raya, a woman married to a French doctor in *An al Anwan / The Time has Come*, who has forgotten Arabic and now speaks only French – all of these characters are suffering from the same identity crisis. This is a countrywide crisis, not an individual one.

There has been much speculation on why cinema is not more important in the Arab world and the usual answer is some variation on the idea that, since Islam is hostile to images, that includes moving pictures, so there is a religious or cultural taboo against 'representations of life'. Another problem specific to cinema is that it requires both technical equipment and the skills to operate that equipment. Thus a stint overseas to learn the technical aspects of film-making was usually a prerequisite for Middle Eastern film-makers. In addition, especially in the early days of film, acting was often considered inappropriate behaviour.

Perhaps the French colonial influence encouraged the Lebanese to make movies. Certainly enough foreign film-makers used Lebanon as a scenic backdrop to make them consider making their own movies. Many of the countries that have been most active in making films since gaining their independence – places like Algeria, Morocco and Lebanon – were previously the site for at least heavy film viewing by the colonials.

The earliest movie from Lebanon is usually considered to be *Moughamarat Elias Mabrouk / The Adventures of Elias Mabrouk*, directed in 1929 by Jordano Pidutti, who was Italian by birth. This was a silent comedy that followed the progress of Elias Mabrouk, an emigrant returning from a long sojourn in the United States. The theme of the return of the emigrant also fascinated Lebanese directors and recurs often. The motives for emigration change through the decades, but the impetus is still there. In 1931 Pidutti filmed a second movie, *Moughamarat Abu Abed / The Adventures of Abu Abed*, about a Lebanese emigrant who returned to his homeland from Africa.

The next film, *Bayna Hayakel Ba'albek / In the Ruins of Ba'albek* (1933) is cited by some authors as the first Arab film produced entirely in an Arab country. This film, directed by Julio De Luca and Karam Boustany, featured spoken Lebanese with French subtitles. The cinematographer of this production was George Costi, a Lebanese citizen whose six-month study of film-making at Pathé Studios in Paris was underwritten by Lumnar Film Co., a concern begun by a German-Lebanese woman. *Bayna Hayakel Ba'albek* was an international project in the sense that Costi photographed it and there was Arabic dialogue with French subtitles; it was sold throughout France, the other Arabic countries and Africa. The Lebanese film industry was paralyzed by World War II until 'Ali al-Ariss made *Bayyaat al-Ward / The Flower Seller* (1943) and *Kawkab Amirah al-Sahra / Kawkab, Princess of the Desert* (1946). So, in its early days, Lebanese films were the products only of disjointed individual efforts. At the same time, Lebanon became a favourite setting for Egyptian directors because of its natural beauty, and later for Western directors because of its exotic location. George Nasser's 1957 film *Ila Ayn / Toward the Unknown* was the first of many Lebanese films that were well received at film festivals outside the country but failed to be shown in Lebanon. *Ila Ayn* was the story of a Lebanese emigrant to Brazil; it was hailed at the Cannes, Moscow and Beijing Film Festivals, but little screened in Lebanon. Nasser followed up with *Le petit étranger / The Little Stranger*, the story of a Lebanese boy's coming of age, filmed in French and shown at Cannes in 1961. This film was not screened at all in Lebanon, while foreign films, whether American, Italian or French, were screened for audiences that were ravenous for movies.

In the late 1950s production increased. Mohammed Selmane invented a formula that would prove very successful commercially when in 1957 he filmed *al-Lahn al-Awal / The First Melody*, starring the singer Najah Salam (his wife). *al-Lahn al-Awal* was a musical comedy, with the photography ably directed by George Costi, and commercial success followed. Selmane went on to make many movies of different types. First he made a group of films about musical revues, including *Lubnan Fi al-Layl / Lebanon at Night* (1963). In *Lubnan Fi al-Layl* he toured the hot night clubs in Beirut, using his film as a showcase featuring many popular singers and theatrical dancing groups. Next Selmane made Bedouin movies, such as *Badawia Fi Baris / A Bedouin in Paris* (1964) and *Badawia Fi Roma / A Bedouin in Rome* (1965), featuring Samira Toufic, the most famous popular singer of Bedu songs. Finally, he made a wave of *policiers* (detective movies). His first *policier* was *al-Jaguar al-Sawda' / The Black Jaguar* (1965), starring Ihsan Sadek as a detective in the James Bond mould – driving a black Jaguar, fighting drug traffickers and speaking Egyptian Arabic. Arab movies looking for commercial success had to be in Egyptian, both because Egypt was the dominant market and especially because Arab film audiences were in general acclimatized to the Egyptian dialect. A recent example of this was Samir Zikra's *Hadith al-Nusf Metre / The Half-Metre Incident* (1981); it is in Egyptian (rather than Syrian) Arabic, even though Zikra is Syrian and the film is set in Damascus.

In 1965 Youssef Chahine made *Bayya' al-Khawatim / The Seller of Rings*, a vehicle for the famous Lebanese singer Fayrouz. The critics considered this musical comedy 'pure pleasure' and even as prefiguring of some of Chahine's more famous movies, such as *Iskandariyya Lih? / Alexandria Why?* (1978). Another interesting film from 1965 was *Garo* by Gary Garabédian. This took a documentary approach to the *policier* in following the exploits of Garo, a famous criminal whose life of crime was a result of his sufferings at the hands of society. In addition, Baalbek Studios (founded in 1956 by Badih Boulos) had become the pre-eminent Middle Eastern movie studio. Baalbek Studios worked full shifts round the clock and served as a regional centre for the Middle East in general, providing modern equipment and well-constructed studios. Its significance was greatest from 1965 to 1974, and it closed in 1994.

A group of directors – Antoine Rémy, the Rahbani brothers and Mohammed Selmane among them – produced many reasonable, if not terribly memorable, films. At the height of his popularity Selmane, for example, was making several films a year: six in 1965, four in 1966 and so on. Things continued in a generally undistinguished vein until 1975, when two thought-provoking films were released: Soubhi Seifeddine's *al-Rajul al-Samed / The Resister* and Maroun Baghdadi's *Beyrouth ya Beyrouth / Beirut Oh Beirut. al-Rajul al-Samed* portrayed a hero from Ottoman times: Abu Ali Melham Kassem. The film recounts Abu Ali's patriotic struggle against the Turks from 1914 to 1918. *Beyrouth ya Beyrouth*, filmed before the civil war began, shows the social and political conflicts that spawned the war. Consequently the films are considered prescient by some critics, although the Lebanese critic Mohamed Soueid has pointed out that they have no explicit connection to the war. That connection was made retrospectively.

In the 1970s production diminished as Egyptian directors returned to improved conditions in Egypt. Selmane's films, albeit mediocre, continued to be a commercial success and he still found willing producers. At the time, Lebanese directors frequently used a mix of Egyptian and Lebanese actors to assure themselves of an audience. One example of this kind of pan-Arab combination is Samir al-Ghoussayni's 1972 film

Qutat Shari' al-Hamra / Les chats de la rue Hamra / The Cats of Hamra Street, which used Egyptian and Lebanese actors, an Egyptian dialect, and included songs and dances. The film was partly inspired by the 1969 US film *Easy Rider*, bringing 'hippies' to Lebanese film. al-Ghoussayni wanted to make commercial films and followed the example set by Selmane. In 1975 war broke out and cinemas and studios were damaged. It became impossible to run cinemas in central Beirut: famous movie theatres like the Rivoli, Dunia, Empire and Roxy were ruined in the war. A few intrepid film-makers continued to film during the war. Maroun Baghdadi, for example, filmed *Hurub Saghira / Little Wars* in 1982. After making a number of documentaries, including *Lubnan Fi al-Asifa / Lebanon in the Whirlwind* (1975), Jocelyn Saab filmed her first feature, *Ghazal al-Banat 2 / The Razor's Edge*, during the shelling of the city in 1985.

In the 1980s poorly produced action films continued to be made, often suffering (according to one critic) from poor lighting, choppiness of plot and poor soundtracks, among other things. However, Lebanese audiences found the films of Youssef Charafeddine comforting because they showed a secure society, ruled by law and order, which was of course not the case at that time in Lebanon. Such films were heavily derivative of US action films and lacked a Lebanese identity. They were not usually shown in the top movie houses (before they were destroyed); there the audiences preferred Western films. Films like Youssef Charafeddine's *al-Mamarr al-Akhir / The Last Passage* (1981), *al-Qarar / The Decision* (1981) and *Qafzah al-Mawt / The Leap of Death* (1982) were made to poor technical standards which were made worse by the war. Those films that incorporated the war and worked with its unpredictable outcomes were the most visually successful. In them the failures of production (for example, the bursting shells seen through the living-room windows in *Ghazal al-Banat 2*) are merely read as part of the plot. If the lights go out, it is simply what is expected to happen in times of war. It was not possible in war-torn Beirut to make highly polished films, but that lack of polish became part of the success of films like *Hurub Saghira* or *Ghazal al-Banat 2*. However, the Israeli invasion of Lebanon and blockade of Beirut in 1982 nearly finished commercial cinema for a while. Film-making became too expensive: Youssef Charafeddine moved to Egypt, while several other film-makers moved to Paris.

During the war period a number of women film-makers made noteworthy films: in addition to Saab's *Ghazal al-Banat 2* and the documentaries she filmed beginning in 1975, Heiny Srour made *Leila Wa al-Zi'ab / Leila and the Wolves* (1985) and Randa Shahal Sabbag made *Khatwah Khatwah / Step by Step* (1976). More recently Olga Nakkash made *Lubnan Qita, Qita / Lebanon: Bits and Pieces* (1994), which received favourable reviews at the Carthage Film Festival. The collaboration of Jean Chamoun and May Masri has resulted in several films, among them *Zahrat al-Qindul / Women from South Lebanon* (1985). One might well ask, with the critic of *La Revue du cinéma*, not just what other Arab country has so many women directors, but what other country in the world has so many women directors?

Recent films by experienced and young directors show a continuing desire to understand the causes or the roots of the civil war, and to come to terms with the destruction and attitudes that it has left behind. Films such as *Hurubina al-Ta'isha / Our Heedless Wars*, *West Beirut*, *Kharij al-Hayat / Outside Life* and *al-E'sar / The Tornado* show that the war is still at the forefront of the national consciousness. In

Randa Shahal Sabbag's *Hurubina al-Ta'isha* she comments regretfully that 'all we [the Lebanese] want now is mediocrity'. In *al-E'sar* the hero returns to Beirut from art school in Moscow and promptly gets sucked into the tornado of violence – the pointless and sudden violence that has led to death for many of his friends. It will be interesting to see what the film-makers turn to as the war fades from memory and new concerns overtake them.

Censorship and taxation are among the current problems plaguing directors. For example, Habchi's film *al-E'sar* had two scenes cut, one of Christ dressed as a militiaman, because the censors found them offensive. The film was made with the help of the Lebanese government, but banned by that government until the cuts had been made. The Lebanese censors ban violence in Lebanese-produced films, but allow violent US films to be imported – some reasons for this double standard have already been given.

New Lebanese films continue to need funding from Europe – Doueiri's *West Beirut* received funds from France that had been earmarked for Lebanon, and, one might add, despite the film's rather acid presentation of the French school in Beirut. Such directors have also spent time abroad training and working (Baghdadi, for example, spent many years in France), so a question remains about the extent to which their films represent a Lebanese perspective, even when the director has returned to film in Lebanon (as Baghdadi did for *Kharij al-Hayat*).

Orientalism in Lebanese films

There is a great deal of what must be called 'orientalism' in films made both by Arabs and for an Arab audience, particularly those from Lebanon. An orientalist view considers the inhabitants of 'the mysterious East' to be exotic or unknowable merely because of the accident of their location (Said 1979). The fact that the field is usually defined by outsiders, in academic terms, makes matters worse. Arab film-makers appear to be as prone to showing the 'pretty face' or 'exotic face' of orientalism in films as Western film-makers. One could create a scale of orientalism: two points for each scimitar, three points for each poisoning by a woman and one point for each camel (or three points for each camel with no evident connection to the plot). In Lebanon the trend towards orientalism manifested itself in the 1960s. For example, in *Bayya' al-Khawatim* / *The Seller of Rings*, the Rahbani brothers' scripted Lebanon as a utopian mountain village, filled with simple people who loved to sing and dance. Considering that *Bayya' al-Khawatim* was made in 1965, it is not likely that the majority of Lebanese people actually aspired to such an unsophisticated life. Nonetheless, the film was very popular.

The Lebanese director Mohammed Selmane made a number of Bedouin films, starting with *Afrah al-Shabab* / *Joys of Youth* (1964), which featured the Bedouin singer Fahd Ballane. Also in 1964 Selmane made the first of his so-called 'Bedouin wave' movies, *al-Badawia Fi Baris* / *A Bedouin in Paris*, with the popular songstress Samira Toufic, considered the pre-eminent singer of Bedouin songs. She also appeared in the sequel, *al-Badawia Fi Roma* / *A Bedouin in Rome*, the following year. Toufic had already appeared in the 1963 film *al-Badawia al-'Asheqa* / *The Bedouin Lover*. In 1966 Farouk Agrama cast her as a Bedouin in *al-Kahiroun* / *The Conquerors* with Fahd Ballane.

In *Bint al-Shaykh / Daughter of the Sheikh* (1970) the director Halmi Rafleh takes advantage of many orientalist stereotypes that are considered offensive. The Arabs wield large curved daggers beneath their beards and burning eyes, much like the cartoon Arabs that Jayce Salloum and Elias Suleiman use to such good effect in *Muqaddima Li-Nihayat Jidal / Introduction to the End of an Argument* (1994). Salloum and Suleiman create a *mélange* from US cartoons showing Arabs as dark bearded men with burning eyes, clutching curved scimitars, to demonstrate one negative image of Arabs in US movies. The plot of *Bint al-Shaykh* features numerous instances of treachery, which could be seen as mere plot twists but, given the deliberate setting, appear orientalist. Then there are the belly-dancers in revealing costumes, especially one young dancer who wears above the navel only jewelled pasties with tassels. Samira Toufic, starring in this film, appears in many production numbers that make it clear her skill is singing, rather than acting. In one scene a train of camels wander by in the background for no reason. 'The Orient' in this movie exists in the same shadowland as 'the Wild West' does in Hollywood – there is no sense of a real place.

In *Kana Ya Makana Bayruth / Once Upon a Time Beirut* (1994) Jocelyn Saab uses clips from many movies, both Arab and Western, to show the views held of Beirut in the city's heyday. She makes the point in film that others have made in print: many people had orientalist views of Beirut as a city filled with intrigue and spies. Among the twenty plus clips from Arab directors that Saab includes are Barakat's *Bint al-Haris / Daughter of the Guardian*, Garabédian's *Garo* and Mohammed Selmane's *Ya Salam al-Hubb / Hello, Love*.

So many directors include short scenes of women dancing folkloric (oriental) dances in their films that it has become a required element. Saab's heroine Samar performs a 'pretend' seductive belly dance in *Ghazal al-Banat 2 / The Razor's Edge* while she is actually being watched without her knowledge. Likewise, women in Baghdadi's *Hurub Saghira / Little Wars* perform a belly dance during an impromptu party. Women in the prison yard are seen belly dancing in his French film *La fille de l'air / The Girl of the Air*. Even in Habchi's *al-E'sar / The Tornado*, one of the most modern of the recent films, we see a woman performing a belly dance through a window in a neighbouring flat. By showing women not only dancing Middle Eastern dances, but also hidden from the public gaze (though not the camera's view) in the privacy of their homes, the film-maker further reminds the audience of women's identity as hidden from view, secluded, private. Thus using dance, in orientalist practice, defines a private world.

In these films orientalism is used even by the people who might object to it, in much the same way as 'blackness' is utilized in blaxploitation films like *Shaft*, alternately lionizing and mocking the characters. These films emphasize the elements that others see in their culture as seen by those others, and thus acquiesce in the stereotyping of Arab men as violent and women as seductive plotters.

Filmography

al-Ajniha al-Mutakasira / The Broken Wings

1962, 93 mins, black and white, Arabic and French (English subtitles)
Director: Youssef Malouf

Producer: Touric Kairouz, Antoine Khoury
Screenwriter: Saeed Akal
Cinematographer: Antoine Sabagha
Music: Sergei Rachmaninoff
Leading Players: Pierre Borday, Saladin Nader and Nidal Ashkar

The story of the famous Lebanese poet Khalil Gibran's infatuation with a young beauty, Salma Karamy, whose father had promised her to another man. After her marriage they have only occasional meetings, and Salma dies in childbirth. This film looked dated and old-fashioned even when it was first released, and was roundly panned by *Variety* (3 April 1968) during its New York run: it was called a 'turgid antique'. Based on Khalil Gibran's book, it was billed as the first Lebanese movie released for a commercial run in the United States.

This film is mostly of historical interest, since the print was lost during the war years and only resurfaced in Lebanon years later.

An al-Anwan / *Histoire d'un retour* / *The Time has Come*

1994, 83 mins, colour, Arabic and French (English subtitles)
Director / Screenwriter: Jean-Claude Codsi
Producer: Aflam Films (Lebanon), ADR Productions (Paris), Earth Cinema Company (Moscow)
Sound: Dirk Bombey
Cinematographer: Milan Tauk
Editor: Nathalie Goepfert
Artistic Director: Youssef Haïdar
Music: Toufic Farroukh
Leading Players: Simon Abkarian, Darina el-Joundi

Kamil, a ne'er-do-well singer, and Raya, a rich woman married to a French doctor, meet on the Cyprus–Jounieh ferry. Both are returning to Lebanon after a long stay in France, Kamil to write and record a song for International Action Day, and Raya to find her kidnapped son. Eventually Kamil writes a song, which he then refuses to record. Raya's son was not kidnapped at all; she visits him and returns to France. The symbol of Raya's Europeanization is that she has lost her Arabic. Kamil continues to hang out in Beirut, house-sitting in a very nice house whose owners have fled to Canada and pining for Raya to rejoin him. The slenderness of the story is not helped by what one reviewer described as the 'narcissistic' quality of the film (Bitton 1995). It was one of seven Lebanese films presented at the Carthage Film Festival in 1994.

Bayya'al-Khawatim / *Le vendeur de bagues* / *The Seller of Rings*

1965, 95 mins, colour, Arabic
Director: Youssef Chahine
Producer: Nader el-Attasy, Tannous Frangié (Phenicia Films – studios Asry Beirut)

Screenwriter:	Rahbani brothers
Sound:	Stanley Khoury
Cinematographer:	André Domage
Editor:	Sabah Haddad
Designer:	Habib Khouri
Music:	Rahbani brothers
Leading Players:	Fayrouz, Youssef Azar, Nasry Chamsel-Din, Youssef Nassif, Salwa Hadad and the Lebanese Folkloric Troupe

Bayya' al-Khawatim is a happy combination: the legendary Lebanese singer Fayrouz directed to good effect by the equally famous Egyptian director Youssef Chahine. This film opened the Fifth International Film Festival in Beirut (1965), where it was a smash hit. Peter Baker, writing in *Films and Filming* in January 1966, raved that musically it was better than *Les parapluies de Cherbourg / The Umbrellas of Cherbourg* (1964).

The simple storyline is about the Festival of Singles in a small village. There will be thirty single young women and only twenty-nine men looking for wives. Fayrouz is among the single women. At the end of the story her father allows her to move to the next village where she will marry the ring seller. This is a very light, successful movie, with the many songs and folkloric dances seamlessly woven into the story. It includes a village waterfight at the pump in the town square. Chahine shows a puckish attitude in his opening disclaimer: 'This is the story of a village; the story is not true and the village does not exist'.

al-E'sar / The Tornado

1992, 90 mins, colour, Arabic and French (English subtitles)

Director:	Samir Habchi
Producer:	Makmel Film, Strannick
Screenwriter:	Samir Habchi, Ara Manoukian
Sound:	Victor Bruntchuguin
Cinematographer:	Gregori Boulkot, Milad Tawk
Editor:	Natalia Borovskaya
Designer:	Edmond Habchi, Vadim Khatsevich
Music:	Igor Stetsiouk
Leading Players:	Philippe Akiki, Chawki Mata, Julia Kassar, Fadi Abou-Khalil, Farhat Manafov, Samir Sarieldine, Chéhadé el-Hatchiti

Akram prepares to return to Beirut from Moscow, where he is studying art, when he sees the latest car-bombing in Beirut on the Russian nightly news. When he reaches Beirut, he at first does not understand the new relationships that have been caused by the long-term civil war. His old friend Roy has been changed by the war. Initially withdrawn from the action, Akram is sucked into a tornado of violence.

Al-E'sar highlights the senselessness of violence in a long-running civil war. Unlike American westerns in which, at least in fiction, the premise is of honour – men taking ten paces, turning and shooting at each other face-to-face – most of the people in this movie die shot in the back or at close range through a car window or as victims of an anonymous car bomb left in a traffic jam on a busy street. Despite many elements common to Lebanese war movies – guns, bombs and houses furnished with sheeted chairs – Habchi shows his own vision, using El Greco-like images and religious symbolism which perhaps owe something to his Russian education. This film was made during the war, with the approval of the Lebanese authorities, whose censors later forced him to cut two scenes before it could be shown.

A funeral procession of people in black-and-white dress carrying gonfalons and accompanied by triumphal music is a visual homage to Fellini's facist procession in *Amarcord* (1973). In the Fellini movie, black-dressed officials with black gonfalons parade down a plaza with stone buildings on either side and a church belltower in the background. In Habchi's scene, the procession begins with the tolling of a church bell and then the camera finds the procession below, flowing between stone ramparts into a plaza.

Al-E'sar won the special jury prize at the Festival de Bastiz and won the Prix de la Nonviolence in Beirut in 1992.

Garo

1965, Arabic
Director / Producer / Screenwriter /
Cinematographer / Editor: Gary Garabédian
Dance: Nadia Gamal
Leading Players: Mounir Maasri, Samira Baroudi, Samir Chams, Marcelle Marina, Joseph Nano

Garo flees from the police in Damascus, then from Aleppo and finally comes to Lebanon disguised as a Bedouin. There he creates a devoted band who engage in drug-trafficking to survive. The style of the film is 'police documentary' but, of course, there is an oriental dance. As the film progresses an off-screen narrator keeps the audience up to date with the latest news of Garo. The film describes the murder both from the murderer's and from the official point of view, giving it a *film noir* aspect. In a twist, the audience feels sympathy for Garo, who is driven to such deeds to provide for his family: social conditions have forced Garo to become a criminal. One critic described it as 'tender and poetic'.

Garo was shown at the festival of Lebanese film organized by the Centre National du Cinéma in 1967, along with *Bayya' al-Khawatim* / *The Seller of Rings* and others. Mounir Maasri received the prize for best actor at this festival for his role as Garo.

Ghazal al-Banat 2 / *Une vie suspendue* / *The Razor's Edge (a.k.a. The Adolescent Sugar of Love, a.k.a. Hayat Mucallaqat* / *A Suspended Life)*

1985, 100 mins, colour, Arabic and French (English subtitles)
Director: Jocelyn Saab
Producer: Ciné-vidéo, Sigmarc, Centre National de la Cinématographie, Téléfilm Canada
Screenwriter: Gerard Brach

Sound:	Pierre Lorraine
Cinematographer:	Claude La Rue
Editor:	Philippe Gosselet
Artistic Director:	Marc Julian
Music:	Siegfried Kessler
Leading Players:	Jacques Weber, Hala Bassam, Juliet Berto, Youssef Housny, Denise Filiatrault

Ghazal al-Banat 2 was the first feature film by documentary film-maker and journalist Jocelyn Saab, and was named after the 1949 Egyptian film classic *Ghazal al-Banat*, which is about a flirtatious young girl whose old teacher falls in love with her. Samar, a Lebanese adolescent, develops a crush on Karam, a middle-aged artist attempting to hang on in Beirut despite the difficulties of ferrying his large paintings across town to his dealer. Karam lives in a shelled building, although most of the ravaged walls have an artistic patina in this film. Samar's father, formerly a fisherman in the south of Lebanon who was forced to take his family and flee to Beirut, now collects ceramic tiles for rebuilding – because of constant shelling this is a Sisyphean task. For a while Samar is able to pretend that her love for Karam will protect them, but in the end it does not. Samar, about fifteen years of age, is alternately child and woman, sometimes playing at seductive dances with her girlfriend.

The movie is stuffed full of the standard vocabulary of the Lebanese civil war: the old half-mad aristocratic neighbour who mumbles to himself in French, piles of building rubble, families living in half-bombed houses – in fact, Beirut itself is the most interesting character in the film.

The tragedy we see is an entire generation of children growing up illiterate and unschooled; the only game they ever play is war, using sticks or anything else to hand. Love appears to Samar to be a new game that she has discovered.

Hurub Saghira | Petites guerres | Little Wars

1982, 108 mins, colour, Arabic (English subtitles)	
Director:	Maroun Baghdadi
Producer:	SNCT
Screenwriter:	Maroun Baghdadi, Kamal Karim Kassar
Cinematographer:	Edward Lachman, Heinz Holcher
Editor:	Joële Van Effentere, Nelly Neunier
Music:	Gabriel Yared
Leading Players:	Soraya Khoury, Nabil Ismail, Roger Hawa, Reda Khoury, Youssef Hosni, Rifaat Tarabay

On one level this is a story of how a man is forced to take over his father's position when the father is kidnapped. On another level, the film starkly demonstrates how the civil war in Lebanon influenced even the smallest corners of people's lives. Filmed in Beirut during the war, the film is full of cowboys and petty criminals who would be mere thugs were it not for the conflict around them. Given the war, they fight for one militia or another. At the opening of the film, Talal's father (a local strongman) has been kidnapped and the family must try to get him back. Soraya, Talal's girlfriend, has just discovered she is pregnant and, although her friends are all leaving, she is staying in Beirut. Another character, Nabil, is working as a photographer, shooting scenes of war-damaged Beirut, and is also on the fringes of petty crime and drug-dealing.

In a Hitchcockian touch, when the action begins Baghdadi uses a photograph of himself as a stand-in at the funeral of a young militiaman. The young men are all light-hearted and very funny; indeed in one scene the feeling is of Lebanon as a summer camp without rules, a heaven on earth for young males – until they shoot or are shot. Throughout the film the violence is senseless and purposeless. Life no longer seems to mean anything more than a videogame. Everyone is tired of the violence and death, from the personnel at the hospital to the idle young men who shoot people, but no one seems to know how to stop it. Leaving appears to be the only rational option and the airport is a symbol of the way to safety. The contrast between the safety of Europe – a short flight away – and Lebanon where death may strike at any moment is emphasized by the Western journalists flocking to get the story.

Hurubina al-Ta'isha / Nos guerres imprudentes / Our Heedless Wars

1995, 61 mins, colour, Arabic / French / English (English subtitles)
Director:	Randa Chahal Sabbagh
Producer:	Archipel 33, La Sept (Arte & Leil Productions)
Sound:	Pierre Camus, Eric Munch, Nadia Ben Rachid
Cinematographer:	Frédéric Labourasse, Roby Breidi, Hassan Naamani, Lionel Cousin
Editor:	Yves Deschampes, Catherine Barétat
Music:	Franz Schubert, Fayrouz, Umm Kulthum, Ahmed Kaabour, Marcel Khalifé
Leading Players:	Victoria Naaman Chahal, Nahla Chahal, Tamine Chahal (mother, sister and brother of the director)

This film is a collage of the director's family history from old scrapbooks and current interviews, interwoven with the history of the Lebanese civil war. Chahal Sabbagh's family was politically prominent – her father was one of the founders of the communist party in Lebanon and her mother was a journalist by profession and had been jailed a couple of times in her youth. Chahal Sabbagh, however, lived in Paris for much of the war, so this is the record of her family's lives during the war. Her sister, who speaks French, was an organizer and was once arrested by the Israelis when trying to return to Lebanon by boat. Her brother Tamine, who speaks Arabic, said he became a bodyguard for his sister and a thug during the war. Her mother Victoria says she has not lived the life she would have chosen, having been too much alone. Her father, a doctor, had died a few years earlier.

The film-maker's conclusion is that 'the end of war brought the end of the city'. The personal and the political are well connected in this film, which attempts to make the viewers feel the loss of Chahal Sabbagh's city.

al-Jaguar al-Sawda' / The Black Jaguar

1965, 90 mins, black and white, Arabic

Director / Screenwriter: Mohammed Selmane
Producer: Anwar Cheikh Yassine (Baalbek Studios)
Cinematographer: Ibrahim Chamat
Music: Includes cuts from James Bond movies
Leading Players: Ihsan Sadek, Taroub, Rachid Alamé, Samir Chams, Joseph
                            Nano, Mohsen Semrani

Based on a story by Mohsen Semrani, this film represents the Lebanese response to the James Bond movies (which began in 1962 with *Doctor No*). Ihsan Sadek takes the role of the secret agent pursuing a drug-smuggling gang. The title comes from the sleek black Jaguar he drives, although it is never explained how an honest cop can afford such a car.

After an introductory meditation on marriage being the usual trajectory of life, the scene shifts to a nightclub. Anwar (Ihsan Sadek), sent by Interpol, infiltrates a drug gang to find out how they manage their smuggling. Suffice to say the amount of drugs smuggled is tiny, the smuggling always occurs on the coast by Beirut and eventually the bad guys get caught – but not before a runaround with a woman who pretends to be blind. This film was one of the first *policiers* – yet another variety of film from the prodigious Mohammed Selmane. James Bond music, familiar to all from the ubiquitous movies, frequently pops up in the background when Anwar is driving his Jaguar, no matter how unrelated it is to the action.

The film ends with an ineffectual shoot-out in the woods – both sides firing single-action pistols – which is uncannily prescient in view of the civil war.

Kan Ya Makan Bayrut (a.k.a. Qissah Najmah) / Il était une fois Beyrouth, histoire d'une star / Once Upon a Time Beirut (a.k.a. The Story of a Star)

1994, 104 mins, colour / black and white, Arabic and French (English subtitles)
Director: Jocelyn Saab
Producer: Balcon (France), Arte (Hessischer Rundfunk and Stras-
                    bourg)
Screenwriter: Philippe Paringaux, Roland Paringaux, Jocelyn Saab
Sound: Pierre Bouvier
Cinematographer: Roby Breidi
Editor: Dominique Auvray, Isabelle Dedieu
Music: Collage from movies, including 'Don't bogart that joint'
Leading Players: Myrna Makaron, Michèle Tyan, Pierre Chamassian, Nessim
                    Accar, Emile Accar

Saab uses two young women, Yasmine and Laila. They are evenly balanced: one is Christian, one is Muslim, but both speak French, not Arabic. Also they are about fifteen years old – too young to remember Beirut before the war. They visit an old projectionist who shows them old films of Beirut before the civil war. Clips from both Arab films and Western films follow in a dizzying progression. We see such gems as David Niven in *Where the Spies Are* as an example of the Western movie's take on Beirut. *Garo* and *al-Jaguar al-Sawda' / The Black Jaguar* show the Arab film-maker's equally orientalist view of the city. In the end, the clips become repetitive, boring and lacking in continuity.

Kharij al-Hayat / Hors la vie / Outside Life

1991, 97 mins, colour, Arabic and French
Director / Screenwriter:	Maroun Baghdadi
Producer:	Jacques Perrin
Sound:	Guilliaume Sciama, Chantal Quaglio, Dominique Hennequin
Cinematographer:	Arnaud Borrel, Jeanne-Louise Bulliard
Editor:	Luc Barnier
Designer:	Dan Weil
Music:	Nicolas Piovani
Leading Players:	Hippolyte Girardot, Rafic Ali Ahmad, Hussein Sbeity, Habib Hammoud, Magdi Machmouchi, Sabrina Leurquin

Kharij al-Hayat is the fact-based story of a French photo-journalist who was kidnapped in Beirut during the Lebanese civil war and held hostage for 319 days, before eventually being released. Patrick Perrault (the hostage) makes up names for his captors, such as 'De Niro' and 'Frankenstein', but rebels when they try to give him an Arab name. His French nationality is what guarantees his survival in the end. Details of the lives of his captors are shown, as well as of his captivity. He is finally released on the beach, disguised as a woman, dressed in a full veil. After he returns to Paris, Patrick calls the flat in Beirut where he was held, but the phone rings unanswered.

The film focuses on the changing relationships between the hostage and the militia-men who hold him. This film is considered Baghdadi's most important: it won the Cannes Festival Jury Prize in 1991. Since Maroun Baghdadi himself was Lebanese but living in Paris, questions of Arab, Lebanese and French identity and relationships run through the film. (See *L'Avant-scène* 1994, Ra'ad 1996, *Revue du cinéma* 1991, *Sight and Sound* 1992 for more details.)

La fille de l'air / The Girl of the Air

1992, 106 mins, colour, French
Director:	Maroun Baghdadi
Producer:	CIBY 2000, TF1 Films, Investimage 4, Canal+
Screenwriter:	Florence Quentin, Dan Franck, Maroun Baghdadi
Sound:	Jean-Pierre Duret, Stephanie Granel, François Groult
Cinematographer:	Thierry Arbogast
Editor:	Luc Barnier
Designer:	Michel Vandestien
Music:	Gabriel Yared
Leading Players:	Béatrice Dalle, Thierry Fortineau, Hippolyte Girardot, Jean-Claude Dreyfus

A woman, Brigitte, and her boyfriend, Daniel, are sent to jail for robbing grocery stores. Brigitte has their illegitimate child while in jail and marries Daniel, despite the fact that he has been sent down for a long prison sentence. Once she is released, she puts all her energy into planning his escape. In the course of committing a crime to finance the escape plan, Brigitte's brother is shot by the police. Eventually she learns to fly a helicopter and snatches Daniel from the prison exercise yard. Their escape is brief, however: they are recaptured within four months.

This is a French film, yet many Baghdadi touches remain: Gabriel Yared's music (the composer also wrote the music for *Hurub Saghira / Little Wars*), women belly-dancing in their prison exercise yard and the French police pictured as little more than militiamen. This was Baghdadi's last film. The critic writing in *Positif* (December 1962) found little to like in the film and was particularly upset that Baghdadi considered this film 'truly French'.

Leila Wa al-Zi'ab / Leila and the Wolves

1984, 93 mins, colour, Arabic (English subtitles)
Director / Screenwriter: Heiny Srour
Producer: BFI Production Board (United Kingdom), Hussein El Sayed (Lebanon) and others
Sound: Eddy Tise, John Anderton and others
Cinematographer: Max Marrable, Sarkis Khoury, Ahmed Mjarkech
Editor: Eva Houdova
Music: Munir Bechir, La Camparsita
Leading Players: Nabila Zeitouni, Rafiq Ali Ahmed

Leila is seen in various situations involving issues for women, then reviews the history of women in the Middle East and particularly the situation of Palestinian women. Archival and old film footage is used. In the end Leila comes to be an Arab every-woman – an archetype rather than a character.

Leila Wa Zi'ab won the Mannheim Film Festival grand prize in 1984.

Lubnan Qita, Qita / Lebanon: Bits and Pieces

1994, 60 mins, colour, Arabic and French (English subtitles)
Director: Olga Nakkash
Producer: Unité de production France 3: Documentaires and maga-zines
Screenwriter: Eliane Raheb
Sound: Marcel Soler
Cinematographer: Philippe Le Nouvel
Editor: Josiane Zardoya

This documentary interviews several of the director's childhood friends and other acquaintances to discover, in their own words, how the war has affected them. Through their conversations Nakkash brings out the questions of religious identity and ethnicity that the Lebanese face. Are they Arab or Lebanese? Her friend Amira says she grew up liberal, but how should she raise her young daughters? 'There should be no difference', Amira says, 'but we live in the Middle East'. This film pictures a society trying to rebuild itself and find security and an accomodation after years of civil war.

al-Risalah | The Message (a.k.a. Mohammad, Messenger of God)

1976, 182 mins, colour, Arabic and English versions
Director: Moustapha Akkad
Producer: Filmco International
Screenwriter: H.A.L. Craig
Sound: Chris Greenham
Cinematographer: Jack Hildyard
Editor: John Bloom
Designer: Tambi Larsen, Maurice Fowler
Music: Maurice Jarre
Religious Adviser: Shaikh Abdallah al-Alayli
Leading Players: Anthony Quinn, Irene Papas, Michael Amara, Johnny Sekka, Michael Forest

Spectacular but not particularly convincing-looking epic about the Prophet's mission and the early history of Islam. The script is lacking a single vision, not surprising given that it was vetted by a commission of experts from al-Azhar. Shooting began in Morocco, but had to be finished in Libya after the film unit was expelled. This US$17 million epic is further frustrated in dramatic terms because the person of the Prophet is not represented on screen (*Monthly Film Bulletin* 1976).

Saat al-Tahrir Dakkat Barra Ya Isti'mar | L'heure de la libération a sonné | The Hour of Liberation has Sounded – the Struggle in Oman

1974, 62 mins, black and white (some tinted), Arabic
Director / Screenwriter / Editor: Heiny Srour
Producer: Srour Films
Sound: Jean-Louis Ughetto, Itzhak Ibrahim Souleily
Cinematographer: Michael Humeau
Music: Written and sung by the People's Army
Leading Players: People of Dhofar, Oman

Heiny Srour spent three months in Dhofar, the Western province of Oman, which was the liberated zone at that time. Srour considers objectivity 'bourgeois' and she rejects it (*Cahiers du cinéma* 1974). Her objective is to show the history of colonialism in Oman and the struggle of the Popular Front for the Liberation of Oman (FPLO). Since Oman was producing a large proportion of the world's oil in the 1970s, with the imperialist powers (the United Kingdom) enjoying fabulous profits, the FPLO's struggle was not without interest. It was not covered in the Western press at the time. Srour particularly focused on the status of women in a traditional Arab society, the issue of women training with the FPLO and how national liberation also improved women's status. The film was shot in 1971.

This film was shown during Critics' Week in Cannes in 1974 and has been banned throughout the Arab world, except in the Yemen. Critics have considered it ragged in technique, but nevertheless interesting.

West Beirut

1998, 105 mins, colour, Arabic and French (English subtitles)

Director / Screenwriter:	Ziad Doueiri
Producer:	Doueiri Films (Lebanon), Ciné Libre Eliane Dubois (Belgium), Exposed Film Productions a.s., Bjorn Eivind Aarskog (Norway), with the participation of the French Ministry of Culture and Ministry of Foreign Affairs
Sound:	Ulrike Laub
Cinematographer:	Ricardo Jacques Gale
Editor:	Dominique Marcombe
Artistic Director:	Hamzé Nasrallah
Music:	Stewart Copeland
Leading Players:	Rami Doueiri, Mohamad Chamas, Rola al-Amin, Carmen Lebbos, Joseph Bou Nassar, Leila Karam

On the first day of the Lebanese civil war in April 1975, Tarek is thrown out of class in his French-style school for his behaviour and from the balcony of the school he accidentally witnesses masked gunmen riddle a civilian bus with bullets. The next day school is closed and Tarek and his friend Omar begin an imposed holiday, at first wonderful but later becoming destructive. Before our eyes we see the fabric of family, marriage and neighbourhood torn apart by the stress of living under a state of siege in the ensuing civil chaos.

In the movie's one memorable scene the two teenagers ogle the new girlfriend of Omar's uncle, whom Tarek considers a real 'lamb'. They lie across Omar's bed, smoking forbidden cigarettes, while Omar spins out a fantasy for Tarek, imagining that Tarek is on a beach with the 'lamb' and she takes off her clothes, prior to giving herself to Tarek. Omar strokes Tarek a bit to demonstrate a point, between puffs on his cigarette, and it is a poignant, true scene of adolescent lust. However, many other scenes (such as the funeral procession that becomes a bloody shooting match and the boys' trip to a brothel) are too familiar. This is a successful, commercial coming-of-age film which just happens to be set in Beirut. The director, who was born in Lebanon, left there at college age and has since worked in film production in Hollywood. The gloss shows.

List of directors

Baghdadi, Maroun (b. 1948 or 1951, Beirut, Lebanon; d. 1993, Beirut, Lebanon)

Baghdadi died on 10 December 1993 in a freak accident. He had returned from Paris to shoot a new film called *Zawaya / Coins / Corners*.

Baghdadi studied at the University of St Joseph in Beirut, continuing to study political science at the Sorbonne in Paris. He also studied cinema at the IDHEC in

Paris. Baghdadi began his career as a television journalist; in 1975 he filmed his first long feature *Beyrouth ya Beyrouth* / *Beirut Oh Beirut*. This film used Egyptian actors in the lead roles and discussed the changes in society in Beirut from 1968–70, in the wake of the 1967 war. While this film is often considered to be prescient regarding the civil war – showing the class struggle, identifying confessional differences and describing the situation in the south of Lebanon – Mohamed Soueid points out that it used prominent Egyptian actors and was filmed before the war broke out (Soueid 1986).

After filming this movie, between 1976 and 1980 Baghdadi made a number of documentaries on the war. In 1982 he directed *Hurub Saghira* / *Little Wars*, which focused on the senseless killings involved in the civil war and how they affected everyone, no matter how they tried to avoid it. Following this film, Baghdadi moved to Paris. However, Lebanese themes were still within his purview: Baghdadi's next film was *L'homme voilé* / *The Veiled Man*, the story of a Lebanese doctor who returns to Paris to see his sixteen-year-old daughter, and the complicated falsehoods and events that result. In fact the violence of the war follows the Lebanese community to Paris and continues there, exacting revenge. One reviewer said that the film 'pulls viewer back to … Beirut with every scene' (*Variety*, 14 October 1987). Baghdadi followed this with *Kharij al-Hayat* / *Outside Life*, about the kidnapping of a French photojournalist in Beirut; it was filmed in Palermo, France and Beirut. His last completed film was *La fille de l'air*, which he considered a totally French effort, although it is studded with references to the Arab community in Paris.

The trajectory of Baghdadi's career took him from Lebanon to Paris and then back to Beirut to direct a film (*Zawaya*) there. Despite his untimely death, Baghdadi remains a seminal figure in Lebanon. Among other awards named in his honour, there is a script prize named after him in the new Beirut Film Festival, which has only recently resumed after the disruption of war. (See al-'Ariss 1994, Ra'ad 1996 for more details.)

Selected feature films: *Beyrouth ya Beyrouth* / *Beirut Oh Beirut* (1975); *Hurub Saghira* / *Little Wars* (1982); *L'homme voilé* / *The Veiled Man* (1987); *Kharij al-Hayat* / *Outside Life* (1991); *La fille de l'air* / *The Girl of the Air* (1992)

Saab, Jocelyn (b. 1948, Beirut, Lebanon)

Saab studied economics at the University of St Joseph in Beirut. She began her career as a journalist at Télé Liban. One of her earliest interests was the Palestinian cause and the relationship between the Palestians and the Lebanon left. She did not study cinema, instead learning in the field. Saab began making documentaries on Palestinan issues for the French television station France 3 in 1973; her programmes were entitled *Magazine 52*. In 1974 Saab became an independent journalist and director.

Ghazal al-Banat 2 / *The Razor's Edge* was her first feature film in 1985. In a 1994 interview, she said that she was moving away from the Middle East as a subject for her film-making and planned her next project to be in Vietnam (*Cinemaya* 1994–5). Saab is now a French citizen.

Selected feature films: *Irak: La guerre au Kurdistan* / *Iraq: The War with Kurdistan* (1973); *Lubnan Fi al-Asifa* / *Lebanon in the Whirlwind* (1975) (winner of the Arab

Critics' Prize at the 1976 Palestine Festival); *Les enfants de la guerre / Children of War* (1976); *Le sahara n'est pas à vendre / The Sahara is Not for Sale* (1977); *Beyrouth, ma ville / Beirut, My City* (1982); *Ghazal al-Banat 2 / The Razor's Edge* (1985); *Kana Ya Makana Bayrut / Once Upon a Time Beirut* (1994).

Selmane, Mohammed (b. 1922 or 1924, Lebanon; d. 1998)

Selmane was an actor, singer and director. In directing, his guiding ambition was initially to make Lebanese films with singing and dancing like the Egyptian musicals of the 1940s. In *Layla Fi al-Iraq / Layla in Iraq*, an Iraqi–Lebanese co-production dating from 1949, Selmane played the male lead. He also appeared in many Egyptian films. However, Selmane was not trained in direction. In 1957 he directed *al-Lahn al-Awal / The First Melody*, which featured his wife, Najah Salam. In addition, he frequently wrote the songs for his own movies. Selmane hired George Costi as director of photography; this was an excellent move, as Costi was a well-known early cinematographer. Selmane's films met with great commercial success, as he appeared to understand the popular taste.

In the 1960s Selmane came into his own. His first big hit was *Marhabane Ayouh al-Hubb / Greetings to Love* in 1962, also featuring Najah Salam. He frequently made more than one movie in a year, making two in 1963, six in 1965 and four in 1966. His films had major distribution throughout the Arab world. Selmane established the wave of musical comedies in the Arab world, continuing to recycle popular singers and dancers in formulaic movies that continued to be successful. Next he shot a wave of Bedouin movies, and then a wave of *policiers*. In 1965 *al-Jaguar al-Sawda' / The Black Jaguar*, Selmane's first *policier*, featured the Lebanese screen idol Ihsan Sadek as the debonair cop driving a black Jaguar. In 1978 *Variety* reported that Selmane had moved to Syria on a permanent basis due to the civil war in Lebanon.

The critic Mohammed Rida has called Selmane the father of Lebanese film because he was so prolific. The B-movie director Samir al-Ghoussayni, whose first film was *Qutat Shari' al-Hamra / The Cats of Hamra Street* (1972), was Selmane's disciple, continuing to follow Selmane's escapist tendencies, which at least – for periods when the cinemas were still open – diverted people's attention from the war (see Sadoul 1966).

Selected feature films: *al-Lahn al-Awal / The First Melody* (1957); *Angham Habibi / The Songs of My Love* (1959); *Marhabane Ayouh al-Hubb / Greetings to Love* (1962); *Hikayat Gharam / A Love Story* (1963); *Lubnan Fi al-Layl / Lebanon at Night* (1963); *Afrah al-Shabab / Joys of Youth* (1964); *al-Badawia Fi Baris / A Bedouin in Paris* (1964); *al-Badawia Fi Roma / A Bedouin in Rome* (1965); *al-Jaguar al-Sawda' / The Black Jaguar* (1965); *al-Dalou'a / The Tease* (1966); *Baris Wa al-Hubb / Paris and Love* (1971); *Guitare al-Hubb / The Guitar of Love* (1973); *The Siren of the Sahara* (1978)

List of actors

Fayrouz (Nohad Haddad) (b. 1934, Beirut, Lebanon)

Fayrouz was a leading lady and singer. She studied song at the National Conservatoire of Music, and married the composer Assi Rahbani in 1955. Assi and his brother

Mansour Rahbani composed more than 300 songs and musical comedies for Fayrouz.

Fayrouz was the leading lady in several film productions, including *Bayya' al-Khawatim* / *The Seller of Rings* (1965) and *Bint al-Haris* / *Daughter of the Guardian* (1968). *Bayya' al-Khawatim* was critically acclaimed for the Rahbani brothers' excellent musical score. It is a cut above the average musical – helped, no doubt, by Youssef Chahine's direction – in the sense that the action is all connected, the songs and the dance numbers fit smoothly and logically into the film's action. The whole is much more than merely a vehicle for Fayrouz, who was already a big star at the time.

Fayrouz's music is found in nearly every Arab film made during the period of her popularity, whether listed on the official credits or incidental. For instance, Dureid Lahham's *al-Hudud* / *Borders* (1984) includes Fayrouz singing 'Watani' / 'My Country' on the taxi radio in an early scene of an abortive border crossing. Similarly *al-E'sar* / *The Tornado* (1992) by the young film-maker Samir Habchi uses Fayrouz's music in the background for its atmospheric value: a Fayrouz song is a shorthand way of showing the viewers where they are.

Fayrouz's popularity increased because she remained in Beirut during the years of the civil war, refusing to take sides, while many rich people fled to Europe. She is now more than a legend: she is an institution. (See Abu Khalil 1998, *Who's Who in Lebanon 1982–1983*: 435–6 for more details.)

Sadek, Ihsan (thought to be over 65 in 1999)

Sadek proved to be a perenially popular screen idol, who worked with many notable directors, including Georges Kahi, Mohammed Selmane and the Rahbani brothers.

One of Ihsan Sadek's earliest movies was *Azab al-Damir* / *Remorse* (1953), directed by Georges Kahi; he also starred in Kahi's *Kalbane Wa Jassad* / *Two Hearts, One Body* (1959). Mohammed Selmane cast Sadek in *Afrah al-Shabab* / *Joys of Youth* (1964) and in *al-Jaguar al-Sawda'* / *The Black Jaguar* (1965), in which he took the lead role as Anwar. Sadek was cast as James Bond by Antoine Remy in that director's take-off of the 007 series: *Beyrouth Sifr Hdaache* / *Beirut 011* (1967). (The music from James Bond movies had also featured in *al-Jaguar al-Sawda'*.) Sadek starred with Fayrouz in a Rahbani brothers production called *Safar Barlek* (1967).

Selected feature films: *Kalbane Wa Jassad* / *Two Hearts, One Body* (1959); *al-Jaguar al-Sawda'*/ *The Black Jaguar* (1965)

SYRIA

This section covers film-making for a small market, the orientation of the Syrian film industry, the importation of foreign (Arab) films, the development of the Syrian domestic industry and censorship.

Against all the odds Syria has produced many vibrant films. Obstacles include being a small country without a large and avid movie-going public, the occasional shortage of film stock, limited budgets, no cinema training available locally and intense government censorship of both scripts and completed films. On the positive side, Syria has produced a number of directors (all male) who were driven to make films; the cities and natural scenery can be visually stimulating if carefully chosen; and the Syrians have developed a tradition of cinematic storytelling. In the Levant, Syria is well placed to become a major cinematic player, partly due to political situations in which their neighbours have been embroiled.

Economic necessity dictates that Syrian films must be exportable or they will never turn a profit. The dialect used, the nationality of actors and the sensitivity to political realities portrayed are all considerations in making a film with wide appeal. Syria was in the political and social orbit of Moscow, until the disintegration of the Soviet Union in the early 1990s. Many directors studied in Moscow. They presented their films at the Moscow Film Festival or at festivals in other Eastern bloc countries. (By contrast, Lebanon turned to Europe.)

Syrian films were often difficult to export to large Arab markets, such as Egypt, because they were filmed in Syrian Arabic, which Egyptian audiences were unaccustomed to. Arab audiences were comfortable with Egyptian Arabic through long exposure, even if they did not understand all the words. The audience in Syria itself is very limited, partly due to the number of cinemas in what is a small country (the population is around 13 million). There are about twenty movie theatres in Damascus and ninety in the entire country, so film-going remains restricted.

The first Syrian film was the silent *al-Muttaham al-Bari / The Innocent Accused*, filmed in 1928 by the Hermon Film Production Company. It featured the actors Ayyub Badri, Ahmed Tello and Mohamad al-Muradi; Rashid Jalal wrote the screenplay. Jalal produced another film, *Tahta Sama Dimashq / Under the Damascus Skies* (1932), which was directed and written by Ismail Anzur who had studied film-making in Austria. This film was a victim of poor timing – an Egyptian talkie was released in Damascus only two months earlier and it suffered big losses. After that audiences had no further interest in silent films, even though another Syrian silent movie was made in 1936.

Nur Wa Zalam / Light and Shadows (1947), the first Syrian talkie, was directed by Nazih Shahbandar. He made much of the equipment used in the production of this film, but the film has not survived. The history of early cinema in Syria consists of many individual failures due to a lack of technical knowledge and experience.

Prior to 1958, owners of movie theatres imported about 450 films per year for fifty-six venues. Of these two-thirds were American and the rest European and Egyptian, with a few Soviet films included. For example, in 1963 Syria was spending US$500,000 annually on importing film. Private companies made a profit importing films, and used this profit to finance their own films, until the state took over importing films and even this avenue of funds disappeared. In 1958 Syria joined with Egypt to form the United Arab Republic. In 1963, following the Syrian revolution, the government created the National Film Organization (also known as the National Organization for Cinema) under the Ministry of Culture. This was the turning point in the history of Syrian film.

A small national cinema emerged to make documentaries on various aspects of Syrian life. The National Film Organization was independently financed and administered, and charged with making long and short feature films, as well as doing anything else necessary to gear up its own movie industry. At first Syrian films were poor copies of Egyptian films. Since the private sector had an aversion to risk, the idea of a state-sponsored cinema that was willing to take a chance on unknown young directors was inspired.

One of the Film Organization's earliest movies, *Sa'iq al-Shahinah / The Truck Driver*, filmed in 1967, was shot by the Yugoslavian director Bosko Vucinitch. *Sa'iq al-Shahinah* dealt with social class and unionism. Although the director was Yugoslavian, the cast and crew were Syrian.

During the early 1970s three very significant films indicated a sea-change in Syrian film: *al-Fahd / The Leopard* (1972), *Kafr Kassem* (1973) and *al-Hayat al-Yawmiyya Fi Qariah Suriyah / Daily Life in a Syrian Village* (1974). Nabil al-Maleh's film *al-Fahd*, set in the late 1940s, dealt with the oppression of the common people by the French colonial army, with the pre-Ba'athist army playing the heavies. It told the heroic story of a peasant's revolt against the feudal land-holding system. The film is noteworthy for its artistic use of Syrian locales and the strong-featured faces of its actors. Visually the film is stunning: Adib Kaddoura gives a convincing portrayal of the peasant as a brutish man-leopard, single-handedly fighting an unjust system. In terms of ideology this film owes much to the American western.

Kafr Kassem, a film by Burhane Alawiya, showed the Palestinians as people – peasants who worked the fields – just like their Syrian neighbours. This effective film re-enacted the massacre of Palestinians in unsentimental documentary style. *al-Hayat al-Yawmiyya Fi Qariah Suriyah* by Omar Amiralay was also filmed in documentary style and showed the life of a poor small village, including the negative effects of the bureaucrats in Damascus. This film is probably the single most influential and rarely seen Syrian film, since the government banned it. *Al-Hayat al-Yawmiyya* has only been screened at festivals; however, numerous articles note the film's style of fictionalized documentary.

Throughout the 1970s and 1980s Syrian films contained interesting ideas and storytelling, despite poor technical conditions. Alawiya said of *Kafr Kassem* that he filled all the important technical posts (camera, sound) with a Belgian crew because of a lack of technical expertise in the Middle East. He further remarked that Eastman Colour 35 mm film lost 60 per cent quality when it was processed in Lebanese studios, compared to Eclair in Paris; he also discussed the difficulties of sound mixing (*Cahiers du cinéma* 1974–5). Many directors, including Abdulatif Abdulhamid, Raymond Bustros and Mohammed Malass studied in Moscow; a few studied in Paris (Omar Amiralay) or Prague (Nabil al-Maleh). A centre for film study in Damascus – which the Film Organization was charged with establishing – had not materialized at this point. Commenting on this state of affairs in a 1982 essay, the Egyptian critic Samir Farid said that film is like any other language, one must study it, and at that time it was not possible to study film in Syria or any other Arab country.

Some of the most successful Syrian film-making was a co-operative venture with other countries, such as *al-Makhdu'un / The Duped* (1974), directed by the Egyptian director Taufiq Salih, and *Kafr Kassem* (1974), directed by Burhane Alawiya with a Belgian crew. As was the case in Lebanon, Egyptian directors sometimes came to make movies in Syria as a working holiday – or because the political climate at home was hostile.

In 1984 the appearance of Mohammed Malass's *Ahlam al-Madina / Dreams of the City* marked the beginning of an individualized, *auteur* style in Syrian film. Beautifully realized, it shows the director's recollection of his childhood in Damascus. The character of Dib, the boy, is an individual, not a type. Although the hero in *al-*

Fahd was noble, he was not an individual; he served instead as a stand-in for abused peasants everywhere.

Recently, production has decreased to two, three or four films annually, rather than the target of twice as many. Nevertheless, the National Film Organization continues to sponsor some amazing movies.

The only challenge to the state monopoly on film-making has been from Dureid Lahham, who began as an actor but went on to direct *al-Hudud / Borders* (1984), *al-Taqrir / The Report* (1986) and *al-Kafrun / The Infidels* (1990). *Al-Hudud*, in particular, is a sharp and funny examination of the failures of Arab governments to co-operate on questions of stateless persons. Lahham's films are all extremely funny.

The major influence on Syrian cinema has been exerted through two governmental institutions: the National Film Organization and the Damascus Film Festival. The Syrian government is poor, not being an oil-garchy, but it has dealt with its limited funds and film stock by allowing directors to make movies on a rotating basis. This has the unfortunate effect of leaving directors idle for years between films, with no opportunity to develop their craft. Although the directors are legally limited to one long film per year, decreed in 1974, according to the Syrian film critic Salah Dehni they actually direct considerably less, often waiting many years between films. Thus many Syrian directors emigrate to the Gulf countries, France or the United States.

The Censor Board operates a separate office which must give a licence to all films, foreign and domestic. Although the Censor Board officially censors films with extreme violence, US and Hong Kong films are currently very popular – these films are known for action and violence. In another case, Taufiq Salih received a licence to show *al-Makhdu'un* in Damascus on 4 March 1972, which was revoked on 11 March for further consideration. His previous film, *Sayed El-Bolti* (1969), which he had made in Egypt, was pulled from public viewing after three days, for reasons of 'morality'. More recently, the censors removed the action in *Rambo: First Blood, Part II* (1985) from Vietnam to the Philippines in World War II, because at that time Syria was a Soviet client state and the depiction of Russians is anything but kind in the movie. This led to the substitution of 'Guadacanal' for 'Nam' in the subtitled line, 'You made a hell of a reputation for yourself in 'Nam' (*The Times*, 4 December 1985: 10). Usually censorship falls more heavily on local than on foreign film-makers. Oussama Mohammed is a good example. Six years after making *Nujum al-Nahar / The Stars in Broad Daylight* in 1988, Mohammed was still waiting for a licence to release it in Damascus, even though the film has been critically acclaimed at festivals and was made under the auspices of the National Film Organization.

The Damascus Film Festival began in 1979. Films shown in competition had to be in Arabic, English or French; filmed within the previous two years; and each country was limited to two entries. However, the director of the festival could add films as they saw fit.

Filmography

Ahlam al-Madina / Dreams of the City (a.k.a. City Dreams / Les rêves de la ville)

1984, 120 mins, colour, Arabic (French subtitles)

Director: Mohammed Malass
Producer: National Film Organization
Screenwriter: Mohammed Malass, Samir Zikra
Cinematographer: Ordigan Angin
Editor: Haitham el-Kwattly
Leading Players: Bassel al-Abiad, Hicham Chkhreifati, Yasmin Khlat, Rafiq
                       Sbai, Naji Jabr, Ayman Zeydan

Ahlam al-Madina tells the story of Dib, an orphaned boy whose mother moves the family to Damascus after the father's death in Kuneitra. In addition to Dib's experiences, the story follows the political developments in Syria during the 1950s, the time of Nasser's nationalization of the Suez Canal, and the lives of Dib's neighbours in their small quarter. Dib flourishes despite living with a strap-wielding grandfather and despite his mother leaving him for 'temporary marriage'.

The film is significant as an early Syrian *auteur* film in which the director revisits his own boyhood. *Ahlam* is attractively framed, showing the neighbourhoods of Damascus to advantage. Khlat is believable in her role as Hayat, a beautiful, frustrated young woman, condemned to non-life in a patriarchal society when her protector dies. In many ways, an interesting slice-of-life film, notable for its picture both of Syrian society and of the inability of people to express their feelings to those closest to them. Malass's first feature, it played in the Cannes Critics' Week in 1984.

Haditha al-Nusf Mitr / The Half-Metre Incident

1981, 110 mins, colour, Arabic
Director / Screenwriter: Samir Zikra
Producer: National Film Organization
Sound: E. Sa'adeh
Cinematographer: Abdul Kadar al-Shurbagy
Editor: Antonette Azarieh, Hanna Ward
Set Designer: A. Farhoud
Music: Marcel Kalipheh
Leading Players: Abdul Fatah al-Mozaeen, Gyana Ide, Ali Assed, Hassan
                       Yoness, Nizar Charaby

Haditha al-Nusf Mitr takes as its starting point a man, Ahmed, who lusts after a woman, Wafet, whom he sees on a city bus every morning a half-metre away. One day he is by chance thrown against her. The action takes place in 1967, after the Arab defeat in the Six Day War. Already defeated in war, he will now be defeated in his relationship with a woman.

Ahmed is a small-time bureaucrat. Wafet is a physical education teacher at a school. His inability to deal with women is shown at an early stage in their relationship – first he slaps her, then he kisses her. Wafet had previously had a soldier lover, which she confesses to Ahmed. Then they have sex in front of a fire symbolizing love.

Wafet becomes pregnant; faced with her pregnancy, Ahmed decides his career must come first and dumps her. She attempts to abort the foetus with a knitting needle and when she ends up in hospital, haemorrhaging, the doctor takes her under his wing.

This film is told entirely from the male perspective, in that a man falls in love on a bus with a nameless stranger whom he imbues with his ideas. She gets pregnant after one night with him, and he is unable to face reality. Wafet remains a cipher to both Ahmed and the doctor. This well-known film was shown at film festivals in Carthage, Berlin, Nantes and Venice. (See Bose 1995 for further details.)

al-Hayat al-Yawmiya Fi Qaria Suriya / Daily Life in a Syrian Village

1974, 90 mins, black and white, Arabic
Director:	Omar Amiralay
Producer:	Syrian General Organization for Film
Screenwriter:	Sadala Wannous
Cinematographer:	Hazem Bay'a, Abdo Hamze
Editor:	Kaiss Zoubaydi
Leading Players:	The villagers of al-Mouwayleh

Amiralay spent two years making this gritty film, which has many of the characteristics of a documentary, but is much more opinionated than a point-and-shoot film. *al-Hayat al-Yawmiya* is set in al-Mouwayleh, the region of Dayr al-Zawr, in the extreme north-east of Syria. In an interview, Amiralay commented that the film crew were seen as 'foreigners' by the villagers: being 'Syrian' was not important, they were outsiders. Amiralay shows the villagers raging against the government, for its uselessness and bureaucracy, as well against natural hardships (drinking water given to children though it is polluted with deadly bacteria, for example) – ignorance and anger that create a dangerous environment. The power of the film resides in its distance from its subjects and empathy with them, and its starkness in black and white. One critic compares it favourably to Robert Flaherty's *Man of Aran* (1934) and Luis Buñel's *Las Hurdes / Land Without Bread* (1932) (*Cahiers du cinéma* 1977, 1978).

This is one of the most famous Syrian movies ever made – every film article on Syria mentions it and admires the spare technique – but, as it was censored by the Syrian government and has never played in Damascus, it has rarely been seen. One critic said that the censor considered the feudalism portrayed in the village to be unrepresentative of events on the ground. It certainly demonstrated that socialism, the official government policy, had not reached the outlying areas. When it has been screened, such as at the Berlin Film Festival of 1976, *al-Hayat al-Yawmiya* has found appreciative festival audiences.

al-Hudud / Borders

1984, 100 mins, colour, Arabic
Director:	Dureid Lahham
Producer:	National Film Organization
Screenwriter:	Mohammad al-Maghut, Dureid Lahham
Cinematographer:	Mohammad al-Rawash, Haytham al-Maleh
Editor:	Mohamad Ali al-Malih
Music:	Samir Helmi

Leading Players: Dureid Lahham, Raghdah, Hani al-Rumani, Omar Hajaw, Sabah al-Salem

In this acid political comedy Abd al-Wadud is caught up in the government bureaucracies of two neighbouring unnamed Arab states when he loses his passport, and that of his female passenger, while driving from one state to the other. He ends up shuttling between Sharqistan ('Eastland') and Gharbistan ('Westland'), with the woman whom he had picked up hitchhiking. In this film very little is as it appears: the apparently pregnant woman is a smuggler whose 'stomach' contains contraband, border officials want to ply Abd al-Wadud politely with tea while refusing to understand his problem. He tries to sneak across the border using several ruses, including donning a sheepskin and huddling up with the other sheep – but Abd al-Wadud is left behind and ends up looking at the border guard's shoes.

Eventually, he gives up on crossing the border and, realizing that he must live in no-man's land, he builds a hut and then a travellers' restaurant in the stateless zone. His passenger rejoins him, they marry, and guards from both borders come to the wedding reception, after which they go home to their posts and leave the couple to their own devices. Despite diplomatic intervention at the highest levels, including a major celebration, the facts on the ground are not resolved.

Despite the background of romantic comedy, this is a dark movie, pointing a finger at the Arabs own inability to work together to solve their problems. This movie does not focus on any foreign (that is, non-Arab) government, but rather on Arab governments' own failures. Although it contains many elements familiar to Arab film-goers – musical selections, Fayrouz on the car radio, politicos making speeches, nosy journalists looking for the hot story – Lahham has given the story a hard edge.

Kafr Kassem

1974, 120 mins, colour, Arabic and Hebrew (French and Arabic subtitles)
Director / Screenwriter: Burhane Alawiya
Producer: National Film Organization (Syria), Etablissement arabe (Lebanon)
Sound: Henri Morelle
Editor: Eliane Du Bois
Designer: Tajeddin Taji
Music: Walid Gulmiah
Leading Players: Abdallah Abbassi, Ahmad Ayub, Salim Sabri, Shafiq Manfaluti, Charlotte Rushdi, Zaina Hanna, Intissar Shammar

Kafr Kassem dramatizes the apparently unprovoked massacre by the Israeli army of the inhabitants of a Palestinian village in 1956. The film first introduces us to the ordinariness of village life, with the villagers gathering at a café in the evening in groups – the Nasserites, the communists, and the women who listen to a radio separately in their own room. Nasser's nationalization of the Suez Canal forms the political content. Political slogans – 'We live and die on the land' – are written on the café walls. One Arab, who has been working in Tel Aviv as a waiter, has changed his name to a

Jewish one, so his customers feel more comfortable. One day the army declare a curfew for 5 PM that evening, and the soldiers are ordered to shoot anyone in the streets after curfew. They kill forty-seven villagers as they return from their usual daytime jobs – a group cycling home from work, a truckful of women brought back from picking fruit, a shepherd coming down from the hills with his sheep.

The village of Shaykh Saad played the role of Kafr Kassem and the action was filmed in a stark docu-drama style. *Kafr Kassem* was co-winner of the Grand Prix at Carthage in 1974.

al-Kombars | *The Extras*

1992, 110 mins, colour, Arabic (English subtitles)

Director:	Nabil al-Maleh
Producer:	National Film Organization
Screenwriter:	Nabil al-Maleh
Sound:	Emil Saade
Cinematographer:	Hanna Ward
Editor:	Mohamed Ali Maleh
Music:	Vahe Demerjian, Samir Hilmi
Leading Players:	Samir Sami, Bassam Koussa, Mohamed al-Sheikh, Wafaa Mouselly

Salem, a part-time theatre extra and full-time petrol pump attendant, is about to live out a fantasy. Most of Salem's acting is imagined, with him picturing himself as a tough guy with a gun or as a stud in bed with three women. Adel loans Salem his apartment for an assignation with Nada, an attractive widow who sews in a factory. After months of public courtship in parks, Salem hopes they will become intimate during her visit. A string of visitors, including Adel's fiancée and the secret police investigating a neighbour who is a blind musician, destroy this hope and the relationship.

This film shows the destructive effects of sexual and political repression. Due to sexual repression, Salem nearly attacks Nada, then engineers a home marriage; we see his lack of experience and complete inability to deal with a live woman. *al-Kombars* also demonstrates the corrosive effects of a repressive state in which neighbour spies on neighbour and the secret police pursue citizens at the most anonymous level of society. It is surprising to that such a film could be made under the auspices of the National Film Organization, Syria's official film board: the way the story plays out is a tremendous indictment of the Assad regime. One can only wonder what the censors were thinking when they approved it, although after the film's screening at the Montpellier Festival it was banned and the government asked for the print to be returned. Instead, *al-Kombars* was sent on to its London Film Festival date. Although the alienation of the hero from his fellows is one of Maleh's primary themes, his secondary characters here, especially the women, are cardboard cut-outs who only serve to actualize the male character. This is particularly apparent in Salem's sexual fantasy of Nada – he focuses on Nada's legs, imagining her skirt becoming transparent, while the camera only shows her from the waist down; Nada's individuality is thereby completely lost. The feeling of the film is at once surreal and claustrophobic, as the action takes place in one small set.

Layala Ibn Awa / *Nights of the Jackal*

1989, 104 mins, colour, Arabic and French (English subtitles)
Director: Abd al-Latif Abd al-Hamid
Producer: National Film Organization
Screenwriter: Abd al-Latif Abd al-Hamid
Cinematographer: Abdo Hamzeh
Editor: Antoinette Azarieh
Designer: Muwaffak Kaat
Leading Players: As'ad Feddah, Najah al-Abdullah

Layala Ibn Awa tells the story of a man who loses or destroys his whole family through his will to dominate. In the film we see this as a reaction to his upbringing in a patriarchal society and as a fear of the unknown, represented by the howling of unseen jackals. At night his sleep is disturbed by the howling of jackals in the woods behind his farm. Abu Kamal wakes his wife, who magically quiets the jackals with her whistle. He first alienates his oldest son after an unannounced visit to the son's rented room in Latakia, where Kamal finds pin-ups of busty women, and shirts and cologne bought on the father's credit at a local shop. The alienation progresses through the family, as another son is killed while in the army. Finally Kamal's wife dies, perhaps of exhaustion.

   Abd al-Hamid has portrayed life for a rural family, in which only the men direct fate. The radio, which participates like another actor, moves the action along, driving Abu Kamal to despair by reporting the fall in the price of his freshly harvested tomatoes and by giving news of army battles. *Layala Ibn Awa* tells a strong story of a man who loses his family because he could not deal with them as people.

al-Makhdu'un / *The Duped*

1974, 107 mins, black and white, Arabic (English subtitles)
Director / Screenwriter: Taufiq Salih
Producer: National Film Organization
Sound: Zoheir Fahmy
Cinematographer: Behgat Haidar
Editor: Farin Dib
Music: Solhi El-Wadi
Leading Players: Mohamed Kheir Helwani, Abdel Rahman al-Rachi, Bassam
                         Loutfi, Sakeh Kholoki

This film is an adaptation of Ghassan Kanafi's book *Rijal Taht al-Shams* / *Men under the Sun*. Three men try to leave their impoverished and hopeless lives to get work in Kuwait. They hire a water-truck driver to transport them illegally across the border in the tank of his truck. The oblivious teasing of the driver by officials at the Kuwaiti border leaves them in the empty water tank for too long, with fatal results. Although the film is formulaic in some senses, showing a young man, a middle-aged man and an old man trying to emigrate to Kuwait, Salih's direction is clear and unsentimental. Marwan's father, who can no longer stand living in a mud hut, left his family for a one-legged woman whose house has a real roof. Marwan's brother, who had been sending money to his mother, is saving to get married. So now Marwan must support them. The old man, who is Palestinian and has been stuck hopelessly in the refugee camps, must get to Kuwait to support his family. There we see the results of US aid, but such charity cannot compensate for the loss of homes and land. The truck driver, who seems fortunate enough at first, has been emasculated in battle by a land mine and now cares only about money.

Al-Makhdu'un was shown in 1972 at the end of the Young Cinema Festival in Damascus, where it aroused controversy, and at the Carthage Film Festival, receiving the Tanit d'Or for long films. Although the film initially received permission to be screened in Damascus, the permission was withdrawn after a week to allow further study of the film. *Al-Makhdu'un* was controversial because of its depiction of the treatment of Arabs by other Arabs and their relationships with Palestinians. However *al-Makhdu'un* continues to appear on critics' lists of the most important Arab films.

Nujum al-Nahar / The Stars in Broad Daylight (a.k.a. Stars of Midday)

1988, 105 mins, colour, Arabic
Director / Screenwriter: Oussama Mohammad
Producer: National Film Organization
Sound: Emile Saade, H. Salem, A. Kaook
Cinematographer: Abdel Kader Charbaji
Editor: Antoinette Azaria
Music: Traditional
Leading Players: Abd al-Latif Abd al-Hamid, Zouher Ramadan, Zouher Abdelkarim, Maha Ala Saleh, Saba al-Salem, Saddim Bakdounes

The story of *Nujum al-Nahar* revolves around a peasant's plot to regain the family land by marrying his sister to his cousin Marouf. The peasant's brother is to cement the bond by marrying Marouf's sister. Both siblings refuse to go along with the marriage plans: the sister Sana runs away to the city with Khalil. The film focuses on social issues – both in city and country.

Abd al-Hamid, the director of *Layala Ibn Awa / Nights of the Jackal*, stars in this film. *Nujum al-Nahar* was shown in the Directors' Fortnight at Cannes Film Festival in 1988 and won the Golden Palm at Valencia in Spain the same year. Although it also won prizes at film festivals in Carthage and Nantes, and was picked to open the 1989 Damascus Film Festival, *Nujum al-nahar* was censored by the government and has not been screened publicly in Syria. The film was widely praised in the Western press for its strong condemnation of 'patriarchal oppression' (Thoraval 1994), but this quality made it too politically sensitive for the government censorship board at home. As of 1994, it had still not received authorization to be shown in Syria.

List of directors

Malass, Mohammed (b. 1945, Kuneitra, Syria)

Malass was educated at VGIK in Moscow in 1974 and is a director with the National Film Organization of Syria. He has been regarded as the first of the *auteur* directors in Syria, following his important film *Ahlam al-Madina / Dreams of the City* (1984). *Ahlam* tells the story of a young boy, Dib, growing up with his widowed mother and harsh grandfather in Damascus in the 1950s. The screenplay, which he also wrote, is heavily autobiographical, but elements of political action (such as Nasser's nationalization of the Suez Canal) are also included. In addition, the film observes the lives of Dib's neighbours and of his co-workers at the laundry. Malass's film *al-Layl / The Night*, which received the Tanit d'Or at the Carthage Film Festival in 1991, was adapted from his own novel. It deals with the Palestinian issue by showing the destruction of Kuneitra from the Arab point of view. Like his characters, Malass's own father died at Kuneitra while the director was a child, and he has again mined his memories of the past for the film.

Malass made a short film *al-Manam / The Dream* (1986), which was shot before the Israeli massacres in the refugee camps of Sabra and Shatila in 1982, but which he edited five years after the massacre. Throughout his career Malass has been driven by his father's early death and the destruction of his hometown, Kuneitra.

Selected feature films: *Ahlam al-Madina / Dreams of the City* (1984); *al-Layl / The Night* (1991)

Selected short films: *al-Manam / The Dream* (1986)

IRAQ

Iraq makes an interesting case study to compare with Syria. There was a moment when Iraq was poised to become a major player in Arab cinema, ready to take advantage of the anti-Egypt boycott, but the destructive war with Iran (1980–8) sapped its reserves. This was followed by a shattering economic boycott, initiated by the United Nations in 1991 and continuing after the Gulf War. However, for the first four decades of the twentieth century, Iraq was a consumer of films, not a producer.

From 1948 until 1968 about thirty-seven feature films were produced by Iraqi filmmakers. In 1968 the state established the General Organization for Cinema and Theatre to produce movies. According to a report in *Variety*, from 1968–80 only thirty films were produced and, in the opinion of the reporter, these were not at the level of achievement as the previous films. A few films, several of them serving propaganda purposes, were made in the 1980s and 1990s. The boycott has led to Iraq's cultural, as well as economic, isolation.

The first Iraqi cinema was built in Baghdad in 1909, although the first Iraqi film was not made until 1946. The earliest Iraqi efforts, *al-Qahirah – Baghdad / Cairo–Baghdad* (1946) and *Ibn al-Sharq / Son of the Orient* (1946), were co-productions with Egypt. Such films were individual efforts made by independent producers. These first two films, despite initiating Iraqi cinema, depended entirely on Egyptian expertise, as there were no studios, equipment or technicians in Baghdad. In 1948 the Studio of Baghdad was created to produce films. *'Aliya Wa 'Issam / 'Aliya and 'Issam* was its first film, telling the story of two young lovers – like Romeo and Juliette – who belonged to rival tribes. It was very popular for its accurate depiction of the Iraqi milieu. The Studio of Baghdad's second film, *Layla Fi al-Iraq / Layla in Iraq* (1949), was a co-production with Lebanon. The Egyptian director Ahmed Kamal Morsy directed it, while Mohammed Selmane played the male lead; Selmane went on to become one of the most prolific Lebanese directors. In 1953 Haydar al-Omar directed *Fitna Wa Hassan / Fitna and Hassan*, another tale of ill-starred love like *'Aliya Wa 'Issam*, this time transported to a Bedouin setting, with many songs. It was wildly successful, demonstrating once again that the home audiences were hungry for local fare.

The 1960s saw a movement towards social realism in Iraqi film. This direction actually began in 1957 with the release of *Sa'id Effendi / Mr Sa'id*, a film by Kameran Hassani. The film was shot on location in the old section of Baghdad, in a house the producer rented for that purpose. The hero was an ordinary man, a schoolteacher, and the film was praised for its veracity. Despite the commercial and critical success of *Sa'id Effendi*, many of the movies made in the next few years featured stories of impossible love, Bedouin songs and dance, and the scenic countryside – although none of these themes had a particular resonance for city-dwelling Iraqis.

Al-Haris / The Night Watchman (1968) by Khalil Shawki told the story of a night watchman who falls in love with a widow, but is unable to marry her due to social pressures. *Al-Haris* was included in the Festival of Iraqi Films at al-Rashid Cinema and won the Tanit d'Argent at the Carthage Film Festival of 1968. This film is not a documentary, but it is known for its unblinkingly accurate description of social problems, including the fate of widows, poverty and differences in social stature. *al-Jabi / The Conductor* (1967) by Ja'far 'Ali showed the trials and tribulations in the daily life of a bus conductor. Although the storyline lacked dramatic tension, it is considered a realistic depiction of life for the lower classes.

In 1962 one of the great Iraqi directors, Mohammed Shukri Jamil, made his feature debut with *Abu Haylah*. Shukri Jamil began his career in 1953 as an aide in the film department of the Iraqi oil company. In 1958 he travelled to London, where he studied at the Technical Film Institute. Shukri Jamil studied and worked in London for three years, returning to Baghdad in 1963. In 1971 he directed his first noteworthy film, *al-Zama'un / The Thirsty*, which included many documentary elements. It told the story of a group of semi-nomadic Bedouins who finally leave their parched lands, except for a man and his son who try to dig a well. *Al-Zama'un*, which had its international premiere at the Moscow Film Festival in 1973, demonstrated the Iraqi bid for cinematic prominence had teeth. From 1968 to 1975 Iraqi directors concentrated on documentaries.

In this brief moment, before the wars and Iraq's economic isolation deflated their ambitions, Iraq seemed poised to become a major cinematic contender. Following Egypt's signing of the Camp David accords in 1978, Arab leaders called for a boycott against Egypt. At the time Egypt was producing the majority of films screened throughout the Arab world, so this left an opportunity for others to sell their films. Baghdad attempted to position itself to take over as a major supplier of films to the Arab world. As *Variety* reported in 1979, oil revenues gave Iraq a financial edge in trying to corral the film market. Films such as *al-Ra's / The Head* (1978) by al-Yassiri and Mohammed Shukri Jamil's *al-Aswar / The Walls* (1979) made this a possibility.

The Baghdad Film Festival of 1978 focused on the Palestinian issue. It was the city's third festival and the top prize was given to a Dutch documentary, Johan van der Keuken's *The Palestinians*, a balanced historical review of the Palestinian situation. Italy, Sweden and West Germany also participated. However, in 1980 the Iraq–Iran war began to evolve from border skirmishes into a major drain on both countries' economies. Abdul Amir Mu'alla, director of the General Organization for Cinema and Theatre, announced plans to build a US$35 million cinema city, according to reports published in *Variety*. But later reports (1988) indicated that Iraq had dropped plans to build a new studio. At the same time Iraq scaled back large productions like *al-Qadassiyah* and *al-Mas'ala al-Kubra / The Big Question*.

The fourth Iraqi Film Festival in Baghdad in 1980 continued to focus on the Palestinian issue; the slogan of the festival was 'The Liberation of Palestine is the Cornerstone of World Peace'. Organizers required entries in the competition to be on this theme and films not dealing with this theme were shown outside the competition.

In the late 1970s and 1980s Iraq began to make feature films under the aegis of the General Organization, although a political and sometimes propagandist component was frequently evident, as for example in *al-Ayyam al-Tawila / Long Days* (1980), the story of an attempted Ba'ath assassination and Saddam Hussein's flight to the desert. Directed by the famous Taufiq Salih, *al-Ayyam al-Tawila* drags, especially in the second half when the hero is making his endless flight through the countryside and the desert to the border with Syria.

Filmography

al-Aswar / Les murs / The Walls

1979, 94 mins, colour, Arabic

Director:	Mohammed Shukri Jamil
Producer:	General Organization for Cinema and Theatre
Screenwriter:	Sabry Moussa, Fawaz Mouaffar Khidr
Cinematographer:	Rifat Abdel-Hamid, Hatim Hussen
Editor:	Amir al-Haditi, Mohammed Shukri Jamil
Music:	Abdul Amir al-Saraf
Leading Players:	Ibrahim Jalai, Sami Abdul Hameed, Tuama al-Tamini, Ghazi al-Kinani, Saleema Khudayir, Saidia al-Zydi

Based on a novel by Abdul Rahman al-Rubayi, *al-Aswar* takes place in the 1950s and features three *lycée* students, Abbas, Naji and Yassine, and their relationship with their history professor, Hatef, as they become politically aware. The story continues with their reactions to the call for an uprising against the Hashemite monarchy. The professor, a committed Ba'athist, encourages their political development. The ideology of the Ba'athist party was Arab and socialist. The students all react in different ways to the events that transpire. Abbas is accused of murder, thrown into prison and tortured by the regime; Naji is killed by the police during a demonstration; and

Yassine abandons the struggle, reverting to the reactionary path followed by his father. The 'walls' of the title refer to the walls of the monarchy, which must fall for reform to take place.

The film won the Golden Sword (first prize) in the first Damascus Film Festival (1979).

al-Ayyam al-Tawila / Long Days

1980, 150 mins, colour, Arabic and French (English subtitles)
Director / Screenwriter: Taufiq Salih
Producer: General Organization for Cinema and Theatre
Cinematographer: Nihad Ali
Editor: Irina al-Adadh
Music: Solhi al-Wadi
Leading Players: Saddam Kamel, Nada Siham, Mohsin al-Azzawi, Ibrahim Jalal, Salman al-Jawhar

In 1959 underground revolutionaries try to assassinate Prime Minister Abd al-Karim Kassem in Baghdad. News reports claim they have failed, and at first the revolutionaries lie low, but as the secret police continue to comb neighbourhoods with house-to-house searches, they flee to the countryside. Among those fleeing is Saddam Hussein, the future president of the republic.

The urban action that comprises the first half is reasonably well paced, apart from a scene in which a bullet is dug out of a wounded revolutionary's leg without anaesthesia, but the film loses its way in the desert in the second half, becoming a long day indeed. One of the director's less impressive outings.

al-Haris / Le veilleur de nuit / The Night Watchman

1968, 90 mins, Arabic
Director / Screenwriter: Khalil Shawki
Producer: Compagnie Aflam Alyom
Cinematographer: Nahad Eli
Editor: Najib Araboo
Music: Ahmed al-Khalil
Leading Players: Zaynab Kassem Haoui, Maki al-Badri, Abdelbaqui Douri

Adapted from a story by Qassim Hawal, *al-Haris* is the story of a night watchman who falls in love with a widow, but is unable to marry her due to social pressures. Widows are not expected to remarry and, in any event, the poor watchman does not have the social status to court his beloved. He therefore makes do with a portrait of her, lovingly ensconced in his house. When his house burns down, he tries to rescue the portrait, which is all he feels he has of her.

Al-Haris won the Tanit d'Argent at the Carthage Film Festival in 1968. The film is seen as an example of the social-realist school in Iraqi film-making, dealing with social issues, such as poverty, loneliness and the taboos on male–female relationships in traditional society.

al-Hudud al-Multahibah / Flaming Borders

1986, 90 mins, colour, Arabic

Director / Editor:	Sahib Haddad
Producer:	General Organization for Cinema and Theatre
Screenwriter:	Qassem Mohamed, Sahib Haddad
Cinematographer:	Nihad Ali
Music:	Solhi al-Wadi
Leading Players:	Kan'an Ali, Saadia al-Zaydi, Hamded, Hind Kamel, Sami Qaftan

The primary storyline concerns Mansour, an archeology professor, who has to leave behind his student sweetheart when he is called up for service. The film is interesting for its shots of prosperous Baghdad, of conditions in a bomb shelter and even of the archeological museum in Baghdad. It also realistically portrays the waves of suicide soldiers, often children, that the Iranians sent against Iraqi trenches along the border. The greatest suspense is provided when Mansour nearly trips a pressure landmine and has to stand frozen while his buddy defuses it.

The Iraqi soldiers are ostentatiously shown following the Geneva Conventions for POWs: accepting their surrender, giving them water, treating their officer with respect and giving him cigarettes, never mistreating any prisoners. This war movie dates from the Iran–Iraq war and serves as Iraqi propaganda for that war.

al-Mas'ala al-Kubra / La grande question / The Big Question (a.k.a. Clash of Loyalties)

1983, 170 mins, colour, Arabic and English versions

Director:	Mohammed Shukri Jamil
Producer:	General Organization for Cinema and Theatre
Screenwriter:	Lateif Jorephani, Mohammed Shukri Jamil, Ramadan Gatea Mozan, Roger Smith
Cinematographer:	Jack Hildyard, Majid Kamel
Editor:	Bill Blunden
Sound:	Feisal al-Abbasy, Norman Bolland
Music:	Ron Goodwin
Designer:	Frank White
Leading Players:	Oliver Reed, Ghari al-Takriti, James Bolam, Helen Ryan, Yousef al-Any, Sami Abdul Hamid

Al-Mas'ala al-Kubra covers the Iraqi Liberation Movement in the 1920s and particularly the leadership of Shaykh Dari Mahmud. The Iraqis were rebelling against British occupation. This is a historical chronicle and action film. It is unusual in that it shows a period of colonial history from the point of view of the colonized but with the participation of British actors in the British parts.

The presence of the renowned director Mohammed Shukri Jamil and the British actor Oliver Reed signal the serious intent of this film. It was screened at the Moscow Film Festival in 1983.

al-Zama'un | Les assoiffés | The Thirsty

1972, black and white, Arabic

Director:	Mohammed Shukri Jamil
Producer:	General Organization for Cinema and Theatre
Screenwriter:	Thamir Mahdi
Cinematographer:	Hatim Hussen, Talib Amin
Leading Players:	Khalil Shawki, Nahida Alramah

Based on the novel by Abderrazak al-Mutalibi, *al-Zama'un* tells the story of a group of semi-nomadic Bedouins who finally leave their parched lands to find work in the city, except for a man and his son who try to dig a well. The events take place in a small village in southern Iraq during a drought. The pair are opposed by a corrupt village official who spreads discord in encouraging the inhabitants to leave their native village. At one point the villagers as a collective whole come to the aid of the two well-diggers.

 Al-Zama'un, which had its international premiere at the Moscow Film Festival in 1973, is considered very powerful for its austere, documentary style, avoiding sentimentalism and the general view that life in the Third World is full of misery. Instead it is a black-and-white paean to the beauty of the land and the battle of humans against unrelenting natural forces, and a consideration of the difficulties faced by women in a patriarchal society.

KUWAIT

The film world was astounded when Khalid al-Siddiq's first feature, *Bas Ya Bahr | The Cruel Sea*, appeared in 1972. Kuwait was a country with practically no cinematic tradition, but al-Siddiq's film demonstrated great artistry.

Filmography

Bas Ya Bahr | The Cruel Sea

1972, 120 mins, colour, Arabic

Director:	Khalid al-Siddiq
Producer:	Falcon Production
Screenwriter:	Khalid al-Siddiq, Rahman Saleh, Saeed Farap, Wala Salahdin
Cinematographer:	Taufiq Ameer
Music:	Bo Tarik
Leading Players:	Mohammad Mansour, Amal Baker, Saad Faraj, Hayat Fahad

Bas Ya Bahr is the story of a crippled pearl diver who forbids his son Mussaid to go to sea to dive for pearls. However, the boy cannot see any other way to make enough money to marry Nura, his beloved. Finally, his father gives Mussaid permission to go to sea, and he works with the man to whom his father owes money; while Mussaid is away, Nura is forced by her family to marry a rich, older suitor. Nura is the daughter of a merchant who wants her to marry for money. The story ends in tragedy – Mussaid dies in a diving accident and Nura is raped by her husband on her wedding night.

Bas ya Bahr was co-winner (with two other films) of third prize at the 1972 Carthage Film Festival.

Acknowledgements

Thanks to Mohamed Soueid, Women Make Movies, Walid Ra'ad, Akram Zataari, Omar Amiralay, August Light Productions and the librarians at the Oriental Room of the New York Public Library (especially Gamil Youssef) for all their assistance.

References and further reading

Abu Khalil, A. (1998) 'Fayrouz', *Historical Dictionary of Lebanon*, London: Scarecrow Press.
Aliksan, J. (1962) *Arab Cinema and Culture Round Table Conference*, Beirut: Arab Film and Television Centre.
—— (1987) *Tarikh al-sinima al-Suriyah, 1928–1988*, Damascus: Wizarat al-Thawafah, al-Jumhuriyah al-Arabiyah al-Suriyah.
Arasoughly, A. (ed. and trans.) (1996) *Screens of Life*, St-Hyacinthe: World Heritage Press, vol. 1.
al-'Ariss, I. (1994) *al-Hulm al-mu'allaq: sinima Maroun Baghdadi*, Beirut: Dar al-nahar li-l-nashr.
L'Avant-scène (1994) 'Hors la vie', 431 (April). Special issue on *Kharij al-Hayat*, with screenplay and stills.
al-Bindari, M., Qasim, M. and Wahbi, Y. (eds) (1994) *Mawsu'at al-aflam al-cArabiyah*, intro. Salah Abu Sayf, Cairo: Bayt al-Macrifah.
Bitton, S. (1995) 'Cinéma libanais: La relève des militants', *Le Monde Diplomatique* January: 21.
Bose, S. (1995) 'Samir Zikra: Themes that Dare' (interview), *Cinemaya* 27: 44–7.
Cahiers du cinéma (1974) 'Interview with Heiny Srour', 253 (October–November): 48–51.
—— (1974–5) 'Entretien avec Borhan Alaouié [Burhane Alawiya]', 254–5 (December–January): 59–72.
—— (1977) '*People's War* (Newsreel); *La vie quotidienne dans un village syrien* (O. Amiralay)', 277 (June): 61–2.
—— (1978) 'Entretien avec Omar Amiralay', 290–1 (July–August): 79–89.
Cinéma (1975) 'L'experience cinéma en Syrie', 197 (April): 98–115.
Il Cinema dei paesi arabi (1997) 4th edn, Bologna: Mostra, internazionale del Cinema libeo.
Cinemaya (1994–5) 'Interview with Jocelyn Saab', 25–6 (autumn–winter): 14–16.
Cluny, C.M. (1978) *Dictionnaire des nouveaux cinémas arabes*, Paris: Sindbad.
—— (1995) *Cine e Islam*, Nosferatu no. 19, Barcelona: Edicións Paidós.
Comolli, J.-L. and Daney, S.(1978) Interview with Omar Amiralay, *Cahiers du cinéma* 290–1 (July–August): 79–89. Interview conducted in French, includes stills.
Cowie, P. (ed.) (1994) *Variety International Film Guide*, London: Hamlyn.
Darraj, M. (1995) 'Omar Amiralai: The Cinema I Make is Disturbing', *Alif* 15: 138–47. Interview in Arabic.

Dehni, S. (1987) 'Quand cinéma et télévision se regardent en chiens de faience', *Cinémaction*: 72–72.

Institut du monde arabe (1987) *La semaine du cinéma arabe du 14 au 21 décembre 1987*, Paris: Institut du monde arabe.

Kamalipour, Y. and Mowlana, H. (1994) *Mass Media in the Middle East: A Comprehensive Handbook*, Westport: Greenwood Press.

al-Kasan, J. (1987) *Tarikh al-sinima al-suriyyah, 1928–1988*, Damascus: Ministry of Culture.

Malkmus, L. and Armes, R. (1991) *Arab and African Film Making*, London and Atlantic Highlands: Zed Books.

Monthly Film Bulletin (1976) 43, 512 (September): 187–8.

Morini, A., Rashid, E., Di Martino, A. and Aprà, A. (1993) *Il Cinema dei paesi arabi*, Venice: Saggi Marsilio.

Mufarriji, A.F. (1981) *Masadir dirasat al-nahat al-sinimai fi al-Iraq, 1968–1979*, Beirut: al-Muassasah al-Arabiyah li-Dirasah wa-al-Nashr.

Nuri, S. (1986) *A la récherche du cinéma irakien: histoire, infrastructure, filmographie (1945–1985)*, Paris: L'Harmattan.

Ra'ad, W. (1996) '*Beyrouth ya Beyrouth*: Maroun Baghdadi's *Hors la vie* and Franco–Lebanese History', *Third Text* 36 (autumn): 65–82.

Revue du cinéma (1991) Review of *Kharij al-Hayat*, 472 (June): 18–19.

Saab, J. (1976) *Paroles ... elles tournent!*, Paris: Editions des femmes.

Sadoul, G. (1966) *The Cinema in the Arab Countries*, Beirut: Inter-Arab Centre of Cinema & Television.

Said, E. (1979) *Orientalism*, New York: Vintage.

Shafik, V. (1998) *Arab Cinema: History and Cultural Identity*, Cairo: American University in Cairo Press.

Sight and Sound (1992) Review of *Kharij al-Hayat*, 1, 10 (February): 47.

Soueid, M. (1986) *al-Sinima al-mu'jallah aflam al-harb al-ahliyyah al-lubnaniyyah*, Beirut: Mu'assasa al-'arabiyya.

Suwayd, M. (1996) *Ya Fu'adi: sirah sinama'iyah can salat Bayrut al-rahilah*, Beirut: Dar al-Nahar.

Thoraval, Y. (1993) 'Films Rather than Cinema', *Cinemaya* 21: 12–15.

—— (1994) 'Syrian Cinema: A Difficult Self-Assertion', *Cinemaya* 22: 49–50.

—— (1994–5) 'Interview with Jocelyn Saab', *Cinemaya* 25–6 (autumn–winter): 14–16.

Who's Who in Lebanon 1982–1983 (1983), 8th edn, Beirut: Publitec Publications.

Zaccak, H. (1997) *Le cinéma libanais itinéraire d'un cinéma vers l'inconnu (1929–1996)*, Beirut: Dar el-Machreq.

Cinema in Libya

Amal Sulayman Mahmoud al-'Ubaydi

The emergence of cinema in Libya resembles to a large extent the beginnings of cinema in the other Arab countries, starting a few years after the appearance of cinema in the world as a whole. By the beginning of the twentieth century, before the rise of local production, Libyan cinema emerged in the form of silent imported movies. In general, the historical development of cinema in Libya had started by 1910.

Most of the efforts made in this field were focused on documentary films. Attempts to produce drama from the 1970s came to little, in spite of serious efforts to establish support for a local cinematic industry (some in the form of shared production with other Arab states, along with international and local production). An important reason is the lack of technical ability in the country, together with the absence of a private sector and a lack of administrative stability in the various bodies that are interested in this sector. This is manifest in resolutions to variously eliminate, assimilate and merge the companies and institutions that were interested in film production.

The historical development of cinema in Libya

It is possible to divide the historical development of cinema in Libya from the time of its emergence (in the form of foreign silent films and cinemas to screen those films) to the beginning of local production into two phases. The first phase stretches from 1910 to 1973, the second phase from 1973 to 1990 (al-Farjani 1996: 14).

The first phase: Libyan cinema from 1910 to 1973

When examining the historical development of cinema in Libya from 1910 to 1973, its development is seen to have two aspects. The first concerns the showing and importing of films, the second involves film production. About the former it may be said that the emergence of cinema in Libya started with the establishment of primitive movie theatres by foreigners who screened imported silent movies. The first cinema in Libya appeared in Tripoli (the old city), before the Italian invasion in 1911, in the Bab al-Bahr area.[1] The Italians demolished it after their occupation of the country.[2]

During the period of the Italian occupation (from 1911 until World War II), and with the spread of the Italian settlement movement in Libya, the Italians established cinemas in major cities. Most of these restricted their shows to Italian drama, documentaries and news releases, and most of those who frequented these cinemas were Italian settlers, since most of the cinemas prohibited access to Libyan citizens (al-Farjani 1996: 15).

From the end of the 1920s and during the 1930s some modern cinemas started to appear, like the Bernitch in Benghazi and Mari Mario in Tripoli. Until the end of World War II, these cinemas used to show contemporary Egyptian films, along with fascist Italian and German propaganda. The Italians, followed by the Germans and English, documented most of their battles on Libyan territory. These films were later useful as historical documents depicting Libyan urban society, showing clothing styles and jewellery, and marketplaces of the period. Such films presented a vivid recording of the agony of the Libyan people and how they suffered under Italian occupation (al-Zaruq 1994: 6).

After the defeat of the Italians in World War II and the advance of the allied British, French and US troops into Libyan territory, cinema was used by the Allies as an active tool of propaganda and intellectual and cultural domination. Mobile cinematic units became widespread, some of which were affiliated with the British Information Office, while others were linked with the American Cultural Center.[3] Films from these units were added to the regular screenings of documentaries and cinematic drama that were presented by cultural centres linked to foreign embassies.

During the 1950s and the 1960s, the Egyptian cultural centre became prominent in Tripoli and Benghazi through its weekly presentations of Egyptian drama and documentaries. These cinematic shows attracted a lot of people, especially during the period of Nasser's rule. This period also saw a rise in the activities of oil companies with the establishment of special cinematic units showing drama and documentaries to their employees, especially in regions of heavy oil production.

In 1959 a cinema division (linked to the Ministry of News and Guidance) was formed which, in addition to production facilities, comprised mobile film units equipped with 16 mm cameras and sound-recording equipment, and showed documentaries and news in various regions of Libya (al-Farjani 1996: 20). During the 1960s cinema was also used in Libya as an educational tool, through audio-visual divisions that were linked to the Ministry of Education and Learning. In addition, further cinema divisions were established, along with mobile film units, that were linked to ministries like the Ministry of Agriculture and the Ministry of Health; these were equipped with 16 mm projectors and Arabic movies appropriate for orientation, awareness and guidance purposes (al-Farjani 1996: 18). Of the old public cinemas, some are still operating to this day after improvements and renovation, while others were closed or demolished. Many of these cinemas used to operate as theatres as well. During this period, the ownership of cinemas in Libya was divided between municipalities, individuals and companies. This remained the case until a resolution was issued by the Public Popular Committee (Ministerial Council) on the 21 July 1979, which declared all cinemas in Libya would be linked to the General Company for Cinema (al-Sharika al-'Amah lil-Khayala).[4] Most movies shown during this phase of development were dubbed Italian films, along with some from Egypt, the United Kingdom and the United States.

Local production during this phase was non-existent.[5] Until 1943 the production of news releases was only possible through foreign press agencies. These news releases showed the activities of the Italian occupation force, in addition to documentaries on the aspects of Libyan life, especially focusing on the desert, oases and ancient archeological sites. Some film dramas were also filmed on Libyan soil, but were conducted by foreign production companies with the help of some Libyan labour.

Fouad al-Ka'bazi was one of the Libyan film pioneers. He had begun documentary film production in Libya by the end of the 1940s and the beginning of the 1950s in co-operation with some Italians who were residing in Libya. The first film-making opportunity was offered to Fouad in 1947. An old colleague called Enrico (who was born in Libya) had borrowed a mobile film camera from the University Film Club of Padua where he had studied medicine (al-Farjani 1996: 21).

Fouad and Enrico produced a documentary on the activities of the mystic Asmarian order, focusing on the *al-wali* (holy man) Master 'Aba al-Salam al-Asmar who was famous in Italy.[6] (It was well known that King Victor Emmanuel III used to send annual gifts to *al-wali* in order to curry favour with the Libyans.) The movie was directed and filmed by Fouad and enjoyed some success in film competitions in Italy. The collaboration between Fouad and Enrico was strengthened by the rise of the idea of producing and directing tourist documentaries in Libya using coloured Cinemascope techniques. In 1954 the Italian Company produced four documentaries. These were *'Aruss al-Bahr al-Abyad al-Mutawasit / The Bride of the Mediterranean*, *Ghadamis Durat al-Sahra' / Ghadamis, the Jewel of the Desert*, *Hayat Fi al-Sahra' / Life in the Desert* and the archeological *Wahat Min Rakham / Oases of Marble*. These films were made in Italian and some of their scenes were used in international film dramas (al-Farjani 1996: 22).

Some international directors made film dramas in Libya, including the American Hathway who produced and filmed *Tinbaktou* using Libyan landscapes. Many companies from France, Italy, the United Kingdom and the United States filmed whole dramas or some scenes in Libya.

As for the local production of films, from the end of the 1950s through the 1960s production was restricted to news releases and 35 mm documentaries. There were, however, some developments (al-Farjani 1996: 23–7). In particular:

1   At the beginning of the 1960s a cinematic production division affiliated to the Ministry of Media and National Guidance in Tripoli was established. This division produced about ten documentaries a year. Fifteen Libyans worked in this division in the areas of direction, cinematography, editing and acoustics, and this division may be considered as the first real local film industry. The artists and technicians working in this division were pioneers in this field in Libya. They produced more than eighty documentaries and news releases. Most of the technical manufacturing operations were conducted in developing and printing laboratories in London, Italy or Egypt.

2   The role of large oil companies operating in Libya in establishing film production divisions involved them in making advertising and documentary films about their work. These films were produced by foreign film-making companies and technicians.

3   A number of people were involved at this stage in the development of the film industry. In 1964 the theatre director 'Abed al-Hamid al-Jarab merged cinematic techniques with those from the theatre in his theatrical work *Zalam fi al-Zahira / Darkness at Noon*. With the assistance of the cinematic division of the Ministry, he projected shots onto a background screen above the stage during his play.

An attempt was made in 1967 by the director and cinematographer Mohamad al-Farjani to produce a short drama entitled *Sa'id al-Hut / The Whale Hunter*, in which the actors Isma'il Rihan and al-Zaqzuqi appeared. Unfortunately the film was ruined while it was being developed and printed abroad.

The main step in the history of the Libyan film industry was taken in 1970 with the establishment of the Administration of Cinematic Production, which was affiliated with the Media Ministry. This institution was equipped with the most up-to-date technolgy needed for film-making. It also was provided with a complete black-and-white developing and printing laboratory, in addition to a library and special archive of important documentary films and news releases on Libya that had been filmed in various historical periods. During the period of 1970–3, the following developments were made:

1   Educational films were produced for the first time locally and in such a way as to accord to the teaching methods in Libya.
2   A new attempt to produce a long drama (*Thawra Fi al-Qulub / Revolution in the Hearts*) started in October 1970. It was supposed to be produced by the Libyan Company for Cinematic Production and a group of Libyan actors were to appear in it, including 'Amr al-Shuwayrif, al-Dukali Bashir, 'Umran al-Jazuwi, Fatima al-Haji and Khadujah Sabri. However, the film was never realized.
3   In 1971 Sharikat al-Sharq lil-'Amal al-Sinama'iya (a Libyan private-sector film company) produced a joint Libyan–Egyptian film entitled *Kalimat Sharaf / Word of Honour*. Egyptian actors like Farid Shauqi, Ahmad Mazhar and Hind Rustum starred in it, under the direction of Husam al-Din Mustafa. In 1972 the same company produced a drama entitled *Abu Rabi' / Father of Rabi'*, starring Farid Shauqi, Nagla' Fathi and Mukhtar Aswad, and directed by Nader Jalal.
4   In 1973 Idarat al-Sinama (the administrative body for cinema in the Ministry of Media and National Guidance) produced the film *al-Tariq / The Road*. It was devised by Ahmad al-Darnawi, directed by Yusif Sha'ban and starred Libyan actors like Yusif al-Ghiryani. In August of the same year, the first Libyan long drama was shown under the title *'Indama Yaqsu al-Dahr / When Fate Becomes Hard*. The story was written by 'Amr al-Shuwayrif and the film was directed by 'Abdallah al-Razuq and produced by al-Sharika al-'Arabiya lil-Intaj al-Sinama'i (Arab Company for Cinematic Production). In the cast were 'Amr al-Shuwayrif and Zahrah Musba. It was neither a technical nor a popular success.

The second phase: Libyan cinema from 1973 to 1990

In December 1973 a law was issued that decreed the establishment of the first General Foundation for Cinema in Libya. This foundation for cinema started its operations at the beginning of 1974, assimilating all the capabilities and technical elements of the previous production administration. Besides the efforts to provide more modern technical film-making equipment, the foundation generated the technical cadre needed in all the divisions of film-making. This was done by sending a large number of Libyan nationals to study film-making abroad, in addition to local training courses (al-Farjani 1996: 28).

The planning department of the General Foundation for Cinema prepared a study of the needs of various regions of Libya for cinemas. Within its plan for the years between 1976 and 1980, it proposed the establishment and construction of thirty-five new cinemas, with their location determined by population density. The execution of this plan was assigned to the Social Security Board and the Housing Ministry. The capacities of these cinemas differed according to the population density in their area. Some of these cinemas seated 400–500 people, while others seated 500–700 or 800–1,000. The cinemas built during this period were equipped with the newest film, sound and light equipment, and with modern and comfortable seating, and were generally used for international conferences and various meetings, as well as for screenings of selected films and film festivals (al-Farjani 1996: 31).

In July 1979 the General Popular Committee (Ministerial Council) reached a resolution to assimilate all cinemas in all regions with the Public Company for Cinema (al-Sharika al-'Ama lil-Khayala), which would become the designated responsible entity for every activity related to cinema. This involved production, the establishment and construction of new cinemas, and the import, distribution and marketing of films everywhere in Libya. With regard to imported films, these came from many different Arab and foreign states. Some 2,650 films were imported between 1974 and 1990, of which 2,050 films were approved for showing. These included Arabic, English, Indian, Pakistani, Italian, French, Russian, US and Yugoslavian films.[7] The General Company for Cinema was the organization responsible for the import of film drama of all sorts, and the period for leasing a film ranged from three to five years (al-Farjani 1996: 127).

In terms of local film production during this period (1973–90), the General Foundation for Cinema[8] contributed to various documentaries and news releases, as well as producing a film magazine with sound and long film dramas, both through co-productions and national or local production. Libyan co-production and local production are discussed below.

Libyan co-production

Co-production comprises two different types of co-operation in the production of film drama. The first is Arab co-production, where Libyans work with Arab specialist technical elements. The second refers to Libyan production at an international level, in co-operation with international specialization in all the arts involved in the film-making industry. The works that were co-produced in 1973–90 are *al-Risala* / *The Message* (1975–6), *al-Daw' al-Akhdar* / *The Green Light* (1976), *al-Sufara'* / *The Ambassadors* (1976), *Ayna Tukhabi'un al-Shams?* / *Where Do You Hide the Sun?* (1977), *'Umar al-Mukhtar: Asad al-Sahra'* / *'Umar al-Mukhtar: The Lion of the Desert* (1978–80), *Faqid al-Dhakira* / *The Person Who Lost His Memory* (1989) and *al-Bahth 'An Layla al-'Amiriya* / *Searching for Layla al-'Amiriya* (1990) (al-Farjani 1996: 80–4).

National and local production

This kind of production relies in its stories on topics related to the causes and struggles of the Libyan people. It is realized by national elements with local capabilities. Some of the main attempts at local and national production of this period are *'Indama Yaqsu al-Zaman* / *When Fate Hardens* (1973), *al-Tariq* / *The Road* (1973), *Ma'rakat Taqraft* / *The Battle of Taqraft* (1981), *al-Shaziya* / *The Splinter* and *Hub Fi al-Aziqa al-Dayiqa* / *Love in Narrow Alleys* (1986?) (al-Farjani 1996: 86–93).

The use of literature

Some of those interested in the cinema in Libya attempted to make use of literature in films. One of the main attempts was that of the late director Muhamad 'Ali al-Farjani, who wrote a scenario based on the short story *al-Shaziya* (1983) by Ibrahim al-Kawni.[9] al-Farjani directed the film and realized his artistic interpretation of the story. In *al-Shaziya*, al-Kawni deals with issues of mortality: the story ends with one of the characters being killed by a World War II landmine. In the film adaptation, this story is used to condemn those who planted the landmines in Libyan territory and thus spread death over the landscape long after the end of the war.

A second film is *al-Bahth 'An Layla al-'Amiriya / Searching for Layla al-'Amiriya*, which is based on work by the Libyan author Ahmad Ibrahim al-Faqih.[10] The film's events revolve around an Arab woman, her status and varying roles, examined through a historical evocation of the poet Layla al-'Amiriya.

Cinema for children

There are few Libyan children's films. However, two attempts are worth mentioning. The first is a documentary entitled *al-Fusul al-Arba'a / The Four Seasons*, which was produced in 1990. The story is by Salem al-Barudi, and the script and direction again by the late Muhamad 'Ali al-Farjani. The film presents, with a musical narration, the succession of the four seasons of the year. This is presented in the form of a musical dialogue between the children and each of the seasons, which talk about what happens to each season in terms of their distinguishing natural phenomena. Each of the seasons evaluates these phenomena in a beautiful speech with an appropriate tune. This film was Libya's entrant for the Second Egyptian International Children's Film Festival in 1991.

The second film, entitled *To Whom It May Concern*, was produced by the General Company for Cinema and the High Committee for Children in 1993, with a running time of thirty minutes. The story focuses on the destruction of social relations within the family, whereby children become the victims of violent parental struggles that force them to search out an escape route. The film was directed by 'Abdallah al-Zaruq, the assistant director was 'Abd al-Nur Ahmad and the actors were Khdujah Sabri, 'Ali al-Qablawi, Huda al-Latif and two children, Shakir al-Maghbub and Ahlam al-Zlaytni.

War films

'Umar al-Mukhtar: Asad al-Sahra' / 'Umar al-Mukhtar: The Lion of the Desert reflects the agony of the Libyan people during the Italian occupation from 1911 until the fall of the leader of popular resistance, 'Umar al-Mukhtar, in Barqah in 1931. The story of the film was based on the historical fact, and the film shows most of the battles and various aspects of popular resistance. The battles between the Libyans and the Italians were filmed at various sites in Libya, and reveal the military might of the Italians in comparison to the simple weapons owned by the Libyans.

Similarly, *Ma'rakat Taqraft / The Battle of Taqraft* is a lively demonstration of the main military battles of Libyans against the Italian occupation in 1928.

Dubbing foreign films

The authority for importing Arabic and foreign films is the General Foundation for Cinema (al-Mu'assasah al-'Amah lil-Khayalah), which acts in accordance with the principles it laid down for that purpose. These principles require that the subject matter of the film complies with the general conceptions outlined by the government in its cultural plan and policy, according to which subject matter should not contradict religious law or differ from national conceptions and objectives.[11] As most of the production of films in Libya concentrates on documentaries, with very few dramas being produced, most of the films that are shown in Libya are imported. In most cases, the General Company for Cinema (al-Sharika al-'Ama lil-Khayala) gives preference to films produced in Arabic countries, while films in other languages must have Arabic subtitles.[12] As for dubbing, the only film worth mentioning is *al-Risalah* / *The Message*, to which Libya contributed. Two versions of this film were produced: one in Arabic with Arab actors and the other in English with foreign actors. *'Umar al-Mukhtar: Asad al-Sahra'* / *'Umar al-Mukhtar: The Lion of the Desert* provides a prominent example of dubbing into Arabic.

Documentary films

The most prominent cinematic activity in Libya is the making of documentaries. Before 1963 documentary production was irregular and undertaken by the oil corporations working in Libya, the British administration, the UN media administration, the publications and press administration within the Libyan Media Ministry, and other foreign production companies and press agencies. Even then documentaries were regarded as the most active and successful of all production activities in Libya. This is was even more true after the regularization in 1963 of the production of news releases and documentaries, whereby the cinema division in the Ministry of Media and National Guidance started broadcasting its magazine *al-Khayalah al-Natiqah* ('Speaking Cinema').

   The active production of documentaries continued apace in Libya from 1974, following the establishment of the General Foundation for Cinema in 1973. These documentaries covered all aspects of culture, focusing on particular subject areas like agriculture, industry, health and projects under the transformation plan for Libya. Good examples of these are *Risalah Min Libya* / *A Message from Libya* and *Kifah Sha'b* / *The Strife of a People*.

Social realism

Cinema in Libya relies extensively on social realism, in both the few films that have been produced locally and in those co-produced with other countries. Most of the storylines of these films rely on issues that interest ordinary people and reflect their suffering in one way or another. Some of the more prominent films of this type are *al-Tariq* / *The Road* and *Hub Fi al-Aziqa al-Dayiqa* / *Love in Narrow Alleys*.

Filmography

Ayna Tukhabi'un al-Shams? | Where Do You Hide the Sun?

1977, colour

Director:	'Abdallah al-Mubahi
Assistant Director:	Ahmad Wajih al-Sab'awi, Muhamad Sabri
Producer:	Ahmad al-Quraysh, General Foundation for Cinema
Cinematographer:	William Iskandar
Leading Players:	Adel Imam, 'Ali Ahmad Salim, Nur al-Sharif, Nadia Lutfi, 'Abd al-Hadi bil-Khayat, 'Abd al-Wahab al-Dukali, Layla Hamadah, Mushirah Isma'il

This film was produced and directed by the Moroccan director 'Abdallah al-Musbahi, with the support of the General Foundation for Cinema in Libya. Filming started in mid-1976, with the finished film screened in 1977, and took place in Libya, Egypt, Spain and Saudi Arabia. The cast were from Libya, Egypt and Morocco. The film centres on the effects of corruption on young people and on society. *Ayna Tukhabi'un al-Shams?* aimed to prevent the corruption of Libyan youths by conserving Islamic customs and teachings.

al-Bahth 'An Layla al-'Amiriya | Searching for Layla al-'Amiriya

1990, colour

Director / Screenwriter:	Qassem Hawl
Producer:	General Company for Media Services, General Company for Cinema
Cinematographer:	'Abd al-Majid Hamid
Leading Players:	Darina al-Jundi

This full-length drama centres on a historical evocation of the poet Layla al-'Amiriya, through which questions are raised about the status and changing role of the Arab woman. The woman in this film is at one point taken to be Layla, at another to be the Lebanese militant Sana' Mhaydli; at other times she appears in the harem of the palaces of oil princes or is a military officer, soldier, doctor, lawyer and so on.

The film is based on a story by the Libyan writer Ahmad Ibrahim al-Faqih and the filming was done on location in Greece and Lebanon, as well as in Libya.

al-Daw' al-Akhdar | The Green Light

1976, colour

Director:	'Abdallah al-Mubahi
Assistant Director:	Ahmad al-Sab'awi
Producer:	General Foundation for Cinema
Screenwriter:	Sharif al-Mahnawi, Fawzi al-'Umari
Leading Players:	Farid Shawqi, al-Tahir al-Qaba'ili, Layla Tahir, Sou'ad Amin, Zahra al-Ghayzi, Sa'd al-Jazwi, Mukhtar al-Aswad,

‘Abd al-Wah‘b al-Dukali, Muhamad bin ‘Ali, ‘Ali al-Qablaw, Michel Thabit

The events of this film occur around the socio-political struggle in Libyan society before the revolution of 1969. The story depicts Libyan society burdened by a repressive property distribution and colonialist collaborators who are not concerned with the rights of their people and their homeland. The film also deals with the role of a younger generation, in revolt against backwardness and oppression, striving to save their homeland while looking forward to a bright future.

The production of this film started in July 1975 and filming took place in Libya, Tunisia and Cairo. The original story was written by the Palestinian Fawzi al-‘Umari. The technicians who worked on the film were from Libya, Egypt and Morocco, while the actors were from Egypt, Libya, Tunisia, Morocco and Lebanon.

Faqid al-Dhakira / The Person Who Lost His Memory

1989, colour
Director: Jaji Narlev
Cinematographer: Borlev Nortari
Leading Players: Amido Kamayga, Tahir Narlev, Salem Bu-Khashim, Mustafa Qanaw, Narlev Hood Jadozdio

This 35 mm film was co-produced by Libya, Turkey and the Soviet Union.

Hub Fi al-Aziqa al-Dayiqa / Love in Narrow Alleys

1986?, colour
Director: Muhamad ‘Abd al-Jalil Qanidi
Screenwriter: Midhat Bakir, Muhamad Qanidi
Leading Players: ‘Ali Muftah al-Shawl, ‘Ali al-Warshafani, Kariman Jabr, Yusif al-Kurdi, Su‘ad Faraj Shatwan, Sa‘d al-Jazawi, Najah ‘Abd al-‘Aziz, Fatimah ‘Abd al-Karim, ‘Ali al-Qablawi, Ibrahim al-Khamsi, Zahrah Salam, Na‘imah Bu Zayd, Muhamad al-Qadari, Bashir al-Shaykh, Hasan ‘Abd al-Salam, Ramdan Da‘dush, ‘Issa Abu al-Qasem, ‘Ayad al-Zlaytini

Based on a story by the Libyan writer Bashir al-Hashimi, the action of this film (set in 1956 and the years following) unfolds in the alleys of the old city of Tripoli during the period of monarchical reign. The story reveals several of the practices of the former regime towards the people, including many expressive scenes showing the repression by the security forces and police of citizens who have expressed their opposition to the presence of foreign military bases in Libya. The film focuses on how Libyan citizens interacted with national events during that period, their loathing for the tripartite aggression (British, French and Israeli) against Egypt in 1956 and their support for the Egyptian leader Nasser. Filming for *Hub Fi al-Aziqa al-Dayiqa* started in Tripoli in 1986.

'Indama Yaqsu al-Zaman / When Fate Hardens

1973, colour
Director: 'Abdalla al-Zaruk
Producer: Libyan Company for Cinematic Production
Screenwriter: 'Amr Shuwayrif
Leading Players: 'Amr Shuwayrif, Zahra Musba, 'Abdallah al-Shawish, 'Abdallah
                 Hafuza

This film is the only production among the attempts by the Libyan Company for Cinematic Production (al-Sharika al-Libiya lil-Intaj al-Sinama'i) to establish local production through the private sector to have been completed and ready for showing. The film deals with an international theme, reflected in the story of the love between a young man and a young woman. Fate is hard on the young man, whose mother's death is followed by the death of his lover. He remembers the miseries inflicted on humanity in India, Vietnam and other parts of the world that are subject to pain and suffering. The film is full of symbolism, reflecting the psyche of Arab youth after the strife of 1948 and 1967, but it has plenty of comedy also.

Ma'rakat Taqraft / The Battle of Taqraft

1981, colour
Director: Khalid Mustafa Khashim, Mahmud 'Ayad Drayzah
Producer: Administrative Committee of Revolutionary Media,
                           Orientation Administration of the Armed Forces
Production Management: Salem Muhamad Mussa
Screenwriter: Ahmad al-Zawi, Khalid Khashim, Mahmud
                           Drayzah
Cinematographer: 'Abd al-Majid Hmayid, Muhamad Budayri, Faraj
                           Khalil
Editor: Oversize (London)
Music: 'Ali Mahir
Leading Players: al-Amin Nasif, Hamidah al-Khujah, 'Ali Qadah,
                           Khadujah Sabri, al-Mabruk al-Maj'uk, 'Abd al-
                           Nabi al-Maghribi, Yusif Khashim, 'Issa 'Abd
                           al-Hafiz, Faraj al-Rab', 'Abd al-Rahim 'Abd al-
                           Mawla, Salih Nadrat

The filming of this movie started in 1978, but its first showing was in March 1981. Most of the filming took place at the sites in the Taqraft region where the events portrayed actually happened. The plot revolves around a battle from 1928, part of the people's struggle against the Italian invasion.

al-Shaziya / The Splinter

Director: Muhamad 'Ali al-Farjani
Assistant Director: Naji Bu-Sab'ah, Ghayth al-Shames
Producer: General Company for Cinema

Screenwriter: Muhamad al-Farjani, 'Abed al-Salam al-Madani
Cinematographer: Muhamad Musbah Budayri
Leading Players: al-Tahir al-Qaba'ili, 'Ali al-'Aribi, Kariman Jabr, 'Ali al-Warshafani, Anwar al-Tarabulsi, Ramdan Nasir, Um al-Sa'd 'Ali, Ahmad Bakir, 'Abd al-Salam al-Warfali, Najah 'Abd al-'Aziz, Salih Bu Ghazil

This film is considered to be the first comprehensive Libyan production undertaken by the General Company for Cinema. *Al-Shaziya* was also the first long drama to be edited locally.

The film's plot was originally based on a short story by the Libyan writer Ibrahim al-Kawni. This story indirectly treats the issue of landmines planted by the states that fought on Libyan territory during World War II. These caused injury to many innocent victims and extensively damaged the national economy. The film expresses this through the actions of a lumberjack, who collects firewood in dangerous areas in the heart of the desert (which is full of fatal landmines), and a murderer, who has escaped into the desert elude the police and his tribe. After initial enmity, the two become friends, but they are both subsequently killed by the landmines.

The filming took place in different regions of Libya, including the desert area of Maghraw (which is 400 kilometres from Tripoli), the Sarman region, the Green Mountain, al-Kuf valley and the waterfall of Darnah.

al-Tariq / The Road

1973, black and white
Director: Yusif Sha'ban Muhamad
Screenwriter: Ahmad al-Darnawi, Yusif Sha'ban Muhamad
Music: 'Atiyah Muhamad
Leading Players: Yusif al-Gharyani, Mustaf al-Masrati, 'Aiyad al-Zlaytini, Sa'idah Abu Rawi, Salem Bu-Khashim

This film treats issues related to roads, their importance and the extent to which they are needed by the inhabitants of villages and remote areas. This is enacted by a meeting of the inhabitants of one remote village to study and discuss this problem, and the extent to which they need a road that links their remote village to the main road. The inhabitants of the village find the solution by relying on themselves and local co-operation in levelling and paving a new road.

The film shows the difficult living conditions experienced by the villagers, due to the geographic isolation of their village. Their suffering increases when the sheikh of the village falls ill and it proves impossible to take him to the city for treatment because of the lack of a paved road. The sheikh, who is in great pain, is eventually transported in a carriage pulled up rough mountainous paths by a donkey. This incident provokes the inhabitants into making a concerted effort to change their reality: at this point in the film they show a new self-reliance, starting to plough through the mountain and open a gap there that will break their siege (al-Ja'fari 1974).

'Umar al-Mukhtar: Asad al-Sahra' / 'Umar al-Mukhtar: The Lion of the Desert

1978–80, colour
Director: Moustapha Akkad
Producer: Falcon
Leading Players: Anthony Quinn, Oliver Reed, Irene Babass, Rod Steiger, John Gablegood, Bijoni

'Umar al-Mukhtar: Asad al-Sahra' reflects the agony of the Libyan people following the Italian occupation of Libya in 1911, following the story as far as the fall of the popular resistance leader 'Umar al-Mukhtar in Burqah in 1931. The storyline closely follows the actual historical account of the al-Mukhtar's life (al-Din Ghalib al-Kayb 1986: 9). The film embodies the strife of a whole people in its depiction of this great leader.

Acknowledgements

Many thanks to Nader El-Bizri at the University of Nottingham for translating this chapter.

Notes

1 A photograph of this cinema, 'Cinematograph Bab al-Bahr', appeared in the Italian magazine *La Lettura* on 1 September 1916.
2 See *The Arabic Libyan Cinema: Its Emergence, Activity and Development*, p. 2. This is an unpublished, undated report by al-Lajna al-Sha'biah lil-I'lam wal-Thaqafa, al-Sharika al-'Amah lil-Khayala.
3 One of the main propaganda news releases that was broadcast by the American Cultural Center in Tripoli was the newsreel *Libya Today*, which was shown in public- and private-sector cinemas and through the mobile cinematic units.
4 *The Arabic Libyan Cinema*, p. 2.
5 The film historian George Sadoul asserts that until 1966 there was no attempt to establish an Arabic national film industry, not even at the level of short films (Sadoul 1968: 544).
6 The Asmarian order is a religious order connected to the righteous 'Aba al-Salam al-Asmar in the western region of Zlaytin in Libya.
7 *The Arabic Libyan Cinema*, p. 5.
8 From its establishment in December 1973 until 1990, the General Foundation for Cinema (al-Mu'assasa al-'Amah lil-Khayalah) passed through various phases of development. In December 1979 the government issued a resolution to establish an incorporated general Libyan society called the Public Company for Cinema, which was affiliated with the Ministry of Media and National Guidance. This company received all the rights and properties of the General Foundation for Cinema. The aims of this new company were to produce films with subtitled copies of them or copies in various original languages. It also aimed at dubbing and translating films, importing and distributing various foreign films, and doing anything else related to the domain of cinema, including the supervision of societies and amateur clubs in Libya. The new company was merged with the Media Services Company, following a government resolution in December 1989. The General Foundation for Cinema was regained its former status in August 1990. While these administrative changes aimed at improving cinema in Libya, the instability of the Foundation may have had a negative influence on the film industry in the country.
9 Other works by al-Kawni include the short-story collections *al-Salat Kharij al-Awqat al-Khamsah* (1974), *Shajarat al-Ratm* (1986), *Ruba'iyat al-Khusuf* (1989), *al-Qafas* (1990) and *Diwan al-Nathr al-Bari*; the novels *al-Bi'r*, *al-Wahah*, *Akhbar al-Tawafan al-Thani*, *Nida' al-*

Waqwaq, *al-Tabr*, *Nazif al-Hajar*, *al-Majus* (in two parts), *al-Rabah al-Hajariya, Kharif al-Darwish*, *al-Fam* and *al-Saharah* (in two parts).

10 Some of the main works of Ahmad Ibrahim al-Faqih are *Fi'ran Bila Juhur* and a novel in three parts: the first called *Sa'ahibuka Madina Ukhra*, the second *Hazihi Tukhum Mamlakati* and the third *Nafaq Tudi'uhu Imra'a Wahidah*.

11 All sorts of imported films are examined by the censorship committee, which approves or prohibits their showing, or deletes scenes or parts of scenes according to the discretion of the censorship committee members. After the monopoly on film imports was given to the General Foundation for Cinema, some conditions on imports were issued. These included the following: not defaming Arab and Muslim heritage, not containing scenes of sex and violence, having a humanist objective, battling evil and siding with goodness, avoiding racism, complying with technical and trade specifications, and not violating the ban on Israel (*maktab muqata'at Isra'il*). (These details are from *Halaqat al-Khayala fi al-Watan al-'Arabi fi al-Fatra Min 21–28 Yunyu 1975 / The Circle of Cinema in the Arab World During the Period of June 21–28, 1975*, Tripoli: al-Sharika al-'Ama lil-Nashr wal-Tawzi' wal-I'lan, pp. 58–9, jointly written by several authors and undated.)

12 *Halaqat al-Khayala fi al-Watan al-'Arabi*, p. 33.

References and further reading

al-Din Ghalib al-Kayb, N. (1986) *Nazarat fi al-Khayala al Mua'sira* (*Critical Views of Contemporary Cinema*), Tripoli: al-Munisha' al-'Ama lil-Nashr wal-Tawzi' wal-I'lan.

al-Farjani, M. (1996) *Kisat al-Khayala al-Arabiya al Libyia 1910–1990* (*The Story of Arab Libyan Cinema 1910–1990*), Tripoli: al-Sharika al-'Ama lil-Khayala.

al-Ja'fari, A. (1974) 'al-tariq wa al-tajraba al-Libiya fi maidan al Khayala: Rw'aya tahliliya lil-Sharit al-Libiyi al-Awal' ('*The Road* and the Libyan Experience in the Arena of Cinema: A Critical View of the First Libyan Film'), *al-Thaqafah al-'Arabiyah* 8: 101–2.

al-Ka'bazi, F. 'Dhakirat al-Kalimat' (The Memory of Words), *Majalat al-Fan al-Sabi'* 4–5.

al-Kawni, I. (1983) *Jar'a Min Damm, Qisas Qasirah* (A Sip of Blood: Short Stories), Tripoli: al-Munsha'a al-'Amah lil-Nashr wal-Tawzi' wal-I'lan.

Sadoul, G. (1968) *The History of Cinema in the World*, trans. I. Kilani and F. Naqsh, Beirut: Manshurat 'Uwaydat wal-Bahr al-Mutawasit.

al-Zaruq, A. (1994) 'On the History of Arab Libyan Cinema', *Sahifat al-Shams*, 7 December.

Cinema in the Maghreb

Roy Armes

Amateur film-making

There was some amateur film-making in the Maghreb both before and after the first professional features were produced. In Morocco, for example, Mohamed Osfour (b. 1927) – who was later to make one of the pioneering Moroccan features, *al-Kinz al-Jahannamy* / *Le trésor infernal* / *The Devil's Treasure* (1970) – was active from the 1940s, transposing figures from international mass culture (such as Robin Hood or Tarzan) into local settings. Later, in Algeria in the 1980s, Abdelhamid Benamra attracted attention with a number of Super 8 films made while he was still a teenager.

But amateur film-making was strongest and most influential in Tunisia, where the Association des Jeunes Cinéastes Tunisiens (AJCT) was set up in 1961 to promote amateur film and to provide a focus for the flourishing Tunisian amateur film-making movement, which had clubs throughout Tunisia: Hamman-Lif, Kaïrouan, Tunis, Sousse, Jemmal, Le Kef, Bardo, Monastir, Sfax, Ksar Hellel, Radès, Hammanmet, El-Menzah and Kélibia.

The AJCT, which in 1968 was restructured as the Fédération Tunisienne des Cinéastes Amateurs (FTCA), played a key role in the founding and organization of the biennial amateur film festival, the Festival International du Film Amateur de Kélibia (FIFAK), held in that town from 1964 and still in existence in the 1990s. The history of the festival is the history of the varying technologies available to amateur film-makers: initially (until 1981) 16 mm film, then half-inch black-and-white video, then (from 1979) Super 8 film and finally a return in the 1990s to 16 mm film and some limited Betacam colour video. The high point of the FTCA's existence was the late 1960s, when it received substantial government aid and when a number of future feature film-makers made their first amateur films, among them Omar Khlifi, Ridha Behi, Ferid Boughedir, Selma Baccar, Moncef Dhouib, Abdelhafidh Bouassida and Ahmed Khéchine. But even in the late 1990s there are still enthusiasts, such as Ridha Ben Halima, active within FTCA and concerned with the progress of FIFAK.

'Beur' cinema

Films made in France by film-makers of North African origin or descent have generally been considered by critics under two headings, which correspond broadly to those used to classify the corresponding literary works. In post-war North African literature in French there is a clear contrast in both the style of, and the critical approach applied to, the books of the 1960s and 1970s by such writers as Mouloud Feraoun,

Mohammed Dib, Driss Chraïbi and Albert Memmi (generally considered in terms of the problems of colonialism and post-colonialism) and those of later writers such as Kateb Yacine, Rachid Boudjedra and Nabile Fares (whose work throws up very different questions of form and style).

In cinema in the 1970s the key term was 'cinémas de l'émigration' and the focus was on the work in France and Belgium of North African-born film-makers, usually treating social or political subjects. The French-made works most discussed included the early films of the Algerians Ali Ghalem (*Mektoub?*, 1970; *L'autre france / The Other France*, 1975) and Ali Akika (*Voyage en Capital / Journey to the Capital*, 1977; *Larmes de sang / Tears of Blood*, 1980), both with Anne-Marie Autissier. In Belgium at the beginning of the 1970s two Algerians produced films of a similar kind as part of their studies at the Institut National des Arts du Spectacle et Techniques de Diffusion (INSAS): Mohamed Ben Salah (b. 1945 in Oran) made two shorts (*Accident*, 1970; *Il faut, il faut / You Must, You Must*, 1971) and a very low-budget feature-length work (*Les uns et les autres / Some People and Others*, 1972) as part of his studies, while Malek Kellou made the short, *Vidange perdue / Lost Sewage*, in 1974.

Virtually all these works, like the studies of North African communities by Ahmed Rachedi (*Un doigt dans l'engrenage / A Finger in the Works*, 1974; *Ali Fi Bilad al-Sarab / Ali au pays des mirages / Ali in Wonderland*, 1979) and Naceur Ktari (*al-Sufara' / Les ambassadeurs / The Ambassadors*, 1975), were first-hand accounts of the problems and pressures of émigré life, and they were generally considered in relation to the work of contemporary French film-makers, such as Michel Drach and Yves Boisset, whose films contained images of Maghreb emigrants living in France. Questions of nationality, like those concerning the film-makers' places of birth and residence, were generally considered secondary to the social message.

By contrast, since the 1980s the perspective shifts to the 'immigrant' community when one considers the films of a new generation of young film-makers, who were either born in France or had reached France as children and had grown up there. The customary term adopted for films by film-makers with Maghreb connections is 'beur' cinema, the product of a slang inversion of the consonants RB in 'Arab' to give BR. A surprising number of films have been made by this group.

The key film-makers in this classification are Benayat, Charef, Bahloul, Bouchareb, Touita, Hakkar, Chibane, Dridi and Belghoul. Mohamed Benayat – born in Algeria in 1944, of Algerian nationality and brought to France at the age of four – was active in the 1970s and 1980s: *Le masque d'une éclaircie / The Mask of an Enlightened Woman* (1974), *Barricades sauvages / Savage Barricades* (1975), *Les nouveaux romantiques / The New Romantics* (1979), *L'enfant des étoiles / Child of the Stars* (1985) and *Stallion* (1988). Mehdi Charef, born in 1952 in Algeria and living in France from the age of ten, though still an Algerian citizen, is the director of *Le thé au harem d'Archimède / Tea at Archimedes' Harem* (1985), *Miss Mona* (1987), *Camoumille / Camomile* (1988), *Elles / Women* (1991) and *Au pays des Juliets / In the Land of the Juliets* (1992). Abdelkrim Bahloul, born in 1950 in Algeria and an Algerian citizen who went to France in his teens, has made *Le thé à la menthe / Mint Tea* (1984), *Un Vampire au Paradis / A Vampire in Paradise* (1991), *Les soeurs Hamlet / The Hamlet Sisters* (1996) and *La nuit du destin / The Night of Destiny* (1997). Rachid Bouchareb, born in 1953 in France and a French citizen, has directed *Bâton Rouge* (1985), *Cheb* (a Franco-Algerian co-production, 1990), *Segou* (1992), *Des années déchirées / Shattered*

Years (a study of post-revolutionary Algeria that had to be shot in Tunisia, 1992). After a study of Vietnam orphans called *Poussières de vie / Life Dust* (1994), Bouchareb returned to the subject of the immigrant community with *L'honneur de ma famille / My Family's Honour* (1997). Okacha Touita, who was born in 1943 in Algeria and is of Algerian nationality, has made *Les sacrifiés / The Sacrificed* (1982), *Le rescapé / The Survivor* (unreleased, 1986) and *Le cri des hommes / The Cry of Men* (a Franco-Algerian co-production, 1990). Alone among the group, Touita has made films which deal centrally with the Algerian conflict. Amor Hakkar, born in 1958 in Algeria and brought up in Besançon, is the director of *Sale temps pour un voyou / Bad Weather for a Crook* (1992). Malek Chibane made *Hexagone / Hexagon* (1993) and *Douce France / Sweet France* (1997). Karim Dridi, of Tunisian origin, has made three films: *Pigalle* (1994), *Bye Bye* (1995) and *Hors Jeu / Out of Play* (1998). Farida Belghoul, born in 1958 in France but possessing dual nationality (French and Algerian), is one of the few female directors in the Maghreb. She has to date made only medium-length video pieces, *C'est madame la France qui tu préfères? / You Prefer Madame France?* (1981) and *Le départ du père / Father's Departure* (1985), though she has also published a French-language novel called *Georgette*.

Many of the works produced by the 'beur' group of film-makers are of considerable interest in their own right. The continuing strength of this new cinema is exemplified in the late 1990s by two acclaimed documentaries: *Mémoires d'immigrés / Immigrants' Memories* (1997) by Yamina Benguigui (born in Paris but of Algerian descent) and *Dans la maison de mon père / In My Father's House* by Fatima Jebli Ouazzan (who was born in Morocco in 1959 but has lived in the Netherlands since 1970). Equally remarkable is *Vivre au paradis / Living in Paradise* (1998), a fictional study of life in the shantytowns of Nanterre at the beginning of the 1960s. This first feature, shot in Tunisia by Bourlem Guerdjou (a director of Algerian descent), beat all the Maghreb opposition to win the Tanit d'Or at the Carthage Film Festival in 1998. All these films serve as examples of the extremely fruitful cultural interaction of France and the Maghreb, but labels such as 'beur' and conventional classificatory terms help little, since they tend to blur the very significant differences among those thus grouped. Certainly in the 1980s and 1990s the work produced in France by film-makers with links to the Maghreb went far beyond the mere treatment of the theme of emigration, extending to embrace the fictional expression of a great many of the forms of alienation found in modern urban society.

Carthage Film Festival

The Journées Cinématographiques de Carthage (JCC), which is the leading film festival in the Arab world, has been held every two years since 1966 and complements the Festival Panafricain du Cinéma de Ouagadougou / Panafrican Film Festival of Ouagadougou (FESPACO), the leading festival in sub-Saharan Africa, founded in 1969 and likewise taking place in alternate years. The key figure in its founding was Tahar Cheriaa, director for the first four meetings (1968–72). It was at the third meeting of the JCC in 1970 that the Fédération Panafricaine des Cinéastes / Panafrican Federation of Film-makers (FEPACI) was founded. The JCC provides a unique focus and meeting place for Arab film-makers and each festival offers a number of events, including an official competition (at which the Tanit d'Or is awarded to the best film), an information section, one or more homages to film-makers or national cinemas, an international film market and a colloquium. Brief details of the various meetings are as follows:

JCC 1 (1966)
Director: Tahar Cheriaa
Tanit d'Or: *La noire de … / Black Girl …* (Ousmane Sembene, Senegal)
Colloquium: 'Mediterranean and Arab Cinema' / 'Cinéma méditerranéen et arabe'.

JCC 2 (1968)
Director: Tahar Cheriaa
Tanit d'Or: Not awarded
Colloquium: 'Traditional Oral Arts in Africa and their Relationship with Cinema and Television in Africa' / 'Arts traditionnels oraux en Afrique et leurs relations avec le cinéma et la télévision en Afrique'.

JCC 3 (1970)
Director: Tahar Cheriaa
Tanit d'Or: *al-Ikhtiyar / The Choice* (Youssef Chahine, Egypt)
Colloquium: 'The Soundtrack in African and Arab Films' / 'La bande sonore dans les films africains et arabes'.
                 Fédération Panafricaine de Cinéastes / Panafrican Federation of Film-makers (FEPACI) founded.

JCC 4 (1972)
Director: Tahar Cheriaa
Tanit d'Or: *al-Makhdu'un / The Duped* (Taufiq Salih, Iraq)

JCC 5 (1974)
Director: Moncef Charfeddine
Tanit d'Or: *Kafr Kassem* (Burhane Alawiya, Lebanon)
Colloquium: 'Film Distribution and Production in Africa and in the World' / 'Distribution et production de films en Afrique et dans le monde'.

JCC 6 (1976)
Director: Moncef Ben Ameur
Tanit d'Or: *al-Sufara'/ The Ambassadors* (Naceur Ktari, Tunisia)
Colloquium: 'Cinema, Literature and Popular Heritage' / 'Cinéma, littérature et patrimoine populaire'.

JCC 7 (1978)
Director: Hamadi Essid
Tanit d'Or: *Mughamarat Batal / The Adventures of a Hero* (Merzak Allouache, Algeria)
Colloquium: 'Film Distribution and Production in Africa and the World' / 'Distribution et production de films en Afrique et dans le monde'.

JCC 8 (1980)
Director: Hassen Akrout
Tanit d'Or: '*Aziza* (Abdellatif Ben Ammar, Tunisia)
Colloquium: 'Cinema and Television: Competition or Complementarity' / 'Cinéma et télévision: concurrence ou complémentarité'.

JCC 9 (1982)
Director: Rachid Ferchiou
Tanit d'Or: *Finye / The Wind* (Souleymane Cisse, Mali)
Colloquium: 'Arabo-African Cinema: Creation and Creativity' / 'Cinéma arabe-africain: création et créativité'.

JCC 10 (1984)
Director: Rachid Ferchiou
Tanit d'Or: *Ahlam al-Madina / Dreams of the City* (Mohammed Malass, Syria)
Colloquium: 'JCC Colloquia: Retrospectives and Perspectives' / 'Colloques des JCC: rétrospectives et perspectives'.

JCC 11 (1986)
Director: Moncef Ben Ameur
Tanit d'Or: *Rih al-Sad / Man of Ashes* (Nouri Bouzid, Tunisia)
Colloquium: 'The New Circuits of Film Distribution' / 'Les nouveaux circuits de distribution du cinéma'.

JCC 12 (1988)
Director: Ali Zaiem
Tanit d'Or: '*Urs al-Jalyl / Wedding in Galilee* (Michel Khleifi, Palestine)
Colloquium: 'For an Inter-Maghreb Common Market for Film and Television' / 'Pour un marché commun intermaghrebin de films de cinéma et de télévision'.

JCC 13 (1990)
Director: Ezzedine Madani
Tanit d'Or: *Halfawin 'Usfur Stah / Halfaouine* (Ferid Boughedir, Tunisia)
Colloquium: 'The Audiovisual Market between Northern Transformations and South–South Cooperation' / 'Le marché audiovisuel entre les mutations du Nord et la coopération Sud–Sud'.

JCC 14 (1992)
Director: Ahmed Attia
Tanit d'Or: *al-Layl / The Night* (Mohammed Malass, Syria)
Colloquium: 'Film Creation in the South Face-to-Face with Northern Markets' / 'La création cinématographique du Sud face aux marchés du Nord'.

JCC 15 (1994)
Director: Ahmed Attia
Tanit d'Or: *Samt al-Quousour / Silences of the Palace* (Moufida Tlatli, Tunisia)

Colloquium: 'Southern Cinemas Face-to-Face with Cultural Exclusion' / 'Les ciné-matographies du Sud face à l'exception culturelle'.

JCC 16 (1996)
Director: Abdellatif Ben Ammar
Tanit d'Or: *Salut cousin! / Hello Cousin!* (Merzak Allouache, Algeria)
Colloquium: 'The Script – What's at Stake?' / 'Le scénario – quels enjeux?'.

JCC 17 (1998)
Director: Ali Zaim
Tanit d'Or: *Vivre au paradis / Living in Paradise* (Bourlem Guerdjou, Algeria)
Colloquium: 'Cinemas of the South and What's at Stake with Globalization?' / 'Les cinématographies du Sud et les enjeux de la mondialization'.

Childhood

The characteristic image of childhood in Algerian cinema is that of the child as victim of the liberation struggle. Examples can be found from the very first post-liberation feature, *Une si jeune paix / Such a Young Peace*, directed by the French FNL activist Jacques Charby in 1964, and the early set of five stories, *L'enfer à dix ans / Hell for a Ten Year-Old* (1968), through to the former editor Rachid Benallal's debut feature, *Ya Ouled* in 1993. Aside from mainstream Algerian production there are the innovative features of Tsaki: the three-part study of children at work and play, *Abna al-Rih / Les enfants du vent / Children of the Wind* (1981), and his touching story of the encounter between two deaf-mutes from very different cultures, *Hikaya Liqa / Histoire d'une rencontre / Story of a Meeting* (1983). In the current national crisis, it is significantly a child who offers the moral condemnation in Chouikh's *L'arche du désert / The Desert Ark* (1997).

With the exception of Mohamed Abazzi's *De l'autre côté du fleuve / From the Other Side of the River* (1982), which traces an eight-year-old's trip from Salé to Rabat, and Ahmed Kacem Akdi's *Ce que les vents ont emportés / What the Winds Have Carried Away* (1984), where a twelve-year-old conducts a personal battle against drugs after the death of his brother, most Moroccan studies of childhood are totally bleak. Characteristic examples are the tormented Messaoud in Benani's *Weshma / Wechma / Traces* (1970) and the persecuted trio of orphans in Farida Bourquia's *al-Jamr / La braise / The Embers* (1982). Often in Moroccan film narratives, a tormented childhood is chronicled to explain later problems and failures: Ferhati's *Araîs Min Qasab / Poupées de roseau / Reed Dolls* (1981), Saad Chraïbi's *Waqai'a Min Hayat Adia / Chronique d'une vie normale / Chronicle of a Normal Life* (1991) and Noury's *Atoufoula Almortasaba / L'enfance volée / Stolen Childhood* (1993).

The image of childhood in Tunisian cinema, on the other hand, is remarkably optimistic, with the young protagonists experiencing problems but finally emerging more determined and secure. The pattern is set in Hamouda Ben Halima's *Khalifa al-Aqra' / Khlifa le teigneux / Khlifa Ringworm* (1969), where Khlifa uses his baldness to his own advantage (particularly in terms of access to women). He ends lamenting that his hair has started to grow again. In Ben Mabrouk's *al-Sama / La trace / The Trace* (1988) the young Sabra succeeds in acquiring the education she strives for and in Tlatli's *Samt al-Quousour / Les silences du palais / Silences of the Palace* (1994) the mature Alia takes new strength especially from the example of her mother as a servant in the palace of the beys, as she looks back to her own childhood. Most optimistic of all is Boughedir's *Halfawin 'Usfur Stah / Halfaouine l'enfant des terrasses / Halfaouine* (1990), in which a young boy's increasing interest in women and sexuality is ultimately rewarded with a dream encounter.

Colonial heritage

There had been a history of cinema in Algeria during the colonial era, but there was no Algerian cinema in any true sense, since Algerians themselves had played very little part in it. At the time of independence, for example, there were over 300 film theatres operating with 35 mm equipment, but these were mostly located in the cities of Algiers and Oran – where over half the European settlers lived – and were designed to serve the entertainment needs of this settler community. Of the 1,400 feature films handled by the thirty-seven Algiers-based film distribution companies in 1955, just seventy were Egyptian films and these were subject to higher rates of taxation than imported European or Hollywood films. This was merely one end-point of a colonial system which had ignored the needs (and in a sense the very existence) of native Algerians.

Towards the end of the nineteenth century the Algiers-born Félix Mesguich had shot a number of street scenes in Algiers and Tlemcen for Louis Lumière and no doubt these formed part of the first Lumière screenings – for settler audiences in Algiers and Oran – in the autumn of 1896. Subsequently, during the period between World War I and the beginning of the war of liberation, over fifty fictional feature films were shot by foreign companies – mostly French – in Algeria, but few featured Algerian players even in minor roles. During World War II the French authorities set up a distribution network, the Service de Diffusion Cinématographique (SDC), to take films to the rural masses for propaganda purposes, and established a parallel production unit for the same propaganda purpose, the Service Algérien du Cinéma (SAC). After independence these functions were taken over in 1964 by the newly formed Centre National du Cinéma (CNC).

In Morocco there is also a history of film production under colonialism that does not involve the Moroccans themselves. The Lumière brothers shot a number of tiny films in Morocco in 1896 and the first showings took place at the royal palace in Fez the following year. French aggression in the run-up to the establishment of the protectorate was again filmed by Félix Mesguich. In 1919 the first of some fifty features to be shot under colonial rule was made in Morocco. A solid infrastructure of production facilities was established to support this: a first film laboratory, Cinéphane, was set up in Casablanca in 1939, and the privately owned Souissi studio and laboratory at Rabat opened in 1944. The same year an administrative structure, the Service du Cinéma, was established within the Ministry of Information, and the Centre Cinématographique Marocain (CCM) was set up to make both informational documentary films (particularly films of a tourist nature) and, from 1953, newsreels for the state, in collaboration with a French production company. During the immediate postwar years a number of major international productions were shot in Morocco – André Zwoboda's *La septième porte / The Seventh Door* and *Noces de sable / Desert Wedding* (both in 1948), Orson Welles's *Othello* (1949), Jacques Becker's *Ali Baba et les quarante voleurs / Ali Baba and the Forty Thieves* (1954) and Alfred Hitchcock's *The Man Who*

Knew Too Much (1955) – but films made by the Moroccans themselves were slow to appear.

The number of film theatres rose during the period preceding independence from around 80 in 1945 to some 150 in 1956. This expansion has continued, so that there were around 250 cinemas – mostly in urban areas – at the beginning of the 1990s. Moroccan film-makers do not draw the full benefits from this exhibition infrastructure, since film screens continue to be dominated by imported films.

Tunisia had the firm beginnings of a film culture even before independence was granted by France in 1956. In production terms there were the pioneering silent films of Albert Samama-Chikly and two feature-length fictional films with sound, Abdelaziz Hassine's *Tergui* (1935) and the Frenchman M.J. Creusi's *Majnun al-Kairouan / Le fou de Kairouan / The Madman of Kairouan* (1939). After World War II a Frenchman, Georges Derocles, established the Studios Africa, which produced documentaries and (from 1953 to 1954) a regular newsreel *Les Actualités Tunisiennes*. When the Studios Africa moved to Algiers in 1954, newsreel production was taken over by a new, Tunisian-owned company, Al-ard al-jahid. The growth of filmic awareness in Tunisia was reflected in the pioneering ciné-club movement, which had begun as early as 1946, leading to the creation of the Fédération Tunisienne de Ciné-Clubs (FTCC) in 1950 and, eventually, to the opening of the Cinémathèque Tunisienne in 1954. The main, and continuing, structural weakness of the situation in Tunisia has been the paucity of film theatres compared with either Morocco or Algeria. At the time of independence there were only around seventy-five cinemas, mostly situated (as elsewhere in the Maghreb) in urban areas, a figure which remains virtually unchanged in the 1990s, creating a market insufficient to support the full costs of local film production.

Comedy

The thread running through Algerian film comedy is the series of films featuring the actor-playwright Rouiched as his 'little man' hero, Hassan. Making his first appearance in Mohamed Lakhdar Hamina's tale of an unlikely liberation fighter, *Hasan Tiru / Hassan Terro* (1967), the character reappeared in Mustapha Badie's *Hurub Hasan Tiru / Hassan Terro's Escape* (1974), Moussa Haddad's six-part television series *Hassan Terro au maquis / Hassan Terro in the Resistance* (1978), Mohamed Slim Riad's *Hasan Taxi / Hassan-Taxi* (1981) and Ghaouti Bendeddouche's *Hassan Niya* (1989). Otherwise comedies are rare, Haddad's farcical *'Utla al-Mafattish Tahar / Les vacances de l'inspecteur Tahar / Inspector Tahar's Holiday* (1973), Zemmouri's acerbic view of liberation-struggle heroics in *Sanawat al-Twist al-Majnouna / Les folles années du twist / The Crazy Years of the Twist* (1984) and Benamar Bakhti's well-observed study of a taxi-driver, *Le clandestin / Moonlighting* (1991), being among the best examples.

Comedies are rare in Moroccan cinema too. The biggest popular success in the genre is Tazi's *Bahthan 'An Zawj Imra'ati / A la recherche du mari de ma femme / In Search of My Wife's Husband* (1993), a film about the problems of a polygamous husband with a spirited young third wife, to which the director made the sequel *Lalla Hobby* in 1997. Otherwise it is largely playwrights turning to cinema who have provided the principal comic films. Nabyl Lahlou began by adapting his own work and then produced a string of original sardonic tales about a world full of unfathomable contradiction, such as *Brahim Yash? / Brahim qui? / Brahim Who?* (1982), a satire on bureaucracy and film-making. A lighter touch was displayed by Tayeb Saddiki in *Zeft* (1984), a comedy about tradition and modernity that was adapted from his play *Sidi Yassine Fi Trik*.

As elsewhere in the Maghreb, comedy is comparatively rare in Tunisia, though a tentative start was made with Abderrazak Hammami's sole feature, *Ummy Traky / Ommi Traki* (1973). Ali Mansour's farcical *Farda Wa Liqat Ukhtaha / Deux larrons en folie / Two Thieves in Madness* (1980) was not well received, but a dozen years later Mohamed Ali El Okbi was more successful with *al-Zazuwwat / Les zouzous de la vague / The Teddy Boys* (1992) which offered both plenty of laughs and a fresh portrait of Tunisian youth. But the comedy specialist is Ferid Boughedir, who contributed the satirical sketch 'The Picnic' to the collectively made *Fi Bilad al-Tararani / Au pays de Tararani / In the Land of Tararani* (1972), and returned to fictional film-making in the 1990s with the internationally successful *Halfawin 'Usfur Stah / Halfaouine l'enfant des terrasses / Halfaouine* (1990) and its more uneven successor *Salfun Fi Halq al-Wadi / Un été à La Goulette / One Summer at La Goulette* (1995).

Co-productions

A very large proportion of North African films are made as co-productions with European film and / or television companies; indeed in Tunisia, with its distribution base of just seventy cinemas, some form of foreign distribution is a necessity. What is of interest – as indicative of an official attitude to cinema – is the relationship of the state organizations, principally ONCIC in Algeria, CCM in Morocco and SATPEC in Tunisia, towards overseas producers.

In the period after independence in Algeria, ONCIC's forerunner CNC co-produced one film with France: Denys de la Patellière's *Soleil noir / Black Sun* (1967). *La Battaglia di Algeri / Ma'rakat al-Jaza'ir / The Battle of Algiers* (1965), directed by the Italian Gillo Pontecorvo, was typical of the output of the only private film production company, Casbah Film, which was geared towards foreign markets. Other international products for which Casbah Films was responsible were Ennio Lorenzini's *Mains libres / Free Hands* (1965), Enzo Pero's *Trois pistolets contre César / Three Guns against Caesar* (1966) and Luchino Visconti's *L'étranger / The Outsider* (1967) – an adaptation of Albert Camus's novel. Generally, Algerians were employed only in subsidiary roles on these films, though Moussa Haddad is credited as co-director of *Trois pistolets contre César*.

There was considerable criticism in Algeria of ONCIC's initial policy of expensive co-productions with France and Italy, films such as Costa-Gavras's *Z* (1968), Michel Drach's *Elise ou la vraie vie / Elise or Real Life* (1970), Jean-Louis Bertucelli's *Remparts d'argile / Clay Ramparts* (1971), Eduoard Molinaro's *Les aveux les plus doux / The Most Gentle Vows* (1971), Mario Monicelli's *Brancaleone aux croisades / Brancaleone on the Crusade* (1971) and Sergio Spina's *L'âne d'or / The Golden Ass* (1971). Later in the 1970s ONCIC's co-production policy shifted towards the establishment of a new Arab identity. Among the films co-produced in the mid-1970s were three films by the great Egyptian film-maker Youssef Chahine – *al-'Usfur / The Sparrow* (1973), *'Awat al-Ibn al-Dall / The Return of the Prodigal Son* (1975) and *Iskandariyya Leh? / Alexandria Why?* (1978) – and one film, *'Aziza* (1980), by the

Tunisian director Abdellatif Ben Ammar. ONCIC was dissolved in 1984 and its various successors have been principally concerned with seeking overseas partners for Algerian film-makers.

In a similar way Moroccan distributors have shown more interest in contributing to the funding of foreign films whose titles speak for themselves – *Ali Baba, Maroc 7 / Morocco 7*, *Marie Chantal contre Docteur Kha / Marie Chantal versus Dr Kha*, *Requiem pour un agent /Requiem for an Agent* and *Mission à Casablanca / Mission in Casablanca* – than to supporting talented local film-makers. The state organization CCM made just one venture into foreign co-production in the 1970s, the Moroccan–Romanian *Les bras d'Aphrodite / The Arms of Aphrodite* (1978), directed by Mircea Dragan. In the 1990s, however, CCM and certain independent producers have adopted an innovative policy of co-production with Mali (Djibril Kouyate's *Tiefing, le dernier rempart / Tiefing, the Last Rampart*, 1993; Abdoulaye Ascofare's *Faraw, une mère des sables / Faraw, Mother of the Sands*, 1997), the Ivory Coast (Henri Duparc's *Une couleur café / Coffee Coloured*, 1997), Tunisia (Keltoum Bornaz's *Kiswa, al-Khayt al-Dhai / Keswa: Le fil perdu / Keswa: The Lost Thread*, 1997; Taïeb Louhichi's *'Urs al-Qamar / Noces de lune / Moon Wedding*, 1998) and Spain (Liorenç Soler's *Saïd*, 1998).

In Tunisia, the participation of SATPEC (set up in 1957 and dissolved in 1994) in foreign co-productions was at best questionable, as with Francisco Arrabal's 1970 production of *Viva la muerte* which could not be screened in Tunisia for censorship reasons. At worst, the choice has been disastrous, as with the two French co-productions made in the early 1970s: Daniel Moosman's *Biribi* and Jacques Poitrenaud's *Mendiants et orgueilleux / The Beggars and the Proud*. But a few significant Arab films were also supported, such as Borhan Alawiya's *Beirut al-Liqa / Beyrouth: La rencontre / Beirut: The Meeting* (1982).

Exile

Algerian cinema is firmly inwardly focused, concentrating on the national situation, and only Rachedi, with the low-budget 16 mm *Un doigt dans l'engrenage / A Finger in the Works* (1974) and the 35 mm feature *Ali Fi Bilad al-Sarab / Ali in Wonderland* (1979), has tackled the subject of exile head-on. But Algerian-born film-makers working in France have given numerous vivid images of immigrant life: Abdelkrim Bahloul's *Le thé à la menthe / Mint Tea* (1984), *Les soeurs Hamlet / The Hamlet Sisters* (1996) and *La nuit du destin / The Night of Destiny* (1997); Mehdi Charef's *Le thé au harem d'Archimède / Tea at Archimedes' Harem* (1985); Rachid Bouchareb's *L'honneur de ma famille / My Family's Honour* (1997); Okacha Touita's *Les sacrifiés / The Sacrificed* (1982); Malek Chibane's *Hexagone / Hexagon* (1993) and *Douce France / Sweet France* (1997), and the debut film of Bourlem Guerdjou, *Vivre au paradis / Living in Paradise* (1998), about life in the Nanterre slums in the 1960s.

In Moroccan film narrative the voyage to Europe is always an endpoint and usually an impossibility. For Abdelwahad in al-Maânouni's *al-Ayyam al-Ayyam / O les jours! / The Days, the Days!* (1978) it is a dream he *may* perhaps accomplish after the end of the film. But the lorry driver at the end of Tazi's *Ibn al-Sabil / Le grand voyage / The Big Trip* (1981) realizes with certainty that he will not see land again, the polygamous husband in Tazi's *Bahthan 'An Zawj Imra'ati / A la recherche du mari de ma femme / In*

Search of My Wife's Husband (1993) is last seen trying desperately to reach Belgium as an illegal immigrant, and, most poignantly of all, the two main protagonists in Ferhati's *Kuius al-Has / Chevaux de fortune / Make-Believe Horses* (1995) die attempting the narrow crossing from Tangier in a seaside pedal boat. Returnees are also rare: in Benlyazid's *Bab al-Sama' Maftuh / Une porte sur le ciel / A Gateway to Heaven* (1987) Nadia returns to devote herself to Islam and women's education, while in Najib Sefrioui's *Shams / Soleil / Sun* (1985) a young intellectual returns from Europe to confront his traditionally minded father.

There is only one film-maker of Tunisian origin active in France, Karim Dridi, most of whose features deal with specifically French themes, but whose *Bye Bye* (1995) gives a vivid picture of immigrant life. One Tunisian look at immigrants in Paris is Lotfi Essid's *al-Sabt Fat? / Que fait on ce dimanche? / What are We Doing this Sunday?* (1983), which is about a Tunisian and an Algerian who spend the weekend looking for female company; far more insightful is Ktari's masterly *al-Sufara' / Les ambassadeurs / The Ambassadors* (1975) which takes on board the problems and challenges of solidarity against racism. The most sophisticated and universally relevant parable about exile, borders, rules and bureaucracy is Ben Mahmoud's *'Ubur / Traversées / Crossings* (1982), where two passengers are trapped in a cross-channel ferry, while the most pessimistic view of exile is to be found in Louhichi's *Dhil al-'Ardh / L'ombre de la terre / Shadow of the Earth* (1982), which ends with the frozen image of the coffin in which the body of young man who has chosen exile is returned to his family.

Experiments in narrative

The structure of the Algerian film industry up to 1993 and the chaos endured by the country since 1992 have done nothing to encourage an experimental approach to narrative. Neither Allouache's fairy-tale *Mughamarat Batal / Les aventures d'un héros / The Adventures of a Hero* (1978) nor Bouamari's two stylized features *al-Khutwat al-Ula / Premier pas / First Step* (1979) and *al-Raft / Le refus / The Refusal* (1982) are generally considered to rank as their best works. Most of the best Algerian features are those that, while remaining basically realist in style, avoid the twin threats of didacticism and self-censorship. Among the few truly distinctive Algerian approaches to film narrative are Zinet's use of his narrator in *Tahia Ya Didou / Alger Insolite* (1971), Allouache's direct-to-camera style in *Umar Gatlatu / Omar Gatlato* (1976), Beloufa's play with complex narrative in *Nahla* (1979) and Tsaki's use of space and silence in *Hikaya Liqa / Histoire d'une rencontre / Story of a Meeting* (1983).

Moroccan cinema, however, established its international reputation in the 1970s with Benbarka's early political films and a number of highly original experiments in film narrative, including films by three directors trained at the Institut des Hautes Etudes Cinématographiques (IDHEC) in Paris and one at the Polish film school in Lodz: Benani's *Weshma / Wechma / Traces* (1970), Derkaoui's *Anba'dh al-Ahdâth Biduni Ma'nâ / De quelques événements sans signification / About Some Meaningless Events* (1974), Smihi's *Charqi Aw al-Çoumt al-'Anif* (1975); and *Al-Sarab / Le mirage / The Mirage* (1980), the debut of the editor and short film-maker Bouanani. Subsequently, Bouanani returned to film editing, Benani had to wait twenty-five years to make a second feature and Smihi moved towards mainstream film-making, but Derkaoui kept the experimental approach alive with a series of complex and innova-

Figure 43 Umar Gatlatu / Omar Gatlato

tive films during the 1980s and early 1990s, beginning with *Ayyam Chahrazad al-Hilwa / Les beaux jours de Chahrazade / The Beautiful Days of Sheherazade* (1982). The new generation of film-makers – such as Daoud Aouled Sayed and Nabil Ayouch – which emerged in the 1990s have adopted a more conventional approach.

In Tunisia, the two poles of the experimental approach to film narrative could hardly be more different. At one extreme are the theatrically trained collaborators from the Théâtre Nouveau de Tunis – Fadhel Jaïbi, Fadhel Jaziri and their colleagues, Mohamed Driss, Jalili Baccar and Habib Masrouki – who have developed a quite distinctive style, much influenced by twentieth-century European drama, in their two complex theatrical adaptations *al-'Urs* / *La noce* / *The Wedding* (1978) and *'Arab* / *Arab* (1988). By contrast, another Tunisian film-maker not trained professionally in a European film school, Naceur Khemir, in his two features *al-Haimun Fi al-Sahra'* / *Les baliseurs du désert* / *The Drifters* (1984) and *Tawq al-Hamama al-Mafqûd* / *Le collier perdu de la colombe* / *The Lost Collar of the Dove* (1990) creates a dream image of Andalusia using methods and approaches drawn from the Arab oral tradition (Khemir is a storyteller and sculptor as well as a film-maker).

Foreign productions

Since before World War I, North Africa has constantly been used as a film location by foreign film crews. Of course many of the most famous films dealing with fictional happenings in North Africa are purely study productions, among them the most celebrated of them all: *Casablanca*. Nevertheless, the study *Le cinéma colonial* (Boulanger, 1975) lists some some 210 feature films shot wholly or partly in the Mahgreb between 1911 and 1962, 'from *L'atantide* to *Lawrence of Arabia*'. Since independence, foreign producers have been actively encouraged by governments to shoot in both Morocco and Tunisia. This has allowed a number of future feature film-makers to supplement their film-school training abroad with practical experience in the Maghreb of Hollywood and European production methods. Among those who took this opportunity are the Moroccans Mohamed Abazzi, Souheil Benbarka, Mohamed Osfour and Mohamed Abderrahman Tazi, and a great many Tunisians, including Ali Abdelwahab, Ahmed Attia, Brahim Babaï, Abdellatif Ben Ammar, Kaltoum Bornaz, Ferid Boughedir, Nouri Bouzid, Mohamed Ali el-Okbi, Naceur Ktari and Mohamed Zran.

Well over 130 feature films have been shot in Morocco since independence. Most of these are routine productions of little lasting interest, but among the major film-makers to have filmed there are Pier Paolo Pasolini (*Edipo Re* / *Oedipus Rex*, 1967), John Huston (*The Man Who Would Be King*, 1975), Blake Edwards (*The Return of the Pink Panther*, 1975), Raúl Ruiz (*L'île au trésor* / *Treasure Island*, 1986; *Derrière le mur* / *Behind the Wall*, 1988), Martin Scorsese (*The Last Temptation of Christ*, 1987), Bernardo Bertolucci (*The Sheltering Sky*, 1989) and Jean Delannoy (*Marie de Nazareth*, 1995). More than sixty foreign feature films have been shot in Tunisia and among the directors to have worked there are Alain Robbe-Grillet (*L'Eden et après*, 1969), Fernando Arrabal (*Viva la Muerte!*, 1970), Claude Chabrol (*Les magiciens*, 1975), Roman Polanski (*Pirates*, 1985), Roberto Rossellini (*The Acts of the Apostles*, 1968; *The Messiah*, 1978), Monty Python (*The Life of Brian*, 1979), Franco Zeffirelli (*Jesus of Nazareth*, 1981), Steven Spielberg (*Raiders of the Lost Ark*, 1981), George Lucas (*Star Wars*, 1977) and Anthony Minghella (*The English Patient*, 1997).

Gender

Algerian cinema is a resolutely masculine cinema. Though Algerian film-making began in the maquis and women participated in the armed struggle, their stories are recorded only in films made by foreign directors, Gillo Pontecorvo in *La Battaglia di Algeri* / *The Battle of Algiers* and Youssef Chahine in *Jamila*. Women appear largely as mothers (as in Mohamed Lakhdar Hamina's powerful first feature, *Rih al-Awras* / *Le vent des Aurès* / *The Wind from the Aurès*, 1966) or as wives (Ali Ghalem's *Zawja Li Ibny* / *Une femme pour mon fils* / *A Wife for My Son*, 1982). Powerful domestic tensions are traced in Lakhdar Hamina's timeless *Rih al-Rimâl* / *Vent de sable* / *Sandstorm* (1982) and working women appear tentatively in Bouamari's *al-Faham* / *Le charbonnier* / *The Charcoal Burner* (1972) and more forcefully in Mazif's *Leila Wa Akhawatuha* / *Leila et les autres* / *Leila and the Others* (1978). After the break-up of the state system, women appear as suffering protagonists in Rachid Benhadj's *Touchia* / *Tushia* and Zinai-Koudil's *Le démon au féminin* / *The Female Demon* (both 1993). But some of the most sensitive portrayals are in short films: Ahmed Lallem's *Elles* / *Women* (1966), updated as *Algériennes, trente ans après* (1996), and Kamal Dehane's *Femmes d'Alger* (1992).

Since the stories of male protagonists in Moroccan cinema tend to end in disaster, it is not surprising that narratives with female protagonists have traditionally tended to be totally pessimistic. The tone is set in Smihi's *Charqi Aw al-Çoumt al-'Anif* (1975), where Aicha's efforts to deal with the problem of her husband taking a second wife lead only to her death, and continues through Tazi's *Badis* (1988), where the two women seeking to escape from oppression are stoned to death by villagers. In Ferhati's *Shatiu al-Atfal al-Mafqudin* / *La plage des enfants perdus* / *The Beach of Lost Children* (1991) an abandoned pregnant woman is driven to murderous violence, while in Noury's *Atoufoula Almortasaba* / *L'enfance volée* / *Stolen Childhood* (1993) the heroine R'kia struggles hard but ends as a prostitute. More recently, however, the picture has begun to look somewhat brighter. Mouna Fettou gives spirited, independent-minded performances as the youthful heroine of both Lagtaa's *Hubb Fi al-Dar al-Bayda* / *Un amour à Casablanca* / *A Love Affair in Casablanca* (1991) and Tazi's *Bahthan 'An Zawj Imra'ati* / *A la recherche du mari de ma femme* / *In Search of My Wife's Husband* (1993). The female protagonist, Saida, finally obtains her divorce at the end of Noury's *Destin de femme* / *A Woman's Fate* (1998) and the four women in Saâd Chraïbi's *Femmes … et femmes* / *Women … and Women* (1998) offer each other spontaneous viable support in a male-dominated world.

Tunisian cinema is full of powerful depictions of women. The year 1972, for example, offered both Rachid Ferchiou's image of the dream woman (played by a European actress of course) in *Yusra* / *Yusra* and also Omar Khlifi's powerful depiction of women's exploitation, *Surakh* / *Hurlements* / *Screams*, in which two young women are condemned either to death or to madness by male prejudice. By contrast, Abdellatif Ben Ammar offered a totally positive image of a contemporary young woman in *'Aziza* (1980) and a new image – that of a female protagonist created by a woman director – was already being pioneered by Selma Baccar in her first feature *Fatma 75* (1978), which was held back by the censors. The late 1980s and 1990s have seen a certain breakthrough by women directors looking at women's lives from a woman's perspective: Neija Ben Mabrouk's *al-Sama* / *La trace* / *The Trace* (1988), Moufida Tlatli's *Samt al-Quousour* / *Les silences du palais* / *Silences of the Palace* (1994), Baccar's *Habiba M'Sika* / *La danse du feu* / *The Fire Dance* (1995) and Keltoum Bornaz's *Kiswa, al-Khayt al-Dhai* / *Keswa: Le fil perdu* / *Keswa: The Lost Thread* (1997). Nouri Bouzid has also moved from his studies of tormented male figures to an image of female solidarity in *Bent Familia* / *Tunisiennes* / *Girls from a Good Family* (1997).

Liberation struggle

The liberation struggle dominates the early years of Algeria's state-controlled cinema and persists as a favoured subject into the 1990s. This is hardly surprising since authentic Algerian film-making began in the maquis and many pioneer film-makers had first-hand experience of the struggle. Beginning with Rachedi's *Fajr al-Mu'adhdqabin / L'aube des damnés / The Dawn of the Damned* (1965), there were a number of compilation films: *The War of Liberation* (1973, a collective reworking of Beloufa's censored *L'insurrectionelle*), Mohamed Slim Riad and Ghaouti Bendeddouche's *Morte la longue nuit / Dead the Long Night* (1979) and Azzedine Meddour's *Le colonialisme sans empire / Colonialism without Empire* (1978), made for television. The fictional features, beginning with Lakhdar Hamina's *Rih al-Awras / Le vent des Aurès / The Wind from the Aurès* (1966) and culminating with the same director's award-winning *Waqa'a Sanawat al-Jamr / Chronique des années de braise / Chronicle of the Years of Embers* (1975), constitute a remarkable national effort, but one which is marred by simplistic plotting and over-reliance on the positive, flawless hero – as, for example, in the two 1969 films, Tewfik Fares' *al-Kharijun 'Ala al-Qanun / Les hors-la-loi / The Outlaws* and Rachedi's *al-Afyun Wal-'Asa / L'opium et le bâton / Opium and the Stick*.

Morocco's progress towards independence does not offer the same dramatic possibilities as the Algerian war of independence, but it does form the subject of a handful of films, such as Smihi's *Quarante-quatre ou les récits de la nuit / Forty-Four or Tales of the Night* (1981), Lahlou's *Nahiq al-Ruh / L'âme qui brait / The Soul that Brays* (1984) and Larbi Bennani's *Le résistant inconnu / The Unknown Resistance Fighter* (1995). It also forms the background setting for a number of other films: Smihi's *Charqi Aw al-Çoumt al-'Anif* (1975), set in Tangier in 1950, Ahmed Yachfine's *al-Kabus / Cauchemar / Nightmare* (1984) and Mohamed Ismaïl's *Aouchtam* (1998)

Omar Khlifi, the Tunisian pioneer film-maker, made a trio of films which deal

Figure 44   Waqa'a Sanawat al-Jamr / Chronicle of the Years of Embers

directly with the complex issues of resistance and collaboration, and which established his reputation: *al-Fajr / L'aube / The Dawn* (1966), *al-Mutamarrid / Le rebelle / The Rebel* (1968), set in the late nineteenth century, and *al-Fallâga / Les fellagas / The Fellagas* (1970). He was less successful when he returned to the era of 1950s struggle with *al-Tahaddi / Le défi / The Challenge* (1986). A wider perspective on Tunisian moves towards autonomy in the 1920s is chronicled from a woman's perspective in Selma Baccar's *Habiba M'Sika / La danse du feu / The Fire Dance* (1995). The 1950s provide the background for a number of other Tunisian films: Abdellatif Ben Ammar's *Sejnan / Sejnane* (1974), Moufida Tlatli's *Samt al-Quousour / Les silences du palais / Silences of the Palace* (1994) and Ali Abidi's *Redeyef 54* (1997).

Literary adaptations

The links between film-making and literature are not close in North Africa, partly because of the economic situation of the film-maker who is usually constrained to be their own producer and scriptwriter, as well as the principal promoter of the film at international festivals and with foreign television companies. The cost of film rights to French-language novels is also prohibitive; mostly, when a novel has been adapted, the film-maker is a personal friend of the novelist concerned.

In the early years of Algerian cinema, the actor Rouiched had two of his plays adapted: *Hasan Tiru / Hassan Terro* (Mohamed Lakhdar Hamina, 1967) and *al-Ghula / El Ghoula* (Mustapha Kateb, 1972). Novels by Mouloud Mammeri, who wrote the commentary for *Fajr al-Mu'adhdqabin / The Dawn of the Damned*, were the source of Ahmed Rachedi's *al-Afyun Wal-'Asa / Opium and the Stick* (1969) and Abderrahmane Bouguermouth's *La colline oubliée / The Forgotten Hillside* (made in the Berber language, 1996). Ali Ghalem adapted his own novel (*Zawja Li Ibny / Une femme pour mon fils / A Wife for My Son*) in 1982, Mohamed Slim Riad adapted Abdelhamid Ben Hedouga's *Rih al-Janub / Vent du sud / Wind from the South* (1975) and Mahmoud Zemmouri made a version of Rachid Mimouni's *Sharaf al-Qabilu / L'honneur de la tribu / The Honour of the Tribe* (1993). Other literary figures who have become involved with cinema include the novelist Rachid Boudjedra wrote three original scripts: *Nahla* (1979) for Farouk Beloufa, *Un doigt dans l'engrenage / A Finger in the Works* (1974) and *Ali Fi Bilad al-Sarab / Ali in Wonderland* (1979) for Ahmed Rachedi. Two women novelists also directed 16 mm films for television from their own original scripts: Assia Djebar with *Noubat Nissa Jabal Chnouwwa / La nouba des femmes du Mont Chenoua / The Nouba of the Women of Mount Chenoa* (1978) and *Zerda Wa Aghani al-Nisyan / La zerda et les chants de l'oubli / The Zerda and the Songs of Forgetfulness* (1982), and Hafsa Zinai-Koudil with *Le démon au féminin / The Female Demon* (1993).

In Morocco links between film and literature have been particularly tenuous. Souheil Benbarka made free adaptations of Federico García Lorca's play *Bodas de sangre / Blood Wedding* as *'Urs al-Dam / Noces de sang* (1977) and Alan Paton's novel *Cry, the Beloved Country* as *Amok* (1982). Moumen Smihi based *Qaftân al-Hubb / Caftan d'amour / Caftan of Love* (1987) on Mohamed M'rabet's story 'The Big Mirror' and Hamid Benani made a screen version of Tahar Ben Jelloun's *Sirr al-Majarra / La prière de l'absent / A Prayer for the Absent* (1995). Mustapha Reggab's *Hallaq Darb al-*

Figure 45   Noubat Nissa Jabal Chnouwwa / The Nouba of the Women of Mount Chenoa

Fouqara / Le coiffeur du quartier des pauvres / The Barber of the Poor Quarter (1982) was adapted by Youssef Fadel from his own play, Tayeb Saddiki used his own play as the basis of *Zeft* (1984) and his fellow dramatist Nabyl Lahlou wrote and directed a number of original scripts.

The first Tunisian adaptation came with Hamouda Ben Halima' *Khalifa al-Aqra' / Khlifa le teigneux / Khlifa Ringworm* (1969) from a story by Bechir Khraieff, whose novel *Barg Ellil / Nocturnal Lightning* was filmed by Ali Abidi in 1990. Both Brahim Babai's fictional films are adapted from novels, *Wa Ghadan … ? / Et demain … ? / And Tomorrow … ?* (1972) after Abdelkader Ben Cheikh and *Laylat al-Sanawât al-'Achr / La nuit de la décennie / The Night of the Decade* (1991) after Mohamed Salah Jabri, who also provided the source for Ali Abidi's *Redeyef 54* (1997). In addition, Taïeb Louhichi's *Majnun Leila / Leila ma raison / Leila My Reason* (1989) used André Miquel's French-language version of the legend. The Nouveau Théâtre de Tunis also adapted two of their stage successes, *al-'Urs / La noce / The Wedding* (1978) and *'Arab / Arab* (1988).

Masculinity

The state-controlled Algerian cinema was unique in the the Maghreb in demanding a positive male hero, whether in its depiction of the freedom fighter in the liberation struggle or the urban intellectual intervening in rural life by participating in the agrarian reform movement. Each is given a stereotyped opponent, the violent torturing French soldier in the former case and the still powerful but backward-looking landowner in the latter. The result is the paradox of a would-be revolutionary cinema following the plot patterns and final resolutions of Hollywood cinema, opening up a gap between the film rhetoric and the actual experience of the audience, which increasingly came to comprise a new generation with no personal experience of the independence struggles. This is what made the hesitant, defeated hero of Allouache's *Umar Gatlatu / Omar Gatlato* (1976) such a key figure. But often, in the background of these films, is the figure of the 'holy fool', the madman who sees the truth. With the break-up of the state industry and the breakdown of social order, this figure comes splendidly to the fore in Chouikh's *Youcef Kesat Dekna Sabera / Youcef ou la légende du septième dormant / Youssef: The Legend of the Seventh Sleeper* (1993) to uncover the truth beneath the state rhetoric. Since the collapse of the state funding structure, the new protagonists of films by Chouikh, Belkacem Hadjadj and Abderrahman Bouguermouh are heroes who struggle but face ultimate defeat.

For the Moroccan male film protagonist, the action of the film is almost always a journey to defeat, whether the setting is in the city or in the countryside. The pattern begins with the early experimental narratives: Benani's *Weshma / Traces* (1970) and Bouanani's *al-Sarab / The Mirage* (1980). The same is true of most of the socially committed work in a more realist style: all Benbarka's films from *Alf Yad Wa Yad / Mille et une mains / A Thousand and One Hands* (1972) to *Les cavaliers de la gloire / Horsemen of Glory* (1993), Reggab's *Hallaq Darb al-Fouqara / The Barber of the Poor Quarter* (1982), Noury's *Sa'i al-Barid / Le facteur / The Postman* (1980) and *Un simple fait divers / A Simple News Item* (1997), Tazi's *Ibn al-Sabil / The Big Trip* (1981) and Ferhati's *Kuius al-Has / Make-Believe Horses* (1995). The same is true of the work of the best of the younger directors, such as Daoud Aouled Sayed's *Adieu forain / Goodbye Travelling Showman* (1998) which, like Ferhati's work, is a chronicle of failed dreams.

Death is the fate of all the heroes in Omar Khlifi's depictions of the liberation struggle and this sets a pattern for Tunisian cinema's portrayal of the male protagonist. Tahar struggles in vain against the forces of 'modernization' in Ridha Behi's *Shams al-Diba / Le soleil des hyènes / Hyenas' Sun* (1977), just as the aging patriarch fails to preserve his traditional lifestyle in Taïeb Louhichi's *Dhil al-'Ardh / Shadow of the Earth* (1982) and the overwhelming love of Qaïs drives him to madness in the same director's *Majnun Leila / Leila My Reason* (1989). The two male protagonists in Mahmoud Ben Mahmoud's *'Ubur / Crossings* (1982) are irrevocably trapped aboard the cross-channel ferry. Similarly, Nouri Bouzid's three studies of male identity – *Rih al-Sid / L'homme de cendres / Man of Ashes* (1986), *Safa'ih Min Dhahab / Sabots en or / Golden Horseshoes* (1989) and *Bezness / Business* (1992) – are all stories of defeat. The same theme is picked up by newcomer Mohamed Ben Smaïl in *Ghoudwa Nahrek / Demain je brûle / Tomorrow I Burn* (1998), where the protagonist is doomed from the very first sequence and goes slowly towards his death.

Production and distribution structures

Film was seen to form a vital part of the Algerian liberation struggle by the Front de Libération Nationale (FLN), the army, the Armée de Libération Nationale (ALN) and the Algerian provisional government in exile (Gouvernement Provisoire de la République or GPRA). The army set up a documentary film unit headed by the

French documentarist and FLN supporter René Vautier, whose best-known film of the period is *Algérie en flammes / Algeria in Flames* (1959). The GPRA also set up a photo and film service in Tunis. After independence, virtually all feature films were state produced and – unlike the situation in Morocco and Tunisia – the film directors became salaried state employees.

The first context of production for post-independence Algerian cinema was the Centre Audio-Visuel (CAV) set up by the Algerian Ministry of Youth and Sport in 1962. For two years CAV provided the basis for the film-making collective set up by René Vautier which produced a number of short documentaries and one feature-length work: *Peuple en marche / A People on the March* (1963). It also participated in what was ultimately to prove an unsuccessful attempt to establish a network of ciné-clubs across the country, the Fédération Algérienne de Cinéma Populaire, generally known as the *ciné-pops*. At the beginning of 1963, the Algerian Ministry of Information set up the Office des Actualités Algériennes (OAA) to produce a regular weekly newsreel. A third production context was the Centre National du Cinéma (CNC), set up by the Ministry of Information and Culture in 1964. The organization had a wide remit: the responsibility for supervising film distribution and exhibition, the provision of a rural ciné-bus film-distribution system, the creation of a film archive (the Cinémathèque Algérienne) and the establishment of the new professional film-training programme at the Institut National du Cinéma d'Alger (INC), where students in its sole year of operation included Merzak Allouache, Sid Ali Mazif and Farouk Beloufa. In addition, the company was concerned with the production of short and feature films. Alongside these state organizations, the only private company active in 1965–7 was Casbah Films, founded by the former FLN activist Yacef Saadi, whose own story formed the basis of the company's best-known feature, *La Battaglia di Algeri / Ma'rakat al-Jaza'ir / The Battle of Algiers* (1965).

The other key mid-1960s production organization – set up when the television system was nationalized in 1962 – was Radio-Télévision Algérienne (RTA) which co-produced the first Algerian fictional feature, *al-Lailu Yakhaf Ash-shams / La nuit a peur du soleil / The Night is Afraid of the Sun* (1965). Though never lavishly funded, RTA pursued an ambitious programme of feature-length film production for television, with its directors usually working in black and white, shooting on 16 mm film, often on location. A number of these productions received a wider distribution and some were shown in foreign film festivals.

In 1967–8 the film industry was radically reorganized. OAA and CNCA were disbanded, and two new organizations set up. The Centre de Diffusion Cinématographique (CDC) was established to take over the ciné-bus role initially established by the colonial SDC, and the Centre Algérien de la Cinématographie (CAC) was set up to take on the administrative roles: controlling access to the profession, supervising film theatres, running the Cinémathèque and so on. In 1967 the monopoly of film production and – from 1969 – of film import and distribution was taken over by the Office National du Commerce et de l'Industrie Cinématographique (ONCIC). This production monopoly meant that ONCIC was responsible for virtually all Algerian feature-film production from 1968 until it was dissolved in 1984, except for the television works produced by RTA (mostly in black and white on 16 mm) and a tiny handful of independent works.

The 1980s saw further reorganizations. ONCIC was dissolved in 1984 and its functions split between two separate organizations, with Entreprise Nationale de Production Cinématographique (ENAPROC) being responsible for production and Entreprise Nationale de Distribution et d'Exploitation Cinématographique (ENADEC) for distribution, and the state monopoly of film production was abolished, so that film-makers could now set up their own production companies. In November 1987 there was another decisive reorganization, with the setting up of the Centre Algérien pour l'Art et l'Industrie Cinématographiques (CAAIC) to replace both ENAPROC and ENADEC and to take over all the activities previously undertaken by ONCIC.

A parallel step was taken with respect to television production when RTA resources were regrouped in the same year (1987) to form Entreprise Nationale de Productions Audiovisuelles (ENPA). The new organization offered support for a wide range of film-makers and participated in numerous co-productions with CAAIC, blurring the boundaries which had separated RTA from ONCIC.

An even more radical step was taken in October 1993 when the state-employed directors were given the equivalent of thirty-six months' salary and invited to form their own audio-visual production cooperatives for future film production. CAAIC continued to offer production support and to administer a new system whereby film-makers could receive state support for specific projects on the basis of scripts read by a commission initially chaired by the writer Rachid Mimouni. The new privatization, combined with the increasing political turmoil and waves of mass killings, seriously disrupted Algerian cinema and its links with the outside world. Only four Algerian features were seen abroad in 1995–7: one in 1995, one in 1996 and two in 1997. Many film-makers have been forced into exile.

In Morocco, the Centre Cinématographique Marocain (CCM) had considerable experience of short film-making before feature-film production began in 1968, twelve years after independence. The delay in undertaking such production had its origins largely in the attitude of the government. Whereas in Algeria the government had been keen from the outset to promote feature film-making, in Morocco the authorities seemed initially indifferent to the medium. The CCM had been created in the 1940s as an essentially colonial organization, yet it was allowed to continue to exist with virtually unchanged functions after independence – though with the newsreel service restructured in 1958 as an independent production facility, the *Actualités Marocaines*. Significantly, CCM is responsible not – as is usually the case with state film-production organizations – to the Ministry of Culture, but to the Ministry of Information and the Interior. After independence the state took no powers to control film import, distribution or exhibition, and Morocco's 250 35 mm cinemas (mostly in urban centres) were left in the private sector. Inevitably they favoured imported foreign films.

Though the CCM funded or co-funded the first three Moroccan feature films in the late 1960s, it did not immediately continue this support in the following decade: it was not until 1977 that at least partial funding by the CCM became the norm. Even then CCM's sortie into foreign co-production – *Les bras d'Aphrodite / The Arms of Aphrodite* (1978), directed by the Romanian Mircea Dragan – was perhaps as ill-judged as the European co-productions undertaken by the Algerian state production company, ONCIC, in this same period. The advances in the provision of facilities for laboratory and dubbing work – with the opening of new studios at Aïn Chok (Casablanca) in 1970 to supplement those in existence at Souissi since 1944 – had little or no impact on the level of production, which remained low throughout the 1970s. The situation changed radically in 1980 when the government introduced a system of assistance for production (the so-called 'fonds de soutien'), which had the effect of greatly stimulating production activity in Morocco. Initially, the 1980 scheme paid no attention to quality, but it did serve to foster production. The 1980s saw an upsurge in film-making with the production of thirty-eight feature films, twenty-one of them made by new directors. The plan was undoubtedly well-intentioned, but the sums offered were small and they were paid only after the completion of the film. Moreover, the scheme was not supported by any system to control imports or to organize distribution, so that the result was the production of a large number of films for which there was virtually no audience, either inside Morocco or abroad.

In 1988 the scheme was modified again to offer funding largely on the basis of scripts submitted by film-makers. The level of funding increased in the 1990s and new tax concessions were offered to film producers and, for the first time, Moroccan films – especially those with sexual themes and offering a touch or two of nudity – began to attract substantial local audiences.

After independence in Tunisia, the two key organizations which shaped film production and film culture in general were SATPEC and SEACI. The Société Anonyme Tunisienne de Production et d'Expansion Cinématographique (SATPEC) was the state-owned company set up in 1957 to manage production, import, distribution and exhibition of films. In the early 1960s SATPEC attempted to confront the multinational distribution companies whose films dominated the Tunisian domestic market, but a boycott by the foreign majors eventually led to capitulation by the Tunisian government in 1965. Undeterred, in 1966 SATPEC established a film production complex at Gammarth, an ambitious development which, until 1983, unfortunately could only process black-and-white films. The costs and losses incurred were to lead eventually to the virtual bankruptcy of the parent company in the 1980s and to its closure in 1994.

The Secrétariat d'Etat aux Affaires Culturelles et à l'Information (SEACI) was the government organization set up to supervise culture and information, the cinema division of which was headed by Tahar Cheriaa from 1961 till 1969. In the early 1960s SEACI pioneered the rural distribution of films, setting up a number of cultural centres equipped with 16 mm projectors and organizing a ciné-bus distribution system. It also produced two films directed by foreign film-makers: Mario Ruspoli's documentary *Renaissance* and Jean Michaud-Mailland's fictional feature *H'mida*. Moreover, it was thanks to Cheriaa (and SEACI) that the biennial Arab film festival, the Carthage Film Festival (the Journées Cinématographiques de Carthage or JCC), was founded in 1966. In the 1960s the amateur film movement was also strengthened by the founding of the Association des Jeunes Cinéastes Tunisiens (AJCT) in 1961, the creation of the film review *Goha* (later *SeptièmArt*) in 1964, the establishment of the first amateur film festival FIFAK at Kélibia (also in 1964) and the opening of the first art cinema ('cinéma d'art et d'essai'), Le Globe, in Tunis in 1965.

The 1970s saw the establishment of the Association des Cinéastes Tunisiens (ACT), which in 1971 presented its 'Reform Plan for a Viable Tunisian Cinema'. Under the leadership of Hamadi Essid from 1971 to 1979, however, SATPEC followed a quite contrary policy, buying out foreign distribution companies, sponsoring ambitious conferences (such as the Congress of the International Newsreel Agency and the

Confédération Internationale des Cinémas d'Art et d'Essai in 1976) and turning the seventh session of the JCC in 1978 into a festival for the whole of the Third World, a policy opposed by the ACT, FTCC and FTCA (Fédération Tunisienne du Cinéma Amateur). Essid's policy led to the virtual bankruptcy of SATPEC, but the appointment of Hassen Akrout as his successor in 1979 opened a new era of optimism for Tunisian film-makers, as the government abandoned SATPEC's monopoly of the import and distribution of films and instigated a new system of state aid for short- and feature-film production.

Since the mid-1980s there has been a new and marked emphasis on international co-production and the role of independent producers in Tunisian film-making, in part due to the 1981 law which introduced a system of aid for film producers based on a 6 per cent levy on box office receipts. Key developments have been: the introduction of colour facilities at the Gammarth complex in 1983 and the eventual privatization of the whole production set-up; the opening of the new studios of Carthago Films by Tarak Ben Ammar at Sousse in 1985; the emergence of Ahmed Attia as a major Tunisian film producer with his company Cinétéléfilms in the late 1980s; and the closing of SATPEC in 1994, when it was absorbed into Canal Horizon.

Rural life

The Algerian countryside formed the location for much of the resistance to the colonizer between 1954 and 1962, and many of the war films reflect this. The land reforms of 1972 gave added impetus to the depiction of rural communities, beginning with Bouamari's *al-Faham* / *Le charbonnier* / *The Charcoal Burner* and Tolbi's *Noua* / *Nua* (both 1972), and backed up by many features destined solely for television. Other key works of the 1970s with rural settings include Bouamari's *al-Irth* / *L'héritage* / *The Inheritance* (1974), Riad's *Rih al-Janub* / *Vent du sud* / *Wind from the South* (1975), Mazif's *Masirat al-Ruh* / *The Nomads* (1975) and Amar Laskri's *al-Mufid* / *El Moufid* (1978). Many of these directors themselves came from rural backgrounds, but the narratives tended to be shaped by a simplistic division, depicting the peasants torn between tradition (the wealthy landlords) and new ideas (brought to the community by urban intellectuals). Often contentious issues could only be raised by setting the films – as in the case of *Nua* – in the last years of colonialism. One problem of the rural films – the question of language – was resolved only in the 1990s, when it became possible to make films in the Berber language: Belkacem Hadjad's *Machado* (1995), Abderrahman Bouguermouh's *La colline oubliée* / *The Forgotten Hillside* (1996) and Azzedine Meddour's *Djebel Baya* / *La montagne de Baya* / *Baya's Mountain* (1997).

An interest in rural life dates back to the very beginnings of Moroccan cinema, with the flood of documentaries produced immediately after independence by the CCM being the forerunners for Abdelaziz Ramdani and Larbi Bennani's feature *Hinama Yandhuju al-Tamr* / *Quand murissent les dattes* / *When the Dates Ripen* (1968). Usually depicted as a place of tradition and backwardness, the countryside is the central focus of a wide range of features: al-Maanouni's *al-Ayyam al-Ayyam* / *O les jours!* / *The Days, the Days!* (1978), Mohamed B.A. Tazi's *Lalla Shafia* / *Madame la guérisseuse* / *Medicine Woman* (1982), Mohamed Abdoulouakar's *Hadda* (1984), Mohamed Abazzi's *Kounouz Latlas* / *Les trésors de l'Atlas* / *The Treasures of the Atlas*

Mountains (1997) and Daoud Aouled Sayed's *Adieu forain / Goodbye Travelling Showman* (1998). Whereas the trip from countryside to the city usually ends in disaster, the voyage from the city to the rural south is generally seen as a voyage of reconciliation, as in Hamid Bencherif's *Khutawat Fi Dabab / Des pas dans le brouillard / Steps in the Mist* (1982) and Nabil Ayouch's *Mektoub* (1997).

Tunisian cinema is predominately an urban cinema, focused on Tunis, but on occasion rural settings are used to convey strong social messages, as in Brahim Babaï's *Wa Ghadan … ? / Et demain … ? / And Tomorrow … ?* (1972) and Ridha Behi's *Shams al-Diba / Le soleil des hyènes / Hyenas' Sun* (1977). Occasionally the village or rural community is firmly located in time, as with Ali Abidi's *Redeyef 54* (1997), but usually (as is so often the case with urban films) the time is imprecise, as with Taïeb Louhichi's poetic vision *Dhil al-'Ardh / L'ombre de la terre / Shadow of the Earth* (1982). Often the rural landscape is a timeless poetic setting for a parable: as with Fitouri Belhiba's *Ruqayya / Coeur nomade / Wandering Heart* (1990), Louhichi's *Majnun Leila / Leila ma raison / Leila My Reason* (1989) and Naceur Khemir's *al-Haimun Fi al-Sahra' / Les baliseurs du désert / The Drifters* (1984) and *Tawq al-Hamama al-Mafqûd / Le collier perdu de la colombe / The Lost Collar of the Dove* (1990).

Urban life

The opposition of urban and rural life – as sites of modernity and tradition, corruption and virtue – is fundamental to all African cinema.

Depictions of contemporary urban reality, beginning in the 1970s with Zinet's *Tahia Ya Didou / Alger Insolite* (1971) and Allouache's *Umar Gatlatu / Omar Gatlato* (1976), are comparatively rare in Algerian cinema, but include some major works: Mazif's *Leila Wa Akhawatuha / Leila et les autres / Leila and the Others* (1978), Rabah Laadji's *Saqat Wa'aila / Un toit, une famille / A Roof, a Family* (1981), and a number of studies of the urban troubles of the post-1988 period: Malik Lakhdar Hamina's *al-Kharif – October Fi al-Jaza'ir / Automne – Octobre à Alger / Autumn – October in Algiers* (1991), Chouikh's *Youcef Kesat Dekna Sabera / Youssef: The Legend of the Seventh Sleeper* (1993) and Allouache's *Bab el-Oued City* (1994).

The lure of city life for those living in the countryside, despite its threats and mysteries, is apparent from the very first Moroccan feature, Mohamed B.A. Tazi and Ahmed Mesnaoui's *Intisar al-Hayat / Vaincre pour vivre / Conquer to Live* (1968), and continues with such features as the collectively made *Ramâd al-Zariba / Les cendres du clos / Cinders of the Vineyard* (1977), Bouanani's *al-Sarab / Le mirage / The Mirage* (1980) and Mustapha Khayat's *al-Wata / L'impasse / Dead End* (1984). Yet, for those who live there, the city is often a place of loss and despair – for Hadi in Latif Lahlou's *Shams al-Rabi' / Spring Sunshine* (1969), for Zakaria in Noury's first film *Sa'i al-Barid / Le facteur / The Postman* (1980) and for Miloud in Reggab's *Hallaq Darb al-Fouqara / Le coiffeur du quartier des pauvres / The Barber of the Poor Quarter* (1982) – or a corrupting force that destroys people's ideals – as in Lahlou's *al-Musawama / La compromission / The Compromise* (1986) and Saad Chraibi's *Waqai'a Min Hayat Adia / Chronique d'une vie normale / Chronicle of a Normal Life* (1991). While the enclosed world of the traditional souk features in a number of films, such as Tazi's *Bahthan 'An Zawj Imra'ati / A la recherche du mari de ma femme / In Search of My Wife's Husband* (1993), a special fascination is exercised by contemporary Casablanca, as in Lagtaâ's

Hubb Fi al-Dar al-Bayda / Un amour à Casablanca / A Love Affair in Casablanca (1991) and *Les Casablancais / The Casablancans* (1998).

Tunisian cinema has few examples of the traditional African journey from countryside to city. In Ben Mabrouk's *al-Sama / La trace / The Trace* (1988) a young country girl acquires an education in the city and in Aly Mansour's *Farda Wa Liqat Ukhtaha / Deux larrons en folie / Two Thieves in Madness* (1980) two farcical peasants make their way to the capital. What Tunisian cinema does offer, however, is an analysis of urban spaces, beginning with Ben Ammar's *'Aziza* (1980), which depicts a family which moves from the shelter of the medina to a new development on the outskirts of Tunis. Specific areas of Tunis, such as the medina with its traditions and myths, become a focal point of many 1980s and 1990s films: Boughedir's *Halfawin 'Usfur Stah / Halfaouine l'enfant des terrasses / Halfaouine* (1990), Moncef Dhouib's *Ya Sultan al-Madina / Soltane el Medina / The Sultan of the Medina* (1993), Tlatli's *Samt al-Quousour / Les silences du palais / Silences of the Palace* (1994). More recently new urban spaces have been explored in Mohamed Zran's *al-Sayida / Essaida* (1996) and Louhichi's *'Urs al-Qamar / Noces de lune / Moon Wedding* (1998).

Social realism

The dominant style of the state-run Algerian cinema is a conscious didacticism, whether in depicting total national unity in the liberation struggle or in praising the incontestable advantages of the proposed land reforms of the 1970s. The style has inherent weaknesses: Manicheism, flawless heroes, stereotyped villains, predictable endings. It is therefore to works on the margins of the government's concerns that one has to look for a realist approach capable of depicting if not flaws, at least ambiguities, in society. Works which implicitly or explicitly question the ideological norms of the one-party state include Zinet's *Tahia Ya Didou / Alger Insolite* (1971), Tolbi's *Noua / Nua* (1972), Allouache's *Umar Gatlatu / Omar Gatlato* (1976) and *Bab el-Oued City*

Figure 46 Samt al-Quousour / Silences of the Palace

(1994), Beloufa's *Nahla* (1979), Rachedi's *Tahunat al-Sayyid Fabre / Le moulin de Monsieur Fabre / Monsieur Fabre's Mill* (1982) and Chouikh's *Youcef Kesat Dekna Sabera / Youcef ou la légende du septième dormant / Youssef: The Legend of the Seventh Sleeper* (1993).

Moroccan film-making has a multi-faceted identity but from early on realism was an important feature. The strong strand of realist film-making had its tentative beginnings with Latif Lahlou's *Shams al-Rabi' / Soleil de printemps / Spring Sunshine* (1969), but reached its full flowering with the socially committed studies of urban poverty and oppression by Ferhati (*Arais Min Qasab / Poupées de roseau / Reed Dolls*, 1981; *Shatiu al-Atfal al-Mafqudin / La plage des enfants perdus / The Beach of Lost Children*, 1991), Noury (*al-Mitraqa Wa Alk-sindan / Le marteau et l'enclume / The Hammer and the Anvil*, 1990; *Atoufoula Almortasaba / L'enfance volée / Stolen Childhood*, 1993) and Tazi (*Ibn al-Sabil / Le grand voyage / The Big Trip*, 1981; *Badis*, 1988). There are parallel strands of politically committed film-making, also using a realist style, exemplified by the early work of Benbarka, especially *Alf Yad Wa Yad / Mille et une mains / A Thousand and One Hands* (1972) and *Harb al-Bitrul Lan Taqa' / La guerre du pétrole n'aura pas lieu / The Oil War Will Not Happen* (1974), and also the more documentary approach of al-Maanouni (*al-Ayyam al-Ayyam / O les jours / The Days, the Days!*, 1978).

There are numerous examples in Tunisian cinema of films – whether depicting urban or rural subjects – which are not precisely located in time or place, but instead allude to an ill-defined epoch viewed or remembered with nostalgia. But there are also powerful examples of a socially committed realist approach, beginning with Ahmed Khéchine's *Tahta Matar al-Kharif / Sous la pluie d'automne / Under the Autumn Rain* (1970), Brahim Babaï's *Wa Ghadan … ? / And Tomorrow … ?* (1972), Abdellatif Ben Ammar's *Sejnan / Sejnane* (1974) and Ridha Behi's *Shams al-Dibâ / Hyenas' Sun* (1977). Highpoints of the Tunisian social realist approach, offering acute insights into vital contemporary issues, include Ben Ammar's *'Aziza* (1980), Naceur Ktari's *al-Sufara' / Les ambassadeurs / The Ambassadors* (1975) and four striking features by Nouri Bouzid that treat issues rarely confronted in Arab cinema.

Women film-makers

Among the 250 or so directors to have made a feature film in North Africa, only a handful have been women. Of these, several have experienced considerable difficulties with the state production companies and only one has been able to go on to make a second feature. All have produced films in which women's issues are central, but this in itself does not distinguish them from their male counterparts who have also shown a distinct predilection for making women's role and status in Islamic society a central focus of their films. Like the men, most of the women film-makers were born in the 1940s, before independence, and most have spent long periods in higher education in Europe, before returning to North Africa with their diplomas. The women film-makers in no way form a coherent group, being totally diverse in background, approach and style.

Despite the rhetoric of women's emancipation after Algerian independence, no woman has made a 35 mm feature film for cinema release in Algeria. The two figures of note are both French-language novelists who received funding from the television authorities to make feature-length 16 mm works. Assia Djebar (b. 1936) made two highly personal evocations of women's lives – *Noubat Nissa Jabal Chnouwwa / La nouba des femmes du Mont Chenoua / The Nouba of the Women of Mount Chenoa* (1978) and *Zerda Wa Aghani al-Nisyan / La zerda et les chants de l'oubli / The Zerda and the Songs of Forgetfulness* (1982) – for RTA. Although not conventional feature films, these two works obtained screenings at various international festivals. Hafsa Zinai-Koudil (b. 1951) had published four novels and worked for a time as assistant director when she made the controversial 16 mm feature *Le démon au féminin / The Female Demon* (1993), dealing with a woman who is tortured by fake exorcists when her husband thinks she is possessed by devils. The film was disowned by the production company, ENPA. Zinai-Koudil now lives and works in Paris. A third important figure is Yamina Benguigui, born in Paris but of Algerian descent, who made the highly successful documentary *Mémoires d'immigrés / Immigrants' Stories* (1997) through her own production company in France.

In Morocco in the 1980s two women film-makers each made a single feature film for commercial release. Farida Bourquia (b. 1948), who studied drama in Moscow in the early 1970s, made *al-Jamr / La braise / The Embers* (1982). It is the story of the difficulties encountered by three village children after the deaths of their parents. Four years later, Farida Benlyazid (b. 1948) produced *Bab al-Sama' Maftuh / Une porte sur le ciel / A Gateway to Heaven*, which told of a young woman's return to Morocco to work with other women there, after a period of exile in Paris. In 1988, when the film appeared, Benlyazid (who had studied at the Paris film school IDHEC) was already known as the scriptwriter for two films directed by her husband, Jillali Ferhati. She has since gone on to write two further scripts, this time for Mohamed Abderrahman Tazi, and she shot a second feature – as yet unreleased – in 1998. In Europe, Fatima Jebli Ouazzani (b. 1959, Morocco, but living in the Netherlands since 1970) made a highly successful documentary about the issue of virginity, *Dans la maison de mon père / In My Father's House* (1997).

In Tunisia four women directors have made features over a period of twenty years. The pioneer is Selma Baccar (b. 1945), who studied at the Institut Français du Cinéma (IFC) in Paris. After having problems with the release of her first feature, *Fatma 75* (1978), she continued making short documentaries and working as a producer, before completing a second feature *Habiba M'Sika / La danse du feu / The Fire Dance* (1995). Nejia Ben Mabrouk (b. 1949), who studied at the Belgian film school INSAS, had extreme problems with her sole feature, *al-Sama / La trace / The Trace* (1988) – the film's release was delayed for six years because of a dispute with the state production company SATPEC. In contrast, Moufida Tlatli's *Samt al-Quousour / Silences of the Palace* (1994) swiftly gained an international reputation. The most recent woman to break through is another IDHEC graduate, Kaltoum Bornaz (b. 1945), with *Kiswa, al-Khayt al-Dhai / Keswa: Le fil perdu / Keswa: The Lost Thread* (1997).

ALGERIA

Film was seen as forming a key part of the Algerian liberation struggle and in the mid-1960s the new Algerian government played the major part in the organization of all aspects of cinema, maintaining a monopoly on production, distribution and exhibition through an often bewildering succession of bureaucratic organizations. Given this direct involvement and the fact that Algerian cinema was born out of the war, it is not surprising that the thematic focus of virtually all film-making in the early years was the war of liberation itself, a subject of vital concern to the first generation of Algerian film-makers, many of whom had been active in the struggle.

In all, three features were made by the Centre National du Cinéma (CNC), founded in 1965. *Une si jeune paix / Such a Young Peace* (1965), was a fictional story of the impact of war on the young, directed by the French FNL activist Jacques Charby. Ahmed Rachedi (b. 1938) made his first feature, *Fajr al-Mu'adhdqabin / L'aube des damnés / The Dawn of the Damned* (1965), a compilation film which put the Algerian war within the context of contemporary Third World struggles. Mustapha Badie (b. 1928) made the ambitious *al-Lailu Yakhaf Ash-shams / La nuit a peur du soleil / The Night is Afraid of the Sun* (1965), a three-hour epic study of the origins, unfolding and outcome of the war.

Simultaneously, the newsreel organization, the Office des Actualités Algériennes (OAA), became the base for Mohamed Lakhdar Hamina (b. 1934) who was director of the organization from 1963 until it was dissolved in 1974. Under his leadership the focus shifted, first from newsreel production to short documentaries and then to fictional feature films. Lakhdar Hamina's own first three features offer very varied approaches to the war of liberation. *Rih al-Awras* (or *Asifa al-Uras*) */ Le vent des Aurès / The Wind from the Aurès* (1966), a powerful if conventionally structured dramatic tale of a family destroyed by war, established Lakhdar Hamina's reputation as Algeria's leading film-maker. By contrast, *Hasan Tiru / Hassan Terro* (1967), which was adapted from his own play by the actor Rouiched (who plays the lead), was the comic tale of a little man who becomes a hero by accident, while *Décembre / December* (1972) looked at the issue of torture, not from an Algerian perspective, but through the eyes of a conscience-stricken French officer. Lakhdar Hamina also produced *al-Ghula / El Ghoula* (1972), directed by Mustapha Kateb. The latter had made his acting debut in the FLN theatrical company and had become director of the Algerian national theatre in 1963, before starring in several key post-independence Algerian features.

Alongside these state organizations, the only private company active in 1965–7 was Casbah Films, which specialized in foreign co-productions. Its founder was the former FLN activist Yacef Saadi, whose own story formed the basis of the company's best-known feature, *La Battaglia di Algeri / Ma'rakat al-Jaza'ir / The Battle of Algiers*, directed by the Italian Gillo Pontecorvo.

The other key mid-1960s production organization – set up when the television system was nationalized in 1962 – was Radio-Télévision Algérienne (RTA) which co-produced the first Algerian feature, *al-Lailu Yakhaf Ash-shams / The Night is Afraid of the Sun* (1965) and made numerous 16 mm black-and-white feature-length television films. Among the RTA film-makers who later went on to contribute to the international reputation acquired by Algerian cinema were Abdelaziz Tolbi, Mohamed Ifticène and Mohamed Lamine Merbah.

Though the production context was altered with the founding of the Office National du Commerce et de l'Industrie Cinématographiques (ONCIC) in 1968, the thematic focus remained initially unchanged, with the war at first remaining the dominant topic for treatment, though the approaches to it were many and varied. *Al-Tariq /*

La voie / The Way (1968), ONCIC's first feature, directed by Mohamed Slim Riad (b. 1932) set the pattern. For his sole feature Tewfik Farès (b. 1937), who had scripted Lakhdar Hamina's *Rih al-Awras*, made the Hollywood-style *al-Kharijun 'Ala al-Qanun / Les Hors-la-loi / The Outlaws* (1969). Ahmed Rachedi adopted a blockbuster approach in his first fictional feature, *al-Afyun Wal-'Asa / Opium and the Stick* (1969). Two collectively realized films used an episodic format: *L'enfer à dix ans / Hell for a Ten-Year-Old* (1968) offered six stories dealing with children's experience of the war and *Histoires de la révolution / Stories of the Revolution* (1969) contained three stories of the resistance in action.

Three things are notable about this first Algerian group of film directors in the context of Maghreb film-making. The first is the closeness of their personal links to the liberation struggle. René Vautier and Jacques Charby were both French FLN activists. Ahmed Rachedi had worked with Vautier in the army film unit and followed him to the Centre Audio-Visuel (CAV), where the collective documentary feature *Algérie en flammes / Algeria in Flames* (1959) was made. Mohamed Lakhdar Hamina had worked for the provisional government's film unit in exile in Tunis; Mohamed Slim Riad had been interned in France for his political views. The second is their age. Born in the 1930s, they are, on the whole, slightly older than most of those who were subsequently to dominate Maghreb film-making. Third, they mostly lack formal film-school training. Lakhdar Hamina rapidly abandoned his studies at the Prague film school, FAMU, for trainee work in the Barrandov film studios. Riad and Badie trained in French television at ORTF. Kateb was a professional actor on stage and screen, Farès had collaborated on short films and wrote scripts, Rachedi had participated in the various collectives formed by Vautier.

In the early 1970s ONCIC continued to foster films dealing with the liberation struggle. Amar Laskri's *Dawriyyah Nahwa al-Sharq / Patrouille à l'est / Patrol in the East* (1973) and Ahmed Lallem's *al-Faiza / Zone interdite / Forbidden Zone* (1974) offered dramatic stories of the revolutionary struggle, while Sid Ali Mazif's *al-'Araq al-Aswad / Sueur noire / Black Sweat* (1972) showed a group of miners driven to political awareness by the repression of a strike in 1954. A film to some extent aside from the dominant 1970s trend of treating almost exclusively national subjects, though still a story of armed conflict, is Mohamed Slim Riad's tale of the Palestinian struggle *Sa Na 'Ud / Sanaoud* (1972). But the two compilation films made in the 1970s followed the dominant trend: *La guerre de libération / The War of Liberation* (collective, 1973) retold the whole story of the war through archive footage and *Morte la longue nuit / Dead the Long Night* (1979), co-directed by Riad and Ghaouti Bendeddouche, dealt with the wider struggle against neo-colonialism. In a comic vein, Mustapha Badie's ONCIC feature *Hurub Hasan Tiru / L'évasion de Hassan Terro / Hassan Terro's Escape* (1974) and Moussa Haddad's six-part television serial *Hassan Terro au maquis / Hassan Terro in the Resistance* (1978) for RTA continued the adventures of Rouiched's comic hero, previously chronicled by Lakhdar Hamina. And it was Mohamed Lakhdar Hamina who outshone all these tales of resistance and rebellion with his own epic account of fifteen years of struggle, *Waqa'a Sanawat al-Jamr / Chronique des années de braise / Chronicle of the Years of Embers* (1975), which was the first African or Arab film to win the Palme d'Or at the Cannes Film Festival.

Given that ONCIC was a state organization, it is hardly surprising that the agrarian revolution of the early 1970s found an immediate reflection in the cinema and formed the second collective focus for Algerian cinema. Mohamed Bouamari's *al-Faham* / *Le charbonnier* / *The Charcoal Burner* (1972) and Abdelaziz Tolbi's *Noua* / *Nua* (1972), the latter made by RTA but distributed by ONCIC, began a whole series of films with rural themes. These came to include Bouamari's second feature, *al-Irth* / *The Inheritance* (1974), though his third (*al-Khutwat al-Ula* / *Premier pas* / *First Step*, 1979) was more overtly experimental. Following the main trend, however, were Riad's *Rih al-Janub* / *Vent du sud* / *Wind from the South* (1975), Mazif's *Masirat al-Ruh* / *The Nomads* (1975), Mohamed Lamine Merbah's two features *al-Mufsidun* / *Les spolia-teurs* / *The Plunderers* (1972, made for RTA but given an ONCIC release) and *al-Muqtala'un* / *Les déracinés* / *The Uprooted* (1976), Haddad's *Min Qurb al-Saf Saf* / *Au près du peuplier* / *Near the Poplar Tree* (1972, also made for RTA), Ghaouti Bendeddouche's *al-Shabaka* / *Les pêcheurs* / *The Fishermen* (1976), Lallem's *al-Hawâjiz* / *Barrières* / *Barriers* (1977) and Laskri's *al-Mufid* / *El Moufid* (1978). Another film which belongs broadly to this trend, though adopting a very distinctive approach, is *L'olivier de Boul'hilet* / *The Olive Tree of Boul'hivet* (1978), directed by Mohamed Nadir Azizi. The collectively made *Pour que vive l'Algérie* / *So that Algeria May Live* (1972) drew attention to a whole range of government programmes and achievements, of which rural reform was one.

The sense of conformity to a centrally determined set of themes was strong in the 1970s. When Ahmed Rachedi wanted to deal with emigration, he had first to make the independent low-budget 16 mm film *Le doigt dans l'engrenage* / *A Finger in the Works* (1974) for l'Amicale des Travailleurs Algériens en France. Only then was he able to explore the same subject for ONCIC in the 35 mm feature *Ali Fi Bilad al-Sarab* / *Ali in Wonderland* (1979). *Al-Usar al-Tayyibah* / *Les bonnes familles* / *The Good Families* (1973), a feature made independently on behalf of the FLN by a collective headed by Djafar Damardji, was completed but apparently never distributed by ONCIC.

Throughout the 1970s, however, isolated works of distinctive quality, aside from the prevailing style and mood, were made and distributed. Mohamed Zinet's portrait of Algiers, *Tahia Ya Didou* / *Alger Insolite* (1971), Merzak Allouache's picture of Algerian youth, *Umar Gatlatu* / *Omar Gatlato* (1976) and Farouk Beloufa's *Nahla* (1979), set in Lebanon and produced by RTA for distribution by ONCIC, are films that stand out in the 1970s. Unfortunately neither Zinet nor Beloufa was given the resources to make a second feature, but Allouache did pursue his distinctive path with a succession of further remarkable films in the 1980s and 1990s.

The 1970s were also a period of cross-fertilization between ONCIC and RTA. A number of RTA films were given cinema release, including Tolbi's *Noua* / *Nua* and Merbah's *al-Mufsidun* / *The Plunderers*. Two 16 mm RTA features made by the novelist Assia Djebar – *Noubat Nissa Jabal Chnouwwa* / *The Nouba of the Women of Mount Chenoa* (1978) and *Zerda Wa Aghani al-Nisyan* / *The Zerda and the Songs of Forgetfulness* (1982) – were shown at international festivals. RTA participated in a number of co-productions of films for cinema release, including Allouache's *Mughamarat Batal* / *Les aventures d'un héros* / *The Adventures of a Hero* (1978), Riad's *Autopsie d'un complot* / *Autopsy of a Plot* (1978) and Mazif's *Leila Wa Akhawatuha* / *Leila et les autres* / *Leila and the Others* (1978). Several directors established at RTA were able to direct films for cinema release. Moussa Haddad, for example, made *'Utla al-Mafattish Tahar* / *Les vacances de l'inspecteur Tahar* / *Inspector Tahar's Holiday* for ONCIC in 1973. Films by television directors helped shape foreign perceptions of

Algerian filmic identity, but did not create institutional unity between film and television at home.

Algeria made considerable progress in film-making in the 1970s. Four directors from the 1960s continued to be active and fifteen new film-makers made their debuts. But overall only thirty-three features were made in the decade. The ages and backgrounds of many of the 1970s film-makers were very similar to those of their 1960s predecessors. Mohamed Bouamari (b. 1941) and Mohamed Nadir Aziri (b. 1941) had no formal film training. Abdelaziz Tolbi (b. 1937) had studied film in Cologne but also worked as a trainee in German television, and Moussa Haddad (b. 1937) was a trainee in French television and assistant on foreign co-productions in Algeria. Mohamed Zinet (b. 1932), like Mustapha Kateb, was an actor associated with the beginnings of the Algerian national theatre, Djafar Damardji (b. 1934) had studied theatre in what was then East Berlin, while Assia Djebar (b. 1936) was a novelist who had studied literature in Paris. But there were an increasing number of new directors with at least some formal film-school training, particularly those born in the 1940s. Mohamed Lamine Merbah (b. 1948) and Sid Ali Mazif (b. 1943) were graduates of Algeria's own film school, INC, as were Merzak Allouache (b. 1944) and Farouk Beloufa (b. 1947), who both also completed further studies at IDHEC in Paris. Ghaouti Bendeddouche (b. 1936) was a graduate of IDHEC and Ahmed Lallem (b. 1940) also studied there, albeit for just eight months. Amar Laskri (b. 1942) spent many years studying theatre, radio, television and film-making in Belgrade and Mohamed Ifticène (b. 1943) followed production courses at the Polish film school in Lodz.

In the 1980s the veterans of Algerian cinema continued their careers despite the disruption to production structures in 1984 (when ONCIC was dissolved) and in 1987 (when its successor, ENAPROC, was itself replaced). If the two Hassan Terro sequels – Riad's *Hasan Taxi / Hassan-Taxi* (1981) and Bendeddouche's *Hassan Niya* (1989) – were minor works, the latter director's *Moissons d'acier / Harvests of Steel* (1982) was a more substantial work. Rachedi's *Tahunat al-Sayyid Fabre / Monsieur Fabre's Mill* (1982) was a work showing all the director's communicative vigour. Bouamari's *al-Raft / Le refus / The Refusal* (1982), by contrast, was a more esoteric effort (echoing *al-Khutwat al-Ula / First Step*) which found a less responsive audience in Algeria. Mazif followed *J'existe / I Exist* (1982), a compilation film on women's issues that was co-produced with the Arab League, with a return to fiction in *Huria / Houria* (1986). Allouache made *Rajul Wa Nawafidh / L'homme qui regardait les fenêtres / The Man Who Watched Windows* (1982), before leaving Algeria to make *Hubbub Fi Baris / Un amour à Paris / A Parisian Love Story* (1986) in France. Lakhdar Hamina's two 1980s films, *Rih al-Rimâl / Vent de sable / Sandstorm* (1982) and *al-Sura al-Akhira / La dernière image / The Last Image* (1986), show the continuing pull of Europe and international audiences for Algeria's leading director. After a break of ten years, Laskri completed *Abwab al-Soumt / Les portes du silence / Gates of Silence* (1987).

Two further directors previously active with RTA turned to films for cinema release in the 1980s. Mohamed Chouikh made *al-Inqita' / La rupture / Breakdown* (1982) and *al-Qal'a / La citadelle / The Citadel* (1988). The IDHEC-trained Abderrahmane Bouguermouh contributed *Ourakh al-Hajar / Cri de pierre / Cry of Stone* (1986).

The ranks of directors were reinforced in the 1980s by eleven further recruits. Ali Ghalem (b. 1943) returned from film work in exile in France to make a rather muted version of his own novel, *Zawja Li Ibny / Une femme pour mon fils / A Wife for My*

Son (1982). Tayeb Mefti directed *Le mariage de Moussa / Moussa's Wedding* (1983). Ghalem and Mefti are self-taught film-makers, but most of the other newcomers were film-school graduates.

Rabah Laradji (b. 1943), who had studied at INC in Algiers, made *Saqat Wa'aila / A Roof, a Family* (1981). Brahim Tsaki (b. 1946), who was trained at INSAS in Brussels, made two highly original studies of children: *Abna al-Rih / Children of the Wind* (1981) and *Hikaya Liqa / Story of a Meeting* (1983). Jean-Pierre Lledo (b.1947), who had studied at the State Institute of Cinema (VGIK) in Moscow, made his debut with *Mamlakat al-Ahlam / L'empire des rêves / Empire of Dreams* (1982). Mahmoud Zemmouri (b. 1946), an IDHEC graduate who had directed a feature in France, went on to make the first of three Algerian features, *Sanawât al-Twist al-Majnouna / Les folles années du twist / The Crazy Years of the Twist* (1984), which brought a quite new tone to the depiction of the liberation struggle and of contemporary Algeria. Mohamed Meziane Yala (b. 1946), who had studied at Lodz in Poland, made *Ughniyat al-Kharif / Chant d'automne / Autumn Song* (1983). Sid Ali Fettar (b. 1943), who had enrolled at INC in Algiers and completed his studies in Lodz, made a family drama: *Rai* (1987). Mohamed Rachid Benhadj (b. 1949), who had trained as an architect and worked at RTA, made his feature-film debut with *Louss / Rose des sables / Desert Rose* (1989) which received wide acclaim. In addition two young directors, Mustapha Mengouchi and Rabah Bouchemha, completed four episodes for a film on children's role in the liberation struggle as *Nous irons sur la montagne / We Shall Go Onto the Mountain* (1987).

The 1980s marked a first slight falling off in the level of Algerian production from thirty-three features and nineteen active film-makers in the 1970s to twenty-seven features and eighteen active film-makers in the 1980s. None of the Algerian film-makers, whether veteran or newcomer, was able to make more than two films in the ten-year span, and for the first time Moroccan production outstripped Algerian output. A new generation of feature film-makers made its appearance, all (except for Boughermouh) born in the 1940s and all (except for Ghalem and Mefti) film-school trained. But the opportunities offered to them were very limited.

Initially the 1987 reforms seemed to favour Algerian production and fifteen features were released in 1990–3 – an average of almost four a year. The early 1990s saw new films from a number of established directors of the 1970s and 1980s. ENPA co-produced *Les enfants des néons / The Neon Children* (1990), made by Brahm Tsaki in France, and *Le cri des hommes / The Cry of Men* (1990), which was the second film of Okacha Touita (b. 1943) who had previously made *Les sacrifiés / The Sacrificed* (1982) in France. Mahmoud Zemmouri made a further satire, *De Hollywood à Tamanrasset / From Hollywood to Tamanrasset* (1990), Jean-Pierre Lledo completed his second feature, *Adhwa' / Lumières / Lights* (1992), Sid Ali Fettar directed *Amour interdit / Forbidden Love* (1993), and the new head of ENPA, Mohamed Lamine Merbah, made a 16 mm feature, *Radhia* (1992). Djafar Damardjji, whose first film dates from 1972, finally completed a second, *Errances / Wanderings*, also known as *Terre en cendres / Land in Ashes* (1993).

A new generation, quite literally, emerged with the feature debut of Mohamed Lakhdar Hamina's son, Malik Lakhdar Hamina (b. 1962): *al-Kharif – October Fi al-Jaza'ir / Automne – Octobre à Alger / Autumn – October in Algiers* (1991). Many of the other 1990s newcomers making cinema films came from the old RTA. Mohamed

Hilmi (b. 1931) wrote and directed *El Ouelf Essaib* (1990), the IDHEC-trained Benamar Bakhti (b. 1942) made the highly successful *Le clandestin / Moonlighting* (1991), Rabah Bouberras (b. 1950), who had studied at VGIK in Moskow and made a number of RTA television features, directed *Sahara Blues* (1991), followed by *La nostalgie du monde / Nostalgia for the World* (1994), Rachid Ben Brahim (b. 1951), who trained in France, directed *Le troisième acte / The Third Act* (1992), Hadj Rahim made *Le portrait / The Portrait* (1994) and Abderrazak Hellal directed *No. 365* (1994) and *Question d'honneur / Question of Honour* (1997).

Other early 1990s debuts include those of journalist Saïd Ould Khelifa with *Ombres blanches / White Shadows* (1991), Rabie Benmokhtar (b. 1944) with *Marathon Tam* (1992), and the IDHEC-trained film editor-turned-director Rachid Benallal (b. 1946) with *Ya Ouled* (1993). ENPA also initially supported the female novelist Hafsa Zinai-Koudil, whose controversial *Le démon au féminin / The Female Demon* (1993) led to a dispute with the producers.

The year 1993 saw yet another – even more radical – reorganization of film production, when production was privatized and film directors were given three-years' salary and invited to set up their own companies and seek state support for specific projects on the basis of script proposals. This reorganization, coinciding with widespread political upheaval, seriously threatened Algerian film output.

The confusions within the film industry and the chaos within society at large, as Islamic fundamentalists continued their war on politicians, intellectuals and foreigners, were clearly reflected in a number of films of 1993–4. In Mohamed Rachid Benhadj's second film, *Touchia / Tushia* (1993), a woman trapped in her flat by Islamic demonstrators in 1991 recalls a parallel disillusionment when her 1950s dreams of independence ended in rape and the death of her closest friend. Mahmoud Zemmouri's *Sharaf al-Qabilu / L'honneur de la tribu / The Honour of the Tribe* (1993) begins as an apologia for the new Islamic force for change, but ends with a caption that contradicts the whole logic of the narrative: 'Djamel and his friends have now shown their true faces. People die every day in Algeria.' In Mohamed Chouikh's *Youcef Kesat Dekna Sabera / Youssef: The Legend of the Seventh Sleeper* (1993) an amnesiac travels through the country failing to find in contemporary Algeria any of the ideals for which he and his colleagues fought during the liberation struggle. Perhaps the clearest depiction of the Algerian predicament is Merzak Allouache's *Bab el-Oued City* (1994) which depicts unemployed young men who find a sense of direction in the new rigid Islamic attitudes and young women whose lives are stifled in the new environment.

Since 1995 production in Algeria has been reduced to a mere trickle of one or two films a year, most of them French co-productions exploring the strengths and contradictions of traditional attitudes. They mark a retreat from the urban environment and a shift from realistic narratives to fables and allegories. Some film-makers have turned to the Atlas mountains. The first three films in the Berber language were released in 1995–7. The INSA graduate Belkacem Hadjhad (b. 1950), who was well-known for short films (such as *La goutte / The Drop*, 1989) and who had made three feature-length television films for RTA (including a collection of five short films called *El Khamssa*, 1988), led the way with *Machado* (1995). Abderrahman Bouguermouh followed with his long-delayed *La colline oubliée / The Forgotten Hillside* (1996), based on the novel by Mouloud Mammeri. Another film to depict a mountain community and to use the Berber language was *Djebel Baya / La montagne de Baya / Baya's Mountain* (1997), a first fictional film by Azzedine Meddour (b. 1947) – a documentarist who had studied at the Moscow film school VGIK. Other film-makers, such as Mohamed Chouikh with *L'arche du désert / The Desert Ark* (1997), have looked instead at remote desert communities and explored the validity of their values and traditions.

But for many other film-makers the only choice has been exile. Merzak Allouache has made two films in France *Salut cousin! / Hello Cousin!* (1997) and *Alger – Beyrouth: Pour mémoire / Algiers – Beirut: In Remembrance* (1998). Mahmoud Zemmouri directed his musical film, *100% Arabica* (1997), in France and Mohamed Rachid Benhadj shot *L'Albero Dei Destini Sospesi / The Tree of Suspended Fates* (1997) in Italy.

Filmography

Abna al-Rih / Les enfants du vent / Children of the Wind

1981, 75 mins, colour
Director / Screenwriter: Brahim Tsaki
Producer: ONCIC
Screenwriter: Mustapha Belmihoub
Music: Djillali
Set Design: Larbi Chenit
Editor: Tachid Soufi
Leading Players: Djamel Youbi, Benanni Boualem, the children of Sidi Yacoub

Abna al-Rih, Brahim Tsaki's remarkable first film, shows his characteristic insight into the lives of children and sympathy for the disabled. It comprises three stories, each of which shows the difficulties confronted by children in contemporary Algeria. 'Boiled Eggs' / 'Les oeufs cuits' is about the disillusionment with the world about him experienced by a boy, whose job is to sell eggs in the bars of Algiers. In 'Djamel in the Land of Images' / 'Djamel au pays des images', a boy struggles to come to terms with the world offered to him daily by the television. By contrast, 'The Box in the Desert' / 'La boîte dans le désert' shows the creative ingenuity of children building fantastic toys for themselves from scraps of wire and metal.

al-Afyun Wal-'Asa / L'opium et le bâton / Opium and the Stick

1969, 127 mins, colour
Director / Screenwriter: Ahmed Rachedi
Producer: ONCIC
Cinematographer: Rachid Merabtine
Editor: Eric Pluet
Music: Philippe Arthuys
Designer: A. Bouzid
Set Design: Sidi Boumediene

Leading Players: Mustapha Kateb, Ahmed Rouiched, Mohieddine Bachtarzi, Abdelhalim Rais, Sid Ali Kouiret, Marie-José Nat, Larbi Zekkal

Ahmed Rachedi's first fictional feature, adapted from a novel by Mouloud Mammeri (who wrote the commentary for the director's earlier feature-length documentary *Fajr al-Mu'adhdqabin / The Dawn of the Damned / L'aube des damnés*) is a classic example of Algerian cinema's depiction of the liberation struggle. Set during the war of liberation, it tells of a young doctor who leaves Algiers for his native village of Thala in Kabylia, where he finds his family divided, one brother fighting in the resistance, the other collaborating with the French. Shot in colour with a comparatively large budget, the film turns the liberation struggle into a Hollywood-style action film, lauding the positive doctor hero and obliterating any ambiguities.

Bab el-Oued City

1994, 90 mins, colour
Director / Screenwriter: Merzak Allouache
Producer: Flash-Back Audiovisuel (Algeria), Matins Films (Paris), La Sept Cinéma (Paris), ZDF (Germany), Thelma Film AG (Switzerland)
Cinematographer: Jean-Jacques Mréjen
Editor: Marie Colonna
Music: Rachid Bahri
Set Design: Philippe Sénéchal
Leading Players: Nadia Kaci, Mohamed Ourdache, Hassan Abdou, Nadia Samir, Mabrouk Ait Amara, Messaoud Hattou, Ahmed Benaissa, Mourad Khen, Simone Vignote

Merzak Allouache's fifth feature film is a return to the quarter of Algiers which had formed the setting of *Umar Gatlatu / Omar Gatlato*, but which has now been totally transformed by the new and violent force of Islamic fundamentalism. Allouache's sharp social and political insights are, as always, accompanied by humour, as the film traces the tragic outcome of a seemingly minor incident: the destruction of a loudspeaker from the mosque that had been placed outside the hero's window. Boualem is driven into exile, his girlfriend abandoned and sequestered, and the marginalized are terrorized as the local thugs – behind whom lurk mysterious forces – take over the quarter.

Charaf al-Qabilu

See *Sharaf al-Qabilu*.

al-Faham / Le charbonnier / The Charcoal Burner

1972, 100 mins, black and white

Director / Screenwriter: Mohamed Bouamari
Producer: ONCIC
Screenwriter: Daho Boukerche
Editor: Ali Medaoui
Music: Ahmed Malek
Set Design: Rachid Bouafia
Leading Players: Fattouma Ousliha, Youcef Hadjam, Ahmad Hamoudi,
                         Mustapha El Anka

Mohamed Bouamari's first feature is one of the films which inaugurated the cycle of films about the agrarian revolution in early 1970s Algeria. It tells of a charcoal burner who loses his livelihood with the introduction of gas into the countryside and who tries to find work in the city. There he finds that his situation as a former fighter in the liberation struggle offers him no advantage. Obstructed everywhere, he also has to come to terms with his wife, who sides with the new order, particularly because of the opportunities it gives to women. Shot simply with a low budget, *al-Faham* – while remaining positive about Algeria's future – raises many issues of immediate concern.

Fajr al-Mu'adhdqabin / L'aube des damnés / The Dawn of the Damned

1965, 100 mins, black and white
Director: Ahmed Rachedi
Producer: CNCA
Cinematographer: Nasreddine Guenefi
Editor: Rabah Dabouz
Commentary: Mouloud Mammeri

Ahmed Rachedi's pioneering feature is a compilation film which looks at the liberation struggle from a pan-African perspective. With a commentary by the novelist Mouloud Mammeri, *Fajr al-Mu'adhdqabin* looks at the whole history of the African continent using a wide variety of materials: books, documents, photographs, enacted scenes and newsreel film footage, much of the latter previously unedited. The struggle is seen as one that concerns the whole of Africa and there is a constant concern to make links between Arab and Black Africa, Francophone and Anglophone areas. This is a powerful celebration of victories and statement of African issues and inherited problems in the light of an emerging sense of a distinct Third World identity.

Leila Wa Akhawatuha / Leila et les autres / Leila and the Others

1978, 85 mins, colour
Director: Sid Ali Mazif
Producer: ONCIC, RTA
Screenwriter: Hamid Ait Amara, Sid Ali Mazif
Cinematographer: Rachid Merabtine
Editor: Anna Ruiz
Music: Ahmed Malek

Set Design: Kamel Messeker
Leading Players: Nadia Samir, Aida, Chafia Boudra

Mazif's *Leila Wa Akhawatuha* tells the stories of two women who are friends and neighbours and who struggle to reshape their role and status as women. Myriem, a young schoolgirl, refuses the marriage arranged for her by her parents, preferring to continue her studies. Leila, a married woman, works in a factory where she struggles for respect, dignity and recognition. Leila organizes a strike which at first causes dissension among her colleagues but is finally supported by all, as the workers recognize their common rights.

Nahla

1979, 165 mins, colour
Director: Farouk Beloufa
Producer: RTA
Screenwriter: Farouk Beloufa, Rachid Boudjedra
Cinematographer: Allel Yahiaoui
Editor: Moufida Tlatli
Music: Ziad Rahbani
Set Design: Kamel Mekesser
Leading Players: Yasmine Khlat, Lina Tebbara, Nabila Zitoumi, Youcef Salah, Roger Assaf, Fayek Hamissi, Ahmed Meehrez

Produced by Algerian television, but in colour and on 35 mm film and intended for cinema release, Beloufa's only feature film to date is a unique and powerful examination of Arab society. It is unusual in being set in Lebanon in 1975, at the time of the civil war. The central narrative thread explores questions of Arab identity through the story of the relationships between an Algerian journalist and three women: the singer Nahla, the journalist Maha and the Palestinian activist Hind. Shot deftly and elliptically narrated, the film captures graphically the confusions of civil conflict and, in retrospect, offers clear insights into and parallels with the developing situation in Algeria. Though eventually shown abroad, it had major initial problems with the censors.

Noua / Nua

1972, black and white, 90 mins
Director / Screenwriter: Abdelaziz Tolbi
Producer: RTA
Cinematographer: Noureddine Adel
Editor: Arezki Haddadi
Set Design: Caoui
Leading Players: Non-professionals

Based on a story by Tahar Ouatar and one of the few television films to obtain international festival screenings, Tolbi's *Noua* gives an explicit picture of the sufferings endured by the peasantry under French rule – high taxation, land seizure, the eviction of the sick, forcible enlistment of young men for military service in Indo-China, imprisonment of those too poor to pay taxes – but ends with the emergence of Algerian rebels who give the people new hope and kill their principal oppressors, the rich landowners. Though ostensibly dealing with the situation in 1954, the film raises issues very relevant to the agrarian reforms of the early 1970s. The film uses a realist style and striking black-and-white images to make its forceful and explicit denunciation of the landowners and their French-educated sons.

Noubat Nissa Jabal Chnouwwa / La nouba des femmes du Mont Chenoua / The Nouba of the Women of Mount Chenoa

1978, 115 mins, colour
Director / Screenwriter: Assia Djebar
Producer: RTA
Cinematographer: Ahmed Sedjane
Editor: Arezki Haddadi, Nicole Schlemmer
Music: Bela Bartok, popular songs
Leading Players: Sasan Noweir, Mohamed Haymour

Assia Djebar was already established as a major French-language novelist when she made *Noubat Nissa Jabal Chnouwwa*, one of the very few Algerian films to be written and directed by a woman. This television-funded film tells the fictional story of Leila – an architect who returns to the family home to investigate once more the circumstances of her bother's death. Her story is interwoven with the documentary accounts of six old women who recall the events of the war and with a section devoted to the legends and battles of the distant past (such as the 1871 nationalist revolt in the area of Mount Chenoua).

al-Qal'a / La citadelle / The Citadel

1988, 95 mins, colour
Director / Screenwriter: Mohamed Chouikh
Producer: CAAIC
Cinematographer: Allel Yahiaoui
Music: Jawad Fasla
Set Design: Rachid Bouafia
Editor: Yamina Chouikh
Leading Players: Khaled Barkat, Djillali Ain-Tedeles, Fettouma Ousliha, Momo, Fatima Belhadj, Boumediene Sirat, Nawal Zaatar

Though originally scripted four years earlier, Mohamed Chouikh's second feature found an immediate response from audiences in Algeria when its release coincided with the October 1988 uprisings. The film paints a claustrophobic portrait of a village on the brink of explosion. Society is rigidly divided: between the haves and have-nots, the polygamous rich and the wifeless poor, the separate worlds of men and women. When the central character Kaddour creates tensions in this community, where men and women keep to their traditional roles, by loudly proclaiming his passion for the shoemaker's wife, the elders, with whom all power resides, inflict a terrible lesson on him by their choice of a bride for him.

Rih al-Awras (or Asifa al-Uras) / Le vent des Aurès / The Wind from the Aurès

1966, 90 mins, black and white

Director:	Mohamed Lakhdar Hamina
Producer:	OAA
Screenwriter:	Tewfik Fares
Cinematographer:	Jovanovic
Editor:	Yazid Khodja, Hamid Djellouli
Music:	Philippe Arthuys
Set Design:	Sidi Boumediene
Leading Players:	Keltoum, Mohamed Chouikh, Hassan El Hassani, Omar Tayare, Ahmed Boughrir, Tania Timgab, Mustapha Kateb

Mohamed Lakhdar Hamina's first fictional feature film is a key work in the history of Algerian cinema. Unlike most Algerian films dealing with the liberation struggle it focuses on a female protagonist, an indomitable mother (played by the celebrated actress Keltoum). The film tells the story of a family destroyed by the war – the father killed while taking part in a resistance attack and the son imprisoned for his own political activities. Its picture of colonial barbarity is unrelenting and the mother dies electrocuted on the barbed wire of her son's prison, vainly trying to reach him.

Sharaf al-Qabilu / L'honneur de la tribu / The Honour of the Tribe

1993, 90 mins, colour

Director / Screenwriter:	Mahmoud Zemmouri
Producer:	Neuf de Coeur Productions, BFK Productions (Algeria), Fennec Productions (France)
Cinematographer:	Mustaph Belmihoub
Editor:	Jacques Caillard
Music:	Jean-Marie Sénia
Designer:	Amielle Belmihoub
Set Design:	Philippe Sénéchal
Leading Players:	Said Amadis, Rabah Louci, Maurice Chevit

Adapted from a novel by Rachid Mimouni, *Sharaf al-Qabilu* is a bleak – if often farcical – look at the impact of twenty-five years of FLN rule, which reflects in revealing fashion the confused situation of Algeria in the early 1990s. Djamel, the film's positive hero, studies law and espouses Islamic values to oppose the corruption of the ruling elite, embodied in the figure of his father. But during the filming the situation changed and the film ends with a caption accusing 'Djamel and his friends' of daily killings.

Tahia Ya Didou / Alger Insolite

1971, 120 mins, colour
Director / Screenwriter: Mohamed Zinet
Producer: City Administration of Algiers
Dialogue: Mimoud Brahimi
Cinematographer: Ali Marok
Music: Hadj M'Hamed El Anka
Leading Players: Mimoud Brahima, Mohamed Zinet, Georges Arnaud, Suzie
                         Naceur, N. Draïs

Mohamed Zinet's film is one of the few 1970s features not produced by the state film
organization and has a very distinctive style and approach. Shaped loosely around the
wanderings of two French tourists, the film begins lightly but takes on a very different
hue when the Frenchman, an ex-serviceman, finds himself unable to endure the stare
of an Algerian he once tortured (but who is in fact now blind). Alongside this very
unheroic view of the war of liberation, *Tahia Ya Didou* also offers a very unofficial
portrait of Algiers, celebrating its poetry and dialect, its city spaces and its ordinary
citizens with a total freshness and a sharp insight.

Tahunat al-Sayyid Fabre / Le moulin de Monsieur Fabre / Monsieur Fabre's Mill

1982, 100 mins, colour
Director: Ahmed Rachedi
Producer: ONCIC
Screenwriter: Commandant Azzedine, Ahmed Rachedi, Boukalfa Hamza
Cinematographer: Rachid Merabtine
Editor: Rachid Mazouza
Music: Noubli Fadel
Leading Players: Jacques Dufilho, Ezzat el-Allali, Sid Ahmed Agoumi,
                         Hassan El Hassani, Catherine De Seynes, Mustapha Halo

Ahmed Rachedi's fourth fictional feature is a brave work, being a ferocious satire on
both the inanities of bureaucracy and (by implication) the stupidities of a one-party
state. It is set one year after independence, when there was a wave of nationalizations
throughout Algeria. The mayor of a remote village is in despair: a high official from
Algiers is coming on a visit and there is nothing for him to nationalize. The film pits
the mayor and his supporters against a Polish immigrant, Monsieur Fabre, whose mill
is targeted. The problem for the mayor is that Monsieur Fabre is known as both an
opponent of French colonial policy and a strong supporter of the FLN.

Umar Gatlatu / Omar Gatlato

1976, 80 mins, colour
Director / Screenwriter: Merzak Allouache
Producer: ONCIC

Cinematographer:	Smaïl Lakhdar Hamina
Editor:	Moufida Tlatli
Music:	Ahmed Malek
Leading Players:	Bennani Boualem, non-professional actors

Merzak Allouache's debut film is a key date in the history of Algerian cinema, marking an end to the endless tales of revolution and agrarian reform, and offering instead an amusing and very unofficial view of the post-revolutionary generation growing up in Algiers. In addition to its vivid portrayal of everyday life in a poor suburb of Algiers, *Umar Gatlatu* is a penetrating examination of the consequences of the segregation of the sexes in Arab society. Omar becomes obsessed with a girl whose voice he hears on tape, but confronted with her in the flesh he can only turn and run. Like most of Allouache's work, the film is shaped as a comedy but still full of particular insights that illuminate the wider issues of Arab life.

Waqa'a Sanawat al-Jamr / Chronique des années de braise / Chronicle of the Years of Embers

1975, 195 mins, colour

Director:	Mohamed Lakhdar Hamina
Producer:	ONCIC
Screenwriter:	Mohamed Lakhdar Hamina, Tewfik Fares
Cinematographer:	Marcello Gatti
Editor:	Youssef Tobni
Music:	Philippe Arthuys
Leading Players:	Jorgo Voyagis, Larbi Zekkal, Mohamed Lakhdar Hamina, Sid Ali Kirouet, Nadia Talbi, Leïla Shenna, Taha El Amiri

Lakhdar Hamina's *Waqa'a Sanawat al-Jamr* is a monumental epic tracing the main events in Algeria's history between 1939 and 1954. The film interweaves two stories, those of the knowing madman (played by Lakhdar Hamina himself) and the mythologized figure of Ahmed, an uneducated peasant transformed into master swordsman and revolutionary. Designed as a flamboyant celebration of the Algerian revolution, the film succeeded in being the first Arab or African film to win the Palme d'Or at the Cannes Film Festival. But beneath the vivid surface, the film offers less political insight than purely lyrical protest, with poverty and suffering presented in lushly beautiful images.

Youcef Kesat Dekna Sabera / Youcef ou la légende du septième dormant / Youssef: The Legend of the Seventh Sleeper

1993, 105 mins, colour

Director / Screenwriter:	Mohamed Chouikh
Producer:	CAAIC, ENPA
Cinematographer:	Allel Yahiaoui
Music:	Khaled Barkat
Set Design:	Rachid Bouafia

Editor: Yamina Chouikh
Leading Players: Mohamed Ali Allalou, Selma Shiraz, Youcef Benadouda,
                      Dalila Helilou, Mohamed Benguettaf, Azzedine Medjoubi

A variant of the traditional tale of a warrior who sleeps for centuries, Chouikh's *Youcef Kesat Dekna Sabera* tells of an amnesiac who has spent decades in hospital. Emerging, he can find no trace of the new society for which he and his colleagues fought against the colonizers, as he wanders through contemporary Algeria. Indeed, he is convinced that Algeria is still under colonial rule. How can independence have been won when everywhere he finds exploitation, poverty, suffering, humiliation, injustice? A rambling, episodic film, *Youcef* gives the clearest possible portrait of the political void in 1990s Algeria that allowed the upsurge of Islamic fundamentalism.

List of film-makers

Allouache, Merzak (b. 1944, Algiers, Algeria)

One of Algeria's leading directors since the mid-1970s, Allouache was a graduate of the short-lived film school Institut National de Cinéma d'Alger (INA) at Ben Aknoun, studying in 1967 alongside such future feature film-makers as Farouk Beloufa and Sid Ali Mazif. His graduation films (*Le voleur* / *The Thief* and *Pensée Intime* / *Intimate Thought*) were never given a soundtrack but, along with the first works of his fellow graduates, they formed part of the programme *Alger vu par ...* / *Algiers Seen By ...*, which was given one or two showings at the Cinémathèque Algérienne in the late 1960s. Allouache subsequently completed his studies at IDHEC in Paris. He worked first for the newsreel office, the OAA, and later for the CNC within the Ministry of Information and Culture, where he was involved with the ciné-bus service and its support for the agrarian revolution. He made his first documentary, *Nous et la révolution agraire* / *Our Part in the Agrarian Revolution* (1975), for the Ministry. He also worked as assistant on Mohamed Slim Riad's *Rih al-Janub* / *Le vent du sud* / *Wind from the South* (1975). On joining ONCIC, he co-directed a further 16 mm documentary, *Tipasa l'ancienne* / *Ancient Tipasa* (1975).

In the late 1980s, after returning from shooting a feature in Paris, Allouache began a projected series of fifty-minute video documentaries with *Ba'ada Uctubar* / *L'après-octobre* / *After October* (1989) and *Femmes en mouvement* / *Women on the Move* (1990), the latter co-directed by Assia Djebar and Hamid Djellouli. He has subsequently made other documentaries: *Voices of Ramadhan* (1991, for BBC2 in London) and *Jours tranquilles en Kabylie* / *Quiet Days in Kabylia* (1994). He has also made some shorter fictional works: *Caméra interdit* / *Cameras Forbidden*, *Donyazad et Mordjane* / *Donyazad and Mordjane* (1996), *Dans le décapotable* / *In the Convertible* (1996).

Allouache's international reputation as one of North Africa's leading film-makers rests on six very varied and original features made in Algeria and France. His debut with *Umar Gatlatu* / *Omar Gatlato*, made for ONCIC in 1976, is a key date in the history of Algerian cinema. *Umar Gatlatu* marks an end to the endless tales of national liberation and the agrarian revolution, offering instead an amusing and very unofficial view of the post-revolutionary generation growing up in Algiers. *Mughamarat Batal* / *Les aventures d'un héros* / *The Adventures of a Hero* (1978) is a philosophic fable, the story of a young peasant, Mehdi, who is given the role of confronting twentieth-century oppression and injustice, and who roams through time and space, reality and legend. *Rajulun Wa Nawafidh / L'homme qui regardait les fenêtres / The Man who Looked at Windows* (1982), a brooding view of contemporary Algeria, comprises the dark visions of a middle-aged bureaucrat whose life is over-turned when he is transferred to the film-book section of the library where he works and whose path leads him eventually to commit murder. *Hubbub Fi Baris / Un amour à Paris / A Parisian Love Story* (1986), a French-language feature shot in Paris, tells the doomed love story of a French Jewish woman from Algiers and an Algerian youth, born in Clichy, which contrasts their dreams (becoming a model, training as an astro-naut) with the bleak reality of their lives. *Bab el-Oued City* (1994) is a return to the quarter of Algiers which had formed the setting of *Umar Gatlatu*, but which is now totally transformed by the new and violent force of Islamic fundamentalism. The film is a major statement about contemporary Algiers. Forced into exile, Allouache completed his sixth feature in France. *Salut cousin! / Hello Cousin!* (1996) is a much more light-hearted study of the lives and adventures of two cousins, one a thoroughly Parisianized second-generation immigrant and the other newly arrived from Algiers. Allouache's subsequent feature-length work was the French television film, *Alger – Beyrouth, pour mémoire / Algiers – Beirut, In Remembrance* (1998), in which a French journalist, on a visit to Beirut, revives a romance with an acquaintance from Algiers but only succeeds in reactivating the man's sense of guilt and driving him suicidally back to his native city.

Beloufa, Farouk (b. 1947, Oued Fodda, Algeria)

Beloufa received his film training at both the short-lived INC at Ben Aknoun (along-side Merzak Allouache and Sid Ali Mazif) and at IDHEC in Paris, from which he graduated in 1967. Subsequently he studied under Roland Barthes at the Ecole Pratique des Hautes Etudes in Paris, completing a thesis on film theory. From his early shorts, *Situation de transition / State of Transition* (1966) and *Travesties et cassures noir sur blanc / Disguises and Fractures in Black and White* (1967), both made during his studies at IDHEC, his strong aesthetic sense is apparent. His strong political views caused his compilation film, *Insurrectionelle / Insurrectionary* (1973), to be re-edited by the Algerian authorities and released as a collective work under the title *La guerre de libération / The War of Liberation*. In 1976 he worked as assistant to the great Egyptian director Youssef Chahine on the feature film *'Awat al-Ibn al-Dall / The Return of the Prodigal Son*, which was made as a co-production with the Algerian state film corporation, ONCIC.

Beloufa's sole fictional feature is *Nahla* (1979), produced by RTA but shot on 35 mm and intended for a cinema release. One of the few Algerian films to look at problems outside the national framework, *Nahla* is set in Lebanon at the outbreak of the civil war and paints a vivid picture of Lebanese life at the beginning of 1975. The film follows the relationships between an Algerian journalist and three women: the singer Nahla, the journalist Maha and the Palestinian activist Hind. Shot deftly and elliptically narrated, the film captures graphically the confusions of civil conflict. Despite the critical success which the film achieved, Beloufa has not as yet made a second feature.

Bouamari, Mohamed (b. 1941, Sétif, Algeria)

Bouamari received no formal training in film-making. He worked as assistant director for ONCIC on *Fajr al-Mu'adhdqabin / The Dawn of the Damned* (Ahmed Rachedi, 1965), *Rih al-Awras / The Wind from the Aurès* (Mohamed Lakhdar Hamina, 1966), *al-Tariq / The Way* (Slim Riad, 1967), *Z* (Costa-Gavras, 1968), *Remparts d'argile / Ramparts of Clay* (Jean-Louis Bertucelli, 1969). Simultaneously he began a career as a short film-maker, directing *Conflit / Conflict* (1963), *L'obstacle / The Obstacle* (1966), *La cellule / The Cell* (1967) and *Le Ciel et les Affaires / Heaven and Business* (1967).

Bouamari achieved a considerable reputation with his first two features. *al-Faham / The Charcoal Burner* (1972) is the story of a charcoal burner who loses his livelihood with the introduction of gas into the countryside and who tries to find work in the city. Obstructed everywhere, he also has to come to terms with his wife, who sides with the new order – particularly the opportunities it gives to women. *al-Faham* has considerable historical interest as the film which began a cycle of works devoted to the agrarian revolution. *Al-Irth / The Inheritance* (1974), a further contribution to the agrarian revolution, deals with the heritage of colonialism, focusing on the plight of Belkacem, driven to madness by torture by the French, and his wife, who both restores his sanity and leads the progressive forces in rebuilding the village.

In these first two films, both starring his wife Fattouma Ousliha, Bouamari's formal concerns are balanced by his engagement with social problems and issues in Algeria. But his subsequent two features, *al-Khutwat al-Ula / The First Step* (1979) and *al-Raft / The Refusal* (1982) are more esoteric and formalist works – akin to some of the contemporary film work in Morocco. *al-Khutwat al-Ula*, for example, is a complexly structured tale of a woman who becomes a leader in her community, as Algerian society takes its first step towards the emancipation of women. The story may be a conventional moral tale, but the style is unorthodox: the actors are introduced to us as themselves before being assigned their roles and proceed to act out variations on the scenes in which they are to appear. Neither of these films found critical acclaim nor a positive audience response in Algeria, and with them Bouamari's career seems to have come to an end.

Chouikh, Mohamed (b. 1943, Mostaganem, Algeria)

Chouikh began his career as an actor, joining the Algerian national theatre in 1963. In addition to his stage work, Chouikh starred in several of the key pioneering Algerian films of the late 1960s, including *Rih al-Awras / The Wind from the Aurès* (Mohamed Lakhdar Hamina, 1966) and *al-Kharijun 'Ala al-Qanun / The Outlaws* (Tewfik Fares, 1969). He also appeared in short films which marked the emergence of other key film-makers: Mohamed Bouamari's *L'obstacle / The Obstacle* (1966) and Ahmed Lallem's *Lauriers roses / The Pink Laurels* (1968). He continued his acting career into the 1970s, appearing in the French director Michel Drach's ONCIC co-production *Elise or Real Life / Elise ou la vraie vie* (1970), Sid Ali Mazif's *Masirat al-Ruh / The Nomads* (1975), Amar Laskri's *al-Mufid / El Moufid* (1978) and the television serial, *Es Silane / Barbelés / Barbed Wire* (1981), directed by Ahmed Rachedi. He also wrote the commentary for Annie Tresgot's *Les passagers / The Passengers* (1971).

Chouikh was writer-director of two feature-length television films for RTA: *L'embouchure / The Mouth* (1972–4) and *Les paumés / The Wrecks* (1974). He was assistant director for Mohamed Lakhdar Hamina's *Rih al-Rimal / Vent de sable / Sandstorm* (1982) and subsequently wrote and directed films for cinema release. *Al-Inqita' / La rupture / Breakdown* (1982), produced by ONCIC, was set in colonial times and told of a young man who escapes from prison with his poet friend, abducts the woman he loves, but is eventually recaptured by the colonial forces. *al-Qal'a / The Citadel* (1988), produced by CAAIC, deals with the love of Keddour for the shoe-maker's wife, which creates tensions. In a community where men and women keep to their traditional roles, this love can lead only to disaster. *Youcef Kesat Dekna Sabera / Youssef: The Legend of the Seventh Sleeper* (1993), a CAAIC–ENPA co-production, is a vivid portrait of the confusions in Algeria at the beginning of the 1990s. An amne-siac who has spent decades in hospital can find no trace of the new society for which he and his colleagues had fought against the colonizers, as he wanders in a stupor through contemporary Algeria. The Franco-Algerian co-production, *L'arche du désert / The Desert Ark* (1997), is an allegory on the origins of violence. An innocent embrace between two young people who love each other plunges the community into a crisis that leads eventually to death and destruction.

Djebar, Assia (b. 1936, Chercheli, Algeria)

Djebar's real name is Fatima Zohra Imalayen. She studied at the Ecole Normale Supérieure de Sèvres in Paris. Best known as a French-language writer, she has published numerous novels and collections of stories – *La soif / Thirst* (1957), *Les impatients / The Impatient* (1958), *Les enfants du nouveau monde / Children of the New World* (1962), *Les allouettes naïves / The Naïve Seagulls* (1967), *Femmes d'Alger dans leur appartements / Algerian Women in Their Apartments* (1980), *L'amour, la fantasia / Love, Fantasia* (1985), *Ombre sultane / Shadow Sultaness* (1987), *Loin de Médine / Far From Medina* (1991), *Vaste est la prison / Vast is the Prison* (1995), *Le blanc de l'Algérie / The White of Algeria* (1996), *Les nuits de Strasbourg / Strasbourg Nights* (1997), *Oran, langue morte / Oran, Dead Language* (1997) – as well as a collection of poems, *Poèmes pour une Algérie heureuse / Poems for a Happy Algeria* (1969), and the essay *Chronique d'un été algérien / Chronicle of an Algerian Summer* (1993).

One of the few women film-makers in North Africa, she has made two poetic docu-mentary feature films for RTA. *Noubat Nissa Jabal Chnouwwa / The Nouba of the Women of Mount Chenoa* (1978) is an innovative work that explores time, legend and collective memory, bringing together a number of narrative threads. The fictional story of Leila – an architect who returns to the family home to investigate once more the circumstances of her bother's death – is interwoven with the documentary accounts of six old women who recall the events of the war, and a section devoted to the legends and battles of the distant past, such as the 1871 nationalist revolt in the area of Mount Chenoua. *Zerda Wa Aghani al-Nisyan / The Zerda and the Songs of Forgetfulness* (1982) was a similarly original personal and meditative work, giving a view of women's place in history and society, and focusing on music as a unifying factor of Maghreb life. In 1990 Djebar co-directed a fifty-minute video documentary with Merzak Allouache, *Femmes en mouvement / Women on the Move*.

Lakhdar Hamina, Mohamed (b. 1934, M'sila, Algeria)

The most forceful of all Algerian film-makers, Lakhdar Hamina originally followed somewhat turbulent studies in France, first of agriculture and then of law. Conscripted into the French army in 1958, he deserted after two months and fled to Tunis. There he worked first in the Information Ministry of the Provisional Algerian Government in Exile (GPRA), then as a trainee in the Tunisian newsreel company Actualités Tunisiennes. In 1959 he went to study at FAMU, the Czech film school in Prague, at a time when the students included future directors such as Jaromil Jirès, Evald Schorm and Vera Chytilova. He abandoned his studies for practical work in the Barrandov studios, specialising in camerawork. He wrote and co-directed three short films: *Homer's Island*, *In the Kingdom of Neptune* and *The Treasures of Mahdia*. On visits to Tunis he photographed several shorts for Djamal Chanderli: *Yasmina* (1961), *Saout Eshaab / The Voice of the People* (1961) and *Banadiq al-Huria / The Guns of Liberty* (1962). After the Evian Agreements in 1962 he made a number of documentaries on pre-independence and independence issues, then returned to Algeria with some of his Tunis-based colleagues to set up the OAA, the new Algerian newsreel office, of which he was director from February 1963 until it was dissolved in 1974.

The OAA formed the base for his production activity throughout the early period of his production career. He began by shooting reports and documentaries, before going on to make fictional films. His shorts include *July's Promise* (1963), *Light for All* (1963), *Once More* (1963), *You are Looking for Science* (1963), *War on Slums* (1964), *The Tree Campaign* (1964), *Take Care* (1964), *But One Day in November* (1964) and his first fiction *Le temps d'une image / The Time of an Image* (1964).

The first of his three features produced by OAA was *Rih al-Awras / The Wind from the Aurès* (1966), a powerfully dramatic story scripted by Tewfik Fares. The film tells the story of a family destroyed by the war – the father killed while taking part in a resistance attack, the son imprisoned for his political activities and the mother electrocuted on the barbed wire of her son's prison. The film's use of linear narrative and a basically Western style of dramatic structure set the pattern for Lakhdar Hamina's subsequent work and established him as one of Algeria's most forceful and talented directors. *Hasan Tiru / Hassan Terro* (1967) was a work of a very different kind, a comic tale adapted from one of his own plays by the actor Rouiched, who plays the lead. It is a humorous tale of misunderstandings and problems of identity, dealing with a little man who gets caught up in the events of the revolution and becomes a hero against his will. *Décembre / December* (1972) returns to the serious tone of Lakhdar Hamina's first film. It explores the use of torture as a weapon of war by examining the inner struggles of a French officer confronted with the reality of its use by his own side in the war against the Algerian people. In addition to his own work, Lakhdar Hamina also produced the sole feature film of the actor Mustapha Kateb (who had appeared in *Rih al-Awras* and *Hasan Tiru*) *al-Ghûla / El Goula* (1972).

Lakhdar Hamina subsequently joined ONCIC, of which he became director from 1981 to 1984. His most celebrated work is *Waqa'a Sanawat al-Jamr / Chronicle of the Years of Embers* (1975), which was the first African film to win the Palme d'Or at Cannes and a film of considerable visual imagination and power. A monumental epic tracing the main events in Algeria's history between 1939 and 1954, the film interweaves the story of a knowing madman (played by Lakhdar Hamina himself) with that of the mythologized figure of Ahmed, an uneducated peasant transformed into a master swordsman and revolutionary. Made in colour, in a wide-screen format with stereophonic sound – again from a script by Tewfik Fares – *Waqa'a Sanawat al-Jamr* is a remarkable technical achievement, but its narrative stance turns the epic national struggle for independence into lushly lyrical protest which, though emotionally powerful and visually exciting, offers limited political insight.

Both Lakhdar Hamina's subsequent features are expensive, lavishly produced works which show Lakhdar Hamina's ambition to become a sort of Algerian David Lean. *Rih al-Rima / Sandstorm* (1982) is a melodramatic tale of an isolated rural community battered both by the violence of nature and by the more private conflict between men and the women who bear the brunt of the men's anger and frustration. *Al-Sura al-Akhira / The Last Image* (1986), a French-language film with European actors, is further proof of the lure of internationalism for the director. Set in an Algerian village on the eve of the outbreak of World War II, the film shows the disruption caused in the village by the arrival of a new teacher from the metropolis, Mademoiselle Boyer.

Mohamed Lakhdar Hamina's son, Malik Lakhdar Hamina, appeared as a child in several of his father's films, as well as in Costa-Gavras's *Z*. In 1992 Malik directed his own first feature: *al-Kharif – October Fi al-Jaza'ir / Autumn – October in Algiers*.

Mazif, Sid Ali (b. 1943, Algiers, Algeria)

Mazif was assistant on Marc Sator's *Vingt ans à Alger / Twenty Years Old in Algiers*, before joining the short-lived Algerian film school, INC, at Ben Aknoun in 1964. There he made three shorts: *La vie à deux / Life as a Couple*, *Les deux soldats / The Two Soldiers* and *Touhami*. His fellow students at INC included Merzak Allouache and Farouk Beloufa. Mazif joined the CNC just before it became part of ONCIC and made further shorts: *La cueillet des oranges / The Orange Harvest* (1967), *Le paludisme en Algérie / Paludism in Algeria* (1967), *Sucotries el Khemis / Sugar* (1968), *Nifta* (1968) and *Volontariat / Voluntary Service* (1973). He began as a fiction film-maker by contributing episodes to two collective works: 'La rencontre' / 'The Meeting' (one of five stories depicting the war as seen through the eyes of young children) to *L'enfer a dix ans / Hell is Ten Years Old* (1968) and 'Le messager' / 'The Messenger' (one of three stories showing the first days of the new order in a village in the Aurès) to *Histoires de la révolution / Stories of the Revolution* (1969).

Mazif's first solo feature film, *al-'Araq al-Aswad / Black Sweat* (1972), was a story of growing political awareness, set during the period of French rule. The film focuses on a young man, excluded from the education his family had intended for him, who learns the necessity of revolt by working as a miner and experiencing the full force of French repression. *Masirat al-Ruh / The Nomads* (1975), a more overtly propagandistic work, preaches the advantages of collective farming for Algerian peasants. It is the story of three sons who, on the death of their father, each choose different ways of proceeding: one of them leaving for the city, the second trying to continue in the old ways and the third joining one of the new farming collectives. *Leila Wa Akhawatuha / Leila and the Others* (1978), co-produced by ONCIC and RTA, looks at the problems and opportunities for women in Algerian society through the stories of two women – Myriem, a student who refuses an arranged marriage, and Leïla, who struggles for respect and recognition in her workplace. Mazif followed this with *J'existe / I Exist*

(1982), a three-part compilation film which looks at many aspects of women's role in society: women's own aspirations, the role of the state and the contribution of the organizations created during the struggle for emancipation. Subsequently Mazif went on to make another fictional feature, this time a love story called *Huria / Houria* (1986). Set in Constantine, this is the story of the unhappy love affair of two young students whose relationship meets with parental disapproval.

Rachedi, Ahmed (b. 1938, Tebessa, Algeria)

It was in Tebessa that Rachedi joined the first film element of the FLN, the 'groupe Farid', together with the Frenchman René Vautier. Rachedi subsequently reached Tunis where he acquired a professional training. In 1962 he was one of the founding members of the collective CAV, set up by Vautier. From 1964 to 1966 he was director of the Centre de Diffusion Nationale. Director-general of ONCIC from the time it was set up in 1967 until 1971, Rachedi acted in a production capacity for Costa-Gavras's *Z* (1969) and for Youssef Chahine's *al-'Usfur / The Sparrow* (1973) and *'Awat al-Ibn al-Dall / The Return of the Prodigal Son* (1976). For the CAV collective he worked on the short films *Référendum / Referendum* (1962), *Dimanches pour Algérie / Sundays for Algeria* (1963), *Comités de gestion / Management Committees* (1963), *Tébessa année zero / Tebessa, Year Zero* (1963), *Cuba Si* (1964), *La campagne de l'arbre / The Tree Campaign* (1964), *Les Ouadhias* (1964), *Problèmes de la jeunesse / Youth Problems* (1964) and *Les mains comme des oiseaux / Hands like Birds* (1964), and on the feature-length *Peuple en marche / A People on the March* (1963). For the CNC he directed *La commune / The Commune* (1967) and for ONCIC *Les élections / Elections* (1967), *L'informatique en Algérie / Computer Science in Algeria* (1973) and *Les transports / Transportation* (1973). He also contributed to the collective film *Pour que vive l'Algérie / So that Algeria May Live* (1972, co-directed by Sid Ali Mazif, Mohamed Nadir Azizi, Rabah Laradji and Ahmed Kerzabi).

His first solo feature film was the well-received compilation film *Fajr al-Mu'adhdqabin / L'aube des damnés / The Dawn of the Damned* (1965), which looked at the liberation struggle from a pan-African perspective. The commentary of *Fajr al-Mu'adhdqabin* was written by the novelist Mouloud Mammeri, and it was to Mammeri's 1965 novel that Rachedi turned for his second feature and first fictional work, the big-budget production *al-Afyun Wal-'Asa / L'opium et le bâton / Opium and the Stick* (1969). Set during the war of liberation, the film tells of a young doctor who leaves Algiers for his native village of Thala in Kabylia, where he finds his family divided, with one brother fighting in the resistance and the other collaborating with the French. Attracted by question of emigration, Rachedi worked with the novelist Rachid Boudjedra on two feature-length works. *Un doigt dans l'engrenage / A Finger in the Works* (1974) was a low-budget piece, shot in 16 mm, which combines documentary and interview footage with fictional sequences depicting an emigrant who arrives in Paris and promptly gets lost in the *métro*. It was followed by *Ali Fi Bilad al-Sarab / Ali au pays des mirages / Ali in Wonderland* (1979). This 35 mm feature, funded by ONCIC, offers a caustic picture of the situation confronting emigrants in France: Ali is a crane operator who uses a pair of binoculars to study the world below him, into which he is never invited. The film shows Rachedi's skill in handling actors and Boudjedra's gift for finding an original angle on the subject matter. *Tahunat al-Sayyid Fabre / Le moulin de*

Monsieur Fabre / *Monsieur Fabre's Mill* (1982) is perhaps Rachedi's finest work – a formidable satire on populist politics set in 1963. The film pits Monsieur Fabre, a Polish immigrant who has supported the FLN, against the local party bureaucrats who want to take possession of his mill so as to have something for a visiting dignitary from the capital to nationalize. The film is excellently structured, the tone is well-sustained and Jacques Dufilho gives a powerful performance in the lead role.

Rachedi has also worked more recently in television. For RTA he directed the twelve-part series *Es Silane* / *Barbed Wire* (1981), an epic tale of a border village before, during and after the war of liberation. Subsequently he co-directed, for Antenne 2, *C'était la guerre* / *It Was the War* (1992), which intertwines the stories of two men whose destinies come together in the Algerian conflict: a young Algerian who joins the resistance and a French schoolteacher who is recruited into the French army.

Tolbi, Abdelaziz (b. 1937, Temlouka, Algeria)

Tolbi fought in the ranks of the ALN and was sent to Tunis when wounded. He completed his secondary education in Damascus and studied film at the University of Cologne. He worked in German television for some time before returning to Algiers to join RTA, for whom he made a series of feature-length works: *Alger et l'Algérie* / *Algiers and Algeria* (never shown, 1966), *Rendez-vous au Tropique du Cancer* / *Appointment on the Tropic of Cancer* (five one-hour episodes, 1968), *L'homme traqué* / *The Hunted Man* (1969), *L'homme au pilon* / *The Man with the Wooden Leg* (incomplete, 1969), *La cagoule* / *The Hood* (1970), *La clef de l'énigme* / *The Answer to the Problem* (1971). His best-known feature is *Noua* / *Nua* (1972), which was made for RTA but distributed in a film version by ONCIC and shown abroad. Set in 1954, it is a forceful work offering an explicit picture of the sufferings endured by the peasantry under French rule – high taxation, land seizure, eviction, forcible enlistment for military service in Indo-China and so on – but ends with the emergence of Algerian rebels who give the people new hope and kill their principal oppressors.

Tsaki, Brahim (b. 1946, Sidi Bel Abbes, Algeria)

Tsaki began studying drama (both acting and direction) in his home town. Later he pursued further studies at INSAS in Brussels, graduating in 1976. His first film was *Gare de tirage* / *Marshalling Yard* (1975). In 1978 he joined the documentary section of ONCIC. His three features are all studies of children and all privilege the image. *Abna al-Rih* / *Les enfants du vent* / *Children of the Wind* (1981) is a seventy-five-minute compilation of three stories, all giving a precise insight into the particular worlds of children. 'Les oeufs cuits' / 'Boiled Eggs' is about the disillusionment with the world about him experienced by a boy whose job is to sell eggs in the bars of Algiers. In 'Djamel au pays des images' / 'Djamel in the Land of Images' a boy struggles to come to terms with the world offered to him daily by the television, while 'La boîte dans le désert' / 'The Box in the Desert' shows the creative ingenuity of children building fantastic toys for themselves from scraps of wire and metal. *Hikaya Liqa* / *Histoire d'une rencontre* / *Story of a Meeting* (1983), an eighty-minute feature, tells of the encounter between two children from totally different backgrounds who share a common fate: being deaf-mutes. For a while they are able to communicate across the cultural barriers that separate the daughter of an American oil engineer from the son of an Algerian peasant, but eventually they are separated as the girl's father moves on. In 1990 Tsaki went to France to direct the Franco-Algerian co-production *Les enfants des néons / The Neon Children*, the story of two boys (one of them a deaf-mute) and an older French girl with whom the other boy falls unhappily in love.

Zemmouri, Mahmoud (b. 1946, Boufarik, Algeria)

Zemmouri studied film-making at IDHEC in Paris. He then worked as assistant director on two feature films made in France by Ali Ghalem: *Mektoub?* (1970) and *L'autre France / The Other France* (1975). He began his directing career in France with the short film *La brèche / The Breach* (1978) and his first feature *Prends dix mille balles et casses-toi / Take a Thousand Quid and Get Lost* (1981), a sardonic fictional account of the effects of the French government policy which offered immigrants who agreed to return 'home' the sum of 10,000 francs. Two young Algerians, brought up in France and unable to speak Arabic, take up the French government's offer but find it impossible to adjust to life in Algeria. The film's comic approach set the tone of Zemmouri's career after his return to Algeria. There he first made further features which offered a disenchanted look at the country's past and present. Zemmouri is very much part of a new generation of Algerian film-makers for whom the heroics depicted in the films of the late 1960s and early 1970s are alien. *Sanawat al-Twist al-Majnouna / Les folles années du twist / The Crazy Years of the Twist* (1984) depicts the Algerian struggle for liberation as a boisterous farce, peopled by characters concerned only with their own well-being. The film demystified the notions of heroism and selfless commitment that generally appear in filmic representations of Algerian history in this story of a community torn between the demands of the FLN and those of the French army. *De Hollywood à Tamanrasset / From Hollywood to Tamanrasset* (1990) was an equally questioning look at contemporary Algeria. The film deals amusingly with the alienating influence of foreign television on a community in rural Algeria, where the director was born and grew up. The production was hindered by often violent interventions by Muslim fundamentalists. Zemmouri subsequently made a third feature in Algeria: *Sharaf al-Qabilu / L'honneur du tribu / The Honour of the Tribe* (1993). This film is a bleak – if often farcical – look at the impact of twenty-five years of FLN rule, which clearly reflects the confused situation of Algeria in the early 1990s. Zemmouri has since worked in France, completing *100% Arabica* (1997), which combines a satirical look at a poor Parisian suburb with the *rai* music of Khaled and Cheb Mami.

Zinet, Mohamed (b. 1932, Algiers, Algeria; d. 1995, Paris, France)

Zinet was a actor from his teens and had his play *Tibelkachoutine* performed in Tunis when he was just twenty-one. An officer in the ALN during the war of liberation, he was wounded and sent in 1958 to Tunis, where he founded what was to become the Algerian national theatre. In Tunis he also appeared in the play *Le cadavre encirclé / The Encircled Corpse* by Kateb Yacine. He was trainee at both the Berliner Ensemble in what was then East Berlin and at the Kammerspiele in Munich. In 1962 he also worked in theatre in Paris, invited by Jean-Marie Serreau to appear in Jean Genet's *Les bonnes / The Maids* and Eugène Ionesco's *Comment s'en débarasser / How to Get*

Rid of It. Zinet also toured in Scandinavia. On his return to Algeria, he was one of the founders – with Yacef Saadi – of Casbah Films for which he worked for a number of years, including serving as assistant to Ennio Lorenzini (*Mains libres* / *Free Hands*, 1965) and Gillo Pontecorvo (*La Battaglia di Algeri* / *The Battle of Algiers*, 1965). He worked as an actor in two twenty-minute shorts directed by René Vautier, *Les ajoncs* / *The Adjuncts* (1968) and *Trois cousins* / *Three Cousins* (1970), as well as a number of French feature films: *Monagambée* (Sarah Maldoror, 1970), *Le bougnole* (Daniel Moosman, 1974), *Dupont Lajoie* (Yves Boisset, 1975), and the Tunisian film *'Aziza* (Abdellatif Ben Ammar, 1980).

Zinet is best remembered for one unique film, *Tahia Ya Didou* / *Alger Insolite*, in which he also appears. It was produced by the municipal authorities in Algiers in 1971 but not released by ONCIC until five years later. Shaped loosely around the wanderings of two French tourists, the film begins lightly but takes on quite a different hue when the Frenchman, an ex-serviceman, finds himself unable to endure the stare of an Algerian he once tortured (but who is in fact now blind). The film – a homage to Algiers and evocation of the recent war – is an unclassifiable collage of documentary footage, enacted scenes and gags, held together by the music of Hadj Mohamed El Anka and the poetic observations of the eccentric Momo (Himoud Brahimi), who hardly moves from his position on a pier in the harbour but knows the whole action unfolding in the city.

MOROCCO

Though independence was achieved in 1956, it was not until twelve years later that the first feature films directed by Moroccan film-makers were made. The first two Moroccan feature films were both produced by the Centre Cinématographique Marocain (CCM), set up under the Protectorate in 1944 and directed by its employees. These employees had previously made documentaries: *Intisar al-Hayat* / *Vaincre pour vivre* / *Conquer to Live* (1968), co-directed by Mohamed B.A. Tazi (b. 1936) and Ahmed Mesnaoui (b.1926), and *Hinama Yandhuju al-Tamr* / *Quand murissent les dattes* / *When the Dates Ripen* (1968), by Abdelaziz Ramdani (b. 1937) and Larbi Bennani (b. 1930). These initial features were followed in 1969 by *Shams al-Rabi'* / *Soleil de printemps* / *Spring Sunshine*, made by another CCM employee: Latif Lahlou (b. 1939), who had studied at the French film school, IDHEC, in Paris.

The limited state interest and involvement in film-making led to a paucity of films in the 1970s, though during this period two film-makers, Souheil Benbarka (b. 1942) and Abdallah Mesbahi (b. 1936), managed to establish themselves with three and four feature films respectively. In some respects they represent the two opposing poles of Moroccan cinema. Mesbahi followed the pathway opened up by Tazi and Mesnaoui in their first Moroccan feature, *Intisar al-Hayat*, adopting the model of the Egyptian musical melodrama for his first feature-length film *Sukut, al-Ittijah al-Mannu'* / *Silence, sens interdit* / *Silence, No Entry* (1973). Subsequently, in the 1970s Mesbahi made other commercial efforts: *Ghadan, Lan Tatabaddala al-Ardh* / *Demain la terre ne changera pas* / *Tomorrow the Land Will Not Change* (1975) and *Où cachez-vous le soleil?* / *Where Are You Hiding the Sun?* (1979), as well as *al-Daw' al-Akhdhar* / *Feu vert* / *Green Fire* (1976), a co-production with Libya. He also worked for a time in the

Egyptian studios. Similarly, the purely commercial route of Ramdani and Bennani in *Hinama Yandhuju al-Tamr* was followed by the veteran amateur film-maker Mohamed Osfour (b. 1927) in his sole feature-length film, *al-Kinz al-Jahannamy / Le trésor infernal / The Devil's Treasure* (1970).

Benbarka, in contrast, represents a more intellectual strand that runs through the whole history of Moroccan film-making. Trained in film-making at the Centro speri-mentale di cinematografia in Rome and in sociology at the University of Rome, Benbarka worked for five years in Italy as assistant to, among others, Pier Paolo Pasolini. His first feature, *Alf Yad Wa Yad / Mille et une mains / A Thousand and One Hands* (1972), made with some European funding and widely acclaimed on the festival circuit, was an attack on the impact of tourism. He followed it with two further ambi-tious features in which a strong European influence is apparent: *Harb al-Bitrul Lan Taqa' / La guerre du pétrole n'aura pas lieu / The Oil War Will Not Happen* (1974), a political tract in the contemporary manner of Elio Petri or Francesco Rosi, and an adaptation of a play by García Lorca, *'Urs al-Dam / Noces de sang / Blood Wedding* (1977).

A highly intellectual approach and a self-conscious play with narrative form are also apparent in the work of three Moroccan film-school graduates from IDHEC in Paris whose careers also began in the 1970s: Hamid Benani (b. 1940), whose debut film was the highly impressive *Weshma / Wechma / Traces* (1970), Moumen Smihi (b. 1945), whose first film was *Charqi Aw al-Çoumt al-'Anif / El Chergui: Le silence violent / El Chergui* (1975), and Mustapha Derkaoui (b. 1941), whose first feature was *Anba'dh al-Ahdath Biduni Ma'na / De quelques événements sans signification / About Some Meaningless Events* (1974). Derkaoui followed this (unreleased) debut work with the collective feature *Ramad al-Zariba / Les cendres du clos / Cinders of the Vineyard* (1977), made with a group of young film-makers, most of whom eventually directed feature films of their own. They included his brother, the director of photography Mohamed Abdelkrim Derkaoui, Mohamed Reggab, Nour Eddine Gounajjar, Abdellatif Lagtaa and Saad Chraïbi.

Equally distinctive personal paths were also chosen by the Belgian film-school graduate Ahmed al-Maanouni (b. 1944) with *al-Ayyam al-Ayyam / O les jours! / The Days, the Days!* (1978); by Jillali Ferhati (b. 1948), who studied literature and soci-ology in France and began his career with *Sharkhun Fi-l Ha'it / Une brèche dans le mur / A Hole in the Wall* (1978); by Ahmed Bouanani, who followed a series of noted short films with *al-Sarab / Le mirage / The Mirage* (1980), a black vision of the ensnarements of city life set in the 1940s; and by the dramatist-turned-film-maker Nabyl Lahlou (b. 1945), who began with a theatrical adaptation *al-Kanfoudi* (1978).

There is no sense of continuity in terms of personnel, since none of the five direc-tors involved in the three 1960s films worked again on a feature in the 1970s. Some key films – Ferhati's *Sharkhun Fi-l Ha'it*, Benbarka's *'Urs al-Dam*, Bouanani's *al-Sarab*, Nabyl Lahlou's *al-Kanfoudi* and the collectively made *Ramad al-Zariba* – received CCM support. But the crucial experimental first features of Benani, Benbarka, Derkaoui and Smihi were given no state funding and, in all, only fifteen feature films were made in the whole decade of the 1970s.

The increase in production during the 1980s, after the introduction by the govern-ment of the 'fonds de soutien' funding scheme, had a sharply differing impact on

Figure 47   al-Ayyam al-Ayyam | The Days, the Days!

experienced Moroccan film-makers. Abdallah Mesbahi and Souheil Benbarka, who had been the two most prolific Moroccan film-makers of the 1970s, directed just one feature each in the 1980s: Mesbahi making *Ardhu-l Tahaddi | La terre du défi | Land of Challenge* (1989) and Benbarka producing *Amok* (1982), an ambitious anti-apartheid drama made with funding from Senegal and Guinea as well as Morocco.

Other established directors had more production opportunities. Nabyl Lahlou directed four features in the 1980s: *al-Hakim al-'Am | Le Gouverneur-Général de l'Île de Chakerbakerben | The Governor-General of Chakerbakerben Island* (1980), *Brahim Yash? | Brahim Qui? | Brahim Who?* (1982), *Nahiq al-Ruh | L'âme qui brait | The Soul that Brays* (1984) and *Komany* (1989). Mohamed B.A. Tazi (co-director of the first Moroccan feature) made three features: *Amina* (1980), *Lalla Shafia | Madame la guérisseuse | Medicine Woman* (1982) and *Abbas ou Jouha n'est pas mort | Abbas or Jouha is not Dead* (1986). But others could not manage more than two features in the same decade: Mustapha Derkaoui directed *Ayyaam Chahrazad al-Hilwa | Les beaux jours de Chahrazade | The Beautiful Days of Sheherazade* (1982) and *'Unwanun Mu'aqqat | Titre provisoire | Provisional Title* (1984); Moumen Smihi had to wait six years after his first feature before he could make *Quarante-quatre ou les récits de la nuit | Forty-Four or Tales of the Night* (1981) and then a further six before completing *Qaftan al-Hubb | Caftan d'amour | Caftan of Love* (1987).

Other film-makers who had previously shown promise completed only one further feature. Sixteen years after his debut with *Shams al-Rabi'*, Latif Lahlou made his second feature, *al-Musawama | La compromission | The Compromise* (1986). Ahmed al-

Maanouni quickly followed his widely seen first feature *al-Ayyam al-Ayyam* with *al-Hal / Transes / Trances* (1981), but then fell silent. Jillali Ferhati made *Arais Min Qasab / Poupées de roseau / Reed Dolls*, a study of female oppression which set the tone for his mature style, in 1981, but had to wait a further ten years before he worked again.

Over half the thirty-eight films produced in the 1980s were the works of newcomers and many of them did not go on to make a second film. Film-directing debuts came at a rate of two or three a year and in general we find solitary debut films of quite variable quality with strikingly differing themes and subjects. Abdou Achouba (b. 1950) made *Tarunja* in 1980 and Hamid Bensaïd (b. 1948) directed *L'oiseau du paradis / The Bird of Paradise* in 1981. Mustapha Reggab directed, as his only solo feature after his participation in the collectively made *Ramad al-Zariba*, the widely praised *Hallaq Darb al-Fouqara / Le coiffeur du quartier des pauvres / The Barber of the Poor Quarter* (1982). Also in 1982, Hamid Benchrif (b. 1948) directed *Khutawat Fi Dabab / Des pas dans le brouillard / Steps in the Mist* and Hassan Moufti (b. 1935) made *Larmes de regret / Tears of Regret*. In 1983 Driss Mrini made *Bamou*. In the following year, Mustapha Khayat (b. 1944) directed *al-Wata / L'impasse / Dead End*; the Moscow film-school graduate Mohamed Aboulwakar (b. 1946) made *Hadda*, a visually resplendent study of rural life; the dramatist Tayyeb Saddiki (b. 1937) adapted one of his own plays to produce *Zeft*, a quite unclassifiable fantasy about a peasant whose life is threatened by both past and future; and the Lodz-trained director of photography Mohamed Abdelkrim Derkaoui (b. 1945) and Driss Kettani (b. 1947) co-directed *Yawm al-'Id / Le jour du forain / The Travelling Showman's Day* (1984). In 1985 Najib Sefraoui (b. 1948) directed *Shams / Soleil / Sun*, an allegorical tale of a young intellectual's return to confront his feudally minded father, and Said Souda (b. 1957), a martial arts specialist, made the action-drama *Dhil al-Haris / L'ombre du gardien / Shadow of the Guardian*.

There were also two isolated features made in the 1980s by women directors: *al-Jamr / La braise / The Embers* (1982) made by Farida Bourquia (b. 1948), who had studied drama in Moscow, and the striking *Bab al-Sama' Maftuh / Une porte sur le ciel / A Gateway to Heaven* (1987) directed by the IDHEC graduate Farida Benlyazid (b. 1948). Benlyazid, the wife of Jillali Ferhati, had previously scripted her husband's films *Sharkhun Fi-l Ha'it* (1978) and *Arais Min Qasab* (1981), and in the 1990s she co-scripted two of Mohamed Abderrahman Tazi's features.

Three of those newcomers who made just a single feature in the 1980s returned in the 1990s, though in all cases only after a considerable gap. Hakim Noury (b. 1952) had to wait ten years after *Sa'i al-Barid / Le facteur / The Postman* (1980) before he was able to direct again. Ahmed Yachfine (b. 1948), who had studied film in Los Angeles, made *al-Kabus / Cauchemar / Nightmare* (1984), a troubling nightmare vision of the Moroccan past from which the protagonist cannot free himself, but then had to wait eleven years. Mohamed Abbazi (b. 1938), who directed *De l'autre côté du fleuve / From the Other Side of the River* in 1982, did not get a second chance for fifteen years.

Few of the new film-makers of the 1980s were able to make two features in the decade. Ahmed Kacem Akdi (b. 1942), however, followed *Le drame des 40,000 / The Drama of the 40,000* (1982) with *Ce que les vents ont emportés / What the Winds Have Carried Away* (1984). Abdallah Zeroualli (b. 1939) began a first feature, *Le tourbillon / The Whirlwind* (1980), which was left uncompleted until 1995 when it emerged as *Moi l'artiste* / *I'm the Artist*. Zeroualli's second 1980s film, *Rifaq al-Nahar* / *Les copains du jour* / *Pals for the Day* (1984), was completed but failed to be released. By far the most important of the newcomers to make two features in the 1980s is Mohamed Abderrahman Tazi (b. 1942), who followed *Ibn al-Sabil* / *Le grand voyage* / *The Big Trip* (1981) with *Badis* (1988). Both films received foreign festival screenings and Tazi continued his career successfully into the 1990s.

The early 1990s saw the flow of productions continue at almost four films a year, but with far fewer new directors making their debuts and established directors often experiencing long gaps in output. A real sense of continuity is hard to perceive. Of those who made features early in the 1990s, Nabyl Lahlou followed his four 1980s features with *Laylat Qatl* / *La nuit du crime* / *The Night of the Crime* (1991) but was then reduced to silence. Another established director, Moumen Smihi, completed only *Sayidat al-Qahira* / *La dame du Caire* / *The Lady from Cairo* (1991) in eight years. Mohamed Abderrahman Tazi was more fortunate, being able to follow his highly successful comedy *Bahthan 'An Zawj Imra'ati* / *A la recherche du mari de ma femme* / *In Search of My Wife's Husband* (1993) with the sequel *Lalla Hobby* (1997).

Many other established film-makers succesfully continued their careers in the new decade, but again only after a long break between films. After an eight-year gap, Mustapha Derkaoui emerged as the most prolific of all Moroccan film-makers, directing *Riwaya Ula* / *Fiction première* / *First Fiction* (1992), *Je(u) au passé* / *(Ga)me in the Past* (1994), *Les sept portes de la nuit* / *The Seven Gates of the Night* (1994) and a sixty-minute piece called *La grande allégorie* / *The Great Allegory* (1995) in quick succession. After a ten-year gap Jillali Ferhati followed *Shatiu al-Atfal al-Mafqudin* / *La plage des enfants perdus* / *The Beach of Lost Children* (1991) with *Kuius al-Has* / *Chevaux de fortune* / *Make-Believe Horses* (1995). After a similar gap and in a similar realist vein Hakim Noury made *al-Mitraqa Wa Alk-sindan* / *Le marteau et l'enclume* / *The Hammer and the Anvil* (1990), *Atoufoula Almortasaba* / *L'enfance volée* / *Stolen Childhood* (1993) and *Le voleur de rêves* / *The Dream Thief* (1995).

Souheil Benbarka, also after a gap of over ten years, made the historical drama *Tubul al-Nar* / *Les tambours du feu* / *Drums of Fire* (1991; later re-edited as *Les cavaliers de la gloire* / *Horsemen of Glory*, 1993). This was followed in 1996 by another ambitious superproduction: *Delo Pheraoun* / *L'ombre du pharaon* / *Shadow of the Pharaoh*. Mohamed Abbazi had to wait fifteen years before he could make his second film: *Kounouz Latlas* / *Les trésors de l'Atlas* / *The Treasures of the Atlas Mountains* (1997). No less than twenty-five years separate Hamid Benani's debut film *Weshma* from his second feature *Sirr al-Majarra* / *La prière de l'absent* / *A Prayer for the Absent* (1995), an adaptation of Tahar Ben Jelloun's novel, and Larbi Bennani (co-director of the second Moroccan film in 1968) returned to film-making after twenty-seven years with *Le résistant inconnu* / *The Unknown Resistance Fighter* (1995). Equally remarkable was the film-directing debut, at the age of fifty-eight, of experienced producer Mohamed Lotfi (b. 1939) with *Rhésus − Le sang de l'autre* / *Rhesus − Another Person's Blood* (1997).

Another characteristic feature of the early 1990s was the debut as directors of a number of members of the collective that had produced *Ramâd al-Zariba* in 1977. Saad Chraïbi (b. 1952) made *Waqa'a Min Hayat Adia* / *Chronique d'une vie normale* / *Chronicle of a Normal Life* (1991) and *Femmes … et femmes* / *Women … and Women* (1998), Nour Eddine Gounajjar (b. 1946) directed the video *La mémoire bleue* / *Blue*

Memory (1991) and the 16 mm feature *La salle d'attente* / *The Waiting Room* (1991). Abdelkader Lagtaa (b. 1948), who had trained in Lodz, attracted considerable attention with his first feature *Hubb Fi al-Dar al-Bayda* / *Un amour à Casablanca* / *A Love Affair in Casablanca* (1991), which was followed by *al-Bab al-Nasdud* / *La porte close* / *The Closed Door* (1994) and *Les Casablancais* / *The Casablancans* (1998).

Among the debut films by other newcomers of the 1990s was *La fête des autres* / *Other People's Celebrations* (1990), directed by the Paris-trained Hassan Benjelloun (b. 1950), who went on to make *Yarit* (1993) and *Les amis d'hier* / *Yesterday's Friends* (1997). The 16 mm experimental feature *Ymer ou les chardons florifères* / *Ymer or the Flowering Thistles* (1991) proved to be the only film made by Tijani Chrigui (b. 1949), a painter who had earlier co-scripted Aboulwakar's *Hadda* (1984). In 1991 Naguib Ktiri Idrissa returned from teaching in the United States to show his 16 mm production *'Aziza Wa Ittu* / *Azis et Ito: Un mariage marocain* / *Aziz and Itto: A Moroccan Wedding*.

Finally, in 1997, a truly new generation emerged with *Mektoub*, the commercially successful first feature of Nabil Ayouch (b. 1969) who had previously made three fictional shorts. This was followed by debuts from two other younger directors: *Aouchtam* (1998), made by producer Mohamed Ismaïl (b. 1951), and *Adieu forain* / *Goodbye Travelling Showman* (1998), the debut film of Daoud Aouled Sayed (b. 1953) who had previously made several short documentaries.

Filmography

Alf Yad Wa Yad / *Mille et une mains* / *A Thousand and One Hands*

1972, 90 mins, colour

Director:	Souheil Benbarka
Producer:	Euro-Maghreb Films
Screenwriter:	Ahmed Badry
Cinematographer:	Girolamo Larosa
Editor:	Souheil Benbarka
Music:	Abdou Tahar
Leading Players:	Aïcha El Ghazi, Abdou Chaibane, Mimsy Farmer, Si Ahmed

Souheil Benbarka's first feature inaugurates a whole series of Moroccan films showing a concern with social issues which continued into the 1990s. Shot with evident social and political commitment, *Alf Yad Wa Yad* contrasts the beauty and colour of Moroccan carpets with the grim reality of their production, which involves thousands of children whose pitiful wages have to help support their families. While visually opulent, the film confronts head-on the factors that underlie this exploitation: the greed of foreign capitalists and the complicity of the national authorities.

Arais Min Qasab / *Poupées de roseau* / *Reed Dolls*

1981, 88 mins, colour

Director: Jillali Ferhati
Producer: Heracles Productions
Screenwriter: Farida Benlyazid
Cinematographer: Mohamed Abdelkrim Derkaoui
Editor: Jillali Ferhati
Music: Zineb Alaoui, popular songs
Designer: Jillali Ferhati
Set Design: Abderrahmane Khabbaz
Leading Players: Châaibia Adraoui, Souad Ferhati, Souad Thami, Jillali Ferhati, Ahmed Ferhati, Ahmed Boudouadi, Btissam Moutalib

Arais Min Qasab, scripted by Ferhati's wife Farida Benlyazid, follows the customary pattern of Moroccan realist cinema in telling the story of a woman destroyed. Aicha, while still a child, is betrothed to her cousin. As soon as she menstruates, she is married and swiftly has three children. But when her husband dies, her brother-in-law reduces her to poverty and then rejects her when she becomes pregnant. Deprived of her children and her home, she has nowhere to turn. *Arais Min Qasab* is one of the few North African films scripted by a woman and offers a moving picture of female solidarity – between Aicha and her aunt / mother-in-law – and a clear sympathy for those who find themselves outside the bounds of marriage. But it can offer no solution to Aicha's problems in a society depicted as both repressive and exploitative of women.

Atoufoula Almortasaba / *L'enfance volée* / *Stolen Childhood*

1993, 90 mins, colour
Director / Screenwriter: Hakim Noury
Producer: MPS (Sarim Fassi Fihri)
Cinematographer: Girolmao Larosa
Editor: Allal Sahbi
Music: Moncef Adyel
Set Design: Faouzi Thabet
Leading Players: Fadila Mansour, Touria Alaoui, Zhar Slimani, Mustapha Zaâri, Ahmed Saari, Saadia Azgoun, Mohamed Mrani, Fairouz

Hakim Noury is one of the leading Moroccan realist directors, making closely observed studies of the poor and underprivileged. *Atoufoula Almortasaba* is the story of R'kia, a child bought from her peasant family to work in Casablanca. We see her life in three stages: a ten-year-old working as a maid, a teenager experiencing her first love before being betrayed when pregnant and, ultimately, a whore on the Casablanca streets. The fragmentation – with an eight-year gap in the middle of the film – is a little awkward, but the first part in particular is full of acute and well-realized observation of childhood sufferings and dreams.

al-Ayyam al-Ayyam / O les jours! / The Days, the Days!

1978, colour, 90 mins
Director / Screenwriter: Ahmed al-Maanouni
Producer: Rabii Films, CMM
Cinematographer: Ahmed al-Maânouni
Editor: Martine Chicot
Music: Nass El Giwane
Set Design: Ricardo Castro
Leading Players: Non-professionals

Ahmed al-Maanouni's first feature was based on three months' research and shot with a crew from INSAS, the Belgian film school where he had studied. At the centre of the film is the young peasant who wishes to achieve his independence and sees only one way of doing this: emigration to Europe. The director uses the real words and gestures of the peasants to animate his script. Drawing on the real problems and conflicts of rural life that he discovered, the film emerged as a close, perceptive and realistic look at everyday life in a Moroccan village, depicted without any trace of folklore or exoticism.

Ayyam Chahrazad al-Hilwa / Les beaux jours de Chahrazade / The Beautiful Days of Sheherazade

1982, 97 mins, colour
Director / Screenwriter: Mustapha Derkaoui
Producer: Mustapha Derkaoui, Art 7
Cinematographer: Mohamed Abdelkrim Derkaoui
Editor: Mohamed Meziane
Designer: Bachir El Fassi
Leading Players: Meryem Fakhreddine, Mohamed Khalfi, Abdelwahab Doukkali, Fouiza Aaoui, Farid Belkahia, Naïma Lamcharki

All of Mustapha Derkaoui's films are experimental, exploring both the question of storytelling and the nature of cinema, and he is as interested in the inner lives of his characters as in their overt actions. *Ayyam Chahrazad al-Hilwa* is a complex work. It is partly a tale about a woman singer, partly the story of a man who becomes rich, partly the account of a film-maker who fails to make his film. The film constantly shifts registers of time and reality, mixing actuality and fiction in ways that deny the viewer the pleasure of a single extractable meaning.

Bab al-Sama' Maftuh / Une porte sur le ciel / Gateway to Heaven

1987, 100 mins, colour
Director / Screenwriter: Farida Benlyazid
Producer: Interfilm (Morocco), SATPEC (Tunisia), France Média (France)

Cinematographer:	Georges Barsky
Editor:	Moufida Tlatli
Music:	Annouar Braham.
Set Design:	Fawzi Thabet
Leading Players:	Zakia Tahiri Gompertz, Chaaibia Adraoui, Eva Saint Paul, Ahmed Bouanani, Bachir Skirej

After scripting two features by her husband, Jillali Ferhati, Farida Benlyazid turned to directing with this story of a young woman, Nadia, who – after returning home from France to attend her father's funeral – discards her French boyfriend and rediscovers her Islamic identity as a woman working with women in Morocco. The theme of the generation gap – traditionally minded elders and Westernized young people – is a common one in Maghreb cinema, but usually, though the West is criticized, part of the focus is on the limitations of a traditional society. Here Benlyazid advocates a positive vision of a tolerant Islam, through which a woman finds her true place.

Badis

1988, 90 mins, colour

Director:	Mohamed Abderrahman Tazi
Producer:	Arts et Techniques Audiovisuels (ATA) (Morocco), TVE (Spain)
Screenwriter:	Nour Eddine Sail, Farida Benlyazid
Cinematographer:	Federico Ribes
Editor:	Angela Barragan
Music:	Tawfiq Ouldomar
Designer:	Farid Belkahia
Leading Players:	Jillali Ferhati, Maribel Verdu, Zakia Tahiri, Bachir Skirej, N. Lancharki, Aziz Saad Allah, Miguel Molina

Tazi's film is set in a small, remote community living alongside the fortress of *Badis* where Spanish political prisoners are held. The focus is on the friendship between two women: one oppressed in her domestic life, the other (a peasant girl) persecuted because of her love for a Spanish soldier. As their closeness and the pressures grow, they plan to flee together. But when they are discovered to be missing the whole village takes up the chase and they are caught and stoned to death for their actions. Tazi depicts a cruel world in which it is the village women who cast the first stones.

Bahthan 'An Zawj Imra'ati / *A la recherche du mari de ma femme* / *In Search of My Wife's Husband*

1993, 88 mins, colour

Director:	Mohamed Abderrahman Tazi
Producer:	Arts et Techniques Audiovisuels (ATA)
Screenwriter:	Farida Benlyazid
Cinematographer:	Federico Ribes

Editor:	Kahena Attia
Music:	Abdelwahab Doukkali
Designer:	Abdelkrim Akellah, Naïma Bouanani
Set Design:	Christian Baldos
Leading Players:	Bachir Skirej, Mouna Fettou, Naïma Lemcherki, Amina Rachid

Tazi's third feature, scripted by Farida Benlyazid, is one of the rare Maghreb comedies and enjoyed great popularity in Morocco. To expose the contradictions of polygamy, Tazi has built his film around a fairly obscure point of Islamic law. Hadj Ahmed Ben Moussa, a wealthy polygamous jeweller in Fez, repeatedly repudiates (and then reconciles himself with) his beautiful young third wife, Houda. He then discovers – on the third occasion – that he can only take her back if she has meanwhile been married to another husband and the marriage has been consummated.

Brahim Yash? / Brahim qui? / Brahim Who?

1982, 100 mins, colour

Director / Screenwriter:	Nabyl Lahlou
Producer:	Loukkos Film
Cinematographer:	Mustapha Marjane
Editor:	Nabyl Lahlou
Music:	Mohamed Belkhayat
Set Design:	Yahia Abdessalam
Leading Players:	Larbi Dogmi, Allal Saadi, Nabyl Lahlou, Mustapha Belhadj, Nadia Atbib, Latefa Ahandouz

The characteristic tone of the work of the playwright-turned-film-maker Nabyl Lahlou is derisive. *Brahim Yash?*, Lahlou's third feature, is full of sardonic insights and bitter ironies in its satire on both bureaucracy and film production. The film's pensioner hero, Brahim Boumalfi, is robbed of his pension when his papers are lost and, when they are found, by the misspelling of his name. His travails are parallelled by those of Jalili, a film-maker in search of finance – a situation familiar to Lahlou himself. Both die, only to find the same constraints in the afterlife.

Delo Pheraoun / L'ombre du pharaon / Shadow of the Pharaoh

1996, 100 mins, colour

Director:	Souheil Benbarka
Producer:	Le Dawliz, CCM (Morocco), MG Films (Italy)
Screenwriter:	Adriano Bolzer, Souheil Benbarka
Cinematographer:	Girolamo Larosa
Editor:	Ahmed Darif
Music:	Richard Horowitz

Leading Players: Helmut Berger, Florinda Bolkan, Hassan Joundi, Orso Maria Guerrini, Philippe Leroy, Alessio Naguas, Mohamed Miftah

Souheil Benbarka is unique in North African cinema for the resources he can command for his productions. He has of late looked abroad for players, subjects, distribution and co-production funding. *Delo Pheraoun* shows perfectly the director's epic ambitions. He is far more interested in marshalling a thousand horsemen than in probing individual human complexity. His characters are little more than ciphers caught up in complex political manoeuvrings. Here the pharaoh's son, Anhur, overcomes the opposition of the fanatics in order to succeed his father, but only after the death of the recognized heir, his twin brother.

Hallaq Darb al-Fouqara | Le coiffeur du quartier des pauvres | The Barber of the Poor Quarter

1982, 105 mins, colour
Director: Mohamed Reggab
Producer: Reggab Films, Omar Akouri
Screenwriter: Youssef Fadel (from his own play)
Cinematographer: Mohamed Reggab, Mustapha Stitou
Editor: Mohamed Reggab
Music: Mohamed Jouay
Set Design: Hasan Amiri
Leading Players: Mohamed Habichi, Hamid Najah, Khadija Khammouli, Omar Chenbout, Mohamed Tajer, Salah Eddine Benmoussa

Reggab's *Hallaq Darb al-Fouqara* is one of the few North African films to be adapted from a play and this origin is apparent in the episodic structure, the handling of the action and the nature of the dialogue. The film traces the manoeuvring of a rich former collaborator, Jalloul, to acquire the property (and the wives) of the inhabitants of the poor quarter. The central figure is Miloud, the barber of the title, who is deprived of everything, including his shop and his wife. At the same time his friend Houmane is driven to murder his wife by the lies spread by Jalloul. The action is restricted to Casablanca, but Reggab includes regular radio news broadcasts to set the action in the wider context of the Israeli invasion of the Lebanon.

Hubb Fi al-Dar al-Bayda | Un amour à Casablanca | A Love Affair in Casablanca

1991, 90 mins, colour
Director / Screenwriter: Abdelkader Lagtaa
Producer: Cineastar
Cinematographer: Mohamed Abdelkrim Derkaoui
Editor: Abdelkader Lagtaa
Music: Abdelouhab Doukkali

Set Design: Najib Chlih
Leading Players: Ahmed Naji, Mouna Fettou, Mohamed Fouzi

Lagtaa's *Hubb Fi al-Dar al-Bayda* has a complicated plot concerning Saloua, an eigh-teen-year-old schoolgirl, who (feeling oppressed at home) plunges into sexual relationships: first with a fifty-year-old official, Jalil, and then with a young photogra-pher of her own age, Najib. Tragedy ensues when the young man is confronted with the fact that Saloua's other lover is his own father. The film, which shows a very contemporary world of drink, drugs and sex, and deals directly with the frustrations of young women in a society where men make all the rules, was one of the first Moroccan films to achieve box-office success to rival that of imported Hollywood features.

Ibn al-Sabil / *Le grand voyage* / *The Big Trip*

1981, 87 mins, colour
Director: Mohamed Abderrahman Tazi
Producer: Nour Eddine Sail
Screenwriter: Nour Eddine Sail
Cinematographer: Mohamed Abderrahman Tazi
Editor: Allah Sayed
Music: Omar Sayed
Designer: Larbi Yacoubi, Mustapha Mounir
Leading Players: Ali Hassan, Nadia Atbib, Abdallah Serouali, Jillali Ferhati

This first film by Mohamed Abderrahman Tazi was scripted by the former film-club activist and critic Nour Eddine Saïl, who was also its producer. Like all the films the pair have made together, it offers precise insights into contemporary Moroccan society. *Ibn al-Sabil* utilizes the classic motif of the journey – in this case the trip is that undertaken by a lorry-driver who drives from the south to Casablanca. Everywhere along the way he is cheated and robbed. He decides to emigrate, but real-izes too late – when already at sea – that he is about to be cheated again.

Kuius al-Has / *Chevaux de fortune* / *Make-Believe Horses*

1995, 83 mins, colour
Director / Screenwriter: Jillali Ferhati
Producer: Heracles Productions
Cinematographer: Gilbert Azevedo
Editor: Hélène Muller
Music: Ali Souissi, Hassan Souissi
Sound: Faouzi Thabet
Leading Players: Nezha Rahil, Jillali Ferhati, Hamid Zoughi, Brigitte Rouan, Jean-Louis Richard, Driss Karimi, Larbi Yacoubi, Hicham Ibrahimi

Ferhati's *Kuius al-Has* focuses on an ill-matched group of individuals who meet up in Tangier, all nursing hopeless dreams of going to Europe: Mohamed to see a horse race, Ali to have an operation to restore his sight, Fatima to rejoin her mother. Mohamed enters a fantasy world, pretending to his wife that he is already in Paris, and steals to pay for his visa. Ferhati creates a suffocating world, reminiscent in some ways of the French poetic realism of the 1930s: the enigmatic blind man, rain-swept and darkened streets, characters prevented from achieving their dreams, the opportunity to escape always in view but always just out of reach. The ending, inevitably, is death.

al-Sarab / Le mirage / The Mirage

1980, 100 mins, black and white

Director / Screenwriter:	Ahmed Bouanani
Producer:	Basma, CCM
Cinematographer:	Abdellah Bayahia
Editor:	Ahmed Bouanani
Music:	'Images' (a group from Tarbes), songs by Houcine Slaoui
Designer:	Naïma Saoudi
Set Design:	Yahia Bou Abdessalam
Leading Players:	Mohamed Habachi, Mohamed Saïd Afifi, Fatima Regragui, Mustapha Mounir, Mohamed Slaoui, Mohamed Rzin, Mohamed Idrissi, Abdellah Amrani, Jilali, Eliane Niorte, Amina Saoudi

Ahmed Bouanani's first feature is a major work, helping to establish the experimental thread which runs through Moroccan cinema. Basically it is a fable with a simple storyline: a young peasant sets out for the city, full of hope, to change some money he has found, but meets only disillusionment. However, the telling of this story is complex: the city is a labyrinth, full of detours, surprises and contradictions, where the colonial presence can be felt and heard, but never seen. More important than the storyline is the welter of allusions that it makes – to Moroccan history and its oral tradition, to literature and to film (Chaplin and Fellini being among those cited).

Weshma / Wechma / Traces

1970, 90 mins, black and white

Director / Screenwriter:	Hamid Benani
Producer:	Sigma 3
Cinematographer:	Mohamed Abderrahman Tazi
Editor:	Ahmed Bouanani
Music:	Kamal Dominique Hellebois
Set Design:	Hans Klein
Leading Players:	Mohamed Kadan, Abdelkader Moutaa, Khadidja Moujabid

Along with the first films of Hamid Benani and Moumen Smihi, Bouanani's *Weshma* is one of the films which opened up the experimental tendency in Moroccan cinema. The film, shot in black and white, tells the story of an orphan who is adopted and given a harsh traditional upbringing to which he responds with minor delinquency. As an adolescent, he grows increasingly distant from society, moving from one meaningless encounter to another as he drifts seemingly inevitably towards a pointless killing and to his own death. The film begins in a realist style with the symbolic imagery integrated into the narrative, but as the film proceeds the storyline becomes more and more fragmented and the poetic imagery more enigmatic.

List of film-makers

Benani, Hamid (b. 1940, Meknes, Morocco)

One of the pioneers of Moroccan cinema, Benani studied at IDHEC in Paris, graduating in 1967. His graduation film was a short work made in France called *Coeur à coeur / Heart to Heart* (1967). On his return he made a few shorts for Moroccan television and collaborated on the short-lived film journal *Cinéma 3*. He was also instrumental in setting up the film collective Sigma 3, which produced his first feature and involved two other future feature-film directors: Mohamed Abderrahman Tazi and Ahmed Bouanani, as well as Mohamed Seqqat who went on to specialize in the production of advertising shorts through his company Spot 2. Benani's first feature film, *Weshma / Wechma* (1970), is a claustrophobic narrative, more concerned with inner pressures than with an external action. The film tells the story of an orphan who is stifled by his upbringing and who grows from awkward child to delinquent adolescent, following a path of rebelliousness that can only lead to his death. *Weshma* is an important work in the development of Moroccan cinema, opening the way to the kind of narrative experiment also practised by Moumen Smihi, Mustapha Derkaoui and, later, Ahmed Bouanani, who was the editor of *Weshma*. Despite its critical success, particularly abroad, the film did not get a commercial release in Morocco and was not seen there at all until it was shown in a Rabat art cinema in 1980. Benani was unable to find finance for his long-planned project *Sables noirs / Black Sands*. It was not until twenty-five years after his first feature film that he was able to complete his second, *Sirr al-Majarra / La prière de l'absent / A Prayer for the Absent One* (1995), an adaptation of Tahar Ben Jelloun's novel. This film, one of the rare literary adaptations in Maghreb cinema, tells the story of Mokhtar, an amnesiac who undertakes a journey across Morocco in an attempt to recover his past and his memory.

Benbarka, Souheil (b. 1942, Timbuktu, Mali)

Son of a family from southern Morocco, Benbarka has been one of the key figures in Moroccan cinema for over twenty-five years. He followed initial studies in Morocco and a diploma in sociology in Italy with a training in film-making at the Centro sperimentale di cinematografia in Rome, where he graduated in the same class as Bernardo Bertolucci. Five years of work in the Italian film industry followed, during which time he worked as assistant to Pier Paolo Pasolini (*Il Vangelo Secondo Matteo / The Gospel According to St Matthew*, 1964; *Edipo Re / Oedipus Rex*, 1967) and Valentino Orsini

(*I Dannati della Terra / The Damned of the Earth*, 1969). His first three short films were all made in Italy in 1969–71. His first feature film, *Alf Yad Wa Yad / Mille et une mains / A Thousand and One Hands* (1972), was a fictional study contrasting the lives of rich and poor through a look at the misery that goes into the manufacture of exquisite Moroccan carpets. This first feature revealed a political commitment and concern with social injustice that is characteristic of Benbarka's whole career as a film-maker. *Alf Yad Wa Yad* received showings at several foreign festivals, where its professionalism and skilful use of colour as well its message earned it prizes, but it did not receive distribution in Morocco. *Harb al-Bitrul Lan Taqa'* (1974), Benbarka's second feature, was an ambitious study of the struggle which occurs at all levels of society when oil producers are pitted against multinational companies. The film was told in a style that echoed the contemporary French political thrillers of Costa-Gavras and Yves Boisset. This film was hardly screened in Morocco and pushed the director to look towards the possibilities of more international production. His use of a European actor, Sacha Pitoëff, to play the lead in *Harb al-Bitrul Lan Taqa'* anticipated the employment of Irene Papas and Laurent Terzieff – dubbed into Arabic – in *'Urs al-Dam / Noce de sang / Blood Wedding* (1977), a loose adaptation of Federico García Lorca's 1933 play depicting two lovers kept apart by family hatreds. Its hero, Amrouch, is a young peasant who is kept from marrying the girl he loves simply because she is the daughter of a rich man. Equally ambitious was another work with literary inspiration: *Amok* (1982). This was made with production links to Kenya, Tanzania, Zambia and Mozambique, and had Miriam Makeba in a starring role. Set in South Africa, it echoed the basic storyline and themes of Alan Paton's novel *Cry, the Beloved Country*. The story concerns a black school teacher summoned to Johannesburg by news of his sister's illness and confronted there with all the violence, terror and corruption of South African urban life in the 1980s; through this the film deals with the horrors of apartheid.

From the 1980s Benbarka has become more and more interested in production, setting up complex co-production arrangements for his own films, co-producing the work of others (such as Ahmed al-Maanouni's *al-Hal* and Hakim Noury's *Sa'i al-Barid*, both made in 1980) and developing his own Dawliz distribution, production and laboratory complex.

Benbarka's interest in working for the international market was confirmed when he resumed feature-film production in the 1990s. His ambitious period epic set in the mid-sixteenth century, *Les cavaliers de la gloire / Horsemen of Glory* (1993), was a re-edited version of *Tubul al-Nar*, first shown in 1991. This co-production with finance from Italy, France and the USSR told of the Moroccan Prince Abdelmalek who sacrifices everything to recover his father's throne, only to die – poisoned and disillusioned – at the moment of his triumph on the battlefield. Also directed towards an international market was a further 1990s epic: *Delo Pheraoun / L'ombre du pharaon / Shadow of the Pharaoh* (1996). This was co-produced with an Italian company and told of the pharaoh's son, Anhur, who after the death of his twin brother overcomes the opposition of fanatics to win recognition and so to succeed his father as ruler.

Benlyazid, Farida (b. 1948, Tangier, Morocco)

Benlyazid is one of comparatively few women film-makers in the Maghreb and also (with the Tunisian Nouri Bouzid) one of the few Maghreb film-makers to work consistently as a scriptwriter for other directors. She studied film-making at IDHEC in Paris and subsequently worked as a writer and journalist, also making a first short. After scripting *Sharkhun Fi-l Ha'it* (1978) and *Arais Min Qasab* (1981) – the first two films of her husband, Jillali Ferhati – Benlyazid went on to make her own feature-film debut as director with *Bab al-Sama' Maftuh / Une porte sur le ciel / Gateway to Heaven* (1987). This is the story of a young woman, Nadia, who after returning home from France to attend her father's funeral, discards her French boyfriend and rediscovers her Islamic identity as a woman working with women in Morocco.

Subsequently Benlyazid co-scripted Mohamed Abderrahman Tazi's tale of female victims, *Badis* (1988), with Nour Eddine Saîl, and scripted the same director's comedy, *Bahthan 'An Zawj Imra'ati* (1993). She contributed one episode, 'Sur la terrasse' / 'On the Terrace' to a collective film made to celebrate the centenary of cinema: *Cinq films pour cent ans / Five Films for a Hundred Years*. In 1996 she received funding for a second feature, *Kied Ensa / Ruses de femmes / Women's Wiles*, to be produced by her own company, Tingitania Films.

Bouanani, Ahmed (b. 1938, Casablanca, Morocco)

Bouanani was involved with Hamid Benani and Mohamed Abderrahman Tazi in the collective Sigma 3 in the late 1960s and worked as an editor on several films, including Benani's pioneering *Weshma* (1970), Mohamed Osfour's *al-Kinz al-Jahannamy* (1970) and Nabyl Lahlou's *al-Kanfoudi* (1978). He also made a number of short films from the mid-1960s onwards: *Tarfaya or a Poet's Progress* (1966, with Mohamed Abderrahman Tazi), *Six and Twelve* (1968, script only, co-directed with Mohamed Abderrahman Tazi and Majid R'chiche), *Memory 14* (1970), which anticipated many of the formalist aspects of much later Moroccan feature film production, *Sidi Hmad or Moussa* (1972), *Arba'a Yanabi'a / The Four Springs* (1977), *Hill 2,400* (1978), *Visiting Card* (1981), *Sidi Qacem / The Olive Branch* (1982), *Sporting Complex in Casablanca* (1984), *The Child, the Tortoise and the Computer* (1984).

Bouanani's first and (to date) only feature-length work is *al-Sarab / Le mirage / The Mirage* (1980), a self-consciously told allegorical fable set in 1947. It tells of a young man who discovers a sackful of money and sets out to the city, full of hope, to change it. He meets only disillusionment. In the 1990s Bouanani has played an important role in the emergent short-film sector. He wrote the script and dialogue for Daoud Aoulad Sayed's twenty-minute black-and-white short film, *Entre l'absence et l'oubli / Between Absence and Forgetfulness* (1993). He also edited Daoud Aoulad Sayed's *Mémoire ocre / Ochre Memory* (1991) and *al-Oued / Le fleuve / The River* (1995), as well as Hassan Alaoui's *Aidi* (1993) and Jamal Belmejdoub's *Moins une / One Less* (1994). Bouanani received funding for his own short-film project, *Le chômeur / Out-of-Work* in 1995.

Derkaoui, Mustapha (b. 1944, Oujda, Morocco)

Brother of the leading director of photography Mohamed Abdelkrim Derkaoui, Mustapha Derkaoui is Morocco's most prolific film-maker. He studied theatre at the

Conservatoire d'Art Dramatique in Casablanca and then went on to study literature and philosophy in Bordeaux and Rabat. He subsequently studied film-making at IDHEC in Paris, from which he graduated with his first short film: *Les quatre murs / The Four Walls* (1964). Then, in 1965, he went to the film school at Lodz in Poland, where he stayed until he graduated in 1972, specialising in direction. During this period he made four shorts in Poland – *Amghar* (1966), *Adoption* (1967), *Les gens du caveau / People from the Vaults* (1968) and *Un jour quelque part / One Day Somewhere* (1971) – and one in Paris – *Les états-généraux du cinéma / The States General of the Cinema* (1969).

His subsequent films include four documentaries on rural subjects for the Iraq government in 1974–5 and a further short, *Les cent jours de la Mamounia / The Hundred Days of the Manouta* (1978), a play for television called *Deux moins un / Two Minus One* (1979) and a six-part television serial, *L'agonie des fleurs / The Agony of the Flowers* (1980). His first feature film, *Anba'dh al-Ahdath Biduni Ma'na*, was made in 1974 but was apparently never shown in Morocco. It weaves together reflections on the inner life of a film director with his simultaneous investigation of a crime he has uncovered by chance. Derkaoui was subsequently part of the collective which made *Ramad al-Zariba* (1977), the tale of a country boy who has long dreamed of the city but finds the reality of Casablanca to be very different.

In the 1980s and 1990s he has made a series of features, all produced by his company Art 7. *Ayyam Chahrazad al-Hilwa* (1982) is a complex story: partly a tale about a woman singer, partly the story of a man who becomes rich, partly the account of a film-maker who fails to make his film. *'Unwanun Mu'aqqat* (1984) describes the way in which a person tormented by the idea of death learns to endure suffering. In *Riwaya Ula* (1992) two young people – a factory worker, Hilma, and Larbi, a book salesman – meet and fall in love, but find themselves confronted by innumerable problems. *Je(u) au passé / (Ga)me in the Past* (1994) tells of Natalia, a young woman who sets off to find a man her mother had once known and who is remarkably like the Moscow student with whom Natalia herself has fallen in love. In *Les sept portes de la nuit / The Seven Gates of the Night* (1994) Derkaoui chronicles the adventures of a man, Brahim, who sets out in search of his son and also the son's friendship with Kamal. Derkaoui has also made a sixty-seven-minute fiction, *La grande allégorie / The Great Allegory* (1995), which deals with a young woman writer who constructs a story in which she evokes the memory of a young man who died in the war. This was originally intended as an episode in the collective film which became *Cinq films pour cent ans / Five Films for a Hundred Years*.

Following in the experimental style pioneered by Hamid Benani in *Weshma* (1970), Derkaoui's output represents a conscious – often self-conscious – attempt to explore the nature of storytelling, to play games with time and memory, and to use the visual resources of cinema in order to investigate the inner worlds of his characters. Derkaoui also directed one episode, 'al-Samt' / 'Le silence' / 'The Silence', for the collective film produced by the leading Tunisian producer Ahmed Attia, *Harbu al-Khallij Wa B'ad? / La Guerre du Golfe … et après? / After the Gulf War?* (1992).

Ferhati, Jillali (b. 1948, Khemisset, Morocco)

Ferhati is one of a number of Moroccan directors who came to film-making after theatre and drama studies. He studied literature and sociology at the Université de

Paris VIII and then, from 1969 to 1973, followed courses in dramatic art and direction. In all he lived in Paris for ten years. In addition to working as an actor and theatre producer for the Théâtre International de Paris, he made two short films: *Charon / Caron* (1973) and *Bonjour madame / Hello Madam* (1974). Ferhati appeared, along with his brother Ahmed, in his own first feature, *Sharkhun Fi-l Ha'it* (1978). This was made from a script by his wife, Farida Benlyazid (who went on to direct *Bab al-Sama' Maftuh* in 1987), and was filmed by the future documentarist Ahmed al-Maanouni. The film showed life on the margins of Tangier, as seen through the eyes of a deaf-mute. Ferhati's subsequent features show increasing mastery of form, while remaining simple in their narrative construction. *Arais Min Qasab* (1981), also scripted by Farida Benlyazid and in which he again appeared alongside his brother, explores the sufferings of a young woman. Aicha, who is little more than a child, finds herself married, a mother, widowed and then rejected by her brother-in-law when it is discovered that she is pregnant. Deprived of her children and her home, she has nowhere to turn.

While *Arais Min Qasab* is a familiar tale of woman as victim, *Shatiu al-Atfal al-Mafqudin* (1991), which Ferhati both wrote and directed, is a more optimistic tale of a woman's revolt. The heroine finds she is pregnant after the death of her lover but, despite enormous pressure, she finds the strength to stand up to her oppressive father and his antagonistic second wife. *Kuius al-Has* (1995) explores the dreams of a group of characters in Tangier, separated from the Europe they dream of by a thin strip of sea. The attempt finally to take this small step ends in tragedy. Ferhati later contributed one episode, 'Le mouchoir bleu' / 'The Blue Handkerchief', to the collective film made to commemorate cinema's centenary, *Cinq films pour cent ans / Five Films for a Hundred Years* (1995).

Ferhati currently runs a theatre company in Tangier, which provided a number of the players for *Shatiu al-Atfal al-Mafqudin*. Like Hakim Noury, he consistently shows in his work the power of simple well-constructed narratives based on social observation and commitment, moving away from the kind of esoteric narrative experimentation so common in Moroccan cinema and typified by the work of Benani, Smihi and Derkaoui. Ferhati has also appeared as an actor in films by other directors, including the lead role in Mohamed Abderrahman Tazi's *Badis* (1988).

Lagtaa, Abdelkader (b. 1948, Casablanca, Morocco)

Lagtaâ graduated from the film school in Lodz in Poland in 1975, having specialised in directing. He participated in the collectively made *Ramad al-Zariba* (1977) and collaborated on a number of shorts, including *The Rural Woman* (1977, co-directed with Mustapha Derkaoui), and directed a series of short films for Moroccan television: *Rabi and Abstract Painting* (1984), *Chaïbia* (1984) and *Kacimi or the Unveiling* (1985).

Lagtaâ is the author of two feature films. *Hubb Fi al-Dar al-Bayda* (1991) offers a controversial view of city life in Casablanca (drugs, sex, alcohol and so on), telling the story of an eighteen-year-old girl who is oppressed at home and runs off with a fifty-year-old man, only to abandon him for her true love, his son. *Al-Bab al-Nasdud* (1994) is another uncompromising tale of modern-day Morocco, dealing with a young man who frees himself from his oppressive mother and sets out in search of the woman he loves. Lagtaâ contributed one episode, 'Happy End', to the collective film made to celebrate the centenary of cinema, *Cinq films pour cent ans / Five Films for a Hundred Years* (1995). In 1998 he made a further feature called *Les Casablancais / The Casablancans*.

Lahlou, Nabyl (b. 1945, Fez, Morocco)

One of a number of Moroccan directors to come to the cinema from theatre, Lahlou studied drama in Paris at the Académie du Théâtre de la Rue Blanche and then the Ecole Charles Dullin–TNP. For a number of years, while continuing his total involvement with the theatre, he divided his time between France (where he wrote plays in French), Algeria (where he taught at Kordj-el-Kifane) and Morocco (where he wrote plays in Arabic and produced them, sometimes without official permission). Among his plays, *Ophélie n'est pas morte / Ophelia is not dead* (1969) and *Schrischamtury* (1975) are in French, while others are in Arabic: *Les milliardaires / The Millionaires* (1968), *Les tortues / The Turtles* (1970), *La grande kermesse / The Big Fair* (1970), *Stop* (1971), *Le bal aura lieu sur la plage / The Ball Will Take Place on the Beach* (1971), *Asseyez-vous sur des cadavres / Sit on Corpses* (1974) and so on. His first work for the cinema was a medium-length work, *Les morts / The Dead* (1975).

His films are, in a sense, a by-product of his playwriting. They show his caustic and sardonic view of society, and demonstrate his stated view that derision is the only language through which to understand a world that is complex, incomprehensible and full of contradictions. In *al-Kanfoudi* (1978), his first feature-length film, sudden wealth is of no use to a poor musician who wins the lottery. His life becomes no better in a world of greed and ruthless money-making which Lahlou depicts with bitter sarcasm. *al-Hakim al-'Am* (1980) parodies the demagogy of pseudo-democracies in the Third World through the story of a newspaper worker who takes the place of his lookalike, the governor of the island of Chakerbakerben. Lahlou's next two films were both sardonic fables. In *Brahim Yash?* (1982) a man robbed of his pension by the misspelling of his name in his papers finds that, even after his death, bureaucracy defeats him. In *Nahiq al-Ruh* (1984), a tale narrated by a donkey, the unhappy fate of a former resistance fighter is contrasted bitterly with the situation of those who collaborated with colonialism and still remain rich and powerful. Lahlou's subsequent films are *Komany* (1988), a tale of mixed identities in the clash of religion and politics, in which an actor is chosen to play the role of the dictator in films made by a sect wishing to denigrate the leader, and *Laylat Qatl / La nuit du crime / The Night of the Crime* (1992), his last film to date, in which a driver murders his boss after falling in love with his wife. All Lahlou's feature films have been produced by his own company, Loukous Films.

al-Maanouni, Ahmed (b. 1944, Casablanca, Morocco)

Ahmed al-Maanouni studied at the Université Internationale du Théâtre in Paris, from which he graduated in 1970, and subsequently at INSAS in Brussels, where he specialised in camerawork and graduated in 1975. He also studied – from 1975 to 1976 – at the Université de Paris VIII.

He has worked as director of photography on several films, including Jillali

Ferhati's feature *Sharkhun Fi-l Ha'it* (1978) and Izza Genini's short *Cantiquers brodées / Embroidered Canticles* (1991). His own shorts include *Festival de Tabouka / Tabouka Festival* (1975), *Fons de marolles* (1976) and *L'enfance émigré / Emigrant Childhood* (1977). He has also worked in television and made commercials.

Al-Maanouni is one of the few North African film-makers to have made feature-length documentaries for cinema release. His first two feature-length works were made in quick succession: *al-Ayyam al-Ayyam* (1978) was a close and perceptively realistic look at everyday life in a Moroccan village, depicted without any trace of folklore and exoticism; *al-Hal* (1981) was a study of the music group Nass el-Giwane, whose music, based on traditional Arab and African sources, is extremely popular in Morocco. al-Maanouni also made a number of shorter films in the 1990s, including *Les goumiers marocains / The Moroccan Native Troops* (a medium-length documentary for television, 1992) and *Du Maroc au Séville / Morocco to Seville* (1992).

Noury, Hakim (b. 1952, Casablanca, Morocco)

Noury learned how to make films by working as assistant on most of Souheil Benbarka's early feature films. He also made a short film, *Sans paroles / Without Words* (1977), and three films for television. He made his first feature in 1980, but had to wait ten years before resuming his directing career. In addition to his features, he also contributed one episode, 'Cinéma impérial' / 'Imperial Cinema', to the collective feature-length film made to commemorate the centenary of cinema: *Cinq films pour cent ans / Five Films for a Hundred Years* (1995).

All Noury's feature films show a concern for social issues, akin to that of his contemporary Jillali Ferhati, and focus on characters who are defeated by forces outside their control. *Sa'i al-Barid* (1980) relates the tribulations of a young marginalized postman, a dreamer whose dreams are seldom realized – and even then only fleetingly. *Al-Mitraqa Wa Alk-sindan* (1990) is the story of a civil servant whose forced early retirement disrupts his ordered existence and causes him psychological as well as material problems. In *Atoufoula Almortasaba* (1993) a girl of ten sent to work as a maid in Casablanca survives the hardships, only to find her life shattered a few years later when she finds herself pregnant and abandoned. *Le voleur de rêves / The Dream Thief* (1995) traces the friendship of two very different men, an ex-prisoner and a young dropout, who share their fears and dreams. He subsequently directed two further features: *Un simple fait divers / A Simple News Item* (1997) and *Destin de femme / A Woman's Fate* (1998).

Reggab, Mohamed (b. 1942, Safi, Morocco; d. Paris, France, 1990)

Reggab studied at the film school VGIK in Moscow. His short films include *Histoire en verre / History in Glass* (1969) and *Séquestration / Sequestration* (1972) and a series of documentaries made in 1977–80: *Les bidonvilles de Rabat / The Slums of Rabat* and *Le schéma directeur de Beni Mellal / Beni Mellal's Master Plan*. He was part of the collective First Cultural Festival at Asilal which was responsible for *Ramâd al-Zariba* (1977).

His single solo directing effort, *Hallaq Darb al-Fouqara* (1982), adapted from a play by Youssef Fadel, paints a vivid picture of a working-class district. A poor barber is deprived of everything, including his shop and his wife, by the rich man – an ex-collaborator with the French – who now controls the area. The film won awards at several foreign festivals, but the debts incurred in completing it led Reggab to spend some time in prison. Reggab died in 1990, shortly after making an appearance in Saad Chraïbi's first feature, *Waqai'a Min Hayat Adia*, which appeared in 1991.

Smihi, Moumen (b. 1945, Tangier, Morocco)

Smihi studied first at the University of Rabat and then in Paris at the Ecole Pratique des Hautes Etudes, under Roland Barthes. From 1965 to 1967 he studied film-making at IDHEC. He worked as assistant on a few projects for French television and then made a very well-received short: *Si Moh, pas de chance / If Moh, No Chance* (1971), a 16 mm black-and-white documentary which dealt with the problems of North African immigrants in Paris. His other short film, *Couleurs au corps / Colours of the Body* (1972), was a fifteen-minute colour documentary on a studio teaching painting, shot in Paris. He continued making documentaries alongside his features: *Le FAO au Maroc / The FAO in Morocco* (1976), *Amade* (1984), *La santé de vos enfants / The Health of your Children* (1984), *Villes marocaines / Moroccan Cities* (1985), *al-Sinima al-Misriya / Egyptian Cinema* (1986) and *Avec Matisse à Tanger / With Matisse in Tangier* (1993).

Smihi is best known for his feature films, which show a wide range of approaches to the problem of remaining authentically Moroccan and yet finding a wider audience. *Charqi Aw al-Çoumt al-'Anif* (1975), the story of a woman whose efforts to prevent her husband taking a second wife lead only to her own death, is a complex tale set in the last years of the Protectorate. In it, the flow of the narration is disrupted, de-dramatized and wedded to a complex music soundtrack, so that the resulting film emerged as one of the most striking Moroccan experiments with film narrative of the 1970s, following in the line of Hamid Benani's *Weshma* and anticipating the work of Mustapha Derkaoui. *Charqi Aw al-Çoumt al-'Anif* was refused release by Moroccan distributors and all Smihi's subsequent work has been co-produced by his company Imago Films and French companies.

Quarante-quatre ou les récits de la nuit / Forty-Four or Tales of the Night (1981), made after a break of seven years, was a Franco-Tunisian co-production in which many of the Arab roles are played by French performers such as Marie-France Pisier, Pierre Clémenti and Christine Pascal. The 'forty-four' of the title denotes the number of years of Franco-Spanish occupation of Morocco and the film's fragmented narrative chronicles the fate, over a long period, of two families – one living under the French protectorate, the other under Spanish rule. *Qaftan al-Hubb* (1987) is a version of 'The Big Mirror', a story by the Moroccan storyteller Mohamed M'rabet, many of whose oral tales were recorded, translated and published by the American novelist Paul Bowles. It tells of a man who marries the woman of his dreams, only to find that their life together turns into a nightmare. *Sayidat al-Qahira* (1991), co-written with the Egyptian writer-director Bashir al-Dik, is the story of a peasant woman who goes to Cairo to seek her brother and stays on to become a famous singer.

Tazi, Mohamed Abderrahman (b. 1942, Fez, Morocco)

Tazi studied first film-making at IDHEC in Paris and subsequently studied mass-media communication at Syracuse University in New York. He was involved, in the late 1960s, with Hamid Benani and Ahmed Bouanani in the film collective Sigma 3. He was director of photography for the only film produced by the collective, Benani's *Weshma* (1970), and he worked as co-producer of Moumen Smihi's pioneering *Charqi Aw al-Çoumt al-'Anif* (1975). Later he worked as director of photography on Latif Lahlou's *al-Musâwama* (1986). In addition he has assisted various foreign directors working in Morocco, including Robert Wise, Francis Ford Coppola and John Huston (*The Man Who Would Be King*, 1975). He has also directed a number of shorts, among them *Tarfaya or a Poet's Progress* (1966, co-directed with Bouanani), *Six and Twelve* (1967, co-directed by Majid R'chiche, from a script by Bouanani), *Les guérisseurs des Philippines / Filipino Healer* (1976) and *Aux portes de l'Europe / At the Gates of Europe* (1987).

Tazi's first two feature films were both stories of victims and their failed attempts to escape social constraints. *Ibn al-Sabil* (1981), written by Nour Eddine Saîl, is the story of a journey undertaken by a lorry-driver from the south to Casablanca. Everywhere he is cheated and robbed, but when he decides to emigrate he realizes too late – when already at sea – that he is about to be cheated again. *Badis* (1988), a Moroccan–Spanish co-production co-scripted by Sail and Farida Benlyazid, was set during the Franco Era and depicts the friendship between two women: one oppressed by her domestic life, the other a peasant girl persecuted because of her love for a Spanish soldier. Together the pair set out for freedom, but they are caught and stoned to death for their actions. Tazi's third feature, *Bahthan 'An Zawj Imra'ati* (1993), again scripted by Farida Benlyazid, was a new departure – a comedy dealing with the marriage problems of a polygamous jeweller. He repeatedly repudiates and then reconciles himself with his beautiful third wife, until he discovers – on the third occasion – that he can only take her back if she has been married meanwhile to another husband. The jeweller ends up seeking to emigrate illegally to Belgium and the sequel, *Lalla Hobby*, which Tazi completed in 1997, depicts the misadventures of the jeweller in Belgium, still in search of his third wife.

In 1995 Tazi completed a short film, *Images volées / Stolen Images*, originally intended to form part of the collective feature to commemorate the centenary of cinema that emerged as *Cinq films pour cent ans / Five Films for a Hundred Years* (1995).

TUNISIA

As far as film production was concerned, the first decade following the ending of the Protectorate (1956–65) was marked by the production of a considerable number of documentaries made by Tunisian film-makers – some working within the context of the Tunisian amateur film movement – and a few more ambitious works shot by foreign directors. Mario Ruspoli made a documentary on the national liberation struggle, *Renaissance* (1963), and two fictional features were made by French film-makers: Jacques Baratier's internationally distributed *Goha* (1958), which introduced Omar Sharif to worldwide audiences, and Jean Michaud-Mailland's *H'mida* (1965).

The first Tunisian post-independence feature film, *al-Fajr / L'aube / The Dawn* (1966), was directed by the self-taught Omar Khlifi (b. 1934), who went on to make a further 1960s film, *al-Mutamarrid / Le rebelle / The Rebel* (1968), and to complete a trilogy of films on resistance themes as he continued his career into the 1970s. Otherwise the 1960s saw only two other features. A 1950s graduate of the Paris film school IDHEC, Hamouda Ben Halima (b. 1935), made his sole feature *Khalifa al-Aqra' / Khlifa le teigneux / Khlifa Ringworm* (1969) and Sadok Ben Aicha (b. 1936), who worked extensively as an editor, made his first feature with *Mukhdâr / Mokhtar* (1968)

At the beginning of the 1970s, with *al-Fallâga / Les fellagas / The Fellagas* (1970) and *Surakh / Hurlements / Screams* (1972), perhaps his finest and most personal feature, Omar Khlifi reaffirmed his status as Tunisia's most forceful director. Khlifi, an unsophisticated director who had previously made a number of documentaries, came from the flourishing amateur film movement and was a self-taught film-maker. His output, marked by the release of four features in just six years, was virtually unique at the time in North Africa.

In general the overall level of Tunisian feature-film production – less than two films a year from the mid-1960s through to the 1990s – has allowed few similar opportunities for sustained individual output. Other directors of the same generation as Khlifi, who shared the same background in the amateur film movement, were seldom able to complete more than a single feature: Ahmed Khéchine (b. 1940), for example, made just *Tahta Matar al-Kharif / Sous la pluie d'automne / Under the Autumn Rain* (1970); Ali Abdelwahab (b. 1938) made *Um 'Abbas / Om Abbes* (1970), and Abderazak Hammami (b. 1935) completed *Ummy Traky / Ommi Traki* (1973) – and then, in each case, either silence or a shift to a different career. Later in the decade Mohammed Hammami (b. 1941), a graduate of the VGIK film school in Moscow, made his sole feature: *Sira / Mon village / My Village* (1979).

The career of another film-maker without formal film-school training who was active in the 1970s, the critic and documentarist Ferid Boughedir (b. 1944), is more complex and long-lasting. During the 1970s he co-directed just one feature, *al-Mawt al-Akhir / La mort trouble / Murky Death* (1970, with the Frenchman Claude d'Anna), and contributed a single episode, 'Annouzha' / 'Picnic', to another – the collectively made *Fi Bilad al-Tararani / Au pays de Tararani / In the Land of Tararani* (1972). But Boughedir remained influential as a documentary film-maker and as a writer about film, and later returned to the forefront of Tunisian feature film-making. The other episodes of *Fi Bilad al-Tararani* were contributed by two film-makers who had received a formal film training at IDHEC in Paris during the 1950s: Hamouda Ben Halima (b. 1935) and Hedy Ben Khalifa (1937–79). Neither, however, was able to sustain a career in film-making.

But other foreign film-school graduates were able to make a heavier impact on their return to Tunisia. In the 1970s Abdellatif Ben Ammar (b. 1943) made two striking and successful features: *Hikaya Basita Kahadhidhi / Une si simple histoire / Such a Simple Story* (1970) and *Sejnan / Sejnane* (1974). Another IDHEC graduate, Mohamed Ali El-Okby (b. 1948), began his career with *Kurra Wa Ahlam / Un ballon et des rêves / A Ball and Some Dreams* (1978), featuring the 1997–8 Tunisian football team. Brahim Babaï (b. 1936) contributed the widely seen fictional feature *Wa Ghadan ... ? / Et demain ... ? / And Tomorrow ... ?* (1972) and a feature-length documentary, *Intissar Sha'ab / Victoire d'un peuple / Victory of a People* (1975). Rachid Ferchiou (b. 1941), who had studied film in Berlin, made *Yusra / Yusra* (1972) and *Atfal al-Qajaq / Les enfants de l'ennui* / *The Children of Boredom* (1975). Naceur Ktari (b. 1943) studied film in Paris and Rome before making a most striking debut with one of the most successful films on emigration to France: *al-Sufaral'* / *Les ambassadeurs* / *The Ambassadors* (1975). An equally distinctive but isolated work in the decade is *al-'Urs* / *La noce* / *The Wedding* (1978), the film transposition of one of the stage productions of a theatrical collective called the Nouveau Théatre de Tunis, led by Fadhel Jaïbi (b. 1945) and Fadhel Jaziri (b. 1948), who likewise had no formal film training.

The late 1970s show some continuity with the earlier years. Ben Aicha, for example, released his second feature, *'Aridhat al-'Azia* / *Le mannequin* / *The Mannequin* (1978), But the key feature is the emergence of a number of forceful and talented new feature-film directors. One such was Ridha Behi (b. 1947), who had studied social science in Paris and began his career with a widely praised indictment of tourism: *Shams al-Dibâ* / *Le soleil des hyènes* / *Hyenas' Sun* (1977).

The 1970s also saw the appearance of the first Tunisian female feature-film director when Selma Baccar (b. 1945), who had completed her studies at IFC in Paris in 1970, completed her feature-length documentary *Fatma 75* (1978), but found its release blocked by the authorities.

The 1980s began well as Abdellatif Ben Ammar made his finest film, the masterly *'Aziza* (1980), before turning to production activities, and Ferid Boughedir was finally able to complete his long-term documentary project on film-making south of the Sahara, *Kamira Ifriqiya* / *Caméra d'Afrique* / *African Camera* (1983), and then a second documentary, this time on Arab film-making, *Kamira 'Arabiya* / *Arab Camera* / *Caméra arabe* (1987). Ridha Behi contributed a melodrama in the Egyptian style, *al-Mala'ika* / *Les anges* / *The Angels* (1984) and then a feature with French players in the leading roles, *Washmun 'Ala al-Dhakira* / *Champagne amer* / *Bitter Champagne* (1988). Fadhel Jaïbi and Fadhel Jaziri followed *al-'Urs* by completing their second theatrical adaptation: *'Arab* / *Arab* (1988). Omar Khlifi returned to the kind of story of violent action with which he had made his reputation, but *al-Tahaddi* / *Le défi* / *The Challenge*

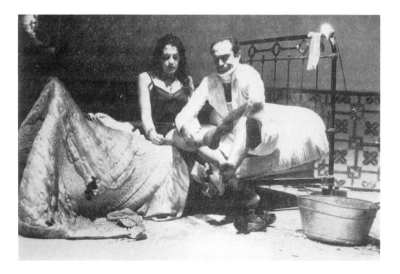

Figure 48 al-'Urs / *The Wedding*

(1986) showed how far Tunisian cinema had developed during his fourteen-year absence.

A further film-maker with a highly personal style but no film-school background who emerged in the early 1980s was the sculptor, writer and storyteller Naceur Khemir (b. 1948), whose first feature, *al-Haimun Fi al-Sahra' / Les baliseurs du désert / The Drifters*, was widely shown and praised at festivals when it appeared in 1984.

The 1980s also saw the production of a first feature by a second woman director, but again her progress was thwarted by the authorities. Neija Ben Mabrouk (b. 1940), a graduate of the INSAS film school in Belgium, had to wait six years for the release in 1988 of her fictional feature *al-Sama / La trace / The Trace*, completed in 1982 but delayed because of a dispute with the state production organization SATPEC. By contrast, two highly talented male newcomers of the 1980s, with similar film-school backgrounds to those of Baccar and Ben Mabrouk, found an enthusiastic international audience for their films. Both *'Ubur / Traversées / Crossings* (1981), directed by the INSAS graduate Mahmoud Ben Mahmoud (b. 1947), and *Dhil al-'Ardh / L'ombre de la terre / Shadow of the Earth* (1982), made by Taïeb Louhichi (b. 1948), a graduate of the IFC in Paris, were highly successful on the international film festival circuit and both directors went on to complete a second feature. Ben Mahmoud had to wait until the 1990s, but Louhichi followed the fifty-minute 16 mm study, *Gorée, l'île de grand-père / Gorée, Grandfather's Island* (1987, shot in Senegal), with a new fictional feature, *Majnun Leila / Leila ma raison / Leila My Reason* (1989). But the dominant figure of the decade is undoubtedly a newcomer whose first feature appeared in 1986. With *Rih al-Sid / L'homme de cendres / Man of Ashes* (1986) and *Safa'ih Min Dhahab / Sabots en or / Golden Horseshoes* (1989), Nourid Bouzid (b. 1945) – a former political detainee – brought a new range of subject matter to Arab film-making and established himself as one of North Africa's major film-makers.

Otherwise most of the films of the 1980s were first features by newcomers who either failed to get subsequent backing or had to wait years for a second opportunity, though most had studied at one of Europe's film schools. The range of background and approach is wide. Ali Mansour (b. 1944), who had studied extensively in France, taking film courses at the Conservatoire Indépendent du Cinéma Français (CICF) in Paris, made a low-budget comedy, *Farda Wa Liqat Ukhtaha / Deux larrons en folie / Two Thieves in Madness* (1980). Abdelhafidh Bouassida (b. 1947), who had spent seven years at the FAMU film school in Prague, made a lavish period drama: *Sarab / La ballade de Mamelouk / The Ballad of Mamelouk* (1981). Lotfi Essid (b. 1952) completed *al-Sabt Fat? / Que fait on ce dimanche? / What are We Doing this Sunday?* (1983), about the adventures of two North African emigrants in Paris. Mohamed Damak (b. 1952) made another comedy, this time about football, called *al-Ka's / La coupe / The Cup* (1985) and Habib Mselmani contributed *Sabra Wa-l Wahsh / Sabra et le monstre de la forêt / Sabra and the Monster from the Forest* (1986).

If the 1980s were a period of renewal for Tunisian film-making, the 1990s have largely been one of consolidation, with the bulk of the films being made by those with a prior experience of feature production. A key figure has been Ahmed Attia, producer of the first features of Bouzid, Boughedir, Tlati and Dhouib. He was also responsible for the collectively made feature, *Harbu al-Khallij Wa B'ad? / La Guerre du Golfe ... et après? / After the Gulf War?* (1992). Among the successes of the new decade were Nouri Bouzid, with *Bezness / Business* (1992) and *Bent Familia /*

Figure 49 Dhil al-'Ardh / Shadow of the Earth

Tunisiennes / Girls from a Good Family (1997), and Ferid Boughedir, who followed his dazzling first feature, a wonderfully humorous fictional evocation of childhood called *Halfawin 'Usfur Stah / Halfaouine l'enfant des terrasses / Halfaouine* (1990), with *Salfun Fi Halq al-Wadi / Un été à La Goulette / One Summer at La Goulette* (1995).

For several other key figures, the early 1990s were also a time when their reputations were consolidated. Naceur Khemir, for example, made a new exploration of the richness of the oral narrative tradition with *Tawq al-Hamama al-Mafqud / Le collier perdu de la colombe / The Lost Collar of the Dove* (1990), and Mahmoud Ben Mahmoud and Fadhel Jaïbi combined to make *Chichkhan / Chichkhan / Poussière de diamants* (1992). Mohamed Ali El-Okbi directed a second, highly successful comedy called *al-Zazuwwat / Les zouzous de la vague / The Teddy Boys* (1992) and Taïeb Louhichi made his third feature, *'Urs al-Qamar / Noces de lune / Moon Wedding* (1998).

Otherwise, however, the results have been mixed. Among the pioneers of the 1970s,

Rachid Ferchiou with *al-Kharif '82 / L'automne '82 / Autumn '82* (1990) and *Kich Mat / Echec et mat / Check and Mate* (1995), and Brahim Babaï with *Laylat al-Sanawat al-'Ashr / La nuit de la décennie / The Night of the Decade* (1991), made welcome reappearances, though without adding substantially to their reputations. Ridha Behi's continued search for international success led him to choose a French lead for his dramatic study of the Palestinian struggle: *al-Khuttaf La Iyamut Fi al-Quds / Les hirondelles ne meurent pas à Jérusalem / Swallows Don't Die in Jerusalem* (1994).

In the early 1990s a number of other new film-makers emerged, many of them having their work previewed at the Tunisian film festival, the Journées Cinématographiques de Carthage (JCC). These included Ali Abidi (b. 1950), who trained in Romania, whose debut film *Barg Ellil / Eclair nocturne / Nocturnal Lightning* (1990), adapted from a novel by Bhechir Khraief, was followed later in the decade by *Redeyef 54* (1997), a study of struggle against the French. Fitouri Belhiba (b. 1950) made *Ruqayya / Coeur nomade / Wandering Heart* (1990). Ahmed Djemaï made his appearance at the JCC with *Rih al-Masa'ir / Le vent des destins / Wind of Destinies* (1993) and Ezzedine Fazai (b. 1957) made his debut with *al-Sahir / Le magique / The Magic Box* (1994). Moncef Dhouib (b. 1952), who was already well known for his short films, achieved less success with his initial feature: *Ya Sultan al-Madina / Soltane el Medina / The Sultan of the Medina* (1993).

As is the case throughout North Africa, the bulk of the film-makers – even the newcomers – are people born in the 1940s. The first newcomer from a younger generation to emerge from short-film production in Tunisia was Mohamed Zran (b. 1959) with *al-Sayida / Essaida* (1996). A second newcomer to make his debut was the actor Mohamed Ben Smaîl (b. 1953) with *Ghoudwa Nahrek / Demain je brûle / Tomorrow I Burn* (1998).

A further key development was the emergence of new women film-makers in the 1990s alongside Selma Baccar, who completed a new fictional feature called *Habiba M'Sika / La danse du feu / The Fire Dance* (1995). The IDHEC-trained former editor Moufida Tlatli (b. 1947) made a striking debut with the feature *Samt al-Quousour / Les silences du palais / Silences of the Palace* (1994) and Kalthoum Bornaz (b. 1945) followed several short films with a first feature: *Kiswa, al-Khayt al-Dhai / Keswa: Le fil perdu / Keswa: The Lost Thread* (1997).

Filmography

'Aziza

1980, 100 mins, colour

Director / Screenwriter:	Abdellatif Ben Ammar
Producer:	SATPEC, Latif Productions (Tunisia), ONCIC (Algeria)
Adaptation / Dialogue:	Taoufik Jebali, Abdellatif Ben Ammar
Cinematographer:	Youssef Sahraoui
Editor:	Moufida Tlatli
Music:	Faouzi Thabet
Leading Players:	Yasmine Khlat, Raouf Ben Amor, Dalila Rames, Mohamed Zinet, Tawfik Jebali, Mouna Noureddine

Abdellatif Ben Ammar's third and most successful feature is a further example of his central concern with Tunisia's national identity, though the film itself was a Tunisian–Algerian co-production. As so often, the film-maker sought to explore contemporary society through a female protagonist: the action here is seen through the eyes of a young orphan, 'Aziza. She lives with a family which moves from the old Arab quarter of Tunis to a new housing development on the outskirts. This physical shift allows Ben Ammar to probe the inevitable changes that population shifts, economic change and consumerism have brought to Tunisia.

Bent Familia / Tunisiennes / Girls from Good Families

1997, 112 mins, colour
Director / Screenwriter: Nouri Bouzid
Producer: Cinétéléfilms, Canal+ Horizons, Lucie Films (Tunisia), SFP
                            Cinema (France)
Cinematographer: Armand Marco
Editor: Kahena Attia
Music: Naseer Shama
Designer: Khaled Joulak
Set Design: Hechmi Joulak, Patrick Colot
Leading Players: Amel Hedhili, Nadia Kaci, Leila Nassim, Raouf Ben Amor,
                            Kamel Touati, Abderrazek Hammami, Wafa Salem,
                            Kaouther Bardi, Hassiba Rochdi

Nouri Bouzid's fourth feature, *Bent Familia*, is the story of three women – Amina, a woman suffering violence at home, Aida, a divorcee, and Fatiha, an Algerian refugee – who come together to offer each other comfort until their lives drive them apart again. The film is a powerful exposition of the injustices suffered by women in Tunisian society; indeed at times it seems almost like a sociological study of all possible injustices. But, as always with Bouzid, the performances are strong and there are many powerfully emotional scenes.

Dhil al-'Ardh / L'ombre de la terre / Shadow of the Earth

1982, 90 mins, colour
Director / Screenwriter: Taïeb Louhichi
Producer: SATPEC, Tanit (Tunis), Les Films Molière (Paris), ZDF
                            (German Federal Republic), NCO (Netherlands)
Cinematographer: Ramon Suarez
Editor: Moufida Tlatli
Music: Egisto Macchi
Designer: Naceur Khemir
Set Design: Fawzi Thabet
Leading Players: Despina Tomazani, Abdellatif Hamrouni, Hélène Catzaras,
                            Mouna Noureddine, Abdelkader Mokdad, Rached Khemis

Louhichi's *Dhil al-'Ardh* is the tale of an isolated rural family community – a patriarchal father with his sons and nephews and their families – whose life is slowly torn apart by natural forces and the impact of the modern world. As natural disasters increase pressure on the group, the young men leave for exile or are conscripted. Life continues, with incongruous intrusions from the modern world – identity cards, conscription, a battery-operated television set – as well as the regular exploitative visit of the carpet merchant. The film is an elegy for the passing of a traditional way of life.

al-Fajr / *L'aube* / *The Dawn*

1966, 95 mins, black and white

Director / Screenwriter:	Omar Khlifi
Producer:	Les Films Omar Khlifi
Cinematographer:	Ezzedine Ben Ammar
Editor:	Omar Khlifi
Designer:	Mohamed Sehili
Set Design:	Moncef Fersi
Leading Players:	Habib Chaari, Mohamed Daragi, Jamila Ourabi, Bchira Hah, Ahmed Hamza

The first Tunisian feature film was made by Omar Khlifi, who came from the Tunisian amateur film movement and had no professional training. Set in 1954, *al-Fajr* traces the story of three contrasting young men who participate in the independence struggle. It traces their adventures – liberating prisoners, seeking weapons, dealing with traitors – which lead to death in combat for two of them and execution in prison for the third. The film ends with a postscript: Habib Bourguiba's triumphal return to Tunis on 1 June 1955. The film, which received support from the Tunisian Ministry of Culture, is a soberly told story of resistance to the French occupiers.

Habiba M'Sika / *La danse du feu* / *The Fire Dance*

1995, 100 mins, colour

Director / Screenwriter:	Selma Baccar
Producer:	Phenicea Films, Intermedia Productions, ERTT (Tunisia), CAAIC (Algeria), Canal Horizons, Auraman (France)
Cinematographer:	Allel Yahiaoui
Editor:	Tahar Riahi
Music:	Hammadi Ben Othman
Set Design:	Fawzi Thabet
Leading Players:	Souad Hamidou, Najib Belkadki, Féodor Atkine, Raouf Ben Amor, Jamil Joudi, Paulette Dubost, Abdellatif Khayreddine, Noureddine Ben Aziza, Hédi Daoud, Samia Rhayem, Mohmed Dhia

Habiba M'Sika, the second film by Tunisia's pioneer woman director, tells the story of Habiba M'sika, a singer and dancer who created her own band of devoted admirers but also scandalized Tunisian audiences in the 1920s. She was a woman caught up in a period of turmoil: a nationalist, but influenced by European ideas; a woman passionate about traditional Arab poetry, but influenced by some of the more outrageous European performers of the time, such as Isadora Duncan. As important as the personal trajectory of the singer are the mutations of Tunisian society, caught between Europe and an emerging sense of its own distinct cultural identity.

al-Haimun Fi al-Sahra' / Les baliseurs du désert / The Drifters

1984, 95 mins, colour
Director / Screenwriter: Naceur Khemir
Producer: SATPEC, Latif Productions (Tunisia), France Média (France)
Cinematographer: Georges Barsky
Editor: Moufida Tlatli
Music: Fethi Zgonda
Set Design: Faouzi Thabet
Leading Players: Soufiane Makni, Naceur Khemir, Hedi Daoud, the inhabitants of the villages of Nefta and Tamagza

Khemir's film, imbued with the atmosphere of the *Arabian Nights* and legends of the lost glory of Andalusia, begins with a young schoolteacher, who is sent to a remote village lost in the desert. Certain themes – the mysterious beauty of women and the power of children's ritual games, for example – are established and then vanish, as if effaced by the moving sands of the desert through which men drift endlessly, but with no evident goal. New narrating voices enter and the pattern shifts to form a new whole, as the film creates a complex multi-layered narrative, which constantly reinvents itself in this dream landscape.

Halfawin 'Usfur Stah / Halfaouine l'enfant des terrasses / Halfaouine

1990, 98 mins, colour
Director / Screenwriter: Ferid Boughedir
Producer: Cinétéléfilms (Tunisia), Scarabé Films, France Média (Paris)
Adaptation: Maryse Leon Garcia, Nouri Bouzid, Taoufik Jebali
Cinematographer: Georges Barsky
Editor: Moufida Tlatli
Music: Anouar Braham.
Designer: Claude Bennys
Set Design: Hechmi Joulak
Leading Players: Sélim Boughedir, Mustapha Adouani, Rabia Ben Abdallah, Mohamed Driss, Hélène Catzaras, Fatma Ben Saidane

Ferid Boughedir's internationally acclaimed film *Halfawin 'Usfur Stah* traces the passage from childhood to adolescence of Noura, a young boy of twelve growing up in the Halfaouine quarter of Tunis, who begins to display an increasingly intense interest in the goings-on in the women's bath house to which his unsuspecting mother still takes him. The film paints a vivid picture of the transition from one world to another, from the feminine world of home and security to the harsher masculine world of the streets. Like all of Boughedir's work, it is a passionate plea for tolerance, respect and *joie de vivre*.

Rih al-Sad / *L'homme de cendres* / *Man of Ashes*

1986, 109 mins, colour
Director / Screenwriter: Nouri Bouzid
Producer: Cinétéléfilms, SATPEC
Cinematographer: Youssef Ben Youssef
Editor: Mika Ben Miled
Music: Salah Mehdi
Designer: Claude Bennys
Set Design: Faouzi Thabet, Mohamed Riadh Thabet
Leading Players: Imad Maalal, Khaled Ksouri, Mouna Noureddine, Yacoub Boheri, Mustapha Adouani, Habib Belhedi, Mohamed Dhraief

Nouri Bouzid's first feature is a powerful work that confronts issues of sexuality seldom dealt with in Arab cinema. The film deals with Hachemi, a young carpenter whose imminent marriage (arranged by his parents) makes him recall his childhood. In particular he remembers the male rape of which he – together with his closest friend – was the victim as a child of twelve. As he celebrates his last bachelor night with his friends, he relives his past, including his friendship with an old Jew called Levy. Powerful performances and precise choice of detail make this an unequalled insight into a damaged male identity.

al-Sama / *La trace* / *The Trace*

1988, 90 mins, colour
Director / Screenwriter: Neija Ben Mabrouk
Producer: SATPEC (Tunisia), Marisa Films (Belgium), ZDF (German Federal Republic)
Cinematographer: Marc-André Batigne
Editor: Moufida Tlatli
Music: François Gaudard
Set Design: Faouzi Thabet
Leading Players: Mouna Noureddine, Fatma Khemiri, Basma Tajin, Othman Khemili, Karim Zakaria

By one of the few women directors in North African cinema, *al-Sama* – Neija Ben Mabrouk's first and to date only feature film – had to wait until 1988 (it was shot in 1982) to receive its first screening because of a dispute the with the Tunisian producers SATPEC. The film tells of the efforts made by a young girl, Sabra, born into a poor family in a remote south Tunisian village, to obtain an independent identity in the face of the nightmare of being reduced to a traditional woman's role in society. The school-girl's efforts are eventually successful and she continues her studies – in exile in Europe.

Samt al-Quousour / Les silences du palais / Silences of the Palace

1994, 127 mins, colour
Director / Screenwriter: Moufida Tlatli
Producer: Cinétéléfilms, Magfilm (Tunisia), Mat Film (France)
Adaptation: Nouri Bouzid
Cinematographer: Youssef Ben Youssef
Editor: Moufida Tlatli
Music: Anouar Brahem
Designer: Claude Bennys
Set Design: Fawzi Thabet
Leading Players: Amel Hedhili, Hend Sabri, Najia Ouerghi, Ghalia Lacroix, Kamel Fazaa, Hishem Rostom, Hélène Catzaras, Sonia Meddeb, Mechket Khrifa

Moufida Tlatli's directing debut – after almost twenty years' work as one of the Arab world's leading film editors – is a clear-sighted view of Tunisia's move to independence and its immediate aftermath. The history and politics are conveyed obliquely through the stories of two women: Khedija, servant in the palace of the beys, and her daughter Alia, who breaks away to become a singer in post-independence Tunis. The film is structured around Alia's return, after a gap of ten years, to the palace where she grew up and paints a vivid picture of women's life during the 1950s, as cut off from the wider world but bound by close female solidarity.

Shams al-Diba / Le soleil des hyènes / Hyenas' Sun

1977, 110 mins, colour
Director / Screenwriter: Ridha Behi
Producer: Newin Film (Tunis), Fugitive Film Production, Zegert Huisman (Netherlands)
Cinematographer: Theo Van de Sande
Designer: Jean-Robert Marquis
Music: Nicola Piovani
Set Design: Ton De Graaf
Leading Players: Ahmed Snoussi, Mourad Methkal, Hélène Catzeras, El Ghazi, Mahmoud Morsi

Ridha Behi's savage denunciation of the impact of European tourism on a Mediterranean village ironically received wide screenings (and numerous prizes) at European film festivals. The opening depiction of life in the isolated fishing village shows that traditional life is by no means idyllic, with the power of rich landlords exercised autocratically. But the impact of German developers, working in collaboration with the local rich, is devastating. Tahar tries to resist, but when he returns from prison he finds a new world in which former values have been turned on their head.

al-Sufara' | Les ambassadeurs | The Ambassadors

1975, 102 mins, colour
Director / Screenwriter: Naceur Ktari
Producer: SATPEC, COCITU (Tunisia), General Organization El Kayala (Libya), Unité Trois, Les Films du Nidal (Paris)
Adaptation / Dialogue: Lise Bouizidi, Christine Jancovici, Ahmed Kassem, Gérard Mauger, Naceur Ktari
Cinematographer: Jean-Jacques Rochut
Editor: François Ceppi, Arbi Ben Ali, Lise Bouizidi
Music: Hamadi Ben Othman
Designer: Denis Martin-Sisteron
Set Design: Antoine Bonfanti, Hachmi Joulak, Auguste Galli
Leading Players: Sid Ali Kouiret, Tahar Kebaïli, Mohamed Hamman, Dynn Yaad, Denise Peron, Jacques Rispal, Marcel Cuvelier

Naceur Ktari's sole feature film is a forceful and committed study of the lives of immigrant workers in France. The ironic title derives from the words of the politician who addresses them as they leave for Europe and in no way reflects their actual status there. The film's strong narrative traces the group's shift from individual concerns to real friendship and, after two racist killings, the move to political action. But here too Ktari refuses rhetorical notions, such as the unity of the workers of the world.

'Ubur | Traversées | Crossings

1982, 90 mins, colour
Director: Mahmoud Ben Mahmoud
Producer: SATPEC (Tunisia), Marisa Films (Belgium)
Screenwriter: Mahmoud Ben Mahmoud, Philippe Lejuste
Dialogue: Fadhel Jaziri
Cinematographer: Gilberto Azevedo
Editor: Moufida Tlatli, Arbi Ben Ali
Music: Francaso Accolla
Designer: Maryse Houyoux
Set Design: Faouzi Thabet, Hechemi Joulek
Leading Players: Fadhel Jaziri, Julian Negulesco, Eva Darlan, Vincent Gras, Christian Maillet, Colette Emmanuel

Mahmoud Ben Mahmoud's *'Ubur* is set on 31 December 1980 and plots the parallel fates of two refugees, a working-class Polish dissident and an Arab intellectual, trapped on a cross-channel ferry. Because they both lack the necessary passport documents, neither the British nor the Belgian authorities will allow them to come ashore. Separated by language, class and culture, they are unable to take a common stand and each goes their separate way: the Pole towards the suicidal killing of a policeman and the Arab, strengthened by a casual sexual encounter, towards an inner world. The film is a major examination of issues of emigration, exile and identity.

al-'Urs / La noce / The Wedding

1978, 90 mins, black and white
Director / Screenwriter: Collectif du Nouveau Théâtre de Tunis (Jalilla Baccar, Mohamed Driss, Fadhel Jaïbi, Fadhel Jaziri, Habib Masrouki)
Producer: Collectif du Nouveau Théâtre de Tunis
Cinematographer: Habib Masrouki
Editor: Arbi Ben Ali
Set Design: Faouzi Thabet, Hechmi Joulak
Leading Players: Jalilla Baccar, Mohamed Driss, Fadhel Jaziri, Fadhel Jaïbi

Al-'Urs is the adaptation of their own successful stage production by the Collectif du Nouveau Théâtre de Tunis. Set after the guests have departed, it depicts the violent and self-destructive interaction of a newly wed couple. The film's theatrical origins are very apparent in both the static action and the symbolic setting of a crumbling mansion. Shot in black and white, the film's strength lies in the power of the performances and the simple but effective direction. Two of the collective, Fadhel Jaïbi and Fadhel Jaziri, went on to direct further features.

List of film-makers

Attia, Ahmed Baha Eddine (b. 1946, Sousse, Tunisia)

Attia began to study modern literature at the Sorbonne before going on to study film direction at the Centro sperimentale di cinematografia in Rome from 1968 to 1970. From 1970 to 1971 he worked for the Italian television service RAI. At the beginning of his career he did a wide range of production work during and after his studies in Europe and Tunisia, before returning home in 1973. He worked from 1974–8 as head of audio-visual services at Office National de la Télévision Tunisienne (ONTT). He occupied a variety of production roles – assistant director, production manager and executive producer – from the late 1960s onwards. Among the feature films to which he contributed as assistant director were Sadok Ben Aicha's *Mukhdar* (1968), George Cukor's *Justine* (1969), Abdellatif Ben Ammar's *Hikaya Basita Kahadhidhi* (1969) and Taïeb Louhichi's *Dhil al-'Ardh* (1982) and a number of French and Italian films. He worked as production manager on several late 1970s films: the English *Life of Brian* (1978), the French *Rodriguez* (1978) and the Italian *Le Larron / The Thief* (Pasquale Festa Campanile, 1979). He also made a number of short films in the late 1960s and

1970s: *Le vendeur d'eau* / *The Water Seller* (1969), *Takrouna* (1969), *Il Bollerino* (1970, his graduation film at the Centro sperimentale), *L'industrie de chaussure* / *The Shoe Trade* (1973), *La colonie de vacances* / *The Holiday Camp* (1973), *L'olivier* / *The Olive Tree* (1974), *L'université de Tunis* / *The University of Tunis* (1974), *Cités ouvertes de Tunisie* / *Open Cities of Tunisia* (1975) and *La côte de corail* / *The Coral Coast* (1980).

In the 1980s he emerged as Tunisia's leading film producer with his company, Cinétéléfilms, founded in 1983. The apparently semi-autobiographical *auteur* cinema Attia advocates and supports – exemplified by the first fictional feature films of Nouri Bouzid (*Rih al-Sid*, *Safa'ih Min Dhahab*, *Bezness* and *Bent Familia*), Ferid Boughedir (*Halfawin 'Usfur Stah*), Moufida Tlatli (*Samt al-Quousour*) and Moncef Dhouib (*Ya Sultan al-Madina*) – has attracted worldwide attention. His company has regularly shown a preference for supporting new talent and has produced numerous short films by young directors. In 1992, with backing from Channel Four in the United Kingdom and Libra Film in Italy, Attia produced *Harbu al-Khallij Wa B'ad?* / *La Guerre du Golfe … et après?* / *After the Gulf War?*, which allowed five Arab film-makers (Bouzid, Neija Ben Mabrouk, the Moroccan Mustapha Derkaoui, the Lebanese documentarist Borhan Alawiya and the New York-based Palestinian Elia Soleiman) to offer short meditations, mixing documentary and fiction, on the aftermath of the Gulf War. In 1992 and again in 1994 Attia was director of the Carthage Film Festival (the JCC – Journées Cinématographiques de Carthage) in Tunis. In 1997 he produced Mohamed Abderrahman Tazi's Moroccan comedy, *Lalla Hobby*.

Baccar, Selma (b. 1945, Tunis, Tunisia)

A product of the Tunisian amateur film movement FTCA, Baccar first made two personal films, *al-Yaqda* / *L'éveil* / *The Awakening* (1968) and *al-Ghurub* / *Le crépuscule* / *The Twilight* (1968), in the context of the ciné-club at Hammam-Lif. She also studied direction at the IFC in Paris from 1968 to 1970. Subsequently she worked as assistant in Tunisian television, RTT, from 1969 to 1976. She was assistant director on Sadok Ben Aicha's *'Aridhat al-'Azia* (1978) and worked in production roles on *al-Zaïtuna, Qalbu Tunis* / *La Zitouna au coeur de Tunis* / *The Zitouna in the Heart of Tunis* (Hmida Ben Ammar, 1982), *'Ubur* (Mahmoud Ben Mahmoud, 1982), *al-Sama* (Neija Ben Mabrouk, 1988), *al-Zazuwwat* (Mohamed Ali el-Okbi, 1992).

In 1978 she completed the first feature-length work directed by a woman in Tunisia, *Fatma 75*, a series of portraits of major Tunisian women from the days of Carthage onwards. The film was censored by the government. She later made the fifty-two-minute documentary *Au pays du Tarayoun* / *In the Land of the Tarayoun* (1985), which was one of the first films produced by Ahmed Baba Eddine Attia's Cinétéléfilms; this film was also distributed in a shortened version under the title *De la toison au fil d'or* / *About the Golden Fleece*. A further short film is *L'histoire des costumes* / *The History of Costume* (1985). Her second feature-length film, *Habiba M'Sika* (1995), was the fictional study of real character, Habiba M'Sika, a singer and dancer who scandalized Tunisian audiences with her Westernized attitudes during the nationalist turmoil of the 1920s.

Behi, Ridha (b. 1947, Kairouan, Tunisia)

Behi studied literature and social science, first in Tunis and then (from 1969–76) at Paris X – Nanterre. In Paris he completed his doctorate with a thesis on 'Cinema and Society in Tunisia during the 1960s' under the supervision of Marc Ferro at the Ecole Pratique des Hautes Etudes in 1977. Meanwhile he had come to film-making through the AJCT and the amateur film movement. In Kairouan he worked on two short films with Ahmed Khéchine, *Sabra* (1966) and *La poupée / The Doll* (1967), and then collaborated on the script of the same director's first feature, *Tahta Matar al-Kharif* (1970). Behi worked for a time as assistant in Tunisian television and made his first first short film, *La femme-statue / The Woman-Statue*, in the context of the Kairouan ciné-club in 1969 – it attracted little attention. He achieved widespread notoriety and won the major short-film prize at the Carthage Film Festival (the JCC), however, with his second short film, *Atabat Mamnu'a / Seuils interdits / Forbidden Thresholds* (1972), a study of sexual frustration featuring a young Arab who rapes a young blonde tourist in a mosque.

Behi's first feature film, *Shams al-Diba* (1977), was co-produced by his production company Newin Production. The film, which had to be shot outside Tunisia – near Agadir in Morocco – with production finance from Germany and the Netherlands, is a lucid and impassioned attack on the impact of tourism on North African life and society. The film was widely and successfully shown in the West, but received distribution in only two Arab countries, Libya and Iraq. Behi made ten documentaries in the Gulf states between 1980 and 1983, and has subsequently struggled to establish his own voice, with the pressures of co-production and internationalism being particularly apparent in his later work. For *al-Mala'ika* (1984), the story of a group of young Tunisian actors and their relationship with a rich businessman, he obtained production finance from Egypt and Kuwait, and used Egyptian stars (Madiha Kamil and Kamal al-Shinawi) and Egyptian dialect, but still failed to get distribution in Egypt. Subsequently, in *Washmun 'Ala al-Dhakira* (1988, also known as *La mémoire tatouée / Tattooed Memory*), he employed international stars (Ben Gazzara and Julie Christie) and the French language, even using French actors to play Arab roles in the story of a settler, forced to break his ties with the past on the eve of independence in 1955, who abandons his Arab mistress. In 1994 he made a further international film, *al-Khuttaf La Iyamut Fi al-Quds*, starring Jacques Perrin and dealing with the problems of a French journalist in Israeli-occupied Palestine.

Ben Ammar, Abdellatif (b. 1943, Tunis, Tunisia)

Ben Ammar studied at IDHEC in Paris, graduating in 1964. He worked for a while as a reporter and cameraman for the Tunisian newsreel company *Les Actualitées Tunisiennes*, then worked as assistant cameraman on *Les aventuriers / The Adventurers* (Robert Enrico, 1966) and *Indomptable Angélique / Untameable Angélique* (Bernard Borderie, 1966), and as assistant director on *Justine* (George Cukor, 1968), *Rebel Jesus* (Buchanan, 1970), *Biribi* (Daniel Moosman, 1971), *Il Messia / The Messiah* (Roberto Rossellini, 1974), *Les magiciens / The Magicians* (Claude Chabrol, 1975) and as director of production on *Jesus of Nazareth* (Franco Zeffirelli, 1977). Ben Ammar also worked as cameraman on the short Tunisian films *2 + 2 = 5* and *Matanza* (both directed by Hassan Daldoul in 1966) and the feature-length *Mukhdar* (Sadok Ben

Aicha, 1968). He made a number of short films of his own, including *The Brain* (1967), *Operation Eyes* (1967), *Espérance / Hope* (1969), *Baal Babylone* (1971) and *Kairouan* (1973).

In the decade 1970–80, Ben Ammar wrote and directed three feature films that are among the major works of Tunisian cinema. *Hikaya Basita Kahadhidhi* (1970) examined the contemporary clash of cultures experienced by a young Tunisian who returns from training in France, told through the stories of two mixed couples both of which relationships end in failure. *Sejnan* (1974) is set in 1952 – the period preceding Tunisian independence – and traces the growth in political awareness of Kemal, who abandons his studies to take up a struggle which culminates in his death, setting this against the story of Anissa, the girl he loves but who is married against her will to a rich neighbour. *'Aziza* (1980), which won the Tanit d'Or at the Carthage Film Festival (the JCC) in 1980, is Ben Ammar's finest film, a depiction of the problems of contemporary Tunisian society – emigration, foreign dominance, speculation and superstition. Contemporary society is seen through the eyes of a young orphan, 'Aziza, who lives with a family which moves from the old Arab quarter of Tunis to a new housing development on the outskirts.

Subsequently Ben Ammar has made publicity shorts and documentaries, and been involved – through his production company Latif Productions, set up in 1972 – with co-productions such as Naceur Khemir's *al-Haimun Fi al-Sahra'* (1984) and Fitouri Belhiba's *Ruqayya* (1990).

Ben Mabrouk, Neija (b. 1949, El-Oudiane, Tunisia)

Ben Mabrouk studied French language and literature in the University of Tunis, before going on to study film-making at INSAS in Belgium from 1972–6. Her graduation film, which she both wrote and directed, was the award-winning *Pour vous servir / At Your Service* (1976). She worked as a trainee in Belgian television (RTBF) before filming *al-Sama* (1988), the first fictional feature film to be made by a woman director in Tunisia. The film, set in a remote south Tunisian village, shows the efforts made by a young girl, Sabra, to keep her independent identity – efforts which eventually drive her into exile in Europe. Because of a dispute with SATPEC, the producer, this film was not shown until 1988, despite having been completed in 1982. In 1992 Ben Mabrouk contributed one fifteen-minute episode, 'Fi al-Bahth An Shaima' / 'In Search of Chaima', to the collectively made *Harbu al-Khallij Wa B'ad? / La Guerre du Golfe … et après / After the Gulf War?*, produced by Ahmed Baba Eddine Attia. Filmed in Baghdad, her contribution was an investigation of the impact of the war on women and children.

Ben Mahmoud, Mahmoud (b. 1947, Tunis, Tunisia)

Ben Mahmoud now lives in Belgium where, after studying film-making at the Belgian film school INSAS from 1967 to 1970, he took diplomas at the Free University of Brussels in both art history / archeology and journalism / social communication (1971–4). He collaborated on the scripts of the first feature films of two of his fellow INSAS graduates: *Le fils de Amr est mort / Amr's Son is Dead* (1972) by the Belgian film-maker Jean-Jacques Andrien and *Kafr Kassem* (1974), directed by the Lebanese documentarist Borhan Alawiya. Later Ben Mahmoud worked on the scripts of Alawiya's *L'Emir* / *The Emir* (1975) and Philippe Lejuste's feature *L'odeur angulaire* / *The Angular Scent* (1975). He also worked as sound recordist on Rachid Ferchiou's Tunisian feature *Yusra* / *Yusra* (1972).

Ben Mahmoud's first and (to date) only solo feature was *'Ubur* (1982), an elegant fable of identity and commitment. The film plots the parallel fates of two refugees, a Polish dissident and an Arab, trapped on a cross-channel ferry because they both lack the necessary passport documents. His second feature, *Chichkhan* / *Chichkhan* (1992), was co-written and co-directed with Fadhel Jaïbi. It is a fable of family rivalries and secrets, built around a stolen bracelet (the Chichkhan of the title) and telling of the doomed love of an old man for a young girl.

Ben Mahmoud subsequently made three video documentaries: a fifty-minute portrait of members of the Italian community in Tunisia, *Italiani del altra riva* / *Italians from the Other Shore* (1992), the twenty-seven minute collective documentary *Les travailleurs émigrés en Belgique* / *Immigrant Workers in Belgium* (1994), a video portrait of Claudia Cardinale called *La plus belle Italienne de Tunis* / *The Most Beautiful Italian Woman of Tunis* (1994) and a documentary study of the pioneer Tunisian film-maker of the 1920s: *Albert Samama-Chikly* (1996).

Boughedir, Ferid (b. 1944, Hammam Lif, Tunisia)

Boughedir has led a varied career as film critic, theorist and historian, as well as working as a film-maker. A product of the Tunisian amateur film movement and member of the Tunis ciné-club, he studied literature at the University of Rouen. He has continued his academic career, teaching film at the Universities of Paris III and Tunis, and completing his doctorate – with a thesis on the thematics and economics of African cinema – in 1986. He has published widely on African and Arab cinemas, writing for numerous magazines (especially *Jeune Afrique*, for which he edited a special number on 'Le cinéma en Afrique et dans le monde' in 1984). He has contributed to collective volumes in the CinémAction series on *Cinémas noirs d'Afrique* (1984), *Les cinémas du Maghreb* (1987) and *Les cinémas arabes* (1987), and produced a solo study of *Le cinéma africain de A à Z* (1987).

His first short films date from the 1960s: *Paris–Tunis* (1963–7), made within the context of the Tunis ciné-club, *Riche pour un jour* / *Rich for a Day* (1964) and *Le roumi* (1969). In the late 1960s he also worked as assistant director on *L'Eden et après* (Alain Robbe-Grillet, 1969) and *Viva la muerte* (Fernando Arrabal, 1970), and his early work shows a self-conscious concern with modernist narrative-structures and a taste for farce and grotesquery. He also worked on two French-language Tunisian features at the end of the 1960s, co-scripting *Mukhdar* / *Mokhtar* (1968), directed by Sadok Ben Aicha, and co-writing and co-directing *al-Mawt al-Akhir* (1970) with the Frenchman Claude d'Anna. The latter film is a complex allegory about colonialism, sexuality, race and power involving three girls, an old man and a servant, all set on an imaginary island. He also contributed one farcical sketch, 'al-Nuzha' / 'Le pique-nique' / 'The Picnic', depicting the misadventures of a family who set out to enjoy a picnic, to the feature-length collective film *Fi Bilad al-Tararani* (1972), which comprised adaptations of stories by Ali Douaji. Subsequently he completed four documentaries about African and Arab cinemas. These were two shorts – *JCC 74* (1974) and *al-Sinima Fi*

Qartaj / Cinéma de Carthage / Cinema at Carthage (1984) – and two more substantial works – the feature-length *Kamira Ifriqiya / Caméra d'Afrique / African Camera* (1983) and the medium-length *Kamira 'Arabiya / Caméra arabe / Arab Camera* (1987) – all of which have received international television screenings.

Boughedir's first solo fictional feature was *Halfawin 'Usfur Stah* (1990), produced by Ahmed Baba Eddine Attia. The central figure is a young boy, growing up in Tunis, who displays an increasingly intense interest in the goings-on in the women's bath house to which his unsuspecting mother takes him. It is a marvellously evocative and humorous portrait of childhood which became not only a critical success but also (to date) the most popular local film with Tunisian audiences. Boughedir's second fictional feature, *Salfun Fi Halq al-Wadi* (1995), is another look back at his youth – this time the port-resort of La Goulette in the 1960s. But the film lacks *Halfawin*'s sureness of touch: its attempt to link the action to the outbreak of the July 1967 war and find a role for Claudia Cardinale are clumsy. But the film's noisy elements of farce and touches of nudity meant that it did find an audience.

Bouzid, Nouri (b. 1945, Sfax, Tunisia)

Bouzid studied film-making at INSAS in Brussels from 1968, graduating in 1972 with the short film *Duel*. He worked as trainee on André Delvaux's *Rendez-vous à Bray / Appointment at Bray* (1972). On his return to Tunisia, he spent some time in 1972–3 working in Tunisian television (RTT). He was arrested and imprisoned for over five years (1973–9) for his participation in the radical Groupe d'Etude et d'Action Socialiste Tunisien (GEAST). Subsequently he worked as assistant director on a number of foreign films, including *Raiders of the Lost Ark* (Steven Spielberg, 1981), *Mieux vaut d'être riche / Better to be Rich* (Max Pécas, 1981), *Le Larron / The Thief* (Pasquale Festa Campanile, 1982), *Anno Domini* (Stuart Cooper, 1984), *The Key to Rebecca* (David Hemming, 1984), *Par où t'es rentré? / Where Did You Come Back In?* (Philippe Clair, 1984).

Bouzid was also assistant on several Tunisian features in the 1980s: *'Aziza* (Abdellatif Ben Ammar, 1980), *al-Zaïtuna, Qalbu Tunis* (Hmida Ben Ammar, 1982), *al-Mala'ika* (Ridha Behi, 1984). In addition, he worked on the adaptation for and/or dialogue of a number of key Tunisian feature films of the 1990s, including Ferid Boughedir's *Halfawin 'Usfur Stah* (1990), Brahim Babaï's *Laylat al-Sanawat al-'Ashr* (1991), Moncef Dhouib's *Ya Sultan al-Madina* (1993) and Moufida Tlatli's *Samt al-Quousour* (1994).

Bouzid's own first three feature films, all produced by Ahmed Attia and made in quick succession, established him as a major figure in Maghreb cinema and confronted themes and issues long ignored or evaded in Arab cinema in general. All have a personal, semi-autobiographical tone which is rare in the Maghreb, where it is more customary for male directors to make sensitive films about female victims than to confront the contradictions of Arab concepts of masculinity. *Rih al-Sid* (1986) was a remarkable debut, a brooding and atmospheric film set in the director's birthplace – the city of Sfax. The film deals with Hachemi, a young carpenter, whose imminent marriage, arranged by his parents, makes him recall his childhood. In particular he remembers the male rape of which he was the victim as a child of twelve, an event he is unable to discuss with anyone within his own family circle. The film deservedly won the top prize, the Tanit d'Or, at the Carthage Film Festival (the JCC) in 1986. *Safa'ih Min Dhahab* (1989) followed in the same semi-autobiographical vein, with its story of a political prisoner unable to reintegrate himself into Tunisian life. The story of a man who emerges from years in prison but is able neither to recognize the society in which he finds himself nor to re-establish relationships with his family. The film ends in suicide. Bouzid's third feature, *Bezness / Business* (1992), was equally controversial with its story of a Western photographer making a report on Tunisian gigolos who prostitute themselves to male as well as female tourists. It showed the contradictions in the life of Roufa, who sells himself to tourists while remaining totally repressive towards his sister and his girlfriend, who loves his country but dreams of Europe.

Bouzid contributed one episode, 'Sakatat Shahrazad 'An al-Kalam al-Aubab' / 'C'est Shérazade qu'on assassine' / 'It's Sheherazade Who's Being Killed', a discussion of where the blame for the Gulf War lies, to the collectively made *Harbu al-Khallij Wa B'ad?* (1992), also produced by Attia. In 1993 he shot a twenty-minute video called *Les mains dans le plat / Hands in the Dish*. He returned to feature-film directing with *Bent Familia* (1997), the story of three women – a battered middle-class wife, a divorcee and an Algerian refugee – whose lives come together in Tunis. The film is a powerful plea for women's freedom.

Jaïbi, Fadhel (b. 1945, Ariana, Tunisia)

Born in Ariana in Tunisia, Jaïbi studied at the Institut des Etudes Théâtrales – Paris Censier from 1967 to 1972, simultaneously working as a trainee at the Université Internationale du Théâtre in Paris from 1969 to 1970. In 1970 Jaïbi was co-founder of the Théâtre de l'Epoque in France and two years later he was co-founder, with Fadhel Jaziri, of the Théâtre du Sud at Gafsa in Tunisia. From 1974 to 1978 he worked as director of the Centre National d'Art Dramatique. In 1976, together with Jaziri, Jalila Baccar, Mohamed Driss and Habib Masrouki, he helped found a theatrical collective called the Théâtre Nouveau de Tunis. For the stage its major productions included *al-'Urs* (1976), *L'instruction / The Order* (1978), *Ghassalet Ennouader* (1979), *'Arab* (1987) and *El Awada* (1989).

For the cinema the collective produced a film version of *al-'Urs* (1978), a claustrophobic tale of unhappy sexual relationships, set in a bleak and crumbling mansion and drawing inspiration in part, it seems, from Bertolt Brecht. Subsequently Jaïbi and Jaziri co-scripted and co-directed the film adaptation of a second Nouveau Théâtre de Tunis stage production: *'Arab* (1988). This was a complex fable dealing, on one level, with an air-hostess from Beirut transported into a world of legend and, on another, with fundamental questions of Arab history and contemporary experience. Later Jaïbi co-directed a new feature, *Chichkhan* (1992), with Mahmoud Ben Mahmoud. This is a darkly brooding tale of family secrets and rivalry, focused on a stolen bracelet (the Chichkhan of the title) and treating the doomed love of an aging aristocrat for a young girl. Jaïbi also co-wrote two other scripts, *Kahla Hamra* (1985) and *Saveur orientale / Oriental Flavour* (1987), that were never produced. With Fadhel Jaziri, he also co-directed video versions of three theatrical productions: *L'instruction* (1978), *Ghassalet Ennouader* (1979) and *El Awada* (1989).

Jaziri, Fadhel (b. 1948, Tunis, Tunisia)

Jaziri was, with Fadhel Jaïbi, one of the founders of the Théâtre du Sud at Gafsa in Tunisia. In 1976, together with Jaïbi, Jelila Baccar, Mohamed Driss and Habib Masrouki, Jaziri was one of the co-founders of the theatrical collective known as the Nouveau Théâtre de Tunis. He was actively involved in a number of the collective's stage productions, including *al-'Urs* (1978), *L'instruction* (1978), *Ghassalet Ennouader* (1979) and *'Arab* (1988).

In 1978 the collective brought to the screen a striking version of one of its productions, *al-'Urs* (1978), a tale of of unhappy sexual relationships, set in a bleak and crumbling mansion, which apparently drew its inspiration from the work of Bertolt Brecht. Ten years later Jaziri and Jaïbi co-wrote and co-directed the screen adaptation of another of the Nouveau Théâtre's productions, *'Arab* (1988), a complex fable dealing, on one level, with an air-hostess from Beirut transported into a world of legend and, on another, with fundamental questions of Arab history and contemporary experience With Fadhel Jaïbi, he also co-directed three video versions of theatrical productions: *The Order* (1978), *Ghassalet Ennouader* (1979) and *El Awada* (1989). In 1982 Jaziri played the lead in Mahmoud Ben Mahmoud's *'Ubur*, for which he also co-wrote the dialogue. He had previously appeared in Abdellatif Ben Ammar's *Sejnan* (1974) and Roberto Rossellini's *Il Messia / The Messiah* (1978).

Khemir, Naceur (b. 1948, Korla, Tunisia)

Khemir has been active as a sculptor, writer and performing storyteller, in addition to his work as a film-maker. He was responsible for the show *Alf Yad Wa Yad*, presented at the Théâtre National de Chaillot in 1982 and 1988. He has also shown his work widely in North Africa and in France, with exhibitions of sculpture at both the Musée d'Art Moderne and the Centre Georges Pompidou in Paris. His books in French include *Ogresse / Ogress* (1975), *Le soleil emmuré / The Walled-In Sun* (1981), *Le conte des conteurs / The Story of Storytellers* (1984), *Schéhérazade / Sheherazade* (with Oum El Khir, 1987) and *Paroles d'Islam / Words of Islam* (1994).

His short films include the animation *al-Haatah / The Woodcutter* (1972), *al-Baghl / Le Mulet / The Mule* (1975), *Hikayatu Bilad Malik Rabbi / Histoire du pays du bon dieu / The Story of God's Own Land* (1976, for INA), *Sum'a / Soma* (1978, with Mohamed Charbagi), *L'ogresse / The Ogress* (1977), a television production for Suisse Romande Television.

He began his feature-film career with *al-Haimun Fi al-Sahra'* (1984), a complex narrative which draws on the Arab oral tradition in its story of a young schoolteacher who is sent to a remote village in the desert, where he experiences a series of stories which successively come into view and then fade from sight. Khemir's second feature, *Tawq al-Hamama al-Mafqud* (1990), further develops the narrative experiments of his first feature. Set in the eleventh century, at the height of Andalusian civilization, the film tells of the mysterious events that result from a young calligrapher's quest for love and knowledge. Khemir subsequently made a two-hour video, co-produced with France and Italy, called *A la recherche des mille et un nuits / In Search of the Thousand and One Nights* (1991). Khemir was also responsible for the design of Taïeb Louhichi's *Dhil al-'Ardh* (1982).

Khlifi, Omar (b. 1934, Soliman, Tunisia)

Omar Khlifi, the great pioneer of post-independence Tunisian cinema, studied both in Tunis and at Nancy in France. He received no formal training in film-making, but emerged from the flourishing Tunisian amateur film-making movement. In 1959 he founded the Association des Cinéastes Amateurs de Tunisie and, in the early 1960s, made a dozen short 16 mm films: *Une page de notre histoire / A Page of Our History* (with Ahmed Rachedi, 1961), *Oncle Mosbah à la ville / Uncle Mosbah in the City* (1961), *Les volontaires / The Volunteers* (1961), *J'ai rencontré deux jeunes filles / I Met Two Young Women* (1962), *Pèlerinage 1963 / Pilgrimage 1963* (1963), *Hlima* (1963), *Le grand air / Fresh Air* (1963), *Pèlerinage 1964 / Pilgrimage 1964* (1964), *Antar, mouton de l'Aïd / Antar, Sheep of the Aïd* (1964), *Khemaïs Tarnan* (1964), *Congrès Uget 1964 / Uget Congress 1964* (1964), *Amour et Jalousie / Love and Jealousy* (1964). His first 35 mm film was a twenty-minute short called *Drame Bédouin / Bedouin Drama* (1965).

Khlifi founded his own production company, Les Films Omar Khlifi, in 1960 and six years later directed the first Tunisian feature film. Set in 1954, *al-Fajr* (1966) traces the story of three young men who give their lives in the independence struggle. This forms a loose trilogy with his two subsequent features: *al-Mutamarrid* (1968), dealing with the struggle against Ottoman rule in Tunisia, and *al-Fallaga* (1970), made in colour as a Tunisian–Bulgarian co-production and depicting the struggle in the 1950s against the French who continued to threaten Tunisian independence. In all three films the themes are passionately nationalist, but the style is deeply influenced by popular Hollywood cinema. By contrast *Surakh* (1972), arguably Khlifi's best film, treats the problems of women in Arab society in a stylistically more interesting way, focusing on two women, one of whom is raped, then disowned and eventually killed by her family, while the other (her sister) is married against her will.

For his return after a fourteen-year break, Khlifi decided to attempt a political thriller in Costa-Gavras's style: *al-Tahaddi* (1986). The film tells of a rising by Tunisian resistance fighters in 1952 which provoked mass arrests and the assassination of political leaders. It has the same commitment as Khlifi's earlier work, but the result was markedly less successful, with the political struggle reduced to a leaden and unconvincing melodrama. In 1970 Khlifi published his own French-language account of the origins of Tunisian cinema, *L'histoire du cinéma en Tunisie*.

Ktari, Naceur (b. 1943, Sayad, Tunisia)

Ktari studied in Paris – at IDHEC, at the Conservatoire du Cinéma Français (CCF) and at the Sorbonne – and in Rome at the Centro sperimentale di cinematografia. He worked as a trainee in the Dino de Laurentis studios, then as assistant to Roberto Rossellini (*Atti degli Apostoli / The Acts of the Apostles*, 1968) and Dino Risi (*Il Giovane Normale / The Normal Young Man*, 1968). He also made a first short film, *Show 5000* (1968), while in Italy. Back in Tunisia he worked both for television and SATPEC, serving as assistant on two fairly insignificant Franco–Tunisian co-productions: *Biribi* (Daniel Moosman, 1970) and *Mendiants et orgueilleux / The Beggars and the Proud* (Jacques Poitrenaud, 1971).

He made a further short film in France, *Prenons la ville / Let's Take the City* (1973), before completing his first, much-acclaimed feature, *al-Sufara'* (1975), which won the Tanit d'Or at the Carthage Film Festival in 1976. This film dealt with emigration; in it

the protagonists move from individuality to friendship and from violence to a realization of the need for unity. It was a committed, closely observed study of Arab
immigrants in France, well acted and with the narrative shape and pace of the action
excellently handled. From 1979–80 Ktari worked in Canadian television and in 1981
worked as assistant director (alongside Nouri Bouzid) on Steven Spielberg's *Raiders of
the Lost Ark*. In the 1980s he made only a handful of short films: *Bonne fête / Good
Holiday* (1981), *Tihi Wa Aziko* (1985) and *JTC* (1985).

Louhichi, Taïeb (b. 1948, Mareth, Tunisia)

Louhichi studied film-making at the IFC and the Ecole de Vaugirard in Paris. He also
studied literature and sociology at Paris VII, completing his doctorate with a sociological
study of his native region. He made short films both in the context of the FTCA and at
film school. His shorts include *Masques / Masks* (1970), *Loge d'artiste / The Artist's Box*
(1971), *Ourakh al-Hajar* (1971), *Labyrinthes / Labyrinths* (1971), *Qariaty Bayna al-Qura /
My Village, a Village like So Many Others* (1972), *Ziara ou visite à l'aïeul Marabout / Ziara
or Visit to the Marabout Ancestor* (1973), *al-Khammas / The Sharecropper* (1975), *Le
temps d'apprendre / The Time to Learn* (1978), *Carthage, an 12 / Carthage, Year 12* (1978),
Gabès, l'oasis et l'usine / Gabès, the Oasis and the Factory (1983), *La famille productive /
The Productive Family* (1990), *Cinéma du sud / Cinema from the South* (1992), *Ecrans
d'Afrique / African Screens* (a study of the invasion of African screens by films from the
north, 1992), *Ker Joe Ouakam* (1994) and *Le chant de Baye Fall / The Song of Baye Fall*
(1994). He has also worked as a producer for French radio.

His first feature, *Dhil al-'Ardh* (1982), is the tale of an isolated rural family community torn apart by natural forces and, to a lesser extent, by the impact of the modern
world. The film has a slow deliberate rhythm and is beautifully shot. *Gorée,
Grandfather's Island* (1987), a fifty-minute 16 mm film shot in Senegal, deals with an
American jazzman who returns to the former slave port to seek out his own origins.
Majnun Leila (1989), his next feature, was a version of the legend of *Le fou de Layla*,
adapted with the French author André Miquel from the latter's novel. The love of the
young poet Qays for the beautiful Layla meets with opposition from her father in this
adaptation of a traditional tale, filmed with considerable visual sophistication in the
Algerian desert. In 1998 he made a third feature, *'Urs al-Qamar*, the urban story of a
group of young people whose friendship is disrupted by an accidental death and its
aftermath.

Samama-Chikly, Albert (b. 1872, Tunis, Tunisia; d. 1934, Tunis, Tunisia)

A businessman who specialized in introducing Western novelties (such as the bicycle,
still photography and the radio) to Arab consumers, Samama-Chikly arranged the
first film showings in Tunis in 1897. Subsequently he made the first Tunisian short
film, *al-Zahara / Zohra* (1922) and the first Tunisian feature, *Ain al-Ghazal / La fille de
Carthage / The Girl from Carthage* (1924), both starring his daughter Haydée Chikli (b.
1906), who also appeared in Rex Ingram's 1924 feature, *L'arabe / The Arab*, which
starred Alice Terry and Ramon Navarro. *al-Zahara / Zohra*, which told the story of a
young French woman shipwrecked on the coast of Tunisia and eventually rescued by a
dashing airman, included scenes of Bedouin life; *Ain al-Ghazal* made strong use of

local colour (palaces, landscapes, local dances and ceremonies) in telling the unhappy tale of young lovers who are separated when the girl is married off to a rich man, and who eventually die in each other's arms.

Tlatli, Moufida (b. 1947, Sidi Bou Said, Tunisia)

Tlatli studied at the IDHEC in Paris, graduating in 1968. From 1968 to 1972 she worked at ORTF in Paris as a scriptwriter (1968–9) and director of production (1969–72). On her return to Tunisia she worked as editor on many major Arab films of the 1970s and 1980s, including the Tunisian films *Sejnan* (Abdellatif Ben Ammar, 1974), *Fatma 75* (Selma Baccar, 1978), *'Aziza* (Abdellatif Ben Ammar, 1980), *Dhil al-'Ardh* (Taïeb Louhichi, 1982), *'Ubur* (Mahmoud Ben Mahmoud, 1982), *al-Sabt Fat?* (Lotfi Essid, 1983), *al-Haimun Fi al-Sahra'* (Naceur Khemir, 1984), *Kamira 'Arabiya* (Ferid Boughedir, 1987), *al-Sama* (Neija Ben Mabrouk, 1988), *Majnun Leila* (Taïeb Louhichi, 1989), *Halfawin 'Usfur Stah* (Ferid Boughedir, 1990) and *al-Zazuwwat* (Mohamed Ali el-Okbi, 1992); the Algerian films *Umar Gatlatu* (Merzak Allouache, 1976) and *Nahla* (Farouk Beloufa, 1979); the Palestinian film *al-Dhikrayat al-Khasibah / Fertile Memory* (Michel Khleifi, 1981); and the Moroccan film *Bab al-Sama' Maftuh* (Farida Benlyazid, 1987).

Tlati made her feature-film debut as a director with *Samt al-Quousour* (1994), produced by Ahmed Attia. In the film, the twenty-five-year-old Alya remembers her upbringing in the bey's palace where her mother was a servant in the 1950s. This eloquent study of women's servitude won the Tanit d'Or at the 1994 session of the Tunisian film festival, the Journées Cinématographiques de Carthage.

MAURITANIA

There is no Mauritanian cinema as such, but a number of Mauritanians are actively involved with cinema, working largely from exile in Europe. The major figure, meriting a place in any list of major African film-makers, is Med Hondo (b. 1936), who has made a number of documentaries and seven feature-length films in the course of thirty years: *Soleil O* (1969), *Les bicots-nègres vos voisins / The Niggers Next Door* (1974), *Nous aurons toute la mort pour dormir / We Shall Have the Whole of Death to Sleep* (1977), *West Indies ou les nègres marrons de la liberté / West Indies* (1979). *Sarraounia* (1986), *Lumière noire / Black Light* (1995) and *Watani: Un monde sans mal / Watani: A World Without Evil* (1997).

In addition, in the 1970s, Sidney Sokhona (b. 1952) made two feature-length studies of the effects of emigration in Paris, *Nationalité: Immigré / Nationality: Immigrant* (1975) and *Safrana ou le droit à la parole / Safrana or the Right to Speak* (1977). More recently Karim Miske (b. 1954), who works in France as a journalist specialising in African affairs, has made a number of solo documentaries – *Culture Hip-Hop / Hip-Hop Culture* (1991), *Afrique de l'Ouest: La presse au pluriel / West Africa: A Press with Many Voices* (1991) and *Enfants et femmes du Burundi / Women and Children in Burundi* (1992) – and three video works with the French television documentarist Brigitte Delpech – *Economie de la débrouille à Nouakcott / The Informal Economy in Nouakcott* (1988), *URSS–Afrique, voyage d'amour / USSR–Africa, a Journey of Love*

(1991) and *Derrière le voile, la séduction en Mauritanie / Behind the Veil, Seduction in Mauritania* (1993).

A further, younger talent is Abderrahmane Sissako (b. 1961), a Mauritanian brought up in Mali, who studied at the State Institute of Cinema (VGIK) in Moscow from 1983 to 1988, making *The Game* (1988) as his graduation film. While working as a trainee cameraman in the Moscow studios, he made a second short, *October* (1993), followed by *Le chameau et les bâtons flottants / The Camel and the Flowing Sticks* (1995), *Sabriya* (1996, shot in Tunisia) and *Rostov–Luanda* (1997). His major work is a sixty-minute reflective piece, *El Aich Ala El Ardh / La vie sur la terre / Life on Earth* (1998), filmed on his return to the Mauritanian village where he grew up.

List of film-makers

Hondo, Med (b. 1936, Aïn Ouled Beni Mathar, now in Mauritania)

Hondo studied in Rabat and worked in Morocco before departing in 1958 to Marseilles, where he did a variety of jobs (working as waiter, docker, cook and so on). He also attended Françoise Rosay's evening courses in drama from 1959 to 1963 in Paris. After a wide variety of acting roles, he founded his own theatrical company Shango which, after four productions, joined forces with another to become Griotshango. He worked as an extra on various films in the late 1960s and founded his own film production company, Les Films Soleil O, in 1969. All his films have been made in exile from his production base in Paris. He began with two 16 mm short films: *Ballade aux sources / Ballad at the Source* (1969) and *Partout ou peut-être nulle part / Everywhere or Perhaps Nowhere* (1969), before making his feature debut with *Soleil O* (1969). This remarkable film, notable for the eloquence of its attack on neo-colonialism, reflects both his ten-year experience of living in France and his involvement there with avant-garde theatre. Though the film has moments of violence and forceful expression, the tone is always assured, showing a willingness to confront points of conflict and controversy. The richness of its audio-visual complexity, mixing narrative and reportage, animation and *cinéma-vérité*, theatre and documentary, nightmare and actuality, makes it a major innovatory work of African cinema. The same stylistic mix found a more uneven synthesis in his second feature, and first in colour, *Les bicots-nègres vos voisins / The Niggers Next Door* (1974), which gives a vivid picture of the realities of life for Africans living in exile in France, treating such issues as exploitation, emigration and the difficulties of retaining cultural traditions. In the mid-1970s he worked on the production of a number of documentaries: the feature-length *Sahel, la faim pourquoi? / Sahel, Why the Hunger?* (1975), co-directed with the Frenchman Théo Robichet; the medium-length *Polisario: Un peuple en armes / Polisario: An Armed People* (1978); and, especially, *Nous aurons toute la mort pour dormir / We Shall Have the Whole of Death to Sleep* (1977), a further feature-length documentary on the Polisario Front, in which the film-maker's sincere commitment again shines through. Taking the form of a lyrical celebration of the popular struggle, the film lacks drama or conflict, seeming to address those already converted and committed to the cause rather than a wider public, but remains an eloquent statement of the movement's cause. *West Indies ou les nègres marrons de la liberté / West Indies* (1979) is another major work, an exuberant, stylized studio movie, shot on a huge set representing a slave ship (built in a disused Paris railway station). Here the unequal relationship over the centuries between France and the Antilles finds vivid expression through the use of music, dance and song. *Sarraounia* (1986), by contrast, is a far more direct work. Set in the late 1890s and tracing the violent disintegration of a French army group, sent out to pacify the territory, which fails in its confrontation with the warriors led by the legendary African queen, Sarraounia. In a surprising turn to his career, Hondo directed the French thriller *Lumière noire / Black Light*, based on a novel by Didier Daeninckx, in 1994. The hero is a Frenchman who tries to find out the truth about the death of a friend, killed in a botched police anti-terrorist action. The search for witnesses takes him to Mali and makes him aware of the reality of the deportation of immigrants, but eventually he is himself eliminated. *Watani: Un monde sans mal / Watani: A World Without Evil* (1997) is virtually a return to Hondo's roots in *Soleil O*. Apart from a powerful opening sequence, using music and coloured African graphics, the film is shot in black and white. It combines documentary, fiction and comedy to look at the rise of fascism and the treatment of blacks in contemporary France.

References and further reading

Ait Hammou, Y. (1996) *Lecture de l'image cinématographique*, Marrakesh: El Watanya.

Allouache, M. (1987) *Omar Gatlato* (script), Algiers: Cinémathèque Algérienne / Editions LAPHOMIC.

—— (1996a) *Salut cousin!* (script), Paris: L'Avant-Scène du Cinéma, no. 457 (December).

—— (1996b) *Bab el-Oued* (novel), Paris: Seuil and Casablanca: Editions le Fennec.

Arab Cinema and Culture: Round Table Conferences (1965), Beirut: Arab Film and Television Center, 3 vols.

Arasoughly, A. (ed.) (1998) *Screens of Life: Critical Film Writing from the Arab World*, vol. 1, Quebec: World Heritage Press.

Armes, R. (1987) *Third World Film-making and the West*, Berkeley: University of California Press.

—— (1996) *Dictionary of North African Film-makers / Dictionnaire des cinéastes du Maghreb*, Paris: Editions ATM.

—— (1998) *Omar Gatlato*, Trowbridge: Flicks Books.

—— (1999) *Omar Gatlato: Film-clef du cinéma algérien*, Paris: Editions L'Harmattan.

Bachy, V. (1978) *Le cinéma de Tunisie*, Tunis: Société Tunisienne de Diffusion.

Belfquih, M. (1995) *C'est mon écran après tout!: Réflexions sur la situation de l'audiovisuel au Maroc*, Rabat: Infolive.

Ben Aissa, A. (ed.) (1996) *Tunisie: Trente ans de cinéma*, Tunis: EDICOP.

Ben Aissa, K. (1990) *Tu vivras, Zinet!: Tahia ya Zinet!*, Paris: L'Harmattan.

Ben El-Haj, B. (1980) *Une politique africaine du cinéma*, Paris: Editions Dadci.

Ben Ouanès, K. (ed.) (1991) *Cinéma et histoire* (Actes du Colloque du Festival International du Film Historique et Mythologique de Djerba: 2ème session), Tunis: Editions Sahar.

—— (ed.) (1995) *Le personnage historique au cinéma* (Actes de Colloque du Festival International de Djerba: 4ème session), Tunis: Editions Sahar.

Berrah, M., Bachy, V. Ben Salama, M. and Boughedir, F. (eds) (1981) *Cinémas du Maghreb*, Paris: *CinémAction* no. 14.

Berrah, M., Lévy, J. and Cluny, C.-M. (eds) (1987) *Les cinémas arabes*, Paris: *CinémAction* no. 43 / Editions du Cerf / IMA.

Bossaerts, M. and Van Geel, C. (eds) (1995) *Cinéma d'en Francophonie*, Brussels: Solibel Edition.

Bosséno, C. (ed.) (1983) *Cinémas de l'Emigration 3*, Paris: *CinémAction* no. 24 / L'Harmattan.

Boudjedra, R. (1971) *Naissance du cinéma algérien*, Paris: François Maspéro.

Boulanger, P. (1975) *Le cinéma colonial*, Paris: Seghers.

Bouzid, N. (1994) 'Sources of Inspiration' Lecture: 22 June 1994, Villepreux, Amsterdam: Sources.

Brahimi, D. (1997) *Cinémas d'Afrique francophone et du Maghreb*, Paris: Nathan.

Brossard, J.-P. (ed.) (1981) *L'Algérie vue par son cinéma*, Locarno: Festival International du Film de Locarno.

Cent ans de cinéma: Cinéma arabe (Bibliographie de la bibliothèque de l'IMA) (1995) Paris: Institut du Monde Arabe.

Cheriaa, T. (1964) *Cinéma et culture en Tunisie*, Beirut: UNESCO.

—— (1979) *Ecrans d'abondance … ou cinémas de libération en Afrique?*, Tunis: Société Tunisienne de Diffusion.

Cinémas des pays arabes: Les cinémas marocain, tunisien, mauritanien (1977) Algiers: Cinémathèque Algérienne / Cinémathèque Française (bound photocopy).

Cinémas des pays arabes: Le cinéma algérien (1977) Algiers: Cinémathèque Algérienne / Cinémathèque Française (bound photocopy).

Cinéma: Production cinématographique 1957–1973 (1974) Algiers: Ministère de l'Information et de la Culture.

Clerc, J.-M. (1997) *Assia Djebar: Ecrire, Transgresser, Résister*, Paris and Montreal: L'Harmattan.

Cluny, C.-M. (1978) *Dictionnaire des nouveaux cinémas arabes*, Paris: Sindbad.

Dadci, Y. (1970) *Dialogues Algérie-Cinéma: Première histoire du cinéma algérien*, Paris: Editions Dadci.

—— (1980) *Première histoire du cinéma algérien, 1896–1979*, Paris: Editions Dadci.

Dahane, M. (ed.) (1995) *Cinéma: Histoire et société*, Rabat: Publications de la Faculté des Lettres.

De Arabische Film (1979) Amsterdam: Cinemathema.

Downing, J. (ed.) (1987) *Film and Politics in the Third World*, New York: Praeger.

FEPACI (1995) *L'Afrique et le centenaire du cinéma / Africa and the Centenary of Cinema*, Paris: Présence Africaine.

Gabous, A. (1998) *Silence, elles tournent!: Les femmes et le cinéma en Tunisie*, Tunis: Cérès Editions / CREDIF.

Gariazzo, G. (1998) *Poetiche del cinema africano*, Turin: Lindau.

Ghazoul, F. (ed.) (1995) *Arab Cinematics: Toward the New and the Alternative*, special issue of *Alif – Journal of Comparative Poetics* 15.

Hadj-Moussa, R. (1994) *Le corps, l'histoire, le territoire: Les rapports de genre dans le cinéma algérien*, Paris and Montreal: Publisud and Edition Balzac.

Hennebelle, G. (ed.) (1972) *Les cinémas africains en 1972*, Paris: Société Africaine d'Edition.

—— (ed.) (1979) *Cinémas de l'émigration*, Paris: CinémAction no. 8.

Hennebelle, G., Berrah, M. and Stora, B. (eds) (1997) *La guerre d'Algérie à l'écran*, CinémAction no. 85 / Paris: Corlet-Télérama.

Hennebelle, G. and Schneider, R. (eds) (1990) *Cinémas métis: De Hollywood aux films beurs*, Paris: CinémAction no. 56 / Hommes et Migrations / Corlet / Télérama.

Hennebelle, G. and Soyer, C. (eds) (1980) *Cinéma contre racisme*, Paris: CinémAction (hors série) / Tumulte no. 7.

Images et Visages du Cinéma Algérien (1984) Algiers: ONCIC.

Jaïdi, M. (1991) *Le cinéma au Maroc*, Rabat: Collection al-Majal.

—— (1992) *Public(s) et cinéma*, Rabat: Collection al-Majal.

—— (1994) *Vision(s) de la société marocaine à travers le court métrage*, Rabat: Collection al-Majal.

—— (1995) *Cinégraphiques*, Rabat: Collection al-Majal.

Khayati, K. (1996) *Cinémas arabes: Topographie d'une image éclatée*, Paris and Montreal: L'Harmattan.

Khelil, H. (1994) *Résistances et utopies: Essais sur le cinéma arabe et africain*, Tunis: Edition Sahar.

Khémir, N. (1992) *Das Verlorene Halsband der Taube*, Baden: Lars Müller.

Khlifi, O. (1970) *L'histoire du cinéma en Tunisie*, Tunis: Société de Diffusion.

Landau, J. (1965) *Etudes sur le théâtre et le cinéma arabes*, Paris: G.-P. Maisonneuve et Larosé.

Maherzi, L. (1980) *Le cinéma algérien: Institutions, imaginaire, idéologie*, Algiers: Société Nationale d'Edition et de Diffusion.

Malkmus, L. and Armes, R. (1991) *Arab and African Film-Making*, London: Zed Books.

Martineau, M. (ed.) (1979) *Le cinéma au féminisme*, Paris: *CinémAction* no. 9.

Megherbi, A. (1982) *Les algériens au miroir du cinéma colonial*, Algiers: SNED.

—— (1985a) *Le miroir apprivoisé*, Algiers: ENAL.

—— (1985b) *Le miroir aux alouettes*, Algiers and Brussels: ENAL / UPU / GAM.

Mimoun, M. (ed.) (1992) *France–Algérie: Images d'une guerre*, Paris: Institut du Monde Arabe.

Morini, A., Rashid, E., Martino, A. and Aprà, A. (1993) *Il cinema dei paesi arabi*, Venice: Marsilio Editori.

Moumen, T. (1998) *Films tunisiens: Longs métrages 1967–1998*, Tunis: Touti Moumen.

Niang, S. (ed.) (1996) *Littérature et cinéma en Afrique francophone: Ousmane Sembene et Assia Djebar*, Paris: L'Harmattan.

Nicollier, V. (1991) 'Der Offene Bruch: Das Kino der Pieds Noirs', *Cinim* 34 (December).

Paquet, A. (1974) *Cinéma en Tunisie*, Montreal: Bibliothèque Nationale de Québec.

Pour une promotion du cinéma national (1993) Rabat: Centre Cinématographique Marocain.

Regard sur le cinéma au Maroc (1995) Rabat: Centre Cinématographique Marocain.

Le rôle du cinéaste africain dans l'éveil d'une conscience de civilization noire (1974) Paris: *Présence Africaine* no. 90.

Sadoul, G. (1966) *The Cinema in the Arab Countries*, Beirut: Interarab Center for Cinema and Television / UNESCO.

Salah, R. (1992) *35 ans de cinéma tunisien*, Tunis: Editions Sahar.

Salmane, H., Hartog, S. and Wilson, D. (1976) *Algerian Cinema*, London: BFI.

Sherzer, D. (1996) *Cinema, Colonialism, Postcolonialism: Perspectives from the French and Francophone Worlds*, Austin: University of Texas Press.

Shiri, K. (ed.) (1992) *Directory of African Film-Makers and Films*, London: Flicks Books.

—— (1993) *Africa at the Pictures*, London: National Film Theatre.

Signaté, I. (1994) *Un cinéaste rebelle: Med Hondo*, Paris and Dakar: Présence Africaine.

Souiba, F. and El-Alaoui, F. (1995) *Un siècle de cinéma au Maroc*, Rabat: World Design Communication.

Taboulay, C. (1997) *Mohamed Chouikh* (long interview plus the script of *L'arche du désert*), Paris: K Films Editions.

Tamzali, W. (1979) *En attendant Omar Gatlato*, Algiers: Editions ENAP.

La Tunisie: Annuaire 1995 (Etats des Lieux du Cinéma en Afrique) (1995) Paris: Association des Trois Mondes / FEPACI.

Vautier, R. (1998) *Caméra citoyenne: Mémoires*, Rennes: Editions Apogée.

Vieyra, P. (1975) *Le cinéma africain des origines à 1973*, Paris: Présence Africaine.

Journals

Adhoua (4 issues, Paris, 1980–1)

Africultures (14 issues, Paris, from 1987)

Cinécrits (16 issues, Tunis, from 1994)

CinémArabe (12 issues, Paris, 1976–9)

Cinéma 3 (3 issues, Casablanca, 1970)
Les Deux Ecrans (monthly, Algiers, 1978–83)
Ecrans d'Afrique / African Screen (bilingual) (23 issues, Milan, from 1992)
Images Nord–Sud (35 isssues, Paris, from 1988)
Mar'a (3 issues as supplements to *Cineaste*, New York, 1979–80)
Médiasud (monthly, Algiers, from 1994)
Qantara (28 quarterly issues, Paris, from 1993)
SeptièmArt (formerly *Goha*) (89 issues, Tunis, 1964–98)
Unir Cinéma (Dakar, from 1973)
Vision (30 monthly issues, Casablanca, 1990–3)

Catalogues

Actes du Festival International de Montpellier (21 issues, 1979–99), Montpellier: Fédération des Oeuvres Laïques de l'Hérault.
Biennale des cinémas arabes à Paris (1992), Paris: Institut du Monde Arabe.
Deuxième biennale des cinémas arabes à Paris (1994), Paris: Institut du Monde Arabe.
Deuxième festival du film arabe (1984), Paris: L'Association pour le Film Arabe.
Festival Cinema Africano (annual, Milan, 1991–9).
Festival: Images du monde arabe (1993), Paris: Institut du Monde Arabe.
Festival National du Film Marocain (Rabat, 1982; Casablanca, 1984; Meknes, 1991; Tangiers, 1995; Casablanca, 1998).
Jeunesse du cinéma arabe (1983), Paris: L'Association pour le Film Arabe.
Journées Cinématographiques de Carthage (biennial, 18 issues since 1966, Tunis).
La semaine du cinéma arabe (1987), Paris: Institut du Monde Arabe.
Quatrième biennale des cinémas arabes (1998), Paris: Institut de Monde Arabe.
Troisième biennale des cinémas arabes (1996), Paris: Institut du Monde Arabe.
Troisième festival du film arabe (1985), Paris: L'Association pour le Film Arabe.

Cinema in Palestine

Viola Shafik

Palestinian cinema is only partly a cinema made by Palestinians, but is to a large extent a cinema which was first and foremost preoccupied by the question of the invaded Palestine, the subsequent resistance and the issue of Palestinian self-representation. It is hardly surprising that Arab Palestinians, due to the political circumstances, did not make any use of the audio-visual media before late 1960s. Until then, the representation (and / or misrepresentation) of Palestine and its people was left to others. At the end of the nineteenth century Palestine was one of the first places in the so-called 'Orient' to arouse the interest of Lumière's and Edison's cameramen, who were eager to bring home exotic footage from the 'Holy Land'. As a whole, the early silent period in Palestine was dominated (just as in other Arab countries) by newsreels, travelogues and documentaries exclusively shot by foreigners (Shohat 1989: 15). The first 'native' film was not produced by Arabs, however, but by Jewish-Ashkenazi immigrants. It was entitled *Haseret Harishon Shel Palestina / The First Film of Palestine* (1911) and was (most likely) directed by Moshe Rosenberg. Other Jewish newsreels and documentaries followed, but until the early 1960s these films remained a synonym for Zionist propaganda (Shohat 1989: 18), aiming to represent the Holy Land as a desert made to bloom by its Jewish settlers and confirm the thesis of 'a land without people for a people without land'. Arab Palestinians, if they were to appear in that scenery, represented nothing more than uncivilized nomadic troublemakers. In the Arab world and particularly in Egypt (which developed the first Arab film industry) the Palestinian question became part of two competing anti-colonial discourses during the 1930s: secular nationalist and Muslim fundamentalist. However, it is only after the proclamation of the Jewish state in 1948 and the subsequent flight of more than 900,000 Palestinians that commercial Egyptian cinema produced its first full-length fiction touching the issue, *Fatat Min Filastin / A Girl from Palestine* (1948) by Mahmud zu-l-Fiqar. During the 1960s, before and after the Arab débâcle in 1967, other Arab countries (such as Syria, Lebanon, Iraq, Algeria and Tunisia) followed the Egyptian example and produced about a hundred documentaries and fiction films tackling the occupation or dealing in general with Palestine (al-'Audat 1987: 104). It was the atmosphere of pan-Arab solidarity prevailing in the 1960s and 1970s that supported this productivity. Some of these solidarity films were highly acclaimed within and even outside the Arab world, including the three Syrian public productions: *Kafr Kassem* (1974) by the Lebanese Borhane Alaouié, *al-Sikkin / The Knife* (1971) by the Syrian Khaled Hamada and *al-Makhdu'un / The Duped* (1973) by the Egyptian Taufiq Salih.

Only in 1968 did Palestinians themselves attempt, under extremely difficult conditions and in the light of the acute political conflict, to make use of cinema. After the defeat of Egypt, Syria and Jordan by Israel during the Six Day War in 1967 and the Israeli occupation of all Palestine, the Palestine Liberation Organization (PLO) decided to take up armed resistance. Thus, born under the auspices of Yassir Arafat's Fatah-movement, the first film unit – founded in Jordan by Mustafa Abu 'Ali, Hani Jawhariyya and Sulafa Jadallah between 1967 and 1968 – was completely committed to national liberation. Its first work, Mustafa Abu 'Ali's documentary *La Li-l-Hall al-Silmi* / *No Peaceful Solution!* (1968), criticized the Rogers plan while challenging the domination of Zionist representation in the media.

The next Palestinian film, *Bi-l Rawh Wal-Damm* / *By Blood and Soul*, by Mustafa Abu 'Ali (again a film unit production) was completed only three years later in 1971. In the same year another Palestinian organization, the PFLP (Popular Front for the Liberation of Palestine), for the first time produced two documentaries: *Alla Tariq al-Thawra* / *On the Way of the Revolution* by Fu'ad Zantut and *al-Nahr al-Barid* / *The al-Barid River* by the Iraqi Qassim Hawwal. Because of the Black September events in 1971, when Jordanian authorities fought the Palestinian resistance movement and drove them out of Jordan, the members of the film unit were (just like other activists) forced to move to Beirut. Some of them continued their work under the name Palestinian Film Organization, which started to produce newsreels along with documentaries in 1972 but never managed to produce them on a regular basis (Madanat 1994: 130). Concentrating now on Lebanon, the years between 1973 and 1977 became the most productive period of Palestinian film-making. In this phase several political organizations, such as the PDFLP (Popular Democratic Front for the Liberation of Palestine), the Samed Organization and the Department for Information and Culture of the PLO showed increasing interest in the media, along with the PFLP (hosted by Syria). Most of the films produced by these institutions showed a clear revolutionary orientation and called for liberation through armed struggle – a fact that is clearly reflected in their titles: for example, *Bi-l-Rawh Wal-Damm* / *By Soul and Blood* (1971) by Mustafa Abu 'Ali, *Limadha Nazra' al-Ward Limadha Nahmil al-Silah* / *Why We Plant Roses, Why We Carry Weapons* (1973) and *Lan Taskut al-Banadiq* / *The Guns Will Never Keep Quiet* (1973) by Qassim Hawwal, as well as *al-Banadiq Muttahidatun* / *The Guns are Unified* (1974) by Rafiq Hajjar.

Works like *al-Irhab al-Suhyuni* / *Zionist Terror* (1973) by Samir Nimr and *Lays Lahu Wujud* / *He Does Not Exist* (1974) by Mustafa Abu 'Ali tried, in a more or less accusatory manner, to describe the desperate situation of Palestinians – the deprivation they suffered, particularly in the refugee camps in South Lebanon – and Israeli abuses. A second category of documentaries was preoccupied with addressing national and cultural identity by portraying Palestinian artists and documenting traditional Palestinian arts – for example, 'Adnan Madanat's *Ru'ya Filastiniyya* / *A Palestinian Vision* (1977).

Working conditions during the early period were disturbed by economic and political restrictions. Banned from their original homeland, actively involved in the liberation movement and financed by political organizations, the cineastes could mainly report on military actions and the situation in the refugee camps. Some of them even risked their lives, including Hany Jawhariyya who was killed by a bullet in 1976 during the early part of the Lebanese civil war (Khayati and Henebelle 1977: 26). Prohibited from entering Israel, film-makers were forced to resort to unconventional means. Ghaleb Chaath (Ghalib Sha'th), for example, sent a European crew to

Nazareth to shot in his absence the requested material for his documentary *Yawm Al-Ardh / Day of the Earth* (1977). Chaath, whose family was exiled to Egypt, had studied cinema in Austria. After the 1967 war he returned to Cairo, where he participated in the foundation of the New Cinema Society in 1969. His full-length feature film *Zilal 'Ala al-Janib al-Akhar / Shadows on the Other Side* (1971) was one of the two films produced by the Society and was banned in Egypt until the October or Yom Kippur War in 1973 because it reflected on the reasons of the Arab defeat by Israel in 1967. Eventually Chaath moved to Beirut in 1974 and stayed there until the Israeli occupation of Lebanon.

During the revolutionary period, Ghaleb Chaath's work was certainly some of the most cinematic. His documentaries had few agit-prop characteristics, but rather seemed descriptive and poetic. In *al-Miftah / The Key* (1976), produced by Samed, Chaath illustrated the personal tragedy of the refugees by using a simple but expressive motif: many Palestinians kept the key of their lost homes in spite of being exiled for decades. Moreover, Chaath's following work *Yawm Al-Ard* was one of the first films documenting the situation of Palestinians who had remained in Israel and the political pressure to which they had been exposed.

In 1982 most Palestinian cinematographic activities were blocked because of the Israeli invasion of Beirut. A large part of the national film archive disappeared at that time.[1] After the transfer of the PLO to Tunis in the same year, its Department for Information and Culture kept on producing films, albeit on a restricted scale. Some of them deserve mention, like Qaiss al-Zubaidi's *Filastin: Sijjil Sha'b / Palestine: Chronicle of a People* (1982) which astonishes with its immense compilation of archival footage recapturing the history of the Palestinian question, as well as *al-Manam / The Dream* (1987) by one of the most distinguished Syrian directors, Mohammed Malas, which features Palestinians recounting their night dreams. Also among these productions was the first Palestinian animation: *al-Tariq Illa Filastin / The Way to Palestine* (1984) by the female director Layali Badr.

During the late 1980s the PLO's production rate decreased further, not least because it decided to support sympathetic Western productions, recognizing the benefits of positive Western presentations of the Palestinian cause. Until 1987 the total output of all Palestinian institutions had been around fifty-two films in all categories, including two full-length feature films, the experimental fiction *Mi'at Wajh Li-Yawm Wahid / The Hundred Faces of One Day* (PDFLP) directed by the Lebanese Christian Ghazi in 1971 and *'Aid Illa Haifa / Back to Haifa* (PFLP, 1982) by Qassim Hawwal.[2]

Because of its institutional character, it is difficult to categorize early Palestinian cinema according to film-maker's nationality. In fact, some of the directors involved in revolutionary Palestinian productions did not come from Palestine at all – to name only the most prolific, these included the two Iraqis Qaiss al-Zubaidi and Qassim Hawwal.[3] However, at the same time as the Palestinians of the Occupied Territories started their latest uprising (the first *intifada*) in 1987, Palestinian film-making shifted gradually from the diaspora to Gaza, the West Bank and to Israel itself.

This geographic shift was anticipated in 1980 by the first documentary by Michel Khleifi (Khalifi), *al-Dhakira al-Khisba / Fertile Memory*, which announced the advent of a new, artistically and technically more advanced 'post-revolutionary' Palestinian cinema. Khleifi, who has been based in Brussels since he studied at the Belgian film-school INSAS, was brought up in Galilee, Israel. After the considerable success of his first full-length fiction, *'Urs al-Jalil / Wedding in Galilee* in 1987, which was co-produced by the German company ZDF (Zweites Deutsches Fernsehen), the Belgian Ministry of the French Community and the French Ministry of Culture, Khleifi became the first internationally recognized Palestinian director. Khleifi's work did not only represent a new Palestinian cinema but also paved the way for the recognition of the subsequent Palestinian generation, represented among others by Elia Suleiman (Iliyya Sulayman) from Nazareth and Rachid Masharawi (Rashid) from a Gaza refugee camp. What they all have in common is their individualism: they are innovative and work as independent director / producers.

Palestinian cinema was for a long time synonymous with documentary film-making. These have reached an international standard, starting with Khleifi's *al-Dhakira al-Khisba*, but continuing with Maï Masri's *Atfal al-Nar / Children of Fire a* (1990) and Rashid Masharawi's *Ayam Tawila Fi Ghazza / Long Days in Gazza* (1991). Nizar Hassan's work, shot on video appears less polished, but creates by showing the director's often funny interaction with his protagonists an individual and rather ironic style. Hassan who was born in Israel tackles among others with *Istiqlal / Independence Day* (1994) and the family-chronicle *Ustura / The Legend* (2000) in a humourous and self-critical way the dilemmas of national identity facing Israeli-Palestinians.

In general, post-revolutionary Palestinian film-making is characterized by a stronger penetration of fictional and experimental elements. Michel Khleifi, for example, created a documentary style of his own by dramatizing his *mise-en-scène* and accentuating it with music. In *Canticle of Stones / Nashid al-Hajjar* (1990) he even started mixing documentary footage with staged scenes performed by professional actors. Similar attempts were undertaken by Majdi Elomari (al-'Umari) in his short *al-Naus / Quiver of a Branch in the Wind* (1988). Raised in Egypt, his films mostly deal with exile, such as his most recent, *Hajar al-Ba'id / Traces in the Rock of Elsewhere* (1999). Others, such as Elia Suleiman (*Takrim bi-l-Qatl / Homage by Assassination*, 1992 and *Cyber Palestine*, 1999) and the Great Britain-based fine artist Mouna Hatoum (*Measures of Distance*, 1988), concentrated on film form as such and developed an analytical, yet (in the case of Hatoum) highly expressive experimental style.

In contrast, Rachid Masharawi's interlude making documentaries is framed by his fictional productions. He started his career in Israel with two short fiction films: *Jawaz Safar / The Passport* (1987) and *al-Malja' / The Shelter* (1989). In 1993 he directed his first full-length feature *Hatta Ish'ar Akhar / Curfew* and two years later *Haifa*. In spite of his simple *mise-en-scène*, Masharawi's films are able to uncover the difficult conditions in the Gaza refugee camps and depict the various survival strategies pursued by their inhabitants with a great deal of humour and by using rather pragmatic realist camerawork. Moreover Masharawi's approach was followed by other young Palestinian film-makers born in Israel, such as Hanna Elias and Hany Abu-Assad (the latter co-produced some of Masharawi's films), as expressed in their short fictions, respectively *al-Jabal / The Mountain* (1991) and *Bayt Min Waraq / The Paper House* (1992).

Since the early 1990s the less expensive electronic and lately digital technology has given an opportunity to an increasing number of young directors to use the audiovisual, to mention only Sobhi Zubeidi (Subhi Zubaisi) with *Khartati al-Khasa Jiddan / My Very Personal Map* (1998) and Azza al-Hassan with *Zaman al-Akhbar / News Time* (2001). This process started with the BBC production *Yawmiyat Filastiniyya /*

Palestinian Diary (1992) which invited several Palestinian youths to present their cinematic vision.

In spite of the relative recognition Palestinian cinema has received lately, it has remained deprived of an own industrial infrastructure – that is, laboratories, equipment and expertise. Even during the Lebanese interlude, Palestinian cinema could only temporarily rely on regional facilities because Lebanon's commercial film industry was destroyed after the outbreak of civil war in 1975. Today film-makers still have, if they do not want to resort to video, to send their stock material abroad for post-production, mainly to Europe, and while shooting have to rely on either expensive foreign technicians or badly trained local ones.

Up to the present day, Palestinian institutions were not able to cope with these deficiencies. Although they financed early Palestinian cinema they showed (according to the film critic and director 'Adnan Madanat) little sense for cinematic requirements and neglected the technical and artistic side of the medium. Hence their support remained sporadic and accidental, and was not based on thorough planning (Madanat 1994: 130). This and the general lack of facilities led the films of the revolutionary period to be repetitive, propagandistic and of poor technical quality. Since the 1980s financial sources for, as well as the audiences of, Palestinian cinema shifted towards the West. European television channels – primarily the BBC and the German ZDF; in sum, cultural Western institutions – became the main producers, supporting Michel Khleifi, Maï Masri, Rashid Masharawi and Elia Suleiman among others. However, the question of whom should be the target audience for Palestinian productions was never really solved (Madanat 1994: 132). Born in exile, Palestinian cinema has remained largely deprived of a native audience. It could not rely on any cultural or commercial distribution system, either abroad or under occupation – particularly after the outbreak of the *intifada*, when the few movie theatres in the Occupied Territories closed down because of the constant curfews.

Thus the screening of early Palestinian films was largely confined to Arab film festivals or, at most, reached anti-imperialist audiences in the West and in Eastern Europe – as in Leipzig, where the documentary film festival of the former German Democratic Republic invited Palestinian works on a regular basis. It is only during the 1990s, since the Oslo peace agreement and the creation of the autonomous territories, that a national Palestinian television channel has started to operate (albeit at a very low level). At the same time, a few cultural initiatives were undertaken by, for example, the Women's Studies Centre in Ramallah, which organized the Arab women's film festival in 1994 and 1995, sending its programme on a tour through several Palestinian cities. But at present Palestinian distribution remains deficient. The most recent Palestinian productions are primarily screened in the West, and gain little access to Arab or Palestinian audiences.

From heroism to pragmatism

A clear distinction can be made between revolutionary and post-revolutionary film-making, on the level of theme and ideology, as well as style. While the former was rather modernist and Third Worldist in its quest for liberty and search for an independant national identity, the latter has tended to undertake pragmatic self-criticism. Revolutionary cinema preferred to display a male-oriented unitarian nationalism *vis-*

à-vis the occupying villain, whereas post-revolutionary cinema turned away from simplified one-sided generalizations of both Palestinian and Israeli society. Focusing to a large extent on gender inequality in Palestinian society, along with the multi-layered effects of political oppression, the new cinema stopped representing any clear-cut groups, stressing local individual experiences instead.

In revolutionary cinema anti-colonial resistance constituted the cornerstone of the cinematic discourse. The films called for armed resistance and discredited Israeli terror against Palestinians. Little attention was paid to internal Palestinian conflicts, such as class, gender or generational differences. Almost every expression was centred around the Palestinian–Israeli conflict. In the course of and after the civil war in Lebanon – culminating in the Israeli invasion, the subsequent horrible massacres in some Palestinian refugee camps and the exodus of the PLO to Tunis – the early aggressive attitude gave way to images of helpless accusations, starting with *Taht al-Anqad /* *Under the Ruins* (1983) by Jean Chamoun and Maï Masri, which depicted the casualties and horrors of the Israeli invasion, and ending with *Lamma Zaffuk / Your Procession* (2001) by Iyas Natur.

Revolutionary Palestinian representation was in general encoded in an antagonistic traditional and genderized iconography. It was centred around the binary opposition of male people and female soil, using the character of the self-sacrificing male resistance fighter, or *fida'i*, as one of its key motifs. His appearance was also adopted and generalized in non-Palestinian Arab film-making, for example in the two commercial Lebanese feature films *Kuluna Fida'iyyun / We Are All Fida'iyyun* (1969) by Gary Garabédian and *al-Filastini al-Tha'ir / The Revolutionary Palestinian* (1969) by Rida Myassar, as well as in the Algerian state production, *Sana'ud / We Will Return* (1971) by Mohamed Slim Riad, which placed the *fida'i*, ultimate representative of his people, as an intrepid supernatural fighter in a western-style plot.

Female resistance fighters appeared only occasionally in revolutionary Palestinian and Arab cinema, as did female experiences of daily life. Women were mostly assigned secondary roles as mothers, wives, daughters and sisters. The strength of women crystallized in their ability to sacrifice their sons or their beloved for the patrimony, as in the Lebanese fiction *Fadak Filastin! / For Your Sake, Palestine!* (1969) by Antoine Rimi and the Palestinian documentary *Umm 'Ali / Ali's Mother* (1983) by Muhammad Tawfik. In them, women who lose their sons in the struggle proudly carry the title 'mother of martyrs' (*umm al-shuhada'*).

An additional crucial motif in the revolutionary discourse was the innocent raped virgin, an allegorical representation of occupied Palestine, which was introduced by, among others, the novelist Ghassan Kanafani. His stories and novels were adapted for several Arab fiction films. In the novel *What Was Left for You* (*ma tabbaqa lakum*), which provided the model for Khaled Hamada's *al-Sikkin / The Knife* (1971), a young girl is seduced and raped by a Palestinian collaborator. Her brother escapes the occupation in desperation, abandoning her as a helpless abused victim.

Palestinian self-criticism made use of the same genderized iconography, as in *al-Makhdu'un / The Duped* (1973) which was produced by the National Syrian Film Organization, directed by the Egyptian Taufiq Salih and adapted from the Kanafani novel *Men under the Sun*.[4] It tells the allegorical story of three Palestinian refugees who try to cross the Iraqi desert into Kuwait. There they hope to find a job that would enable them to support their families back in the camps. A truck-driver and fellow Palestinian offers them a ride. However, he is only interested in their money. When they die in the heat of the desert he just dumps them on the garbage. The driver's selfish attitude is related to the fact that he lost his manhood when he stepped on an Israeli mine. Accordingly, his egocentrism and lack of patriotism are identified with a lack of virility.

Arab women directors were among the first to challenge male-oriented nationalism and show deeper interest in Palestinian women's living conditions. These included the Lebanese-Egyptian Nabiha Lotfi (Lutfi) in her PLO production *Li'an al-Judhur Lann Tamut / Because the Roots Will Not Die* (1977), in which she describes the women of the Tall Za'tar refugee camp. Most recently, the Palestinian Norma Morcos (Murqus) discussed the lives of Palestinian women from different social backgrounds in *L'espoir voilé / Veiled Hope* (1994), while May Masri presented in her *Hanan 'Ashrawi: Imra'a Fi Zaman al-Tahaddi / Hanan 'Ashrawi: A Woman in the Time of Confronation* (1995) a portrait of the well-known politician 'Ashrawi. Active female resistance was also underlined by a Lebanese-European production: the semi-documentary *Layla Wal-Zi'ab / Layla and the Wolves* (1984) by Heiny Srour (Hayni Surur), a classic of Arab feminist cinema. Male directors have also contributed some highly critical works, such as *Nisa' Fi-l-Shams / Women in the Sun* by Sobhi Zubeidi tackling the effect of Islamism on gender politics and *Yasemine* (1997) by Nizar Hassan portraying a women involved in a crime of honor.

However, one of the most powerful representations of the contradictions in the Israeli–Palestinian conflict with reference to the conservative conception of gender is found in Michel Khleifi's work. In his film *al-Dhakira al-Khisba / Fertile Memory* (1980), Khleifi introduces two Palestinian women of a distinct social background: the feminist writer Sahar Khalifa from Nablus in the West Bank and Khleifi's aunt, who lives in Galilee in Israel.

Al-Dhakira al-Khisba uncovers the traces of a double occupation in the life of its protagonists. The women do not only suffer from the effects of Israeli domination, but also from their menfolk's claims of ownership and the restrictions imposed on them by patriarchal society as a whole. Hence in the film the Palestinian male occupies the position of at once culprit and victim. This view corresponds to Sahar Khalifa's opinions, as expressed in her literary and feminist work. Her position opens up the notion of Palestinian resistance and revolution to a critique comprising the entire society and counters the image of the passive abused Palestinian woman.

In Michel Khleifi's films, women like his Galilean aunt have turned into guardians of land and soil and ceased to represent the lost homeland sullied by occupation. Again, in *Nashid al-Hajjar* (1990), Khleifi presents an old unmarried woman, decendant of a rich feudal family, who refuses to sell off her little remaining property to the nearby Jewish settlement in spite of her age and lonely existence. Just like the widow from Galilee, this woman has decided to defend every inch of her ancestral land.

A similar switch of signification from female weakness to power may be found in *'Urs al-Jalil / Wedding in Galilee* (1987), in which the whole narrative is structured around two antagonisms: steadfastness and the desire to dominate. They structure the film's rhythm by a constant rise and fall. Being overwhelmed by the heat, the sumptuous meal and various aromas, an Israeli female soldier faints during the wedding. The Palestinian women carry her into the house, take off her grey uniform and eventually wrap her in a colourful embroidered Palestinian gown. When she wakes up she finds herself surrounded by the magic of the house, subdued light, gentle female voices and soft fabrics. The aggressive male power that the soldier has hitherto symbolized are absorbed by the 'female' interior of the Arab house. When the Israeli's male colleague tries to follow her into the house he finds himself encircled by women and prevented from entering. His vigour is cushioned by their soft but determined movement and challenged by their seductive mockery. Michel Khleifi's binary notion of gender certainly draws from traditional ideas, but invalidates them by changing and twisting their signs.

Like Palestinian cinema in general, *'Urs al-Jalil* underlines the rootedness of Palestinians in their soil. This relation is introduced as early as the opening scene, in which the village *mukhtar* (mayor) receives the military governor's permission to celebrate the wedding of his son in spite of the curfew, but on condition he invites the governor to the wedding. His bus ride home, or, to be more precise, shots of an affluent and blooming rural landscape passing by during the ride, are undercut by his arrival and the subsequent debate with the village's elders who oppose the Israeli presence during the wedding. Furthermore, many of the film's scenes end with a camera movement from within the buildings to an opening where the landscape becomes visible, thus constantly relating the Palestinian home to the land. As Ella Shohat puts it, the imagery 'makes a simple political point: "we are here, and we exist"', refuting 'the Zionist attempt to obfuscate the Palestinian people under such categories as the "natives", or accidental "nomads", in a "land without people"', by associating 'earth, crops, trees, vegetation and abundance of food with the Palestinians' and not with European-Jewish pioneers (Shohat 1988: 45). The question of Palestinian representation in reaction to Israel, as well as to the West, has always been the preoccupation of Palestinian cinema. While revolutionary cineastes chose primarily to respond to Zionist propaganda with counter-propaganda in which Palestinian oppression is simply reduced to the schema of good Palestinians versus evil Israelis, by contrast post-revolutionary film-makers have attempted to dissect the very discourses that form the basis of Western misrepresentation of Palestinians and their problems.

Elia Suleiman and the Lebanese-Canadian Jayce Salloum, in their joint experimental video *Muqadimma Li-Nihayat Jidal* / *Introduction to the End of an Argument: Speaking for Oneself … Speaking for Others* (1990), juxtaposed observations of daily life under occupation with scenes from Hollywood movies depicting Arabs as a bunch of despots, madmen, crooks and terrorists, thus uncovering the biased Western discourse on the Palestinian question. In his second short film *Takrim Bi-l-Qatl* / *Homage by Assassination* (1992), Suleiman reflected on a similar issue. He depicted a Palestinian immigrant to the United States who is condemned to silent voyeurism by electronic media in the midst of the perfect media spectacle of the Gulf War. Nonetheless, the protagonist tries through the same media to grasp bits and pieces of the real but contradictory conditions in the Middle East.

As such, Suleiman's *Takrim Bi-l-Qatl* may be read as an allegory of Palestinian cinema. Being chained since its beginnings to the Israeli–Palestinian conflict, it has struggled hard not only to attain broader recognition but also to liberate itself from the narrow discursive limits set by the political confrontation and to dig deeper into Palestinian reality.

Filmography

Al-Dhakira al-Khisba / *Fertile Memory*

1980, 99 mins, colour, Arabic
Director:	Michel Khleifi
Producer:	Marisa Films, ZDF, NCO, NOVIB, IKON
Cinematographer:	Yves van der Meeren, Marc-André Batigne
Editor:	Moufida Tlatli
Music:	Jacqueline Rosenfeld, Janos Gillis
Sound:	Ricardo Castro

Al-Dhakira al-Khisba is undoubtedly one of the finest works of Arab documentary film-making, not only presenting a vital problem but also telling its stories in a highly visual language. This is achieved through the sophisticated orchestration of interviews and observant images of the Palestinian countryside, as well as cities, with the music of the group Sabrin. The film largely focuses on two women from different backgrounds: first, the now recognized feminist writer Sahar Khalifa from Nablus in the occupied territories; second, the director's aunt from Galilee in Israel. Sahar represents the emancipated woman, having filed for divorce on order to be able to study. The film adopts her political feminism by putting women's liberation on the agenda of national liberation, uncovering the double oppression of Palestinian women. This oppression is most visible in the life of the aunt, a widowed seamstress who has dedicated her life to her children in the traditional way by working for and educating them. She did not, however, lose sight of the national cause: in spite of the pressures related to bringing up children, she did not give up her right to a piece of land that had been confiscated by the Israelis a long time before.

Haifa

1995, 75 mins, colour, Arabic
Director:	Rashid Masharawi
Producer:	Ayloul Film Production, Argus Film Production, Parev Production
Screenwriter:	Rashid Masharawi
Cinematographer:	Edwin Verstegen
Editor:	Hadara Oren
Sound:	Roberto van Eijdeb, Nawal Jabour
Designer:	Saado Masharawi
Leading Players:	Mohamed Bakri, Hiyam Abbas, Fadi al-Ghaoul, Khaled Awad

The small city of Haifa, close to Tel Aviv, is one of the Palestinian traumata – an old charming town that was lost to the Israelis in 1945. It is also where the eponymous protagonist, Haifa, comes from and has made him what he is, though he is now nothing – just a confused refugee, a madman who roams through the streets of a dusty and dreary camp scaring children and swearing at the adults. However, in the middle of the uncertain on-going peace process, Haifa represents to his very few friends (among others a little girl) not only an embodiment of their painful history but also the voice of truth.

Hatta Ish'ar Akhar / Curfew

1993, 75 mins, colour, Arabic
Director:	Rashid Masharawi
Producer:	Ayloul Film Production, Argus Film Production
Screenwriter:	Rashid Masharawi
Cinematographer:	Klaus Juliusburger
Editor:	Hadara Oren
Music:	Sa'id Murad, Sabreen
Sound:	Roni Berger
Leading Players:	Salim Daw, Nayla Zayad, Mahmud Qadh

Hatta Ish'ar Akhar is set in a refugee camp in Gaza: what happens to a family during one of the long and sudden curfews declared by the Israeli army? Where are they to get fresh vegetables for dinner and milk for the children? What happens when their baby suffocates after inhaling tear gas? What happens to their young neighbour who is in labour? How do old and young, parents and adolescents, manage to get on when they are locked up for days in a few square metres? For Masharawi all this is no reason to be solemn. With serenity and considerable humour he describes how people try to cope with the situation: men put on women's clothes to enable them to search out doctors, hidden windows open between houses so that necessary goods can be exchanged or short visits made possible, onions are used against tear gas and endless backgammon matches serve to kill time. Confined to a single major set – the narrow courtyard of the house – *Hatta Ish'ar Akhar* has much in common with the chamber play, unfolding its strength through witty dialogue and performances, but is thus also (probably unintentionally) sadly reminiscent of the Anne Frank story.

Nashid al-Hajjar / Canticle of Stones

1990, 90 mins, colour, Arabic
Director:	Michel Khleifi
Producer:	Saurat Films, ZDF, Channel Four, RTBF
Screenwriter:	Michel Khleifi
Cinematographer:	Raymond Fromont
Editor:	Moufida Tlatli
Music:	Jean-Marie Sénia
Sound:	Ricardo Castro
Leading Players:	Bushra Karaman, Makram Khouri

In the midst of the ongoing *intifada*, two lovers meet after years of separation – the man a political activist who has spent years in Israeli prisons, the woman having lived for years abroad after being repudiated by her family when she had lost her virginity and became pregnant by him, her first and only love. At the same time she tries to understand what is going on in the Holy Land: young people are beaten or die, family houses are deliberately destroyed, pupils are prevented from going to school. The drama of the *intifada* and the occupation are undercut by the memories of the couple, displaying the hardships of exile and displacement in a moment of actual violent reality. The traditional concept of male honour and masculinity that is linked to female virginity is again paralleled and relativized by general political oppression, thereby demanding a cultural change in Arab society.

'Urs al-Jalil / Wedding in Galilee

1987, 112 mins, colour, Arabic
Director: Michel Khleifi
Producer: Marisa Films, ZDF, French Ministry of Culture, Belgian Ministry of Culture
Screenwriter: Michel Khleifi
Cinematographer: Walther van den Ende
Editor: Marie Castro Vasquez
Music: Jean-Marie Sénia
Sound: Ricardo Castro
Designer: Ives Brover, Rashid Masharawi
Leading Players: 'Ali al-'Akili, Makram Khouri, Bushra Karaman, Sonia 'Ammar

The *mukhtar*, the head of a small village put under curfew, has promised to marry his son within a few days and to celebrate the wedding in adequate splendour and according to tradition. However, his plan is not easy to fulfil, as he first has to gain permission from the military governor. When he receives it, it is under the condition that he welcomes the Israeli military as guests during the wedding. His invitation of the Israelis is not supported by the rest of the village. In the end, the wedding is held successfully, but the father's honour is not secured as his son seems unable to consummate the marriage and to deliver the requested public proof of the bride's virginity. The film's *mise-en-scène* concentrates on displaying Palestinian rootedness in their soil and their native culture *vis-à-vis* the occupation (colonialism), while at the same time it challenges traditional concepts of femininity and masculinity.

List of directors

Chaath, Ghaleb (Sha'th, Ghalib) (b. 1934, Jerusalem)

Chaath has directed one feature, four shorts and documentaries. Raised in Egypt, he studied cinema in Austria and is based in Cairo. He participated in the foundation of the New Cinema Society in Cairo in 1969. His graduation film was *Episode* (1967), a short fiction. His first and only full-length feature film, *Zilal 'Ala al-Janib al-Akhar / Shadows on the Other Side* (1971), was one of the two films produced by the Society. The film's story of a young girl, Rose, who fell in love with the student Mahmud but was abandoned by him the moment she became pregnant, is told four times and through different perspectives by different participants, discussing the responsibility and commitment of Arab youth after the Arab defeat by Israel in 1967. The film was banned in Egypt until the October or Yom Kippur War in 1973. Chaath settled in Beirut from 1974 to 1982, where he directed three documentaries: *al-Miftah / The Key* (1976), *Yawm al-Ard / Day of the Earth* (1977) and *Ghisn al-Zaitun / The Olive Branch* (1980). *Al-Miftah* was inspired by the fact that many Palestinians kept the key of their lost homes in spite of being exiled for decades. *Yawm al-Ard* is set in Nazareth and depicts the political struggle of the Palestinians who had remained in Israel. The film is one of the first (and few) documents about the situation of Palestinians in Israel shot from a Palestinian point of view. His last documentary, produced in Beirut, was *Ghisn al-Zaitun*. During the revolutionary period of Palestinian cinema, Ghaleb Chaath's work was certainly some of the most cinematic. His documentaries are sophisticated, and emphasize observation and lyricism.

Khleifi (Khalifi), Michel (b. 1950, Nazareth)

Director, producer and one of the most important Palestinian film-makers, Khleifi has directed three feature films, one docu-drama, three documentaries, one short and several reports for Belgian television. Khleifi is based in Brussels in Belgium. He trained in directing at the Belgian INSAS, from which he graduated in 1977. His films marked the beginning of the phase of individual film-making in Palestinian cinema. His first film, the documentary *al-Dhakira al-Khisba / Fertile Memory* (1980), portrays the life of two Palestinian women, including the feminist writer Sahar Khalifa. It was one of the first Palestinian documentaries to develop a personal atmosphere and use a quasi-fictional film style. Khleifi's following film, the short documentary *Ma'lul Tahtafil Bi-Damariha / Ma'lul Celebrates its Destruction* (1985), focuses on a group of Palestinian villagers who were displaced from their home village, which was destroyed by the Israeli military and transformed into a park, and come back every year to celebrate its memory. *'Urs al-Jalil / Wedding in Galilee* (1987) has thus far remained the most outstanding Palestinian fiction film, touching on important issues such as gender equality, as well as the persistence of native culture, mythologies and traditions, vis-à-vis political occupation. *Nashid al-Hajjar / Canticle of the Stones* (1990) is a touching and poetic docu-drama that combines a staged love story with observations from daily life under Israeli military occupation. *Hikayat al-Jawahir al-Thalath / The Three Lost Jewels* (1995) is almost a children's film, displaying a certain naïvety in its fairy-tale story of a little boy from a Gaza refugee camp who has to find three jewels in order to marry his beloved girlfriend. In his documentary video *al-Zawaj al-Mukhtalat Fi-l-Ard al-Muqadassa / Forbidden Marriages in the Holy Land* (1995). Khleifi reflects the complex cultural, ethnic and religious diversity of the so-called 'Holy Land' by portraying various examples of mixed marriages in Israel, the West Bank and Gaza, and the problems these couples face from the fundamentalism and ethnocentrism of the opposed communities. Michel Khleifi's films do not only convince by their sophisticated use of a solid but nonetheless innovative and visually aesthetic film language, but also by their 'political correctness' – that is, his intellectual support for gender equality, cultural diversity and political co-existence.

Masharawi, Rashid (b. 1962, al-Shati' Refugee Camp, Gaza)

Masharawi has directed two feature films, seven shorts and documentaries. Having started as a foreign labourer himself, commuting from Gaza to Israel, Masharawi touches in all his works, fiction and documentary, on the situation of Palestinian refugee camp dwellers in Gaza and their various survival strategies. *Jawaz Safar / The Passport* (1986) and *al-Malja' / The Shelter* (1989), two fictional shorts, were produced by Masharawi in Israel with the help of Israeli cineastes and tackled the social and political insecurity of Palestinian foreign labourers who are allowed to work in Israel but not to stay overnight. The documentary *Dar-U-Dur / Merry-Go-Round* (1990) takes up a similar subject: it is a portrait of a worker from Gaza who has to support a large family and whose existence, relying on his work in Israel, is constantly threatened. *Ayam Tawila Fi Ghaza / Long Days in Gaza* (1991), *al-Sahir / The Magician* (1992) and *Intizar / Waiting* (1994) all depict the situation in Gaza partly from the personal point of view of the director. *Hatta Ish'ar Akhar / The Curfew* (1993) and *Haifa* (1995) are Masharawi's two full-length feature films, both set in Gaza refugee camps. The first shows the situation of a family in a refugee camp and how its members all try to cope in a different way with the occupation, whereas the second is centred around a madman called Haifa who is waiting to return to his city – a city that was taken over a long time ago by the Israelis. Masharawi's *mise-en-scène* cannot be compared with the sophistication and aestheticism of a Khleifi or a Suleiman; however, his depictions are the most humorous and accurate account of the actual deprivation experienced in the Occupied Territories, particularly in the refugee camps. In his more recent work the director has remained shifting between short fictions and short documentaries, to mention only *Khalf al-Aswar / Behind Walls (1998)* on East Jerusalem and Maqluba (1999)

Masri, Maï (b. 1959, Amman)

A director, camerawoman and producer, Masri studied at the Cinema Department of San Francisco University and is now based in Beirut. She co-directed and produced five documentaries with her husband, the Lebanese Jean Chamoun. Their first joint documentary was *Taht al-Anqad / Under the Ruins* (1983), shot in the destroyed Beirut; others followed, such as *Jil al-Harb / War Generation* (1986) and *Ahlam Mu'alaqa / Suspended Dreams* (1992), all tackling the situation of Lebanon during and after the civil war. In addition, Masri directed two documentaries on her own, both related to Palestine: *Atfal al-Nar / Children of Fire* (1990) and *Hanan 'Ashrawi: Imra'a Fi Zaman al-Tahaddi / Hanan 'Ashrawi: A Woman in the Time of Confrontation* (1995). The first film deals with social and psychological problems of children born under occupation and the second is a portrait of the Palestinian scholar and politician Hanan 'Ashrawi. Maï Masri's documentaries are direct and acute, her topics socio-political. Masri's last documentaries, *Atfal Shatila / Children of Shatila* (1999) and *Ahlam al-Manfa / Frontiers of Dreams and Fears* (2001) remain much in the style of Atfal al-Nar, focussing on Palestinian children's plight.

Suleiman, Elia (b. 1960, Nazareth)

A director and producer, Suleiman studied cinema first in London, then in New York (where he was based from 1982 to 1993). He has directed one feature film and three shorts. *Mukadimma Li-Nihayyit Jidal / Introduction to the End of an Argument:*

Speaking for Oneself … Speaking for Others (1991) was Suleiman's first film, an experimental video that was co-directed by the Canadian-Lebanese Jayce Salloum. It
contrasts clips of Hollywood movies depicting Arabs with real footage from the
Occupied Territories, thus deciphering the negative image of Arabs in the West and
relating this image to the present political situation. A similar topic recurs in
Suleiman's *Takrim Bi-l-Qatl / Homage by Assassination* (1992), a short episode from
the compilation *Harb al-Khalij Wa Ba'd / The Gulf War and After*, about a Palestinian
immigrant to the United States who is condemned to silent voyeurism by the electronic media in the midst of the perfect media spectacle of the Gulf War. The
protagonist was performed by the director himself. *Waqa'i' Ikhtifa' / Chronicle of a
Disappearance* (1996), a full-length feature film that again stars the director, ironically
displayed the situation of Arab Israelis. *Al-Hulm al-'Arabi / The Arab Dream* (1998) is
a short in which the director travels through the Occupied Territories asking questions
about the future of Palestinian citizen in Israel. Suleiman's narrative style is experimental, his work is concerned with questions of cultural and ethnic representation and
the deconstruction of dominant discourses related to the conflict, as he showed once
more in his short fiction *Cyber Palestine* (1999).

al-Zubaidi, Kaiss al- (b. 1939, Baghdad)

A director, cameraman and editor, al-Zubaidi studied editing and camera in
Babelsberg, in the former German Democratic Republic. He graduated in 1968,
worked in Syria from 1969 and is now based in Berlin. He directed one feature film
and many shorts and documentaries. He edited numerous Arab films, such as Nabil
Maleh's *Aklil al-Shawk / Crown of Thorns* (Syria, 1969), Omar Amiralay's *al-Hayat al-
Yawmiyya Fi Qarya Surriya / Daily Life in a Syrian Village* (Syria, 1974), Maroun
Baghdadi's *Bayrut Ya Bayrut / Beirut, Oh Beirut* (Lebanon, 1975), Ghaleb Chaath's
Yawm al-Ard / Day of the Earth (Palestine, 1977) and *al-Layl / The Night* (Syria,1993)
by Mohamed Malas. Al-Zubaidi directed his first film in 1968: *Möwenflug der Jahre /
Gull's Flight of the Years*, which was his graduation film. It was followed by his Syrian
shorts and documentaries *Ba'id 'An al-Wattan / Far Away from the Native Country*
(1969), *al-Ziyara / The Visit* (1970), *Shihadat al-Atfal Fi Zaman al-Harb / Children's
Testimony in Times of War* (1972), *Za'id Alwan / Plus Colours* (1973) and *Nida' al-Ard
/ The Call of the Earth* (1976), mostly dealing with the Palestinian question. In Syria
he also directed one feature film that was produced by the National Syrian Film
Organization, *al-Yazerli* (1974), an adaptation of Hanna Mina's novel *On the Sacks*.
The basic realist narrative – a materially and sexually deprived youth is moreover
confronted with oppressive working conditions – is relativized and elevated to a more
fictional level by the flashbacks, dreams and visions of the adolescent protagonist,
which constantly break the action's linearity and give the film an expressionist air. Al-
Zubaidi also directed numerous documentaries produced by Palestinian institutions,
such as *Sawt Min al-Quds / A Voice from Jerusalem* (1977), *Hisar Mudad / Counter
Siege* (1978) and *Wattan al-Aslak al-Sha'ika / Native Country of Barbed Wire* (1980).
His two most acclaimed films are *Filastin Sijil Sha'b / Palestine: Chronicle of a People*
(1982) and *Malaf Qadiyya / A File on Issues* (1984), both archival compilation films
that summarize the political history of Palestine since the turn of the century. One of
al-Zubaidi's recent videos is *Stimme der Stummen Zeit / Voice of the Silent Time*

(1990), a German production, in which he portrays the exiled Israeli lawyer and human rights activist Felicia Langer. In almost all his work, al-Zubaidi has proved to be outspoken in addressing the Palestinian question and a good film craftsman. He has rarely attempted to develop a particularly individual film language and style, but tried to go in that direction in his one fiction film.

Notes

1   Author's interview with Ghaleb Chaath, Cairo, 14 January 1988.
2   Madanat states that there was even a third fiction film financed by PFLP, *Kifah Hatta al-Tahrir / Struggle until Liberation*, which was directed by the Palestinian 'Abd al-Wahhab al-Hindi in Jordan in 1969. It had no further institutional support (Madanat 1994: 134).
3   Two co-productions with the former German Democratic Republic were carried out: Qassim Hawwal's *Limadha Nazra' al-Ward Limadha Nahmil al-Silah / Why We Plant Roses, Why We Carry Weapons* (1973) and *Mawlud fi Filastin / Born in Palestine* (1975) by Rafiq Hajjar.
4   The Arabic title (*Rijal Fi-l-Shams*) literally means 'men in the sun'.

References and further reading

Afya, M. (1985) 'Mishal Khalifi (Michel Khleifi) wa khitabuh as-sinima'i', *dirasat sinimia'iyya* 1 (June): 16–20.

al-'Audat, H. (1987) *al-sinima wa-l-qadiyya al-filastiniyya*, Damascus:al-Ahali.

de-Baecque, A. (1987a) 'L'architecture des sens: *Noce en Galilée*', *Cahiers du cinéma* 77 (401, November): 45–7.

—— (1987b) 'La force du faible: *Noce en Galilée*, entretien avec Michel Khleifi', *Cahiers du cinéma* 77 (401, November): Roman III.

Hawwal, Q. (1979) *as-sinima al-filastiniyya*, Beirut: dar al-ahdaf and dar al-'awda.

Khayati, K. and Henebelle, G. (1977) *Le Palestine et le cinéma*, Paris: E 100.

Madanat, 'A. (1994) 'al-sinima al-filastiniya', in S. Farid (ed.) *tarikh al-sinima al-'arabiyya al-natiqa*, Cairo: al-ittihad al- 'am li-l-fananin al- 'arab/mihrajan al-Qahira.

Shafik, V. (1991a) *Zensierte Träume. 20 Jahre syrischer Film*, Hamburg: Kinemathek Hamburg, Initiative Kommunales Kino Hamburg.

—— (1991b) 'Film in Palästina – Palästina im Film', *Die siebten Tage des unabhängigen Films* 13–17 March: n.p.

Shohat, E. (1988) '*Wedding in Galilee*', *Middle East Report* September / October: 44–6.

—— (1989) *Israeli Cinema: East / West and the Politics of Representation*, Austin: University of Texas Press.

Shohat, E. and Naficy, H. (1995) 'The Cinema of Displacement', in J. Friedlander (ed.) *Middle Eastern Identities in Transition*, Los Angeles: Center for Near Eastern Studies, UCLA.

Turkish cinema

Nezih Erdoğan

Deniz Göktürk

The first years

Cinema, as a Western form of visual expression and entertainment, did not encounter resistance in Turkey, a country culturally and geographically bridging East and West. It perfectly represented the ambivalent attitudes of the national / cultural identity under construction. On one hand, cinema came as a sign of modernization / Westernization, not only for the images of the West being projected onto the screen, but also for the conditions of its reception. Cinematography was a technological innovation imported from the West and the ritual of going to the movies became an important part of the modern urban experience. On the other hand, cinema offered possibilities for the production of a 'national discourse'. Many of the early feature films reflect the 'birth of a nation' or resistance to the Allied Forces during World War I. The audience was already familiar with the apparatus (theatre, screen, figures, music and sound, light and shadow), which bore some resemblance to the traditional Turkish shadowplay *Karagöz*, one of the most popular entertainment forms of the past.

Ayse Osmanoğlu, the daughter of Sultan Abdülhamid II, remembers that the French illusionist of the palace used to go to France once a year and return with some novelties to entertain the palace population; a film projector throwing lights and shadows on a wall was the most exciting of these spectacles. The first public exhibition took place in 1896 or 1897 in the Sponeck pub, which was frequented by non-Muslim minorities (namely Levantines), as well as Turkish intellectuals infatuated with the Western civilization in Pera (today Beyoğlu), a district in the European part of Istanbul known for its cosmopolitan character. The film, probably projected by a D. Henri, was the sensational *L'arrivée d'un train en Gare* (Lumière brothers, 1895). Ercüment Ekrem Talu, a famous writer and journalist of the time who was present in the audience, reports how the flickering image of a train approaching the camera scared away the viewers, an effect similar to that experienced by the audience at the Grand Café in Paris in 1895.

It was Sigmund Weinberg, a Polish Jew from Romania, who organized the first regular commercial screenings as the authorized exhibitor of Pathé and Lumière films. In 1908 he began to run the first movie theatre – Pathé. In order to outflank his competitors, he continually upgraded the projection machines, showed longer films with better image quality, and hired someone to stand up during the projection and explain the meaning of what the audience saw.

Until recently the first film to be shot by an Ottoman citizen was generally accepted to be *Ayastefanos Abidesinin Yıkılışı / The Demolition of the Monument St Stephen*

(1914) by Fuat Uzkınay, an army officer who had taken an interest in cinematography. Curiously, this film is not thought to have survived and it is unclear whether it ever existed. A recent discovery suggests that it was the brothers Milton and Yanaki Manaki (Ottoman citizens of Greek origin, who feature in *Ulysses' Gaze* by Theo Angelopolous 1995)) who made the first Ottoman film in 1911. Their film showed Sultan Reshad V arriving at Bitolia.

Just before 1915 the infamous General Enver had spent some time in Germany, where he observed the propaganda value of newsreels. When he became the minister of defence in 1915, he gave orders to establish a film department in the army. Weinberg served as head of the department, filming military, royal and other official visits, as well as Enver's much-admired horses and new-born babies. Weinberg had to quit when Romania and Turkey declared war on each other. His assistant, Uzkınay, having learned all the tricks of the trade from Weinberg, took over the department and continued to make war documentaries. Weinberg, after two unsuccessful attempts, completed the feature film *Himmet Ağanın İzdivacı / The Marriage of Himmet Agha* (1916). A young journalist, Sedat Semavi, followed with two features: *Pençe / The Claw* (1917) and *Casus / The Spy* (1917). The veteran stage actor and director Ahmet Fehim made three films: *Mürebbiye / The Governess* (1919), *Binnaz* (1919) and *Bican Efendi Vekilharç / Custodian Bican* (1921). These were mostly adaptations from stage or literature, and the stars were either amateurs or professional players from the theatre.

The domination of theatre and the first 'cinematographers'

After the founding of the Republic in 1923, a nationalist discourse that had already been gaining power in the final years of the Ottoman Empire was disseminated directly by the state, aiming to legitimize a transition from *ummet* (from *umma*, meaning the Islamic community or population) to *millet* (from *mille*, meaning nation). This transition also brought about a conscious distancing from other Islamic countries that had been part of the Empire for centuries. It further led to a romanticizing admiration for 'contemporary [that is, Western] civilization' which, despite all its imperialist and colonialist attitudes, promised technological progress and offered a model for a better political structure, especially secularism. The films that were made in those years display both an effort to construct a national identity and the heavy influence of the West.

Muhsin Ertuğrul represents the 'cinema' of the newly founded Republic. He was mainly a man of the theatre, but also employed his resources in a wide range of cinematic attractions, such as multinational productions, colour films and adaptations. Turkish film historians define an opposition between a group of film-makers coming from the theatre (Refik Kemal Arduman, Talat Artemel, Mümtaz Ener, Kani Kıpçak, Sami Ayanoğlu, Ferdi Tayfur, Seyfi Havaeri and Hadi Hün) and a mixed group called the 'cinematographers'. The cinematographers were Faruk Kenç and Şadan Kamil, who studied film in Germany; Baha Gelenbevi, who worked in France as an assistant to Abel Gance; Turgut Demirağ, who studied film at the University of Southern California and worked for Leo McCarey and Cecil B. DeMille at Paramount; Vedat Örfi Bengi, who worked in France and Egypt; and, finally, Aydın Arakon, Çetin Karamanbey and Şakir Sırmalı.

The years between 1940 and 1948 are described as the 'transition phase'. It began with a certain enthusiasm on the part of the film-makers, whose styles were by and large influenced first by Ertuğrul and then by Egyptian and Western films which were very popular in those years. Film production proceeded in a somewhat naïve manner, trying various genres and diverse methods of storytelling, and casting inexperienced actors and actresses. But this did not result in an avant-garde movement, independent from commercial interests. Film-makers made every attempt to attract an audience.

In 1948 the municipal tax on domestic films was reduced to 25 per cent, while the tax on foreign films remained at 70 per cent. The Turkish film business was now open to anyone who sought profit. Besides, film companies did not have to compete with US films anymore and they could risk money on adventurous projects. The beginning of this period is marked by the arrival of the cinematographers, who would finally shake off the deadening weight of Ertuğrul and his disciples.

This was still primarily a 'cinema of attraction'. Fight and chase scenes scarcely served the plot and posters show that the performances of belly dancers and orchestras were given special credit, promising entertainment. However, the cinematographers gradually learned how to tell a story coherently. Particularly, Lütfi Ömer Akad, Orhan Arburnu, Metin Erksan, Atıf Yılmaz and later Memduh Ün developed new forms of expression and achieved a degree of unity in narrative structure.

The contemporary Turkish cinema

Yeşilçam

The period from the mid-1960s to the mid-1970s is marked by a mode of production and film performance that is unique in the history of Turkish cinema. Continually increasing demand from the audience caused a rapid expansion of the film business. While the film directors were at pains to reconcile the rules of commercial success and personal style, film production increased enormously. In 1961 the number of films made was 116, twice the figure of previous year, while in 1972 it reached its peak with 298 films. Production companies on Yeşilçam Street in the Beyoğlu district of Istanbul (hence 'Yeşilçam', literally 'Green Pine', cinema) went to the regional film distributors and haggled over plots and stars. Having a clear idea of their audiences' taste, the distributors could demand revisions to plot and casting. For instance, to guarantee profit the distributor of the Adana region might require two fight scenes if Cüneyt Arkın was to be cast in the leading role.

Table 4 Distribution and exhibition in the early 1970s

Regions	Towns	Movie theatres	Admissions
Adana	21	463	37,335,472
Izmir	12	646	51,427,031
Ankara	6	216	29,474,552
Samsun	16	238	20,420,363
Marmara	9	343	27,288,164
Zonguldak	2	82	13,149,007
Istanbul	1	436	67,402,721

Source: Abisel 1994: 100.

The film industry was not capable of catching up with the speed of production; there was no capital reserved for the cinema, no investment was made in studios or even technical equipment. From the 1940s dubbing was standard practice, saving money on actors and studio time. Screenplays were written in a rush – sometimes on the spot – just before shooting started. In order to avoid changing lighting and camera set-ups, every object in the studio was given the same amount of light and the shot-reverse system was abandoned almost entirely. That led to a hybrid visual convention that found a compromise between the tradition of two-dimensional Turkish minia-tures or shadowplay and the Western regime of perspective. Thus the image lacked the dialectics of figure-background and visual depth, due to flat lighting. In addition, when conversing the actors did not face each other, but rather the camera, thus making full identification impossible for the spectator.

Genres of Yeşilçam

Yeşilçam, by deploying the powers of genre and stardom, set a horizon of expecta-tions for its audience. This did not only guarantee commercial success, but also formed well-established conventions of storytelling. It must be noted, however, that in the mid-1980s these conventions collapsed with the emergence of the director as *auteur*. The *auteur* directors, instead of exploiting generic templates, primarily attempted to institute their own individual style.

Melodrama   Melodrama is one of the most popular and powerful genres of Yeşilçam. In fact, the melodramatic mode runs across almost all genres. Yeşilçam's main audience was the family. Family melodramas play on a formula of disequilibrium–equilibrium. In the beginning the family splits up due to some kind of misunder-standing or intrigue, but then reunites at the end thanks to the efforts of the children (Orhan Elmas, *Adını Anmayacağım / I Shall Not Recall Your Name*, 1971; Ülkü Erakalın, *Afacan Küçük Serseri / Afacan, the Little Tramp*, 1971; Metin Erksan, *Feride*, 1971). Other melodramas focus on heterosexual couples, underlining socio-cultural conflicts on a number of axes: poor versus rich, rural versus urban, lower class versus bourgeois, Eastern versus Western. These conflicts are resolved in the realm of fantasy. In a typical plot, the downtown boy would seduce the poor girl from a village, the girl would then go to the city, disguised as a modern and rich woman, and take revenge (Metin Erksan, *Dağdan İnme / Down from the Mountains*, 1973; Orhan Aksoy, *Kınalı Yapıncakı / Golden Red Grape*, 1969).

Comedy   Another popular genre of Yeşilçam was comedy, which was primarily based on gags and puns. Comedy can also use other genres (especially gangster films or science-fiction) to mock familiar elements. Many comedies were produced in series with the same cast playing characters-as-stereotypes. There are parallels between these films and situation comedy. However, Yeşilçam comedies bore melodramatic overtones at climactic points. Examples are the *Hababam … / Carry On …* series (six films between 1975 and 1981) by Ertem Eğilmez, starring Kartal Tibet, and the *Turist Ömer / Ömer the Tourist* series (seven films between 1964 and 1973), directed by Hulki Saner with Sadri Alışık in the title role. Although comedy, like melodrama, reasserted values of family and home, it subtly produced points of resistance to power. In particular the

Şaban series (eight films directed by the former star Kartal Tibet and partly inspired by the folk-hero Keloğlan) centres on a kind of village idiot (played by Kemal Sunal) undoing the conspiracy of a group of people in power who are aiming to abuse him. Finally it should be noted that parodies of US popular films and television series with a slight taste of trash (for example, *Star Trek*, *Bewitched* and *The Pink Panther*) made good box office, becoming *Turist Ömer Uzay Yolunda / Ömer the Tourist on Star Trek*, *Tatlı Cadı / Sweet Bewitched* and *Pembe Panter / The Pink Panther*.

Historical action / adventure   Yeşilçam introduced a series of historical action heroes to the audience. Tarkan, Karaoğlan, Malkoçoğlu, Kara Murat and Battal Gazi are openly chauvinist superheroes, fighting in the name of their country or for some oppressed community against an enemy. Their actions are justified by the enemy's initial move (massacre, torture, breaking an oath and so on). These films produced sites of identification mainly for adolescents who assumed a national identity by imagining fights against the enemy.

Interestingly, these films often centre around a woman. When the hero is caught and put in the dungeon, the enemy's woman (having fallen for the hero) comes to his rescue, risking / sacrificing her own life. Cüneyt Arkın (who played Kara Murat, Malkoçoğlu and Battal Gazi) and Kartal Tibet (Karaoğlan and Tarkan) are the icons of historical action films. A strong appeal to heroism can be traced in other genres as well, but it can work in different ways. For instance, the 'tough guy' character (*kabadayı*) is a very common figure, whose distinguishing marks are still perpetuated today (particularly in television series). He comes from uptown and dutifully protects the poor and the weak from evil forces, demonstrating his power only when needed. His own interests (love for the girl-next-door or the opportunity to lead a decent life) are always subordinate to his concern for others (Yavuz Yalınkılıç, *Cesur Kabadayı / The Brave Swasher*, 1969; Yılmaz Duru, *Erkek Gibi Ölenler /Dying as a Man*, 1970; Cevat Şahiner, *Dört Kabadayı / Four Swashers*, 1970; Kemal Kan, *İstanbul Kabadayısı / The Swashes of Instanbul*, *Kara Murat / Dark Murat*, 1972).

Detective / gangster movies   Detective and gangster movies that were heavily influenced by US films initially appealed to audiences, but were eventually overtaken by a domestic version of Hong Kong karate films. In these films the family is only a pretext for revenge, and the chaste woman disappears in favour of the vamp in order to justify sexually suggestive scenes (Savaş Eşici, *Şimşek Hafiye / The Bright Detective*, 1970; Çetin İnanç, *Zehir Hafiye / The Sharp Detective*, 1971; Kaya Ererez, *Çılgın Gangster / Crazy Gangster*, 1973; Müjdat Saylav, *O Bir Gangsterdi / He was a Gangster*, 1973). The hero is usually a Mike Hammer lookalike who is always on the run, in sharp contrast with the committed male character of melodramas. While Yılmaz Köksal was the exponent of these roles, Yılmaz Güney also largely owes his fame to a melancholic variation on this type of character.

New Turkish Cinema

After the mid-1970s the family gradually vanished from movie theatres due to a combination of the socio-political catastrophe shedding blood in the streets and television now broadcasting entertainment to safe homes. Yeşilçam turned to a lumpen crowd and, in order to survive the economic crisis, started a career in pornography which would last until the military coup in 1980.

Regional distributors who provided money for production were replaced by video distributors who were willing to buy every film that a company stocked. Video distribution was primarily aimed at Turkish migrant workers living in Germany and other Western European countries. Thus, in order to exploit this new market abroad, film companies changed medium. They not only sold all of their films, but also began to produce films (mostly 16 mm) and videos directly for the video market, which would soon include Turkey as well. Due to the drastic fall in the number of movie theatres during the late 1970s, lack of popular films, poor projection and the single state television channel which was still broadcasting in black and white, the early 1980s witnessed video shops mushrooming to the extent that hundreds of films never hit cinema screens. Video business soon began to function as a channel for piracy: in addition to Turkish features, US and even European videos were copied under dubious circumstances and circulated across the country until the government agreed to take action in the late 1980s over the copyright of foreign films.

The new liberal economy policy which was imposed after the 1980 coup gave way to an advertising boom, with significant consequences for feature production. Advertising companies established international connections and benefited from foreign expertise, both in management and in production. A number of Yeşilçam directors, as well as newcomers, were involved in the business, which promised more money than they could ever hope to make in Yeşilçam. At the same time they learned how to convey a message in a thirty-second commercial and how to devote utmost care to each frame. Working with foreign directors, art directors and directors of photography was valuable training for lighting and camera crews. This experience would eventually have an impact on feature-film production.

The directors of the post-1980 period were at pains to formulate their individual style of expression. For the first time in Turkish cinema, the marketing campaigns conceived and introduced the director as an *auteur* (although Metin Erksan is the first real *auteur* of Turkish cinema). Lighting, colour, editing and camerawork gave films a European look, different from the genre cinema of both Hollywood and Yeşilçam. Arguably one can observe the emergence of a New Turkish Cinema after the 1980s.

The cinema now formulated new problems and introduced new concepts. Two major trends emerged in the New Turkish Cinema. Films centred on women and attempted to study them in their own right or questioned the conventions of female representation. Women in the cinema were shown to express desires of their own, with the female protagonist struggling to solve her problems by herself. In *Mine* (Atıf Yılmaz, 1982), Mine (Türkan Şoray) begs the male character to sleep with her; in *Dağınık Yatak / The Unmade Bed* (Yılmaz, 1984), Benli Meryem (Müjde Ar), the mistress of a businessman, falls in love with a young waiter and takes him with her to a holiday resort; in *Dul Bir* Kadın / *A Widow* (Yılmaz, 1985) and *Bez Bebek / Rag Doll* (Engin Ayça, 1987), a mature woman discovers her sexual desires. *Kadının Adı Yok / Woman's Got No Name* (Yılmaz, 1987) is an adaptation of a best-selling feminist novel and tells the story of a woman (Hale Soygazi) in search of her identity, while the heroines (Füsun Demirel, Hande Ataizi, Sevtap Parman) of *Mum Kokulu Kadınlar / Wax-scented Women* (İrfan Tözüm, 1995) get rid of their oppressors (all played by the same actor, Halil Ergün) and start a new life.

Another trend is a preoccupation with the possibilities of the medium itself. Self-reflexive films appeared, focusing on the production process, problems of representation, and the pleasures of voyeurism and exhibitionism. *Adı Vasfiye / Vasfiye is Her Name* (Yılmaz, 1985) tells the story of men telling the story of Vasfiye (Müjde Ar), an enigmatic woman who refuses to speak about herself. *Aaahh, Belinda! / Oh, Belinda!* (Yılmaz, 1986) is about an actress (Müjde Ar) who agrees to perform in a shampoo commercial and all of a sudden finds herself in the fictional world of the petit bourgeois screen family. In *Hayallerim, Aşkım ve Sen / My Dreams, My Love and You* (Yılmaz, 1987), the stereotypical characters played by a Yeşilçam star (who is ironically played by the Yeşilçam icon Türkan Şoray) plague a young man who is writing a screenplay for her. *Gizli Duygular / Secret Feelings* (Şerif Gören, 1984) plays on the notion of voyeurism, with allusions to Hitchcock's *Rear Window*; *Film Bitti / The Film has Ended* (Yavuz Özkan, 1989) is a film about making a film, and *Arabesk* (Ertem Eğilmez, 1988) is a pastiche of Yeşilçam melodramas. *Gece Yolculuğu / Night Journey* (Ömer Kavur, 1987), *Üçüncü Göz / The Third Eye* (Orhan Oğuz, 1988), *Su Da Yanar / Water Also Burns* (Ali Özgentürk, 1986) and *Camdan Kalp / Heart of Glass* (Fehmi Yaşar, 1990) are all about the sufferings of a film director or scriptwriter, in search of himself or of some other kind of truth. *Amerikalı / The American* (Gören, 1993) parodies the climactic scenes of US blockbusters (*Home Alone*, *Basic Instinct*, *Pretty Woman* and so on) and questions the ways in which they have been integrated into the Turkish imagination. *Cazibe Hanımın Gündüz Düşleri / The Daydreams of Miss Attraction* (İrfan Tözüm, 1992) shows a sexually voracious female character (Hale Soygazi) sitting in a rocking chair and restlessly watching images of Istanbul coming from a slide projector.

The industry and audience today

Production

Today, the main funding sources for film-makers are (1) producers (some of whom are US companies) who can risk money on indigenous films, (2) major firms that sponsor production entirely or partially, (3) the ministry of culture which provides loans, (4) television stations which support production on the condition that the broadcasting rights for the film be given to the station, and (5) 'Eurimages' which supports co-productions with partners from at least two other European countries. Not all of these sources are totally reliable: for example, the Ministry of Culture will not support every project and it may have to cut funding according to political decisions or to the budget allocated by the government.

Censorship

Censorship has been a matter for the police from the very beginnings of Turkish cinema and it defines one of the major ways in which the state has interfered with the industry. Although there was no law regulating the production, distribution, exhibition and import of films until 1932, the city governors of the Ministry of the Interior were felt to be fully authorized on the matter. In 1934 the Regulation on the Control of Films and Film Screenplays was formulated as part of the Police Duty and Authorization Law, and it was applied with minor revisions until 1977. The Board of Censors consisted of five main members (two from the Ministry of the Interior, one from the Ministry of Tourism, one from the Ministry of Education, one from the police). Depending on the content of the film, other members coming from the General Staff of the Army, the ministry of commerce and so on might join the Board, albeit on a temporary basis. The Board examined screenplays prior to the production of any film and had to announce the result of their deliberations within a certain time period (this also covered foreign films that were to be produced in Turkey). They might authorize a film, ban it or request revisions on the grounds that films should avoid (1) political propaganda about any state, (2) degrading an ethnic community or race, (3) 'hurting the feelings' [*sic*] of fellow states and nations, (4) propagating religion, (5) propagating political, economic and social ideologies that contradicted the national regime, (6) contradicting national and moral values, (7) denigrating the military forces and reducing their dignity and honour, (8) being harmful to the discipline and security of the country, (9) provoking crime, and (10) criticizing Turkey. The owner of a film and the representatives of ministries could also raise objections, which were addressed to the Ministry of the Interior, and ask for another meeting. The ministry would then forward the request to the Committee of Central Control, which was authorized to give a final decision. However, the Ministry of the Interior reserved the right to censor or ban a film, even if it had been approved by the Board of Censors. In 1977 the law was reformulated in such a way as to express concern for the mental health of juvenile audiences and loosely suggest a rating system be introduced.

Although great efforts were made to overthrow the tyranny of censorship, it remained virtually untouched until 1985. This prevented film-makers from promoting challenging ideas or developing any explicit social or political critique. In order to be able to produce and show their films, they took indirect routes. When they feared a film might be censored, they would submit a screenplay specifically prepared for the Board and produce their film based on a different screenplay, in the hope that the Board would not check the completed film against the previously submitted screenplay. The history of censorship is one of interference, interruptions and paranoid anecdotes. The year 1985 marked a return to a relatively democratic system which afforded 'freedom of speech' as a norm. In 1986 the Ministry of Culture became responsible for affairs of censorship, which brought about a considerable relaxation.

Distribution and exhibition

There were 2,242 movie theatres in 1970 (Abisel 1994) and, according to the results of research conducted by Nezih Coş, this figure soon reached 3,000 (Coş 1969). Most of these theatres exhibited Yeşilçam films, produced at an average rate of 200 films a year. By the mid-1970s the number of theatres began to drop rapidly. Many were converted into apartment buildings, business centres, carparks or small shopping centres. It was recorded that there were only 674 movie theatres left by 1986. In 1995, when the population of Turkey reached 60 million, the number of theatres had dropped further to 363 (half as many as in Greece, where the population was then only 10 million). Today a gradual increase is being observed, due both to rising demand from vast numbers of university students and to the popularity of the shopping centres with cineplexes that have been appearing in many big cities. However, 37.5% of all theatres still show foreign soft-porn films. Interestingly, these cinemas are concentrated in the most conservative regions of the country. Today there are at least 450 theatres, and this figure is likely to grow as international cinema chains (for example, Cineplex Odeon Corporation of Canada and Cinemax of Germany) expand in Turkey.

Audience

An increase in the number of cinemas does not, of course, necessarily mean that Turkish films reach the domestic audience. Film-makers repeatedly complain about the difficulty of booking theatres for their films. Even when they do manage to squeeze their own work in between films from the United States, their films are quite likely to crash at the box office and be withdrawn immediately – perhaps partly due to their failure to meet the expectations of a movie audience whose taste has, to a large extent, been shaped by Hollywood.

Table 5 Audience loss

Year	Movie theatres	Admissions to domestic films	Admissions to foreign films
1959	285	–	–
1970	2,242 / 3,000	–	–
1978	1,285	–	–
1980	938	–	–
1983	975	35,835,614	45,133,962
1984	854	26,753,374	29,562,237
1985	767	21,284,575	21,386,030
1986	674	20,345,721	19,857,030
1987	460	11,734,923	13,097,248
1988	424	7,736,401	12,553,466
1989	383	7,165,710	13,882,149
1990	354	5,668,705	13,565,271
1991	341	4,135,653	12,408,040
1993	320	15 million	
1995	363	1,574,492	7,825,302
1998	450	data unavailable	data unavailable

Source: Data compiled from UNESCO Statistical Yearbooks 1963, 1973, 1981, 1983, 1987, 1993, 1998, Turkish Statistical Yearbooks 1990 and Türsak Yearbooks 1993, 1995/6, 1996/7, *Variety* (various issues).

Table 6 Fall in production

Year	Turkish films in exhibition	Year	Turkish films in exhibition
1991	17	1996	9
1992	10	1997	14
1993	11	1998	10
1994	16	1999	13
1995	10	2000	15

Source: Data compiled from A. Özgüç, *Turk Filmleri Sölüğü 1991–1996*, and *TÜRSAK Sinema Yıllığı 1997–1998*

Note: There may be a significant difference between production and exhibition figures. In 1993, for example, only eleven films out of eighty-two could be screened.

After the mid-1980s the audience (now largely from a younger generation) returned to the cinema to see not indigenous films but Hollywood blockbusters. Discussions about applying quotas to imported films faded when President Bush invited Turgut Özal, then Turkish prime minister, to the White House and converted him to the virtues of a liberal trade policy. In order to bring in foreign money, the 'off-shore media project' launched in 1988 by the liberal government allowed US film distribution and exhibition companies to operate in Turkey. Almost all the movie theatres in the country were booked up by foreign companies, particularly the 'majors' (Warner Bros and UIP); they also began to control the video market, which was already declining because of the increasing number of state and private television channels. A positive result of this cultural invasion, however, was that theatres were renovated in order to catch up with 'global' standards of film viewing: comfortable chairs, air conditioning, digital Dolby-stereo sound systems and high-quality projection equipment were all installed.

According to statistical data provided by Fida Film, which in 1997 ran a survey of 2,438 viewers from ten leading cities, there is a more or less even balance between male and female film-goers (51.11% and 48.89% respectively). Generally, audience-members are young (between 19 and 35), single (77.2%) and either university graduates (41.18%) or have completed their secondary schooling (40.44%) (TÜRSAK 1997). Looking at the top grossing films of 1995–8, however, it is clear that children's films (*Pocahontas*, *The Lion King*, *Richie Rich*, *Casper*, *101 Dalmatians* and *Free Willie 2*) are always at the top of the lists, and children are always accompanied by adults when they go to the cinema. Thus children form a most reliable segment of the audience. Another significant result of this research is that housewives are the least likely to go to a film (10.30%). In part this might be due to the neglect of female audiences by both Hollywood and the New Turkish Cinema. What seems to be far more important in keeping the Turkish housewife at home, however, is television. There are more than fifteen national channels in Turkey, broadcasting old Yeşilçam films and 'female-friendly' soap operas during the daytime, and the frequency of commercial breaks suggests that they receive very high ratings. The situation is reminiscent of the 1970s, when film exhibitors arranged daytime 'women only' screenings. Although Yeşilçam cinema did not achieve full product diversification, it was nevertheless able to address a diversity of audiences, with melodramas for single women and parents, adventure / action films for teenagers, kids films with child stars for children and parents, and comedy for just about everyone. Even now children, housewives and elderly people have yet to receive careful consideration as potential viewers in the marketing audience profiles.

This situation provoked the claim that Turkish films should bring the audience back to the cinemas. In recent years some productions have proved that a film can be both sophisticated and popular. The box-office successes of Yavuz Turgul's *Muhsin Bey / Mr Muhsin* (1986) and *Eşkiya / The Bandit* (1996); Ertem Eğilmez's *Arabesk* (1988); Sinan Çetin's *Berlin in Berlin* (1993) and *Propaganda* (1999); Şerif Gören's *Amerikalı / The American* (1993); Mustafa Altıoklar's *İstanbul Kanatlarımın Altında / Istanbul Beneath, Down Under My Wings* (1995) and *Ağır Roman / Cholera Street* (1997); and Ömer Vargı's *Herşey Çok Güzel Olacak / Everything Will Be Fine* (1999), along with the long-expected re-release of Yılmaz Güney's *Yol / The Way* (1981), arouse the hope that other films may follow in the near future. John Nadler of *Variety* observed in May 1998:

After being virtually eclipsed by free TV and US theatrical releases for most of the decade, Turkish film is resurrecting itself, and the country's producers, distributors and exhibitors have exhibited a new-found respect for domestically made movies.

(Nadler 1998: 61)

Turkish cinema: transnational perspectives

As mentioned already, the percentage of Turkish films shown in Turkish cinemas is relatively small in comparison to imports from Hollywood. Reception of films has always been international to varying degrees. Turkish cinema has developed a transnational presence for itself, as well as through the Turkish diaspora to Germany (where the resident population includes over 2 million people of Turkish origin) and other Western European countries. This expatriate population has formed a non-domestic market, particularly for the consumption of videos (and, more recently, satellite television) but also in terms of film production (by opening avenues to secure funding outside Turkey).

Figure 50 Metin Akpınar (left) and Kemal Sunal (right). Two veteran comedians of Turkish theatre and cinema meet in *Propaganda*.

Migration and cinema

From the early 1960s, migration did not only lead from Turkey to Western Europe, but occured primarily within the country itself, from poor rural areas to the big cities. The population of Istanbul, for example, has grown from 2.5 million to approximately 16 million over the last thirty-five years. Considering the extent of social change brought about by this massive displacement of population, it is not surprising that migration has been an important theme in Turkish cinema. Melodramas or comedies often feature characters who have moved to the city and find it difficult to adjust to being there. Halit Refiğ in *Gurbet Kuşları / Birds of Exile* (1964) or Ömer Lütfi Akad in his trilogy *Gelin / The Bride* (1973), *Düğün / The Wedding* (1973), *Diyet / Blood Money* (1974) explored the experience of migrants. More recently, films like *Yol / The Way* (1981) or *Güneşe Yolculuk / Journey to the Sun* (1999) have focused on mobility and rootlessness as common experiences of people in Turkey. Oğuz Makal (1994) lists further examples in his book about the 'seventh man' in cinema, a study that covers migration both within Turkey and abroad.

Following the labour migration from Turkey to Western Europe, primarily to Germany, film-makers have started making 'expatriate' films, set in the diaspora and partly produced and distributed outside Turkey. Tunç Okan's *Otobüs / The Bus* (1976) features the strange encounters of a group of migrant workers on the road to Sweden, depicting them as speechless victims, much in the style of John Berger and Jean Mohr's text and photograph book *A Seventh Man* (1975). A focus on alienation and incompatibility was to become the prevalent mode in depictions of migrants in the years to follow. The representation of Turkish women in the diaspora, in particular, centred around fantasies of subordination, confinement in claustrophobic spaces, rescue and liberation. In Germany, a kind of ghetto culture emerged that fed on well-meaning discourses of integration and on a system of public funding. German film-makers, such as feminist director Helma Sanders (*Shirins Hochzeit / Shirin's Wedding*, 1975) or Hark Bohm (*Yasemin*, 1988), engaged in this victimizing depiction, as well as Turkish film-makers working within German structures of subsidy. Tevfik Başer, for example, moved from Eskişehir to Hamburg, where he could realize his films with regional film funding. In his *40 QM Deutschland / 40 Squaremeters of Germany* (1986), Turna (Özay Fecht) is brought to a flat in Hamburg and kept confined there by her husband for months. This film was nominated for a German national film prize (the Bundesfilmpreis). In *Abschied vom Falschen Paradies / Farewell to a False Paradise* (1988), Elif (Zuhal Olcay) ends up in a German prison for having killed her oppressive husband, but paradoxically her experience of imprisonment turns into an experience of liberation and integration. The spatial closure is conveyed through the *mise-en-scène* and framing. Characters are depicted in open spaces only in their subjective visions, mostly nostalgic memories of their home villages.

Only a few films – mostly produced in Turkey – transcended the prevalent rhetoric of social work in a more satirical and playful manner. Şerif Gören, who had focused on the problems of Turkish migrants in *Almanya Acı Vatan / Germany, Bitter Home* (1979), proceeded to make *Polizei / Police* (1988), a comedy starring Kemal Sunal as a streetcleaner who adopts the role of a German policeman in an amateur theatre performance, but becomes so fond of the uniform that he continues to wear it on the street, going around Turkish shops to ask for baksheesh. *Mercedes Mon Amour* (1992) is a black comedy about a *Gastarbeiter* ('guest worker'), in love with his yellow

Mercedes, and his hazardous journey back home. The film is based on a novel by Adalet Ağaoğlu and directed by Tunç Okan and contains some moments of humour. Sinan Çetin's *Berlin in Berlin* (1993) has so far probably been the most adventurous exploration of intercultural encounters.

'Europuddings' with Turkish ingredients

The Council of Europe's film-funding scheme Eurimages was established at the end of 1988. The condition for funding any feature film is that independent producers from at least three different member-states participate in the project. The funding programme also offers assistance for distribution. Since the early 1990s about thirty-six Turkish co-productions have been funded by Eurimages, including *Mavi Sürgün / The Blue Exile* (Erden Kıral, 1993), *İstanbul Kanatlarımın Altında / Istanbul, Beneath My Wings* (Mustafa Altıoklar, 1995), *Ağır Roman / Cholera Street* (Mustafa Altıoklar, 1998), *Ustam Beni Öldürsene / Sawdust Tales* (Barış Pirhasan, 1998), *Eşkiya / The Bandit* (Yavuz Turgul, 1996), *Hamam / The Turkish Bath* (Ferzan Özpetek, 1997), *Güneşe Yolculuk / Journey to the Sun* (Yeşim Ustaoğlu, 1999). European funding initiatives like Eurimages are part of a cultural policy scheme that was designed to reinvent Europe. Turkey, which is not yet a full member of the European Union, is nevertheless included in efforts to create a European cinema. An inclusive European space can best be imagined through travel, and consequently quite a few so-called 'Europuddings' have been about journeys. *Mavi Sürgün* is about a journey of exile within 1920s Turkey, from the capital to a remote village on the Aegean coast; *İstanbul Kanatlarımın Altında* about learning to fly in sixteenth-century Istanbul; *Ustam Beni Öldürsene* about the desires and destinies of circus acrobats; *Eşkiya* about a bandit of the old school who feels displaced in the modern metropolis; *Hamam* about a busy Italian who travels to Istanbul because he has inherited an old building from a deceased aunt, and gets increasingly entangled in this foreign place; *Güneşe Yolculuk* about uprooted Turkish and Kurdish characters and a journey to a home which no longer exists. Overall, European funding seems to have contributed to opening up broader horizons and paving the way for a Turkish cinema that travels – possibly beyond Turkey.

New German Cinema – made by young Turks

Recently there have been some new departures in diaspora film production. A new generation of Turkish–German film-makers and actors is emerging, mostly based in Hamburg or Berlin. *Kurz und Schmerzlos / Short Sharp Shock*, a fast-paced thriller which was the debut of Hamburg-based director Fatih Akın and nominated for the German Film Prize, was shown in London in December 1998 at the German Film Festival in the West End, as well as the Turkish Film Festival at the Rio Cinema in Dalston, both within the same week – an interesting overlap which points to the transnational potential of films like this. *Aprilkinder / April Children* (1998), directed by Yüksel Yavuz, is a trilingual melodrama that depicts a Kurdish immigrant family and their somewhat wayward offspring. Meanwhile the discourse of victimization of Turkish girls 'between two cultures' still persists. *Yara / The Wound* (1998), a German–Turkish–Swiss co-production (with Eurimages funding) by director Yılmaz Arslan, is the story of a fragile young girl who is taken back to Turkey against her will to stay with some relatives, runs away and winds up in a psychiatric clinic, disorientated and distraught. *Ich Chef, Du Turnschuh / Me Boss, You Sneaker* (1998), directed by Hussi Kutlucan (who also plays the main part), is one of the few comedies in this area, notable for scenes that foreground masquerade and the performance of ethnicity. The adventures of the asylum-seeker Dudie take us from a refugee-camp in Hamburg to a building site right in the centre of Berlin.

At the Berlin Film Festival in February 1999, when debates about double citizenship were at their peak, many of these films were shown as 'New German Films' and two brand-new productions were presented with great critical acclaim: Thomas Arslan's new film *Dealer*, which offers a rather unglamourous, minimalist vision of Berlin, staging the main character against the background of housing estates, green parks or pointilistic traffic lights; and Kutluğ Ataman's *Lola und Billidikid*, which opened the Panorama section of the festival, is a flamboyant family melodrama and thriller set in the gay and transvestite scene of Berlin. The world distribution of this film is handled by Good Machine International, the same company that distributed Ang Lee's *The Wedding Banquet* – another signal perhaps that Turkish–German film is venturing into the realm of transnational cinema.

Reception of Turkish cinema abroad

'Expatriate' films for and about the diaspora population, European funding and co-productions have challenged the definition of Turkish cinema in simply national terms. Meanwhile, Turkish films have become a more noticeable presence at international festivals. Since 1993 the Turkish Film Festival in London has been presenting a good selection of films (both indigenous and expatriate productions). Over the past couple of years a few films (*Eşkiya* and *Hamam*) have gained wider distribution in Europe. At the Berlin Film Festival in 1999 *Güneşe Yolculuk* and other films by young Turks received critical acclaim and awards. For a long time the only cinematic images of Turkey retained in the cultural memory were based on *Midnight Express* (Alan Parker, 1978) and *Yol* – images of imprisonment, cruelty and oppression. Today there seems to be hope that Turkish cinema is becoming more multi-faceted.

Filmography

Adı Vasfiye / Vasfiye is Her Name

1985, 90 mins, colour, Turkish
Director: Atıf Yılmaz
Producer: Estet Video (Cengiz Ergun)
Screenwriter: Barış Pirhasan
Cinematographer: Orhan Oğuz
Music: Atilla Özdemiroğlu
Art Director: Şahin Kaygun
Leading Players: Müjde Ar, Aytaç Arman, Yılmaz Zafer, Macit Koper, Erol
                             Durak, Suna Tanrıverdi, Oktay Kutluğ, Ali Rıza Tanrıverdi

A young writer goes in search of a woman and meets the men in her life. Each tells the writer their own part of her story, until the man realizes that they are actually their stories and not hers. He finally succeeds in locating her in a nightclub. He begs her to tell him the truth about herself, but Vasfiye keeps silent. At the end of the film he understands that his encounter with her was not real, although he is still carrying the flower she gave to him. The stories told by the male characters are parodies of various genres of Yeşilçam: children falling in love, a young man beating up the men who damaged his honour, a man kidnapping his beloved, a paramedic making love to the women who called for him to give her an injection, a young doctor falling for the plain small-town girl – all male fantasies, repeatedly reproduced and presented by Yeşilçam. The film catches the audience red-handed: it first promises fantasy and then shows its impossibility – in the end, the frame freezes and breaks into pieces like a shattering mirror, which reminds the audience that what they have been watching was their own projection. *Adı Vasfiye* announced the death of Yeşilçam and its audience. Ironically, the release of this film coincided with Turkish cinema losing its audience.

Berlin in Berlin

1993, 117 mins, colour, Turkish
Director:	Sinan Çetin
Producer:	Plato Film Production
Screenwriter:	Sinan Çetin, Ümit Ünal
Cinematographer:	Rebekka Haas
Music:	Nezih Ünen
Art Director:	Zeynep Tercan
Leading Players:	Hülya Avşar, Cem Özer, Armin Block, Aliye Rona, Eşref Kolçak

A genre mix that incorporates elements of the thriller, melodrama and comedy, this film offers a rather bizarre vision of cross-cultural encounters, set in the reunified Berlin. The camera playfully engages in an investigation of voyeurism and dissects the power of the ethnographic gaze. The story begins on a building site. Thomas (Armin Block), a German engineer and amateur photographer, follows the wife (Hülya Avşar) of a Turkish colleague with his camera and takes photos of her without her noticing. When her husband sees the photos he is infuriated, assuming that she has deliberately posed for the camera and exposed herself to the gaze of a stranger – an offence against his honour. In the resulting row the husband is pushed against an iron bar and thus killed by accident. Thomas's attempts to apologize lead him into the home of the husband's family in Kreuzberg. His discovery gives rise to turmoil. Mürtüz, the angry young man (played by popular talk show star Cem Özer), claims that the stranger has murdered his brother and threatens to kill him with his pistol. The chase is stopped, just in time, by the father and the grandmother (Aliye Rona) who pronounce that Thomas is a guest, 'sent to them by God' as a 'trial', and therefore cannot be harmed while inside their home. Thus Thomas is given asylum in the Turkish family home – a reversal of the situation of foreigners seeking asylum on German territory. He settles on the floor for a life in 'Berlin in Berlin' or '4 squaremetres of Germany' and is gradually incorporated into family life. When relatives come to visit, Thomas is the chief attraction. It is now the Turks who are watching the German, almost like a circus animal, and who stare at him in claustrophobic close-ups. Described as a 'multicul-tural melodrama' in Germany, *Berlin in Berlin* was a box-office hit in Turkey, predominantly because it featured Hülya Avşar, an actress and singer popular on Turkish television, in a masturbation scene.

Canlı Hedef / Live Target (a.k.a. Kızım İçin / For My Daughter)

1970, 88 mins, colour, Turkish
Director / Screenwriter: Yılmaz Güney
Producer: İrfan Film (İrfan Atasoy)
Cinematographer: Ali Yaver
Leading Players: Yılmaz Güney, Hülya Darcan, Yıldırım Gencer, Bilal İnci, Danyal Topatan, Erdo Vatan, Peri-Han, Melek Görgün

Asım Mavzer (Yılmaz Güney), an ex-gangster, returns from Europe. An army of enemies is waiting for him to seek vengeance for various affronts. Bilal (Bilal İnci) sends his man Jilet (*Gillette*: razor) to see if Asım's old friends know his whereabouts. Jilet leaves a scar on the face of everyone he visits, but finds out nothing. Asım's best friends, Aspirin (Danyal Topatan) and Korsan (Yıldırım Gencer), two social drop-outs, scare Jilet away and then run into Cino (Erdo Vatan), a classy enemy of Asım who is determined to duel with him. Bilal kidnaps Asım's daughter and one of his men rapes her before his eyes. Asım breaks his word and begins to take revenge. In the ensuing shoot-out, Cino joins Asım and they together demolish the gang. Aspirin and Cino die. Asım and Korsan surrender to the police.

Güney made *Canlı Hedef* the year he produced *Umut / Hope*, a much admired film shot in a style reminiscent of Italian neo-realism. Savaş Arslan has argued that film critics and historians favoured Güney's *Umut* and other art films at the expense of his more entertaining action / adventure movies. It was these films, however, that made Güney popular with the masses, and cinematically they are equally well-crafted as those that brought him international recognition. Asım wears an extravagant outfit for the shoot-out: black shirt and trousers, red scarf and a black hat with a red band around it. Aspirin explains how he got his epithet: 'whenever a woman had a headache, toothache, whatever, she seeks me out first, because the moment I kiss her the pain disappears just like that.' He often asks his comrades to listen to his dirty stories, but they always hush him. In the finale, when he is mortally wounded, he wants to tell his story again. This time Korsan says he wants to hear it. Aspirin begins but cannot continue. So, in a sense, the film ends with an untold story.

Eşkiya / The Bandit

1996, 121 mins, colour, Turkish
Director: Yavuz Turgul
Producer: Filma-Cass (Mine Vargı), Artcam, Geopoly
Cinematographer: Uğur içbak
Editor: Onur Tan, Selahattin Turgut
Music: Erkan Oğur
Art Director: Mustafa Ziya Ülkenciler

Leading Players: Şener Şen, Uğur Yücel, Kamuran Usluer, Necdet Mahfi Ayral,
Kayhan Yıldızoğlu, Şermin Şen Hürmeriç

Baran (Şener Şen) is a bandit who was in prison for over thirty years. After his release
he goes to his village, only to see that it is now flooded because a new dam has been
built. He meets the old woman of the village who has not moved out. She gives him an
amulet, implying that his ordeal is not over. Baran finds out that it was his friend,
Berfo (Kamuran Usluer), who turned him in, in order to marry Baran's fiancée, Keje
(Şermin Şen Hürmeriç). Baran takes a train to Istanbul where Berfo, now called
Mahmut Şahoğlu, lives as a powerful businessman. On the train he makes friends with
Cumalı (Uğur Yücel), a young drug dealer who is dreaming of making his way to the
top. After they arrive in Istanbul Cumalı helps Baran and a father–son relationship
starts to develop. Baran finds Keje, who has refused to speak since she married Berfo.
They decide to leave Istanbul together, but Baran learns that Cumalı is in trouble, so
he and Keje make a deal with Berfo: Keje will stay with him on condition that Berfo
provides the money that will save Cumalı. But Berfo cheats them and eventually
Cumalı gets killed by his own boss, Demircan. Baran takes revenge, killing Demircan
and his men, and then Berfo. He hides on the roofs of Istanbul, just as he hid in the
mountains thirty years earlier, but cannot escape death.

Some of the themes and issues raised by this film are (1) socio-cultural and even topo-
graphical change (Baran cannot cope with the changing morals of the big city; Baran's
village is now underwater); (2) love for its own sake (Berfo loves Keje more than anything
– his love transcends the codes of law, friendship, loyalty, faith and so on – but he gives up
Keje in return for Cumalı's life); and (3) family reunion (Cumalı finds his long-dead
father in Baran and Baran sees Cumalı as his unborn son). The film can also be read as a
metaphor for Turkish cinema's attempt to survive: being the most expensive production
ever, *Eşkiya* is a post-Yeşilçam film that challenges and mocks Hollywood. The cinematography, soundtrack, special effects and editing display a technical perfection that
was compared by critics and audiences to that of Hollywood. There are some moments
when the film parodies scenes from US films: Cumalı kills his treacherous girlfriend in a
style reminiscent of Tarantino; the rooftop encounter between Baran and the rising
police helicopter is a recurrent scene in US action films.

Gelin / The Bride

1973, 97 mins, colour, Turkish
Director / Screenwriter: Lütfi Ömer Akad
Producer: Erman Film (Hürrem Erman)
Cinematographer: Gani Turanlı
Music: Yalçın Tura
Leading Players: Hülya Koçyiğit, Kerem Yılmazer, Ali Şen, Kamuran Usluer,
Kahraman Kıral, Aliye Rona

Gelin is about internal migration from rural areas or provinces to the big city. Veli, his
wife Meryem and their son arrive in Istanbul to join his parents and elder brother,
Hidir, who are working hard to make a fortune in the 'big city which is made of solid

gold'. They are so carried away with their dreams that they cannot see that the little boy, who is in poor health, is dying. The film is important as it is succeeds in presenting the conflicts arising from migration without lapsing into melodrama. It subtly depicts the crisis in the values of the extended family that was brought about by industrialization. They look in disgust at their neighbour who lets his wife work in a factory and refuse to pay for the recommended operation for the ill child. Interestingly, however, it is the woman (Meryem) who acts as an agent of modernization. Against the will of her family, she takes her son to the doctor, demands money for medical treatment and, when the child dies, burns down the shop and leaves home to work in a factory. In the finale, the husband, who has been ordered to kill Meryem for the dishonour she brought to the family, finds her and asks if there is a job for him, implying that he wants a reunion (hence the emergence of the nuclear family in industrial society).

Güneşe Yolculuk / Journey to the Sun

1999, 104 mins, colour, Turkish / German / Dutch
Director / Screenwriter: Yeşim Ustaoğlu

Figure 51 Gelin / The Bride

Producer: Ifr (Behrooz Hashemian), The Filmcompany Amsterdam, Medias Res Berlin, Fabrica, Arte / ZDF
Cinematographer: Jacek Petrycki
Music: Vlato Stefanovski
Leading Players: Newroz Baz, Nazmi Qirix, Mizgin Kapazan, Nigar Aktar, İskender Bağcılar, Ara Güler

Güneşe Yolculuk is an accomplished production, which received funding from Eurimages and television channels Arte and ZDF. The film is a courageous exploration of ethnic segregation and its fatal, often absurd, consequences. It is also the first Turkish film since Yılmaz Güney's *Yol* to engage explicitly with Kurdish issues. The story of a friendship between two young men, a Turk (with 'Kurdish' looks) and a Kurd, is powerfully performed by amateur actors Newroz Baz and Nazmi Qirix. The story begins in the milieu of poor migrants living on the fringes of Istanbul. After the death of the Kurd at a public protest, his friend sets out on a journey through Turkey to take his coffin back home to the Kurd's village – only to find that his home no longer exists. The village has been demolished and deserted. Beautifully photographed, the film shows a refined sense of space and architecture. At the Berlin Film Festival in February 1999 it was awarded the Peace Prize and the Blue Angel Prize.

Figure 52 Sevmek Zamanı / Time of Love, an exploration of love and the problem of representation.

Figure 53 The bandit of the mountains goes to the city. Şener Şen in *Eşkiya / The Bandit.*

Sevmek Zamanı / Time to Love

1965, 90 mins, black and white, Turkish
Director / Screenwriter: Metin Erksan
Producer: Troya Film (Metin Erksan)
Cinematographer: Mengü Yeğin
Music: Metin Bukey
Leading Players: Müşfik Kenter, Sema Özcan, Süleyman Pekcan, Fadil
                           Garan, Adnan Uygur

Sevmek Zamanı is a film more talked about than seen. A house painter falls in love
with the enlarged photograph of a girl, but refuses to love the girl herself. The film is
considered to be an allegorical study of the image / referent distinction, a very
commonly used concept in the esoteric teaching of Sufism. The hero cannot transcend
the illusion that the photograph offers and acquire the truth to which it refers.
However, the film is open to alternative readings, one of which could be psychoana-
lytic. What is common to almost all of Erksan's films are fetish objects and men
obsessively enjoying these objects. *Sevmek Zamanı* runs along the same lines, and calls
for an examination of the psychological structuration of Erksan's filmic discourse.

Sürtük / Streetwalker

1965, 94 mins, black and white, Turkish
Director: Ertem Eğilmez
Producer: Arzu Film
Screenwriter: Sadık Şendil

Cinematographer:	Cahit Engin
Music:	Metin Bukey
Leading Players:	Türkan Şoray, Cüneyt Arkın, Ekrem Bora

Ekrem (Ekrem Bora), a tough, self-made man and the owner of a music-hall chain, wagers with his girlfriend that he can make anyone a star. He happens to hear Türkan (Türkan Şoray) sing in an underrated place and picks her to win the bet. He hires a piano player (Cüneyt Arkın) to give her music lessons. Unaware of the fact that Ekrem is also determined to possess what he has created, Türkan falls in love with Cüneyt. They attempt to escape, but no one in the entertainment business dares to employ them. When Ekrem finally threatens Türkan with murdering Cüneyt, she agrees to leave him. They arrange a small scene to convince Cüneyt that Türkan never loved him. But Ekrem now understands how much she loved him, so he regrets what he did to them. The damage can be repaired: in the finale, Ekrem brings the lovers together in a music hall and then goes into the lonely streets. Playing on the theme of sacrifice, *Sürtük* presents a typical plot in melodrama: the woman not only wins her lover back when she agrees to sacrifice her body, but she is also able to reform the bad. In melodramas, love must transcend the body, but the sacrifice of the body puts everything back in order. Eğilmez filmed a remake in 1970.

Teyzem / My Auntie

1986, 102 mins, colour, Turkish

Director:	Halit Refiğ
Producer:	Burç Film (Fedai Öztürk)
Screenwriter:	Ümit Ünal
Cinematographer:	Ertunç Şenkay
Music:	Atilla Özdemiroğlu
Leading Players:	Müjde Ar, Yaşar Alptekin, Mehmet Akan, Tomris Oğuzalp, Necati Bilgiç, Serra Yılmaz

This post-coup film narrates the story of Uftade from her nephew's point of view. She is a member of a middle-class family that perfectly mirrors the paranoia of the political atmosphere of the 1980s. Uftade's boyfriend Erhan disappears when she expresses her desire to marry him. Her elder brother goes to Germany to work and later returns as a religious man. Her father has died and her mother has married an ex-army officer, a despotic man who begins to make sexual advances to Uftade. Her mother cannot do anything about it, because she has been paralyzed by a stroke. Uftade marries a young man who treats her badly to cover up his sexual impotence. He manages to have sex with her only when his mother has commanded him to do so. Having divorced her husband, Uftade returns home, only to go through a series of ordeals which finally drive her to madness. Finally, she sees Erhan in a dream. He is dressed in a sultan's costume and says: 'I will come in lights and take you away with me'. One night she rushes out into the street and sees him approaching in lights. It turns out to be a truck, which kills her. As Deniz Derman argues:

Teyzem was produced in the 1980s after the military intervention and the mother stands for the silent people who are not allowed to speak, but must obey the step-father's rules. The stepfather stands for the military government, the dead father stands for democracy and Uftade's voice for the rebel.

(Derman 1996: 109)

The film goes into the details of social life and strikingly reveals how fascism operates from within, as if to prove the point that 'the political is personal'.

Yol / *The Way*

1981, 111 mins, colour, Turkish

Director:	Şerif Gören
Producers:	Güney Film /Cactus Film
Screenwriter:	Yılmaz Güney
Cinematographer:	Erdoğan Engin
Music:	Sebastian Argol, Kendal
Leading Players:	Tarık Akan, Şerif Sezer, Halil Ergün, Meral Orhonsay, Necmettin Çobanoğlu, Semra Uçar, Hikmet Çelik, Sevda Aktolga, Tuncay Akça, Hale Akınlı, Turgut Savaş, Hikmet Taşdemir, Engin Çelik, Osman Bardakçı, Enver Güney, Erdoğan Seren

Although this may be the only Turkish film known to an international audience, it was not released in Turkey until 1999. *Yol* received much acclaim, including the Palme d'Or at the Cannes Festival in 1982 (co-winner with Costa Gavras's *Missing*), but it remained banned in Turkey, primarily because of its explicit references to Kurdistan. *Yol* confronted the audience with harsh realities about their country. It presents five parallel stories, following the journeys of five prison-inmates who are released for ten days and travel back to their families, only to discover that life outside the prison is as harsh and oppressive as it is inside. The military presence after the 1980 coup is very noticeable throughout the country. Shootings are common along the south-eastern border where one of the men returns. There he rides his horse but must sacrifice his beloved because custom requires him to 'take over' his dead brother's wife. Generally, family relations come across as oppressive and cruel, especially with regard to women: one woman is frozen to death in snowy mountains, another is killed on a train by her brother for refusing to separate from her husband. Due to the strong performances of the actors and the epic scale of the cinematography, this film remains very powerful.

List of directors

Akad, Lütfi Ömer (b. 1916, Istanbul, Turkey)

Akad is the most prominent director of the cinematographers period. Originally a designer, he took up film-making in the 1940s and began a brilliant career that lasted until the mid-1970s. His films reveal a departure from the theatrical style (he asked his actors not to perform as if on stage) and the search for a individual cinematographic

Figure 54 Yol / The Way

style. The audience warmly welcomed his first film, *Vurun Kahpeye / Strike the Whore* (1949), which was an instant blockbuster. He later made *policiers* (detective films) under the influence of US films, usually depicting the male hero as a wounded man on the run, who is drawn into crime due to his innocence or to social conditions. Akad successfully stages the action against the cityscape of Istanbul, showing the hero's inevitable destruction in the end (*Kanun Namına / In the Name of the Law*, 1952; *Öldüren Şehir / Murderous City*, 1954; *Katil / The Murderer*, 1953; *Üç Tekerlekli Bisiklet / Tricycle*, 1962). He mastered his style in his first trilogy: *Hudutların Kanunu / The Law of the Borders* (1967), *Ana / Mother* (1967) and *Kızılırmak Karakoyun / Red River Black Sheep* (1967), this time far removed from urban territory. His second trilogy is a study in migration from rural areas to the big city. *Gelin / The Bride* (1973), *Düğün / The Wedding* (1973) and *Diyet / Blood Money* (1974) explore the family at the centre of the cultural conflicts and disintegrating forces of the city, interweaving social and human themes in a delicate manner. Akad also tried his hand at documentaries and short television films. He retired from directing features in the mid-1970s and currently teaches film at the Mimar Sinan University in Istanbul.

Çakmaklı, Yücel (b. 1937, Afyon, Turkey)

Çakmaklı wrote film reviews before he began directing feature films (although his first film was a documentary on pilgrimage). His early films criticized Westernization, promoting religious and national values instead. Characters who lead a Western lifestyle find themselves in a cul-de-sac until they discover religion (*Birleşen Yollar* / *Crossroads*, 1970; *Çile* / *The Passion*, 1972; *Oğlum Osman* / *Osman, My Son*, 1973; *Memleketim* / *My Homeland*, 1974). After directing some very successful historical television serials, Çakmaklı returned to film-making, this time concentrating on the theme of the tortured Muslim. His films (*Minyeli Abdullah* / *Abdullah from Minye*, 1989; *Minyeli Abdullah 2*, 1990; *Kanayan Yara Bosna* / *Bosnia, the Open Wound*, 1994; *Bosna, Mavi Karanlık* / *Bosnia, the Blue Darkness*, 1994) were highly popular with large religious audiences at a time when commercial cinema was rapidly declining.

Çetin, Sinan (b. 1953, Van, Turkey)

Çetin started his career in painting, photography and graphic design. He entered the film world as an assistant director on Zeki Ökten's comedy *Hanzo* (1975) and went on to work with Şerif Gören and Atıf Yılmaz. Çetin graduated from the Art History Department at Hacettepe University in Ankara in 1977 and directed two documentaries within the same year: *Baskın* / *The Raid* and *Halı Türküsü* / *Carpet Song*. In 1980 he directed his first feature film, *Bir Günün Hikayesi* / *Story of a Day*. Other

Figure 55 Lütfi Akad: In search of a cinematic language

features followed: *Çiçek Abbas / Abbas in Flower* (1982), *Çirkinler de Sever / Ugly but in Love* (1982), *14 Numara / No. 14* (1984), *Prenses, Gökyüzü / Princess, Heaven* (1986). In the 1980s he also directed commercials for television which helped him to develop his cinematic style. The sophisticated cinematography and fast-moving pace of his more recent, commercially successful films *Berlin in Berlin* (1993) and *Bay E / Mr. E* (1994) bear traces of this training in advertising. His latest film is *Propaganda* (1999).

Eğilmez, Ertem (b. 1929, Istanbul, Turkey; d. 1989, Istanbul)

Formerly a publisher of bestsellers and humorous magazines, Eğilmez began to make films in 1964. His *Sürtük / Streetwalker* (1965), an adaptation of *Pygmalion*, was an immediate blockbuster and he produced a remake in 1970. He followed Hollywood's narrative logic (he had a handbook on screenwriting translated into Turkish which he lived by) but nevertheless his films had an exclusively indigenous quality. They may be considered 'folk films' in the sense that he made films about the people who filled the cinemas. His melodramatic comedies particularly are vivid illustrations of the life of the lower middle class (characters showing solidarity against a contractor who offers the locals good money for their houses, women preparing the meal for a picnic in the countryside, local football players breaking the neighbour's glass windows, secret

Figure 56 Ertem Eğilmez: movie mogul and film director

lovers exchanging glances, harmless neurotics in funny situations, and so on). His *Hababam … / Carry On …* comedy series (*Hababam Sınıfı / The Carry On Students*, 1975; *Hababam Sınıfı Sınıfta Kaldı / The Carry On Students Fail*, 1975; *Hababam Sınıfı Uyanıyor / The Carry On Students Wake Up*, 1975; *Hababam Sınıfı Tatilde / The Carry On Students on Holiday*, 1977; *Hababam Sınıfı Güle Güle / Farewell, Carry On*, 1981) appealed to younger generations and presented the audience with some of the most successful stars of Turkish cinema (Tarık Akan, İlyas Salman, Şener Şen and Kemal Sunal) who are still working today. Interestingly, his last film before his death (*Arabesk / Arabesque*, 1988) is a comic pastiche of Yeşilçam melodramas, including his own most successful films.

Erksan, Metin (b. 1929, Çanakkale, Turkey)

Erksan attracted attention with social realist films set in a rural environment: *Karanlık Dünya: Aşık Veyselin Hayatı / The Dark World: The Life of Veysel the Poet* (1952), *Dokuz Dağın Efesi / The Swashbuckler of Nine Mountains* (1958), *Yılanların Öcü / The Revenge of Snakes* (1962), *Susuz Yaz / Dry Summer* (1963) and *Kuyu / The Well* (1968). *Susuz Yaz* received the Golden Bear at the Berlin Film Festival in 1964. Erksan is the first *auteur* and star-director of Turkish cinema, and founded the Film Industry Workers' Union in 1962. His critique of the hegemony of the upper classes over the disposessed went hand in hand with a search for a personal style of expression. Unusual camera angles, geometrical compositions and the excessive use of fetish objects (such as big portraits dominating the filmic space) are characteristic of his less commercial works like *Suçlular Aramızda / Criminals Among Us* (1964) and *Sevmek Zamanı / Time to Love* (1965). In *İntikam Meleği / Angel of Revenge* (1976), Hamlet (who is played by female star Fatma Girik) listens to classical Turkish music records on a bed outdoors. *Sensiz Yaşayamam / I Cannot Live Without You* (1977) tells the story of a businesswoman who hires a professional killer when she learns that she is mortally ill and subsequently falls in love with him.

Ertuğrul, Muhsin (b. 1892, Istanbul, Turkey; d. 1979, Izmir)

In the first years of the Republic film production was monopolized by a single man: Ertuğrul. He was an actor / director with international connections who came to be remembered as 'the father of Turkish cinema'. He had worked in Germany and the former USSR, and made friends with the celebrities of the film and theatre worlds (he even brought Greta Garbo and Mauritz Stiller to Turkey for one film production). In Germany he directed and acted in three films: *Samson* (1920), *Das Fest der Schwarzen Tulpe / The Black Tulip Festival* (1921) and *Die Teufelsanbeter / Devil Worshippers* (1921). He returned to Turkey and began to work for the first private studio, Kemal Film, founded by the brothers Kemal and Şakir Seden in 1922. The first films he made in Turkey are important because, for the first time in the history of Turkish cinema, Muslim women appeared on the screen (Bedia Muvahhit, Neyyire Neyir). As the director of Municipal Theatre of Istanbul, Ertuğrul staged plays during the winter that he would be able to film during the following summer. His most successful films were *Ateşten Gömlek / Shirt of Fire* (1923), an adaptation from the female novelist Halide Edib; *Bir Millet Uyanıyor / A Nation is Awakening* (1932), in which Atatürk (the President and the Founder of the Republic) and General Kazım Özalp played small roles; *Bataklı Damın Kızı Aysel / Aysel, the Daughter of the Swampy House* (1934), adapted from a Lagerlof novel and creating the atmosphere of Russian rural dramas; and *Bir Şehvet Kurbanı / Victim of Lust* (1940), a remake of Victor Fleming's *The Way of All Flesh*. He made *İstanbul Sokaklarında / In the Streets of Istanbul* (1931), the first co-production (Turkish, Egyptian and Greek) and post-sync film (it was dubbed in Paris). *Spartakus* (1926), which he made in the USSR, is considered by Jean Mitry the first revolutionary epic, but an average work. Ertuğrul also won the first international prize for Turkish cinema with a remake: *Leblebici Horhor Ağa / Lord Leblebici Horhor* (1934), which he first shot in 1923. It was awarded the diploma of honour at the second Venice International Film Festival in 1934, although the film failed at the box office. His *Halıcı Kız / The Carpet Weaver* (1953) was the first Turkish colour film to be exhibited, although it was Ali İpar's *Salgın / The Plague* (1952) that was the first film shot on colour stock (*Salgın* was not released until 1954 because of a two-year wait in film laboratories in the United States). *Halici Kiz* was not well received by the audience, which brought his career in cinema to an end. Film critics and historians have criticized Ertuğrul, not only for his monopolization of Turkish cinema from 1922 to 1939, but also for his lack of a sense of cinematography. It is true that Ertuğrul was not a committed cinematographer; however, his camera set-ups and editing show some effort to develop a specifically cinematic language.

Güney, Yılmaz (b. 1931, Adana, Turkey; d. 1984, Paris)

Güney, the legendary actor-director of Turkish cinema, was able to break free from the restrictions of Yeşilçam, while establishing a longstanding relationship with the audience. The roles he played in *Ben Öldükçe Yaşarım / I Live as Long as I Die* (Duygu Sağıroğlu, 1965), *Hudutların Kanunu / The Law of the Borders* (Akad, 1966) and *Kurbanlık Katil / The Murderer is the Victim* (Akad, 1967) brought him fame. He was particularly admired by lower middle-class audiences in Anatolia. He was given the epithet 'Ugly King', thus shaking the reign of the *jeune premier* as the male lead character. *Umut / Hope* (1970), which opened the doors of international reputation to him, tells the story of a cab driver desperately seeking treasure said to be buried in the country and ending up in lunacy. As a devout Marxist, Güney's films tended towards socialist realism. He related the problems which he exposed in his films to social injustice and its economic underpinnings and, as Roy Armes has put it, showed the 'failure of the individual acting alone' (Armes 1981: 10). He used elements familiar from melodrama to strengthen the total effect of his films. In *Baba / The Father* (1971), the eponymous father accepts the blame for a crime committed by his boss' son and is put in prison. When he is released, he searches for the members of his family, which had broken up years ago, running into his daughter in a brothel and in the end being killed by his son. *Arkadaş / Friend* (1974) is another sensational film, contrasting the idealist engineer Âzem (played by Güney himself) with his classmate Cemil (Kerim Afşar), who represents the corrupt and malfunctioning bourgeoisie. Güney, who had been repeatedly in prison on the charge of spreading communist propaganda, was convicted of murder in 1974 after killing the judge Safa Mutlu in Yumurtalık in Adana as the result of an unfortunate argument. In prison, he wrote the scripts for three films that were directed by others: *Sürü / The Herd* (Zeki Ökten, 1978), *Düşman / Enemy* (Ökten,

1979) and *Yol / The Way* (Şerif Gören, 1981), probably the best-known Turkish film in the West. *Yol*, a drama about five prisoners who go on leave from prison and find that the world outside is no better than life inside, bears resemblance to Güney's own life after shooting was completed: he took leave from prison and never returned. Güney edited *Yol* in France and shared the Grand Prix at Cannes with Costa Gavras in 1982. In 1983 he lost his Turkish citizenship. His last film *Le mur / Duvar / The Wall* (1983), another bleak prison drama, was produced in France, where he died in 1984.

Gürses, Muharrem (b. 1913, Amasya, Turkey; d. 1999, Istanbul)

Gürses is a director of the 1950s who is noteworthy for developing an indigenous version of melodrama. He exercised his craft by exploiting the formulas of a genre ('Gürses melodramas') that was attached to his name for more than a decade. Between 1952 and 1988 he made some eighty-two films that remain untouched by academic

Figure 57 Yılmaz Güney: the legendary figure of Turkish cinema

research. Gürses mainly directed rural and small-town melodramas, historical and religious films, all of which were extremely popular with audiences because of his excessively tragic tone. They include *Zeynep'in Gözyaşları* / *The Tears of Zeynep* (1952), *İhtiras Kurbanları* / *Victims of Lust* (1953), *Gülmeyen Yüzler* / *Stern Faces* (1955) and *Yetimler Ahı* / *The Cry of the Orphans* (1956).

Heper, Alp Zeki *(b. 1939, Istanbul, Turkey; d. 1984, Istanbul)*

Heper, who was an exemplary case of the tormented artist and failed genius, graduated from the Institut des Hautes Etudes Cinématographiques in France. His short films (*Bir Kadın* / *A Woman* and *Şafak* / *Dawn*) won awards from IDHEC and the Ministry of Culture of Austria. After his return to Turkey he worked as an assistant to Akad. He began to direct films for his own company in 1964. His first feature-length film, *Soluk Gecenin Aşk Hikayeleri* / *Love Stories of a Pale Night* (1966), heavily influenced by surrealism, was banned by the censors and never commercially exhibited. After that, he made some more commercial films (*Dolmuş Şoförü* / *Dolmuş Driver*, 1967; *Eşkiya Halil* / *Halil the Bandit*, 1968; *Kara Battal'ın Acısı* / *The Agony of Black Battal*, 1968), but ultimately failed to achieve success. His unstable mental condition led him to isolation and distress. According to his will, Heper's films cannot be distributed and may be screened for audiences of no more than three people.

Kavur, Ömer *(b. 1944, Ankara, Turkey)*

Kavur is probably Turkey's most philosophical film-maker. He went to France after secondary school, graduated from the Conservatoire Indépendant du Cinéma Français and took a Master's degree in film history at the Sorbonne, as well as a degree in social sciences at the Institut des Hautes Etudes du Journalisme. He also worked as an assistant to Bryan Forbes and Alain Robbe-Grillet. After his return to Turkey, he first made documentary films: *Istanbul, Atatürk ve Ankara* / *Istanbul, Atatürk and Ankara* and *İzmir ve Boğaziçi Köprüsü* / *Izmir and the Bosphorus Bridge*. In 1974 he directed his first long feature, *Yatık Emine* (1974), based on a novel by Refik Halid Karay. After a five-year pause, he started directing again and worked with Atıf Yılmaz on some joint projects. In 1978, he established his own independent production company Alfa Film and has since produced his own films: *Yusuf ile Kenan* / *Yusuf and Kenan* (1979), *Ah Güzel İstanbul* / *Oh, Beautiful Istanbul* (1981), *Kırık Bir Aşk Hikayesi* / *A Broken Love Story* (1981), *Göl* / *The Lake* (1982), *Körebe* / *Blind Man's Buff* (1985) and *Amansız Yol* / *Hard Way* (1986). His *Anayurt Oteli* / *Motherland Hotel* (1987), based on a novel by Yusuf Atılgan, is one of the most original literary adaptations of Turkish cinema, filmed in a style that might best be described as magical realism. *Anayurt Oteli* received various awards at international festivals, including the Fiparesci International Screenwriters' Award at the Venice Film Festival. *Gece Yolculuğu* / *Night Journey* (1987) is a self-reflexive film about a screenwriter who runs into a creative crisis. *Gizli Yüz* / *The Hidden Face* (1990) was based on a scenario by Orhan Pamuk and continued along the lines of *Anayurt Oteli* in depicting a dream-like reality, albeit not quite as successfully as its predecessor, appearing slightly contrived, static and uncinematic at times. It got controversial responses, but once again won awards at various international festivals (including the best film award at both the New Cinema

Festival in Montreal and the Istanbul Film Festival). *Akrebin Yolculuğu / Clock Tower* (1997) explored the philosphical dimensions of time.

Kıral, Erden (b. 1942, Gölcük, Turkey)

Kıral graduated with a degree in ceramics from the Academy of Fine Arts in Istanbul. He wrote about cinema in various journals and worked as an assistant to Osman F. Seden, Bilge Olgaç and Yılmaz Güney. He also worked for television stations, directing commercials. After making some short films (*Kumcu / The Sound Seller*, *Unutulmuşlar / The Forgotten People*, *Haşhaş / Poppy*), he directed his first long feature *Kanal / Canal* (1978). *Bereketli Topraklar Üzerinde / On Fertile Soil* (1979) followed. His films tend to focus on the harsh experiences of rural people, attempting to render these from a modern perspective. Kıral lived in Berlin for some years. His *Hakkari'de Bir Mevsim / A Season in Hakkari* (1982), the story of a school teacher who spends a winter teaching in a very poor village in eastern Turkey, was awarded the special jury prize at the Berlin Film Festival in 1983. *Ayna / Mirror* (1984) also received awards at international festivals in Luxembourg, Portugal and Istanbul. Further films were *Dilan* (1986) and *Av Zamanı / Hunting Time* (1987). His *Mavi Sürgün / The Blue Exile* (1993), based on the autobiography of the 'Fisherman of Halikarnassos' Cevat Şakir Kebaağaçlı, was heavily funded by Eurimages. The film begins promisingly with documentary footage depicting Turkey after World War I, but develops into a rather lengthy and melodramatic exploration of the male artist's problematic psyche and the healing powers of rural life.

Figure 58 Ömer Kavur: the philosophical mind of Turkish cinema

Refiğ, Halit (b. 1934, Izmir, Turkey)

Champion and theoretician of a 'national cinema', Refiğ first wrote film reviews and screenplays, and then made his first film, *Yasak Aşk / Forbidden Love*, in 1961. His *Gurbet Kuşları / Birds of Exile* (1964), which focuses on the sufferings and dissolution of a family in the big city, is now regarded as a classic. He made films in a wide range of genres: social realism (*Şehirdeki Yabancı / A Stranger in Town*, 1962; *Gurbet Kuşları*), folk and fairy tales (*Atsız Cengaver / A Warrior without a Horse*, 1970; *Leyla ve Mecnun / Leila and Majnun*, 1982), historical 'costume' dramas (*Haremde Dört Kadın / Four Women in the Harem*, 1965; *Çöl Kartalı / Desert Eagle*, 1972) and melodramas (*Sevmek ve Ölmek Zamanı / Time to Love and Time to Die*, 1971; *Fatma Bacı*, 1972). He developed an indiviual style, which gave added impact to his narratives. He ably handled the most topical stories (such as drug addiction in *Beyaz Ölüm / Death in White*, 1983), as well as the most psychological ones (the young woman going mad in *Teyzem / My Auntie*, 1986; *Köpekler Adası / The Isle of Dogs*, 1997).

Turgul, Yavuz (b. 1946, Istanbul, Turkey)

Turgul began to work as a screenwriter for Ertem Eğilmez in 1976. He made his name writing screenplays for a number of directors who followed the tradition of Eğilmez. His scripts included *Sultan* (Kartal Tibet, 1978), *Çiçek Abbas / Abbas in Flower* (Sinan Çetin, 1982) and *Zügürt Ağa / The Penniless Lord* (Nesli Çölgeçen, 1986). He made his directorial debut with *Fahriye Abla / Sister Fahriye* (1984), telling the story of a young girl going through stages of emancipation. His *Muhsin Bey / Mr Muhsin* (1986) and *Aşk Filmlerinin Unutulmaz Yönetmeni / The Unforgettable Director of Romantic Movies* (1990) focus on the theme of a solitary man who cannot catch up with socio-cultural change. Mr Muhsin is a music producer whose ambition of preserving Turkey's cultural heritage prevents him from making a living. Hasmet Asilkan, the eponymous unforgettable director of romantic movies, makes a political film in order to get the plaudits of the intellectual elite, but goes bankrupt. Turgul's *Eşkiya / The Bandit* (1997) is a phenomenal film. It was screened for more than twelve months all over Turkey, beating films from the United States (including the much admired *Braveheart*). It stirred heated discussions about the possibility of Turkish cinema winning its audience back.

Ustaoğlu, Yeşim (b. 1960, Sarıkamış, Turkey)

Ustaoğlu is one of the promising new women directors of Turkish cinema. She studied architecture at Karadeniz Technical University and took a post-graduate degree at Yıldız University in Istanbul. She wrote articles on cinema in various art journals, and started her career in film-making with the short films *Bir Anı Yakalamak / To Catch a Moment* (1984), *Magnafantagna* (1987), *Düet / Duet* (1990) and *Otel / Hotel* (1992). Her first feature was *İz / The Trace* (1993), a detective film with a twist and somewhat surreal elements. Her latest film, *Güneşe Yolculuk / Journey to the Sun* (1999), the story of a Turkish–Kurdish friendship, was awarded the Peace Prize and the Blue Angel Prize at the Berlin Film Festival.

Figure 59   Yavuz Turgul: the revival of Turkish popular cinema?

Yılmaz, Atıf (Batibeki) (b. 1926, Mersin, Turkey)

Yılmaz began his directing career in 1952 with *Kanlı Feryat / The Bloody Lament*. Director of some 110 films and winner of more than twenty awards, he mastered his craft in a wide range of genres (melodrama, children's films, *policiers*, psychological films, historical 'costume' dramas, epics) and textual modes (realism, fantasy). Yılmaz is called the 'youngest film-maker of Turkish cinema' for his continuous search for new themes and stylistic innovations, although he has never concealed his concern for commercial success. In *Yedi Kocalı Hürmüz / Hürmüz with Seven Husbands* (1971), he attempted the risky task of reviving the visual style of miniature paintings with the narrative running with the rhythm of classical Turkish music; *Ne Olacak Şimdi? / What Now?* (1979) and *Asiye Nasıl Kurtulur / How to Save Asiye* (1986) are exemplary studies in Brechtian alienation effects; the women of *Mine* (1982) and *Bir Yudum Sevgi / A Sip of Love* (1984) dare to violate the norms of society in order to meet their need for love and even sexual desire; *Adı Vasfiye / Vasfiye is Her Name* (1985) and *Aaahh, Belinda! / Oh, Belinda!* (1986) question the ways in which the concept 'woman' is constructed and represented in the media; *Düş Gezginleri / Dream Wanderers* (1992) depicts a lesbian relationship ruined by power games; and his latest film *Nihavent Mucize / Miracle Ma Non Troppo* (1997), co-funded by Eurimages and starring once again Türkan Şoray, is an anti-œdipal comedy about a beautiful woman who returns from the dead to prove to her son that she is really no different from other women.

List of actors

Ar, Müjde (b. 1954, Istanbul, Turkey)

Formerly a stage actress and fashion model, Ar was seen as a more sensual version of Türkan Şoray: straightforward and challenging, but still reserved. She first appeared as the lustful young wife of an old man in a television serial (Halit Refiğ's *Aşk-ı Memnu / Forbidden Love*, 1974) and continued to play film roles with a strong emphasis on her sexuality. Ar became a sex symbol and eventually a bankable star in the mid-1970s, an advantage which was to be enjoyed by film-makers even in post-1980 films that focused on problems of sexuality or the representation and cultural role of women. She played a woman enslaved to the perverse fantasies of her husband (*Asılacak Kadın / The Woman to be Hanged*); the bourgeois prostitute in a parody of Buñuel's notorious *Belle de Jour* (*Maça Kızı / Queen of Spades*); the victim of her own family (*Teyzem / My Auntie*); the high-society prostitute fallen prey to the illusion that she has found the love of her life (*Dağınık Yatak / The Unmade Bed*); the mature widow who cannot break the sexual spell of a male chauvinist (*Dul Bir Kadın / A Widow*); a woman as constructed by the fantasies of the men in her life (*Adı Vasfiye / Vasfiye is Her Name*); and a working girl fascinated by the possibilities of voyeurism (*Gizli Duygular / Secret Feelings*).

Arkın, Cüneyt (b. 1937, Eskişehir, Turkey)

When he first appeared in the movies, Arkın played the naïve and handsome young man. He was either deceived and exploited by the lead female character or loved by a powerful city girl who was fed up with the spoilt men around her (Halit Refiğ, *Gurbet Kuşları / Birds of Exile*, 1964; Ülkü Erakalın, *Gözleri Ömre Bedel / Her Eyes are Worth a Life*, 1964; Nuri Ergün, *Fakir Bir Gencin Romanı / The Story of a Poor Young Man*, 1965; Ülkü Erakalın, *Ayrılık Şarkısı / A Farewell Song*, 1965). As he grew older, he began to play the rich rascal who fell for the naïve and poor girl (*Aşk Mabudesi / Love Goddess, 1969*). He is now primarily remembered for his superhero roles in cop series (*Cemil*, 1975; *Cemil Dönüyor / Cemil Returns*, 1977) and historical action movies, some of which are adaptations of popular comics (*Hacı Murat*, 1967; *Hacı Murat Geliyor / Hacı Murat is Coming*, 1968; *Hacı Murat'in İntikami / The Revenge of Hacı Murat*, 1972; *Kara Murat*, 1972; *Kara Murat Devler Savaşıyor / Kara Murat: Titans Clash*, 1978; *Kara Murat Fatih'in Fermanı / Kara Murat: The Order of Fatih the Conquerer*, 1973; *Kara Murat Kara Şövalyeye Karşı / Kara Murat against the Black Knight*, 1975; *Malkoçoğlu*, 1966; *Malkoçoğlu Kara Korsan / Malkoçoğlu, Black Pirate*, 1968).

Alışık, Sadri (b. 1925, Istanbul, Turkey; d. 1995, Istanbul)

Alışık is noteworthy for his roles as the ordinary man on the street who can be dangerously daring when necessary. His character is self-contained and leads a moderate life until something (mostly a woman in need or a child to be taken care of) knocks him off balance (*Ah Güzel İstanbul / Oh, Beautiful Istanbul*, 1966). In this sense he is very Chaplinesque; however, his characters like to make speeches about the virtues of honesty and a simple life when they are defeated, and lack the economy of Chaplin's minimalist expressions. Just like many other Turkish actors who feel at home with both melodrama and comedy, Alışık made some very popular comedies: the *Turist Ömer / Ömer the Tourist* series (between 1964–71) being the most successful among them.

Işık, Ayhan (b. 1929 Izmir; d. Istanbul 1979)

Işık was the first male star of Turkish cinema, playing the lead role in the early films of Akad. His handsome looks and good performances in *Kanun Namına / In the Name of the Law*, *Öldüren Şehir / Murderous City* and *Üç Tekerlekli Bisiklet / Tricycle* put him in a position to arrange contracts according to his own rules, a sign of stardom and an example that was soon followed by other actors and actresses. Initially he established himself as the serious character who falls prey to the snares of women or society by, for example, risking his life for his homeland. In later years, however, he played a range of diverse characters: a witty chauffeur driving and taming the lady of the house (Nejat Saydam, *Küçük Hanımın Şoförü / Little Lady's Chauffeur*, 1962); a smart and chivalrous thief (Safa Önal, *Cingöz Recai / Shrewd Recai*, 1969). In the early 1970s, he sought international roles, but was only able to make cut-price horror films. He co-starred with Richard Harrison in *Lamico del Padrino / The Godfather's Friend aka The Revenge of the Godfather* (Frank Agrama, 1972) and with Klaus Kinski in both *La Mano che Nutre / The Hand that Feeds Death* (Sergio Garrone, 1974) and *Le Amanti del Mostro / The Love of the Monster* (Garrone, 1974).

Koçyiğit, Hülya (b. 1947, Istanbul, Turkey)

Koçyiğit first studied theatre and ballet, before winning a contest organized by a film magazine in 1963 and making her debut in Metin Erksan's classic *Susuz Yaz / Dry Summer* (1963). She also played in the prestigious Akad trilogy (*Gelin / The Bride*, *Düğün / The Wedding*, *Diyet / Blood Money*, 1973–4). One of the four first actresses of Turkish popular cinema (along with Türkan Şoray, Fatma Girik and Filiz Akın), she is distinguished from the others by her relatively more academic performances. In contrast with Şoray, for example, Koçyiğit skilfully orchestrates her facial features in a slightly self-conscious manner.

Şen, Şener (b. 1942, Adana, Turkey)

Coming from the theatre, Şen attracted attention as the neurotic physical trainer in the *Hababam … / Carry On …* series. He soon began to play the lead in comedies. Şen is able to play completely opposite characters: the civil servant who cannot cope with the demands of his social environment (*Namuslu / Honourable*, 1984) or the sneaky driver who can easily exploit his devout assistant (*Çiçek Abbas / Abbas in Flower*, 1982). His strength lies in the way he keeps a balance between the comic and melodramatic. His collaborations with Yavuz Turgul (former scriptwriter to Eğilmez) made him an established star, mostly acting as an agent of resistance against social and cultural corruption: a manager, himself a fan of Turkish classical music, who is forced to produce a trashy music album (*Muhsin Bey / Mr Muhsin*); an impoverished feudal lord who has to migrate to Istanbul and ends up in the streets selling food (*Züğürt Ağa / The Penniless Lord*); a popular film director who attempts to make an art film in order to be approved by the cultural elite but fails in the attempt (*Aşk Filmlerinin Unutulmaz*

Yönetmeni / *The Unforgettable Director of Romantic Movies*); a stand-up comedian who is determined to become rich at all costs but cannot leave his friends (*Gölge Oyunu* / *Shadow Play*); a noble bandit from south-eastern Turkey who gets lost in the jungle of the big city (*Eşkiya* / *The Bandit*).

Sonku, Cahide (b. 1916, Yemen – part of the former Ottoman Empire; d. 1981 Istanbul)

Muhsin Ertuğrul introduced the first star of Turkish cinema: Sonku, a peroxide blonde from Yemen who quickly became a cult figure in high society. She played a wide range of roles in her films: fallen angels (*Aysel Bataklı Damın Kızı* / *Angel from the Swamps*, 1934), *femme fatales* (*Şehvet Kurbanı* / *Victim of Lust*, 1940) and, in later years, affectionate mothers (*Beklenen Şarkı* / *The Expected Song*, 1953). However, she is now better remembered for the way in which her star persona was overshadowed by images of a scandalous later life (failed marriages, alcoholism, poverty and even homelessness).

Şoray, Türkan (b. 1945, Istanbul, Turkey)

The icon of melodramas and 'Sultaness of Yeşilçam', Şoray started her acting career in the early 1960s. Her clumsy and tomboyish manners in the early films were transformed after she lost weight, changed her hairstyle and had cosmetic surgery on her nose. Still well-built, but elegant and swift, she felt at home in diverse roles, ranging from a jubilant gypsy girl with a certain degree of eroticism (Ülkü Erakalın, *Hapisane Gelini* / *The Jail Bride*, 1968) to a virtuous lady determined to keep faith in her husband (Safa Önal, *Bir Kadın Kayboldu* / *A Woman Vanished*, 1973). Her characters, however, had to obey the rules of chastity. She was seldom seen kissing a man on screen and she never deceived her lover / husband; even when she was involved in a non-matrimonial act, this was only implied (never shown) to serve as a pretext for having children (Nejat Saydam, *Ayşem* / *Ayshe Mine*, 1968). After the 1980s, she changed her star image. Her characters were now more sexually active. There has even been a change in her acting: the slightly exaggerated facial expressions (movement of eyes, the use of lips and eyebrows), which were perfectly in harmony with the style of melodrama, are now controlled by an economy of realism. Şoray has also directed some films: *Dönüş* / *The Return* (1972), *Azap* / *Suffering* (1973), *Bodrum Hakimi* / *The Ruler of Bodrum* (1976) and *Yılanı Öldürseler* / *Kill the Snake* (1981).

Sunal, Kemal (b. 1944, Istanbul, Turkey; d. 2000 Istanbul)

Sunal is one of the most popular stars of Turkish cinema and television. Television channels repeatedly show his films, and he completed a master's thesis on the sources of his popularity. Like many other comedy stars, he first appeared on stage. Sunal then played the unforgettable half-wit character İnek Şaban in the *Hababam ...* / *Carry On ...* series. His performances rely heavily on the possibilities of his face (he once said that he felt lucky because he was ugly) and the vulgar use of language. Following *Hababam ...* he played the lead role in the *Şaban* series. Şaban is a character type inspired by the folktale hero Keloğlan: he is poor, powerless and society looks down on him, but in the end he defeats powerful enemies who have attempted to abuse his good will.

Figure 60 Yeşim Ustaoğlu – architect turned film maker

List of institutions

University programmes

Anadolu Üniversitesi, İletişim Fakültesi, Sinema–TV Bölümü

26470 Eskişehir
Phone: +90 222 335 05 81
Fax: +90 222 320 45 20
B.A. programme in English

Ankara Üniversitesi, İletişim Fakültesi, Radyo–TV–Sinema Bölümü

Cebeci, Ankara
Phone: +90 312 319 77 14
Fax: +90 312 362 27 12

Figure 61 Kemal Sunal: the village idiot pointing the way to resistance

Dokuz Eylül Üniversitesi, Güzel Sanatlar Fakültesi, Sinema–TV Bölümü

Şehitler cad. no. 12, Alsancak, İzmir
Phone: +90 232 421 36 47
Fax: +90 421 57 20

Gazi Üniversitesi, İletişim Fakültesi, Sinema–TV Bölümü

Ankara
Phone: +90 312 212 64 95

İstanbul Bilgi Üniversitesi, Sinema–TV Bölümü

İnönü cad. no. 28, Kuştepe 80310, Şişli-İstanbul
Phone: +90 212 216 22 22
Fax: +90 212 216 24 00
Website: http://ibun.edu.tr
Offers graduate programmes in English

İstanbul Üniversitesi, İletişim Fakültesi, Radyo–TV–Sinema Bölümü

Vezneciler, İstanbul
Phone: +90 212 512 52 57
Fax: +90 212 526 91 94

Marmara Üniversitesi, Güzel Sanatlar Fakültesi, Sinema–TV Bölümü

Haydarpasa Kampüsü, İstanbul
Phone / fax: +90 216 336 84 24

Mimar Sinan Üniversitesi, Sinema–TV Merkezi

Kışlaönü, 80700 Beşiktaş, İstanbul
Phone: +90 212 274 98 70, 267 04 94
Fax: +90 212 211 65 99

Organizations

GİSAM (Görsel İşitsel Sistemler Araştırma ve Yayınlama Merkezi / Audio-Visual Systems Research Centre)

Orta Doğu Teknik Üniversitesi 06531 Ankara
Phone: +90 312 210 29 34
Fax: +90 312 13 27

SE-SAM (Türkiye Sinema Eseri Sahipleri Meslek Birliği / Turkish Producers Organization) and TÜRSAV (Türk Sinema Vakfı / Turkish Cinema Foundation)

İstiklal cad. 122 / 4, Beyoğlu İstanbul
Phone: +90 212 245 46 45
Fax: +90 212 245 27 47

TÜRSAK (Türkiye Sinema ve Audiovisuel Kültür Vakfı / Turkish Foundation of Film and Audiovisual Culture)

Gazeteci Erol Dernek sok. 11 / 2 Hanif Han 80072, Beyoğlu İstanbul
Phone: +90 212 244 52 51 / 251 67 70
Fax: +90 212 292 03 37

T.C. Kültür Bakanlığı, Telif Hakları ve Sinema Müdürlüğü / The Ministry of Culture, Directorate of Copyrights and Cinema

Necatibey cad. 55 / 5, Necatibey, Ankara
Phone: +90 312 231 79 62
Fax: +90 312 231 96 94

Archives

Mimar Sinan Üniversitesi, Sinema–TV Merkezi, a member of FIAF, has the largest film archive. The Film Department (Sinema Dairesi) of the Ministry of Culture in Ankara keeps a video copy of the films that it sponsored. TÜRSAK can also provide video copies, as well as documents and other archive materials. The film and television departments of universities run small archives with limited facilities.

International festivals

Ankara Uluslararası Film Festivali / Ankara International Film Festival

Dünya Kitle İletişim Vakfı, Dünya Ticaret Merkezi, Tahran cad. no. 30, 06700 Ankara

Phone: +90 312 468 38 92–468 77 45
Fax: +90 312 467 78 30

Avrupa Filmleri Festivali / Festival of European Films

Bülten sok. no. 13, Kavaklıdere Ankara
Phone: +90 312 468 71 40
Fax: +90 312 468 71 39

İstanbul Uluslararası Film Festivali / International Istanbul Film Festival

İstanbul Kültür ve Sanat Vakfı, İstiklal cad. 142 Luvr apt, Beyoğlu İstanbul

Phone: +90 212 293 31 33
Fax: +90 212 249 77 71

İstanbul Uluslararası Kısa Film Festivali / International Istanbul Short Film Festival

İFSAK, Ayhan Işık sok, Özverim apt 34 / 2, Beyoğlu İstanbul

Phone: +90 212 243 14 01
Fax: +90 212 252 44 61

İzmir Uluslararası Film Festivali / International Izmir Film Festival

Oğuz Makal, Dokuz Eylül Üniversitesi, Güzel Sanatlar Fakültesi, Şehitler cad. no. 12,
        Alsancak, İzmir
Phone: +90 232 421 36 47
Fax: +90 232 421 57 20

London Turkish Film Festival

Rio Cinema, 107 Kingsland High Street, London E8, England
Phone: +44 0207 254 66 77

References and further reading

Abisel, N. (1994) *Türk Sineması Üzerine Yazılar*, Ankara: İmge.

Armes, R. (1981) 'Yılmaz Güney: The limits of individual action', *Framework*, 15–17 (summer): 9–11.

Coş, N. (1969) 'Türkiye 'deli Sinemalarin Dağılışı ve Bu Dağısın Sebepleri', *As Sinema Dergisi* 2: 12.

Cullingworth, M. (1989) 'On a first viewing of Turkish cinema', in C. Woodhead (ed.) *Turkish Cinema: An Introduction*, London: SOAS, pp. 11–18.

Derman, D. (1996) 'Mother–daughter relationship in the family melodrama: *Teyzem*', in D. Derman and Ross, K. (eds) *Gender and Media*, Ankara: Med-Campus no. A126, pp. 100–15.

Dorsay, A. (1989) 'An overview of Turkish cinema from its origins to the present day', in C. Woodhead (ed.) *Turkish Cinema: An Introduction*, London: SOAS, pp. 21–33.

Erdoğan, N. (1998) 'Narratives of resistance: National identity and ambivalence inTurkish melodrama between 1965 and 1975', *Screen* 39, 3 (autumn): 259–71.

Erdoğam, N. (2001) 'Violent Images: Hybridity and Excess in *The Man Who Saved the World*', in *Medicated Identities*, ed. by Karen Ross, Deniz Derman, Nevena Dakovic, Istanbul: Bilgi University Press, pp. 115–129.

Göktürk, D. (2001) "Turkish Delight – German Fright: Migrant Identities in Transnational Cinema", in *Medicated Identities* (see above), pp. 131–149.

Makal, O. (1994) *Sinemada Yedinci Adam: Türk Sinemasında İç ve Dış Göç Olayı*, Izmir: Ege.

Mehmet, B. (ed.) (1996) *Le Cinema Turc*, Paris: Centre George Pompidou.

Nadler, J. (1998) 'Pic Renaissance' and *Variety* (18–24 May): 61.

Özgüç, A. (1995a) *Türk Film Yönetmenleri Sözlüğü*, Istanbul: AFA.

—— (1995b) *80. Yılında Türk Sineması 1914–1994 / Turkish Cinema at its 80th Anniversary 1914–1994*, Ankara: Ministry of Culture. (In both Turkish and English.)

—— (1997a) *Türk Filmleri Sözlüğü 1914–1973*, Istanbul: SESAM.

—— (1997b) *Türk Filmleri Sözlüğü 1974–1990*, Istanbul: SESAM.

—— (1997c) *Türk Filmleri Sözlüğü 1991–1996*, Istanbul: SESAM.

Özgüven, F. (1989) 'Male and female in Yeşilçam: Archetypes endorsed by mutual agreement of audience and player', in C. Woodhead (ed.) *Turkish Cinema: An Introduction*, London: SOAS, pp. 35–41.

Scognamillo, G. (1990) *Türk Sinema Tarihi 1896–1986*, vols 1–2, Istanbul: Metis. (Includes a short summary in English.)

TÜRSAK (1994) *Sinema Yıllığı 93 / Film Year Book 93*, Istanbul: TÜRSAK. (Includes short summaries in English.)

—— (1995) *Sinema Yıllığı 95–96 / Film Year Book 95–96*, Istanbul: TÜRSAK. (Includes short summaries in English.)

—— (1996) *Sinema Yıllığı 96–97 / Film Year Book 96–97*, Istanbul: TÜRSAK. (Includes short summaries in English.)

—— (1997) *Sinema Yıllığı 97–98 / Film Year Book 97–98*, Istanbul: TÜRSAK. (Includes short summaries in English.)

General index

Page numbers in bold denotes main reference

Name Index

Page numbers in *italics* refers to illustrations
Page numbers in **bold** refers to a main reference on subject

Film index

Page numbers in *italics* refers to illustrations
Page numbers in **bold** refers to a main reference on subject